☆ ☆

My Ayres ~Wood Ancestry

From the 7th Century to the 20th Century

Second Edition

Noreen Ayres Craig

☆ ☆

Library of Congress Control Number: 2017957729

CreateSpace Independent Publishing Platform, North Charleston, SC

U.S.A.

*N*one can understand history without continually relating the long periods which are constantly mentioned to the experiences of our own short lives. Five years is a lot. Twenty years is the horizon to most people. Fifty years is antiquity. To understand how the impact of destiny fell upon any generation of men one must first imagine their position and then apply the time-scale of our own lives. Thus nearly all changes were far less perceptible to those who lived through them from day to day...when the salient features of an epoch are extracted by the chronicler. We peer at these scenes through dim telescopes of research across a gulf of nearly two thousand years.

Winston S. Churchill[1]

---

1 *The Birth of Britain*, A History of English-Speaking Peoples (Toronto, 1956, McClelland & Stewart Ltd.) p.47

Contents

PART TWO

Forward

Noreen worked on this book for many years. On a couple of occasions she asked me to print out a hard copy to proofread. When I would tell her I thought it was supposed to be a genealogy book rather than a history book she would go back to the computer to take out a lot of the history. Her discarded files contain a lot of European history.

Noreen died 1 April 2017 after being ill since suffering congestive heart failure in 2014, probably due to a congenital heart defect. During the last few years of her life she had not been well enough to pursue this work. After she died I felt it would be a shame to trash what she had spent hundreds of hours creating. Accordingly, I have tried to assemble the various files, do a little proofreading, and do the indexing necessary to complete the work. I hope she would approve the result you see here.

Robert Craig

ACKNOWLEDGEMENT

I wish there was some way that I could personally express my thanks to the many court house staff members that provided assistance in this research. Also other diligent researchers and the use of the Family History Libraries. I have been fortunate to have family letters and documents available. I can only posthumously thank my Father, my sister Jean, and my sister Lucille, executrix of our father's estate, who gave me many of the family materials used in this book. Also Paul J. Ayres who let me copy material in regard to his side of the family. And the National Archives for copies of my Grandfather's Civil War Records and those employees who offered personal assistance and interest in helping me regarding them when visiting in Washington, DC. Lastly my beloved husband without whom this would never have been accomplished.

Prolgue

A few minutes past one a.m. of the last day of summer in 1928 an infant female took her first breath. It was in an upstairs bedroom in her maternal grandparent's home at 621 Baker Street in Lansing, Michigan. Did she cry? I do not know but she was lovingly washed by her grandmother with readied heated water and wrapped in a warm blanket. The family doctor, after filling out a birth form, packed his black bag and departed to get some needed sleep in hopes he would get no further calls that weekend. That was not the last family service he would provide. What lies ahead for any newborn is unknown. At some time in an infant's life familiar voices and faces come into focus. Her parent's home at the time was located next door to her father's parents. Her grandfather had built it as well as the one where they lived. She never met this grandfather because he died the year before she was born but she would get to "know" him through family photos, stories about him, the letters he left behind, and her genealogy research. She often spent time during her early years with this Grandmother playing cards, learning how to crochet, and watching her "talk" with her yellow canary named Billy. Each morning Billy took his bath, then she let him loose to fly about the house as she cleaned his cage and gave him new seed and water. He obviously adored her as he would happily continue singing when back in his cage.

A few weeks short of her 5th birthday it was time to enter the big world of kindergarten. The next older sister was put in charge of getting her to school. She and her neighbor girlfriend always walked to school together. With new Buster Brown shoes and a rag rug tucked under her arm she was off for the big event of a half day in kindergarten. The three trekked home for lunch. On the way her sister said now that you know the way to school, you are on your own, but "don't tell Mother." And that's how it was. The next year her Grandmother died in April. It was 1934 and the family moved into her much larger home. Month's later Billy was found dead in his cage one Sunday morning. He missed Grandmother also. A day at a time, year after year, life unfolded. But it was her father's tales that started her on this family research venture.

Her father liked to read for relaxation after a late dinner due to his business. Donning his worn brown leather slippers, he would sit in his favorite chair located in front of a tall walnut secretary his father had built. On a stand beside him sat a radio. It occupied the space where large carved oak doors had once separated the parlor from the living room. He usually read until he listened to the 11 pm news. Then he was off to bed. On the opposite side of the archway was his mother's more petite desk. Located near it was a register in the floor through which heat from the coal furnace in the basement barely warmed the house in winter. The brick exterior however kept it cool in summer but its large windows added to winter's coldness. Lying on the floor by her grandmother's desk was a place to gather some heat while reading or drawing pictures. Occasionally her father would chat about the family ancestry, saying we were Scotch, English, Irish, Dutch and Danish. After my research, others could be added. When the mood struck, he would talk about his father's youthful days growing up in Ohio or fighting in the Civil War. He and his older cousin Seymour A. Ayres had made a trip to Ohio to visit relations there. Seymour was gathering information on the family among which was information copied from a letter written by her grandfather, Charles Wesley. He had copied it from his grandfather's Bible that was among the items when the family moved to Ohio from New Jersey. Charles Wesley's Uncle Enos Ayers remained in Ohio and acquired that Family Bible. Where it is today is unknown. Following is the copied information. Note the surname spelling of Ayers. It was changed by my family to Ayres around the Civil War era.

Thomas Ayers born Aug. 16, 1775
Mary (Ross) Ayers, wife born Feb. 20, 1780
Harriet Ayers born Oct. 18, 1804
Augustus Ayers born Apr. 17, 1807
Henry Cook Ayers born Oct. 9, 1812
William Ross Ayers born Jul. 26, 1815
Mary (Ross) Ayers, wife died Aug. 15, 1815
William Ross Ayers died Sep. 15, 1815
Thomas Ayers died Feb 16, 1864 in Marengo, Ohio

Seymour eventually compiled a family history and gave a copy to my father. At the time I was very young and it was fascinating to read. It was a fairy tale with armored men crossing the English Channel from Normandy to England with William the Conqueror in 1066. My father's interest in reading, his family history stories, and a large collection of National Geographics magazines inspired my curiosity and enjoyment in reading. Separating fact from myth or guessing became a challenge. In the process I found that the John Ayer who died in Haverhill, Massachusetts, and ancestor of many by the name of Ayer, Ayers, and Ayres was not the son of Thomas Eyre and Elizabeth Rogers in Salisbury, England, as claimed. Details of this discovery are extensively covered in Appendix C. Finding three ancestors on the *Mayflower* was a bonus. The accidental find of another branch of the family led me further back into history than one could imagine and back to my studies of the early feudal period in 10th grade world history class. This family history starts with the ruling Carolingians on the European continent that eventually led to an individual who settled in early Massachusetts. It is about kings, earls, lords and ladies, barons and baronesses, dukes and duchesses, armored knights and castles but their lives were not *Camelot* ! What was in their genes that made them seek power, prestige and wealth as they plotted against family members and others often resulting in murder. Yet they were patriarchs of monasteries and abbeys. Was their God fame and fortune so their statues or effigies could lay in perpetuity for future generations to see? I'll never know.

Ancestral Lineages

Carolingians

Carloman[1] of Landen m. Gertrude of Bavaria b. c. 590 - d. 645

Pepin[2] of Landen m. Saint Itta/Ida

Begga[3] m. Ansegisel

Pepin[4] of Heristal mistress Alpaida

Charles[5] Martel m. Rotrude of Treves

Pepin[6] the Younger mistress Bertrada

Charles/Charlemagne[7] m. Hildegard

Louis[8] the Pious m. Ermengarde of Hasbaigne

Lothair I[9] m. Irmengarde of Tours

Ermengarde[10] of Loraine m. Giselbert of Darnau

Regnier I[11] of Loraine m. Alberada of Mons

Regnier II[12] of Hainaut m. Adelaide of Burgundy

Regnier III[13] of Hainaut m. Adele of Dagsbourt

(1) Regnier IV[14] of Hainaut m. Hedwig of France d/o Hugh Capet of Robertian Ancestry

Beatrice[15] of Hainaut m. Ebles I

Adele[16] de Roucy m. Haidouin II de Rameru

Marguerit[17] e de Roucy m. Hugh de Beauvais

Adeliza[18] de Clare m. Aubrey II de Vere s/o Alberic de Vere I

(2) Juliane[19] de Vere m. Hugh Bigod

Bigod

Thurston[1] le Bigot m. Judith de Montanolier b. c. 995 - d. 1041

Robert[2] Bigod m. ?

Roger[3] Bigod m. Adeliza/Ida de Tosny

(2) Hugh[4] Bigod I m. Juliane de Vere

(3) Roger[5] Bigod II m. Ida/Isabella de Warenne

(4) Mary[6] Bigod m. Ranulf FitzRobert of the FitzRandolph Family

Robertian/Capetians

Robert II[1] of Hesbaye m. Waldrada Wiltrud of Orleans b. c. 780 - d. 840

Robert III[2] of Worms m. Waldrada of Worms

Robert IV[3] the Strong m. 2nd Adelaide of Tours

Robert I[4] m. 2nd Beatrice ofVermandois

Hugh[5] the Great m. Hedwige of Saxony

Hugh Capet[6] m. Adelaide of Aquitaine

(1) Hedwig[7] of Mons m. Regnier IV a Carolingian

Angevins/Plantagenets

Ingelgar[1] m. Adelais of Neustria b. c. 845 - d. 888

Fulk I[2] *the Red* m. Roscilla deLoches

Fulk II[3] *the Good* m. Gerberga

Geoffrey I[4] *the Greymantle* m. 1st Adela of Meaux

Fulk III[5] *the Black* m. 2nd Hildegard of Sundgau

Ermengarde[6] of Anjou m. Geoffrey of Gâtinais

Fulk IV[7] *le Réchin* m. Bertrade de Montfort

Fulk V[8] *le Jun* m. Ermengarde de la Flèche

Geoffrey[9] *le Bel* & mistress

Hameline[10] of Surrey m. Isabella de Warenne

(3) Isabella[11] de Warenne m. Roger II Bigod

FitzRandolph

Nominoe[1] de Bretagne m.Argentaela de Brittanyb. 790 -d. 851

Erispoe[2] de Bretagne m. Marmohee de Poher

Daughter[3] m. Gurvand of Rennes

Judicael/Juhel I[4] of Rennes m. Gerberga

Conan I[5] le Tort m. 2nd Ermengarde of Anjou

Geoffrey[6] of Brittany m. Hawisa of Normandy, great granddaughter of Viking Rollo/Rolf the Ganger

Eudes/Odo[7] of Penthievre m. Anges de Cornouaille

Ribald[8] of Middleham m. Beatrix of Lincolnshire

Ralph/Randolph[9] FitzRibald m. Agatha de Brus

Robert[10] FitzRalph m. Helewisa d/o Ralph de Glanville

(4) Ranulph[11] FitzRobert m. Mary Bigod

Ranulf[12] FitzRanulf m. Bertrama

Ralph[13] FitzRanulf m. Tiffany de Lascelles

<u>FitzRandolph Con't.</u>

Ranulph[14] FitzRalph m. Isabel

John[15] FitzRandolph m. Maud de Campania

Randall/Ranulf[16] FitzJohn m. ?

John[17] FitzRandall/Ranulf m. ?

Ralph[18] FitzJohn m. Elizabeth Scrope

John[19] FitzRandolph m. Joan Conyers

John[20] FitzRandolph m. ?

Christopher[21] FitzRandolph m. Joane Langton

Christopher[22] FitzRandolph m. ?

Edward[23] FitzRandolph m. 2nd Frances Howes

Edward[24] FitzRandolph m. Elizabeth Blossom

Hope[25] FitzRandolph m. Ezekiel Bloomfield

(5) Mary[26] Bloomfield m. Obadiah Ayers III

<u>Ayers/Ayres</u>

John[1] Ayers m. Hannah Evered als Webb b. c. 1600 - d. 1657

Obadiah[2] Ayers I m. Hannah Pike

Obadiah[3] Ayers II m. Joanna Jones

(5) Obadiah[4] Ayers III m. Mary Bloomfield

Daniel[5] Ayers m. Elizabeth (?Webb)

Thomas[6] Ayers m 1st Mary Ross

(6) Henry[7] Cook Ayers/Ayres m. Lydia Wood

Charles[8] Wesley Ayres m. Mary F. McNeil

Eno[9] Richmond Ayres m. Clara M. Woolcock

Author[10]

<u>Wood</u>

John[1] Wood m. 1st Margaret

William[2] Wood m. M. Earle

William[3] Wood m. Mary ?

Jonathan[4] Wood m. Peace Davis

Daniel[5] Wood m. Susannah Chase

David[6] Wood m. Rest Macomber

Jonathan[7] Wood m. Martha Reynolds

(6) Lydia[8] Wood m. Henry Cook Ayers

Charles[9] Wesley Ayres m. Mary F. McNeil

Eno[10] Richmond Ayres m. Clara M. Woolcock

Author[11]

<u>*Mayflower*</u>

*William Warren

*Francis Cooke m. Hester Mayhieu

*John Cooke m. Sarah Warren

Mary Cooke m. 1st Philip Taber

Lydia Taber m. Joseph Mosher

Philip Mosher m. Abigail Tripp

Caleb Mosher m. Elizabeth Wilbur

Elizabeth Mosher m. Amos Reynolds

Martha Reynolds m. Jonathan[7] Wood

Lydia[8] Wood m. Henry[7] Cook Ayers

Charles[8] Wesley Ayres m. Mary F. McNeil

Eno[9] Richmond Ayres m. Clara M. Woolcock

Author

*Indicates those that came on the Mayflower

PART ONE

Ayres Ancestry

In the Beginning

Michigan, the place of my birth, is mitten shaped and surrounded by lakes. Growing up in its capitol had its benefits. The State's museum and library was near the grade and junior high schools I attended. School trips there were frequent and many were made on my own. Among the many displays, were maps and models showing retreating glacial ice that scoured out land that filled with melting water forming the Great Lakes and other slender long lakes and rivers in numerous states and Canada about 26,000-13,000 BC. Other continents were also affected by retreating glaciers. One was the European continent where this family history begins. A sad part of my past happened when an unhappy young man started a fire in a men's rest room resulting in a great loss to the State Museum building and its contents. That was in February 1951.

To continue, since most of this early family history begins in France and northern Britain, my initial focus will be on those areas. Any early dating of time can only be approximate. Ages ago the British Isles were connected to the western European continent. There was no English Channel or North Sea. Around 75,000 BC Ice Age glaciers began in Europe known as the Pleistocene Ice Age. There were cycles of cooling and warming with advancing and retreating glaciers. In Europe, ice covered Scandinavia and extended south and east across Germany and southwest to what is today the British Isles. Glacers reached their maximum around 18-16,000 BC, then began their very slow retreat. During ice ages, continental shelves are exposed. Any dry land reaches the glacier's edges. Its water is dark, deep and cold. However, rising waters encourage life to develop. Salmon can ascend upriver to spawn. Birds can nest in marshlands and grains can grow in the marshes which eventually encouraged plant cultivation and domestication of animals. Due to the area's closeness to the north pole, summer daylight is long. Winter days are long but dark. The retreating glaciers left the British Isles a land of tilted mountains, slow rivers, open downs, and wooded valleys in undulating land on its eastern coast making it accessible to friend and foe. It is in Britain's northeast where this story begins.

Yorkshire, Britain's largest county, has a varied topography with its northeasterly Moors and westerly Pennine chain of hills made of carboniferous material. In the southeast are the Yorkshire Wolds of Cretaceous chalk uplands, and a central valley. There are also numerous rivers.

Opinions differ among those who study the history of weather and man. Consensus is that the Paleolithic or old stone age man is divided into lower or early, middle or Mesolithic, and upper, the latter being small bands of hunters and gatherers who improved tool making them less dependent on the earlier use of one's teeth and robust bodies for tools. Once man started using fire in stone pits for heating and cooking, digestion of foods improved. As his digestive system decreased man's brain size increased.

In Northeast Derbyshire there is evidence of occupation in the cliffs at Creswell Crags during the Holocene warm period about 12,000 years ago (BP) or earlier. A cave in Yorkshire has yielded projectile points and a bone head of a harpoon from the Old Stone Age. Around 8,000 BC or earlier, some say 9,000 BC, rising sea levels created the chilly North and Irish Seas and the English Channel. A Mesolithic site was found on the eastern shore of glacial Lake Pickering. In the northern Pennines near Malham a cave held flint trapezoidall microliths used on wooden shafts as arrows. Animal bones there included fox, deer, badger and a large bird as well as fish scales. This was a seasonal hunting camp area. The North York Moors have yielded flint tools and their flakes. Also the area at West Heslerton is evidence of dwellings and occupations since 5,000 BC.

Then came the New Stone Age whose people started growing grain and raising cattle, pigs and sheep. Around 3,000 BC farming and domestication of animals began in the Vale of Pickering, its arable land was in the fertile part of a limestone belt. These people were the first to destroy the forests of North York Moors. They were skilled in making tools and pottery. Their dead were buried in long burial mounds on the moors. Its populace didn't fly around like the Flintstones of early TV but built stone monuments like Stonehenge near Salisbury, England, and the Ring of Stones of Stenness off the tip of Scotland. The East Yorkshire Wold Valley was a place of worship and there the numerous monuments were built near Rudston dating around 3,100 BC nearing the end of the Neolithic era. The tallest monument at Rudston is over 25' tall. Close to Masham in North Yorkshire are the Thornborough Henges consisting of three aligned Henges.

Newcomers brought about major changes with the beginning of making implements of bronze refined from copper and tin, one too soft, the other brittle. They discovered if blended they could be hammered into shapes. It gave them an edge over those still using flint arrows. Another major change in Yorkshire was its burials. Circular mounds of earth called barrows were built over the bodies and often accompanied by bronze artifacts. Most are found in the Wolds, Moors and Pennine areas. The Iron Age brought mostly a change in burials and the building of coastal and inland promontories for defense. Around 700 BC the Iron Age began in Yorkshire. The La Tène culture [Gaels] had dominated western Europe before the people known as Celts arrived in Albion [Britain] about 500 BC from Brittany in coastal France. They consisted of several tribes and built carts, ships, and worked in metal and named the land Britain. East Yorkshire burial sites became square with grave goods consisting of carts or chariots. Between the Tyne and Humber Rivers lived a large Celtic group called Brigantes. Other tribes were the Parisii and Cervetii. The Brigantes' villages were small and they raised the common livestock of today. They were noted for their fortifications. Stanwick was its tribal center. New vegetables were introduced and their clumsy iron plow managed to change agriculture. Eventually they mingled with the bronze metal users who made better weapons and jewelry. Other tribes from Europe came to Britain. Druids came from southern Germany. Belgic Gaul, today's Belgium had related tribes that began their invasions into Britain about 100 BC. They lasted several centuries and like Romans, rode in chariots, made coins, and spread throughout Britain's valleys.

Meanwhile, near Reims in eastern France, a Roman General named Julius Caesar lived there during winters that were unusually warm at that time. In 55 BC he decided to send some spies into Britain to learn about their situation. These spies didn't like facing the Channel's tides and fogs and lost numerous vessels in doing the job. But we know what was on Caesar's mind. They reported back to Caesar that the tribal people were simple farmers either wearing tightly fitted leather and fur apparel or colorful woven attire adorned with gold arm bands and jewelry. Some of the men seeking to conquer wore tightly woven felt clothing, no armor. Over the winter Caesar ordered all sorts of sailing vessels to be made for an invasion the next year. During the invasion many of the vessels that lay at anchor at Deal were wrecked in a storm while Caesar was busy with his marching army.

Centuries of Roman occupation would change Britain with the introduction of previously unknown vegetables, herbs, imported nuts and oils, and enclosed parks for deer. The building of roads increased tradeing of foods but it had little effect on populations living far from a city. Meanwhile Rome found itself in the midst of a bloody civil war. Caesar had grandiose ideas for himself but he had to face his own problems in Gaul/Normandy. He ordered his men to decimate Gaul, killing millions in the process. Now Gaul was Caesar's and he established his base there with his Legions. Then he was off to Rome in 49 BC where a few years later he cowed the Senate to declare him a dictator for ten years, later for life. Nervous Senators gave in to his every whim. Just before his death in 44 BC, Caesar made his grandnephew 18 year old Octavian his heir. Octavian, aka Augustus Caesar, took over Caesar's reign as general and continued Caesar's expansionist policy ruling for 44 years.

After a new millennium arrived, Rome decided to enslave Britain. This conquest began on

Britain's southern border when Emperor Claudius sent a large Legion of young warriors there in 43 AD. Britain was organized as a Roman province with its capitol in Arles, France. It took eight more years to defeat Britain's tribes. Then Romans called the Isles Britannia as part of their Roman Republic. However, it did not include Ireland or Scotland. Small tribal groups lived in different parts of Britannia. One tribe named the Iceni lived in what is present day Norfolkshire. Its king was Prasutagus who, in order to retain some rule over his tribal area, made a land agreement with the Romans. His wife was named Boadicea. The Romans meant to stay and establish a strong military presence but they needed food for its army resulting in heavy taxes imposed on all the tribes. This created hardships for the Iceni and other tribes. Back in Rome, the Emperor ordered his men to rescind the agreement with Prasutagus (Iceni). Hoping to resolve the change, Prasutagus made a will that gave Nero, now Emperor, half his kingdom. Since Prasutagus had only two daughters and no son to inherit his land, his wife received the other half. After he died, Boadicea was arrested and beaten and their two daughters raped. While Britannia's Roman governor Paulinus was leading a campaign on an island off the northwest coast of Wales in 61 AD, Boadicea organized her Iceni and other tribes in a revolt. Their massive army with faces painted with woad, a plant that served as a blue dye until indigo was discovered, destroyed three cities known today as Colchester, St. Albans, and London. Eventually Boudicca was defeated but she did not allow herself to be captured. Some say she took poison but no one really knows. A large monument of her riding in a chariot pulled by two horses is located in a small park by the Westminster bridge on the Thames River opposite Westminster Abbey.

Romans recovered and headed north toward Brigantian territory. The Brigantian Queen Cartimandua was not like Boadicea. She sought help from the Romans to fight her estranged husband, Venutius' army. Things were at a stalemate for the Queen until the 9th Legion under Quintus Petillius Cerialis moved in and ended the couple's reign. Then the Romans built a fort at Doncaster in 71AD and advanced to Lincoln, crossed the Humber River, then headed for the Parisii capital at Brough. In 74AD they defeated the Brigantian's at Stanwick and completed their conquest by 77AD. They hit the jackpot when they discovered iron being smelted. Another Legion was brought to the area to curb insurrections from the Brigantians and a massive wall was built on the northern border to curb Pict invasions.

The Roman occupiers preferred to live in a city [civitas in Latin] with town houses and nice estates. But they needed even more money to support this life style. Controlling so much territory from their barbaric westwardly conquests, dealing with slavery, mobs erupting in Rome over its political corruption, and class envy over lavish lifestyles eventually caused economic chaos so Rome just debased its currency creating inflation. Sound familiar?

After 3½ centuries of Roman rule Britannia's cities had become Roman in food, housing, and custom. The people probably had a better life than those in the coming centuries. Around 426 Romans gathered all the gold, buried some, and took the rest with them to Gaul. What followed was some of Britannia's roads becoming overgrown with trees and its towns crumbling. Britannia lay prey to plundering tribes. Picts came down from the north. Saxons came from the mouth of the River Elbe and settled in the Thames valley. The Angles from Sleswick moved into the Midlands and North which was isolated from the rest of Britannia by thick forests and marshlands. Jutes from the Rhineland inhabited Kent and the Isle of Wight. With this mixture of tribes there were also differences in their beliefs, especially that of Christ. So two French Bishops were sent to Britain in 429 to resolve the discord. One was St. Germanus from Auxere. What little of the area he saw he spoke about positively except being at war with invading armies, some in an ill-assorted alliance. The next year he faced an uprising and the Bishop, being a distinguished general, gathered some local forces and drove the Picksand The people were rural and lived in small villages surrounded by a stockade. Inside were markets for their farm goods and a vulnerable mint for coinage. Their cities names ended in *ing, ham, ton, stowe, and stead*. They took over a limited number of Roman cities that included London and Bath. Britain had no further invasions for the time being but plenty of battles among themselves.

As Christianity gained a foothold, around 523 cooler temperatures arrived due to numerous volcanic eruptions in Central and South America that veiled out the sun's rays. Britain had its worst weather beginning in 535 due to solar inactivity with ocean cycles in constant fluctuations. It ushered in another period of constant wars, famine, plagues, and chaos as frightened people fled westward to no avail. Others went to Breton/Brittany in modern coastal France where the weather wasn't much better. Another decade brought an improvement in the weather. The 600's brought the deaths of Pope Gregory I, Bishop Paulinus, and many kings of whom several were killed. There was little change in the 700's.

On the other side of the North Sea Danish Vikings, who were long distance traders, started the profession of plundering. They first stuck their toe on Britain's eastern shore six years before their men attacked the monastery of Lindisfarne in January 793. The news of it spread far and wide, even to Charlemagne in current France who had been buying woolen cloaks and blankets from Mercia. Early in 796 he wrote to Offa, Mercia's king, complaining about the irregular size of the goods. It isn't known if Offa replied since he died that July.

The weather began cooling again when Mercia's army invaded its neighbor Wessex in 825 and Mercia was overthrown. It's southern and eastern shires came to terms with Wessex's King Egbert creating a much needed bond to fight invading Danes. Ten years later hundreds of Viking vessels rowed up the rivers in southern Britain occupying London. At the time, it was neither a large city nor capitol. For thirty years these hardy and agile murdering thieves invaded and demanded tribute [Danegeld] from the Saxons. Britain's monasteries, churches, and cathedrals were easy picking for the invaders. They were filled with gold, silver, jewels, wine and food for the taking, much that came from the local people paying for their absolution of sins. Town after town was at the mercy of the Danes who killed with their forged steel long broad swords and spears. They were nothing like the comic strip *Hagar the Horrible* and didn't wear clumsy horned helmets. Saxon Kings sought help from each other and formed an alliance under Alfred of Wessex in 849. Alfred had made numerous changes in the army, local government, schools, and laws. But the Danes kept coming and staying longer. The fleets continued the invasions and finding little resistance they began bringing their families. Females were earlier banned from any raids. The men became warrior settlers in fortified towns causing the economy to crumble leaving the old Roman roads, walls, baths, and villas to further deteriorate. Hodgkin wrote: *The schools and monasteries dwindled into obscurity or nothingness; and the kingdom which had produced Bede and Alcuin, which had left the great stone crosses as masterpieces of Anglican Art, and as evidences of Anglican poetry, the poems of Caedmon and the Vision of the Rood, sank back in the generation following the defeat of the Northumbrians in the year 867 into the old life of obscure barbarism.*[1] In January 871 at Ashdown, the Danes clashed with the West Saxons under brothers Ethelred and Alfred. The fight was brutal leaving the Berkshire hills strewn with bodies. It was a victory of sorts for the Saxons but the Danes persisted and the war continued the rest of the year with the Danes getting new forces from home. Eventually the two came to a truce on condition the Danes depart. But they hung around for a few months waiting for tribute to be paid. They also kept their grip on London and eventually gained control of East Anglia, Essex, the eastern half of Mercia, and the southern part of Northumbria which included the towns of York, Lincoln, Derby, Nottingham, Leicester, Brunanburg, Stamford, Maldon as well as London. The names of Viking settlements end with *by, thorpe, toft* and *scale* as in Thurnby and Woodthorpe near

---

1 Hodgkin, *History of the Anglo-Saxons*, vol. II, p. 525

Leicester. Alfred's Wessex men could not be subjugated so the Danes decided to settle on the lands they held. Eastern Briton found itself with these warriors becoming yeomen and tillers of the soil. They ruled by Danelaw and brought their methods for storing cheese and butter. They made dried hung beef and smoked and dried fish. Their staple diet was stews or pottage made of deer, elk, and boar with seaweed, onions, and cabbage cooked in a cauldron and eaten with flat bread. Nothing was wasted. Briton lay divided. Its lands in ruin once again from 120 years of fighting and paying tribute. Meanwhile on the European Continent, its Frankish cousins had blossomed after 100 years of Viking settlements into a feudal society based on Rome's having bound its agricultural laborers and tenants as *coloni* or serfs under proprietors of large estates. Beginning in 1066 Briton became influenced by these Frenchmen that led to another change in life style, diet, and overpopulation. They even brought rabbits for their meals since Britain had none.

Backing up a few centuries, numerous Germanic barbarian tribes had invaded Rome's western territory. Tacitus wrote in 98AD that these Germanic tribes were illiterate and ignorant of the arts. Even though they had some knowledge of agriculture, plundering seemed easier. Their dwellings were built of rough timber plastered with mud. When not fighting or hunting, their time was spent sleeping and carousing. When it came to marriage, they were monogamous with an occasional political exception for a chief. Divorce was almost unknown and in some cases widows were forbidden to remarry. Its military leaders were elected and lost their authority when a campaign was over. They were called Franks.

Edward James in his book *The Franks* explains this complex situation is based on various authors who wrote on the Peoples of Europe. His own findings are based on archeology, language, burials, clothing, weapons and Roman authors up to the beginning of the Carolingian empire. The Salian Franks were one group of undistinguished barbarians from the marshy lowlands on the Rhine. The enforcement of Salic law depended on family and kinship that differed from Roman Gaul in which the state was the enforcer. Salic Law considered women as prized possessions and bearers of children. Females were forbidden to inherit land and excluded from succession to the crown. They were disposable either by divorce or repudiation. Women gained their power at home and in the Church as aristocracy's power increased. The most stable kingdom was later achieved in the Merovingian dynasty established by Clovis I, a petty chieftain, who had defeated Sygrius at Soissons in 486 ending Rome's hold on Gaul. From this came the origin of France. The Franks power developed in Brittany, Burgundy, and Gothia, a later southern province of France whose people survived mostly in Sweden. By 536 Roman Gaul was controlled by the Franks except Brittany and Septimania. These Gauls were called Celts and considered to be tall, fierce, blond haired barbarian Germans located in the north and east of the lower Rhine, the Netherlands, and the northwest part of Germany. They were adept in using ships in their raids as were the Vikings centuries later.

James makes interesting points in his book about linguistics and commonalities often imposed by language. The most direct descendants of the Franks today are linguistically the Dutch and those who speak Flemish in Belgium. Confusion exists due to fixed ideas of what constitutes a people or nation and is overly simplified by historians. He notes that people are not biological entities and commonalities that are often imposed by language, culture, or dress either by conquest or cultural domination. Most people do not refer to themselves by labels which have been attached to them by others. The term Franks in the German language meant *fierce* and later, *free.* James states that perceptions of people are mostly derived from outsiders. The implication today is that the Franks spoke a Germanic language and lived in a defined area in the Roman Empire. The term Franks was not used in Roman writings and perhaps many tribes or groups became collectively referred to as Franks by historians. The term has no meaning and changes with circumstances.

Tribal unification came under the rule of Clovis I (481-511) who led the people into many military campaigns. By the 6th century it was fashionable for Romans to adopt Germanic names and customs as the Franks adopted the Latin language and Roman ways thus changing the meaning of Franks. Neustrians spoke Latin/French and its lands consisted of today's northern part of France excluding Brittany. Neustrians located around Paris preferred to call both lands Francia. The Austrasians were mostly German speaking and came to Neustria from the eastern lands around the Meuse, Moselle and Rhine Rivers. Literature ceased to describe Germanic speaking people about the time the ruling Merovingians were superseded by the Carolingians in the 7th century.

Tribal rulers preferred living in rural villas to city life. They concentrated on controlling Francia's heartland between the Seine and Rhine Rivers. This area became subdivided and the lands divided among their heirs with each asserting their independence. Clovis I's descendants became the Merovingian kings who were at constant odds among themselves and killing family members to gain control. The central government was out of control and of its officials, the most important was the Mayor of the Palace. It is here that begins the Pippinid dynasty. This dynasty descended from a marriage between the son of the Bishop Arnulf of Metz and a daughter of Pippin I, the lay aristocrat and Mayor of the Palace of Austrasia. Arnoulf was a major Bishop, aristocrat, and adviser to Merovingian Dagobert I and became one of the largest land owners in the north. Arnoulf founded a Basilica in Paris and the Abbey of St. Denis where he eventually died. He also founded a castle in Meersburg. The Mayor of the Palace was in charge of the administration acting as the king's deputy. He also represented the nobility's interests. They built their own power as hereditary Mayors. Due to the discord within the Merovingian families it slowly deteriorated and the Mayor of the Palace, aristocrat Pippin of Landen, began the reconstruction of the Frankish kingdom.

Used in this book are passages from *The Chronicles of Fredegar*[1] written in Latin with subsequent translations. They date from 584 to about 641. The Continuations of The Chronicles are based on the *Liber Historiae Francorum* up to the year 721 when they stop. Thereafter The Chronicle was continued up to the year 751 on the orders of Charles Martel's half brother Count Childebrand. Nibelung, Childebrand's son, had the work carried on to 768 when it ends. Its time frame places events close to their occurrence although the dating can be confusing due to the use of statements like "The next year" with no reference.

Pippinid & Carolingian Ancestries

Initially Mayors of the Palace were under Merovingian kings of Austrasia, Neustria, and Burgundy. They became more important than kings by controlling the purse strings and could come from the same lineage and be mayor in the different Frankish areas. Carloman[1] of Landen was an aristocrat[2]. His wife was Gertrude of Bavaria. They had a son, Pippin I or Pepin of Landen[3] who was appointed in 623 by king Dagobert I to govern Austrasia as Mayor of the Palace.

Dagobert's father, Chlotar II, had three sons: Merovach, Dagobert I, and Charibert II. In making Dagobert I ruler over Austrasia, Chlotar II reserved certain Austratian lands for himself. Dagobert

---

1 J. M. Wallace-Hadrill, *The Fourth Book of the Chronicle of Fredegar*, Toronto, Thomas Nelson & Sons Ltd, 1960

2 Superscripts numbers after a name denotes the generation of that person. These numbers correspond to the numbers shown in *Ancestral Lineage*.

3 Oman, Charles. The Dark Ages 476-918. London: Rivingtons, 1914.

I's advisor was the Bishop Arnoulf of Metz, son of Baudgise II of Aquitaine and Oda. Arnoulf first served in the Merovingian court of king Theudebert II, son of Childebert II, of Austrasia. Later as Bishop of Metz under Dagobert I. Three days after Dagobert I married in 625 he argued with his father Chlothar II over the Austrasian lands. Dagobert I wanted to rule all of Austrasia. They agreed that twelve lords would resolve the issue. One was Arnoulf who eventually reconciled the situation by having the father cede most of Austrasia to his son Dagobert I, keeping only the Austrasian territory beyond the Loire River valley in Provence for himself. Things went well for Dagobert I until he started getting greedy, even wanting his father's home. This dismayed Pippin I and the Austrasians. Then Bishop Arnoulf got into politics when Dagobert I's son Clovis II's foreign wife, queen Brunhilda/Baldechildis, ordered the killing of the parents of a friend of Arnoulf. A revolt of Frankish nobles led to her overthrow, subsequent death, and reunification of Frankish lands under Chlotair II who died in 629 and buried in the church of St. Vincent outside Paris. According to his desires, Aquitaine was granted as a subkingdom to his younger son Charibert II. In 632 Charibert II died and his infant son, Chilperic, was ordered by Dagobert I to be assassinated in order to keep all of Austrasia under his control. But the strong aristocracy forced him to make his own son Sigebert III his subking.

Bishop Arnoulf gave up politics and managed to retire in a hermitage located on a mountain in the Vosges desiring only to be a monk and hermit. His friend, Romaric, whose parents were killed preceded him to the mountains where he established the Benedictine Remiremont Abbey. Arnoulf settled into the Abbey where he died around 640 and was buried in the Monastery. About twelve years later he was subsequently declared a Saint and his remains removed to the Cathedral in Metz. There are several legends about Arnoulf's guilt and repenting over his actions while in the political realm.

King Dagobert I fell ill at his villa of Épinay-sur-Seine near Paris. Feeling the end was near, he was carried to the Church of St. Denis on Jan 19th 639 where he shortly died and was buried in the Basilica. Pippin I and some Austrasian dukes got together and decided they wanted Dagobert I's son Sigebert III for their king rather than his son Clovis II. Taking advantage of the situation, Sigebert III asked for his share of Dagobert I's treasure from his brother Clovis II. That involved Pippin and others in settling the request. Dagobert I's treasure was subsequently divided in thirds. One to Sigebert III, the others to Dagobert I's 3rd consort queen Nantechildis, and Clovis II. Pippin I died the next year.

Pippin I's[2] wife, Itta von Swaibia, had founded a nunnery at Nivelles and helped found an Irish monastery at Fosses that was governed by Abbess Dominica. Itta and Pippin I had two daughters and two sons. Their enterprising son, Grimoald I, became the next Mayor of the Palace of Austrasia. It was a time of intrigue, murder, and fighting armies. Sigebert III's tutor tried to displace Grimoald I while Sigebert III and his army were on the move. This concerned the Dukes Grimoald I and Adalgisel who realized the dangers Sigebert III was making for himself. A large battle ensued with some traitors and Sigebert III saw many of his followers slain including Adalgisel's son Duke Bobo. Although Grimoald I was kind and gentle, he had his share of enemies but managed to keep his position as Mayor of the Palace. Grimoald I convinced Sigebert III to adopt his son Childebert as his heir. Grimoald I was deposed and killed around 657 by Sigebert III's brother, Clovis II King of Neustria and Burgundy, who felt the adopted Childebert had usurped the throne. One of Pippin I of Landen's daughters was:

Begga[3] who married Ansegisel C, the second son of Bishop Arnoulf of Metz and his wife Dode/Doda. Ansegisel served king Sigebert III of Austrasia (634-656) as a dux (military leader) and domesticus. Ansegisel was slain in a feud by his enemy Gundewin sometime before 679. After the death of her husband, Begga made a pilgrimage to Rome and upon her return founded seven churches and a convent at Andenne sur Meuse where she spent the rest of her days as Abbess. Begga died Dec 17th 693 and was buried in Begga's Collegiate Church in Andenne. Later she was commemorated a Saint. St. Begga's Feast Day is Dec 17th.[1] Begga and Ansegisel's children were: +1) Pippin II of Heristal, 2) Martin of Laon, and 3) Clotilda of Heristal who married Clovis II'son, king Theodoric III of Neustria. Begga and Ansegisel's eldest son:

Pippin II[4] of Heristal became Mayor of the Palace of Austrasia in 680. His mother had become a Saint and his grandfather was a Bishop and also declared a Saint. Would Pippin be as saintly? Pippin II held Austrasia's purse strings and managed to get into a fight with king Theuderic III of Neustria and Berchar, Mayor of the Palace, defeating them at Testry in 687. Both fled and Pippin II gave chase and subjugated the region of Neustria. Pippin II secured Theuderic III and his treasure, then departed after making administrative plans for its palace. He appointed his young son Grimoald II by his wife Plectrude its Mayor of the Palace. His elder son, Drogo who was married and had sons Hugo and Arnoulf, was given the duchy of Champagne. He died of a fever in 708 and buried in the church at Metz. After the Franks took the city of Utrecht in the Netherlands around 696, Pippin II, at his wife's request, gave Archbishop Willibrord land there for his episcopal see. He had the Church of St. Savior built and rebuilt the smaller St Martin's Church. A cathedral now stands on the latter site. From Utrecht, Willibrord carried out his missionary tasks among them. He also founded a school where the clergy were educated. The school was known far and wide for its high standard of education. Pippin II became ill at Jupille near Liège. His son Grimoald II came to visit him and was murdered by Rantgar while on his way to prayer in the Church of St. Lambert. Grimaold's young son Theudoald became Mayor but that didn't stop the feud between the two Frankish lands. Pippin II died Dec16[th] 714. His 1st wife was the intelligent Plectrude who took control and opened the door for the Franks to revolt. Since Salic law considered women as property, Pippin had taken a 2nd wife, the lovely Alpaida by whom he had a son Charles Martel.[2] The Church also banned divorce. Plectude put Charles Martel in confinement but ultimately set him free. "His diebus Carlus dux a praefata femine Plectrude sub custodia detentus Dei auxilio liberatus est." Plectrude was just trying to keep the position of Mayor of the Palace of Neustria for her grandchildren. Pippin II and Alpaida's son:

Charles Martel[5] was born in August 686 and became known as the *hammer*. Despite Plectrude's efforts, Charles Martel became the Frankish Mayor of the Palace in 715. He initiated a period of military conquests, some previously noted, that continued under his descendants. He waged wars against the Saxons, Burgundians, and Frisians adding to the family's prestige in military strength. The wars in this era were fought when weather was compatible for travel. Martel was liked by his Austrasians. His military adroitness and captured booty kept the Austrasians happy and well supplied. When Charles Martel learned in 725 that Eudo broke the treaty, he hastened his army across the Loire River and sent Eudo fleeing. According to The Chronicles, Eudo decided to get even by seeking the help of the Saracen Abdul Rahman to fight Martel.

It may have seemed insignificant at the time in northern Francia while dealing with their own atrocious invasions, that aggressive Muslims since Mohammed's death in 632 were slowly devouring

---

1 *Butler's Lives of the Saints*, Continuum International Publishing Group, 1995, p 146

2 "Igitur praefatus Pippinus aliam duxit uxorem nobilem et eligantem nomine Chalpaida, ex qua genuit filium uocauitque nomen eius lingue proprietate Carro; creuitque puer, eligans atque egregius effectus est."

the old Roman Empire. The lands around the Mediterranean were flying a crescent flag along with Palestine, Persia, and much of the Byzantine Empire. In 721 Duke Eudo of Aquitaine defeated them at Toulouse forcing them out of his territory. At the time Aquitaine was not part of the Frankish kingdom. They returned a decade later crushing Eudo in the Battle of Garonne river. Eudo and his men fled north to meet with Charles Martel seeking help. Eudo agreed to submit to the Franks so Charles Martel began gathering an army to fight the Muslim horsemen. Paired stirrups had been in use across China from around 477 and eventually spread westward into Europe. It made horse and rider a more effective fighting unit enabling the thrust of the horse to aid the rider in striking an adversary with his weapon. Charles Martel recognized its proficiency. Despite the expense of horses and armor, Charles Martel gathered and trained a large group of men in using stirrups. They were called Retainers, later known as Knights. They had no political power so were not of the noble class. Their lords gave them benefices for their service that included estates (feifs) whose income would benefit their families. Later they were required to take an oath of fealty to their particular lord. However, Charles Martel's retainers would not be used to fight at Tours. With their sabers in hand, thousands of stirrup mounted Umayyads led by Abdul Rahman Al Ghafiqi headed into Francia in 732. Charles Martel had enough time to select the battlefield. He chose a high wooded plain between Poitier and Tours and gathered a massive infantry that slowly defeated Rahman's cavalry. Charles Martel almost lost his life on the 7th day of fighting. Earlier he had sent some infantry to the enemy's camp to free his men held prisoners. Believing they were being plundered, Abdul Rahman and his cavalry raced back to protect their camp. During the retreat Abdul Rahman was surrounded and killed. Charles Martel regrouped expecting an attack. It never came. Abdul Rahman's men were in full retreat. It took two more battles in 736 and 739 to end Muslim expansion at that time into western France. Charles Martel used Retainers in these battles. Eudo died in 735. Upon this news reaching Charles Martel, he hastened across the Loire to Bordeaux and the stronghold of Blaye on the Garonne, and proceeded to occupy the whole area, its cities and strongholds.

Conditions were becoming perilous for Christianity due to change in political and social order. Pope Gregory was most grateful to Charles Martel sending him a letter, preserved in the *Codex Carolinus*, and many costly gifts. Politically, wealthy Counts held the high offices and ruled local courts. They dispensed justice, waged war, and collected taxes. In other words, Counts were the government. It was not an hereditary office but tended to stay in the same family. In 740 harbingers of misfortune in the sun, moon, and stars was the subject on the date of the most holy celebration of Easter. Shortly thereafter Charles Martel fell ill of a fever upon arriving at the palace of Quierzy on the Aisne and there died in the peace of the Holy Church on Oct 22nd 741 and buried at Paris in the Church of St. Denis. His empire was divided between Pippin III and Carloman on advice of his magnates, his sons by his wife Plectrude of Treves, and their half brother Grifo by his 2nd wife Swanhild. Carloman to rule over Austrasia, Swabia, and Thuringia; Pippin over Burgundy, Neustria and Provence. The two brothers put Grifo in confinement and sent Grifo's mother to a nunnery. His daughter, Chiltrudis, followed her step-mother's advice and secretly went over the Rhine to Duke Odilo of the Bavarians who married her without the permission of her brothers. For a while the brothers worked together fighting for independence. Duke Odilo rose in revolt and his army was slaughtered in an ensuing fight as he slinked away. Since Charles Martel had confiscated some church property to pay his army, their was enough land to pay their Retainers. Ironically, Charles Martel supported the Anglo-Saxon Wynfrith, i.e., Boniface and the Church. Charles Martel's son Carloman was a religious man, Pepin III a pragmatic ruler. Carloman donated land for Boniface's monastery at Fulda. The Rule of St. Benedict had been established by Charles Martel in all the monasteries he had founded or reformed. Boniface preached against divorce by mutual consent, polygamy, and incest which at the time was widespread. But when it came to rebellions, Charles Martel could be ruthless. Carloman left his heir Drogo with Pippin III and renounced his position as major domo to live a monastic life at Monte Cassino, a Benedictine community. Charles Martel and Rotrude's son:

Pippin III[6] was a runt. As an adult he was barely over 4 feet tall. But that didn't deter his ambition. He helped his father bring Germanic tribes under their jurisdiction. Meanwhile, back in Rome the Pope and Emperor were still in conflict. The Pope sought the help of Charles Martel but he had died before he could help. Pippin III made use of the situation. By political moves he was ruling like a monarch. His half-brother Grifo escaped from captivity in 747 with the assistance of their sister's husband, Duke Odilo of Bavaria, and attempted to seize its duchy. Pippin III invaded Bavaria and installed Odilo's infant son Tassilo III as duke. Grifo's continual rebellion led him to be killed in the battle of Saint-Jean de Maurienne in 753. Meanwhile, Pippin III had married in 748 his mistress, Bertrada of Laon, to legitimize his son Charles. Then he went after his cousin Drogo's territory. The Holy See was asked to comment on kingship. His opinion was that he who has the power was entitled to be king. So Pippin's family was raised to kingship of the Franks in November 751 ending Merovingian rule and beginning Carolingian rule. The Merovingian king, Childeric III, was sent to a monastery for the rest of his life. The Saxons broke their oath of fealty to their king in 753. Pippin III was furious and gathered his army. They crossed the Rhine and plundered and laid waste the Saxon's lands. The poor Saxon people were grief-stricken and promised they would not rise again against their king and would pay heavier tribute. Pippin III headed for home where news reached him that his brother Grifo had been slain by Counts Theudoenus of Vienne and Frederic of Transjura who also lost their lives. The next year Pope Stephen II traveled all the way to Paris to anoint Pippin III a 2nd time in a lavish ceremony at the Basilica of St Denis making him *patricius Romanorum* [Patrician of Romans]. It was the first recorded crowning of a civil ruler and his two sons by a Pope. The Pope was still having problems with Aistulf, king of the Lombards. Later that year the Pope begged Pippin III to come to his aid. Pippin III's brother Carloman left the monastery to ask Pippin III not to march on Italy. Unmoved, he imprisoned Carloman in Vienne where he died the following Aug 17th and was buried in Monte Cassino monastery. Then Carloman's son Drogo demanded from his uncle Pippin III his father's share of the family inheritance. His request was swiftly rejected and Pippin III went off toward Italy. They made quarters at Saint-Jean-de-Maurienne. Due to narrow passes over rocky heights, his main army could not go forward. The Lombards swiftly took up arms and advanced on his troops. Due to heavy losses, the Lombards withdrew. Pippin's army went on to ravage and defeat the Lombards. Later the Lombards broke their oath and Pippin III headed back to face the Lombards on Jan 1st 756 and repeated the battle giving their estates to the Holy See. Those Papal States existed until 1870 when abolished under a new Italy. Pippin III brought back a Lombard mistress for his son Charles. Then he faced difficulties at home. His army was burning and plundering in Aquitaine. A fortress that burned killed many men, women and children in 762. Year after year his troops faced battles. There were oaths made and broken and giving of gifts and making repairs. In Feb 768 his wife, Bertrada, arrived at Maine-et-Loire. Pippin was informed and he went to meet her, then departed and won control of Aquitaine. Then he returned to Bertrada. Pippin III acquired a fever and departed for the monastery at Tours where he sought help. Joined by Bertrada and his sons, they departed for the monastery of St. Denis in Paris. Realizing he was not going to recover from the illness, he summoned counts, bishops, priests and the Frankish nobility who granted approval of his dividing his kingdom between his quarrelsome sons. Charles to be king of Franks of Neustria and Carloman as king of Franks of Austrasia. Pippin III died on Sep 24th 768 and was buried in the Church of St. Denis in Paris. On Oct 9th his sons were consecrated by the Church and given their kingships. Mother Bertrada's role was trying to maintain a precarious peace between her sons to save Francia from ruin. Carloman was just twenty when he died in 771 leaving two sons who were recognized as lawful heirs by Desiderius, the Lombard King. Carloman's widow Gerberga asked for Desiderius' protection. After Pope Stephen died in 772, Gerberga assailed the new Pope for refusing to crown her sons as kings.[1] Pippin III and Bertrada's son:

Charles[7] was born at Ingelheim on Apr 2nd 742. His first wife, a Frank, bore him a son. He was named after Charles' brother Carloman. At his christening in Rome on Easter 781 he was renamed Pippin (the Hunchback). Sounds like a spinal problem ran in the family. In 768, the year his father Pippin III had split his kingdon, Charles married Desiderata, daughter of King Desiderius, to keep peace with the Lombards. Pope Stephen who favored Charles' brother Carloman opposed the marriage. Three years later after his father, brother Carloman, and Pope Stephen died, Charles at age 29 seized control of Austrasia and became the sole king of the Franks. He ruled like his father and grandfather in military expansion and diplomatic policies. His visions for the territory were large as he tried to repair the Roman road system and build new ones by appointing a road commission and commanding feudal lords to comply with it. It took ten years to have a wooden bridge built across the Rhine River at Mainz. Three hours after its completion it was destroyed by fire. He also attempted to have a canal built to link the Rhine and Danube rivers at their headwaters but was thwarted by cold weather and inexperienced engineers.

His biographer Einhard paints a picture of Charles who was...*large and strong, and of lofty stature, though not disproportionately tall...the upper part of head was round, his eyes very large and animated, nose a little long, fair hair, and face laughing and merry. Thus his appearance was always stately and dignified...although his neck was thick and somewhat short, and his belly rather prominent; but the symmetry of the rest of his body concealed these defects. His gain was firm, his whole carriage manly, and his voice clear, but not so strong as his size led one to expect. In accordance with the customs, he took frequent exercise on horseback and in the chase, accomplishments in which scarcely any people in the world can equal the Franks. He enjoyed the exhalations from natural warm springs, and often practiced swimming, in which he was such an adept that none could surpass him. As to his clothing he wrote: Next to his skin he had a linen shirt and linen drawers; and then long hose and a tunic edged with silk. He wore shoes on his feet and bands of cloth wound round his legs. In winter he protected his chest and shoulders with a jerkin made of otter skins or ermine. He wrapped himself in a blue cloak, and always had a sword strapped to his side, with a hilt and belt of gold or silver...He hated clothes of other countries, no matter how becoming they might be, and he would never consent to wear them...On feast days he walked in procession in a suit of cloth of gold, with jewelled shoes, his cloak fastened with a golden brooch and with a crown of gold and precious stone on his head. On ordinary days his dress differed hardly at all from that of the common people* who wore a shirt, drawers, long hose and tunic, and cloaks and furs in cold weather. He was a great warrior and fought in more than fifty campaigns.

Lombards took up arms again in 772 threatening the papacy. Adrian, the new Pope, sought Charles' help. Charles obliged. He and his men swept down the mountainous Alps, seized King Desiderius at Pavia and this time claimed Lombard lands for himself in June 774. Then he banished the Lombard king to the Abbey of Corbie in Francia and proceeded to Rome where he was welcomed by the Pope. After returning home, he sent his Lombard wife packing since a Lombard alliance was no longer necessary. Northern Italy was now part of Charles' Empire. Charles' many bloody conquests added most of central and western Europe to his domain. In addition to the Lombard region were the southern Pyrenees, Saxon Rhine, Elbe, Bavaria and Corinth. Alliances were also formed with other

---

1 Photos: bing.com.images and Wikipedia

large territories. Conquests required considerable effort and money. Governing vast lands is difficult. Ask the Romans. Then Charles made a disastrous campaign in 778 against the Muslims in Spain. You can't win them all.

One enduring legacy was bringing Briton's Northumbrian scholar Alcuin to his court at Aachen in 781. Alcuin was his chief adviser on religious matters and leader of the palace school. Charlemagne was semi-literate and wanted to halt the threat of illiteracy among his people. The various groups were unable to communicate with each other. Alcuin encouraged the completion of Boniface's work and the Christianization of northern Europe with its concern with the poor, sick, and downtrodden. Herbal medicines, diet, and hygiene were encouraged to overcome the use of charms, amulets, and incantations used in healing. Charlemagne even forbad the stomping of grapes by foot in making wine. Boniface and Charlemagne's approach were very different. Boniface was gentle, Charlemagne's iron fisted. In defeating the Saxons he decreed that any who refuse baptism or behavior unbecoming to the Church was to be executed.

On Apr 30th 783 Charles young wife Hildegard died followed by their infant daughter. She was the daughter of Gerold I, Count of Vinzgau and his wife Emma. Hildegard had given Charles four sons (one set of twins) and five daughters in twelve years of marriage. Einhard wrote: *He paid such attention to the upbringing of his sons and daughters that he never sat down to table without them when he was at home and never set out on a journey without taking them with him. His sons rode at his side and his daughters followed behind. Hand picked guards watched over them...*Charles and Hildegard's sons were: 1) Charles, +2) Louis; 3) his deceased twin; and 4) Lothair. Their sisters were: 5) Adelaide; 6) Rotruda; 7) Bertrada; 8) Gisla; and 9) Hildegarde who died an infant.

It was a clear pleasant day in Jan 6th 793 when out of the east came a long, low, black ship with a tall curving prow and broad red and white sails that plunged onto the beach of Lindisfarne Island off Britain's Northumbria coast. A Christian monastery stood on the island. It contained relics of gold, silver, ivory, silk and linen tapestries, paintings, and illuminated books encrusted with precious stones brought by Benet Biscop who had raided Italian libraries. To them, it was more than a repository of worldly wealth, it was a center for learning and contemplation. Vikings, whose belief came from Odin and other gods, had no knowledge of Moses, Exodus XX, 13 & 15. They attacked, killed, looted, and loaded booty into their vessels and took prisoners for the slave market. This was their idea of redistribution of wealth. Then they vanished into the dark waters of the North Sea. News of this atrocity flew as fast as foot, messengers on horses, or ships could spread it throughout scattered kingdoms. Eventually small Viking groups would settle in Russia to France, the British Isles and Iceland. They preferred to live in sparsely inhabited lands where they could quickly assimilate with locals.

When news finally reached Aachen aka Aix-la-Chapelle, Lindisfarne's monk and ranking scholar, Alcuin, was teaching at Court. Alcuin expressed his dismay in writing: *It is nearly 350 years that we and our fathers have inhabited in this most lovely land, and never before has such a terror appeared in Britain as this that we have just suffered from a pagan race.* He likened it to Jeremiah 50:3 *For out of the north there cometh up a nation against her, which shall make her land desolate, and none shall dwell therein...* And they came, and they came.[1]

Charles main residence was in Aachen [New Rome], where Alcuin lived. Charles liked being around learned people and a good education was provided for his children. It also had warm springs

---

1 The Anglo Saxon Chronicle translated stated: "In this year portents appeared in Northumbria, and miserably afflicted the inhabitants: there were exceptional flashed of lightening, and fiery dragons were seen flying in the air, and soon followed a great famine, and after that in the same year the harrying of the heathen miserably destroyed God's church in Lindisfarne by rapine and slaughter.

where he, his friends and officials, his children and grandchildren could swim. Obviously he enjoyed companionship but disliked marital alliances, so he kept his daughters at home having them study under Alcuin. But that did not stop them from having children. Charles was close to his sister Gisla who was Abbess of Chelles near Paris. She visited him regularly. As a workaholic, his day began with matins, then handling business, followed by noon Mass and his main meal with his family. He never overindulged in food or beverage, but did overlook fast days. He also liked to be read to when eating. After he finished his meal, others in the palace ate in order of rank. Despite claims that he had a hoard of children by concubines, no evidence exists.[1] Shortly after Hildegard died, he married youthful Fastrada by whom he had two daughters. During the next decade his reign was the least stable. Emperor Constantine VI was blinded and deposed by his mother, the Byzantine Empress Irene, who refused to recognize Charlemagne.

Pope Leo III was beaten and driven out of Rome in 799. People had enough of his tyrannical ways. Leo struggled over hill and dale to reach Charles for help. Charles being a devout person helped the Pope return to Rome. In gratitude, on Christmas at Rome in 800 Pope Leo crowned Charles as Emperor over a vast territory. It was the central event of the Middle Ages and said that if it had not happened, the history of the world would be different. Each possessed an undercurrent of material interests and mastery. The Pope was concerned for the land of the Church and a lust for worldly wealth and pomp while Charles began making laws for those under his rule. He eliminated the power of tribal dukes and installed his own appointees as Counts. He also abolished the office of Mayor of the Palace. Sorry Grandad. A grand jury system developed from Charles' re-establishing the Roman sworn inquest. This would serve as a basis for the later grand-jury system in England. Charles then began reversing the decline in trade. He devised an administrative and legal system that united most of Western Europe beginning a feudal system "in which political power was treated as a private possession and divided among a large number of lords" (suzerains) that would last four centuries.[2]

Charlemagne's royal estates were called vills. Each had its own manor house with surrounding lands. Lacking a financial system, vills were too often haphazardly administered by its vassals who often pocketed its profits. Some were even merciless to its peasants called villeins. Vassals vs Villeins. Observing these conditions, Charles decreed an end to negligence and cheating in vills. His vills evolved into a duality in which men would submit themselves as knights to a lord who had resources to support them. Those officials (lords and counts) ruled feudal principalities. All were supposedly to live to serve God. Goods could not be seized nor any servant of the crown, widows, orphans, strangers, or the church molested. Jewish people were also welcome. Incest was prohibited. If a wife was adulterous her husband might leave and she punished, but the husband could not marry in her lifetime. Men were also punished for adultery.

Bee-keeping was regulated, fruit raised, and seventy-four types of seeds and herbs were selected for growing in gardens. Fish ponds were ordered stocked, flowers grown for decorating church altars, and exotic birds kept "for the sake of ornament." Although Charles traveled from vill to vill, due to the largeness of his domain vassals did not always abide by his decrees. Any complaints required a visit and reprimand. Thou shall obey. In the fall of 800 he visited Rome, then in 804 took on the rebellious Saxons north of Austrasia. In 810 disaster struck. Charlemagne's lands were hit by a bovine epidemic killing virtually all the cattle. That created a great loss of milk, cheese and meat for the people. His son Pepin also died that year followed in a few months by son Charles. That left

---

1 Derek Wilson, *Charlemagne*, Doubleday, Ny, NY, 2000, pp. 48-51

2 J. R. Strayer, *Medieval Statecraft and the Perspectives of History*, Princeton U. Press, 1974, p.63,

Charlemagne's least favorite son as heir. Charles began tidying his affairs to assure succession. At a major assembly in Aachen, he crowned his son Louis as joint emperor. Charles' could only hope that Louis could control regional loyalties and rivalry between the aristocrats. Charles then focused on maintaining peace with the Danes and Byzantines. The following map shows his Empire, the inset is after it has been divided among threes grandsons, children of Louis the Pious. Emperor Charles was 71 when died on Jan 28th 814 and buried in Aachen's church basilica. Charles's son:

Louis I[8] the Pious was age 26 when his father died. Although well educated and very religious, he could not retain the loyalty of the aristocracy who were vital to his administration. He also lacked his father's energy and personality that caused the beginning of the disintegration of an empire made up of a collection of tribes who wished to advance their own local positions. Louis I divided the empire among his sons in 817 who were caught up in a family conflict. To resolve that issue, Louis I put his own sisters and half brothers in religious houses and murdered his nephew, Bernard, King of Italy. His father's large domain was now filled with ruffians and pirates rummaging its waterways. Its lands run by tribal groups headed by aristocratic warrior leaders. Their only interest was in social and financial positions to pass on to their heirs. Yet they were also the benefactors of the great Abbeys and Monasteries. The clergy's interest was little different and each managed to govern in their particular area. Louis did keep the fortresses and coastal watchtowers his father erected manned. Louis' first wife was Ermengarde of Hasbaigne who died Oct 3rd 818. His sons were quarrelsome like their grandfather and his brother. Louis died on Jun 20th 840 near Mainz, Germany. His sons were: +1) Lothair I of Italy; 2) Charles the Bald of Aquitaine; and 3) Ludwig the German of Bavaria. Each were dissatisfied with their lot which led to a three year war. In 843 the empire was dismembered at the Treaty of Verdun, the first division of the Carolingian empire which ended Europe's political unity. Charles the Bald received West Francia (modern France), Lothair the middle Kingdoms with the empty title of emperor, and Ludwig the German East Francia. Charles the Bald died in 877 and Charles III (the Fat) ruled France beginning in 884 until he died in 888.

The next year after the beginning of his reign an immense fleet of 700 Viking vessels led by Viking chieftains, Sigfred and Orm, sailed up the Seine River in mid November penetrating the heart of France. They concentrated at first on the Ile de la Cité in the middle of the Seine. They shot arrows, hurled stones and spears, and flung flaming torches setting the isle ablaze. Three days later they turned on Paris. Meanwhile Muslims were striking from Africa into Lothair's domain where they found little of interest. Before the century ended, Magyars came from the east into the middle and eastern lands. These invasions helped speed up the development of feudalism. Small farmers sought protection from their neighbors who had armed retainers [knights]. Louis the Pious' eldest son continues the family line.

Lothair I[9] married 1st Irmengard of Tours and Orleans Oct 15th 821. He became Emperor of the West in 824 and subsequently divided his realm between his three sons: Louis II, Lothair II, and Charles. Lothair I died in Sep 855 at Pruem, Germany. Lothair's daughter:

Ermengard[10] of Loraine married Giselbert, Count of Darnau. Their son, Regnier I became Duke of Lorraine and Count of Hainaut. He died after Jan 19th 915/6. His 1st wife was Alberada of Mons and their son, Regnier II, Count of Hainaut married Adelaide of Burgundy, daughter of Richard the Justicar, Duke of Burgundy and Adelaide Welf (Guelph). Their son, Regnier III, Count of Hainaut married Adele of Dagsbourt who died in 961. Regnier III died about 973. Regnier III and Adele's son, Regnier IV, Count of Hainaut married Princess Hedwig of France, daughter of Hugh Capet, King of France and his wife Adelaide of Aquitaine. Hugh Capet was the first of the Capetian dynasty. His ancestors were known as Robertians.

Robertian & Capetian Ancestries

While little is known about the beginnings of the Robertian or Robertine family, evidence deduces that its origins were in Hesbaye, Belgium, with one named Robert II[1] of Hesbaye (770-807) also known as Rodbert or Chrodobert, a Frank who was Count of Worms and Rheingau. He became Duke of Hesbaye in 732. His wife was Waldrada or Wiltrud of Orleans and they had a son, Robert III[2] (800-834) of Worms, who was also known as Rutpert, Count of Worms and Rheingau. His wife was Waldrada of Worms.

Their son, Robert IV[3] the Strong (820-866) or Rutpert was Count of Anjou and Margrave in Neustria. During the reign of Charlemagne's grandson, Ludwig the German, king of the East Francia, the Robertian family left East Francia and moved to West Francia. Upon their arrival, Ludwig's brother, Charles the Bald, assigned Robert IV to the lay abbacy of Marmoutier in 852 in honor of his defection. The next year the position of "missus dominicus" in the provinces of Maine, Anjou, and Touraine was granted to Robert IV resulting in his having "de facto" control of the large duchy centered in Le Mans, Neustria, displacing the established Rorigonid family. The position was created to curb Rorigonis's regional power and defend Neustria from Viking and Breton raids. In 856 Robert IV had to defend Autun from Ludwig the German following the death of Lothair I.

A revolt in 856 was sparked by a marriage alliance between Charles the Bald and Erispoe and by the investment of Louis the Stammerer with the title of "regnum Neustriae." This tied Robert IV with the early FitzRandolph family member Erispoe who was assassinated on Nov 2nd 857 by Salomon. Robert IV joined Salomon in a rebellion in 858 against King Charles of Provence. That September Ludwig the German reached Orléans and received delegations from the Breton and Neustrian leaders as well as from Pippin II. These actions curtailed any influence of Salomon and Robert IV. Charles the Bald compensated Robert for the losses suffered in this civil war by giving him the counties of Autun and Nevers in Burgundy which greatly enlarged his land holdings. Neustrian rebels had chased Charles' eldest son Louis the Stammerer from Le Mans, his capitol, earlier that year. Robert IV and the Frankish nobles of Neustria with Duke Salomon and his Bretons asked Ludwig the German to invade west Francia. Despite Robert IV's involvement, Charles the Bald made Robert, Count of Anjou in 861. As Count of Anjou, Robert IV was able to defend the northern coast against Viking invasions. Charles the Bald granted the lay abbacy of Saint Martin of Tours to his son Louis in 862. It was a small benefice compared to the kingdom he had received in 856 and lost two years later. The young Louis rebelled and was joined by Salomon who supplied him with troops for a war against Robert IV.

Two fleets of Vikings, one larger, were forced out of the Seine River in 862 by Charles the Bald. The other fleet returning from a Mediterranean expedition converged on Brittany where one was hired by Salomon to ravage the Loire valley. Robert IV captured twelve of their ships killing all on board except the few who fled. He then negotiated with the former Seine Vikings and hired them to go against Salomon for £6,000 of silver. That placed a heavy tax burden on the populace. Vikings made out well in disputes between the leaders of any region. The treaty between the Franks and Vikings did not last very long for in 863 Salomon made peace with the Vikings and ravaged Neustria as Robert IV was defending Autun again from Ludwig the German, this time after the death of Charles the Bald. Then Robert was made lay abbot of the abbey St. Martin of Tours. Robert IV was in Neustria during 865 and 866 when Bretons and Vikings ravaged Le Mans. Robert IV was killed at the Battle of Brissarthe in 866 while defending Francia against a joint Breton-Viking raiding party led by Salomon and the Viking chieftain Hastein. During the battle Robert IV had trapped the Viking commander in a nearby church. Thinking he was not in danger, Robert removed his armor and began to besiege the church. The trapped Vikings launched a surprise attack and killed unarmored Robert IV before he had time put on his armor. His success against Vykings led to his heroic characterization as "a second Maccabaeus" in the "Annales Fuldenses." Salomon met his demise in 874. Robert IV's 2nd wife was probably Adelaide/Adela of Tours. Their sons were 1) Eudo (860-898), and +2) Robert I. The brothers both became kings of western Francia. Robert IV's son:

Robert I[4] (866–923) was also called Rutpert. He was born shortly after his father died in 866. At age 19 Robert I and his brother, Count Eudo, faced a Vikings siege on Paris in 885. On a warm day late in November Viking ships arrived outside Paris and demanded tribute. Count Eudo said no to any tribute even though he knew his army was small. Aboard the ships were a variety of siege engines which they used to attack. After several days they failed to break through the city's walls. Count Eudo had convinced the Parisians to fortify the city. A thirteen month siege ensued with near starvation for the city. Eudo sneaked out one stormy night and went to see the King who in response raised an army and marched to Paris. But most of the Vikings had left Paris to pillage further upriver. Charles III, son of Louis the Stammerer, was crowned monarch in 893 at Reims Cathedral by a faction opposed to Eudo. However, he was a non-effective monarch until Eudo died in 898. Meanwhile, Count Eudo appointed his brother Robert I as Count of Poitier and Paris, and Marquis of Neustria and Orleans, also abbot of many abbeys plus the military office of "Dux Francorum." All those titles did not assure Robert getting his brother's position. Robert I did recognize Charles III, the Simple, who confirmed his appointed offices and expected him to defend northern Francia from Viking attacks. Robert I and Charles III's relationship went well until around 922 when the leaders of western Francia revolted against Charles. On Jun 29th 922 Robert and his men drove Charles into Lorraine and Robert I crowned himself "rex Francorum" at Reims. Charles, not to be outdone, gathered an army and marched against Robert on Jun 15th 923 near Soissons. Although Robert I was killed, his army routed and captured Charles III. Viking attacks on northwestern Europe were always violent. Once the Vikings realized that returning home was folly, they began to establish themselves on easily defended islands at the mouths of major rivers. An ever growing number of men in their long boats began to conquer and rule, rather than plunder. Male Norseman and French women blended as Vikings settled in Francia. These mingled lines of French speaking men with light hair and blue eyes would be those that would invade Britain in 1066 ending the rule of Germanic Saxons and Danes and also leave their mark in France and Germany. The so called Danes in Britain came from Denmark, Sweden and Norway. Norwegian Vikings were urged to marry and settle in Ireland. It was through them that Ireland acquired its name, Eire, an old Gaelic name with the Scandanavian word, "land," added. Dublin was founded in 841 by the Norse King Thurgesius.

Robert I left a 2nd wife, Beatrice of Vermandois, daughter of Herbert I of Vermandois, a Carolingian. Their children were: 1) Adela who married Herbert II, Count of Vermandois, and +2) Hugh, a son who became Hugh[5] the Great or Hugues le Grand (898-956), Duke of the Franks and Count of Paris. With so many Roberts, generation after generation, we know why they were called Robertians.

At his father's death in 923, Hugh refused his father's crown. Hugh's brother-in-law, Charles III, the Simple, had fled his kingdom and sought help in regaining his crown from his grasping brother-in-law Herbert II, Count of Vermandois. So here we have Herbert II a cousin to Charles the Simple and brother-in-law to Hugh the Great. But Charles the Simple died in 929 leaving Hugh to face Rudolph, king of western Francia. The two men came to an agreement in 935. The next year Rudolph died leaving Hugh in possession of most of the region between the Loire and Seine rivers (ancient Neustria) except the Norman territory of Anjou. When Hugh married his 3rd wife in 937, Hedwige of Saxony, the daughter of Henry the Fowler of Germany and Matilda of Ringelheim, quarrels ensued with Louis IV, King of western Francia. Louis began attacking lands held by his mother's father. In 939 Louis IV attacked Hugh the Great and William I, Duke of Normandy. Hugh and his father-in-law, Duke William, and the Count of Flanders supported Emperor Otto the Great against his struggles with Louis IV. Normandy captured Louis in 945 and gave him to Hugh in exchange for young Duke Richard. Louis was released in 946 on condition he surrender the fortress of Laon. Two years later the church council of bishops at Ingelheim excommunicated Hugh who retaliated by attacking Soissons and Rheims. Eventually Hugh made peace with Louis, the Church, and Otto the Great. When Louis IV died in 954, Hugh recognized Lothair as his successor. Lothair then invested Hugh with the duchies of Burgundy and Aquitaine. Hugh the Great died on Jun 16th 956 in Dourdan. Hugh's first two wives died childless. Hedwige had five children. Among them was their eldest son:

Hugh[6] Capet (939-996) was born in Paris. He was age 17 when his father died and he inherited his father's estates but being a minor, his mother acted as his guardian. Taking advantage of the situation, Theobald I of Blois and Fulk II of Anjou took portions of the lands. Hugh's uncle, who was acting as regent until Hugh was coronated the 1st King of France at Noyou on Jul 3rd 987, didn't do a very good job in keeping Hugh's lands in tact. Kings as the time were actually "rex Francorum" (Ruler of the Franks) with limited sovereignty unlike later Capetians who ruled the Duchies and Kingdoms until 1328. Fortunately, most were mature males and only sons when acquiring the throne. They did not have to put up with quarrelsome brothers or disgruntled relatives claiming the throne. Once crowned, Hugh Capet began to push for the coronation of his son Robert since the position was not hereditary. Robert was crowned on Dec 25th 987. Hugh ruled over estates amounting to about 400 square miles. Outside that perimeter there were risks of his capture for ransom. There was a plot in 993 that failed but no one was punished. The various areas were in constant power struggles with different laws, currency, and languages and limited military power. Hugh could rule only with moral authority and influence. When Hugh appointed Arnulf, Archbishop of Rheims in 988, Charles of Lorraine, Arnulf's uncle, captured Rheims and took Arnulf as a prisoner. Charles of Lorraine was a rival of Hugh and considered Arnulf a turncoat. He demanded Pope John XV depose Arnulf. Getting a message off to Rome took considerable time. An event caused Hugh to convoke a synod at Rheims in June 991 to depose Arnulf. When the news reached the Pope he called for another synod at Aachen to reconsider but it met with refusal. The Pope's demand for them to come to Rome also met with protest so he sent a council of French and German bishops to meet at Mousson. The French were stopped by Hugh Capet and his son Robert. The Germans pronounced the deposition illegal. Nothing happened until Hugh Capet died on Oct 24th 996 at age 56 and buried in St. Denis Basilica in Paris. Arnulf was released and restored as Archbishop of Rheims and Robert continued to reign.

Hugh Capet had married Adelaide, daughter of William III, duke of Aquitaine, in 970, and had three known children: +1) Princess Hedwig[7] Countess of Mons who married Regnier IV[14], Count of Hainaut of the Carolingian line; 2) Gisèle, Countess of Ponthieu who married Hugh I, Count of Ponthieu; and 3) Robert II who succeeded him (996-1031) and had wives: Bertha, daughter of Conrad of Burgundy and Constance, daughter of William count of Toulouse. Hugh Capet's daughter, Princess Hedwig and her husband had a daughter:

Beatrice[15] of Hainaut who married Ebles I, Count of Rheims and Roucy and Archbishop of Rheims from 1021 until his death May 11th 1033. Ebles was the son of Giselbert, Count of Roucy and Rheims who died Apr 19th 990 at Reims. Beatrice and Ebles daughter, Adele[16] de Roucy married Hildouin II de Rameru, Count of Montdides and Roucy. Adele died in 1062. Their daughter, Marguerite[17] de Roucy married Hugh de Beauvais, Count of Clermont and had a daughter, Adeliza[18] de Clermont who married Sir Gilbert FitzRichard, 2nd Earl of Clare. Their daughter, Adeliza[19] de Clare married Aubrey II de Vere, Lord of Hedingham. Their daughter, Juliane de Vere married Hugh[4] Bigod, Earl of Norfolk & Suffolk, and had a son, Roger II[5] Bigod, who married Isabel/Ida de Warenne, daughter of Hamelin Plantagenet and Isabel de Warenne. Their daughter, Mary Bigod[6] married Ranulf[10] FitzRobert of the

FitzRandolph lineage. Mary Bigod brings an end to the Carolingians and Robertians in this ancestry. The FitzRandolph family begins with one named:

FitzRandolph Ancestry

Nominoé[1] de Bretagne who was commissioned in 831 as "missus dominicus" (one who regularly supervised the parts of Louis the Pious' domain that he felt were too distant to personally visit). Some have suggested that this meant Nominoé was the 1st Duke of Brittany. Nominoé, a staunch supporter of the deeply religious Louis I, found his job a challenge. On Nov 22nd 845 Nominoé defeated Louis' son Charles the Bald whose men he had lured into marshland near Ballon Abbey to settle some family differences. Two years later Nominoé was defeated in a major Viking raid. He died in 851, the year his son fought against Charles the Bald at Jengland. Nominoé and his wife Argentaela de Brittany had a son:

Erispoé[2] de Bretagne who was born in 794 and joined his aging father fighting their foe Charles the Bald in addition to fending off renewed Viking raids on Brittany. In settling their differences, Charles the Bald granted Erispoé the counties of Rennes, Nantes, and Payz de Retz in Poitou as far as the river Mayenne to be held in fee [a fief]. By switching loyalty this let Erispoé to be able to consolidate the borders of his father's expansionist policy of medieval Brittany. The next year one named Salomon became a loyal follower of Charles the Bald and he and Erispoé were the "dominatores" of Rennes in 853. Salomon became the most powerful aristocrat at Erispoé's court but this apparently did not satisfy him. On Nov 2nd 857 Salomon seized an opportunity to assassinate Erispoé in the city of Cousin as he was kneeling at the alter in a church. Erispoé by his wife Marmohec de Poher had a son, 1) Nominoé, and 2) a daughter whose name is unknown. Erispoé and Marmohec's unnamed:

Daughter[3] married Gurvand, Count of Rennes, who was apparently later implicated with Pascweten, Count of Vannes, in the death of Salomon in 874 who had earlier assassinated Erispoé. One could say Gurvand got even for Erispoè's death. Civil war erupted and the unity of Brittany collapsed as Gurvand and Pascweten divided and ruled the area. Gurvand became the ruler of Brittany. Then he divided it giving the larger eastern part to Pascweten. They too had a falling out over who was to rule Brittany. By late 870's both were dead and Gurvand's son:

Judicael/Juhel I[4] de Rennes became the ruler of western Brittany. Pascwetan's brother, Alan I, ruled eastern Brittany. The two fought like their fathers but found it necessary to set aside their differences to fight a series of battles against invading Vikings. Judicael died in the battle of Questembert in 888 after which Alan ruled as Duke of Brittany. He continued battling the Vikings vanquishing them by 900. Then Alan ruled the Frankish territories. His strongest opponent was Fulk I of Anjou who disputed Alan I's control of Nantes. But Alan seems to have had the upper hand. His power base remained in southeastern Vannes and Nantes. After Alan I died in 907, Brittany was again overrun by Vikings who held the region until 936 when Alan I's son Alan II, who had fled to England, returned. On Aug 1st 939 Alan II defeated the Vikings with help from Judicael II of Berenguer, Count of Rennes, and Hugh I, Count of Maine, in the battle of Trans-la-Fôret and expelled all the Vikings from Brittany. Alan II re-established a new duchy with its rulers no longer called "kings." A network of powerful lords emerged with a loose feudal loyalty to its dukes. This form of feudalism would be brought to England in 1066.[1] After Alan II's death in 952 his son Drogo succeeded him. The duchy under Drogo continued to experience political instability. After Drogo died in 958, two of Alan II's illegitimate sons, Hoel and Guerich, who served as Counts of Nantes, tried to no avail lay claim to Brittany. Judicael and his wife Gerberga's son:

Conan I[5] *le Tort*, Count of Rennes, became the next Duke of Brittany in 990. As Duke he gave the lands of Villamée, Lillele, and Passille to Mont Saint-Michel Abbey on Jul 28th 990. Later they became part of the seigneury of Fougères. Conan I had m. 2nd Ermengarde/Gerberga of Anjou in 973 daughter of Geoffrey I, Count of Anjou and Adele of Vermandois and had children: +1) Geoffrey; 2) Judith who married Richard II of Normandy; 3) Judicael, Count of Porhoët; and 4) Hernod. Conan I died fighting against his brother-in-law Plantagenet Fulk Nerra *the Black*, Count of Anjou, at the Battle of Conquereuil on Jun 27th 992 and was buried at Mont Saint-Michel Abbey. Conan's eldest son:

Geoffrey[6] succeeded his father as Duke of Brittany. Although their reigns were brief, both brought stability to Brittany which included an alliance with Normandy. Geoffrey from the House of Nantes made an alliance with Rollo and Poppa's grandson, Richard I the Fearless, Duke of Normandy, in a diplomatic double marriage between the two houses. Their church sanctioned marital ceremonies were held at Mont Saint-Michel Abbey located at the mouth of the Couesnon River off the northern coast of Normandy. Geoffrey married Hawisa/Hedwig of Normandy, daughter of Richard I and his Danish mistress Gunnora. Richard I eventually married her to legitimize their children. Richard I's son, Richard II the Good, married Geoffrey's sister Judith of Brittany. Since the two areas were often fighting, this alliance was made to provide a safety net for the two families of Brittany and Normandy.

Geoffrey and Hawisa had four children: 1) Alan III of Brittany (997-1040); 2) Evenus (c.998-aft. 1037); +3) Eudes/Odo[7], Count of Penthièvre (d. 1079); and 4) Adela, Abbess of St. Georges. Geoffrey died on Nov 20th 1008 and was buried with his father at Mont Saint-Michel Abbey. His children were minors. His eldest son Alan III succeeded him as Duke of Brittany with mother Hawisa acting as Regent of Brittany. Her brother, Richard II of Normandy, protected Geoffrey's sons by playing a major role in governing Brittany during their minority. In 1010 a peasant revolt spread from Normandy into Brittany. Alan III, encouraged by his mother led the nobles to quash the rebellion. Around age 35 Alan III was named a primary guardian of young William of Normandy, later known as William the Conqueror. Alan III and his younger brother Eudes also had dispute over land. After arbitration with the Bishop of Vannes, Alan had to give Eudes the bishoprics of St. Bricuc, St. Malo Tréguier and Dol de Bretagne. Also the counties of Penthièvre, Goëlo, Avaugour and Lamballe. Mother Hawisa died on Feb 21st 1034 and three years later relations between Normandy and Brittany again became unstable.

Viking Ancestry

Rolf/Rollo, was a Viking chieftain and Hawisa's great grandfather. It is unknown what part of Scandinavia he was born. Some claim he was Danish, others say he was the son of Rognvald and Christian Poppa of Bayeaux, of French aristocracy. Rollo was known in Norse as Rolf, the Ganger

---

1 The order was: Emperor/king, dukes, margraves, counts/earl, barons, and knights. However, it has undergone changes

[Walker] since he was unusually tall. It was said he could not find a horse strong enough to carry him. Stories are well known of Viking raids on Britain and northern Europe. Britain and the territory of the Franks were hit the most. At home these men were raising families and called Norsemen by outsiders because they came from the north. When several Viking chiefs with a large fleet sailed up the Seine river to capture Paris in 885, at Rouen, Rolf a lesser leader, took possession of Rouen before departing for Paris to join the rest of the fleet. But Sigfred, the Viking leader, had already retreated for tribute from Charles III. The Vikings went on to sack Burgundy, then back home and disappeared from the area. "Blackmail" seems to work since it is still in effect today by nations around the world. In 911 Rolf again left the North to sail up the Seine plundering along the way. A large part of France now known as Normandy was attacked by Rolf and his men. King Charles III was its West Frankish ruler and none too happy with Norsemen. So Charles struck a deal with Rolf called the Treaty of Saint-Clair-sur-Epte. It is said that the beginning of Norman history started with this Treaty which affirmed the suzerainty of the King Charles and defined the boundaries of the Duchy of Normandy.[1] Normans had a penchant for law, logic, and patrons of monasteries. These attitudes would eventually come to Britain. Rolf pledged allegiance to Charles and assumed the Frankish name Rollo. He was granted a title for Rouen and its neighboring lands providing he keep the territory free of Viking assaults. Rollo had much to gain by consenting. Whether he was actually considered a Duke or Count is unknown. This feudal arrangement meant Rollo would have to fight for the king when requested. He would need armed men, so Rollo established a class of nobles and knights who pledged military service for their lands. They could sublet their lands to lesser tenants on the same basis. He and his men became Christians, rebuilt the churches they sacked and kept future Viking attackers paid off although he was still somewhat pagan in his beliefs. Hollywood loves the pagan god Thor. After Charles III was deposed, Rollo felt the treaty null and started a westward expansion dividing the lands among his chieftains. By Poppa of Bayeux, his wife of questionable heritage, they had, +1) William the Longsword; 2) Gerloc/Adela, wife of William III of Aquitaine; and possibly 3) Kadlin, a daughter.

It is also said he had a second wife, Gisela, daughter of Charles III. Before aging Rollo died around 931, he requested to be buried in Rouen's Cathedral. More than one statue exists of Rollo. There is one in Rouen, France, with its replica in Fargo, ND. Rollo left Normandy with an excellent army and societal rules. His descendants would also change England dramatically. Rollo and Poppa's son:

William the Longsword, Hawisa'a grandfather, was a pagan Norse Chief named Vilhjálmr Langaspjót. In 912 both he and his father, Rollo, were baptized by the Archbishop of Rouen. Before his father died William assumed his leadership role as principes [Norse chieftain] in 927. Six years later he accepted Raoul, who was trying to assert his authority in Northern France, as King of Western Francia. A good gesture deserves a good deed so Raoul made him a lord over many of Brittany's lands. Resistance was led by Alan Wrybeard, Duke of Brittany and Count Berenguer of Rennes but ended with Wrybeard fleeing to Britain. Count Beranguer sought reconciliation. William then married Luitgarde of Vermandois in 935 daughter of Herbert II. Her dowry gave him even more lands. At the same time he also arranged a marriage for his sister Adela/Gerloc with William, Count of Poitou. These alliances were with leaders his father Rollo had opposed. After that he faced a Norman rebellion due to claims that he was becoming too timid a leader. His wife Luitgard had no children by William. His mistress Sprota, a Brittany captive who was bound to William in a Danish

---

1 Churchill, p. 143

marriage, was pregnant and he sent her to Fécamp where a son named Richard was born. After the rebellion with the Norman rebels was settled, William was told of the birth of a male. When he met his infant son, he kissed Richard declaring him his heir and sent him to be raised in Bayeux. In 939 William attacked Flanders only to have its Count Arnulf of Flanders and King Louis of France retaliate. It was all about capturing castles. For this venture he was excommunicated for destroying several estates of Count Arnulf. He made peace with King Louis in 940 and the lands his father had given him were returned. Arnulf's revenge came on Dec 17th 942 when William was ambushed and killed by Arnulf's supporters while attending a peace conference at Picquigny on the Somme to settle their differences. Sprota then married a wealthy miller named Esperleng and bore a son named Rodulf. William the Longsword and his father's 14th century funerary monuments are in the Cathedral of Rouen, France. William and Sprota's son:

Richard I of Normandy aka Richard the Fearless, Hawisa's father, became Duke of Normandy in 942 after his father William was killed. He was a lad about age ten or less. King Louis IV seized Normandy and took Richard from his mother, Sprota, and put him in confinement at Lâon under the care of the Count of Ponthieu. Then Louis divided Longsword's lands giving the Robertian Hugh the Great lower Normandy. With help from family friends Richard escaped from Lâon. In 946 he agreed to "commend" himself to Hugh, now Count of Paris. Then Richard allied himself with Norman and Viking leaders, drove Louis out of Rouen, and took back Normandy by 947. Most children had no teen years to enjoy. Theobald I, Count of Blois, attacked Richard at Rouen in 962 but his Norman army defeated Theobald who fled for safety. Lothair, King of the West Franks, moved to prevent any further war between the two. Richard I concentrated on Normandy and less in participating in Frankish politics and petty wars until his death in 996. Instead of expanding the Norman Empire, he stabilized it and united his followers into a cohesive and formidable principality. Richard also used marriages to build the strong alliances noted earlier. Richard I's first marriage in 960 to Emma, daughter of Hugh the Great of France and his wife Hedwige of Saxony, connected him to the Capet family. Emma died in 968 childless. By his Danish wife Gunnora, they had children: 1) Richard II the Good, Duke of Normandy who m. Judith daughter of Conan I of Rennes & Ermengarde of Anjou; 2) Robert, Archbishop of Rouen, Count of Evreux; 3) Mauger, Earl of Corbei; 4) Emma of Normandy, wife of two kings of England: (Ethelred II & Cnut the Great, son of Sweyn Forkbeard of Denmark and England's Northumbria, Mercia and Wessex[1]); 5) Maud of Normandy, wife of Odo II of Blois, Count of Blois, Champagne and Chartres; +6) Hawisa[4] who m. Geoffrey, Duke of Brittany; 7) Papia of Normandy; and 8) William, Count of Eu. By the end of Richard I's reign in 996 important landholders were in feudal tenure. Hawisa of Normandy and Geoffrey Duke of Brittany's third and youngest son:

FitzRandolph Continued

Eudes[7] or Odo, Count of Penthièvre, was born about 999. After his brother, Duke Alan died in 1040, Eudes became the ducal regent for Alan's young son Conan II and took custody of him. When Conan II became old enough to be Duke of Brittany a conflict arose because Eudes refused to relinquish his power but Conan's supporters freed him in 1047. Ambitious Conan II was fighting the

---

1 Social structure divided Northumbria from Kent, East Anglis from the west Midlands, and Danelaw from the rest of England.

Geoffrey III, Count of Anjou, an enemy of William, Duke of Normandy. Eudes was on Geoffrey's side. In Feb 1054 Eudes fought on the side of King Henry I of France in the Battle of Mortemer against Duke William. Even though William won Eudes kept his alliance with Geoffrey III of Anjou. Sometime afterward, Eudes granted land in Beauvais, Picardy, to the Abbey of Angers Saint-Aubin which his wife and five sons witnessed. Around 1056 Conan II acquired the upper hand in Brittany and captured his uncle Eudes in 1057 who was put in chains in a prison. But Eudes oldest son Geoffrey continued the fight. In the midst of these struggles, Conan II and Geoffrey resolved their differences in 1062 and Eudes was finally set free. Meanwhile Brittany was facing threats from Duke William of Normandy and the Normans who were living in Brittany. This led to the Breton-Norman war between the two starting in 1064.

Conan II had a legitimate claim for the title of Duke of Normandy which concerned Duke William of Normandy. Since William was planning an invasion of Britain, he told those Normans living in Brittany and Anjou to stop their attacks. So Conan II used the time to consolidate his authority by neutralizing Anjou and Maine. Then he went after Normandy in William's absence in 1066. During a siege on Angers, Conan II was found dead of poisoning. He was succeeded by his sister as Duchess of Brittany which was now divided into six independent regions. She had married Hoèl of Cornouaille who ruled as Duke over their personal lands. However, Hoèl also had bigger ideas and reignited the feud between Brittany and Normandy. Meanwhile Eudes helped Duke William in his quest for Britain by training and equipping soldiers for William's army. Some were professionals comprised of light and heavy cavalry, archers, crossbowmen and axemen. He also conscripted spearmen. They were put on ships under the command of Eudes' sons Alan Rufus, Stephen, and Brien and set sail to join William's Norman forces at a staging point to get ready to cross the English Channel. Eudes felt he was too old to join in the invasion of Britain.

Eudes had married Agnes de Cornouaille, daughter of Alan Cognairt, Count of Cornouaille. Among his children, probably not all were hers, were: 1) Geoffrey I, Count of Penthièvre; 2) Alan Rufus, 1st Earl of Richmond with most of his manors in East Anglia; 3) Guillaume/William who went to Switzerland to serve the Holy Roman Emperor and helped suppress the revolt of Agaunum (Saint-Maurice-en-Valaisz) receiving a castle for his service; 4) Robert, priest in Yorkshire; 5) Richard, canon of Bayeux; 6) Stephen, Count of Tréguier who married Havise of Guingamp; 7) Bardolf, lord of Ravenstock in Britain and ancestor of the FitzHugh family; +8) Ribald[8], lord of Middleham; 9) Matilda, wife of Walter D'Aincourt; and 10) Brien, Earl of Cornwall. Eudes died about age 80 on Jan 7th 1079 in Cesson-Sévigné, a suburb of Rennes. He was buried in Saint-Brieuc Cathedral in Brittany.

Before the arrival of Duke William and his supporters, a manorial system existed in Anglo-Saxon Britain with its own form of government, especially in southern Wessex. It's king, Edgar the Peaceful (959-975) was sixteen when he became king of the House of Wessex. His policy of peace was mostly non-interference except when Saxons ill treated some Yorkshire merchants. Peace allowed him to make changes in England's administrative structure by dividing Britain into shires, each of which were divided into hundreds. His laws were used by future generations. Edgar encouraged trade and protection of currency. As a believer of monasticism, he was severe on those that withheld their church tithes. The head of a manor was based on personal terms with his men who, if they chose, could leave his manor for another and transfer any land. Taxes were based on land ownership and the number of hides owned which included making a list of the manors and its tenants. Commissioners followed up by visitation to assess any changes. Some of this would change under Duke William.

The Ely Inquest existed before the Domesday survey was taken in 1086. It consisted of many questions asked by commissioners which included: the manors name, who held it in the time of

Norman Edward the Confessor (1043-66), who holds it now, how many villeins [wealthy unfree peasants who pay rent], the number of slaves, freemen, and sokemen [a freeman owing dues to the lord for his land], the number of cottars [unfree peasants holding land up to 5 acres], the number of ploughs owned by the lord and those belonging to peasants, the number of carucates of woodland, meadow, and pasture, the number of mills and fisheries, the amount added or taken away from the estate, its former and present worth when granted, and lastly whether more taxes were taken in the past than is being taken currently.

Unlike Saxon policy, William I invoked a harsh feudal system based on military service. Not all countries practiced the same form of feudalism, a system of rights and obligations. Initially landowners who showed William no opposition kept their lands. Castles were ordered built everywhere that served as William's military outposts. They often resulted in the destruction of housing in some villages and exploitation of the people. The castles were nothing more than wooden houses built on a mound. Northern England's Saxon lords were defiant and sent their sons to French monasteries for an education. Then William and his army headed north leaving a trail of devastation. Land north of the Humber River was now in William's hands. After a rebellion in 1069, William I reorganized the institutions of church and state and redistributed the lands. The tenants were mostly a large miscellaneous class with less than 180 holding estates whose value was more than £100 per year. About half of the land was granted to ten of William's most trusted men from Normandy, two from Brittany. Among them was William of Warenne and Count Alan Rufus from Brittany of the FitzRandolph lineage and one of the King's counselors. Some of the most powerful men of Brittany were Richard Count of Evneux, William fitz Osbern, Robert of Beaumont, Hugh of Grantmesnil, William Malet and Ralph of Tosny. Tosny's daughter married Roger Bigot. William Warren married Isabel, widow of Robert of Beaumont, daughter of Hugh, Count of Vermandois.[1] Intermarriages were important in retaining wealth and power.

It took him twenty years to Normanize England at the point of a sword. Life never was idyllic and living conditions for even the richest were poor. Although food was plentiful, it was not very appetizing. There was ample meat and fish served with cabbage, turnips, carrots, onions and legumes for vegetables. The King did like a particular stew. Thanks to the Romans they had apples and wine or mead. He also imposed a 11 pm curfew that required all fires doused and lights extinguished or shuttered. Normans spoke in their native tongue. England's people spoke in different tribal languages. Norman attitude about language was: *For unless a man knows French, one accounts him little.* It wasn't until Richard I became King (1189-1199) that grammar schools began teaching in English.

William I still had to deal with the King of France over his lands in France. When William decided to separate his Norman and English land holdings, turmoil erupted among the barons who also owned land on both sides of the English Channel. They found themselves owing allegiance to two overlords, so they played one against the other. Even William's sons disliked the division. Fraught with problems abroad with his sons, in 1087 he and his men headed for the town of Mantes. Fire broke out amid the sacking and William's horse stumbled in burning ashes and threw William off his back. He was taken to Rouen and lay in summer's heat fighting his injury. Just before he died, his sons came to him and he appointed William Rufus to succeed him and gave Robert Normandy. His youngest son Henry received £5,000 of silver. Early morning Sep 9th William I and his power died with him. How would his English subjects and its subdued nearby areas react? Time held the answer.

---

1 David C. Douglas, Ed., English Historical Documents, 1042-1189, NY, Oxford Univ. Press, 1953, p.23

Normandy had been undergoing a religious revival with the building of Benedictine monasteries. Within their walls were notable scholars and administrators. Baronial families were their benefactors. After arriving in England the barons continued this practice with the building of monasteries and cathedrals everywhere. William's Norman noble friends were like little provinces with the king's officers heading each area. Everyone owed someone else a form of service. The lords or barons had to provide a set quota of knights to serve the king at his command. Each knight was given enough land with its revenue to support himself for which he was also to provide the baron forty days of military service known as knight's fees. Revenues from Knight's fees went to the King. Manor lands consisted of petty farms, a common forest and pasture lands, a church, and the lord's demesne lands. The farm lands were defined strips that were planted in spring and fall, one left fallow. They were plowed and planted by peasants known as villeins or serfs who first had to maintain their lord's choice property. In addition they were subject to a head tax, rent, and a percentage of all their produce. Fees were also charged for using the village mill, wine press, brewery, oven, and occasionally well water. These hard working individuals were mostly uneducated and very superstitious. While these oppressed individuals toiled, nobles and knights played at warfare, adventure, and sport. Waging war on each other was for a love of fighting. To curb these war like activities, the Church intervened prohibiting nobles and knights from fighting from Wednesday vespers to sunrise on Monday and from Christmas to Epiphany. They also had to allow the peasants time to plant and harvest. Don't bite the hand that feeds you. With the Pope's blessing, William had focused on the Church. Since Saxons were lax in paying tithes, it became an excuse to destroy or remodel their churches. Normans were given any high post in any Church held by a Saxon. At the time the populace was more concerned about life after death which added to the Church's coffers. The price of salvation was one tenth of all wood, corn, milk, eggs, and any increase in their livestock. A law enforcing tithing had been passed in the 9th century which lasted until 1836 when payment was changed to rent, then cash in 1936. Business was good for the Church. By 1087 seven new cathedrals were under construction.

Eudes son, Alan Rufus, had accompanied Duke William for which he received about 100,000 acres lying in northern England. These lands had been under the control of the Saxon Ghilpatric during the reign of Edward the Confessor (1042-1066). Alan Rufus was the First Earl of Richmond and built a wooden tower on a mound [motte] linked to land within an inner wall [bailey]. By 1086 Alan had granted to his brother Ribald several estates in Yorkshire including Middleham, Bolton, Spennithorne, Thornton, Watlass, Scrastone, Havogswell, and two others. Spennithorne consisted of a manor and 8½ carucates. Middleham consisted of a manor and 5 carucates[1] and other lands. Middleham's motte-and-bailey castle was located 500 yards southwest of a site known as William's Hill. It's purpose was to guard Coverdale and to protect the road from Richmond to Skipton. Both estates became prominent in the FitzRandolph family history. Alan Rufus died in 1089 without children. His brother:

FitzRandolphs of Middleham

Ribald[8], Lord of Middleham, married Beatrix, daughter of Norman Ivo de Taillebois and his 1st wife whose name is unknown. Taillebois is a small hamlet in Saint-Gervais de Briouze, Calvados. Ivo sold land at Villers to the Abbey of Saint-Étienne, Caen, where William the Conqueror is buried in

---

1 An old English land measurement that varied from 60 to 160 acres.

its church. He also donated a Church of Christ in Calvados attested by his brother Robert. Ivo had participated with Duke William for which he received many lands with subsequent titles. He became High Sheriff of Lincolnshire shortly after the conquest. In the Domesday Book Ivo appears as a tenant-in-chief holding Bourne and many of its manors. In 1071 Ivo led an army with William I and besieged the Isle of Ely where the rebel leader Hereward *the Wake* was based. Hereward was caught and imprisoned. Ivo's 2nd wife was Lucia of Bolingbroke, daughter of Turold, Sheriff of Lincolnshire. It was her first of three marriages. Ivo's brother, Ralph, was High Sheriff of Bedfordshire who died shortly before 1086 and was succeeded by Ivo. King William Rufus further endowed him with the lands of Ribblesdale and Lonsdale in Cumbria on the border with Scotland and the Barony of Kendal consisting of a sizable portion of Westmoreland. Ivo died in 1094.

Ribald and Beatrix had at least three sons: +1) Ralph/Randolph b. 1080; 2) Hervey; and 3) Henry. After Beatrix died, Ribald gave Abbot Gosfrid perpetual alms for the soul of Beatrix. Aging Ribald disposed of his lands, then became a Monk in the Benedictine Abbey of St. Mary's in York where he died in 1121. It was the richest abbey in the north of England. William Rufus [King William II] endowed it in 1088 with Alan Rufus laying the foundation stone. The ceremony was attended by bishop Odo of Bayeux and Archbishop Thomas of Bayeux. The monks had come to York from Lastingham in Ryedale in the 1080s as noted in Domesday. After a dispute and riot in 1132 at St Mary's Abbey, 13 monks were expelled for their attempts to return to the 6th century Rule of St Benedict. The Archbishop of York provided them with land in the valley of the River Skell, a tributary of the Ure River. After enduring the harsh winter of 1133, they applied to join the Cistercian order at Fountains Abbey in 1135 but subjected themselves to Clairvaux Abbey in France under the rule of St Bernard. Ribald and Beatrix's son:

Ralph[9] or Randolph FitzRibald married Agatha, daughter of Robert de Brus or Bruis, 1st Lord of Annandale in Yorkshire East Riding. Little is known about Ralph FitzRibald. It was his wife, Agatha, who inherited the Lordship of Allewic, Hartness.

Ralph's father-in-law, Robert de Brus, had two wives named Agnes: Agnes, daughter of Geoffrey Bainard, Sheriff of York; and Agnes, daughter and heiress of Fulk de Pagnall, Lord of Carleton, North Yorkshire. He also had two sons: Robert, 2nd Lord of Annandale, and Adam, Lord of Skelton. De Brus' father was a landowner in Normandy. Some historians claim that Robert may have come from Brix, Manche, near Cherbourg in the Cotentin Peninsula and came to Britain after King Henry I of England's conquest of Normandy and that de Brus' presences and absences at Henry's court coincide. De Brus went to Scotland where King David I made him Lord of Annandale in 1124 but apparently he never lived there. De Brus was granted 80 manors in Yorkshire and later 13 manors around Skelton. King David of Scotland became embroiled in King Stephen and Matilda's fight for the English throne. He entered England to support his niece Matilda's claim to the throne and to enlarge his kingdom. David had acquired the Scottish throne due to help from King Henry I. Matilda was Henry's daughter and he wished her to succeed him and in 1127 made his barons and magnates take an oath to that effect. Some were opposed because she had married Geoffrey V, Count of Anjou. Once Henry I died, differences erupted in war and King David invaded England. De Brus was on King David's side until David refused to withdraw his troops. Emissaries accomplished little and on Aug 22nd 1138 the Battle of the Standard or the Battle of Northallerton began at Cowton Moor near Northallerton in Yorkshire. After a 3½ hour fight beginning at sunrise, King David's troops retreated. Due to Matilda's position, there were negotiations that ended with King David's son, Henry, given the lands of Northumberland, Huntingdon and Doncaster. King David kept Carlisle and Cumberland with the promise to remain loyal to Stephen. The resources of northern England benefitted David. The Pennines lead mines gave David silver from which he made his own coins.

Robert De Brus died in 1142 and King David did not get involved in the later disputes. David's son Henry died in 1152 and David the next year. King Stephen died in 1154. These deaths brought 14 year old Malcolm IV of Scotland to face young Henry II of England.

In the interim, Ralph FitzRibald founded an Augustinian Priory in 1129 at Giseburne, York. It was dissolved in 1540.[1] At Middlesburgh, York, he also founded a Benedictine Cell around the same time. Its monks were dependent on the Benedictine Abbey at Whitbey, York, built in the early 1100's.[2] The importance of the early church at Middleburgh, later known as Middlesburgh Priory, a Benedictine Cell, is indicated by the fact that in 1452 it possessed four altars.[3] Ralph FitzRibald and Agatha's children were: +1) Robert, 2) Agnes, 3) Ribald, and 4) Randulph. Their eldest son and heir:

Robert[10] FitzRalph was born in 1110. He was about age 60 when he started to build a new castle at Middleham. It was a structure 180x210 feet with a deep moat overlooking the Ure River between Masham and Leyburn. Its Norman keep was used as a fortress. Most early castles's interiors were dark, damp and cold, its floors covered with rushes. Needless to say, rushes invited an unhealthy situation with the need of constant replacement. A fortress was not princely enough for the Neville family who later added its towers with connecting buildings. The early keep became isolated in the center. Now in ruins, the building had a magnificent hall and chapel with most of the remaining walls of great height. A large gateway on the north side consisted of a circular arch similar to the gateway of Easby Abbey. Its quadrangle is almost fully dark in an already dark interior. Despite its early gloominess, it became the fairest castle in Richmondshire. Later it was home to the powerful lords Salisbury, Warwick, Richard Duke of Gloucester, and King Richard III (1483-1485) whose son Edward was born and died in the Prince's tower, the round southwest tower. After Richard III was killed at Bosworth in 1485, Henry VII (1485-1509) claimed Middleham castle. It was partially destroyed by Oliver Cromwell (1563-1568) and the later Tudors let it fall into disrepair. James I (1603-1625) granted it to Sir Henry Linley in 1604 who occupied it until he died in 1610. His daughter Jane, wife of Edward, 2nd Viscount Loftus, occupied it until 1644 when it became a prison during England's civil war (1642-1651). Two years later Parliament ordered the east wall destroyed with most of its wall walks, leaving it a shell. It was sold in 1662 to Edward Wood, then again in 1889 to the Masham family. In 1925 it became an English Heritage site and is presently open to the public.

Robert FitzRalph married Helewisa, daughter of Ralph de Glanville, Lord of Coverham and Lord Justiciar of Henry II. They were known to have three daughters and three sons. In 1190 Helewisa founded an Abbey at Swainby whose monks later moved to Coverham or Corham Abbey in Yorkshire founded by her son Ranulf FitzRobert, Lord of Middleham, in 1214/5. Helwisa was originally buried at Swainby but Ranulph had her re-interred in the Chapter house at Coverham. It was in use until Henry VIII sold it in 1536 to Humphrey Orme, MP, and it too quickly fell into ruins. Portions of the church remain and several old stone effigies from the reigns of Henry III and Edward II (1216-1307) are there. It is not accessible to the public but its ruins can be seen from the town's old medieval churchyard. Son Ranuph continues later and Helewisa de Glanville, wife of Robert FitzRalph, ancestry follows:

---

1 Elizabeth I granted it in 1562 to Sir Thomas Chaloner valued at £14,246.10s..

2 It was granted to John, Earl of Warwick, in 1465.

3 Elizabeth I granted it in 1564 to Thomas Reve valued at £433.13.04

Glanville/Valognes Ancestry

Ranulf de Glanville, father of Helewisa, was born at Stratford in Suffolk around 1112. Nothing is known of his parents or early life. He became Sheriff of Yorkshire, Warwickshire and Leicestershire in 1163 to 1170 when he was removed from office for corruption with the majority of High Sheriffs. An Augustine Priory was established by Ranulph in 1171 at Butley in Suffolk.[1] In 1173 he was appointed Sheriff of Lancashire and custodian of the honour of Richmond. When he was Sheriff of Westmorland, Ranulf was a major English leader at the small Battle of Alnwick on Jul 11th 1174 in which the King of Scotland, William the Lion, had tried to regain his inherited title as Earl of Northumbria that Henry Plantagenet (1154-1189) rescinded. Sorry, no Scots allowed. This was while Henry II was busy fighting his rebellious sons. The next year Ranulf was reappointed Sheriff of Yorkshire and became justice of the king's court and a justice itinerant in the northern circuit in 1176, then Chief Justiciar of England in 1180. He assisted Henry II to complete his famous judicial reforms although many had been carried out before he came into office in 1154. Glanville became Henry II's right-hand man and during Henry's frequent absences Ranulf was in effect regent of England. He became custodian of Queen Eleanor in 1176 when she was confined to her quarters in Winchester castle. When Henry II died in 1189, Glanville was removed from his office by Richard I (1189-1199) on Sep 17th 1189 and imprisoned until he had paid a ransom, according to one authority, of £15,000. The legal treatise of Tractatus de Legibus et Consuetudinibus Angliae known as "Glanville" which concerned the Laws and Customs of the kingdom of England and Methods of Trial in operation was written during the reign of Henry II. It is traditionally assigned to Ranulf de Glanville, justiciar, but there is no certainty that he was the author of the work. This work was related to the initiation and procedure of litigation and trial in both in civil and criminal law and its relevance or validity to a 12th century form of proof/witness earlier introduced by Norman Henry II.

Glanville founded two abbeys in Suffolk: An Augustine Priory at Butley[2] in 1171 [only the gatehouse remains] and St. Mary's Abbey at Minsmera in 1182. In 1363 it was transferred to Leyestone/Leiston on the coast of Suffolk.[3] Only its chapel remains. He also built a leper hospital at Somerton, in Norfolk. Ranulf de Glanville married Bertha de Valoins, daughter of Theobald de Valoins, Lord of Parham, Suffolk. Their daughters were: 1) Maud/Matilda who married Sir William de Auberville; 2) Mabel/Amabella who married a de Arden; and +3) Helewisa who married Robert FitzRalph; and sons: 4) William and 5) Osbert de Glanville.

Ranulf de Glanville died in 1190 at Acre, Palestine, shortly after his release from prison, from a sunstroke when on the Third Crusade with Richard I. After his death, son William de Glanville held the wardship to Wensleydale forest with its common pasture for his nephews, sons of Helewisa, until she was deceased. Ranulf de Glanville's wife and Helewisa's mother, Bertha's family history dates back to Peter de Valognes/Valoines:

Peter or Pierre de Valognes was a nephew of the Conqueror and from a Norman baronial family. He probably did not initially fight with Duke William because the lands granted in the counties of

---

1 Henry VIII granted it in 1545 to William Forth.

2 Henry VIII granted it to William Forth in 1545.

3 Henry VIII granted it to Charles Bryndon, 3rd Duke of Suffolk in 1537.

Hertfordshire, Cambridgeshire, Norfolk, Suffolk, Essex and Lincolnshire had only 17 manors between 1070-76. The Domesday book noted that the Rysing/Rubirgh lands of Peter had been taken from the Saxon lord, Goerth. They consisted of 2 carucates of land held by one villain and 11 bordarers, and 4 servi, 2 carucates in demean, and one among the men, paunage for 40 swine, 6 acres of meadow, a mill, &c. which Ralph Facto was enfeoffed of it by his lord, Peter de Valognes. A beruite belonged to it, Toftes, and valued with that, was worth in King Edward's time (1300s) £4 per annum, now at £5. Ryburgh was 7 furlongs long, and 5 broad and paid 9¼ d gelt. Peter was sheriff of the counties of Essex and Hertfordshire and farmed the boroughs of Havering and Benington, and Hertford. Peter and his wife Albreda were probably middle aged when they founded Binham Priory in North Norfolk in 1091 on land originally the property of a freeman named Esket according to the Domesday Book. Like many others being built at the time, it took lots of money and people willing to undertake the project. Monastery history notes that the formal ceremony with presenting the charter to the monks took place at the parish church of St. Mary at a mass celebrated by the abbot of St. Albans with all the members of the de Valognes family, knights, friends, abbots of Bury and St. Benet's, and priests of 16 local manors involved plus the parish priest of Binham. Said endowment included the Binham estate [the manor], ⅔ of the tithes of Dersingham and Ingoldisthrope [churches in Peter's hands], and ⅔ tithes of each church on the manors that Peter's military knights held directly, 12 in all. The tithes came from the produce of the villages that were diverted from local parish churches. It is estimated that Peter died around 1109. Monastery records indicate that Peter and Albreda had sons: 1) William, and +2) Roger de Valognes.[1] They also had two daughters. Their son:

Roger de Valognes was an Anglo-Norman nobleman who held lands around Benington in Hertfordshire. Either he or his father built a castle. Roger married Agnes, daughter of John fitzRichard. A grant made after 1158 by the prior of the convent of Binham identifies Lady Agnes de Valognes as Agnes, sister of Payn and Eustace fitz John and widow of Roger de Valognes and mother of his sons and heirs, Peter and Robert who acquired his father's estates near Benington. Roger and Agnes had sons: 1) Peter, 2) +Robert, 3) Geoffrey, 4) Roger and 5) Philip. Roger died around 1141/2. The heir to Roger's lands near Benington was his eldest son, Peter de Valognes who m. Gundrea and died without children about 1158. The next in line was:

Robert de Valognes who appears on documents connected with King Stephen's (1135-1154) first Easter court in 1136 where Roger is listed with other barons supporting Stephen gaining the throne. Robert was lord of Benington and held the barony of Valognes and the lordship of Parham. He died about 1194 and his daughter Gunnora who married Robert fitzWalter succeeded Robert carrying on the Valognes name. Robert's son:

Theobald de Valgones, Lord of Parham, was sheriff of Norfolk and Suffolk. He founded Hickling Priory in Norfolk in 1185 endowing it with the churches of Parham in Suffolk, His two daughters, Jane and Agnes founded an Augustine Nunnery in Campress, Suffolk, on land he gave them for that purpose in 1195.[2] He was among the barons who rebelled against King John (1199-1216) but died around 1209 before war erupted. He was the father of Bertha who married Ranulf de Glanville which takes us back to Helewisa who married Robert[10] FitzRalph whose third son:

---

1 Binhampriory.org

2 Henry VIII granted it to Sir. William Willoughby in 1544.

FitzRandolph Continued

Ranulph/Ralph[11] FitzRobert became the next Lord of Middleham. He acquired lands from his father including Spennithorne. Besides Coverham Abbey, Ranulph also founded a Premonstratensian Abbey at Corham, Yorkshire, which was valued at £4,151.13.04 during the Reformation. Ranulph died in 1251 and was buried with his mother at Coverham. Ranulph's wife was Mary Bigod, daughter of Roger Bigod, Duke of Norfolk, and Isabelle de Warenne. This was an important alliance as Bigod was the Constable of Norwich Castle, a founder of Norwich Cathedral, and one of the great leaders against absolute Papal domination in England.

Middleham Castle passed into the possession of Robert de Neville, who had married Mary, eldest daughter of Robert FitzRalph and Helewisa. These arranged marriages for wealth sometimes didn't work out well. Robert de Neville began seeing a married woman in Crayen. Her husband caught them and beat Neville so badly that he died of his wounds in June 1271. Mary remained a widow until she died in 1320 and was buried with her husband at Coverham. Their son, Ralph de Neville inherited Raby Castle in Durham County but he was so financially careless that his mother left Middleham to her grandson Robert Neville. The Neville family's power fell in 1569 when Northern Barons plotted in Raby castle's Barons Hall to put Mary Queen of Scots on the English throne. When the plot failed, Raby castle was forfeited to the Crown. Its exquisite interior eventually became a great country home within its rectangular stone structure with nine towers. Ranulph FitzRobert's wife Mary Bigod ancestry also begins back in Normandy.

BOGOT/BIGOD ANCESTRY

Thurston[1] le Bigot and his wife, Judith de Montanolier lived in Normandy. They had a son, Robert[2] Bigot who had a a position in Duke William's household and was granted a small parcel of land in western Normandy in 1055 by the Duke for telling him of a pending rebellion by the Duke's cousin. Slightly built Robert came to Hastings with the Duke and proved to be a brave knight despite his stature. He chose to return to Normandy where he died about 1071. His son:

Roger[3] Bigot served the Duke, now King William I of England (1066-1087), as Sheriff of Norfolk. Roger married Adeliza, daughter of Ralph II of Tosny of central Normandy,[1] a companion of Duke William at Hastings. Ralph was the son of Roger de Tosny from Normandy. Ralph's wife was Isabel de Montfort, daughter of Simon I de Montfort and his 1st wife, Isabel de Broyles. Simon died in 1087 was buried in Epernon, France. Roger Bigot was given the Earl of Norfolk's fortified estates making him one of the largest landowners in Norfolk. Roger, now a feudal baron, held one hundred eighty seven lordships in Norfolk, six lordships in Essex, and one hundred seventeen in Suffolk as noted in Domesday. Roger then granted the church of St. Felix, a Benedictine Priory, to the town of Rochester in Kent around 1090.[2] Roger and his wife Adeliza had two sons: the eldest named William; the other Hugh. His eldest son William Bigot became Lord Steward in King Henry I's household. In

---

1 David Dougles, Ed., *English Historical Documents, Vol. II, 1042-1189*, p. 23

2 The Cell was granted to Thomas Sexford by Elizabeth I in 1552.

that period the Lord Steward had authority over legal and judicial matters. The counting house or Board of Green Cloth with its coffers was overseen by the Lord Steward. He controlled expenses and provisions for the royal household. Also anyone who broke the peace within a twelve mile radius of the King's palace was dealt with by the Lord Steward and his board. It was also a position where one could acquire vast lands. But Roger's son William drowned with Henry I's only legitimate son and heir, William Adelin, in the wreck of the *White Ship* after which his brother Hugh Bigot became Lord Steward for Henry I.

By 1086 there were 170 tenants-in-chief or barons who held 50% of the land. Another quarter was held by the Church, 8% by minor officials, the rest the King's. About 200 barons held lands up to the 14th century. English knighthood was a non-inherited professional career. As time progressed lands changed thru inheritance and with the arrival of professional armies few were interested in knighthood preferring to pay a fine. Kings didn't mind. Either way it was a source of revenue for them. By the late 12th century the Bigod family had come to dominate Suffolk, holding the title of the Earl of Norfolk and owning castles at Bungay, Walton, Thetford, and Framlingham. Bungay Castle was built to take advantage of the protection given by a curve in the Waveney River. Walton Castle was initially a fort built by early Romans. Roger Bigod used the Sussex land as the bailey for a castle built of stone. It was strengthened by his son Hugh and later confiscated and garrisoned by King Henry II (1216-1272). It was dismantled and its stone used by Henry II in 1175-76 for his new castle at Orford. In the process some of its early walls were left standing.

Framlingham Castle was an early fortification that existed before Domesday and was held by the Saxon Thane, Aelmer, with 24 villagers. Roger Bigot was later awarded the Framlingham estates with 32 villagers. It passed onto his son Hugh Bigod and it became the family's stronghold. Around 1190 Roger granted the Church of St. Felix to Rochester. It ended up in the hands of Thomas Sexford by Queen Elizabeth 1st in 1577.

Roger rebuilt the motte and bailey castle at Thetford in 1100 placing it to guard both the town and local crossing of Icknield Way over the Rivers Thet and Little Ouse. Then Roger Bigod founded a Cluniac Priory at Thetford in 1104[1] where he was buried in Sep 8th 1107. The Bigot/Bigod family continued to hold their grip on the region by taking advantage of their powerful castles as tensions persisted throughout the land. The family also built and Augustine Priory at Weybridge, date unknown. Centuries later, Henry VIII granted it to Richard Fulmerstone. Roger Bigod and Adeliza's son:

Hugh[4] Bigod became the 1st Earl of Norfolk and Suffolk. He married Juliane de Vere, daughter of Aubrey II de Vere and Adelize de Clare. Little is known of Hugh's early years so I'll begin with his wife's ancestry:

de Vere'Ancestry

Alberic/Aubrey I de Vere fought at Hastings and by 1086 according to the Domesday Book, he was overlord of Count Alan Rufus' Saxon estates in Essex which had belonged to Wulfwine/Ulwin a Saxon nobleman. Also lands in Suffolk, Cambridgeshire and Northampton, about nineteen in all. At Hedingham Castle in Essex he ordered vineyards to be planted. His wife, Beatrice, held land at

---

1 In 1541 Henry VIII gave the Priory to Thomas, Duke of Norfolk

Aldham, Essex, in her own right in 1104 and was accused by Domesday jurors of expanding into Little Maplestead.

A manor at Kensington, Middlesex, was granted by King William I to Geoffrey de Montbray/Mowbray, the warrior Bishop of Coutances and one of the King's inner circle of advisors and wealthiest men in post-Conquest England. Bishop Mowbray in turn granted the tenancy of Kensington manor in west London to Aubrey I de Vere. After Bishop Mowbray and his nephew, Robert de Mowbray, rebelled against King William II (1087-1100), his vast barony was declared forfeit and said lands held by Aubrey I de Vere's were forfeited and converted to a tenancy in-chief with the king's approval.

Aubrey and his wife Beatrice founded a Benedictine Priory[1] at Earls Colne, Essex, in order to have the monks near them and its Abbey to serve as a family mausoleum. Their eldest son Geoffrey had died earlier and was buried there. Just before Geoffrey died at Abingdon, he bequeathed to the town the church and lands at Kensington. The grant was confirmed by his parents and of course King Henry I (1100-1135). The Abbey at Earls Colne was the primary burial place of the Earls of Oxford. Its surviving tombs, some with effigies, were removed to St. Stephen's Chapel near Bures, Essex, in the 1930's. Once the de Veres became the Earls of Oxford in 1110, their estate at Kensington was known as Earls Court. Abingdon lands were called Abbots Kensington and the church, St Mary Abbots. Aging Aubrey and Beatrice were fond of Abingdon but traveling there proved difficult for them. Aubrey I and Beatrice's children were: 1) Geoffrey; +2) Aubrey II; 3) Roger, 4) Robert; 5) William; and 6) Adeliza. After Beatrice died, Aubrey I retired to the priory and was joined by his youngest son, William, both of whom died shortly afterward. Aubrey I and Beatrice's son:

Aubrey II de Vere was born at Hedingham. He was awarded the hereditary office of Lord Great Chamberlain in 1133 first held by Robert Malet whose estates and position were forfeited by Henry I. It is a position in the monarch's household different from the Lord Chamberlain of the Household. The title was held by a de Vere with a couple of exceptions until 1625 when the last 18th Earl of Oxford, a de Vere, held Hedingham Castle. Since he was also a great Baron, deputies performed the financial work. His functions became mainly in regard to ceremony. The office bearer still wears a distinctive scarlet court uniform and bears a gold key and a white stave as the insignia of this office.

Hedingham, the ancestral seat of the de Veres, is today a small village in northeast Essex County situated in Colne Valley on the ancient road from Colchester to Cambridge. Aubrey II was in his 80's when construction of Hedingham castle began around 1140. He represented King Stephen at a church council in 1139 to answer why castles held by Roger, Bishop of Salisbury, were seized. The King couldn't keep track of all his lands. Aubrey II was killed in a riot in London on May 15th 1141 and buried in Colne Priory. The Castle was completed under his sons Robert and Aubrey III. Aubrey III was made 1st Earl of Oxford in 1141 by Empress Matilda of Boulogne, wife of King Stephen. The castle was surrendered to Stephen in 1143 but later returned to de Vere. Empress Matilda died there from the many fevers due to poor sanitation on May 3rd 1152 and was buried in the abbey which she helped to found. Hedingham was attacked in 1216/7 during King John's reign (1199-1216) when the barons rebelled. The more famous of the long line of de Vere Earls of Oxford were Robert the 3rd Earl, Robert the 9th Earl, John the 13th Earl, and Edward the 17th Earl each having served as Lord Great Chamberlain.

Aubrey II de Vere and Adelize de Clare had sons: 1) Aubrey III, 1st Earl of Oxford to 1194; 2) Geoffrey; 3) Robert; 4) William, Bishop of Hertford; 5) Gilbert, prior of Knights Hospitaller; and

---

1 During the Reformation Henry VIII granted the Priory to John de Vere, 15th Earl of Oxford, in 1536.

daughters: 6) Alice of Essex; 7) Rohese, Countess of Essex; +8) Juliane, Countess of Norfolk; and 9) a daughter who married Roger de Ramis.

Their grandson, Robert, 3rd Earl of Oxford, son of Aubrey III became a Magna Carta signer in 1215, d. 1221. Adeliza died in 1163 at Hedingham and buried at St. Osyth's Priory, Essex. Due to its becoming a pilgrimage site, those buried there were removed to a secret site in 1500.

The 9th Earl, Robert de Vere, was the nephew of another Aubrey de Vere. Robert was five years younger than King Richard II and became one of the King's inner circle conducting royal affairs He was appointed Duke of Ireland by the King in 1386. The next year he was installed Justice of Chester. His too close relationship with the King led many in the political establishment to dislike Robert which culminated in his having to escape England for France where he died. Even though he was assumed dead, in Feb 1388 he was sentenced to death in absentia by the Merciless Parliament. Robert had married twice with no children by either wife.

In 1703 the de Vere name became extinct with the death of Aubrey, 20th Earl of Oxford. Ten years later Hedingham was purchased by Sir William Ashhurst. His great granddaughter, wife of Lew Majendie, acquired the estate. It stayed in that family for 250 years when Musette Majendie left it to her cousin Thomas Lindsay, a de Vere descendant. His son Jason and wife Demetra now own the castle and live there with their family. The castle's Norman keep is 110 feet high. There are four floors to explore, including a Banquet Hall spanning a remarkable 28 foot arch, one of the largest English Norman arches. A good view of this room can be obtained from the Minstrels' Gallery built within the thickness of 12 foot walls. Today a visit to the castle and its beautiful grounds makes an excellent family outing. During summer a variety of events bring its colorful history alive with jousting tournaments and other entertainments. One can marry in a candle light civil ceremony in its medieval Banquet Hall. Hedingham was one of the largest manors among those acquired by the de Veres. Aubrey's wife, Adelize de Clare's family follows:

De Clare Ancestry

Godfrey/Geoffrey was the eldest born to one of many mistresses of Richard the Fearless of the de Clare family from county Eu in France. He married, Hawisa, a legitimate daughter of Richard. Refer to Hawisa's Viking Ancestry (Pg. 23). Godfrey and Hawisa's son:

Gilbert Crispin became Count of Brionne and head of the county of Eu. When Robert, Duke of Normandy died in 1035, Gilbert became one of the guardians of the Duke's illegitimate 7 year old son William, the future Duke of Normandy and King William I of England. He paid the price as one of William's guardians when he was murdered near Eschafour in 1039/40 by those who were offended over young William's illegitimacy. Gilbert left two young sons: +1) Richard and 2) Baldwin. The boys fled to Flanders with their guardians, returning as young men in 1053 when William became Duke of Normandy. They joined him in 1066 to invade England. The brothers did well. Baldwin received estates in the shires of Devon and Somerset and was known as Baldwin the Sheriff. He died in 1090 and his three sons died childless. Baldwin's brother:

Sir Richard fitz Gilbert of Clare was granted 176 lordships including Tunbridge in Kent and Clare in Suffolk where 95 of the lordships were attached to Clare castle. The Domesday book noted their name as "de Clare of Suffolk" which was the source of their name de Clare. In the Conqueror's absence Richard was his Chief Justicar. Clare Castle was built as a motte and bailey castle shortly after 1066. Today its attached lands, about 20 plus acres, are a park. In 1075 there was a revolt which Richard helped suppress. Richard married Rohese de Giffard, born 1034 daughter of Sir Walter Giffard, Lord of Longueville and his wife Agnes/Ermentrude[2] Flaitel, daughter of Gerold Flaitel of Normandy. Richard and Rohese built a priory at St. Neots which was dedicated in 1100. Rohese died in 1113 at Clare. They had sons: 1) Walter, Lord of Nether Swent; 2) Richard, Abbot of Ely; 3) Roger d. 1131 without issue; +4) Gilbert; and daughters: 5) Rohese; and 6) Adelize.

Some of these sons managed through intrigue to make the family one of the wealthiest in England. Son Richard seemed content as Abbot of Ely. Son Gilbert was involved in the 1088 and 1095 rebellions. Gilbert and his brother, Roger, were hunting in New Forest with William Rufus, King William II (1087-1100), and the king's younger brother Henry when a "stray" arrow struck the King in the chest on Aug 2nd 1100 killing him. Henry took off to seize the royal treasury at Winchester, Hampshire. It was there Henry buried his brother. Was this another Cain vs Abel incident? Three days later Henry was crowned at Westminster Abbey as King Henry I (1100-1135). To appease the nobles, Henry issued a Charter of Liberties stating he would not confiscate church property or levy unfair taxes. He was also famous for having the most illegitimate children of any English king. It was not uncommon for a lord or earl to place a daughter in the king's household to gain favor and afterward marry one of rank.

Sir Richard fitz Gilbert died in 1091, three years after the first rebellion against King William II and was buried in St. Neot's Priory. Richard and Rohese's son:

Gilbert fitz Richard, 2nd Earl of Clare, was granted the lordships of Clare, Tunbridge, and Cardigan (Wales) by King Henry I. He acquired his father's lands in England, his brother, Roger, acquired those lands in Normandy in 1088. The castle at Tunbridge was fortified against William Rufus' forces (William II) before it was stormed and Gilbert wounded. Gilbert and Roger were in attendance at King William's death in August 1100. Gilbert was with King Henry I at his Christmas court at Westminster in 1101. Henry gave Gilbert Cardigan Castle in Wales in 1110 that he had retrieved from its occupants for misdemeanors. Gilbert founded a college in 1124 at Stoke, Suffolk.[1] His brother Roger founded a Benedictine Nunnery in 1163 at Little Marcis, Yorkshire.[2]

Gilbert had married Adeliza de Clermont, daughter of Hugh, Count of Clermont and Margaret de Roucy. They had six known children born at Tunbridge, Kent: +1) Adeliza de Clare; 2) Richard FitzGilbert de Clare, 3rd Earl of Hertford, d. in 1136 fighting in Wales. His grandson Richard de Clare, 3rd Earl of Hertford was a signer of the Magna Carta, d. 1217; 3) Baldwin FitzGilbert de Clare who m. Adeline de Rollos; 4) Margaret de Clare, m. Sir William de Montfitchet, Lord of Stansted Mountfitchet; 5) Gilbert de Clare, 1st Earl of Pembroke in Wales who m. Isabel of Beaumont, d/o Robert of Beaumont, her 1st marriage. She m. 2nd William de Warenne, 2nd Earl of Surrey;[3] and 6) Rohese de Clare m. Baderon of Monmouth; and possibly 7) Walter de Clare who d. 1149 and 8) Hervey de Clare, Lord of Montmorency. Gilbert and Adeliza's daughter:

Adeliza de Clare m. Aubrey II de Vere, Lord of Hedingham (See de Vere). It was their daughter, Juliane, Countess of Norfolk who married Hugh Bigod I, Earl of Norfolk and Suffolk, son of Roger Bigod. Their son:

---

1 The college was granted in 1549 Edward VI to Sir John Cheke and Michael Mildmay.

2 It was granted to Robert Holgate, Bishop of Landoff in 1544 by Henry VIII.

3 In 1268 Gilbert de Clare, Lord of Glamorgan, began building Caerphilly Castle in Wales. It was half done when knocked down by Llywelyn ap Gruffydd, the last native Prince of Wales and Gilbert had to start over. It is the next largest castle to Windsor.

Bigod Ancestry Continued

Hugh[4] Bigod I was age 25 when inherited the family properties in 1120 under the reign of Henry I (1100-1135). Bungay castle was his base and he became a bold leader among local barons. Around 1122 he was appointed Constable of the royal Castle at Norwich and Governor of the city, the second largest city in England at the time. Then Hugh became involved in the dispute between Matilda and Stephen over the throne in 1141. First he sided with Matilda and raised an army in 1136 against King Stephen (1135-1154) seizing Norwich's royal castle. Stephen, in order to subdue Hugh, marched to Bungay in 1140. During their negotiations Stephen found it expedient to give Bigod the title of Earl of Suffolk to win his loyalty. This resulted in giving Hugh greater respect and support in the region. The next year Hugh donned his armor to fight in the Battle of Lincoln for Stephen. After Stephen died in 1154, Henry Plantagenet became King. Henry had already fought many battles to retain his inheritance. Henry was a freckled red headed man who was facing loss of royal rights thanks to Stephen. The current law consisted of a centralized power based on the judiciary and exchequer that had superceded William the Conqueror's feudal system. Henry preferred English common law. He made his trusted agent, Thomas Becket, Archbishop of Canterbury in 1162. This annoyed the Pope in Rome who felt he should make that appointment. Henry also felt the Church should be run by clergy supervised by him. Here we find disagreement beginning between Kings and Popes.

At the time Hugh Bigod no longer seemed a threat to Henry so in 1164 his earldom and properties at Framlingham, Bungay, Walton, and Thetford were returned to him. Hugh went on to build a large square Norman keep on the Bungay site in 1165. Henry then decided to order a survey of knight's fees on moveable property and income at variable rates, it to be recorded in the Black Book of the Exchequer in 1166. The Bigods were the fifth richest family in England. Marriages usually helped. Hugh Bigod's knights' fee was recorded as 160 which amounted to a huge quantity of land and knights held by Hugh with a hefty tax due the crown. About this time Hugh began building a stone keep. It's walls were about 15-22 feet thick and stood more than 108 feet high. Although it was not one of the largest castles in the country, it was one of the most impregnable fortresses.

Henry II had married Eleanor of Aquitaine who was twelve years older than he. Henry ruled England, Normandy and Anjou. His wife Eleanor ruled Aquitaine. She was five months pregnant by Henry when she asked for an annulment of her marriage to the pious King Louis VII of France. She had given him only two daughters so he did not fight her request. She and Henry were married six weeks after her divorce and she gave birth to a son in 1155 which was named Henry. Later Archbishop Becket turned against Henry II and his authority over the court system. Would church or state rule the courts? Henry VIII settled that centuries later. This shook the ruling class and Becket took off for France. Before leaving he excommunicated some barons including Hugh Bigod. Henry II's response was to crown his eldest son, Henry the young (1170-1183). At the age of five young Henry had been betrothed to King Louis' eldest two year old daughter by his 2nd wife. Not all betrothals ended in marriage but they were married in 1172. Young Henry became 18 the next year and felt he needed some of his inheritance to support his new life style and reward his knights. Instead his father decided to give his younger son, John, for his upcoming marriage three castles which just happened to be located in his older brother's realm. That resulted in young Henry and his mother being encouraged by aristocrats in Poitiers to rebel. But young Henry and two other brothers fled to King Louis's court. Their mother tried to join them but was captured. Normandy and northern England were invaded in Apr 1173 but that mission failed. Negotiations between father and sons slowed the fighting but ended in failure. Then young Henry and his accomplices made alliances with France and Scotland promising them land and revenue from England. Meanwhile Becket returned from France while King Henry II just happened to be in Normandy. News got to him that the Archbishop was going to pull the crown off young Henry's head. Henry's knights who overheard the King lament over the news, crossed the channel to England and confronted Becket at Canterbury and killed him. To many that was a sacrilegious act which horrified the populace. An Archbishop was his own kind of king.

In Apr 1173 Normandy was invaded by the King of France, young Henry, and Bretons. Normandy managed to hold and kicked out the French King and killed the Count of Boulogne. Breton men quickly departed after many losing lives and treasure. Negotiations between father and son also failed. Young Henry's supporter, the Earl of Leicester happened to be in Normandy. He gathered some mercenaries and headed for England to join Hugh Bigod and other barons to rebel against Henry II. Hugh Bigod ended up on the losing side in this Revolt. Hugh's forces with those of the Earl managed to capture the royal castle at Haughley but were unsuccessful in seizing Dunwich and Norwich. It resulted in Henry gathering a massive army against Hugh's men who were encamped. The next offense in the spring of 1174 against the King didn't turn out so well. As his men attacked and burned the city of Norwich, the Earl of Ferrers attacked the royal burgh of Nottingham. Henry II, who was fighting in Normandy, hastened back to England landing on Jul 8th and first did penance for the death of Thomas Becket on the 12th. Then the royal forces destroyed Thetford, Bungay, and other castles as well as towns. The rebel barons and young Henry's advisors were blamed. Did that include the Queen? Wm. Marshall said: *Cursed be the day when traitors scheme to embroil father and son.* On July 13th the king's loyal supporters burned Hugh's castle at Walton. The loyalists then headed for Framlingham where Hugh was forced to surrender to Henry on Jul 25th. In a meeting with the King, Hugh was declared an outlaw and traitor. His armies were disbanded and all properties surrendered. The King had been building a castle at nearby Orford. Once completed, he ordered his men: "tear down the walls of Framlingham." Both Framlingham and Bungay castles were destroyed. Destruction wasn't as fast as today. Hugh eventually managed to save Framlingham from complete destruction on payment of one thousand marks. That was a lot of money (2/3£ sterling per mark) in that century. Hugh's opposition cost him his lands and title of Earl of Norfolk. Henry II rode to each rebel stronghold to receive surrender.

On the last day of September he returned to Normandy to settle with his enemies there including his sons who finally yielded to their father. Their mother's encouragement didn't turn out too well. The eighteenth month revolt ended with destruction of castles, towns, and loss of life over a large territory with Henry II ruling England, Normandy, Brittany, Maine, Anjou, Touraine, Poitou, Aquitaine and Gascony in western France.

Bungay's site was eventually returned to the Bigods and restored. It was further developed in 1294 by Roger Bigod who probably built the massive gate towers on the site. Roger fell out with King Edward I (1272-1307) and after Roger's death the castle reverted to the Crown and falling into ruin. It was described in a document dated 1382 as being "old, and ruinous, and worth nothing a year." After 1483 it was primarily owned by the Dukes of Norfolk, except for brief periods until the 20th century. In 1934 Dr. L. Cane, the Town Reeve of Bungay, organized a program for its excavation and repair. Parts of the decayed walls were rebuilt revealing many hidden features over the past centuries. It was presented to the town by the Duke of Norfolk in 1987 with a preservation endowment. Currently it is owned and administered by the Castle Trust. Castle Visitors Centre called "Jesters" opened in 2000 which provides a visitor center with a café and gift shop with interpretive material.

Hugh Bigod died Mar 6th 1175. Juliane died in 1199. Both are buried at Thetford Priory. Despite appeals from Hugh's son Roger and Roger's mother, the crown held his lands. Wishing to go on a

Crusade, Henry II imposed the Saladin tithe in 1188 to raise funds for the venture. It was levied at 10% on all goods and revenues with exceptions for a knight's horse and armor, plus church vestments. Those who pledged to go with Henry were excluded. But Henry II died at Chinon on Jul 6th 1189 ailing and dispirited over his sons waging war against him. He did leave England with a Constitution and laid the foundation for common law. His trial by jury was different in that the jurymen were witnesses and judges. Hugh I and Juliane's son:

Roger[5] Bigod II was reinstated as 2nd Earl of Norfolk by King Richard I (1189-1199) on Nov 25th 1189. Roger had gained Richard's favor by secreting the King's brother, Prince John, when Richard I was Crusading. In 1194 King Richard was held captive in Germany. That meant raising money for his ransom. A 25% levy on personal property and income was imposed. Despite new taxes, Roger was able to begin building a new castle on the Framlingham site which had been destroyed by Henry II during the revolt. It was completed by 1213 in a new style with no keep. It had an Inner Court defended by 13 towers, an adjacent lower court with smaller stone walls and towers, and a larger bailey with timber defenses. Under a new system, lords provided their knights land for guarding a castle. Roger decided to renovate Hugh's stronghold and obtained a licence to repair it. He erected a gate-house and lofty curtain walls to encircle the original keep. Roger died in 1221 before its completion. Roger had a large group of knights including cavalry contained within its curtain walls laced with strong towers for maximum defense.[1] Bungay remained unoccupied until 1269 when another Roger Bigod inherited the title of the 5th Earl. Roger II donated property to Colne priory for the souls of his father, Hugh, his mother, Juliane, and wife, Ida, which was witnessed by his son, Hugh. Richard I's reign lasted only ten years. Prince John became King (1199-1216) and proceeded to lose Normandy as an English land holding. War needs money so John added an additional new tax on trade in 1202 to 1206. John was facing a French invasion in 1213 or submission to Pope Innocent III. Cunningly, John offered the Pope temporal sovereignty making England a fief of the Papacy. The Pope happily took England under his protection as the barons opposed this new partnership. John was once again demanding money and the barons' service for his military activities. In refusing his demand, royal troops were sent to plunder their lands. John's army arrived at Framlingham on Mar 12th 1215, followed by John on the 13th. Fifty-six men held off the attack for two days. John sent messages the next day to Roger Bigod II, who understood the fate of castles, agreed that his garrison of 26 knights, 20 sergeants, 7 crossbow men and a priest would surrender without a fight. Once again surrender followed but that wasn't the end of King John's fight with the Barons.

On June 15th 1215 John was forced to put his seal on *The Articles of the Barons* written in Latin and signed by 25 Barons, the basis for the *Magna Carta*. Its articles of checks and balances reduced the power of the King upsetting feudal arrangements which subsequently opened up a war for the throne of England. The French were now involved with Prince Louis sending knights to the barons to protect London after which he shortly arrived to claim the throne. Fighting continued in various castles between the rebel Barons and John's supporters, many later requiring costly repairs. King John died in Oct 18th 1216 at Newark Castle in Nottinshamshire. Suddenly Louis seemed more of a threat then 9 year old Prince Henry. William Marshall, young Henry's regent, slowly got the Barons to switch sides. It took until Nov 12th 1216 to get a revised charter approved which regent Marshall signed. But Louis VIII wasn't about to give up and it took until Sep 11th 1217 for him to relinquish his claim by signing the Treaty of Lambeth. Roger Bigod II and Hugh were two of the twenty-five barons who were responsible for the Magna Carta. *Here is a law which is above the King, and which even he must not break. The reaffirmation of a supreme law and its expression in a general charter*

---

1 Warwick Castle was rebuilt in the 14th Century in this manner.

is the great work of Magna Charta and this alone justified the respect in which men have held it.[1]
The Pope responded by excommunicating the barons. However, these events led to the beginning of
Parliament in 1254 and the House of Commons beginnings in the 1260's.

Under Henry III (1216-1272) Framlingham was again returned to the Bigods in May 1221 but
it was short-lived for Roger. He died the following August at age 77 and buried at Thetford Priory.
He was succeeded by his son, Hugh II.

Roger II's grandson, another Roger, inherited Framlingham in 1270 and made extensive
renovations while living in luxury. The home was surrounded by a large park used for hunting.
Although considered wealthy, Roger was borrowing increasing sums from the Jewish community at
Bungay. By the end of the century Roger was heavily indebted to Edward I (1272-1307) as well. As
a result, Roger led the baronial opposition to Edward's request for additional customs and wool taxes
to support his French wars. Edward responded by seizing Roger's lands, only releasing them on the
condition that Roger grant them to the Crown after his death. Roger agreed and Framlingham Castle
passed to the Crown on his death in 1306. With falling revenues, new forms of taxes led to a
Peasants's Revolt in 1381.

In the 15th and 16th centuries Framlingham came into the hands of the Mowbray and Howard
families. Two artificial lakes were built around the castle. Pleasure gardens were added within the
castle and its older parts redesigned to allow visitors to enjoy the resulting views. By the end of the
16th century it fell into disrepair after its last Howard family owner had financial problems. The
castle and surrounding estates were sold. In 1636 Framlingham Castle was given to Pembroke College
after which its internal buildings were demolished to make way for building a poorhouse. In 1839 the
facility was closed. Then the castle was used as a drill hall and a county court. In 1913, the College
donated it to the Commissioner of Works. During World War II, it was used by the military for
regional defense against possible German invasion. Today the Castle is a monument owned by English
Heritage and run as a tourist attraction.

Roger II had married Ida/Isabella de Warenne, daughter of Hamelin de Warenne (Plantagenet),
5th Earl of Surrey and Isabel/Ida de Warenne. Among their children were: 1) Hugh II who married
Maud Marshall; 2) William; 3) John; 4) Ralph; 5) Roger; +6) Mary who married Ranulph
fitzRobert; 7) Alice who married Aubrey IV de Vere; and 8) Margery who married William de
Hastings.[2]

Warenne Ancestry

The first castle at Thetford had been built by William de Warenne, 1st Earl of Surrey, son of
Ranulf and Beatrice from Varenne, Normandy. Ranulf wasn't a major land holder in Normandy so
there was little to pass on to his eldest son, Ranulf. His younger son, William, fought with William,
Duke of Normandy in the Battle of Mortemer in 1054 defeating King Henry I of France. William was
granted castle Mortemer and Bellecombre in Normandy. Then he fought with the Duke William at
Hastings and became a major land holder in England. At the time of the Domesday Book
Conisbrough in Yorkshire and estates in Sussex, Norfolk, Lewes, and Castle Acre were held by
William. Though his wife, Countess Gundrada, he became the 1st Earl of Surrey. She was the sister
of the 1st Earl of Chester. The couple set out for Rome visiting monasteries along the way. Due to

---

1 Winston Churchill, 1956

2 Browning, p. 88

friction between Henry IV, King of the Germans, and Pope Gregory VII in 1077 the trip ended in Burgundy. There they became impressed with a Cluny Abbey and decided to build a priory at Lewes. In 1078 a Cluniac Priory was founded on a pre-existing Sacon shrine to St. Pancras.[1] They sent for monks to come to England. Lazlo was its first abbot. On May 27th 1085 Gundrada died of childbirth at Castle Acre in Norfolk and was buried in the Chapter house at Lewes Priory. William would later be buried beside his wife in 1088.

His heir, William de Warenne, 2nd Earl of Surrey, was seeking a royal bride. Elizabeth de Vermandois was the daughter of Count Hugh of Vermandois, granddaughter of King Henry I of France, and widow of Robert de Beaumont, Count of Meulan, who had just died. William was much older than Elizabeth and they were closely related to the dismay of the church but married in 1118. Her daughter, Elizabeth de Beaumont, married 1st Gilbert de Clare, 1st Earl of Pembroke. She and Wm. Warenne had three sons and two daughters: William, Ralph, Reginald, Gundrada, and Ada who m. Henry, the younger son of King David of Scotland. William and Elizabeth's eldest son, William de Warenne, 3rd Earl of Surrey, inherited his father's property in upper Normandy including the castles after his father died in 1138. Prior to becoming Earl, the young William fought with King Stephen (1135-1154) in Normandy and fled from a battle. He was another Earl who vacillated support for Stephen or Matilda. In 1146 he took up crusading and went on the 2nd Crusade the next year. He had married Adela/Alice, daughter of William Talvas, Count of Ponthieu. Having no sons, their daughter and heiress was Isabel de Warenne, who married 1st William of Blois, Count of Boulogne, who died in 1159. Her 2nd husband, Hamelin Plantagenet, became Count of Surrey. Due to Hamelin's illegitimacy their Plantagenet children took the name of Warenne. Hamelin died at Lewes Priory on May 7th 1202 and buried in its chapter house. Their daughter Isabel de Warenne married Roger II Bigod, 2nd Earl of Norfolk connecting the Warenne and Bigod families.

There are those who claim that Roger's wife Ida, is the supposed daughter of Ralph V de Tosny and Margaret de Beaumont and sister of William de Tosny, lord of Belvoir. Ida Tosny was a mistress of Henry II (1154-1189) and bore Henry a son named William Longspee and is said to have married Roger Bigod in 1181. However, it is written that said marriage to Roger Bigot was around the time of Domesday and she was the daughter (no name) of Ralph de Tosny of central Normandy and the English Midlands.[2]

I don't think the Bigod family would have had much love for Longespee b. 1176, d. 1226. When Hugh Bigod II died in 1175 a third of his estate was set aside for his wife, Maud/Matilda nee Marshall, now wife of William de Warenne who disputed the amount. Hugh's son Roger II, a minor, was heir apparent. Longespee was sent on a military expedition and intended to use money from Bigod lands to defray his costs. It was agreed if young Bigod married during his absence, £100 would be set aside to sustain Longespee. Roger was too young to take over the Bigod estate and came under guardianship of the King who also happened to be a minor. An unexpected opportunity for others to cash in. Differences also arose over Hugh II's original knight's fees. They claimed he hadn't paid enough so the young King's IRS went after his estate. Then it was cunningly arranged for young Roger to marry the King of Scotland's sister, Isabella. That meant paying out a handsome Bigod dower. The King of Scotland agreed to pay any debts from the dower to cover Longespee's debts with the exchequer after a down payment of £1,000. In 1228 Roger left Scotland and returned to Framlingham alone, never having lived in Scotland. There was enough left in the estate for Roger to

---

1 In 1560 Elizabeth I granted the Priory to Richard Baker and Richard Sackville

2 David C. Douglas, *English Historical Documents 1042-1189*, Vol. II, New Yor, Oxford University Press, 1953, p. 23

buy new land and build an estate but he had been forced into a bad deal by Longespee and the King's advisors. In addition, why was there a Bigod named Hamelin? Roger II and Isabella's daughter:

Mary[6] Bigod married Ranulph fitzRobert, the last Lord of Middleham in that line. One can only wonder how she and her siblings grew up in the rebuilt Framlingham castle with all the turmoil going on in the country. Armored knights on horseback and men with crossbows would be occupying the courtyard awaiting battle. There would be meetings of barons plotting their course of action. It is here that Roger II's wife, Isabella de Warrene, connects to the Plantagenets which takes the family back to France in the 900's starting with:

Angevin/Plantagenet Ancestry

Ingelger[1], a minor feudal leader in the province of Gâtinais. He rose to become Viscount of Anger under Robert the Strong's son. They were known as Angevins. Ingelgar was born around 845 in France's Loire Valley possibly a son of Tertullus and Petronilla about the time Charles III became King of France. Ingelgar was a Frankish nobleman who stood at the head of the Plantagenet dynasty. He became a military commander at Tours, France, during the time its territory was in a dispute between the counts of Blois and Anjou with Anjou gaining control. The area was also in a constant battle with Viking invaders. Ingelgar had married Adelais of Neustria whose uncles were the influential Adalard, Archbishop of Tours, and Raino, Bishop of Angier. Ingelgar was in his early forties when he died as prefect in 888 at Tours and buried in the St. Martin church at Châteaunuf-sur-sarthe commune. Ingelgar and Adelais' son:

Fulk I[2] *the Red* expanded their territory and became Count of Anjou and later Viscount and Count of Tours. He must have inherited his father's military ability since his reign was permanently at war with the Normans and Bretons. He occupied Nantes county in 907 but abandoned it to Bretons in 919. He increased the territory by taking part of Touraine for the Viscount of Angers which became a county around 930. His wife was Roscilla[2] de Loches, daughter of Warnerius, Seigneur de Villentrois, and they had children: 1) Ingelger; 2) Guy, Bishop of Soissons; and +3) Fulk II. In March 942 Fulk I died and was buried by his father. Fulk I and Roscilla's son:

Fulk II[3] *the Good* became 2nd Count of Anjou or Angers in 942 after his father's death. Like his father he fought against the Bretons. Despite his warring nature, he was considered "cultured" by the people prospering under him. He was also adept in making marital alliances. He must have learned that from his father who had arranged Fulk II's marriage to Carolingian, Gerberga of Maine, daughter of Ratburnus, 1st Viscount of Vienne. This alliance opened the door for their daughter Adelaide to become married to a future king of France and their son Guy to become Bishop of le Puy. Fulk and Gerberga's children included:

+1.   Geoffrey I, Count of Anjou
2.   Adelaide who married 1st Baron Stephen, Count of Gevaudan and Forez who, after his death, ruled his lands in Aquitaine and eventually her sons became its Counts: Bouchard, Count of Vendomel; and, Humbert d'Anjou. Adelaide had three more marriages including Louis V of France for a short time.
3.   Guy (Dragon) d'Anjou, Bishop of le Puy

After Gerberga died Fulk II married Adelaide, widow of Alan II, Duke of Brittany and Count of Nantes in another influential move to possibly get control of Nantes. Adelaide was the sister of Theobald I, Count of Blois, who permitted Fulk II to form an alliance with the House of Blois. They had no children. It is said Fulk II died at Tours on Nov 11th 958. Fulk II and Gerberga's eldest son:

Geoffrey I[4], Count of Anjou was known as *Greymantle*. He was Count of Anjou from 960 to his death on Jul 21st 987. He succeeded his father Fulk II who passed on a loyal group of supporters to his son. Geoffrey also managed to acquire more followers whose interests were like his own. His father had controlled Nantes through his second marriage and Geoffrey had its Count help him get the Counts of Rennes and Blois to accept him as their overlord. Their alliance also helped Hugh Capet gain the French throne. Geoffrey's power base was Angers with the abbeys of Saint-Aubin and Saint-Serge. Like his father he used marriages to form alliances. He had his eye on Maine and he took advantage of the rift between the Counts of Maine and the Viscounts and Bishops of Le Mans. About 971 Geoffrey secured the See of Le Mans for his ally Bishop Seinfroy. Then in 973 Geoffrey had his daughter Ermengarde marry Conan of Rennes. Two years later he appointed his brother Guy, Bishop of Le Puy. Eventually his son in law Conan I began to oppose Geoffrey. The two met in 982 in the first battle of Conquereuil with Geoffrey defeating Conan. Geoffrey's widowed sister was married to Louis V of France who was only fifteen and the two were crowned King and Queen of Aquitaine. Adelaide was forty-five when the marriage failed. With it went Geoffrey's plans to control Aquitaine. Geoffrey's first wife was Adele of Meaux, daughter of Robert[1] of Vermandois and Adelais de Vergy. Geoffrey I and Adele had three children: 1) Ermengarde-Gerberga of Anjou who married 1st Conan I of Rennes, which happens to be in the FitzRandolph lineage, and married 2nd,William II of Angoulême; +2) Fulk III (970-1040) of Anjou; and 3) Geoffrey of Anjou who died young. Geoffrey I married 2nd Adelaise de Châlons and controlled that county for nearly a decade. Their son: Maurice of Anjou became Count of Châlons. Geoffrey was very aware of what relations could and couldn't do so he advised his sons, Fulk and Maurice, that no house is weak that has many friends and to hold dear those who have been faithful. Geoffrey died in July 987. Geoffrey and Adele's son:

Fulk III[5] *the Black* was 17 when he succeeded his father as Count of Anjou. Immediately he was met with continuous attacks from the Counts of Brittany. After years of fighting, he drove the Bretons beyond Anjou's western borders. Then he went after those on Anjou's eastern borders. They were fighting over the territory of Saumur. He defeated its leader Eudes II at Pontlevoy in 1016 but it took ten years to gain Saumur and part of Touraine. Attacks were endless and despite them he supported its Capetian kings. All this fighting probably affected his temperament which left something to be desired. He was strong, but became violent and cruel. He even pillaged and burned monasteries in the process. Obviously he didn't follow his father's advice. Whether he regretted his actions or felt a Christian need for penitence he built an immense abbey at Beaulieu-les-Loches and others at Angers, Loches and Saumur. A fanatic about defense, he had a great variety of buildings built of stone for that purpose along the border of his territory. He also became known as *the Great Builder*. Obviously he had access to money, like Vikings collecting Danegeld. His exploits were many and he went on several costly pilgrimages to the Holy Land. He had one daughter by his first wife, Elizabeth, heiress of Vendôme. Elizabeth was caught in an affair. Her penalty was to be burned at the stake. His brave second wife, Hildegard of Sundgau, had: 1) Geoffrey Martel, Count of Anjou;[1]

---

1   Geoffrey Martel died in 1060 as did King Henry I of France. King Henry, Geoffrey Martel and Cona, duke of Brittany, were the main opponents of Duke William of Normandy. King Henry had supported William until he married Matilda, the daughter of the count of Flanders, fearing William's potential power. They fought at the battle of Mortemer in 1054 and Varaville in 1057

and +2) Ermengarde. Fulk III died on Jun 21st 1040 at Metz returning from a pilgrimage and was buried in the chapel of the monastery at Beaulieu. He had reigned for 53 years. His daughter carried on this family line.

Ermengarde[6] of Anjou, Duchess of Burgundy and daughter of Fulk III and Hildegard of Sundgau, married 1st about 1035 Geoffrey, Count of Gâtinais, son of Geoffrey, Count of Gâtinais, and Beatrice of Mâcon, daughter of Aubry II of Mâcon. They had children:

1. Hildegarde de Château-Landon.
2. Geoffrey III *the* Bearded.
+3. Fulk IV born in 1043 and later nicknamed *le Réchin* which has numerous interpretations. Since he, like many male siblings, bickered with his older brother Geoffrey, his nickname could translate to quarrelsome.

Shortly after the birth of Fulk IV their father died and Ermengarde married 2nd Robert I, Duke of Burgundy. Ermengarde and Geoffrey's son:

Fulk IV[7] *le Réchin* felt his older brother Count Geoffrey *the Bearded*'s reign "was much ado about nothing." Around 1066/7 Fulk captured Geoffrey but was forced by the Church to release him. Geoffrey's poor management plus a civil war cost the Angevins loss of territory. The brothers' confrontations finally ended with Geoffrey's imprisonment for life in 1068 and Fulk IV becoming Count of Anjou. He had to give up being Gatinais' Count that he inherited from his father to appease King Philip I of France. Fulk IV's life was spent in a struggle with Normandy over Maine and Brittany. The number of his marriages are disputed due to their being close relatives. However, he had a 1) daughter by Hildegarde of Beaugency. His son 2) Geoffrey was the child of Ermengarde de Bourbon. Geoffrey jointly ruled with his father until Count Geoffrey died in 1106. At some point Fulk married Bertrade de Montfort and had a son, +3) Fulk V. When Fulk IV died in 1109 he was succeeded by:

Fulk V, *le Jun*, Count of Anjou, who was born at Angiers. He married 1st Ermengarde de la Flèche in 1109 tying Anjou with Touraine and Maine. She was the daughter of Count Elias I of Maine and Mathilda of Château-du-Loire. Ermengarde became Countess of Maine and Lady of Château-du-Loir in 1110. They had children: +1) Geoffrey of Anjou; 2) Sibyl of Conversano who married William Clito in 1121. After annullment in 1124, she married Thierry, Count of Flanders; 3) Matilda who married William Adelin; and 4) Elias II of Maine. Under Fulk V the lands of Anjou, Touraine, and Maine's resources surpassed or were more than equal to Normandy. He was another one who liked costly Crusading. While he was away for a couple of years King Henry I arranged a couple of marriages for his children. So he supported England's King and abandoned his support of King Louis VI of France. Ermengarde died in 1126 so Fulk went back to Jerusalem. Its King Baldwin II offered Fulk marriage to his heiress daughter, Melisende. But Fulk wanted more than being a Queen's consort and returned to Anjou. When news arrived that he could have his way he made his son Geoffrey Count of Anjou and headed back to Jerusalem. He and Melisende married Jun 2nd 1129 and had two sons. Two years later the couple were joint rulers of Jerusalem after Baldwin's death. When Fulk took control he was met with resistance from the Queen's supporters. After the

---

with Duke William the winner in controlling Normandy. After their deaths, William conquered Maine in 1063. England would be next.

problem was solved in 1136, Melisende had full control. Fulk kept busy securing borders, building forts, and gaining access to the Red Sea. But he failed to adequately defend its northern states that resulted in frequent raids by Syrians and Egyptians on Jerusalem, a never ending problem for the country. In 1143 on a holiday in Acre with Melisende, Fulk met the same fate as the Conqueror. A stumbling horse caused an injury that proved fatal. He died on Nov 13th and buried in the Church of the Holy Sepulchre in Jerusalem. His Plantagenet son:

Geoffrey *le Bel*, was born Aug 24th 1113. To some he was a red haired, jovial warrior. To others he was capable of hiding a cold and selfish nature. His marriage to Empress Matilda in 1128 was arranged to keep peace between two territories making him Count of Anjou, Maine, and Touraine. Matilda was 11 years older than Geoffrey. After Matilda's father William died in Dec 1135, she entered Normandy to claim her inheritance. The border districts submitted to her, but England made her cousin Stephen of Blois its king, Normandy soon followed suit. Then a council of the English church held at Winchester in Apr 1141 declared Stephen deposed and proclaimed Matilda "Lady of the English." But Stephen was shortly back in control. During 1142/43, Geoffrey secured all of Normandy west and south of the Seine River, then on Jan 14th 1144 he crossed the Seine and entered Rouen assuming the title Duke of Normandy that summer and founded an Augustine priory at Chateau-l'Ermitage in Anjou. Geoffrey held the duchy until 1149 when he and Matilda jointly ceded it to their son, Henry, Count of Anjou and Lord of Touraine. It was ratified by King Louis VII of France the following year. Contemporaries in Normandy called his son Henry *Fitz-Empress*. In England Henry carried the emblem *Planta Genesta*. Geoffrey also put down three baronial rebellions in Anjou: 1129, 1135, and 1145–51. He was often at odds with his younger brother, Elias, whom he had imprisoned until 1151. The constant threat of rebellion slowed his progress in Normandy and is one reason he could not intervene in England. Geoffrey was popular with Normans but had to suppress a rebellion of malcontent Angevin nobles. After a brief war with King Louis VII of France, Geoffrey signed a treaty in Aug 1151 surrendering all of Norman Vexin, the border between Normandy and Île-de-France. Geoffrey had been traveling and when he arrived at Château-du-Loire he collapsed from one of the unknown sudden fevers. Feeling the end was near, he made bequests and died on Sep 7th 1151. He was buried in St. Julien's Cathedral in Le Mans, France. Geoffrey and Matilda's children were:

1.   Henry, future King of England.
2.   Geoffrey, future Count of Nantes.
3.   William X, future Count of Poitou.

Matilda died in 1169.

Geoffrey also had a mistress or two and known illegitimate children who were well treated. One of them was named Hamelin. Hamelin's half brother, Henry, was a bit like his father over women. Eleanor, Duchess of Aquitaine, was married to Louis VII, King of France. Crusading was pious Louis' passion. On a second crusade, the lovely Eleanor persuaded Louis to take her along with some other wives. The crusade was a failure and a couple of Eleanor's flirtations led to talk of divorce. She asked the Church for an annulment on the basis that she and Louis were fourth cousins. Louis didn't oppose since they had but two daughters and Eleanor had peculiar ideas about love and matrimony. The Crusade had exposed Eleanor to some silk finery and jewels. She arranged for silk worms and white mulberry trees to be imported to Aquitaine. Earlier she had met Henry Plantagenet which led to their marriage in 1152 stunning the French Court. Henry was nearly nineteen, Duke of Normandy, Count of Anjou, and Lord of Aquitaine controlling most of which is today's France. Eleanor was five month's pregnant. That child died, but she had many more, seven in all. Their children's politically oriented marriages were planned shortly after their birth. Before King Stephen died, Henry and Eleanor headed for England where in 1154 Henry Plantagenet was crowned Henry II (1154-1189) in a pompous ceremony at Westminster. Henry's speech and manners were French and he was sturdily built like a boxer with slightly bowed legs. His hair was worn short and eyes grey and calculating. He had already fought numerous wars defending his inheritance from his grandfather Fulk V of Anjou and re-establishing central power. Thus began the reign of Angevin Kings and the end of Anglo-Norman kings with Henry controlling lands larger than Charlemagne's. Henry II had already been in control of over half of France. Now he faced a land with nearly two decades of anarchy. England was a land in which unlicensed castles owners were robbing the poor. He was passionate about law and order and divided the country in regions in which a judge appointed by him would see that things were run properly. He also went after those unlicensed castles. A license had to be provided or the castle torn down. Henry was also concerned over the proper performance of knight-service of his tenants-in-chief. But it was Eleanor who issued a Charter by writ of the King from over seas, regarding knight service owed to the Abbey of Abingdon in 1156. To those knights and men who hold land and tenures of the Abbey they to do full service to the Abbot Walkelin. And if it is not done, the King and I will cause it to be done.[1] Henry loved to hunt and was not materialistic like his wife, Eleanor. Henry preferred business and travel which caused a rift in their marriage so he confined Eleanor at Winchester. She would re-emerge at his death in 1189. Henry's other loves were deplored by the church and Eleanor. Henry was however kind to his half-brother:

Hameline Plantagenet of Surrey who was born 1129/30 in Normandy, son of Geoffrey Plantagenet and one of his mistresses. King Henry II gave Hameline the hand of the wealthy widowed heiress, Isabella de Warenne, Countess of Surrey. They married in 1163. See Warenne Ancestry.

Isabella inherited Conisbrough castle where an early style castle had been built. Around 1180 Hamelin built its circular keep of fine limestone ashlar with six wedge-shaped buttresses placed equidistantly around its circumference stands close to its original height of 100 feet. The curtain walls were added soon after. Its interior is dark and gloomy due to a lack of windows and its circular shape does not provide very spacious accommodation. Other buildings within the bailey would have provided more pleasant accommodations. A third of the fines levied by Surrey County Courts went into the family's pocket. An endowment of fifty shillings a year was made for a chapel in the castle by Hamelin and Isabel. Hameline was always loyal to Henry II who died in 1189. Hameline and Isabel's children carried the Warenne name. Their son, William Warenne, succeeded as 5th Earl of Surrey. His daughter Isabella de Warenne married Roger II Bigod whose daughter, Mary, married Ranulf FitzRobert of Middleham. When the last Earl Warenne heiress died in 1347, Conisbrough castle reverted to the crown. By 1538 the castle was already in a state of ruin. It was made famous by Sir Walter Scott's book *Ivanhoe*. It is presently an English Heritage site managed today by the Ivanhoe Trust. Ranulph FitzRobert, the last Lord of Middleham, and his wife Mary Bigod's son Ranulf FitzRanulf became the 1st Lord of Spennithorne.

---

1 Douglas, p. 936

FitzRandolph of Spennithorne

Twenty years after the Conquest, the Anglo-Saxon thegns were replaced with a Norman Lord appointed by King William I. The lands in this area were part of the lands held by the Saxon leader, Ghilpatric. Spennithorne village is situated in Richmondshire on a slope above the Ure river and sheltered by high ground from the north and east and has a view of Middleham and its castle. Overlooking the village is the tower of Spennithorne church. Some Anglo-Saxon parts of it are older than Middleham Castle. By the middle of the 12th century the church had been enlarged. Its current tower dates around the 14th century when its aisles were widened to their present width. Within Spennithorne Church the remains of many FitzRandolphs are held. By the 13th century Spennithorne lands had passed to descendants of the FitzRandolphs who held said lands until the 16th century. As time took its toll, the foundations and part of the walls of the old manor house at Spennithorne were later converted into cottages now seen at the east end of the village. This was around the time that the medieval warm period ended and a little ice age began [1250-1300] bringing colder weather. Whether is was caused by lower solar radiation, increased volcanic activity, or a change in ocean currents is unknown. When the last of the FitzRandolphs had no male heirs, Spennithorne passed to the Wyville family through a daughter, Agnes, who married Marmaduke Wyville.

Ranulf[12] FitzRanulf, son of Ranulf FitzRobert and Mary Bigod was the 1st Lord of Spennithorne, as previously noted. He married Bertrama, widow of Sir Roger de Ingoldsby. Their son:

Ralph[13] FitzRanulf, Lord of Spennithorne, married Tiffany/Theophania de Lascelles, daughter and co-heiress of Robert de Lascelles de Kirby Knoll. Their son:

Ranulph[14] FitzRalph, Lord of Spennithorne, married Isabel (?). He died in 1343. Their son:

John[15] FitzRanulph, Lord of Spennithorne, was born about 1325 and married Maud de Campania. He grew up during the first stage (1337-1360) of the so called Hundred Years' War (1337-1453). He was younger than King Edward III (1327/30-1377) of England who was born in 1312. Edward III's mother Isabella and her lover Roger Mortimer deposed Edward in 1327 declaring themselves Regent. Mortimer with his retainers and the young King went after the barons at Lancaster, a southern neighbor of Yorkshire. Edward married in Jan 1328 and a son, Edward, the Black Prince, was born in Jun 1330. The following Oct Edward III seized control at Nottingham Castle. In 1333 Edward repudiated the Edinburgh-Northampton Treaty and war erupted in the north. France supported the Scots and captured some of Edward's French lands. A war of words erupted in 1337. In 1346 Edward invaded Normandy. The long bow took its toll. A treaty was made that cost England much of its French lands as well as paying an indemnity. England had victories in 1346 and (two) 1347. Then in 1348 the Black Death or Great Plague reached England which lasted about two years killing off about a third of its population. With it came loss of manpower, shortage of food, inflation and the end of military campaigns. The manors lost their peasants, small land holdings were deserted, the surviving ploughmen and laborers were in high demand. Their masters resisted paying higher wages so they formed unions to help with the issue. Many villeins fled the manors. Land holders responded by reviving the ancient claim of forced labor. Lacking workers, only the best land was farmed. Livestock was enclosed in the best grazing areas. The Church lost many of its priests and being the largest land holder its manors became the target of attacks. Turmoil reigned. The plague had reached Europe a few years earlier spread by either the Silk Road or merchant ships from Crimea. From Europe it spread to England.

It is not known if John FitzRanulph had to fight in any of Edward's campaigns. He died sometime before 1369 when the 2nd face of the Hundred Year's War began. John and Maud's son was:

Ranulf/Randall[16] FitzJohn, Lord of Spennithorne, wife's name is unknown. He grew up during the fight with France known as the Caroline War, the 2nd phase of the Hundred Years' War which followed the Edwardian War. In May 1369 Charles V of France demanded Edward the Black Prince come to Paris. The Treaty of Brétigny had been made in 1360 in which Edward III retained his French lands by giving up his claim to the French throne. When young Edward refused to go to Paris, Charles V resumed the war in 1369 to regain territorial losses imposed by the Treaty. All was not well for the English in fighting with the French. France felt feudal armies archaic even with the long bow. A new tactic of standing armies was introduced. England's response was to destroy the countryside and its crops. The Black Prince, died in 1376, a year before his father, Edward III. It took until 1389 for King Charles V of France successor to make peace with the Black Prince's 2nd son Richard II, now King of England (1377-1399). Ranulf FitzJohn died in 1388. Ranulf's son was:

John[17] FitzRandall/FitzRanulf, Lord of Spennithorne had grown up late in the reign of Edward III and his son the Black Prince. After the death of childless Richard II, the North Country Earls placed themselves at risk in helping Henry IV, grandson of Edward III by his daughter Blanche and John of Gaunt of Lancaster, acquire England's' throne in 1399. The Earls had been defending northern England from the Scots at their own expense. In asking Henry for reimbursement, they were offered less than the amount they submitted. Archbishop Scrope had also secured loans for Henry's expeditions against the Scots. He received equal treatment from the King. It was the Percy's of Northumberland, of an earlier FitzRandolph connection at Middleham, that gave Henry the most grief. Henry was suspect of the Percy's because they were related to a member of the Mortimer family who had aided the Scots. Edmund Mortimer was an equal to Henry in that he was the husband of Edward III's son Lionel's daughter Phillipa. In 1401 Henry IV passed a terrible statute due to the Lollards growing movement against the Roman Church who regarded them as heretics. They were followers of theologian John Wycliffe. Some Lollard members were knights in the King's court including Sir William Neville, Sir John Montague and Sir William Beachamp. They had been protected by the Black Prince and Henry IV's father, John of Gaunt. The statute stated that heretics were to be burnt alive with judgement solely left to the Church. Sir Henry Percy, *Hotspur*, military and rebel leader died in a battle at Shrewsbury in 1403 led by the King's eldest son Edward. Percy was killed by an arrow in his face, his father rushing to his aid. Henry Percy's uncle Thomas Percy, 1st Earl of Worcester, Sir Richard Venables and Sir Richard Vernon were publicly hanged, drawn and quartered in Shrewsbury on Jul 23rd, their heads displayed in public. Percy's aging father Henry, 1st Earl of Northumberland was found guilty of trespass and given clemency. He was the crown's only means of defending the northern border against the Scots. Two year later, still in mourning, the Earl conspired with Archbishop Scrope of York and Thomas Mowbray of Nottingham seeking reform from Henry IV. It was not over personal issues. Henry IV again marched north and was successful over the reformers. The Earl was driven across the border and his Northumberland estates were forfeited to the crown. Scrope, Mowbray, and Sir John FitzRandall were captured. Scrope and Mowbray were beheaded Jun 8th 1405. After a summary trial Sir John lost his head for treason Jul 20th 1405. However, it would affect his son John wife's family. Sir John's son:

Ralph[18] FitzJohn/Randall, Lord of Spennithorne, married Elizabeth Scrope, daughter of Sir Thomas Scrope of Masham and his wife Elizabeth Greystock of Greystock Manor in Cumberland. This was during the 3rd and last phase of the Hundred Year's War began in 1415 and was known as the Southampton plot. It began to lose support in England due to its cost and loss of French lands held by English nobles. It eventually led to the War of Roses in 1455. Sir Ralph died in Jan 1457/8. The next Lord of Spennithorne was Ralph and Elizabeth's son, John FitzRandolph.

Sir Ralph's wife, Elizabeth Scrope, ancestry follows:

SCROPE ANCESTRY

William le Scrope (pronounced scroop) was born in 1214 at Bolton in Wensleydale, Yorkshire, son of Henry Scrope of Flotmanby and his wife, Juliane, daughter of Roger Brune of Thornton. William served as Bailiff of Richmondshire in 1294 and knighted in 1298 after the battle of Flafirk. By his wife, Constance de Newsom, he had four children including two sons: 1) Sir Henry who served as Lord Chief Justice from 1317–23 and 1329–30; and +2) Sir Geoffrey. William died in 1296 and was buried at Wensley. William and Constance's son:

Geoffrey le Scrope acquired the Manor at Clifton-Upon-Yore in South Wensley and was given license to build a castle in 1318. He was knighted in 1317 and as a lawyer served as Lord Chief Justice in the years 1324-32 and 1337-38. He and his wife Ivetta de Ros of Ingmanthorpe had nine children, five sons and four daughters, born at Masham. In the baronial conflicts of the reign of Plantagenet Edward II (1307-27) Geoffrey was a loyal adherent to King Edward and managed to politically survive Edward's death in January 1327 when he was murdered by his wife, Isabella, making his son Edward III (1327-1377) the new king. Philip IV the Fair of France began supporting Scottish incursions into northern England in 1335. These attacks helped spur the "Hundred Years' War" in 1337 which was over the control of the French throne and partly over the wool trade with the Flemish. Geoffrey Chaucer, son of a London wine merchant, was one of Edward III's administrators. Chaucer's *Canterbury Tales* offer a panoramic view of English life during this era. Geoffrey le Scrope retired as Edward's III's Lord Chief Justice in 1338. After retiring, Geoffrey campaigned with Edward in Flanders and distinguished himself as a soldier. Geoffrey was one of the instigators behind the crown's actions against the very political Archbishop John Stratford who in 1326 served under Edward II as Lord Treasurer and joined Queen Isabella against her husband. Stratford then became a prominent adviser to Edward III as Chancellor in 1330, 1335-37, and briefly in 1340 in addition to being appointed Archbishop of Canterbury in Nov 1333. Meanwhile things were not going well for Edward III who was in Flanders. He returned to England to vent his anger to his Chancellor Robert, the Archbishop's brother. In December 1340 Geoffrey le Scrope died at Ghent, Flanders. His body was returned to England and buried in Coverham Abbey, Yorkshire. This left Geoffrey's sons to deal with Edward III. His eldest son:

Henry le Scrope was born Sep 29th 1312. The early years of his life was spent fighting for Edward III. First in Scotland, then in Brittany, Flanders, and the siege of Calais in 1347. Before he acquired the abeyant title by writ as the 1st Baron Scrope of Masham on Nov 25th 1350, he was in a battle off the coast of Winchelsea. This was the time of numerous battles in the "Hundred Year's War." As an ambassador, he was sent out on several occasions to deal with England and France as well as Scotland. Henry's wife was named Joan. Among his children were:

1. Sir Geoffrey who married Eleanor de Neville, daughter of Lord Ralph Neville and Alice de Audley, daughter of Hugh Audley. Geoffrey was killed on a crusade in Lithuania in 1362 leaving no issue.
2. Henry, 3rd Baron of Revensworth who married Lady Elizabeth de Grey. Henry died 1425.
3. Richard who became Archbishop of Yorkshire and was beheaded Jun 8th 1405 during the reign of Henry IV for his part in the Percy Rebellions in Northumberland. The reaction of the Archbishop of Canterbury and the populace was liken to the murder of Thomas Beckett.
4. Sir John who married Elizabeth Strathbogie.
5. William who fought the Turks and died in that area.
6. Isabel, 1st wife of Sir Robert Plumpton.
7. Joan who married Henry Fitz Hugh, 2nd Baron Fitz Hugh.
+8. Stephen, 3rd Baron Scrope of Masham who died Jan 25th 1406.

Baron Henry Scrope died Jul 31st 1392 the year his son Richard was summoned to Parliament. Henry and Joan Scrope's son:

Stephen Scrope succeeded his father as 2nd Baron Scrope of Masham. He was knighted at Alexandria in 1365 while on a crusade to the Holy Land. His wife was Margery de Welles, widow of John Huntingfield of North Elmsall, Yorks. Her father was the 4th Lord of Welles. Stephen and Margery had children:

1. Henry, 3rd Baron Scrope of Masham, was Counsellor to Henry V and treasurer of the King's Exchequer. For some reason he joined a couple of conspirators against the King. Although he claimed he was trying to foil the plot he was none the less convicted and executed Aug 5th 1415 as a ringleader in the Southampton Plot.
2. Geoffrey.
+3. John, 4th Baron Scrope of Masham, died Nov 15th 1455.
4. Stephen, Archdeacon of Richmond, Chancellor of Cambridge.
5. William, Archdeacon of Durham, died May 12th 1463.
6. Maud, m. Baldwin Freville. Stephen died, Jan 25th 1406 and was buried in St. Stephen's Chapel in Yorkshire. His wife Margery died May 29th 1422.

The Southampton Plot of 1415 was a conspiracy to replace King Henry V (1413-1422), who became king two years earlier, with Edmund Mortimer the 5th Earl of March. Mortimer's claim to the throne was superior in that he was the 2nd surviving son of King Edward III. Henry V and his father, Henry IV's, claim was derived from Henry IV's father who was the 3rd surviving son of Edward III. Moreover, Mortimer's father Roger, the 4th Earl of March, was considered heir presumptive to Richard II as well as Mortimer when a child. The three ringleaders of the plot were Edmund Mortimer's brother-in-law, Richard of Conisburgh, 3rd Earl of Cambridge; Stephen's older brother, Henry Scrope, 3rd Baron Scrope of Masham; and Sir Thomas Grey. The Earl of March informed Henry V of the plot on Jul 31st 1415 saying he had just become aware of it. The three men were promptly arrested with a trial quickly taking place in Southampton. Grey was beheaded on Aug 2nd and the other two on Aug 5th in front of the Bargate. Satisfied Henry V sailed off to France on Aug 11th. The Scrope Baronage title was abolished. Claims of conspiracy and non conspiracy occupied some individuals for some time with nothing resolved. But the beheadings were real. Eventually the event lost interest. Later the War of the Roses between the two houses of York and Lancaster would occupy England. Shakespeare wrote of the offence in Henry V, Act II, Scene 2. The Baron of

Masham's title was restored in 1426 but became abeyant in 1517. Stephen and Margery Scrope's 3rd son:

John Scrope was knighted in 1424 and made a member of the King Henry V's Privy Council, those who advise the king. He was also appointed to the Commissions of the Peace of Essex, Lincolnshire, Nottinghamshire and Yorkshire. These were knights whose job it was to maintain peace. In 1426 he became the 4th Baron Scrope of Masham and was able to acquire the confiscated Scrope lands which had been granted to other knights after his brother Henry's execution. Then John was sent out in 1428 as an Ambassador to the Pope, the King of Spain, the Roman King, and Scotland the next year. John was next appointed Lord High Treasurer of England from Feb 26th 1432 to Aug 11th 1433. Two years later he was an ambassador to the Grand Master of the Order of St John of Jerusalem at Rhodes and in 1439 to the Archbishop of Cologne. His 1st wife was Elizabeth Greystoke, daughter of Sir John Greystoke, was buried St. Stephen's Chapel, Yorks, having no children. His 2nd wife, Elizabeth Chaworth, was the only child of Sir Thomas Chaworth of Wiverton, Notts., and his wife Nicola Braybrokke, daughter of Sir Reynold Braybrooke.

Elizabeth Chaworth's family dates back to Patrick de Cadurcis (Chaworth), a native of Brittany who came with William the Conqueror and made a Baron by King William. The family held lands in Nottinghamshire before the lands at Wiverton came into the possession of Sir William Chaworth in the right of his wife Alice, co-heir of the last Lord Bassett of Drayton in the 1200's. Laurence de Chaworth was a Knight of the Shire in 1313. Thomas de Chaworth was summoned as a Nottingham landowner for military service in 1314 under Edward II. In the reign of Henry VI (1422-1461), Sir Thomas Chaworth by a fortunate marriage, added largely to the family possessions. He became entitled to the inheritance of no less than five families. The acquisition of wealth enabled him to make a park at Wiverton and possibly establishing Wiverton Hall in 1450. Chaworth who died in 1459 left vast estates to his relatives. His possessions in Notts. included property at East Bridgeford, Marnham, Edwalton, Clifton, Wiverton, Langar, Barnstone, Granby, Colston Bassett, Cropwell Butler, Cropwell Bishop, Tithby, Shelford, and Whatton.

John Scrope is said to have three sons & five daughters. Among them was Thomas Scrope. John Scrope died Nov 15th 1455 and was buried in the Scrope Chapel in York Minster. John Scrope and Elizabeth Chaworth's son:

Thomas Scrope became the 5th Lord Scrope of Masham. Apparently he chose to lead a quiet life as little is known about him. He married Elizabeth Greystoke of Greystoke Manor, Cumberland, daughter of Ralph, Lord Greystoke and Catherine Gifford. Thomas and Elizabeth had four sons and three daughters:

1. Thomas who succeeded his father and married Elizabeth Neville.
2. Alice who married James Strangeways.
3. Ralph who married Eleanor Windsor.
+4. Elizabeth who married Ralph[18] FitzRandolph and had son, John.[19]
5. Geoffrey who died unmarried in 1517.
6. Henry who married Elizabeth Percy.
7. Margaret who married Christopher Danby.

Their mother, Elizabeth died on Dec 20th 1490 and was buried at Blackfriars, Yorkshire. Thomas and Elizabeth's grandson John:

FitzRandolph of Spennithorne Cont'd.

John[19] FitzRandolph, Lord of Spennithorne, married Joan Conyers, daughter of Christopher Conyers of Hornby Castle. The initial manor and lands of Hornby belonged to one named St. Quintin who came with the Conqueror. The manor eventually passed to John Conyers by his marriage to Margaret Quintin when the Quintin male line became extinct. John Conyers died in 1422. His son was Christopher Conyers, Lord of Hornby and Sheriff of Yorkshire, who married 1st Elena Rolleston, daughter of Thomas Rolleston, Esq. and Beatrice Haulay of Rolleston, Staffordshire. Elena died Aug 6th 1444 at Hornby Castle. Among their children was Joan Conyers born c. 1420.

The church at Spennithorne was St. Michel the Archangel in which there was a chapel of St. Mary where many of the FitzRanololph family are buried including John FitzRandolph who died Mar 5th 1474/5. Richard Marshall was priest at the time when Christopher Conyers, heir to William Lord Conyers (1468-1524) and his 2nd wife Lady Anne Neville daughter of Ralph Neville, Earl of Westmoreland, made a deed of feoffment on Jan 20th 1496 to pray for John FitzRandolph's soul, his friend's souls, and all Christian souls. John FitzRandolph and Joan Conyer's son:

John[20] FitzRandolph would be the last of this line to die in Yorkshire. His history is very illusive other than he was the father of a son named Christopher. South of Yorkshire is in Nottinghamshire and here we find the next FitzRandolph beginning with John's son:

Christopher[21] FitzRandolph who married Jane/Joane Langton in 1514, eldest daughter and heir of Cuthbert Langton. In 1250 the manor house Westwood or Langton Hall was granted to Geoffrey de Langton by Richard, son of Hugh de Ruddington, who had earlier been granted it by Lord John Stoteville. Thomas de Langton and Robert de Barton paid 20 shilling, the remainder of their account for the Manor in the parish of Kirkby in Ashfield in 1340. It lay on the eastern boundary of Sherwood forest. Before 1066 it was a Danish settlement with Kirkby meaning a village with a church. Ashfeld denotes it was open land with ash trees. At the time of the conquest its landowners were named Levenot and Alvric. The Conqueror gave the lands to the De'stoteville family. In 1340 it was granted to John Darcy. In 1466 it passed to the daughter of Philip Darcy, Elizabeth, who married Sir John Conyers. The manor stayed in that family to Henry VIII's time (1509-1547) until it went to the FitzRandolph's by marriage in 1514.[1]

During the reign of Edward III (1327-1377) the manor belonged to Sir William le Wyne. When he died he left two daughters, one married to Sir Ralph de Langford, knight. In 1431 John de Langton of Kirkby held one messuage called Langton Place and six Closes (an enclosed place near a cathedral or other building) with appurtenances for the daughters, Elizabeth and Margery, heirs of Philip Darcy for which he paid £2.8 yearly rent to them for the service of a hundredth part of a Knights Fee until John died in 1479. His son and heir was Richard Langton. John de Langton had another son named Robert. In 1515 at Middleton, Warwickshire, Gent. Cuthbert Langton, enfeoffed his manor his lands in Huknall Torkard, Durty Huknall, Maunsfeild Woodhouse, Kirkby in Ashfeild and Watnow Chaworth in the county of Notts and Birchwood in County Darby to two knights and

Huknall Torkard was named in 1295 after one of its principal land owners, Torcard. In 1915 its name became simply Huknall. It was known for its parish church St. Mary Magdalene built by Saxons and its thriving market. To its east is the notable Sherwood forest, then a favorite hunting

---

1 Notes from George Gershom Bonser, Nottinghamshire Web Site.

ground for kings. Its hardwood trees were also prized for their timber. A forest consisted of any land that was not enclosed. Only several hundred acres remain of what it was during this period. On Sep 9th 1539 Christopher FitzRandolph and fifteen men called Regarders were appointed to perambulate Sherwood forest in 1251 beginning at the King's Castle at nearby Nottingham. Did the King have them looking for Robin Hood? Actually they were marking the king's bounds and the residences for tax purposes. Since much of the land was used by monasteries, they undoubtedly came under Henry VIII's dissolution policy. Sutton In Ashfield Parish created in 1572 lay further north. Its parish church also named St. Mary Magdalene was built in the 12th century. South of Sutton In Ashfield is Kirkby In Ashfield. Its 11th century church St. Wilfred's was purposely destroyed mid Jan 1907 by an arsonist. Thomas FitzRandolph, son of Christopher and Joane, and his wife Katherine were buried there on Mar 2nd 1593 and Feb 27th 1598, Thomas the latter. On the south wall in the rectory garden is a brass monument written in Latin and dedicated to Thomas and his wife. Christopher and Joane's children were: 1) Thomas; 2) daughter who married Anthony Burgh; 3) Edward; +4) Christopher; and 5) John. Christopher's will dated Jun 1st 1516 was proved the following Jul 17th. His farm went to Anthony Burgh and he to keep son John and his things until son John is age 21. Their third son was:

Christopher[22] FitzRandolph who was born at Sutton-in-Ashfield. His will dated Jun 20th 1588 at Hucknall-under-Huthwaite, Parish of Sutton in Ashfield, Notts., gave his land to his four sons: 1) James; 2) Anthony who was buried Nov 20th 1636, Sutton-in-Ashfield; +3) Edward; and 4) Christopher. Also his lease at Stainesby and 4 kire. To son Christopher £10. To wife (unnamed) his best bed, best pan and best pot plus residue un-bequeathed with sons James, Anthony, and Edward, sole executors. He was buried Jun 28th 1588 in the ancient church of St. Mary Magdalene at Sutton-in-Ashfield. Today Hucknall-under-Huthwaite, now just Huthwaite, is a very small village with few inhabitants that lies west of Sutton In Ashfield. Stainsby is also a very small village on M1 route in Derbyshire northwest of Sutton. Christopher's son:

Edward[23] FitzRandolph was born in Sutton-in-Ashfield. It was recorded in 1612 that he was one of the owners living in Sutton-in-Ashfield as well as Edward Langford and others. On Nov 16th 1589 he married his 1st wife Alice Thompson. She died after the birth of a daughter and buried Dec 27th 1604. Their five children were:

1. Elizabeth, chr. Nov 6th 1590.
2. Thomas, chr. Jan 2nd 1592/3.
3. Richard, chr. Aug 7th 1596.
4. Jane, chr. Jan 1st 1602/3.
5. Catherine, chr. Dec 16th 1604, buried Apr 21st 1610

His 2nd marriage in 1605 was to Frances Howes who was buried Jun 7th 1631 at Kneesall. Edward and Frances had six children:

+6. Edward, chr. Jul 5th 1607.
7. Anthony, chr. Sep 24th 1609.
8. Alice who died an infant.
9. Christopher, chr. May 1613.
10. John, chr. Jan 14th 1615/6.
11. Joseph, chr. Nov 18th 1621.

Edward's will dated Aug 13th 1647 was proved Oct 27th. He gave his son James' four children his house in Hucknall-under-Huthwaite and adjoining property. *To son John my dwelling house in Kirsall, parish of Kneesall on condition he keep my brother Christopher with sufficient meat, drink and lodging during his life. To my children's children 40s each except son Richards. To son Edward[24] £10 if he come to demand it. To son Richard's children: Thomas £20, Elizabeth £10, and Mary £10 if they come to demand it. To William Cooper a piece of land. To daughter Cooper 40s. To Winnifraite Lowe 5s. To Parreill Abbot 5s. To poor of Kirsall 5s, to poor of Kneesall 5s. Residue to son John, executor. Overseers cousin John Kitchin and son-in-law Thomas Trollowe.* Near Sutton In Ashfield, a back road would take one into Kersall then into the village of Kneesall. Today this area is remote with open fields growing crops such as wheat and rape seed with some cattle providing milk for its few inhabitants.

The monarchy and the aristocracy had dominated government for centuries. The Hundred Year's War (1337-1453) had been financially costly for the country causing the ducal houses of York and Lancaster to wage civil war known as the War of the Roses (1455-1485). It ended with Tudor Henry VII, grandson of Henry V, in control. He conserved national finances, encouraged commerce and exploration ending feudalism and the so-called Camelot. England's Renaissance was mostly about philosophy and literature, not jousting and fair maidens. Henry's 6'2" slim son, Henry VIII, with a round face and auburn hair was notably different. He took after his grandfather Edward IV in seeking pleasure. It was Henry's wives that lost their heads. As the people suffered with lost lands, sheep enclosures, fines and heavy taxation that resulted in poverty and poor rates, the crown managed to get these unpopular bills rubber stamped by parliament. The middle class sought government protection which let the monarchy get away with their populace laws. Monasticism crumbled under the Reformation with the establishment of the Anglican Church. Henry VIII died in 1547. His daughter Mary was crowned Queen and left the country more financially sound despite being dubbed *Bloody Mary*. Then Elizabeth I, the last of the Tudors who was like her father Henry VIII, began an extravagant life style that left the country deeply in debt again. Elizabeth was dogmatic about religious practices expanding the Reformation. Wars demanded armies and naval fleets. Spreading commerce bred colonization. All contributed to a rise in royal power with heavy taxation. Despite royal despotism, the ideals of limited government in the Magna Carta couldn't be entirely squelched. In 1625 James I, a stubborn, vane and erudite individual was given the throne with sovereignty over England and Scotland. He was nothing like his mother, Mary Queen of Scots. James soon meddled in business causing citizens to lose their jobs. He raised taxes indiscriminately opposing Parliament. When they protested he dissolved both houses. All this sounds like the USA today. James I hunted, harassed and hung those who opposed the Anglican church and his version of the Bible. So dissidents began fleeing England. Edward FitzRandolph was 18 when James I died in 1625 and King James' son, Charles, became the new monarch (1625-1649). Like his father, Charles would do anything irregular to acquire money. He antagonized religious leaders and Parliament starting a civil war. Parliament briefly ruled until Oliver Cromwell got into the fray in 1653.

The next generation of this FitzRandolph lineage begins with Edward who journeyed to New England which was still under Britain's thumb until the American Revolution. Not being the eldest son, there was little to be gained by staying in England. Edward now at age 26 probably felt New England offered a better life. His real reasons remain unknown.

FITZRANDOLPH'S OF NEW ENGLAND

Edward[24] FitzRandolph was christened Jul 5th 1607 in Sutton-in-Ashfield, Nottinghamshire, eldest son of Edward FitzRandolph and his 2nd wife, Frances Howes of Kneesall. After Edward arrived in New England, he built a house in Scituate. There he met and subsequently was married by Rev. Lothrop on May 10th 1637 seventeen year old Elizabeth Blossom. Edward joined Lothrop's church four days later. Lothrop referred to Edward as "the young Master Fitzrandolphe." Amos Otis wrote that Edward "probably belonged to a good family." Lothrop's group were not appreciated by the established church in New England's colonies. Baptism was a lingering problem and banishment became imposed. Many also opposed the taxes to support the "established" church.

Edward sold his Scituate house to Deacon Richard Sealis in 1639 and moved to Barnstable on Cape Cod where he built a house on an eight acre lot. Elizabeth joined Lothrop's church on Aug 27th 1643. The Barnstable home was sold on Jun 2nd 1649 to Elder John Chipman,[1] a carpenter, and they moved to West Barnstable on a double great lot of one hundred twenty acres. From Scituate to Cape Cod, a virulent outbreak of smallpox and whooping cough swept the area with Nov 15th 1649 being declared a "Day of Humiliation." Early in 1669 they moved to Piscataway, NJ, where Edward was listed as a resident on Jul 28th 1673 and required to take an oath to the Dutch. Edward died shortly before Elizabeth received a land patent in Piscataway on Mar 21st 1675/6 for three hundred acres. He was buried in St. James Churchyard in Stelton, NJ. Many of the FitzRandolph family became Seventh Day Baptists at Piscataway, others Quakers.

Edward and Elizabeth were parents of twelve children, three of whom died young.

1. Nathaniel, bpt. Aug 9th 1640, buried Dec 10th 1640.
2. Nathaniel bpt. May 15th 1642, married Mary Holley.
3. Mary bpt. Oct 6th 1644, died young.
4. Hannah, bpt. Apr 23rd 1648, married Jasper Taylor.
5. Mary, born May 31st, bpt. Jun 2nd 1650.
6. John bpt. Jan 2nd 1651/2, died infant.
7. John born Oct 7th 1653, married Sarah (?).
8. Joseph born Mar 1st 1656, married Joannah Conger.
9. Thomas born Aug 16th 1659, married Elizabeth Manning.
10. Elizabeth born 1657, married Andrew Wooden.
+11. Hope[25] born Apr 2nd 1661, married Ezekiel Bloomfield.
12. Benjamin born 1663, married 1st Sarah Dennis.

Edward FitzRandolph's grandson, Edward, son of Nathaniel was known as the Quaker financier of Woodbridge. In Feb 1701 he described the Jerseys as: *all in confusion for want of Governm't and humbly pray to be taken under his Ma'ties immediate Governm't and Protection being that the area is too large and too few inhabitants.* He proposed East Jersey be annexed to New York and West Jersey to Pennsylvania claiming proprietors had right to the land but not the government. A royal governor was sent who later proclaimed the rights of the proprietors to the land with quit-rents, but not to govern. But that did not end the dispute. In 1707 New Jersey's House of Representatives found that several men had been duped by Richard Saltar into paying Capt. John Bown, who had been arresting innocent persons, £46 for "public good." Among them were John Pike, Hugh Dunn,

Joseph FitzRandolph, John Langstaff, Benjamin Hull, John Drake and Edward Dunham, Pike having given £20 of the total.[1]

There are a couple of interesting stories about later generations of this family. Edward's grandson, Nathaniel FitzRandolph, son of Benjamin was born Nov 11th 1703 at Princeton, NJ. It was reported in the *Pennsylvania Gazette* Aug 16th 1753, that Nathaniel (Benjamin, Edward) was a man of means and offered a £3 reward to whoever secures the thief and his horse, a sorrel pacing gelding six years old which was stolen. In Aug 1755 his six foot Dutch servant man named Christian Luterman ran away and he offered Forty shillings and reasonable charges for his return. His horse was obviously worth more than his servant. The published article described in great detail Luterman's physical appearance. When it was first reported by deputy Gov. Hamilton that a college was to be erected somewhere in New Jersey, Nathaniel was the first to make a proposal for the site. The cornerstone was laid in 1766. In 1905 a descendant gave a gateway known as FitzRandolph Gateway with Princeton's Official Seal patterned after a FitzRandolph Coat of Arms to the college. It is the official entrance to the front campus and Nassau Hall and opened only at Commencement or for receptions of distinguished visitors. When excavation was done in 1909 for Holden Hall several old graves and thirty-two tombs were discovered on the site.

Edward's son Nathaniel had a son, Samuel, who by wife Mary Jones had sons Samuel and Joseph. The younger Samuel was born Dec 16th 1694 at Woodbridge. He was living in New Castle Co., Delaware with his 1st wife Frances in 1719. He returned to Woodbridge around 1726. As Master of the *Seaflower* newspapers printed his inward and outward bounds between Perth Amboy and Boston between 1726-28.[2] Master Samuel married 2nd Joannah Kinsey on Dec 18th 1729 as members of the Quaker Woodbridge Monthly Meeting. Samuel's brother, Joseph was born about 1704 and married Elizabeth Kinsey Jun 17th 1731, sister of Samuel's wife as recorded in Rahway and Plainfield Monthly Meeting records. Joseph was Captain of the sloop *Elizabeth*. The brothers sailed between Amboy and the Carolinas, Jamaica and Curaçoa. Samuel found himself and his mariners in trouble for piracy. In 1749 Samuel was Master of the sloop *Mary*. Arriving in North Carolina, he was met with a petition of his piratical practices. At a Governor's Council held in Burlington, NJ, on Tuesday, Feb 5th 1750, William Waller, mariner of Woodbridge twp. presented the following confession:

> *That on or about the 19th of September past, the examinant sailed out of the Port of Perth Amboy on board the Sloop Mary, Samuel FitzRandolph owner and master. As a sailor he went before the mast and said the sloop was bound to North Carolina where they arrived on Sunday following. They saw a large Spanish ship of about 500 ton at anchor over the bar of Oeracoke inlet and the ship appeared to be in distress, having lost the heads of her fore mast and main mast. Her mizzen mast was quite gone and her rudder. After the gale was over the Boatswain of the Spanish ship came on board the Mary in order to agree with Master FitzRandolph to carry a cargo for the ship to Norfolk in Virginia. The examinant understanding something of the Spanish tongue acted as interpreter. Master FitzRandolph agreed to carry such effects to Norfolk for five hundred and seventy pieces of Eight but there were no articles of agreement signed between the parties. In about a week the Spanish Boatswain came with about fifteen hands in a launch and hawled the Mary alongside. The examinant saw the Master of the Spanish ship (as he was told) on board who ordered the following to be put on board the sloop, to wit, Cocoa, cocheonial, sugars and about fifty chests of money. After the*

---

1 John Brett Langstaff, *New Jersey Generations: Macculloch Hall*, Morristown, NY, Vantage Press, 1964, pp. 161-23

2 Wm. Nelton, Ed., *Colonial Documents of New Jersey, Newspaper Extraces 1704-1739*, Vol. VI (Paterson, NJ, Press Prtg..)

Sloop took on the goods, she hawled off to an anchor. Some words happened in a few days after this between the Master and this examinant and they parted by consent, and this examinant went on board a sloop riding in the harbor bound for Middletown, New Jersey, one Anderson Master. About two or three nights before this examinant left the Sloop, Joseph Jackson, a sailor on board the sloop delivered to this examinant about four hundred and fifty pieces of Eight tied up in an oznaburg bag with a letter directed to the father, James Jackson, the remainder claimed by the examinants share. The examinant believed the money belonged to the Spanish ship and this examinant was informed by Thomas Edwards and Kinsey FitzRandolph [Samuel's son] that they had cut a hole at the foot of the Lar-board cabin through the bulk head into the hold of FitzRandolph's sloop where the money had been lodged. The hatches going into the hold were barred and locked by the Spaniards and they took the keys with them. This examinant never took any money out of the hold but confesses the money was divided amongst the Sloops crew as follows, to wit, Kinsey FitzRandolph, mate, Samuel FitzRandolph, jr., Thomas Edwards, Benjamin Moore, Joseph Jackson and Silas Walker and this examinant. When asked of the examinant if Master FitzRandolph knew anything of the taking of the money, the examinant said not to his knowledge. But when the examinant and the rest of the crew went for water only the Master and his two sons were on board. Kinsey FitzRandolph told this examinant that he had been in the hold and got seven hundred pieces of Eight for his father and also forty pieces for himself. That money was taken twice before out of the hold before this examinant left and he believes that they made two shares amongst the sloop's crew, as aforementioned. That some time in the month of Oct last, this examinant sailed from North Carolina in the middletown sloop and on their voyage, Capt. Anderson discovered that this examinant had Spanish money on board. The Captain told this examinant if he had known it before, he would not have brought him. When they arrived at Sandyhook this examinant went on board a sloop belonging to James Smith of Woodbridge and arrived at Woodbridge on 16 October. The next morning the examinant sent for Mary Jackson, jr., the sister of Joseph Jackson, and gave her the letter directed to her father, James Jackson, and six pieces of Eight. On Monday Sen'night last he delivered to Mary Jackson, jr., two hundred and seven pieces of Eight more, before Robert FitzRandolph, Hartshorne FitzRandolph, Mary Jackson sr., and Mercy Smith. Hartshorne FitzRandolph came as security to the pieces forth coming. This examinant's share of said money he laid out at New York sixty eight pieces, that he lent to James Codington twenty five pieces, to James Pike thirteen pieces, to Robert FitzRandolph five pieces, to Isaac FitzRandolph three pieces, and changed with one Polocks fifteen pieces for Jersey money and the remainder are now at this Deponents place of abode, to wit, the house of Robert FitzRandolph in Woodbridge.

What followed were matters concerning the court findings in that there was sufficient reason to suspect the master and every mariner aboard the sloop was guilty of robbery and piracy and to be brought before the court for examination and any pieces of eight be secured by the court. Nothing further was located as to the legal disposition of this case. One could say that this was a family affair as sons were aboard at the time the coins became missing and later found among family members. Samuel and Joseph's sister, Prudence, had married Shubel Smith. Joseph's children married into the Coddington family. In 1750 James Coddington was loaned 25 pieces of Eight by William Waller of Woodbridge who testified to the theft by the crew of the Sloop *Mary*, Samuel FitzRandolph, owner and Master. A few bad apples didn't spoil the whole basket for some of this family served faithfully during the Revolutionary War.

One of the more revered FitzRandolphs was Captain Nathaniel[28] (Nathaniel[27], Edward[26], Nathaniel[25], Edward[24]) of Woodbridge and Revolutionary War hero known as Natty who married Experience Inslee in 1772, daughter of Jonathan and Grace (Moore) Inslee. British troops consisted of English, Germans, Hessians, and Scot Highlanders. Many were concentrated in Amboy and Brunswick. They would go in large parties to plunder and rob homes. Males being in service were forced to leave wives and children to face these men. Prisoners and wounded were, to put it mildly, ill treated or executed. Natty was revered by his men and fought bravely with them. More than once he was captured and subsequently released on exchange. His home was watched with hopes of capturing or killing him. In a skirmish near Elizabethtown he was wounded, subsequently dying on Jul 23rd 1780. Nathaniel was buried in Woodbridge Cemetery. On May 15th 1788 at Orphans Court in Woodbridge, his widow Experience, now wife of James Coddington, solicited a guardian be appointed for her children Agnes and Nathaniel FitzRandolph, both under 14. Benjamin Manning was appointed guardian to the children with James Dunn, surety. More on the Manning family will come later.

Blossom Ancestry

Elizabeth Blossom, wife of Edward [24] FitzRandolph, and mother of Hope[25] FitzRandolph, was born in 1620 in Leiden, Holland, daughter of Thomas Blossom and Anne Heilsdon, a Huguenot. They were married on Nov 10th 1605 in St. Clement's Church in Cambridge, England. The only remains of the church today is a small plaque marking the spot where the church once stood. Anne had inherited houses in the Parish of St. Giles in Cambridge from her maternal grandfather. Since husbands had control of his wife's property, Thomas gave Anne power of attorney to sell the real estate. About 1608 Thomas and Anne Blossom settled in Leiden, Holland, where they eventually joined the Robinson Separatists. A student in the School of Medicine lived with them in 1609. Thomas and Anne had five children. 1) A child buried Apr 12th 1617; 2) A son who died before 1625; 3) Thomas; +4) Elizabeth; and 5) Peter. Thomas and a son were on the *Speedwell* and among those who returned to Holland. Thomas wrote to Governor Bradford on Dec 15th 1625 the following:

> *Beloved Sir,*
> *Kind salutations, &c. I have thought good to write to you, concerning the case as it standeth both with you and us. We see, alas! what frustrations and disappointments it pleaseth the Lord to send in this our course, good in itself, and according to godliness taken in hand, and for good and lawful ends, who yet pleaseth not to prosper as we are, for reasons best known to himself; and which also nearly concerns us to consider of, whether we have sought the Lord in it as we see, or not. That the Lord hath singularly preserved life in the business to great admiration, giveth me good hope that he will, (if our sins hinder not,) in his appointed time, give a happy end unto it. On the contrary, when I consider how it pleaseth the Lord to cross those means that should bring us together, being now as far off or farther than ever, in our apprehension; as also to take that means away, which would have been so comfortable unto us in that course, both for wisdom of counsel as also for our singular help in our course of godliness; whom the Lord (as it were) took away even as fruit falleth before it was ripe; when neither length of days, nor infirmity of body, did seem to call for his end. The Lord even then took him*

[Mr. Robinson] away, as it were in his anger; whom if tears would have held, he had remained to this day. The loss of his ministry was very great unto me, for I ever counted myself happy in the enjoyment of it, notwithstanding all the crosses and losses otherwise I sustained. Yet indeed the manner of his taking away hath more troubled me, as fearing the Lord's anger in it, that, as I said, in the ordinary course of things, might still have remained, as also, the singular service he might have yet done in the church of God. Alas! dear friends, our state and cause in religion, by his death being wholly destitute of any that may defend our cause as it should against our adversaries; that we may take up that doleful complaint in the Psalm, that there is no prophet left among us, nor any that knoweth how long. Alas! you would fain have had him with you, and he would as fain have come to you. Many letters and much speech hath been about his coming to you, but never any solid course propounded for his going; if the course propounded the last year had appeared to have been certain, he would have gone, though with two or three families. I know no man amongst us knew his mind better than I did, about those things; he was loath to leave the church, yet I know also, that he would have accepted the worst conditions which in the largest extent of a good conscience could be taken, to have come to you. For myself and all such others as have formerly minded coming, it is much what the same, if the Lord afford means. We only know how things are with you by your letters; but how things stand in England we have received no letters of any thing, and it was Nov before we received yours. If we come at all unto you, the means to enable us so to do must come from you. For the state of our church, and how it is with us, and of our people, it is wrote of by Mr. White. Thus praying you to pardon my boldness with you in writing as I do, I commend you to the keeping of the Lord, desiring, if he see it good, and that I might be serviceable unto the business, that I were with you. God hath taken away my son, that was with me in the ship, when I went back again; I have only two children, which were born since I left you. Fare you well.
Yours to his power, Thomas Blossom

The Blossom family arrived at Salem May 15th 1629 aboard another *Mayflower* and set out for Plymouth. Bradford wrote in 1633:

It pleased ye Lord to visite them this year with an infectious fevoure, of which many fell very sicke, and upward of 20 persons dyed, men and women, besids children, and sundry of them of their anciente friends which had lived in Holand: as Thomas Blossome, Richard Masterson, with sundry others, and in ye end (after he had much helped others) Samuell Fuller, who was their surgeon & phisition, and had been a great help and comforte unto them; as is his facultie...and he and ye rest of their brethren much lamented by them; and caused much sadnes & mourning amongst them; which caused them to humble them selves, & seeke ye Lord; and towards winter it pleased the Lord ye sicknes ceased...This disease allso swept away many of ye Indeans from all ye places near adjoyning; and ye spring before, espetially all ye month of May, ther was such a quantitie of a great sorte of flies, like to wasps, or bumble-bees, which came out of holes in ye ground, and replenished all ye woods, and eate ye green-things, and made such a constante yelling noyes, as made all ye woods ring of them, and ready to deafe ye hearers. They have not by ye English been heard or seen before or since. But ye Indeans tould them ye sickness would follow, and so it did in Jun, Jul, Aug, and ye cheefe heat of somer.

Thomas Blossom was age 66 when he died in 1633 after spending a quarter of his adult life in Leiden. His wife, Anne married 2nd Henry Rowley on Oct 17th 1633 and lived in Scituate. Thomas and Anne's daughter Elizabeth was noted in the previous FitzRandolph family history. Thomas Blossom, jr. married on Jun 18th 1645 in Barnstable, Sarah Ewer, with Edmond Freeman performing the ceremony. Thomas' son Peter Blossom married Sarah Bodfish Jun 21st 1666 in West Barnstable, MA.

The Evered/Webb Connection

John Evered als Webb came with his brother Stephen and John Pike in the *James* in 1635. He settled in Boston where he joined Boston's First Church and was declared a freeman on Dec 7th 1636. John Evered married the widow Mary Fayreweather who had a son John. The only mention of Mary's son John is in a deed of gift that she made to him prior to her second marriage. In 1641 John Evered became a merchant involved in a fishing enterprise off the Isle of Sable, Nova Scotia. *A Commission to John Webb als __ of Boston and his company to trade & doe their business at the Isle of Sables & to pass in the barke "Endeavor" of Salem whereof is Master Joseph Grafton.* The sandy half moon shaped Sables Isle lies offshore in the Atlantic where the area is considered the Atlantic's Graveyard due to so many ship wrecks in the area. Seal, cod, and other fish abounded in that area. After leaving Boston, John and Mary Evered moved to suburban Braintree on 90 acres by the Monatiquot River. He became a military officer in 1643. They moved to a farm in 1659 that he was granted by the General Court to military officers at Chelmsford. As Captain his notable duty as the hanging of Mary Dyer in 1660. They moved to Dracut in 1665 where he wrote his will. These towns were located on the Merrimack River which enters Massachusetts from New Hampshire at the town of Tyngsborough and from there, goes past or through Chelmsford, Lowell, Dracut, Tewksbury, Andover, Methuen, Lawrence, North Andover, Haverhill, Groveland, West Newbury, Merrimac, Amesbury, Salisbury and Newburyport into the Atlantic ocean. Timber from New Hampshire was floated down the Merrimack River for commercial purposes. From this one can see that most of the towns settled in northern Massachusetts were located on or near the river. John did a lot of buying and selling land and obviously kept his business contacts with Boston as noted in his will.

The following abstraction of John's Will states that he was related to the Ayers family. Exactly what the relationship is has yet to be discovered due to word usage changes over the centuries.

I Cap[t]. Jn[o] Evered als Webb of Drawcutt upon Mirrimack in the town of Norfolk, late of the town of Boston in New England, Merchant...After payments of debts, to wife, Mary, all my wearing apparel and all my household stuff and ⅓ part of my estate, rest and personal lying in New England and to have during her natural life in loss of her dowery, but also the same to have and enjoy thereafter to prosper and benefit...To the Church of Boston £50 to be paid one year after my decease. To my cousin James Braiden of Boston, merchant, £30. To my brother, Willim Dinsdall of Boston, cooper [a packer of fish and meat], £20. To the pastor of the Church of Chelmsford £20. To my servant, Henry Nolson, his freedom before his term is fully expired and determined, also £10 to be paid to him in three months after my decease. To each of my servants viz: Hugh Stone, Samuel Menter als Watts, John Bennett, Peter Rattlough, and Elizabeth Lilbourus 40 shilling separately to be paid in three months after my decease, and £50 for my body to be buried in Boston. After payment of burial, debts, and legacies aforesaid, I give the remainder of my estate both real and personal (to be equally divided) to my

The term cousin at that time meant some form of a close relative. I suspect they may be his nephews since John Evered said they were his kinfolk and certainly knew the names of most of the Ayer children yet he does not mention their mother in his will. The only indebtedness that comes to mind is the possibility of the payment of their fares to come to New England. On Aug 17th 1668 "John Web, alias, Everit, pursuing a Whale, was caught in ye rope, twisted about his middle, & being drawn into ye sea, was drowned." His earlier will was probated Nov 13th 1668 at Charlestown by Thomas Danforth. Administrator Thomas Hinchman found himself in a difficult situation and made several appearances before the court for determination of payment of debts and legacies. In addition, John's wife Mary was willed goods over and beyond the dower thirds. Thou shall not leave thy wife more than the law states. The results were never located. His inventory, the longest I have seen, and exceeded £2,700.[1]

Ayers Settling On The Merrimack

John[1] Ayer, was born in England and died Mar 31st 1657 in Haverhill, Essex, Massachusetts (HVR 352)[2]. He married in England a woman named Hannah or Anna. The English roots of this couple are illusive although many have made claims about them. In addition the name Ayer appears in documents with numerous spellings. John's wife and their family supposedly came in 1637 on the *Mary Ann* with Capt. Goose. Their names do not appear on the ship's manifest. Some claim Hannah was an older sister of John Evered, others his daughter. Others say she may be John Ayers' second wife.

C. H. Pope stated John Ayer was a merchant from Marlborough Parish in Wiltshire, England.[3] A search of records in the area of Ogbourne St. George and Marlborough Parishes bore no fruit as to John's ancestry or that of his children. Others claim that he was on the *James* that departed England later that year that was caught in a great hurricane on the coast. Torrey published that John was of Norwich. According to C. E. Banks *Topograhical Dictionary of 2885 Emigrants to New England 1620-1650*, John (Ayer) came from Ogbourne St. George Parish and sailed out of Southampton, England, Apr 5th 1635 on the *James* with John Pike and John and Stephen Evered/Webb. Pike was listed as a laborer from Langford on the ship's roll #35 having given Oath on Jun 12th 1635 the day it arrived in New England. The Evereds #5 & #6 were from Marlborough,

---

1 Essex Co, MA, Probate Bk.3, 15,18,133,222.

2 Topsfield Historical Society, Topsfield, MA, Vital Records of Haverhill, Massachusetts (Salem, MA: Newcomb & Gauss Printers, 1910), Vol. *, Births; Vol. II, Marriages and Deaths, hereinafter referred to as HVR with page number following.

3 C.H. Pope, *Pioneers of Massachusetts*, (1900; reprint Boston: Genealogical Publ. Co., 1965), 159

Wiltshire. There is no record of John Ayer being on the *James'* roll. However, the roll may not be complete.

On Sep 4th 1638 twelve men were granted permission to begin a plantation on the Merrimack named Colchester. Two years later on Oct 7th 1640 the name was changed to Salisbury. Exactly when John Ayer and his family arrived in New England remains unknown. He settled on the north side of the Merrimack as he was among "The names of those yt have lotts & proportions granted pr the Toune of Colchester in the first division." On the first leaf of the town's records at Salisbury there is a list of the land grantees in the first division, many of whom owned land in Salisbury prior to 1643. John Ayer, sr. is on this list.[1] There is some confusion in the records exactly which males were in the first division due to the use of the name Colchester or Salisbury. In 1643 the courts placed Salisbury, Amesbury and Haverhill, MA, in Norfolk County, New Hampshire, joining the towns of Exeter and Strawberry Bank (Dover). Its court was held at Hampton. After New Hampshire became a royal province, the General Court passed an act on Feb 4th 1679/80 severing the former Essex County towns from Norfolk County and put them back in Massachusetts for the convenience of its inhabitants to attend public business since they had formerly been represented at Essex courts.[2] John Ayer subsequently left Salisbury and located about ten miles further upriver at Haverhill.

Pentuckett was the Indian name for Haverhill. In May 1640 Mr. Ward and some inhabitants of Newbury had petitioned the General Court to settle at Pentucket. On Oct 7th several men were appointed to view the bounds between Colchester and Mr. Ward's plantation. It wasn't until Jun 2nd 1641 that men were selected to lay out the boundaries. Although there was some settlement at Haverhill, there was no title from the Indians. A deed dated Nov 15th 1642 was given by the Sachems,[3] Passaquo and Saggahew with the consent of Passaconnaway[4] who was friendly with the English Pentucket inhabitants. Ward and five men signed in behalf of the inhabitants for lands that measured eight miles west, six miles north, six miles east including the island in the river fourteen miles in length. The deed wasn't recorded until Apr 27th 1671 into the County Records of Norfolk County (Bk.2, p.209) and later copied into the town records in 1680. Ward, who came from Haverhill, Essex, England later renamed the village Haverhill. Despite the agreement with the Indian Sachems, Haverhill suffered severely from Indians. Before settlement, Haverhill was an immense forest with open meadows and lowlands that Indians had cleared. Its thick grasses lured deer which Indians hunted in the fall. Settlement changed the landscape. The remaining forests afforded a haven for sly attacks so the inhabitants went to work armed and to Church with a psalm book in one hand and a loaded, primed gun in the other.[5] Attacks became more prevalent by the late 1680's but usually they were isolated incidents on the outskirts where one or two men were at work.

Inhabitants called Lake Cochichaweah the Great Pond. Three hundred acres were laid out in 1643 along the Merrimack River in house lots. The first official town meeting was held Nov 6th 1643 and several issues were voted: 1) Any timber on the common that is felled must be used within nine months or forfeited; 2)Three hundred acres and no more were allocated for house lots and those whose worth was £200 have 20 acres added to his house lot; and 3) Everyone under that sum to have acres proportioned for his house lot, marsh, common and planting ground. The land was laid out east

---

1 David W. Hoyt, *Old Families of Salisbury and Amesbury*, (Baltimore, MD: Genealogical Publ. Co., 1982), 7-10

2 D. Hamilton Hurd, *History of Essex County, Massachusetts* (Philadelphia, PA: J.W. Lewis & Co., 1888)

3 Sachem denoted a supreme ruler and the term was used primarily by Indians of Massachusetts.

4 Passaconaway was a chief who lived near the Pennacook, an Algonquian confederacy located on both banks of the Merrimac covering what is Massachusetts, New Hampshire and the southern portion of Maine. Their main village was at present Concord, New Hampshire. Algonquian tribes are a family of linguistic languages. The tribes covered more territory than any other group. They were mainly sedentary and agricultural. Some tribes were the Colorado Plains Arapaho; Blackfoot; Cheyenne of Minnesota and Dakotas; Cree of Canada; Delaware who moved to Ohio, Wyoming and Indiana when settlers and another linguistic group, the Iroquois.

5 Benjamin L. Mirick, *The History of Haverhill, Massachusetts* (Haverhill, MA, A.W. Thayer, 1832) Facimile Reprint (Bowie, MD: Heritage Books, Inc., 1991) 64

of Little River where the village stood. Common or community lands were allocated by Town representatives. Puritans considered it a duty of every male voter to attend town meetings in his community. Neglect to do so deserved punishment. Tardiness merited a rebuke. John Ayer, sr. and James Fiske were fined on Feb 13th 1647 "for not attending the town meeting in season." John became a proprietor and town officer during the era that required evidence of being a respectable member of a Church in order to vote or hold office.

John Ayer's property in the Northwest Parish was valued at £160. It faced the main roadway on the north and the Merrimack River on the south. At least six Ayers generations occupied that property. The nearest fresh water was named Ayers pond, later changed to Plug pond. The stream at the pond's outlet, known as Mill Brook, was where the first gristmill was built. By 1645 there were about thirty-two landowners in Haverhill including John Ayers, sr. and jr.[1] John's sons, Robert, Thomas, and Peter were added to the valuation lists by 1650. In the second land division, John, sr. drew #6 for 8 acres.

On Jan 1st 1650/1 it was determined that the bank in or below the plain butting on the Merrimack River can be fenced for the space of four years. Also those that have land west of the Little River can use the bank up to Thomas Hale's lot. The following Jan 12th the ox-common was reapportioned. Those living west of the Mill Brook were given land for an ox-common to be laid out at a convenient place for as many who will join.[2]

Fisheries were first noted at a town meeting held on Feb 9th 1654 when Stephen Kent was granted the right to place a weir in the Little River to catch alewives or any other fish if he would sell to the town's inhabitants what they needed. Alewives were used as fertilizer for corn. The following May a great mistake surfaced over the boundary between Salisbury and Haverhill. A review of the line was ordered by the general court which resulted in some give and take by both communities. It gave Salisbury rights to Haverhill commons if the swamp stopped the way, the sd way to be forty rods broad. Also a large ox-common was laid out that year.[3]

Houses were generally one story thatched roof structures. Most had one large chimney usually located in the middle of the home. Use of thirty cord of fire-wood was common for a family. Estate inventories paint a picture of what a home was like in that era. John's modest estate showed he had a dwelling house and a barn with implements. The home had three beds with the kitchen supplied with 2 pots, 3 kettles, 1 skillet & frying pan and a warming pan plus pewter dishes.

Children of John and Hannah Ayer were:

1. John[2] Ayer, m. 1st May 5th 1646 Haverhill, Sarah Williams, children: John[3], Zachariah, Nathaniel, Joseph, and Sarah Ayer. John m. 2nd Mar 26th 1662/3 Haverhill, Mary Woodam.
2. Robert[2] Ayer, m. Elizabeth Palmer; children: Elizabeth[3], Samuel, Mehitable, Timothy, Daughter, Hannah, and Mary Ayer.
3. Rebeckah[2] Ayer, m. 1st Oct 8th 1648 John Aslet his 2nd, children: Rebecca[3], Mary, John, Sarah, Ruth, Sarah, Elizabeth, and Samuel Aslet.
4. Thomas[2] Ayer, m. Apr 1st 1656 Elizabeth Hutchins, children: John[3], Elizabeth, Mary, Love, Male twins, Thomas, and Samuel Ayer.
5. Peter[2] Ayer, m. Hannah Allen, children: Ruth[3], Hannah, Abigail, Mary, Martha, Samuel, William, Rachel, and Ebenezer Ayer.

---

1 George W. Chase, *History of Haverhill, Massachusetts* (Haverhill, MA: Author, 1861) 70-71

2 *Ibid.*, 72-73

3 Chase 81

6. Mary[2] Ayer, m. Nathan Parker his 2nd, children: John[3], James, Mary, Hannah, Mary, Elizabeth, and Robert Parker

+7. Obadiah[2] Ayer, m. Hannah Pike.

8. Nathaniel[2] Ayer, m. Tamesin Turloar, children: Hannah[3], Hannah, Elizabeth, Nathaniel, Abiah, Obadiah, Ruth, a child, Benjamin, Mary, and Ruth Ayer.

9. Hannah[2] Ayer, m. Stephen Webster, children: Hannah[3], John, Mary, Stephen, Nathan, and Abigail Webster.[1]

After living approximately 23 years in a new country, John Ayer, sr. died in 1657. He had lived in the colony through hurricanes, viral epidemics, ill treatment of people with different religious practices, the publishing of the Bay Psalm Book on the first printing press in Boston, the beginning of slavery in Massachusetts, the peace treaty with the Narragansett Indians, coins minted in Massachusetts and the colony declaring itself an independent commonwealth. In a little over a month Gov. Bradford would die on May 9th 1657. Only John knows how many of these events affected his life.

John's will was dated Mar 12th 1656/7. He died nineteen days later. The Inventory of his estate was completed Apr 10th 1657 by Robert Clement, James Dennis, Sr., and Henry Palmer and totaled £248.05.00. There is nothing in his will or inventory to suggest that he had a specific trade. Many farmed and sold/ bartered their grains or textiles as did John. He did have considerable land to pass on to his children. His will was attested by Henry Palmer, Oct 6th 1657, at Hampton Court upon his widow's oath as executrix.

Haverhill increasing population in need of necessary housing caused the common lands to become overwhelmed. So Haverhill passed a law in 1660, in the interest of the town's initial inhabitants, preventing anyone that had built houses or occupied one since the town's beginning, has no lawful right to use the commons, its pasture, timber, or wood. Selectmen provided lists of those individuals who had built cottages or houses upon the commons or on their own land that fell under that law. In Jul 1667 more lots of accommodation were laid out. *Oldgood Eyre* (Hannah) was given 8 acres.[2] In Feb 1681 Hannah deeded her common rights in Salisbury to her son, Robert of Haverhill. Hannah died Oct 8th 1688 after living 31½ years as a widow which was unusual at the time since most were remarried in a short time.(HVR 348) Hannah would have seen the banning of Quaker meetings, a major smallpox epidemic, King Philip's War with his subsequent death, another major hurricane and small pox epidemic, and some of her family moving to New Jersey.

John's Ayer descendants were so numerous by 1700 that is was estimated that one-third of the population of Haverhill was of that family. My Ayers ancestors left Massachusetts for New Jersey and then my gt-gt grandfather Thomas left New Jersey for Ohio. They keep moving on when my great grandparents Henry and Lydia and children left Ohio for Michigan.

Nova Cesaria Beckons

New Jersey became part of the Dutch settlement known as New Netherland. The few Dutch settlements were destroyed by fighting with the local Leni-Lenape Indians from 1641-45. Despite a Dutch citizen acquiring a deed in 1651 from Indians for 30,000 acres near South Amboy and northerly, little settlement was made on this land and it remained the Indian hunting grounds. What began as a peaceful agreement turned sour when they tried to collect tribute from the Indians for their trade with Manhattan. In 1660 Peter Stuyvesant ordered any New Jersey settlers to move from

---

1 Further information on these families can be found in the various town records in MA and NJ.

2 Chase., 93,106.

scattered farms to a village or suffer confiscation. The village was known as Bergen, today's Jersey City. Since Dutch settlements were small and scattered, the door was open for England located north and south to gain control of the land. Their legal claim was based on John Cabot's voyage in 1497. All lands that he sailed by was considered the property of the English Crown because it was unclaimed and unknown. On Mar 20th 1664, Charles II of England gave his brother, James, Duke of York, a royal patent for all land between the Connecticut and Delaware Rivers and invested in him the power to govern it.[1] This was in consideration of forty beaver skins annually if demanded. The following June Duke James conveyed a defined portion of the lands to his friends, Sir George Cartaret and John Lord Berkeley in consideration of £40 sterling if demanded. Cartaret and Berkeley were eager to promote this acquisition for settlement to make money but neither were eager to visit it. The next year *The Concessions and Agreements of the Lord Proprietors of New Jersey, etc.* was published and distributed throughout New England. These articles came at a time when people were disheartened and discouraged with Puritan religious intolerance and its Magistrates ruling civil affairs. Their lives were too much like the England they had departed. *The Concessions* twelve articles served as legal basis for its government in defining two settlements. This was a liberal inducement among other things in land and religion that brought a migration into northern New Jersey. Although there was the requirement of an oath of fidelity to the lords proprietors, settlers were assured full freedom of conscience, right of freeholders to choose representatives to a law making assembly, right of jury trial and appeal as well as levying taxes for the support of their government. Quit rents of one-half penny sterling per acre were to be paid to the Lords Proprietors beginning Mar 25th 1670. Land grants varied with each settler depending on arrival, family size and servants. Patent lands were to remain with settlers and their heirs. Sir George Cartaret sent his fourth cousin, Philip Cartaret, to govern the territory. Philip arrived in Aug 1665 with a party of thirty at Elizabeth, NJ, where four log huts awaited the party. They had much work ahead to make the town become their seat of government.

New Jersey, known as *Nova Cesaria.*, was for the most part unexplored wilderness. Tribal warfare left only a few scattered Indian tribes to hunt in the area. The land abounded with deer, berry eating bear, sly fox, shrieking wildcats, pouncing panthers, sly mink, otter, productive rabbits, squirrels and other animals. Northerly winding trails and navigable rivers and southern winding rivers provided the only means of travel.

Cartaret's *Concessions* reached northern Massachusetts in 1665. The response from Newbury was the signing of an agreement on Dec 11th 1666 by Daniel Pierce (blacksmith), John Pike, Abraham Tappen and their associates granting them a tract from the Raritan River to the Rahway River for £80. The land had been purchased from natives in Oct 1664. The tract was approximately one hundred square miles. A week later the associates induced their New Hampshire friends to buy one-third of the tract for £30. John Martin, Hugh Dunn, Benjamin and Hopewell Hull and others responded. This met the first stipulation of *The Concessions* by establishing two plantations or townships with forty families in each. The two plantations would be known as Woodbridge and Piscataway townships. Getting there from the north would be by sailboat down the Atlantic coast since overland journey by foot or horseback would be tortuously slow. Packhorses could carry goods but heavy goods still had to be carried by sailing ships.

It took only two years before the first disputes arose. Cartaret's authority was challenged in 1671 so he hastened back to England for support. In his absence "Declarations" for punishment were imposed on proprietors and settlers by rescinding *The Concessions*. Cartaret returned in Mar 1674 to find a portion of western New Jersey had been sold to Quakers which divided the land into East and West Jersey. East Jersey came under the influence of Scotch Presbyterians. A new governor, Andros, also hampered Cartaret's position. When Sir George Cartaret died in January 1680, Andros

<hr>

1 Walter C. Meuly, *History of Piscataway Township 1666-1976*, [Somerville, NJ, Somerville Press] 7-8

sent the militia to arrest Philip Cartaret. Although acquitted, he had been badly beaten. In Mar 1681 Cartaret assumed his old position over East Jersey. The following Nov he dissolved the assembly who demanded the original *Concessions* be restored. Governor Cartaret died in December 1682 after which the seat of government changed from Elizabeth Town to Amboy. Back in England, Cartaret's widow sold the proprietary rights for £3,400 at a public auction in London in Feb 1682/3 to twelve Quaker Proprietors headed by William Penn. These men's economic interest outweighed any religious concern. Besides the government's exchequer was indebted to William's father, Admiral Penn, for £16,000 plus other considerations. The whole system began to fall apart due to overlapping grants and disputes over land titles with settlers threatened with eviction from their lands. East Jersey was without a central government beginning in 1689 for three years. Any arrangement was of little benefit to settlers or Proprietors. In 1702 the rights were surrendered to Queen Anne and the Jerseys were reunited as a Royal Colony with two capital cities.

Seventy five years later there were still disputes between the Proprietors and Elizabeth Town over land as shown in the following deposition. At a Council of Proprietors held at Perth Amboy on Oct 10th 1740, a deposition was read as follows:

John Worth aged in May last seventy one years, says he was born in Woodbridge, that when he was very young he remembers a great combustion between the Indians and the people of Woodbridge and Piscataway. The Indians alleged that the English cut their trees, mowed their meadows and took their lands from them. And that they threatened to burn the houses of the people that had settled in Piscataway. That the Indians denied that the lands they had sold to Elizabeth Town people had extended so far as Piscataway, that after the corn combustion, the people of Woodbridge and Piscataway agreed to purchase what was not before purchased, that he remembers the people going out to meet the Indians in order for the purchase, And remembers their return and heard them say after their return from the purchasing, that the Indians had gone with them to some place about Kents Neck where the Indians said that they had sold to before and no farther and that the Indians with their King before them went up along Rariton River in Sight of it till they came to Bound Brooke, then went up the Bound Brook to Cedar Brook, then up along Cedar Brook some distance and marked a corner, and then struck off to Minisink Path and marked trees along and then went and marked along Minisink Path to Kents Neck again and the Indians pointing towards Woodbridge said that what was on that side of Minisink Path, they had sold before and pointing to the other side of the Path said what we have now there gone round is the land we have now sold you. Says that Minisink Path came from Monmouth County and crossed Raritan River at Kent's Neck and crossed the County up pretty nigh by John Laings place. Says that Kent's Neck is about two or three miles from Amboy Point up Raritan River. Says further that he remembers Gawen Laurie's purchasing of the Indians. That his purchase contains a large tract of land by the Blue Hills, that at that time not till late, he heard no pretence that that land was purchased of the Indians before nor that any of the Elizabeth Town people pretended it. He remembers the surveying of sundry lands up by the Blue Hills in that purchase. He thinks some by one George Keith and some by John Reed many years ago, and several people settled there upon the Proprietors title and particularly John Barclay. One old Alexander, one Forbes and remembers one Cole and his two sons had head lands and settled there. And they all settled their quietly under the Proprietors and so remained for many years he believes, twenty years,

Others deposed included John Drake of Piscataway, Noah Bishop of Woodbridge, Thomas FitzRandolph of Piscataway, William Bingle of Metuchen, and Jonathan Compton. All were over seventy and eighty years of age.[1]

Woodbridge township contained the towns of Woodbridge, Piscataway, and all plantations on both side of the Raritan River as far east to Chessquake Harbor and southwest to the division line of the Province and northwest to the utmost bounds of the Province. In those early days a plantation contained about 200 acres. Small tracts were called farms or houselots. The people mostly raised peas, Indian corn and grains. The much needed miller in any settlement was privileged with the town supplying money and sod to erect a dam. He usually owned the finest house and was paid in grain like Ministers who were provided a parsonage. Most, if not all towns, had a Commons for grazing stock and gathering firewood. And then there were wolves who killed their stock. Towns often paid several shillings to anyone who killed a wolf. Blacksmiths were also vital and given land to settle on with a condition that he stay at least seven years or lose his land.

Highways were usually laid out by men appointed by the town council. Woodbridge's first highway ran by the Kirk Green over Papiack Creek and beyond. Along it was the grist mill and the Presbyterian Church. What became evident to us when traveling in the eastern states, was these once large creeks were mostly semi-dry small ditches or not visible at all. The 2nd highway ran north from the foot of Strawberry Hill (the Sheep's Common) across Manning's Brook into the common land beyond. It was voted in Aug 1669 to make Strawberry Hill a perpetual sheep common on its west side. Along this road were the house lots of early settlers. John Pike had 10 acres on the east, Obadiah Ayers 16 acres, John Martin 11 acres north of the hill, John Dennis 12 acres, Thomas Bloomfield 17½ acres, his son 11½ acres, Samuel Moore 16 acres, Richard Worth was next to Pike, and others. These settlers were among the patentees of the 1670 freeholders of Woodbridge and each received acreage laid out in plots and drawn by lots. The plots varied in size from 15 to 512 acres. The nine original associates did not receive the greatest acreage due to the method of distribution, the drawing of lots. Land continued to be disbursed in this manner over the years.

Obadiah[2] I, the 7th of ten children was born to John and Hannah Ayer. The record of his birth is an unsolved mystery. Somewhere he met Hannah Pike of Newbury for their marriage was recorded there on Mar 29th 1660/1. She had been born there on Apr 26th 1643, daughter of John Pike and Mary Turvill. Obadiah and Hannah were living in Haverhill. MA, where four children were born of which only the eldest survived before they moved to Woodbridge, NJ. It must have been heartbreaking to lose three children in so short a time. Their children were:

1. John b. 1663 Haverhill, d. 1732 Basking Ridge, m. Mary Walker 1689, children: John, Thomas, Obadiah, Patience, Francis, Benjamin, Nathaniel, Moses, and Aaron Ayers.

---

1 *Minutes of the Board of Proprietors of New Jersey*, 1685-1705, V. II, pp. 104-107

2. Sarah b. 1664 d. Haverhill 1666.
3. Male b. & d. 1666 Haverhill age 2 wks.
4. Samuel b. & d. Haverhill 1667.
5. Samuel b. Woodbridge m Elizabeth ?, children: Rhoda[4], David, Elizabeth, Samuel, twins Rachel & Jacob, Benjamin, & James Ayers.
+6. Obadiah[3] II b. Oct 20th 1671 Woodbridge, m. Joanna Jones Apr 28th 1694 by Justice Hale.
7. Thomas b. Dec 17th 1673, d. Oct 13th 1675;
8. Joseph b. Apr 4th 1674 m. 1st Phebe Camp Jan 5th 1698, children: Phebe, Joseph, Jonathan, David, & Zebulon Ayers. Joseph m. 2nd widow Elizabeth Ayers.
9. Mary b. 1680 Woodbridge m. William Ilsley Jun 18th 1700, daughter: Hannah Ilsley.
10. Sarah b. & d. Nov 8th 1683.[1]

Settlers and freeholders were expected to participate in the governing of individual townships. Township Court Offices voted on were: a President, Assistants, Assistant Justices, Grand Jurymen, two Deputies to the General Assembly, a Town Clerk, a Constable, a Marshall (Sgt. of the Court), Clerk of Courts, Rate Makers (Assessors), Rate Gatherers (Tax Collectors), a Keeper of the Pound, and Military Officers. Others appointed included Jurymen, Overseer of Highways, Meat Packers, Fence Viewers, Lot Layers and Rangers. The earliest record of Obadiah's service in New Jersey began in 1668-70 as a juryman. So we know that Obadiah and his family must have moved to Woodbridge before or in early 1668. He sold his home in Haverhill on May 5th 1669 to his brother Nathaniel. On Mar 18th 1670 Obadiah was patented 171 acres north of Langster's Plain with a Quit Rent of ½ penny Sterling per acre to be paid to the Lord's Proprietors beginning Mar 25th 1670.[2] It included his house lot of 16 acres on the lower east end of Strawberry Hill. Obadiah was elected to serve as Assistant to Pres. John Pike, Sr., his father-in-law on Jan 3rd 1670/71 for a year. That year concerns arose over Indians causing the town to tax its citizens for munitions. In another anxiety the council ordered stockades to be built around the prison which would serve as a safe place for women and children.

Dutch began occupying New York (New Orange) and East Jersey in 1673. On Aug 19th Deputies from the various Jersey towns were ordered to gather its inhabitants and nominate Magistrates (Schepens). Six men's names were submitted with three selected on Aug 24th. Obadiah was sworn in on Sep 1st 1673 with Samuel Dennis and Stephen Kent to represent Woodbridge. Five days later Dutch Captains were sent to the various towns to administer a Dutch oath of allegiance to its inhabitants. A total of 54 adult males in Woodbridge took the oath, one being absent. Said oath served as a census of the heads of households. There were no problems except for anyone who was caught adhering to the Crown of England. Only one was tried and banished.[3] Dutch rule was short for they relinquished the lands at the Treaty of Westminster in Nov 1674.

On Dec 3rd 1685, Obadiah deeded his eldest son, John, ½ of his farm, about 60 acres, lying north of Langster's Farm/Plain, bounded south by a road in the rear of Elisha Elser, west by Joshua Bradly, east by Richard Worth, north by Grantor, plus 15 acres at Rariton River.[4] In Jan 1686 two Constables instead of one were elected for the first time. Obadiah and Nathaniel FitzRandolph held that position. Obadiah bought 8 acres in Woodbridge from Richard Worth.[5] Obadiah's wife, Hannah Pike Ayers, died on May 30st 1689. Four years later he deeded his son Samuel the other ½ of his patented land which lay west by Joshua Bradley, north by the Commons, east a road between the grantor and the deceased Richard Worth. In addition, 8 acres of Rariton Meadows which lay east of his son, John, south by himself, west by a small strip of meadow along the Great Pond, and north by Elisha Parker.[1] Then he purchased a 12 acre house lot, 60 acres of farmland and 6 acres of meadow from Jonathan Clement.[2] The next year Obadiah wrote his will on Nov 10th 1694 that mostly consisted of disposing the rest of his lands to his sons. After debts and funeral expenses his movable were to be divided into five equal shares to be given to his daughter, Mary, and his four sons. He appointed his eldest sons John and Samuel, executors. Obadiah died four days after writing his will. Having disposed of his lands, the inventory, after debts, totaled £51.13.09. In 1695, sons John and Thomas, recorded an account of their father's estate of £50 showing payments to Obadiah's children Mary, Joseph, and Obadiah, and to James Green, Benjamin Grifith, Elisha Parker, Isaac Whitehead, Richard Powell, Sarah Alphin, John Randolf, Ezekiel Bloomfield, Thomas Collier, Thomas Gordin and John Pike.[3]

Pike Ancestry

Hanna Pike, wife of Obadiah Ayers and daughter of John Pike and Mary Turvill, came from Wiltshire, England. The earliest known members of a Pyke family were located in northernmost Wiltshire. They were William Pyke in Hinton, Underditch Hundred, and John, Henry and Simon Pyke in Ashton and Cricklade. These four men were listed on the Tax List of 1332 in Wiltshire County. If there is any connection to the following Pike family, I do not know.

Hannah Pike's ancestors came from Whiteparish in Wiltshire County. The use of the name Whiteparish can be confusing because there is the village of Whiteparish and the Parish of Whiteparish. In the current center of the Parish of Whiteparish was a Benedictine Nunnery built in 871 by King Edgar on the ruins of an Abbey built in 773 that was destroyed by Danes. Centuries later the Nunnery was granted by Henry VIII to Sir William Herbert when Henry dismantled Catholicism. Its location was a mile or two southwest of the present village of Whiteparish. Remains of a chapel can still be seen there. The village of Whiteparish derives its name from its church which was rebuilt in 1190 and later known as White Church. Before the village was consolidated, the area consisted of farmsteads surrounded with cottages. As time passed, its forests were diminished by farmers creating more fields for crops. White Church stood at the edge of the former village green of Frustfield. Later the village was renamed Whitechurch, then Whiteparish a century later. Today remains of the 11th century Norman priest's doorway is concealed by a polygonal vestry. Other pieces of stonework have been reset. The north aisle is 13th century as is the altered chancel arch. The south aisle is partly 14th century. The interior was changed twice in the 19th century. Also a major restoration changed the church's exterior to appear Victorian with limestone and flint chequers and a shingled bell turret under a steep pyramid roof faced with flint and stone. It was dedicated in Feb 1970. A new altar was created in 1987 in memory of the long serving vicar, Rev. Keeley. A new Vicar was there during our visit in 1993. The church registers dating from 1561 of christenings and marriages and from 1560 burials, other than those currently used, are deposited in the Wiltshire and Swindon Record Office. Marriages have also been published. It was here that Pike ancestors were married.

John Pike married Dorothy Daye on Jan 17th 1612/3 in the Church of All Saints, Whiteparish, Wiltshire, England. She was the daughter of Thomas Daye and Jane Morris who were also married there Jun 12th 1589. In my conversation with the vicar's wife at the church she had no knowledge of any named Pike in the area today. John, born about 1592, was the eldest of five children. His siblings were: Robert, Anne, Dorothy and Israel Pike. John, educated and feisty, must have had some reason

---

1 *Ibid.*, p. 407
2 *Ibid.*, Book E, p. 167
3 Middlesex Will Bk. E, pgs. 140-142, 190

to call himself a laborer when he swore allegiance before boarding the ship *James* at Southampton in 1635. The ship's list might be incomplete since John's sons, John and Robert, were among the first settlers at Newbury Old Town.

Before John arrived to settle at Newbury Old Town, the General Court of Massachusetts had granted John Winthrop, jr, and his assigns on Sep 3rd 1633 permission to set up a trading house on the Merrimack River. Subsequently an order was passed stating that Quascacunquen is allowed to be a plantation with three men to set out its bounds or as much as they can with the name to be changed to Newberry. Also said plantation to have sufficient men to make a competent town. Back in Wiltshire, England, others organized a company for raising stock. This was at a time when prices were high for cattle, horses and sheep. They added Flemish stock to their domestic herds and persuaded others to join the enterprise. Many on the earlier *Mary and John* had settled at Ipswich [Agawam] before moving to Newbury in the spring of 1635. They came by water from Ipswich through Plum Island Sound up the Quascacunquen (Parker) River. There had been a few fisherman occupying the banks of the Merrimack and Parker rivers before this, but they were considered intruders by the General Court, not permanent settlers. The secluded area was described as "...Eastward, cold, wide marshes stretched away, dull dreary flats without a bush or tree, O'ercrossed by winding creeks, where twice a day Gurgled the waters of the moon-struck sea; and faint with distance came the stifled roar, the melancholy lapse of waves on the low shore. Inland hills rising above hills stood like sentinels over the almost unbroken wilderness." Centuries before this landing Indians had hunted in these forests and fished in the placid stream that ebbs and flows to the falls of Newbury. Only a few of them remained, smallpox having decimated the population. Each settler was allotted land for a house, a planting lot, and salt meadow. The size depended on the amount of money the individual or family had invested in the venture. Mr. Dummer and his group had the largest acreage, more than a thousand acres up river near the falls for their stock raising. Dummer was granted the right to erect a mill at Newbury falls and given fifty acres of woodland to supply the mill. He was allowed to grind corn if he would grind "all the grain the residents might bring him."[1]

Houses were built on both sides of the Parker River. The principal settlement was around the meeting house on the lower green. When the new settlers arrived, they found that the Bay Colony had established the Congregational form of religion. Everyone was taxed to support the Church and were ordered to attend worship in the meeting house located on the Green. The Reverend Thomas Parker, a member of the stock raising company, was also Newbury's minister. His house lot was closer to the calf common at the west end of town. Those living outside the small settlement had a long trip to Newbury to attend church. They were required to carry their weapons to and from worship due to fear of Indians and wild animals. Sentinels were posted at the meeting house doors.

Before the *James* arrived in June, Gov. Winthrop wrote on May 21st 1635 in his History of New England: *A Dutch ship of one hundred and sixty tons arrived at Marblehead south of Newbury having come from Christopher Island. Aboard was one hundred and forty tons of salt and ten thousand weight of tobacco.* The following Jun 3rd Winthrop noted: *Here arrived two Dutch ships, who brought 27 Flanders mares at £34 a mare, and 3 horses, 63 heifers at £12 the beast, and 88 sheep at 50s. They came from the Tessell in five weeks three days and lost not one beast or sheep. Here arrived also, the same day, the James, a ship of three hundred tons with cattle and passengers which came all safe from Southampton within the same time. On the Lord's day there came in seven other ships, one to Salem, and four more to the mouth of the bay with store of passengers and cattle. They came all within six weeks.* To prevent loss of time and drunkenness which sometimes happened by people running to the ships, it was ordered that one person in each town would buy for all and should sell the lot within twenty days at five per hundred if any came to buy in that time. But most

---

1"Ould Newbury": Historical and Biographical Sketches by John J. Currier (1896), Damrell and Upham, Boston.

of the people would not buy except they buy for themselves. The appointed merchants could not disburse so much money, etc., leaving the seamen discontented. Some of them brought their goods on shore and sold them there.

There were three ships named *James* that sailed out of England in 1635. Besides the Apr 5th departure from Southampton under Master Wm. Cooper, the other departures were May 23rd 1635 under Master Taylor and mid Jul 1635 under Master May. Since these trips took approximately two months to make the journey one way, there is little doubt there were three ships by that name noted in the writings of Govs. Bradford and Winthrop and Richard Mather who kept a diary.

I find it interesting enough to extract some highlights from Mather's diary on a ship named *James* of what it was or could be like making the journey from England to the Colonies. They departed Warrington [London area] on Apr 16th for Bristol arriving there on the 23rd after about a 120 mile journey in seven days. They found themselves having to stay there for a month and two days. Easterly winds were in their favor but the ship was not ready. At King road, a spacious harbor about 5-6 miles wide and 4-5 miles from Bristol they saw the *Diligence* that was heading for Newfoundland at anchor. At King road the *James* passengers were licensed to proceed. The Lord's day brought strong winds and many women and children became sick or light headed riding at anchor. The next day with a good east wind the mariners refused to stir until all the goods were stowed and the deck cleared. Tuesday all were ready to depart but as they weighed anchor the wind turned westerly so they anchored and sat still. The *Diligence* had gone out but returned and the *Angel Gabriel* joined them at anchor. Mather and Taylor boarded the *Angel Gabriel* where many were sick, some with smallpox. They dined with the Captain on cheese, mutton and roast turkey. On Friday morning the wind shifted to southeast but Master Taylor and some crew were ashore to acquire some oats for the cattle, their supply having been used up. The next day found the passengers sitting around while the Master and some crew were ashore. The wind was a strong northwester. Late afternoon it became severe enough to make some passengers seasick. The Sabbath brought an easterly wind but the Master and some crew were once again on shore. Monday's winds were from the west so some went ashore to wash linens and buy hay and provisions. Winds became stronger in the evening and throughout the night. Tuesday a few went ashore for water and hay for their cattle. Wednesday brought good east winds but some crew and the Master left saying they would not leave until the winds settled. Two more ships arrived, the *Elizabeth* or *Bess* and the *Mary*. Thursday the 220 ton *James* was finally to set sail along with the 150 ton *Diligence*, the 80 ton *Mary*, the *Bess*, and the 240 ton *Angel Gabriel*. They got about 35-40 nautical miles before the wind turned westerly with the tide against them forcing them to anchor in the channel between Wales and Winnyard in Somersetshire until 7 p.m. Then the tide turned and they tacked gaining little until 2 a.m. when the tide caused them to anchor again. Friday was much the same with tacking in strong west winds causing many to be sea sick. They set out again at night only to have to anchor on Saturday morning at Lundy. A few of them talked the Master into letting them go ashore where they found only one house. They managed to get some milk, fowl and cheese and went back to the ship. Sunday they lay still at Lundy. Monday they went ashore to get water for the cattle. Tuesday saw no change in the winds. Weary of anchoring there due to its poor harbor and contrary winds, they set out for Milford Haven about 47 nautical miles from Lundy in westerly winds. Their 4th Sabbath was spent ship-board. Monday Mather took his family on shore to Nangle where they got some milk. Tuesday it rained, Wednesday no change in the winds. Thursday a seaman was put on shore for brawling and cursing while drunk. That afternoon Mr. Jessop came aboard from the *Angel Gabriel*. Friday was foggy with west winds. Saturday winds changed little. The Sabbath was a cheerful summer day and many from the *Angel Gabriel* visited them. Monday brought a strong east gale and they departed Milford Haven losing sight of land about noon. Rough seas caused much illness. Tuesday brought rain and losing sight of three other ships. The Master thought they should stay with the *Angel*

Gabriel, a strong ship furnished with ordnance but slow in sailing. Wednesday the east wind died down and they saw an abundance of porpoises playing about the ship. Thursday brought more rain until noon when the sun came out and many came to walk about the deck. Friday brought a north wind and later more westerly as porpoises leaped about the ship. Seaman sounded in the evening and found ground at 50 fathoms. They repeated it on Saturday finding no bottom. A fog lifted and the day became sunny. They were also concerned about water and provisions for the cattle. That evening and Saturday they feasted on three porpoises. Sabbath was fair and sunny with a southerly wind. By afternoon the wind grew stronger. A rough night was spent with wind and rain getting some beds wet. Monday's strong south wind found them filling empty casks with salt water as they were losing ballast. That evening and all night they set forth with good speed. Tuesday became calm and hot in the afternoon causing faintness and sweating. The weather cooled in the afternoon with a northeast wind and a little blue feathered land bird landed on the ship. Wednesday they gained little by tacking north and south in a northwest wind. Thursday afternoon brought a fresh south gale. Large grampushes were tumbling and spewing water beside the ship. Friday's foggy forenoon and west northwest wind gave way to a north by east wind and little was gained. Saturday became cool with a weak north wind. Seaman sounded and found ground at 60 fathom. Another land bird landed on the sails. The calm evening found the seamen fishing for cod as fast as they could get them into the ship. Sabbath was refreshingly cool with a comfortable south gale all day and feasting on the cod. About 3 AM on Monday a rainy storm arrived. The seamen had to let down all the sails and the ship tossed between mountains and valleys of water. By sunrise all was over except the winds were again from the west. Fog and mist kept them from finding land so they lay still with no sails that allowed them to get an abundance of cod and halibut. By Tuesday afternoon the day cleared with a soft south gale so they set about but made little headway. Night brought calm and rain. Wednesday wasn't much better. The afternoon brought sight of a multitude of great whales. Thursday the fog lifted bringing a hot and calm day. Friday's soft west southwest wind gave them some distance but too far north. Saturdays' winds picked up as seamen took and abundance of mackerel. After the fog lifted we had a clear sight of America with its many rocks. The winds were against us but passengers delighted themselves in catching an abundance of mackerel. Sabbath day was clear but winds against us. They tacked about gaining little. Monday morning the seaman were agreeable to anchor off Richmonds Head. Due to winds against us and shoals, a pilot would be necessary to anchor elsewhere. The Penobscot Indians ashore were frightened that we had come to pillage them. Once we anchored off shore they came to us in their shallops. They took some of us ashore to get water and grass for the cattle. They lay at anchor all Tuesday. Wednesday morning brought a north by east gale and they set out from Richmonds Head for Massachusetts Bay. Many fished for mackerel along the way. Toward night the wind calmed so little headway was made. Thursday's winds were against them and they tacked all day gaining little and lay off coast at night. The winds picked up Friday and found them repeating tacking about. Cape Anne was in the eye of the wind and they could not go near it. About 1 in the morning they anchored off the shoals and slept until daybreak. They awoke Saturday to a terrible easterly wind and rain and knew they were in great danger. Three large anchors were lost and cables and their sails like "rotten ragges" blew into the sea. They had no hope of saving themselves from being dashed upon the rocks. *Providence* guided the ship past the rocks giving them a brief respite to fit the ship with other sails. *It was a day much to bee remembered.* Others were not so lucky. Sunday they went on toward Cape Anne in a fresh gale and clear sunny weather. They sailed on down the coast in view of Cape Anne, Saugus Bay, Salem, Marblehead, and other places and anchored at low tide at Nantucket. When the tide turned they set sail in the evening to anchor near Boston. All 100 passengers, 23 seamen, 23 cows and heifers, 3 calves, 8 mares made the trip with no loss of life. They also had no diseases such as smallpox that afflict many on these trips. There was early seasickness, 2 or 3 seamen with flux, and one woman and her child had scurvy. Their provisions were such that they had a variety of food and not restricted to salt fish and beef and biscuits. They had brought along butter, currents and raisins, oatmeal and beer. They managed to get through two storms on Aug 3rd and 13th off the Isles of Shoals. The *Angel Gabriel* was lost at anchor at Pemmaquid off the coast of Maine bursting into pieces. Their journey ended on Aug 17th. Though long, they had anchored in King Road 11 days before setting sail. They spent 3 days at Lundy, 12 days at Milford, 3 days tacking between King Road and Lundy and 1 day between Lundy and Milford, 8 days between Monhegan and Boston. These delays offered them time to acquire hay, oats, fresh water, and other products that allowed them to arrive in good condition on August 17th. The smaller faster ships had outrun the storm.

Governors John Winthrop of Massachusetts Bay Colony and William Bradford of Plymouth Colony recorded accounts of the Great Colonial Hurricane. On Aug 14th 1635 the eye of a great hurricane passed over the area. Winthrop, recalled in his Aug 16th 1635 entry that the winds were kicking up a full week before the hurricane. Once it did arrive, the hurricane: *blew with such violence, with abundance of rain, that it blew down many hundreds of trees, overthrew some houses, and drove the ships from their anchors.* He detailed the deaths of eight American Indians sucked under the rising water while *flying from their wigwams.*

William Bradford, the leader of the Plymouth group, offered a similarly accounting: *Such a mighty storm of wind and rain as none living in these parts, either English or Indian, ever saw. The storm drowned seventeen Native Americans and blew down many hundred thousands of trees turning up the stronger by the roots and breaking the higher pine trees off in the middle. It blew down sundry houses and many houses were flattened.*

Both described high winds, 14 to 20 foot storm surges along the south-facing coasts of Massachusetts and Rhode Island, and great destruction. Much of the area between Providence, Rhode Island and the Piscataqua River was damaged; some damage still noticeable 50 years later. The small barque *Watch and Wait*, owned by Mr. Isaac Allerton, floundered in the storm off Cape Ann with 23 people aboard. The only survivors were Antony Thacher and his wife, who reached an island later named Thacher Island. He wrote an account of the shipwreck. In Narragansett Bay, the tide was 14 feet (4.3 m) above the ordinary tide and drowned eight Native Americans fleeing from their wigwams. The highest ever such recorded value for a New England Hurricane, a 22 foot (6.7 m) storm tide, was recorded in some areas. The town of Plymouth suffered severe damage with houses blown down. The wind cut great mile-long sections of complete blowdown in the woods near Plymouth and elsewhere in eastern Massachusetts. Local crops, along with the forests and many local structures like the Aptucxet trading house on the southwest side [Bourne] of Cape Cod, suffered major damage. Bradford, in his account, predicted signs of the damage would endure into the next century. The Boston area did not suffer from the tide as did areas just to its south. The nearest surge swept over the low-lying tracts of Dorchester, ruining the farms and landscape.

So brutal was the storm that 50 years later, Increase Mather wrote simply, "I have not heard of any storm more dismal than the great hurricane which was in August 1635." His father, the Rev. Richard Mather, was aboard one of the ships nearly sunk at sea by the ferocious weather — but he survived, along with about 100 other passengers. Three years later three more hurricanes came through Massachusetts and Rhode Island.

Modern analysis by The Hurricane Research Division of the Atlantic Oceanographic and Meteorological Laboratory of NOAA has conducted a Re-Analysis Project to re-examine the National Hurricane Center's data about historic hurricanes. In association with the Project, Brian Jarvinen, formerly of NHC, used modern hurricane and storm surge computer models to recreate a storm consistent with contemporary accounts of the Great Colonial Hurricane. Jarvinen estimated that the

GCH was probably a Cape Verde-type hurricane, considering its intensity, which took a track similar to the Great Atlantic Hurricane of 1944 and Hurricane Edna of 1954. The storm's eye would have struck Long Island before moving between Boston and Plymouth. It would likely have been a Category 4 or 5 hurricane further south in the Atlantic, and it was at least a strong Category 3 hurricane at landfall with 125 mph (201 km/h) sustained winds and a central pressure of 938 mbar (27.7 in Hg) at the Long Island landfall and 939 mbar (27.7 in Hg) at the mainland landfall. This would be the most intense known hurricane landfall north of North Carolina. Jarvinen noted that the GCH may have caused the highest storm surge along the east coast of the U.S. in recorded history: 20 feet (6.1 m) near the head of Narragansett Bay. He concluded that "this was probably the most intense hurricane in New England history. So if one chooses to live along the eastern or southeastern coast you can expect hurricanes, some of which can be disastrous. There were 4 major ones on the eastern seaboard in the 1600ˢ, 9 in the 1700ˢ, and 6 in the 1800ˢ. It is little different than living where tornados, drought, floods, or earthquakes can be equally severe. It is the earth's crust of the sphere upon which man lives and one should consider living by the motto "be prepared."

The winter of 1637/8 was so severe that Gov. Winthrop wrote: *The snow lay a half yard deep about the Massachusetts from November fourth till March twenty-third, and a yard deep below the Merrimack, and so the more north the deeper.* Newbury's Town Book recorded on Jun 1ˢᵗ 1638: *Being this day assembled to treat or consider about the well ordering of the affairs of the town, about one of the clock in the afternoon, the sun shining fair, it pleased God suddenly to raise a vehement earthquake coming with a shrill clap of thunder issuing as is supposed out of the east, which shook the earth and the foundations of the houses in a very violent manner to our great amazement and wonder, wherefore taking notice of so great and strange a hand of God's providence, we were desirous of leaving it on record to the view of after ages to the intent that all might take notice of Almighty God and fear his name.* Winthrop also noted: *It came with a noise like continued thunder, or the rattling of coaches in London. The noise and shaking continued about four minutes.* On Aug 3ʳᵈ, Oct 5ᵗʰ & 19ᵗʰ in 1638 more hurricanes blew through the area including Rhode Island.

Massachusetts Bay Colony was well organized and funded. By 1640 its major coastal towns were "modern" and under the control of wealthy merchants. Its merchants enjoyed fine clothing, expensive goods with a good life. England had played a major role in the settlement of the Colonies and as the situation in England improved it slowed down immigration. The lack of these potential consumers in the Colonies created an economic depression which led to its government taking more control over markets. Plymouth Colony's Gov. Bradford complained about the moral decay from materialism. Subsequently both governments became more strict and puritanical.

Shortly after John Pike's arrival on the *James* on Jun 3ʳᵈ 1635, he appeared as a witness in the Court at Cambridge in Massachusetts on Aug 4ᵗʰ 1635. Later as attorney for Mr. Easton at Salem Court Mar 28ᵗʰ 1637. He was fined in Feb 1638 two shillings and sixpence for: *departing from the [town] meeting without leave and contemptuously.* In an argument with Thomas Bloomfield he grabbed Thomas' coat, who slipped out of it and ran away. Enraged at Bloomfield's cowardice, Pike cut the coat to ribbons.

John Pike and his sons, John and Robert, became proprietors and town officers in Newbury, MA, in 1638. John was one of the first to settle as a proprietor in Ipswich where he served as constable in 1648. He moved to Salisbury where he died May 26ᵗʰ 1654. His will dated two days earlier was proved in Hampton court, Aug 3ʳᵈ 1654. His two sons, John and Robert, were appointed executors. He described his lands in Newbury Old Town and lands in New Town each appraised at £60 each. His land at Old Town with rights of Common privilege and his land at Little River to go to his grandson John Pike, son of his eldest son, John, and grandson John Pike, son of Robert Pike with the provision that if either die before age 21 or without children to be divided equally among his siblings and if they didn't have any children it to be divided equally. In other words, keep the lands in the family. His daughter Anne was given £20 to be divided equally between her children. His daughter in law Mary [Turvill], wife of son John, 40 shillings, and 40 shillings each to Mary's children Joseph, Hannah, Mary & Ruth. His daughter in law Sarah, wife of Robert, 40 shillings and children Sarah, Dorothy, Mary & Elizabeth 40 shillings each. He also gave his tenant Samuel Moore *my bedstead that he has.* Interestingly he added that if either of his sons leave the country with their families and my grandchildren are not age 21, his executors to sell the lands for the benefit of his grandchildren. The Inventory taken May 29th 1654 totaled a comfortable £230.06.10. Most people had limited amount of iron cookware used in a fireplace at the time. His were made of brass.

John Pike, eldest son of John Pike and Dorothy Daye, was christened in the village Church in Whiteparish Nov 8th 1613. John Pike's first wife was Mary Turvill who was christened Feb 4th 1615 in a Church at Romsey, Hampshire, daughter of Thomas Turvill and his 1st wife, Dorothy Rogers. Romsey is about 20 miles southeast of Whiteparish. Thomas and Dorothy were married in Romsey Nov 18th 1611. Thomas was christened there Dec 8th 1593, son of Richard Turvill. Richard's other children were: William, Peter, Elizabeth and Joan Turvill. Thomas also had a son, Thomas,3 by his 2nd wife, Mary Claver, whom he married in Romsey Sep 16th 1619. Young Thomas was christened in Romsey Feb 21st 1620/1. This Thomas became a tanner like his father and moved to New England. Thomas died intestate in Newbury May 22nd 1677. An inventory was taken by Caleb Moody and constable, Joseph Pike, who was appointed administrator. *The deceased has been maintained by the Towne neere about foure yeare...and now in his sickness...besides for his funerall neere 40s as we suppose.* The administrator to pay debts so far as the estate would go. His half-sister, Mary Turvill Pike had moved from Newbury approximately ten years before his decease.

John Pike settled with his father in Newbury Old Town where he served as selectman, deputy to the General Court and Lieutenant of the Newbury Company in 1664. In Nov 17th that year settlers could view a comet until the following 4th of Feb. That winter was unusually mild causing grain to mildew. The next year wolves became a problem so the town council voted to pay 40 shillings for every wolf killed. Like many early settlers in Massachusetts Bay Colony, John was a Congregationalist. After being summoned to testify over the teaching of Newbury's church disciplines in a dispute between its pastor and teacher, John took the side of the teacher and joined a Presbyterian Church. He lived briefly in Haverhill, MA, before moving to Woodbridge, NJ, in response to the distribution of the publication *Concessions and Agreements of the Lords-Proprietors.*

There John acquired several parcels of land: a house lot of 10 acres, 180 acres of upland on Langster's Plain, 36 acres of upland on the road to Langster's Plain, 4 acres of meadow north of his house lot, 2 acres of meadow on the eastside of Papiack Creek, 45 acres of meadow on the Raritan river and others totaling 308 acres noted on Aug 20th 1669 by Henry Jaques, sr.[1] July that year brought about a dispute over the boundary between the towns of Piscataway and Woodbridge. Residents of the former destroyed the marks on the trees made by the surveyor. Thomas Bloomfield, sr. who lost his coat to John Pike's father and Stephen Kent sr. were sent to meet with the Piscataway residents; John Pike and Stephen Moore to confer with the Governor. It was concluded sd land belonged to Woodbridge much to the dismay of Piscataway. There must have been a lot of ruffled feathers because some Piscataway residents then pulled up boundary stakes. After months of debate it was finally agreed to create compact town settlements. This affected Strawberry Hill residents where many house lots existed including John Pike's. During these disputes the west side of Papiack Creek by Strawberry Hill, known as the Commons, was ordered by the proprietors to be patented to the

---

1 New Jersey Patents, Bk. 1, p.67.

town as a perpetual sheep common in consideration of a £5 yearly tax.[1] The Common was used by all residents for grazing their flocks of sheep. The means of knowing who owned what animals was by individual earmarks granted by the town to each owner. Earmarks were recorded in town records. Two decades later the Commons was invaded by migrating geese in the fall who were grazing in sheep territory. By then the flocks of sheep had grown so numerous that owners had to take their rams home. As for the geese, it took until the following spring to pass a law that any geese caught nibbling on the grasses be killed. Maybe the residents had already had goose for Christmas.

Two of John Pike's sons and three of his daughters came with their husbands to settle this township. His son, Joseph, stayed in Massachusetts where he was killed in Amesbury by Indians in 1694. John and his male family members were busy with town affairs serving in different capacities. John served as president of the township court in 1669-71 and from 1675-85. In 1672 he was an Asst. Justice, the next year a member of Gov. Cartaret's Council. In 1674 he was a Deputy to the General Assembly, then Assessor in 1679-83. During this time he acquired the title of Captain of the militia and distinguished by that title thereafter but it had little to do with the military. He was a wise man with judicial acumen and heartily helped the township in its business affairs. How he managed all the offices and maintaining a ten acre house lot let alone all the acreage he was patented seems overwhelming.

In the spring of 1684 another dispute arose over taxes. Since East Jersey lands had been purchased from the Indians, some residents felt they were doubly taxed by having to pay the initial Quit Rents plus taxes to the government for the land purchased from Indians which they felt should exempted. John Pike sr. & jr, and John Bishop were sent to discuss the Quit Rents with the Governor and proprietors requesting evidence of the Indians title theory. It took about eighteen months for an agreement at a town meeting in which four of the town's chief men determined that Woodbridge inhabitants pay the Quit Rents and those due the present government.[2]

There were also problems in the household of his John's daughter, Ruth, and her husband, Abraham Tappen/Toppan, a young man that also settled in Newbury Old Town. In a document dated Apr 9th 1678, Abraham agreed that his wife should return to her father's house with her children, taking such articles as she and her father deem necessary in *consequence of the extremity of her distressed condition in respect of sicknesses and illnesses*. At the time they had daughters, Mary and Hannah Tappen, born in Haverhill. On the 14th, witnesses testified that Tappen was then *in his senses*. Captain Pike and his son, John, were convicted in Sep 1684 of secreting goods in their houses. Town records reveal these items. A tin and horn lanthorne [lantern] taken from Holand Sheet, a cushion top worth one shilling, a remnant of homespun [linsey-woolsey] worth four shillings, all the property of his son-in-law, Abraham Tappen. The goods were ordered to be returned and they to pay double the value of the goods as well as fees and court charges. John, jr. lost his position as Clerk of Court. Later records reveal that Abraham was not always sane which gave his family difficulties. During this time Captain Pike's wife, Mary, died and he married 2nd on Jun 30th 1685 in Piscataway, the widow of ancestor Edward FitzRandolph, Elizabeth nee Blossom who apparently was not bothered by his *defamed* character. Being aged there was no further issue. On Dec 23rd 1685, John's son, John, relinquished all claim to the land conveyed to him by his father, Capt. Pike, on Nov 1st 1684.[2] Abraham and Ruth agreed in Jun 1687 to live together again and Capt. Pike gave them a tract of twenty acres of upland and four acres of Raritan meadows. This was a conditional conveyance as noted in a deed dated Nov 21st 1684 from Captain Pike to his son, John. Abraham later returned to Newbury, MA, where he died in Feb 1703/4 having lived with his brother, John, during his old age. He left a small legacy to "a son of his wife."

---

1 Dally, pgs. 40-41.

2 Ibid., pgs. 103-104

Captain John Pike died in 1689 in Woodbridge, NJ, and asked to be buried near his late wife, Mary. Andrew D. Mellick, Jr. in his book, *Story of an Old Farm*, pg. 109 states: *Obadiah Ayres and Richard Worth were sons-in-law of John Pike, who may be called the patriarch of the settlement. Worth, either because of his name or his virtues, seems to have been much more highly esteemed by his father-in-law than was Ayres, as John Pike in his will left the latter six-pence, while the former received the munificent bequest of one shilling.*[1] In the *History of Union and Middlesex Counties, New Jersey*, W. Woodford Clayton, Editor, Everts & Peck, 1882, Philadelphia, pg. 555, it is states: *It is recorded that Capt. John Pike left in his will to Mr. Ayres the sum of one shilling.*

His will dated Jan 24th 1689 written in bold hand reads:

> *Item I give to my Daughter Hanna ten Shillings to Barbara worth one Shilling, to Obadiah Ayres Six pence, to Richard Worth one Shilling, to Abraham Tapping one penney to my daughter Ruth one Shilling to John worth my booke writt by Gillinghast, and all the rest of my estate both real & personall I give vnto my sone John in consideration of my maintenance so long as I do live...*

Most of his real estate went to his sons: John, Thomas and Joseph. Hanna who received ten shillings was Obadiah's wife. John Worth, his grandson, the book. Obadiah & Hannah Ayers' bequest totaled 10 shillings 6 pence, Richard and Barbara Worth's 2 shillings. I need not speculate as to Capt. John Pike's likes or dislikes.

Five years after Captain Pike died, the Assembly enacted in 1694 that the families' name be restored to their former good name and pronounced it lawful for John Pike or his family to commence an legal action for defamation of character against any one reproaching or scandalizing *them as diligent search and inquiry by evidence and clear proof* presented to the Assembly cleared them of any wrong doing. Among his many descendants were Major Zebulon Pike of the Revolutionary War and General Zebulon Montgomery Pike of the War of 1812 and discoverer of Pike's Peak in Colorado.

So I move on to the next Ayers generation of John Pike's daughter, Hannah, who married Obadiah Ayers I and had:

Ayers Ancestry Continued

Obadiah[3] Ayers II born Oct 20th 1671 in Woodbridge, NJ. The first record of him as an adult was on Jan 1st 1693/4 when Samuel Dennis was elected Town Clerk in lieu of Thomas Pike. Dennis was not present at the meeting so Obadiah and two others were sent to locate Dennis and bring him to the meeting to take the oath of office. Dennis refused the job so it was given to Thomas Pike. The following Apr 28th 1694 Obadiah married Joanna Jones in Woodbridge by Justice Samuel Hale.

Joanna was the daughter of Benjamin Jones and his 3rd wife Joanna who came from Huntington and Jamaica, LI, NY. Little is known about Benjamin Jones' early life. His father, Thomas Jones, was a 1666 Patentee at Huntington. Benjamin received an 80 acre patent in 1696 in Huntington where numerous restrictions were in effect over land allotments as well as the marking of livestock, disposing of property, satisfying Indian demands and no marking of wild horses. Benjamin Jones by his wife Sarah Spencer had children:

1. Richard.
2. Benjamin b. Jul 13th 1694.

---

1 Andrew D. Mellick, Jr., *The Story of an Old Farm* (Somerset, NJ, Unionist Gazette, 1889) p. 109

3. Spencer b. Dec 29th 1695 at Springfield.
4. Elifalet b. May 31st 1696
5. Hannah b. Mar 29th 1698/9.
6. Mary who married Charles Salyer/Sallior;
+7. Joanna.
8. Edward Jones.

The first record of Benjamin being in Woodbridge, NJ, was in 1693 with the recording of his earmark. He joined the Woodbridge Presbyterian Church Oct 31st 1708. Benjamin died intestate in mid 1717. The Inventory of his estate which did not include any land dated Jul 2nd 1717 was presented Jul 20th 1717 to John Barclay, Surrogate. Debts of 15 shillings each were due from Richard Jones, Joseph Ayers, and David Alford.

In the year 1695, Woodbridge made it an obligation for all males to attend the town meeting. Due to a lack of attendance, in Jan 1699 a fine of 9 pence was imposed for non attendance. If anyone refused to pay they were not allowed to attend any meeting until their fine was paid. Some thought it of little or no consequence. Obadiah was elected Town Constable at that meeting, not the most beloved job. He joined the Woodbridge Presbyterian Church Nov 6th 1709, Joanna the following Jan 1st. Obadiah became a guardian of two Pike daughters in 1714. From 1706-1758 there were seven more divisions of land. In the drawing on May 8th 1717, Obadiah's drawing netted him 56 acres. Land sizes ranged from 1-69 acres that were distributed to a total of sixty-eight men.

Obadiah and Joanna were parents of:[1]

1. Hannah b. Jan 18th 1694/5.
2. Sarah b. and d. Jan 8th 1696/7.
3. Mary b. Feb 23rd 1698, d. Nov 15th 1704.
4. Rachel b. May 23rd 1701.
5. Joanna b. Dec 25th 1703.
+6. Obadiah[4] III b. Dec 25th 1703.
7. Robert b. Jul 18th 1706 and d. 1740/1 Woodbridge, m. Hume/Hummus Frazee, daughter of Shiphat Frazee. Children: Hume, Frazee, Robert, Huldah, daughter, and ?Reuben Ayers, posthumously. Hume was licensed to marry 2nd on Feb 15th 1743, Peter Knap.
8. Mary b. Sep 29th 1708.
9. Rebeckah b. Nov 14th 1710.
10. Daughter mentioned in Will. [Possibly Sarah who married James Kelly].
11. Benajah b. Nov 17th 1715.

Obadiah II's Will written Oct 27th 1728 was proved May 27th 1729. It noted his occupation was a yeoman, who at that time was a farmer who owned and farmed his own land. He probably died late May 1729 due to the date of proof and inventory dated Jun 2nd 1729 which totaled £60.03.00. He gave his wife use of house and land until son Benejah became of age, then to him. Other lands had already been deeded to his sons Obadiah and Robert. Anything left of his moveable after debts was to be divided between his son Benejah and six daughters at his wife's discretion.

On Nov 27th 1736, Benajah, a yeoman of Woodbridge Twp., sold to his brother, Obadiah Ayers III, a house carpenter of Woodbridge township, for £154 the sundry pieces of lands and meadows in Woodbrige township bequeathed to him by his father, Obadiah Ayers II: one a first division of 8 acres, second 6 acres, third 22.5 acres, also 5 acres being ½ of a third division, plus 4 acres of salt meadow

---

1 Woodbridge Vital Records, pgs. 6,7

at Raritan Meadows, and 3 acres more of salt meadow. Witnessed by John Roy and Thomas Pike.[1] Obadiah II and Joanna's son,

Obadiah[4] Ayers III was born on Tuesday Dec 25th 1703 in Woodbridge, NJ. Although it was Christmas, it would have been an ordinary day in the household except for the birth of Obadiah and his twin sister Joanna. Presbyterians, like Puritans at that time , did not believe in celebrating Christmas. Obadiah had married Mary Bloomfield about 1725 who was born about 1697, the youngest child of Ezekiel Bloomfield and Hope FitzRandolph. Mary's father, Ezekiel, died on Feb 15th 1702 when Mary was five years old. Her mother, Hope, died three years later.

Obadiah and Mary's children born in Woodbridge, NJ, were:[2]

1.   Mary5 b. Apr 13th 1729, was licensed to marry Dec 24th 1750 George Harriot, b. Mar 13th 1720. Mary was listed in Mar 1759 as a member of the First Presbyterian Church of Woodbridge. George served in the 1st and 3rd Regiment of Middlesex County during the Revolutionary War and later became Captain of the North Amboy Militia in 1793. They suffered losses of £47.05.02 during the war in food, bee hives, candles, livestock, glass, fencing and copper weights from the British in 1777. After a break of twenty seven years in the church records both were listed as Communicants in Apr 1786 with George listed as an elder on May 13th 1788. Mary d. Feb 3rd 1794 at age 65 in Woodbridge, George d. Mar 24th 1804, both buried Woodbridge: children: Mary, Ephraim, Samuel, David, James, Joannah, James, Isabel, and Elizabeth Herriott.

+2.   Daniel5 b. in 1732, died Jul 9th 1818 in Perth Amboy, NJ; m. Elizabeth (?), possibly daughter of Abraham & Phebe Webb. Children: Obadiah6, Daniel, Abraham, Phebe, Rachel, Thomas, Elizabeth, and Mary Ayers.

3.   Joanna b. about 1737, m. 1st Jan 26th 1762, William Tappen in Woodbridge, b. Jan 5th 1729 in Woodbridge, son of Abraham4 (Isaac3, Isaac2, Abraham1) Tappen and his 1st wife, Mary Stone who m. Feb 6th 1718. Joanna m. 2nd John Piatt and d. Jan 22nd 1810, age 73: buried Woodbridge.

4.   Susanna b. about 1739. She was about age 11 when the children lost their mother on Jun 21st 1750.

New York, Jul 2. From Amboy, we have Advice, that on Thursday Evening the 21st past, the Wife of Mr. Obadiah Ayers, in that City, was shot dead as she was sitting in her own House, by her own Negro from without, as 'tis thought, in Conjunction with a new Negro belonging to one of the Neighbours: They were both tried on Thursday last, when the new Negro confessed in the best Manner he could express, that the other had persuaded him to lend him his Master's Gun, and go along with him; and that after he had shot his Mistress, he gave him the Gun again, and bid him run into the Woods, and shoot the first Man he met with; which he accordingly attempted the next Day when he was taken; but the Gun would not go off: They were both found guilty and condemn'd to be burnt; and Friday next is appointed the Day of their Execution. – The N.Y. Gazette Revived in the Weekly Post Boy, Jul 2nd 1750.[3]

---

1 Middlesex Deed Bk E$_2$, 44-46.

2 Woodbridge Town Records

3 Wm. Nelson, Ed., *Documents of Colonial History of New Jersey, Extracts from American Newspapers* (Patterson, NJ, Press Prtg. & Publ. Co., Vol XII, 1740-1750) 1895, p. 652

After Mary died Obadiah acquired a license to marry 2nd Mary Wessels, dated Dec 5th 1750 in Perth Amboy, NJ.

East Jersey initially called negros slaves or bonds-people as noted in censuses and tax records. Later records usually referred to them as servants. There were 120 in New Jersey in 1680. Before 1696 Quakers would no longer import or even employ them. The British Royal African Company was engaged in slave trade and Queen Anne encouraged the Royal Governors of New Jersey and New York to get merchants to enter this business. This was in response to the Quakers opposition. The main port of entry was Perth Amboy where barracks housed them. Their number had grown to 10,000 by 1775. The new Continental Congress prohibited trading in slaves and their numbers continued to decline rapidly. East Jersey ranked second to New York in number in the 1790 census. Punishment was severe. In 1791 hangings replaced burnings. As a deterrent servants were made to watch. Once they grew more comfortable with each other servants were treated well, clothed and cared for when sick. But acts of murder or theft were not taken lightly. Also, if found more than five miles from home they were flogged and owners fined by constables for their return. Punishment was swift, as noted in Mary's case. New Jersey Laws starting in 1804 gradually abolished black servants and they diminished in number by 1810. There were none in 1850. Free negroes numbered about 300.

In 1684 the first transportation packet to carry passengers and freight to New York was established by Deputy-Governor Lawrie. It was a stage trip from Burlington to Amboy, then by boat to New York. Connected with the packet was the first public house which opened in Amboy. It became the well known Long Ferry Tavern or "the spot" because it was situated on a beautiful grove of locusts on the river's bank. It was a favorite place for people to stroll and acquired the name "Love-Grove." Alexander Carnes, a man of large stature, kept the tavern for many years. Eventually land in this area would be owned by St. Peter's Church. On Sep 14th 1770 the church Rector, Wardens and Vestry men requested a Warrant from the Board of Proprietors to use a lot 300 feet from the south side of Water street into the river the width of the church lot but not going deep into the river. The request was considered improper. However, the Board did grant 600 feet into the river to E. Bland and H. Johnston and they to convey it to the Church. Said order was then sent to the Surveyor General.[1] On Apr 16th 1785 the Church petitioned the Board to consider giving assistance in completing repairs to the Church and Parsonage. The unusual response was to allocate 100 acres of any unappropriated land, except "Romopock."[2]

In 1695 Inn keepers were taxed £10 for five years for maintaining the road. A general act was passed in 1716 that established travel rates on the route to New York for one man and his horse or just the man. A single passenger paid fourteen pence for the sailing trip. At the time travel from Philadelphia to New York or Staten Island was of great importance and Amboy played its role.

Obadiah III, a yeoman and house carpenter from nearby Woodbridge, purchased from Alexander Carnes for £22.10s a 49½ x 66 ft. lot in Amboy on Aug 23rd 1730. It began on the south side of Smith Street from the northeast corner of Zachariah Week's lot formerly patented to Robert Burnet. Six days later, Obadiah purchased an adjacent lot of the same size from Carnes for £18. Buildings on the north side of Smith Street at its junction with High Street were kept as taverns prior to the Revolution. Travel business was booming.

The March 1732/3 issue of Branford's *Philadelphia Mercury* had an advertisement aimed at merchants, tradesmen, travelers, and others. Two stage wagons intend to go from Burlington to Amboy and back once every week or offt'er if business presents. There was considerable competition for the business. In Apr 1734 a notice was given by Arthur Brown that he would boat between New York and South River in New Jersey and carry goods as cheap as other lines via Amboy or New Brunswick once

---

1 *Minutes of the Board of Proprietors of the Eastern Division of New Jersey, Vol. IV.*, pgs. 210-11
2 *Ibid.*, pgs. 287-288

a week if wind and weather prevail. Boats as well as land stages provided these services. Taverns provided meals and lodging for the travelers as well as their horses if they came in that manner. On May 4th 1743, Obadiah purchased from Thomas Caywood of Woodbridge for £50 a lot of land and dwelling house in New Brunswick being 100 ft. wide and 226 ft. deep. It is not known what he did with this lot but in all probability it was connected to the tavern business or he repaired the house and rented it.

The courts established a uniform rate of charges in Oct 1748 for all taverns in Middlesex County, NJ. Meat, hot 10d, cold 7d; lodging, 4d per night; Lunch 1s.2d; Metheglin, 1s.6d. Beverages served were rum, brandy, wine, strong beer, and cider. Horse provisions included Oats sold by the quart, English hay @ 1s per night, Salt or fresh hay @ 8d per night, ditto for 24 hours at 1s. At the time travel from the major cities was by stagecoach and sailboats. The following was printed in the Penn. Gazette, 25 Jul 1751:

> *Notice is hereby given to all persons that intend to convey themselves, goods, wares or merchandize, from Philadelphia to New York, or from New York to Philadelphia: That there will be a stage-boat, well fitted, and kept by Patrick Cowan, living in Burlington, that will attend every Tuesday in every week at the Crooked Billet Wharff in Philadelphia for the same business, and will proceed the same day up to Burlington, wind and weather permitting. And on Wednesday morning a stage waggon with a good awning kept by Fretwell Wright at the Blue Anchor in Burlington, and John Predmore at Cranberry, and James Wilson at Amboy Ferry; will proceed to Obadiah Ayers's, Inn keeper at Amboy Ferry; where good entertainment for man and horse is and will be kept. And on Thursday, a stage passage boat with a fine commodious cabbin fitted with a tea-table and sundry other conveniences kept by Matthias Ifelstine will be ready to receive the passengers or goods, and proceed directly to New York, and give her attendance at Whitehall Battery...The boat, for the first time, will begin to attend at the Crooked Billet on Tuesday, the 13th day of Aug, 1751, and the waggon will proceed the day following. Further, if the ice, or any thing else, should at any time prevent the passage-boat from going from Burlington to Philadelphia, the stage-waggon will, if requir'd proceed from Burlington Cooper's Ferry.*[1] Obadiah's competitor was John Cluck. The *N. Y. Gazette* or the *Weekly Post Boy*, Jun 4, 1753 noted:

> *That Abraham Webb, being provided with a Boat exceeding well fitted, with a very handsome Cabbin, and all necessary Accommodations; proposes to give his Attendance at the White-Hall-Slip every Monday and Thursday; and the same Day, Wind and Weather permitting, to proceed for Amboy-Ferry to John Cluck's where a Wagon kept by John Richards will be ready to receive either Goods or Passengers and to proceed with them to Borden's-Town, where a Stage-Boat will be ready to carry them to Philadelphia, and the same Method will be followed from the Crooked-Billet Wharf at Philadelphia, up to Borden's-Town, and shall proceed, Load or no Load, twice a Week, by which Means, Passengers or Goods may never be detained on the Road. As the purpose to endeavour to use People in the best Manner they are capable of, they hope all good Persons will give it the Encouragement it deserves. So with Respect they remain Friends to the Publick.*[2]

---

1 Wm. Nelson, Ed., Documents of Colonial History of New Jersey, Extracts from American Newspapers (Patterson, NJ. Press Prtg. & Publ. Co.) Vol. III, pgs. 86-88
2 *Ibid.*, 264-265

By spring of 1754 Obadiah may have felt his health was declining for he wrote his will on April 17th. But it wasn't until Feb 1st 1760 that it was proved, so we can assume he died in late 1759 or in Jan 1760. He had his debts and funeral expenses paid out of his former wife's personal estate that was given to her by her brother, Ezekiel Bloomfield, by his Last Will thus conferring the amounts paid will fully appear and as I am now going to recover and receive all that said estate.

It is my will the same shall pay my debts due after my decease, and if the said estate shall not be sufficient to pay all my Just Debts, my Executrix shall sell a portion of my Lands and Tenements sufficient for the payment of any debts. And the residue of my moveable estate I give unto Mary, dearly and beloved wife for her to dispose of in such a manner she shall deem proper. I also give unto Mary all the accounts and profits of all my Lands, Mortgages and Tenements for maintaining and education of my younger daughter Susannah until she is eighteen years of age and no longer. I give unto my son Daniel Ayres the sum of five pounds to be paid to him by my younger daughters when my youngest daughter Susannah shall be eighteen years of age. I give to my two younger daughters Johannah and Susannah when they shall be of age to possess said lands, but if either of my daughters Johannah or Susannah shall depart this life before my said younger daughter Susannah is eighteen years of age, then all that part of the said land, mortgages and tenements that I have herein given to said daughters shall lawfully devolve unto Mary my wife and my son Daniel and all of my daughters that remain alive to be equally divided among them, and their heirs forever. I give unto Mary beloved wife her choice of dwelling rooms for her to live in as long as she shall remain my widow. And I do make Mary my Sole executrix. And I do hereby give said Executrix to grant bargain and sell any part of my Lands and tenements in the amount of my debts and give good and sufficient Deed or Deeds of Sale as Required. And I hereby utterly ratify this to be my last will and testament. Witnessed by William, Bart and G. Bloodgood.

But wife Mary refused on Jan 31st 1760 to take on the Executorship.

His children: Mary Harriot, wife of George, Daniel and Joanna Ayers requested the Court appoint George Harriot to be appointed Administrator. George Harriot[1] and James Pike, yeoman, posted bond of £500 for sd administration. The estate was sued by John Wattson, Thomas Hadden, Brolifc Kearney, and Joseph Freeman for a total of £511.264.19 and £18.08.07 in damages. The Inventory appearing in the Account Settlement totaled £31.3.4. His burial at £1.12 and legal fees far exceeded the inventory. His lands were publicly auctioned. His son, Daniel, was the highest bidder. Payments and disbursements for the Estate was £114.00.11 in the final accounting.

Obadiah's first wife and mother of his children, Mary Bloomfield, was the daughter of Ezekiel Bloomfield and Hope FitzRandolph. Mary's Bloomfield ancestry follows:

Bloomfield Ancestry

Thomas Bloomfield, a Major in Cromwell's army came with his father, John, to settle in Newbury New Town, MA. After Thomas' father John died, the General Court appointed Thomas Bloomfield,

---

1 George Harriott died in 1802, bur. in Presbyterian Cemetery as a Revolutionary War Burial.

a proprietor in 1638, to administer his father's estate on Mar 3rd 1639/40, he to have the house and grounds. Thomas had a lame sister who was given the over-plus of goods that was not disposed.[1] It is unknown if he brought a bride or met his wife Mary in Newbury. He rented a farm from John Cutting whose will dated Oct 22nd 1659 left the house to his daughter, Mary Noyes, noting that Thomas was in possession. The farm consisted of 70-75 acres. Two years later it was mentioned in the will of Richard Browne...his 8 acres of salt marsh lying...between Mrs. Cuttings and Thomas Bloomfield's marsh.[2] Apparently Thomas continued living there before the family departed for Woodbridge, NJ. We know he was in Woodbridge by July 1669 for in that month he was sent with Stephen Kent to Piscataway to inquire about that town's grievances over the boundary between the two communities. His land patent was for 326 acres. Another patent was for 91½ acres dated Mar 18th 1669/70. His house lot was 17½ acres on Strawberry Hill.

In January 1671 Thomas was elected to serve as a juryman. The following April he was elected a Grand Juryman with John Martin to report on any misdemeanors in the town. At the next Jan (1672) meeting, he was elected Constable serving through 1674. Then he served as a Deputy to the General Assembly and an Assistant Justice. In the early Charter 100 acres had been set aside for educating the children. The land was not initially surveyed so some individuals obtained patents for it and occupied same. In Sep 1682 the aroused community met to claim the patents were illegal and if so determined, the intruders ejected. Capt. Pike, John Bishop, sr., Samuel Moore and Thomas Bloomfield were on committee to represent Woodbridge's claim. The land recovered consisted of 88 acres of upland and 12 acres of marsh land. It took several years before a school and a teacher were elected.[3] This was the last of Thomas' service to the community.

Thomas Bloomfield's children by his wife Mary were born in Newbury where their vital records are located.[4]

1. Mary b. Jan 15th 1641/2, m. Jonathan Singletary aka Dunham, son of Richard and Susanna Singletary. Prior to moving to Woodbridge, he was accused of being a Ranter and disseminating among his neighbors corrupt religious principles not tolerated by Puritan courts. He took on the alias of Jonathan Dunham. On Aug 10th 1672 he was patented 213 acres in Woodbridge and became a respected citizen. Jonathan and Mary's six children were born in Woodbridge.
2. Sarah b. Dec 30st 1643, m. John Dennis 1668: children: John[4], Mary, Sarah, & Elizabeth. John, sr. d. May 8th 1689 and wife Sarah d. a week later on May 15th.
3. John b. Mar 15th 1644/5, m, 1st Sarah Moore: children: Thomas[4] & Sarah.
4. Thomas b. Dec 12th 1648, m, Elizabeth Dennis 1676, no children. Thomas d. Mar 27th 1679.
5. Nathaniel b. Apr 10th 1651, d. May 31st 1689.
+6. Ezekiel[3] b. Nov 1st 1653, m. Hope FitzRandolph.[5]
7. Rebecca b. May 4th 1656, d. Sep 25th 1678.
8. Ruth b. Jul 4th 1659, d. Sep 9th 1678.
9. Timothy b. Apr 1st 1664, d. Dec 28th 1678.[6]

---

1 Essex Co. Probate File, Docket 6984

2 Essex Co. Quarterly Court Files, vol. 6, leaf 139

3 Dally, p. 177

4 Recorded in *Newbury Vital Records*, p. 56

5 Wm. Nelson's *New Jersey Biographical and Genealogical Notes*, reprinted 1989 by Genealogical Publ. Co., Inc. States on page 33 that Ezekiel was the Eldest son of Thomas Bloomfield, etc. This is not consistent with Newbury's Vital Records.

6 Thomas Wilson, Extraction of Rev. Dally's 1873 Records, *Vital Records of Woodbridge, New Jersey* (Lambertville, NJ, Hunterdon House, 1983, pgs 8-10, 15-21.

In 1678/9 there was a major outbreak of smallpox that took the lives of three of their children. More would die ten years later making the Bloomfield family having more than its share of deaths. Thomas Bloomfield's will was located in a NJ deed book and dated Jun 10th 1684. He died Sep 21st 1687 during the second outbreak. His wife Mary and son Nathaniel were executors. His wife was to get half of his homestead and household goods as long as she remained a widow. Nathaniel to get the other half. In addition Thomas mentions his meadows to go to his oldest son John, youngest son Ezekiel, grandson Thomas son of John, grandson Timothy son of Ezekiel. The room by room, yard, cellar, and outyard inventory dated Sep 24th 1687 was made three days after his death by Samuel Moore, Benj. Griffith and Jonathan Dunham [son-in-law]. He had ample land for his heirs and two breeding mares for his grandsons. Unusual items noted were writing paper, ink, and a writing staff in his bed chamber. The inventory totaled £204.12.06[1]

Ezekiel Bloomfield was born Nov 1st 1653 in Newbury, MA. He married Hope FitzRandolph Dec 22nd 1680 in Woodbridge, NJ. Hope was born Apr 2nd 1661 at Barnstable, MA, the youngest daughter of Edward FitzRandolph and Elizabeth Blossom. Ezekiel served as Constable in 1685, Assemblyman in 1687 and overseer in 1689. From 1692-1700 he was keeper of the pound. Records show that many animals were impounded during his term. In Dec 1692 the Woodbridge Meeting house was in need of repairs. Its roof needing shingling and four men needed to work in pairs on each side. No adult male was immune in participating in community work. Ezekiel and Matthew Moore, jr were appointed to do one side, John and Thomas Pike the other. The shingles were required to be made of chestnut boards 5" wide and an inch thick which cost 6 shilling per hundred, the town furnished the nails. The four men were allowed to deduct their costs and labor from their annual tax. There were no stoves in the meeting house at the time. A fireplace was considered sacrilegious. Little choice was left but to shiver through sermons or meet in some hospitable home in the winters. Come Jul 1698 more improvements had to be made. John Pike, Clerk, had to white wash the building. Ezekiel was to build a new Pulpit "forth with."[2] So it can be assumed that Ezekiel was a carpenter. Little else in known about him except in his land disbursements in his will dated Jan 12th 1702/3.[3] He died Feb 15th 1702/3 in Woodbridge, NJ. Hope died three years later leaving minor children.

Ezekiel and Hope Bloomfield had eight children born in Woodbridge.[4]

1. Timothy b. Feb 11th 1681/2, m. Rose Higgins Apr 2nd 1707; children Richard, Rebecca, and Sarah.
2. Ezekiel b. Nov 26th 1683, d. Jan 14th 1748, age 65, m. 1st Hester Dunham Dec 23rd 1706, children: Moses & Hannah.
3. Rebeckah b. Jun 7th 1686, d. Dec 25th 1688.
4. Nathaniel b. Feb 9th 1687/8, d. Oct 15th 1689.
5. Benjamin b. circa 1690 (given 40 acres in Ezekiel's will).
6. Jeremiah b. Jan 28th 1692/3, d. 1746, m. Catherine Weekes, Jan 8th 1722/3, children: Ezekiel, Hannah, Ebenezer, Jeremiah, Eunice, Ursula, Mary, and Katherine.
7. Joseph b. Mar 21st 1694/5, d. May 23rd 1782, m. Eunice Dunham Sep 5th 1721, children: Hannah, Martha, Moses, and Asa.
8. Mary b. 1697, m. Obadiah[4] Ayers III. Their son:

---

1 Middlesex Deed Bk. B: pp. 298-290.

2 Dally, p. 86-87, 116.

3 Middlesex Co. Will Book H, pgs. 127-129.

4 Thomas Wilson, Extraction of Rev. Dally's 1873 Records, *Vital Records of Woodbridge, New Jersey*, Lambertville, N J, Hunterdon House, 1983, pp. 8-10.

Ayers Ancestry Continued

Daniel[5] Ayers was born in 1732 in Woodbridge, NJ. He married Elizabeth about 1759. They had the following children:

1.   Obadiah Ayers, b, Dec 1760 (Ensign, Nov 30th 1793 North Amboy Militia Census), d. before 1850 in New York City; m. about 1789, Catherine Drake of New York City; no children.
2.   Daniel Ayers, b. Mar 31st 1763, d. intestate Feb 12th 1827. (Pvt., Nov 30th 1793 North Amboy Militia Census, Corp. under Capt. Jos. Marsh Co. of Infantry, 3rd Reg. NJ Militia 11 Sep-31 Dec 1794), married 1804, Rhoda Holton, b. 1780, d. 1867. They had five children. On Feb 23rd 1827, Rhoda and son Joseph were declared authorized Administrators. No inventory of his estate was in his file. By 1835 Rhoda had married Venice Talmage.
3.   Abraham Ayers, b. 1766 (Nov 30th 1793 North Amboy Militia Census), m. after 1789 and before 1797, Ann Heath. Mrs. Abraham Ayres was buried Aug 23rd 1826 at St. Peters Church, Perth Amboy, NJ, children: Abraham, Joshua, possibly William, Robert, and George Ayers.
4.   Phebe Ayers, b. Nov 13th 1770, d. Feb 23rd 1815; m. Enos Talmage; b. 1773, d. Nov 3rd 1843, buried in Old Presbyterian Churchyard in Metuchen, NJ, with Phebe and their first three children. Children: Daniel, John, Elizabeth, and Rachel Talmage.
5.   Rachael Ayers, b. 1773, Single in 1819.
+6.   Thomas Ayers, b. Aug 16th 1775.
7.   Elizabeth Ayres, b. Aug 13th 1777, d. Dec 4th 1852 in Perth Amboy (Tombstone), bur. in SW corner of St. Peter's Church Cemetery in Perth Amboy, m. Moses Martin Jan 21st 1807 in Perth Amboy, son of James and Ann Wright Martin. Moses was b. Jan 23rd 1783. Moses Martin's home was on the corner of Smith & State Streets in Perth Amboy. In back of his home was his chair factory where he made lathe turned chairs with rush seats. They became a sought after antique. Children: Nancy, Kimball D. m. Ann Langstaff; Elizabeth d. unm., James Watson and twins Charles and Obadiah Ayres Martin. Obadiah Ayres Martin m. Elizabeth Langstaff. Moses Martin d. Feb 9th 1867. Moses & Elizabeth are buried in the churchyard of St. Peter's Church, Perth Amboy.
8.   Mary Ayers, b. Aug 13th 1777, m. Mr. Crews (possibly Ellis Crow).

My research had led me to believe that Daniel's wife Elizabeth was the daughter of Abraham Webb and Phebe Pindar, but I have not been able to locate a marriage certificate for them or prove this. Daniel and Elizabeth's third and fourth children bear these two names. In addition, Daniel was named an executor of Abraham Webb's estate as well as testifying to the couple's losses during the Revolution. Abraham Webb is noted as having a boat "exceedingly well fitted with a handsome cabin and all necessary accommodations in June 1753 at Perth Amboy.

Abraham's Webb's will dated Sep 29th 1773, states he was of Perth Amboy, NJ.

> *.....to be decently buried at the Discretion of my Executors herein after appointed...I Give...after payment of my Just Debts and funeral Charges...to my son John the sum of five Shillings. Item...all the Residue and Remainder of my Estate both Real and Personal be by my Executors Divided into five Equal parts or shares, one...share...to my Beloved wife Phebe, one...to my son Isaac, one...to my son Pindar, and the other two...shares to my son Abraham...to them their heirs and assigns forever, and in Case of the Death of any or Either of my said three sons*

Abraham Webb's father, John, was a merchant mariner of Perth Amboy and the Barbados. There were numerous people by the name Webb in the Barbados beginning with a marriage recorded in 1645. The 1680 census of St. Peter All Saints Parish in the Barbados lists a John, Nicholas and Thomas Webb. There was also a Mr. Samuel Webb noted in St. George Parish land records and census.

John Webb married Dec 16th 1721 Jane Pinder Mangles in St. Michael Parish where she was born Sep 14th 1701 daughter of John Pinder and Christian Snipes. Her previous mariner husband had died at sea. There was also a Mr. William Snipes listed as a land owner in St. George Parish. John Webb eventually settled in Perth Amboy, NJ. It is known that he came from the Barbados to Perth Amboy on Jul 25th 1725. On Apr 25th 1726 he went back to Barbados on his Brigantine *Jane and Mary* and returned on it the following May 10th. His will dated Jan 19th 1766 arrived at the surrogate's office on Feb 23rd 1767.[2] It is apparent that John brought a number of negros with him from Barbados. His wife, Jane, was given his dwelling house, wharf, and tenement lot in Perth Amboy during her natural life, about 4 acres, household goods, plus negros Betty, Balinda, Dorinda and Abia. His son Abraham was given a house and adjoining lot occupied by a Mrs. Hull plus negro man Anfield, boy Will, and girl Moll plus £50 when he became of age. John's son Isaac was to get the house after his mother's decease and to pay sons, William and John, £75 upon possession. Also negro man Peter and girl Kate. William and John were also given tenements and land. His negro man Quaco and girl Betty were given to William, and boy Coffey and girl Peggy to John. The usual allocations were made in regard to any survivors in regard to negros and sons under age 21. John owned the Brigantine *John and Robert* and ordered it to be dispatched to Ireland. His sloop *Jane* could be either sold or kept, his executrix's decision. A George Webb was one of the will's witnesses.

Daniel Ayers had been deeded on Dec 20th 1751 for the sum of £300.08.00 two parcels of land from his father, Obadiah Ayers I, both listed as of Perth Amboy. All this land was in Woodbridge. One parcel was 79 acres and part of land purchased from Obadiah's Uncle, Thomas Pike. The other, 71½ acres & 20 rods was part of land patented to Capt. John Pike. After Daniel's father Obadiah died, there was difficulty in executing his will due to indebtedness and law suits. His lands were put up for

---

1 Middlesex Co., NJ Will Bk. Book L, pgs. 527-530

2 New Jersey Wills, Bk. H, pgs. 586-88.

auction. Daniel, a party of these parcels in Obadiah's will, secured the lands as highest bidder for £369.16.03 and was deeded same by Samuel Throckmorton, Sheriff of Middlesex County, on Jul 7th 1760. Daniel like his father was listed as a yeoman and house carpenter in the deeds even though his father operated an Inn and died in debt. What is perplexing to me is where Daniel acquired the money to purchase the lands in his father's estate. Could it have been from his wife, Elizabeth? If she were the granddaughter of John Webb, merchant mariner from Perth Amboy and Barbados who was apparently financially well off, and daughter of his son Abraham, money could have come from this family as a dower. One more remaining mystery.

Daniel was 46 years old when he became a Teamster stationed at Morristown in the Revolutionary War. His service record follows:

The Official Register of the Officers and Men of New Jersey in the Revolutionary War, Wagonmaster General's Dept., Oct 23rd 1778, Doc. 5923 Revolutionary; lists Capt. Hallybirt's Brigade with the following Teamsters: Hendry Shoemaker, Davis Moss, Robert Turner, James Beaty, Benjamin Gardner, Albert Henry and Daniel Ayers.

Ayers, Daniel Teamster, Captain Hallybirt's Team Brigade, Wagonmaster General's Department, Oct 23, 1778; stationed at Morristown; carted commissary stores to Kings Ferry; in service in 1780. Received from Edmund Martin, Quartermaster General's Department, Certificate No. 160, dated Feb 8, 1781, for $1024.00, Continental; £10.05.07, Specie. Interest commenced Feb 29, 1780, interest to Jan 1, 1787, £4.04.03¼ - same deposited in the State Treasure, 5957; N.J. Q.M.G. Dept. No 2, Voucher 1961.

In an Alpha listing p. 352 of *Teamster in 1780 Enlisted 9 and 6 months*, Daniel Ayers is 9th followed by, 14 & 15, Silas and Saml B. Ayres, both Majors of Morristown. The Quartermaster Generals Book, Dept. #2, p. 23, voucher No. 1961, Certificate Feb 8, 1781, No. 160, Interest commenced, Feb 9 1780; Amount in Continental, 1024,60; Amount in Special, 10:5:7; Interest to Jan 1787, 4:4:3/4. Robert Ayres and Matthew Eyres are listed on the same page.

After the first shots were fired at Lexington and Concord in Massachusetts on Apr 19th 1775, King George III wrote to Lord Sandwich on Jul 1st 1775 stating: ...*that once those rebels have felt a smart blow they will submit, and no situation can ever change my fixed resolution either to bring the Colonies to a due obedience to the legislature of this Mother Country, or to cast them off...* It started with the King's men trying to confiscate all the weapons in the hands of the local Militia and the people, not about tea. The Dye was cast. When news reached New Jersey shortly afterward, evenings found the locals sipping their beverages at local taverns hoping to hear any news from travelers. The following June Col. Heard and his militia arrested New Jersey's Tory leaning governor in Amboy. Any neighbor bent toward Britain was ostracized by patriot neighbors as all sorts of rumors spread throughout the area. Daniel Ayers' wife Elizabeth was nearing the birth of her sixth child. She and her husband lived on a farm in Middlesex County, NJ, located about two miles north of Perth Amboy City, then known as Amboy, on the Amboy to Woodbridge road. Late 1775 the British began plundering the area for food. The commons at Strawberry Hill in Woodbridge was a choice place for meat. Committees were organized in the various communities to discuss how to deal with the situation as Town meetings carried on their business as usual. In Amboy, artillery was put in place on land by the church that overlooked the mouth of the Raritan River at New York Bay.

It was after the battle at Trenton on Christmas 1776 that East Jersey became terrorized attributed mostly to Germans and Hessians. Once Amboy fell into their hands, their soldier's struck defenseless women, children, and the elderly. No one or nothing was spared, women were violated, many wounded or killed. Any prisoners were poorly fed. That December, Daniel suffered his first material loss due to the War. Items taken from his home included linen yardage, a new striped cotton gown, new yarn and silk stockings, a new worsted cloak, two muskets, a dark brown nine year old mare, and cash from Daniel's pocket. After the battle at Piscataway in February 1777 prisoners were so badly ill-treated that Patriots began arresting their neighbors who sided with Britain and shipped them to Staten Island.

The following June 1777 they destroyed Daniel's crops and took his fencing. Losses also included five milk cows, one yoke of four year old oxen, one yoke of two year old steers, three yearling heifers, a two month old calf, a black mare and two yearling colts, new shoes, new gowns, aprons, linen yardage, bedding, a musket box and a looking glass. These heavy losses of livelihood were enough for him to enter service for support of his family. Being a Teamster was a means of potentially getting some income, especially if they could provide their own team. Some of his cousins were serving at Morristown and his brother-in-law, George Herriot, was also in service. In mid 1780 thousands of British troops moved into New Jersey by way of Staten Island and Elizabethtown. There they hoped to meet Washington and his troops. Daniel was again plundered in July 1780. His 5 year old son Thomas was forced to help the plunderers. Daniel lost a musket to them in 1781. On Nov 19th 1782, Daniel swore before Benjamin Manning to an Inventory for £197.07.06 of damages done by the British in New Jersey to which Aaron Bloodgood swore on his behalf as witness. His daughter, Rachel Ayers, also attested to the inventory and dates of her father's losses. Daniel was a testee to the losses of Abraham and Elizabeth Webb. Despite claims that his son Daniel served in the Revolutionary War, I have found no evidence to support that claim. However, there was a Daniel Ayers who served in the War of 1812 under Capt. Abraham Webb, son of Abraham and Elizabeth. The War cost more than money and many lives. The communities changed. Families that had taken different sides during the war were broken and many no longer friendly neighbors. Gone were "the good old days."

Daniel served as a Commissioner and a Surveyor laying out roads. On Sep 22nd 1809, Daniel pledged timber or stone worth $7.50 toward the building of a parsonage for the new Presbyterian Church of Perth Amboy. His 1809/10 pew rental was $3.50 for a half pew. He decided to make his Will on Feb 6th 1816. The Inventory of his estate taken almost two months after his death was dated Sep 4th 1819. Most significant in the inventory were bonds due from Ephraim Compton Sr. & Jr. in the amount of $264.03. His livestock and horse was valued at $142.00. The Will was proved Mar 21st 1821. Despite all his losses during the Revolutionary War, he left a sizeable estate to his family.

The First Item in his will states:

> *.... all my Debts & Funeral Charges be fully Paid. To my Beloved Wife Elizabeth Ayers all my Estate both Real & Personal as Long as She Remains my Widow...to my Son Daniel Ayers Five Acers of Land Joining Joshuway Bloodgoods Land the Same width that his Lot is...also two Acers of Salt Medow Lying a long Side of Meadow formerly Belonging to John Agguis. After my Wifes Decease the Remainder of my Lands & Salt Medows I Give to my Son Abraham Ayers and my son Thomas Ayers together with all my Moveable Estate to be Equally Divided between them after my Wifes Death. My Son Abraham Ayers & my Son Thomas Ayers Shall Pay all my Debts & Funeral Charges & legesies hereafter named Equally Between them the Legacies to be Paid in Six Months after my Wifes Death. To my Son Obediah Ayers Fifty Pounds. To my Daughter Rachel Ayers Fifty Pounds to her & her Heirs forever. To my Grandchildren Children of Phebe Tammage Twenty five Pounds to be Equally Divided Amongst them. To my Daughter Elizabeth Martin Twenty five Pounds. To my Grandchildren children*

of Mary Crews Twenty Five Pounds to be Equally Divided amongst them & if my Son Obediah Ayers Shoud Die Without Leaving a Lawful Heir or Heirs then what I have left Shall be Equally Divided Amongst my Children & Grandchildren then Living & I herein Appoint my Son Abraham Ayers and my son Thomas Ayers & my Son in Law Enos Tammage Exect[rs] of this my Last Will and Testament. Disanuling all former Wills Testaments & Executors, Confirming this & no Other to be my last Will. In Witness where of I the Said Daniel Ayers hath Set my Hand & Seal the Day & Year first above Written–Signed Sealed & Delivered by him the Said Daniel Ayers in the Presence of us the Witness:

The judges at Orphans Court decreed that Daniel Ayers Will of Feb 6th 1816 made at the township of Perth Amboy *was his last will and testament and that the said Daniel departed this life on Jul 9th 1818 at the township of Perth Amboy without altering the said last will and testament.* One son-in-law was unhappy with the will for on Jul 14th 1818, Moses Martin, one of the heirs of Daniel Ayres deceased, *do hereby Caveat and protest against the proving the Will Testament or Instrument in nature thereof being as pretended to be testaments of and last Will of the said Daniel Ayres until examination thereof in the Orphans Court be had in the County of Middlesex and sentence be thereon pronounced. Witness my hand and Seal this 14th day Jul 1818   Moses Martin* (Folio 524)

Sons Thomas and Abraham renounced administration in September, followed by Enos Talmage on Oct 8th 1818, desiring that Robert Arnold Esq. to administrate the will. (Folio 524).

On Mar 23rd 1820 at Orphans Court, In the matter of Abraham Ayres and Thomas Ayres claiming to be the Executors of the last will and testament of Daniel Ayres deceased and offering the said will for Probate, and on the Caveat filed against the said will by Moses Martin, the Judges of Orphans Court presented as Exhibit A a copy of the said will of Daniel Ayers, and the said Daniel died the 9th day of Jul 1818 without having altered the said last will and testament but leaving the same in full force, *do therefore decree that the said last will and testament be admitted to Probate, and that the affidavits of the executors be accepted, and lastly that the cost of this proceeding and examination be paid as follows viz that each party pay there own share.* Judges were: Robert McChesney, George Boice, Thomas Hance, Joseph McChesney, and J. W. Simpson.

Postmaster Robert Arnold, Administrator of Daniel Ayers estate presented his accounting at Orphans Court on Mar 21st 1821 that totaled $1081.54 which included his 13% commission of $124.41. Costs included printing, tax, copying, appraisals, surveying, witnesses, and court costs. Of note his coffin cost $12.00 and the funeral $14.00 for Daniel and his wife. Thomas Ayers received $255.50, Daniel Ayers $16.53, Abraham Ayers $23.73, Moses Martin $71.96, Enos Talmage $71.82, Rachel Ayers $137.40 and Obadiah Ayers $125.00. On Mar 23rd 1821, Robert Arnold Administrator of Daniel Ayers deposed that the Inventory of the goods, chattels and credits have come to his knowledge or possession or by other persons for his use. His final accounting was presented at Surrogate Court, New Brunswick, Dec 10th 1823, with a balance due of $499.55 and half cent to the accountant.

Daniel and Elizabeth Ayers son:

Thomas[6] Ayers was born on Wednesday, Aug 16th 1775, about four months after the first shots were fired at Lexington and Concord. Infant Thomas lay in a wooden cradle wearing a girlish fine linen shirt and cap trimmed in lace. Later he would still look little different than any of his sisters as a toddler for both wore dresses with fitted bodices that tied in back. Its strings were used to help guide a child learning to walk. Heads were protected by padded pudding caps. Stays underneath supported the back. A straight posture was very important then. What our ancestors didn't realize its price was reduced muscle and dependence on support for women who continued their use. Between ages three to six boy's hair was trimmed and their stays removed. They were then dressed in the newer style trouser suit for boys, not like Dad's knee britches. And he was expected to act like a young adult. Soon Thomas found he would be tested by British soldiers. Thomas was sixteen months old when his father, Daniel, suffered his first material loss to the British in Dec 1776. A month short of Thomas' fifth birthday, Daniel suffered his greatest loss when his homestead was again plundered in July 1780. This time his father was at Morristown carting stores for General Washington. The attack made such an impression on Thomas at the time, he later related to his children the story of being *compelled* to help Tories drive away the cattle from the farm and watch the men tip over the kitchen pie safe with a sword before setting fire to the house. His brave mother and older brothers managed to extinguish the flames.

Even though the family lived near Perth Amboy, the family became members of the First Presbyterian Church at Metuchen. There Thomas Ayers married Mary Ross on Aug 27th 1803 by Rev. Henry Cook. The births of his children were recorded in Thomas' great Bible along with the deaths of Mary and Thomas as previously noted. Their children were:

1.   Harriet b. Oct 18th 1804, d. 1888;
2.   William Augustus b. Apr 17th 1807, d. 1878;
3.   Enos Talmage b. Oct 30th 1809, d. 1889, was named after Thomas' sister Phebe's husband, Enos Talmage;
+4.   Henry Cook, b. Oct. 9th 1812, d. 1886;
5.   William Ross b. Jul 26th 1815, d. the following September after the death of his mother. Mary Ross Ayers died Aug 15th 1815, one day before Thomas' 40th birthday leaving him with four young children.

Ross Ancestry

The Ross name is associated with Scotland. The first mention of the name Ross living in Scotland was in Ayrshire in the 12th century, they having come from Yorkshire, England. Some who came to America settled in the New Jersey/New York area and the Carolinas. On a visit to Scotland a fabric shop gave a program on tartans. I was given a sample of the Ross tartan. The Tartan is a form of what we call a plaid pattern made of vertical and horizontal stripes in multiple colors. In Scotland, plaid is a tartan cloth slung over the shoulder or simply a blanket. Wool Scottish kilts usually use tartan patterns. In 1746 Scotland enacted the Dress Act which the government attempted to control warrior clans by banning the tartan and other aspects of Gaelic culture. By the time it was repealed in 1782, the tartan was no longer ordinary Highland dress, but a symbolic national dress. Until the mid 1800's highland tartans were associated with regions or districts, rather than a specific clan due to their designs being made by local weavers who used local natural dyes for specific area tastes. This made specific tartans becoming associated with Scottish clans, Scottish families or institutions who wished to be associated in some way with a Scottish heritage.

Robert Ross, Mary's grandfather, was born Jun 17th 1731 and lived to be 81 years old. By the time of the Revolution he was a man of wealth as noted in his claim in 1782 for losses suffered by British troops or mercenaries on Feb 4th 1777. It is an assortment of items that included food and other crops, cattle, fencing, 62 glass windows, shutters, saches, hinges, 5 doors, a cupboard, 2 linen wheels, 3 tables, 2 saddles, linen sheets, 2 callico gowns, 2 new petticoats, new silk hat, apron and handkerchief, 3 new shifts and several pair of stockings totaling £242.17.00. From this we can ascertain that he was prosperous, possibly a merchant, a carpenter or spun linen. Even with all these losses he was taxed in 1778 on 210 acres, £254 in interest money, 5 horses, 12 cattle and 3 hogs, the two taxes totaling £11.15.09. In 1779 his tax was based on 210 acres, 5 horses, 10 cattle and 5 hogs, no amount recorded. By 1784 his acreage was reduced to 116 with no livestock. This is evidenced by his will dated 1810. In 1794-5 he served as a Town Clerk and a Commissioner in 1804. The First Presbyterian Church of Metuchen kept records of pew holders of which Robert was one as well as a communicant in the church. Robert also served as a Church Trustee.[1] Robert's children were by his 1st wife Mary ? were:

1. John who m. Catherine Bonney, children: James Bonney, Hannah, Robert L. and Jane Ross.
2. Robert jr. who m. Rebecca Freeman Jan 17th 1816 by Rev. Henry Cook, children: Elizabeth, Mary, Catherine, Robert R., Jonathan, Caroline, Harriet, Hannah & William S. Ross.
3. Elizabeth who m. David Freeman, children: Jonathan, Elizabeth, Mary and Robert Ross Freeman who d. Apr 12th 1784 age 5 mos. 22 dys.
4. William who m. Mary Manning.

In late 1777, Robert m. the widow Mary Perkins Freeman, widow of Jonathan Freeman who d. in Jul 1777. Jonathan Freeman and Mary had a son, David Freeman who m. Robert Ross's daughter, Elizabeth. Jonathan's daughter Hannah Freeman m. Robert Ross's son Robert. Elizabeth Freeman who m. Apr 26th 1798 at Metuchen Richard Ross, son of John and Sarah (Jackson) Ross. In other words, two of Robert Ross' children married his 2nd wife's children.

Robert Ross died Nov 28th 1812, his 2nd wife Mary died Nov 20th 1820. Robert Ross' will was dated Aug 15th 1810, and Proved Dec 1st 1812.[2]

> I Robert Rofs of the Township of Woodbridge in the County of Middlesex...State of New Jersey...do make and publish this my last Will and Testament. I give and bequeath to my beloved wife Mary Rofs the sum of five hundred dollars [$500] to be paid one year from my decease by Executor herein after named but the same to be on Interest from my decease, the above sum I leave her as her right of Dower, but if She my said Wife thinks proper not to take up with the above Sum then in such case I must relinquish the whole of it and take one Third of the Interest of my estate as the law directs during her natural life but if She agrees to the above sum, I then leave her in addition to that Sum my Riding Chair and all my Household furniture to be paid and delivered to her by my Executor herein after named.
> I give and bequeath unto my son, John Rofs the sum of fifty Cents [$.50] together with what he has had. I also give unto James B. [Bonney] Rofs, son of my son John, the sum of fifty cents [$.50]. I give and bequeath unto my son, Robert Rofs the sum of Eight hundred dollars [$800] to be paid in one year from my decease. I give and bequeath unto Elizabeth and Mary Rofs, daughters of my son Robert, the sum of one hundred dollars [$100] each. I give and bequeath unto Robert and Jonathan Rofs, sons of my son Robert, the sum of fifty dollars [$50] each. And I also give unto his daughter, Harriet Ross, the sum of Fifty dollars [$50] the above sums to be paid in one year from my decease. I give and bequeath unto my grandson William M Rofs,

---

1 Presbyterian Church of Metuchen Sessions Records in the Collection of the Dept. Of History, Presbyterian Church (USA), 425 Lombard St., Philadelphia, PA
2 Middlesex Will Bk. A. pp. 497-499.

son of my son, William, the sum of Eight hundred dollars [$800] to be paid in one year from my decease. I give and bequeath unto my granddaughter, Nancy Cook, the sum of Seventy five dollars [$75] to be paid in one year from my decease. I give unto my [step] daughter in law, Elizabeth Rofs, wife of Richard Rofs, the sum of One hundred fifty dollars [$150] to be paid in one year from my decease. I also leave unto Richard Rofs daughters, namely Avaline, Mary and Ann Eliza, the sum of fifty dollars [$50] each when they arrive to age of Eighteen [18] years, Provided my wife Mary Ross takes up with the above sum left her in my Will, but if she does not take up with the above Sum and takes to thirds of my Estate there in such case Cut off the sums to be paid to Elizabeth Rofs and her three daughters and not for my Executor to pay the same to them. I give and bequeath unto my my grandson, Jonathan Freeman, the son of David Freeman, dec^d. the sum of fifty dollars [$50] to be paid in one year from my decease.

I give and bequeath unto my granddaughter Mary Johnson, wife of John Johnson, the sum of one hundred fifty dollars [$150] to be paid to her in one year from my decease. I give and bequeath unto my granddaughter, Frances Bennington, wife of Nathan Bennington, the sum of fifty dollars [$50] to be paid to them in one year from my decease. I give and bequeath unto my granddaughter Mary Ayers, wife of Thomas Ayers, the sum of five dollars [$5]. I give and bequeath unto my son, Robert Rofs, and to my grandson, William M. Rofs, all the residue of my estate both real and personal after my just debts, funeral charges and all the Legacies herein given and bequeathed are paid, unto my son Robert Rofs and grandson William M Rofs, namely Robert Rofs two thirds and William M Rofs one third, the said William Ross share to be paid to him in one from my decease, but if the said Will M Rofs should die before he arrive to the age of twenty one years, then in such case I leave his share as follows to Jonathan Freeman and Mary Johnson Fifty dollars [$50] each and to all the children of my son Robert the residue equal Shares a like. I give unto my Executor herein after named full power to sell all my real and personal Estate not heretofore given away, collect my debts, pay all costs and charges and Legacies as fully and amply as I could were I living. I request my son Robert Rofs to be the Executor of this my last Will and testament and I hereby nominate and appoint him for that purpose, In Witnefs whereof I have hereunto set my hand and Seal this fifteenth day of Aug in the year of our Lord one thousand eight hundred and Ten. Signed:Robert Rofs. Witnessed by: Ezekiel Ayers, William Martin, Neil Campbell.

On Dec 1st 1812 said witnesses appeared before John Heard Surrogate to testify this to be the last Will and testament of Robert Ross as did his son Robert Ross, Sole Executor.

William Ross, Mary's father, died May 20th 1796 and was buried in the First Presbyterian Churchyard at Metuchen. He was the son of Robert Ross by his first wife Mary (?) of Woodbridge. William married 2nd Mary Manning, daughter of Benjamin and Mary (Martin) Manning. Their children were:

1.   Mary who married Thomas Ayers.
2.   Robert m. Rebecka Freeman Jan 17th 1816 by Rev. Cook.
3.   Rachel b. 1796 m. Morse Freeman Mar 6th 1819 by Rev. Cook.
4.   Benjamin b. 1797.

5.   William Manning, m. Margaret Terrill Mar 6th 1813 by Rev. Cook.

After William Ross died, his widow married John Smock on Oct 28th 1802 at Metuchen by Rev. Henry Cook. John Smock was deeded from his parents, Henry and Sarah Smock, 122 acres in Woodbridge twp. which he sold to William Manning Ross for $10,000 on Apr 1st 1816. Said land was bounded on the south and east by Robert Ross.

Manning Ancestry

Jeffrey Manning came from English Saxon stock. He settled first at Hingham, Plymouth Colony. There he married Hepzibah Andrews, daughter of Joseph and Elizabeth Andrews of Hingham and granddaughter of Sir Thomas Andrews, Mayor of London. He and Hepzibah moved to New Jersey around 1668-70 to escape the intolerant established church in Massachusetts. When the Dutch came in control, he gave his oath of allegiance to them on Sep 7th 1673. In 1682 he was appointed to lay out lands in Piscataway including 195 acres for himself. Proprietors had control over the land. Here is one example of how a settler applied for land on which to settle.

Jeffrey petitioned the proprietors at Elizabeth, NJ, on Jan 14th 1685 for 150 acres in Piscataway at a place called Shingle Hill, he was willing to pay quit rents. Proprietor Thomas Warne claimed he already had a claim to that land so the Board said land will not be granted until the proprietors have their land laid out for themselves.[1] The next day, Jeffrey Manning and John FitzRandolph asked for 100 acres each as old settlers and would pay 6 pence per acre quit rent after renouncing their claim in Col. Nicholls' patent and promise to pay their arrears of rent and so it was ordered. The proprietors deeded them the land in 1688.[2] From his will we know that he did acquire land at Shingle Hill and at Dotie's Brook. In the spring of 1689 Jeffrey was among those who formed the First Baptist Church of Piscataway, the settlement consisted of eighty families. Jeffrey and Hepzibah had children:

1.   Elizabeth, m. Thomas FitzRandolph Nov 23rd 1686.
2.   John b. 1670, m. Elizabeth Dennis of Woodbridge Apr 4th 1693.
3.   Joseph b. May 4th 1672, m. Temperence FitzRandolph Nov 23rd 1686.
+4.   James b. Apr 25th 1674, m. Christian Laing Jan 28th 1699/1700.
5.   Benjamin b. Sep 8th 1676, m. Ann Blackford Jan 19th 1698/9. Son Israel b. Dec 30th 1700. Benjamin d. 1702.[3]

Jeffrey d. Jan 26th 1692/3 at Piscataway. His extracted will dated Dec 30th 1692 follows:

And now for the setling of my Temporal Estate and such Goods Chattels and debts and duties I owe....I give... unto my Son John Mannin one hundred acres of land lying at Shingle hill, to him the said John Mannin his Heirs...and Assigns for ever. Item I give unto my said son John Mannin Two Cows two Yearling Steers, and three Ewes, to be delivered to my said son by my Executrix...I give unto my Son Joseph Mannin half of the land at Dates [Dotie's] Brook and my Seventy five acres of land at Ambross brook, with the improvement to...his Heirs...for ever, also I give....unto my Son Joseph Mannin the young Horse that is Now at home and also the old Mare, he giving unto his brother Benjamin the first Colt that the Said Mare

1 Board of Proprietors, *Minutes of the Board of Proprietors of New Jersey* 1685-1705, Vol. I (Perth Amboy, NJ 1949) p. 102

2 *Ibid..*, 108

3 Piscataway, NJ Town Register of Briths, Marriages & Deaths, 1676-1790

The following Aug 3ʳᵈ Hepzibah was among ten people who petitioned the Proprietors for head land as old settlers at Piscataway. The Council determined that all 24 of the first settlers who have not yet had land to appear and acquire 100 acres with quit rent and renounce all claims under Col. Nichols' patents as their neighbors have done.[2] On Apr 20ᵗʰ 1694 Hepzibah petitioned again for 200 acres bounded upon quit rent for her four sons. It was agreed that she have said land at ½ pence per acre paying arrears of rent due from 1675 as others have done. Said deed was recorded in 1695. Jeffrey Manning and Hepzibah Andrews son:

James Manning was born Apr 25ᵗʰ 1674 and married Christian Laing, daughter of John Laing of Piscataway on Jan 23ʳᵈ 1700 at Piscataway. James and Christian had children:

1. James b. May 23ʳᵈ 1700, married Grace FitzRandolph in 1730 daughter of Joseph FitzRandolph and Rebecca Martin. Of their six children, their son James born in 1738 was influenced by Roger Williams and became ordained as a Baptist Minister in 1763. The next year he founded the Baptist Rhode Island College (now Brown University) as the 1ˢᵗ President).
2. Margaret b. Dec 23ʳᵈ 1701 married Jonathan FitzRandolph Dec 3ʳᵈ 1724, children: James b. Sep 26ᵗʰ 1725 and Susannah b. Apr 27ᵗʰ 1727.
3. Ebenezer born Nov 1703 was not mentioned in father's will in 1724.
+4. Nathaniel b. Dec 25ᵗʰ 1707, m. 1ˢᵗ Prudence FitzRandolph who d. Dec 1ˢᵗ 1732. m. 2ⁿᵈ Mary Harris.
5. Isaac, married Catherine Clarkson c. 1732, children: Joseph b. Dec 29ᵗʰ 1733 and John b. Oct 16ᵗʰ 1739.

James' Will dated Oct 31ˢᵗ 1724 in part reads:

---

1 Middlesex C0. Deed Bk. D: 423-4
2 *Ibid..*

Imprimus I give to my son James Manning one quarter part of my moveable estate after all my debts and funeral charges are paid. Item I give to my daughter Margeret Manning one quarter part of all my moveable estate after all my debts and funeral charges are paid. Item I give to my son Nathaniel Manning one quarter part of all my moveable estate after all my debts and funeral charges are paid. Item I give to my son Isaac Manning one quarter part of my moveable estate after all my debts and funeral charges are paid. Item I give to my sons Nathaniel Manning and Isaac Manning the Plantation on which I live together with my Plantations near Dismal to be equally divided between & them their heirs and assigns forever.

And I do constitute make and ordain my brother Joseph Manning, John Laing and William Laing my only and sole executors of this my last will and testament. And also to be Guardians for my two youngest sons Nathaniel and Isaac till they be of age...In witness whereof I have hereunto set my hand and seal the day and year above writte. Signed...by the said James Manning as his last will and Testament in the presence of...Henry Skibbow, Jonathan FitzRandolph and John Manning.

James died at Piscataway Nov 4th 1724. Christian had died earlier. Inventory of James Manning Senior...dated Nov 20th 1724 by Benjamin Hull and John Manning, Prizers, totaled £130.10.00.[1] One can derive from it that he farmed, spun linen, ground grain, sawed his wood and scythed his crops plus other tools. Also a yoke of oxen to pull a plow, owned a cart, sled with a yoke and bells, a chaise and sleigh, a saddle and bridle, tackling, six working horses, four mares, a cole, five sheep and twenty-five hogs, modest clothing, a little cash, one small book and two Bibles, a gun and sword.[2] James Manning and Christian Laing son:

Nathaniel Manning was born Dec 27th 1707 at Piscataway, NJ. After buying 26¾ acres of proprietary and unappropriated land on Jun 28th 1728 including a third right of the woods, trees, mines, minerals, hawkings & hunting & fishings, fowlings, buildings, fences and improvements.[3] Nathaniel married 1st Prudence FitzRandolph the following July 29.th She was the daughter of Joseph FitzRandolph and Joannah Conger. A son, 1) James, was born May 21st 1730 followed by Prudence's death on Dec 1st 1732.[4] Nathaniel married 2nd Mary Harris on Feb 13th 1733/4. She was born in 1714 daughter of William Harris. Six days after the marriage, his brother Isaac, sold him all of his estate right of 40 acres for £30.[5] Nathaniel and Mary Manning had children:[6]

2. Elizabeth b. Sep 7th 1736, m. Meshack Hull c. 1765.
3. Nathaniel b. Aug 19th 1738, m. Mary Hite. Rev. Nathaniel Manning d. 1777 Hampshire Parish, WV. Buried at the Episcopal Churchyard.
4. William b. Jun 8th 1740, m. in 1864 Anna Merrill, d/o Richard Merrill. Apparently they had no children according to his will dated Sep 3rd 1814, proved Oct 10th 1814. It states he was of Piscataway, mentions his wife Anna; nephew W. T. Manning; sisters Sarah Harris, Elizabeth Hull, Rachel Thornal, and heirs of Margaret; Anna Mollorn, Ava Lemmon d/o Nathaniel Mollorn, Henry Boice, Mary Holcom; Nephews: Nathaniel of VA; Lewis Thornel, son of Israel; Meriba Ayres, widow of Ezekiel; Eliza Dunham d/o Benj. Manning; Anna Voorheese, Benj. Harris, Morris Harris, heirs of Benj. Harris dec'd, Presbyterian Church of Metuchen; Grandchildren of Elizabeth Hull: Jeptha, Reuben and Rosannah Randolph; Sarah Wynecope of VA; brother

---

1 NJ Wills 347-349L

2 Piscataway Town Records, pp. 203, 209

3 Middlesex Co. Deed Bk. H$_4$, pp. 58-59

4 Metuchen Presbyterian Church Sessions Records

5 Middlesex Co. Deed Bk. E$_2$, p. 27

6 First 8 children recorded in Piscataway Town Records.

Thomas Manning; Wm. F. Manning son of brother Thomas; Wm. B. Manning, son of Benj. Manning dec'd.[1] William d. Sep 26th 1814 and buried in the Metuchen Presbyterian Church Cemetery. *He was eminently useful in life, and at his death, left a donation of 700 Dollars for the support of the Gospel in this church.*

5. Isaac b. Jun 20th 1742, d. infant.
6. Isaac b. Aug 19th 1743, d. age 22 at Piscataway.
+7. Benjamin b. Aug 12th 1744, m. 1st Mary Martin, and 2nd Rachel Cutter.
8. Margaret b. Sep 20th 1746, m. 1st Jeptha Benajah Martin, 2nd William Lemen. Margaret d. in 1784.
9. Mary b. Jan 5th 1747/8, m. Richard Holcom 1768. Mary d. Jul 10th 1812 in 64th year. Richard d. Feb 5th 1814 in 77th year. Both buried Samptown Baptist Cemetery, S. Plainfield, NJ, with their son, Nathaniel and his wife, Mary.
10. Rachel b. Mar 29th 1751, m. Israel Thornal. Rachel d. Jan 30th 1829, Israel May 9th 1819 in 74th yr. Both buried Metuchen Presbyterian Church Cemetery.
11. Thomas b. Jun 8th 1753, m. Aug 15th 1780 Mary Stelle d/o Isaac Stelle. Thomas d. Oct 21st 1819 an *Elder in this church.* He served in the Middlesex County Militia and State Troops, Sgt. Ballard's Company in the Continental Line. His will proved Nov 10th 1819.[2] Mary d. Mar 29th 1837 age 83y5m. Both buried in Metuchen Church Cemetery with sons: Thomas, who d. Feb 7th 1810 age 25y3m21d; Isaac who d. Feb 7th 1810, age 23y3m21d; and Jephthah who d. Jun 6th 1814 in his 26th yr. and Jepthah's children by his wife, Elizabeth: Anny who d. Mar 31st 1814 age 16m; and John who d. Jan 16th 1814 age 19.
12. Sarah b. Jun 26th 1755, m. Benjamin Harris at Bound Brooke, NJ. Capt. Benjamin d. Apr 14th 1811 age 51y7m 2d. Sarah d. Apr 22nd 1815 in 60th yr. Both buried Bound Brook Presbyterian Cemetery.

Nathaniel Manning's will dated Oct 18th 1765 names his wife Mary, sons: Thomas, Nathaniel, Benjamin, William, and daughters Elizabeth Hull, Margaret, Sarah and Rachel. His tombstone in Piscataway Episcopal Churchyard reads:

Here lies interr'd y Body of Capt. Nathanl Manning, who died - Jany ye 9th 1766 In the 58th Year of his Age. In the virtues of Nathl the Israelite he liv'ed. And in all Christian fortitude Of mind he died.

Mary died Sep 10th 1793 in her 81st year at Piscataway and buried by Nathaniel. Her inscription is from Psalms 116, verse 11. Nathaniel and Mary Manning's son:

Benjamin Manning was born Aug 12th 1744 at Piscataway, NJ. Benjamin's first wife, Mary Martin, daughter of Benajah Martin, d. Apr 2nd 1772 at age 19 after the birth of their daughter and buried in the Piscataway Church Cemetery. Their daughter:

+1. Mary b. 1772, m. William Ross.
By his 2nd wife, Rachel Cutter, he had two sons and one daughter:
2. Nathaniel.
3. William B., b. 1786, d. Jan 2nd 1847 in 61st yr.
4. Elizabeth.

---

1 N.J. Will Bk. B., p. 123
2 N.J. Will Bk. D, p. 419

Benjamin served as a private in Capt. Ward's Company, Eastern Battalion, Morris Co., Militia. Later as recorder and appraiser to the damages by the British during the Revolution. His tax records reveal that he owned 130 acres, 3-5 horses, 7-12 cattle, 8 hogs, a riding chair and sleigh plus 1 servant in the 1780's and 90's. Benjamin's will dated Mar 8th 1794 was proved Jan 16th 1802.

I Benjamin Manning of Piscataway give my sons Nathaniel and William B. all my lands and real estate when they arrive to lawful age and to be divided equally, they paying legacies. The use and profits of 1/3 part is bequeathed to my wife during her widowhood. Also to son William B. a balance of A?sons. To daughter Mary Ross wife of William Ross £94 to be paid by son Nathaniel when he is of lawful age. My said Daughter having already received an out lot out of my estate to the amount of £156. To daughter Elizabeth Manning my second best feather bed, bedding and furniture there unto belonging, also the sum of £250 to be paid as follows. £78 when age 18 by son Nathaniel. And the balance of £172 by son William B. when he arrive at lawful age. Also I give her six silver tea spoons. To wife Rachel Manning and her heirs one horse and riding chair, one milk cow, my best feather bed, bedding and furniture there unto belonging, 2 mahogany tables, 6 chairs and the best looking glass. Also £100 to be paid by executors in one year after my decease provided she should choose to take the value of said £100 out of my moveable estate at appraisal, that then it may be optional with her. Also to her provision sufficient for her use and family for one year. Also the rents of my lands and real estate for her family and my three youngest children for maintenance until my sons shall arrive to age. Also for her use during her life my Big Bible and at her death I devise it to my son Nathaniel. Also during her remaining my widow the use or rents and profits of the 1/3 part of my landed estate so divised to my sons. And the use of 1/3 part of my dwelling house and garden, excepting what is herein willed to her in lieu of dower or power of thirds. Also sale of moveable estate to pay debts is necessary plus disposition if any of the children should die. Wife Rachel, son Nathaniel and brother, Thomas Manning executors. Witnessed by Michael Martin, Samuel Carman and Joseph Mundy.[1]

The inventory totaled £1150.12.06 and was dated Jan 12th 1802. Benjamin died on Christmas day in 1801. Rachel died Feb 11th 1806 age 52.[2] He was buried at Piscataway Church Cemetery with both wives. His tombstone reads:

In memory of BenJamin Manning--who departed this life Decem[r] 25th 1801 in the 58th year of his age. In the cold bosom of the tomb Wrapd in a dark and silent gloom, The husband parent patriot lies Nor knows the grief that makes our eyes Run while his friends and country mourn. And zion weeps upon his urn. Faith looks to heaven wipes off the tear, And smiles to see him glorious there.

Mary Manning was the mother of Mary Ross, wife of Thomas Ayers. She died Jan 3rd 1849 at age 77. She married William Ross as previously noted. Mary Manning's mother, Mary Martin, ancestry follows:

---

1 Middlesex Co. Will Bk. 40: 15-19
2 Middlesex Co. Will Bk. 40: 15-19

Martin - Roberts Ancestry

John Martin was born in Durham, England, and came to Old Dover in New England in 1646. There he married Hester Roberts, daughter of Gov. Thomas Roberts and his wife, Rebecca. John moved to Oyster River around 1659. He was listed as a Stationer, one who sells writing materials.[1] At the time there was an ongoing conflict over Dover Peninsula territory being part of Massachusetts Bay Colony. It took little persuasion to convince John Martin and others to depart New Hampshire. On Dec 18th 1666 Gov. Cartaret's agents, Daniel Pierce and Associates, sold to John Martin, Charles Gilman, Hugh Dunn and Hopewell Hull of New Hampshire for £30 a third of their tract in New Jersey which they named New Piscataqua after the river they had departed. They also agreed to twelve articles of agreement with Cartaret that meant allegiance to England's King and fidelity to the Lords Proprietors by payment of a quit rent to them. They were encouraged to organize a political and religious life as noted in the articles.[2] The land was filled with many rivers and its settlers felt it a buffer between the Massachusetts and Virginia settlements. John Martin sold his New England home and he with the families Hugh Dunn, Hopewell Hull, Charles Gilman and the two young sons of Henry Langstaff sailed down the Massachusetts coast past Long Island to Elizabeth Point, New Jersey. From there they traveled on Indian paths to a spot that became Trenton. More paths led them to their point of settlement they name Piscataway. On the trip young John Langstaff had his eye on John Martin's daughter, Martha.

On Dec 11th 1666 Daniel Pierce, John Pike and seven associates from Newbury, MA, paid £80 for a tract between the Raritan and Rahway Rivers. They made a settlement named Woodbridge after their late pastor. Martin's small group had little difficulty in dealing with the local Raritan Indians who had moved there to escape harassment from other tribes. However after an increase of lost hunting lands, the Indians made a last attempt in 1667 for more payment of the land they deeded to Carteret. A re-purchase was made with the Indians for the land. Lumbering, shipbuilding and fishing became the main source of income. John would play an important role in the new settlement.

Local lumber provided wood for houses which were simple structures. Interior walls were 8-10 inch wide boards plastered inside. The exterior was covered with shingles made from the various trees found there. An ample supply of stone in the area was used in making chimneys. Rooms usually numbered three in poorer houses. Most hired a carpenter who worked with their servants to build a house. Nails were one item that had to be purchased. Local clay soil was made into bricks. In Jan 1686 John Gilman, Hopewell Hull, John FitzRandolph, John Martin, sr., and Edward Slater were responsible for building a meeting house 20x30 feet to be used for church service and town meetings.

When the Dutch took over the area, John Langstaff was commissioned an Ensign in the militia in 1673. Quit rents fell in arrears under the Dutch reign. Then Langstaff became enamored with a daughter of Edward FitzRandolph that complicated his love life. He was age 28 when he finally married Martha Martin. On Feb 11th 1685 John Martin, Hopewell Hull and others complained that Thomas Warne had surveyed part of their warranted land which they were about to lay out lots. They requested the Council that Warne's pretense of claims be revoked. The Council responded that they did not have that power and if the parties cannot agree, "take it to law." The same day John petitioned the Proprietors at Elizabeth Town as an old settler for 200 acres in Piscataway under the Nichol's patent.[3] New Jersey Deed Books show several land transactions for John. He had initially acquired 334 acres. Then he began deeding land to his sons. John and Hester's children were:

1 John Scales, *History of Dover, New Hampshire, Vol I*, (Dover, Authority of City Council, 1923) p. 39

2 Walter Meuly, *History of Piscataway Township 1666-1976*, pgs. 13, 29

3 *Minutes of the Board of Proprietors of New Jersey*, 1685-1705, V. I, pp. 112, 203

+1.   John who m. 1st Dorothy Smith Jun 26th 1677.
2.   Mary who m. 1st Hopewell Hull. Children: Mary, Hopestill, Esther, Martha, Ruth who d. young, Abigail, Ruth who d. age 1 week, Hopewell, Lydia, Joseph, & Benjamin Hull. Mary m. 2nd Justinian Hall.
3.   Martha who m. John Langstaff. Children: Henry, Lucilla, Mary, John, Sarah, Henry, Mary, John, and Priscilla Langstaff.
4.   Lydia who m. John Smalley Oct 18th 1676 at Piscataway. Children: Lydia, John, Jonathan, John, Lydia, Martha, Phebe, Martin, Elisha, and Benjamin Smalley.
5.   Joseph who m. Sarah Trotter Nov 25th 1679 at Piscataway. Children: Joseph, Abigail, David, Josiah, and Moses.
6.   Benjamin who m. 1st Margaret Rennals Oct 24th 1680 at Piscataway. Children: Benjamin, Esther, Benjamin, Jonathan, Mary, and Peter.
7.   Thomas who married Rebecca Higgins Apr 28th 1683 at Piscataway. Children: John, Sarah, Jacob, Rebecca, Zechariah, Anne, and Jeremiah.
8.   James who d. Mar 21st 1676/7, age seven.[1]

John Martin d. Jul 5th 1687 at Piscataway. His will dated Mar 17th 1687 was probated Jul 20th 1687.

Hester d. the following Dec 12th. Her will dated Nov 9th 1687 was probated Dec 20th 1687.[2] Hester Robert's father was:

Thomas Roberts, eldest son of yeoman John Roberts of Woolaston, England was named after his grandfather. Thomas was apprenticed in 1615 at age 15 to William Adys for eight years. Adys admitted the now 23 year old Thomas to the Fishmongers Guild on Apr 29th 1623.[3] Shortly afterward Fishmongers, Thomas Roberts and the Hilton brothers: William and Edward, boarded the *Providence* and sailed for New Hampshire to establish a business in the fishing industry.

Due to Capt. John Smith's earlier trip there in 1614, the area was well known for its abundant fish, timber for shipbuilding, and friendly Indians. A David Thomson had a grant for 6,000 acres in the area. Its indenture provided for seven men in addition to himself to establish a settlement. Other provisions in the indenture dealt with land distribution. By 1623 there was a large settlement. Floating platforms called fishing stages projected from the shore line into the water. They were covered with a shed roof built on the shore end of the platform. The shed was used for splitting and salting fish. The area had a lingering smell of salt and thousands of fish drying further inland. A third of a ship's crew lived ashore for the drying and curing process. Those living aboard ship fished for mackerel or cod. The typical home for those living ashore could be described as a 18 x 40 foot shelter with a large outside chimney with an oven on each side for baking. A kettle placed within the mantle piece was used for brewing or boiling. Another house built at the side was for sieving and milling grain. Inside two chambers held bunks for sleeping and storing ship's sails and dry goods in casks. A kitchen was provided for eating. Drinking with bread and beer was held in a steward's room. Every room was closed with a lock and key.[4]

The three men settled at Dover Point. Sometime after Thomas' marriage to the Hilton's sister, Rebecca, and his farmland cleared, he began construction of a home at Dover Neck on a high bank

---

1 Piscataway Town Records

2 Middlesex Co. Will Bk. A: 107-108

3 Thomas was listed in 1641 on the *List of Emigrant Liverymen of London as members of the Fishmongers Guild* marked *in New England.*. Noyes, Libby & Davis, *Genealogical Dictionary of Maine and New Hampshire* (Baltimore, MD, Genealogical Publ. Co.,1979, p. 589

4 Scles, p. 41

of the Piscataqua or Fore Back River. Dover Neck is a narrow stretch of land between the rivers Piscataqua and Bellamy. Thomas was taught by local Indians how to till the soil and plant corn in the same manner done at Plymouth Colony. There were ample alewives in spring to use for fertilizer. Colonial men were also involved in governing. In 1640 Thomas was made President of the Court to protest against New Hampshire being annexed to Massachusetts Bay Colony and subsequently appointed the 4th Governor of the Colony of Dover succeeding John Underhill. Thomas kept that office until 1643 when Dover became part of the Massachusetts Bay Colony. Like many independent thinking men, Thomas opposed the treatment of Quakers by the orthodox church. He was even fined for attending their meetings and not going to public worship. On Dec 22nd 1662 three female Quaker missionaries were stripped to the waist, tied to the back of an ox cart, and given up to ten lashes as they were led out of Dover. They were pulled behind a cart from town to town throughout the Bay Colony. When they reached Salisbury, MA, going up the Merrimack River, Major Robert Pike, a Quaker sympathizer, took pity and forbad further whippings. A doctor took them in a boat to Maine to the home of another sympathizer out of the colony's jurisdiction. Undeterred, the women later returned to Dover. Thomas' two sons did not acquire his sympathetic nature and became intolerant taking the orthodox church's side in punishment.

Thomas Roberts and his wife, Rebecca, had children:

   1.   John who m. Abigail Nutter.
   2.   Thomas who m. Mary Leighton.
+3.   Hester who m. John[1] Martin.
   4.   Anna who m. James Philbrick.
   5.   Elizabeth who m. Benjamin Heard.
   6.   Sarah who m. Richard Rich.

By 1670 seventy year old Thomas had deeded the last of his lands to his sons.[1] His will dated Sep 27th 1673 was proved on Jun 30th 1674. He named his wife Hester, sons: John and Thomas and daughters: Hester, Anna, Elizabeth, and Sarah. He appointed his son-in-law Richard Rich executor giving him his homestead. Thomas Roberts died at Dover Hill sometime between the date of his will and proof and was buried in the ancient burying ground located on a small piece of his property on Dover Neck with other first settlers. It was his daughter Hester Roberts that married John Martin and had a son James who d. Mar 21st 1676/7 at Piscataway and a son named:

John Martin who was born about 1650 in New Hampshire and moved with them to Piscataway, New Jersey. It didn't take long after the families moved for him to find a wife:

> *Governor of the Provence of New Jersey. Whereas I ave received Information of a mutual Intent and agreement betwene John Martin Junor of Piscataway and Dorothy Smith the Daughter of Richard Smith of the said town planter to solemnize Mariage together for Which they have requested my Lycense and there appeareing No Lawfull Impediment for the Obstructing thereof There are therefore to Require you or Eyther of You to Joyn the said John Martin and Dorothy Smith In Matrimony and them to Pronounce Man and Wife, and to keepe a record thereof according to Law In that case provided, and for the doing thereof this shall be to you Eyther of you, a sufficient Warrant. Given Under my hand and seale of the provence the 15th day of Jun 1677. Ph. Carterett*

---

1 Middlesex Co. Deed Bk. A, pgs. 237,353; Bk. B, p.66

John's wife Dorothy was the daughter of Richard Smith, a planter at New Town (Middleburgh), on Long Island before moving to Piscataway where his patent for 255 acres was dated Jun 6th 1673 and another 120 acres was dated Apr 8th 1676. He owned ½ tract of salt meadow on the Raritan River which he deeded equally between his sons. Then he moved to Woodbridge. His will dated Jul 17th 1692 was probated Apr 30th 1696. At the time of his death he had married 2nd the widow Ellinor Kent. Richard's 1st wife Dorothy had siblings Elizabeth, Richard and Thomas. Dorothy was the youngest of Richard's four children.

John Martin and Dorothy Smith were the parents of:

1. Esther b. Feb 11th 1677/8, d. Apr 9th 1678 age 2 mos.
2. Esther b. Apr 11th 1679, d. Nov 8th 1682.
3. Elizabeth b. Mar 24th 1680/1, m. Hugh Dunn Aug 9th 1697, children: Hugh, Anne, Elizabeth, Martha, Jeremiah, Zecharias, Benjamin, Phinehas, Ruth & Rebecca Dunn.
4. Dorothy b. Jun 7th 1686, m. Benajah Dunham, eldest son of the first pastor of the 7th Day Baptist Church, Sep 21st 1704. Children: John, Benejah, Hezekiah, Martin, Elizabeth, Mary, Esther, Priscilla, Rachel & Elisha Dunham.
5. Patience who m. Daniel Sutton Oct 31st 1704, children: Anne, Zebulon, Zacharias, John, Dorothy, Patience, and Esther Sutton.
+6. John b. Nov 2nd 1691, m. Mary Drake.
7. Richard who m. Mary Salyers Mar 3rd 1713/4; children: Hezekaih, John, Joanna, Patience, & Richard.

On Aug 22nd 1684 John Martin received land from Benjamin Martin and deeded 15 acres of upland in Piscataway to his father who was living in Woodbridge.[2] He petitioned in 1685 for 230 acres as an old settler which was received in 1686 and 1697.[3]

After Dorothy died on Mar 28th 1697/8, John married 2nd Ann Brown, Jan 19th 1698/9. John died May-Jun 1703. John's Will was dated May 21st 1703 and proved Apr 18th 1704.[4] He first bequeathed to his brothers and sisters: Joseph Martin, Benjamin Martin, Thomas Martin and Mary Hull and Lydia Smalley to each one shilling Sterling or in other pay equivalent. To daughter Elizabeth Dunn two shillings and to daughter Ester Martin one shilling to be paid within three months after my decease. After payment of debts and legacies, the remainder shall be deposed as follows:

---

1 *Ibid.*.
2 Middles Co. Deed Bk. B: 78, 219
3 Middlesex Co. Deed Bk. A, p. 352; Bk. F, p.522
4 Middlesex Co. Will Bk 1, pgs. 34-36

brook with 5 acres of meadow joining to my brother Joseph Martin's meadow running from the pond upwards lengthways. To youngest son, Richard Martin, my home lot containing 100 acres with 10 acres of meadow belonging thereto. My wife Ann Martin to enjoy my said home lot with its rights and privileges. His brother Benjamin Martin and friend Samuel Blackford to be sole executors. Witnessed by Benjamin Martin, Joseph Martin, and Stephen Wilson.

His inventory totaled £219.17.6 by John Royse and Edmond Dunham on Jun 12th 1703.[1] John Martin and Dorothy Smith's son:

John Martin (John b. ca 1625, John b. ca 1650, John b. 1691) was born Nov 2nd 1691 at Piscataway. He received a patent of 120 acres on Apr 8th 1676. John married 1st Mary Drake on Jul 16th 1716 at Piscataway.[2] Mary Drake was the eldest child of John Drake and Sarah Compton who married Dec 9th 1697 at Piscataway, NJ. John and Mary Martin had three children born at Piscataway:

1.   Rachel b. Feb 29th 1718.
+2.   Benajah b. Dec 15th 1719.
3.   John b. Dec 22nd 1721.

John, sr., yeoman, died Jul 16th 1721 at Piscataway before the birth of his son, John.[3] John and Mary's son:

Benajah Martin was b. Dec 15th 1718/9 at Piscataway. On Nov 19th 1745 he deeded his brother John *for love and affection about 40 acres at Piscataway located by the southerly corner of the tract my father, John Martin dec'd, bought of Joseph Martin and by the highway and land of John Manning, dec'd.*[4] About that time he married Hannah (?) who was a year younger than he. They had five children:

+1.   Mary who m. Benjamin Manning.
2.   Rachel.
3.   Lewis who died a single man at age 62.
4.   John who m. Sarah Bloomfield.
5.   Michael who m. Eunice (?) and Sarah (?).

Benejah suffered from the British in 1776 and 1777 giving oath on Apr 19th 1783 that he had 7 tons of English Hay, 30 bushels of wheat, 10 sheep, 5 bushels of Indian corn, 10 bushels of rye and 7 tons of Salt Hay stolen amounting to £44.12.00.[5] Tax records in 1782 showed he owned 150 acres, 4 horses, 8 cattle in 1782. By 1784 his acreage was reduced to 119, 4 horses, 9 cattle. Benajah died at age 69 on Jun 21st 1788 at Piscataway.

His will dated Mar 10th 1785 was proved Aug 20th 1788. He named sons, Lewis, John and Michael Martin who received his lands; his wife, Hannah, 2 rooms in dwelling house, negro woman Hester, livestock, beds & bedding, table with cloth & napkins, chairs, cooking vessels, livestock, & ⅓ of real estate to rent for 1 year; daughter, Rachel £100; and grand daughter, Mary Manning £30, daughter

---

1 New Jersey Will Bk..1, pgs. 54-56
2 Piscataway Town Records
3 Ibid.
4 Middlesex Co. Deed Bk. 23: pp 624-5
5 Damages by British, LDS Film No. 699, 888

of Benjamin Manning. Balance of estate: ¾ to son John and ¼ to Rachel. Sons John, Michael, and son-in-law, Benjamin Manning, were named executors. Witnessed by Nicholas Mundy, Reuben Ayres and Phineas Manning, Benjamin and Hannah's eldest child.

Three generations of this family are buried together in the Piscataway Church Cemetery. Michael Martin's wife Sarah d. Dec 13th 1849 in her 80th yr. is next to Michael d. Feb 14th 1826 in his 67th year, then wife, Eunice d. Jul 14th 1796 age 28. Next to Eunice is M. Martin Lupardus b. Oct 18th 1826, d. Sep 20th 1890 and his wife, Ruth A. Dunn b. Mar 5th 1826, d. Mar 16th 1903. Benjah Martin's wife Hannah who d. Nov 28th 1797 age 77 is next to them beside her husband Benajah and then their daughter Mary, her husband Benjamin Manning, then his 2nd wife Rachel, followed by Capt. Nathaniel Manning and his wife, Mary. Benejah and Hannah's daughter:

Mary Martin was the 1st wife of Benjamin Manning. She died Apr 2nd 1772 after the birth of their daughter, Mary Manning. Refer to Manning family.

Other Families connected to the Martin family follow:

Drake/Compton/Trotter/Walker Ancestries

Francis Drake was born in 1615. Many claim he was the son of Robert of Devonshire, England, who settled around 1635 by the Piscataway River, NH. Others say Robert came from Essex and settled first in Exeter, then Hampton where he was selectman, jurist, and freeman. He may have been the son of merchant Augine Drake of Ide, Devonshire, England whose will dated Nov 6th 1644 names his son Francis Drake.

Francis and his wife, Mary Walker, lived at Strawberry Bank on the western side of swift flowing Piscataqua River in New Hampshire. It now divides New Hampshire from Maine. About 1653 Strawberry Bank's name was changed to Portsmouth. On Apr 17th 1654 the town assigned Francis a house lot on Roger Knight's or Noble's Island in the northern part of Portsmouth. In Jul 1655 he obtained another house and lot South of Great Bay, now Greenland. He served on grand juries in 1660, 1661, and 1663. In Jul 1661 he was made an Ensign in the militia and Port Master. The next year he was brought to court for mowing another man's meadow. The year 1663 found him selected as a Surveyor of Highways. Once New Hampshire fell under the control of Massachusetts Bay Colony, discontent erupted among its inhabitants.

Francis was among those who in Jul 1665 signed two petitions to the Commission for Affairs of New England, the governing body of the English colonies in America, and to the King asking that Portsmouth be removed from the jurisdiction of the Massachusetts Bay Colony. That colony was known for its rigid Puritanism and it governed the territories to the north with a heavy hand. In addition, their assertion of jurisdiction conflicted with others, and caused a number of land boundary disputes in the area. The petition to the Commissioners read:

> *The Peticion of part of the inhabitants of Portesmouth and Strawberry Bank, Humbly sheweth: parish have ruled swaied and ordered all offices both civill & military at their pleasures, none of yor Honors peticionrs though Loyall subjects, & some of them well acquainted with the Laws of England, durst make any opposition for feare of great fines or long imprisonment and for want of estates could not peticon home to his Matie for relief, which the contrary party well knoweth, have kept us under hard servitude, and denyed us in our publique*

meeting the Common prayer Sacramts and decent buriall of the dead contrary to the Laws of England & his Maties lre sent by Simon Broadstreet & John Norton in the yeare 1662. And not only so but have also denied us the benefit of freemen, contrary to his Maties said letter and likewise at the election of officers the aforesaid party or the greatest part of them have always kept themselves in offices for the manageing of the gifts of lands & setling them, whereby yor peticoners are not only disabled but also descouraged for continuance in the plantation, & have engrosed the greatest part of the lands within the precincts & limits of this plantation into theire owne hands and other honest men that have been here a considerable time have no lands at all given them, and some that have had lands given & laid out to them, the said contrary party have desowned the grants, and laid it out to others. The premisses considered, we hope your Honors will take it under yor protection, and government & rectifie those miscariages, that thereby his Maties Loyall Subjects may pertake of all such priviledges & liberties, as his Maties gratious pleasure hath bin pleased to confer upon his Subjects in forraigne plantacons and that thereby we may be the more stirred up to glorifie God for his mercies towards us in releasing us out of such great servitude & tirany & your peticoners shall always pray for your Honors happiness in this life, & eternall felicitie in the life to come.

The second petition to the King was similar:

The humble peticon of the inhabitants of Portesmouth and Strawberry Bank Dover: Exiter and Hampton. Humbly sheweth: That yor Maties peticoers were much transported with joy and hope of settlemt when they heard of the care yor Matie had of these plantacions in New England and had heard the power wch yor Matie had given yor Commissioer for the appointing of bounds and gourmt amongst us here. But yor Maties peticoers find to theire great greife that the Masachusetts Denying that authorytie wch yor Matie gave yor Commissionrs hath hindered us from that good wch were Expected from those Commissionrs. Wherefore yor Maties peticoers humbly desire that your Matie would be gratiously pleased to take them into yor Royall Pteccon and gournment and ioyne them to the pvince of Mayne that they may be goved by the knowne lawes of England and enjoy the use of both the sacramts wch they have bin too deprived of. And as in all duty bound, yor peticoers shall dayly pray for the increase of all earthly honor untill you arive at the heavenly kingdome.

Tired with growing intolerance over these conditions, Francis Drake began to cast his eyes elsewhere for a place to live. Shortly thereafter on Dec 18th 1666, four men from the region of New Hampshire took advantage of Carteret's offer and acquired a grant of 40,000 acres on the Raritan River in New Jersey at a place they later called Piscataway. Francis Drake decided to join them. He petitioned for 120 acres at Piscataway, NJ, with warrant on Oct 15th 1665 which was granted.[1]

The East Jersey proprietorship was strictly a business venture with The Board of Proprietors of the Eastern Division serving as the board of directors of a corporation. Land was the commodity. Between 1686 and 1764 at least 17,500 acres were granted as "good rights" or cultivated lands as well as in Perth Amboy "town lotts" or "out lotts." Poor quality wooded lands were known as "pine rights" and sandy coastal land as "barrens". Total dividends were estimated at nearly one million acres.

---

1 *Minutes of the Board of Proprietors of New Jersey, 1685-1705*, V. I, p. 93

Additional dividends were issued from 1764 to 1790. Cartaret and the other eleven proprietors initially paid £284 per share and immediately sold ½ of them. Little is known after that as to prices. The land then went through a series of examinations, then a survey was made. When approved the individual proprietor could devide his land in as many lots he chose for which he charged quit rents. In the 1740's and 50's the Board had to deal with land riots. From 1764-1794 their concern was over settlement of boundaries. After 1780 they moved to divest themselves of the common lands increasing the number of land transactions. There seems to be no doubt that The Board and Proprietors controlled all lands until 1794. The American Revolution disrupted leasing by the Board and ended collection of rents. The war also divided members into patriots, loyalists, and those who were neutral. Lawsuits with mounting expenses and proprietors losing control of their lands caused the Board to sell large tracts of land to meet the expense of having to borrow money.[1] Eventually they met in Perth Amboy.

In preparation for moving to New Jersey, Francis and his wife sold their Greenland property on Aug 5th 1668. They packed their goods and sailed down the Atlantic coast to Elizabethtown, NJ, with their three sons: Francis, John and George, and a daughter Elizabeth. It was here that his son George married Mary Oliver and John married 1st Rebecca Trotter. Roads at the time were mostly foot or bridle-paths used by Indians. Later the Dutch at New Amsterdam used them getting to and from Delaware or Elizabethtown. Paths often followed the rivers making it difficult getting one's goods from Elizabethtown to Piscataway. Creating roads wasn't seriously considered until 1676. Once settled at Piscataway Francis Drake's daughter, Elizabeth, married Hugh Dunn who was another devout settler who departed New Hampshire. Hugh, an exhorter, became instrumental in organizing the Baptist Church with Rev. John Drake, its minister. Hugh died three months after the birth of his and Elizabeth's 9th child in Nov 1694.

Francis Drake was a weaver of cloth by profession. This suggests that he may have come from Essex County in England. At his death, his account books showed that almost all of the prominent families in town owed him money for his work. In addition he was granted a license on Jul 15th 1673 to keep an ordinary/tavern. Two years later on the same date Francis was made Captain of the military company. After nearly three years he requested to be discharged on May 30th 1678. He held a patent for 245 acres in 1675, also a 68 acre right. Two hundred acres were surveyed for him in Mar 1677/8. Francis also served as Justice of Peace and Judge in 1682. He died intestate on Sep 24th 1687 at Piscataway. On Oct 28th 1687 letters of administration were granted to his son George Drake, planter, and Benjamin Hull, gentleman, both of Piscataway.[2] The inventory valued his estate at £67.07.00. An account of the estate dated Aug 20th 1688 included payments to the doctor who attended Francis "in his sickness." Another account was dated Feb 27th 1692/3 by his son George Drake showed payments to brother Hugh Dunn and brother John Drake, totaling £62.14.04. Also payments from the estate by George Drake to his mother, sister Elizabeth Dunn, brother John Drake, Samuel Walker of Boston, merchant, Benjamin Hull, Charles Follet, Walter Robeson, Hugh Stonnels, and John Goning, in all £68.03.06. His wife Mary died Jul 28th 1688. The final account of his estate was dated Feb 27th 1692/3. Francis and Mary Drake's son:

Rev. John Drake settled in Portsmouth, NH, in 1657. Later Rev. Drake became a petitioner in Dover, NH, for protection of his property and religious rights. Since the province's interest was for trade and its laws disregarded, its citizens found the area unendurable and some left in 1668. Among them was John. He married 1st Rebecca Trotter Jul 7th 1677 who was born Jul 5th 1655, daughter of William Trotter and Cutbury Gibbs of Newbury, MA, who had married there on Dec 9th 1652. Trotter

---

1 Ibid., Vol. IV, pgs. xxvi-xxviii, xl, xlii,

2 New Jersey Archives, Vol. 23, pg 142, New Jersey Colonial Documents, Archives XXI, pg 104, Oct 28, 1687

was known for making slanderous speeches and brought to court and required to publicly acknowledge them. One wonders what colorful language he must have used. Trotter's Bridge located in the north part of Newbury's town plot was built over *the Little River* and named for William. He was listed among the settlers of Woodbridge, NJ, in 1665, dying there in 1676. John and Rebecca's sons were John, Francis, Samuel, Joseph, Benjamin, Abraham, Isaac, Jacob and Ebenezer.

Rev. Drake was ordained in 1689 by Thomas Killingworth, a Baptist minister fromNorwich, England. John was one of the original founders of the First Baptist Church of Piscataway and served as its minister until retiring in 1729. He was active in public affairs and a civil magistrate from 1708 to 1714. John died as a lay preacher and yeoman in Sep 1741 in Essex Co., NJ. His will dated Apr 7th 1740 was proved Sep 29th 1741. He does not mention all his children in his will. One can presume he had earlier helped the eldest John. Others were already deceased. In it he gave his children: Benjamin £16, Isaac £19, Abraham £16, Samuel £20 and Sarah Fulsom 7 shilling. His grandchildren: Abraham £7, John £6, Philip £7, and Gershom Drake £7. Also £5 each to Samuel and Thomas and £3 to Mary Davis, children of daughter Mary deceased. Daughter-in-law Patience Drake. Also £6 to Edward Slater, £8 to Allizhiah Skebbo, £3 to Elizabeth, wife of Benjamin Hull, esq., £3 to Filibrates, wife of Benjamin Martin, £30 to Moses FitzRandolph, £5 to Christian Rebout, and £5 to the poor of Piscataqua.

> *I will that if any of the above mentioned Legatorys shall be uneasy turbulent or trouble to my Executors that he or they shall forfeit their Respect Legacies there of which said Legacies shall be disposed of as the rest of my Estate there after mentioned. I will that the remainder of my Estate if any to be divided equally among my own children except my daughter Sarah Fulson which I give nothing but seven shilling. I do hearby appoint my beloved grandsons Samuel Drake and Jonas Drake and their mother Hannah Drake to be my only and Sole Executors of this my Last Will and Testament. Witnessed by James and Grace Manning and David Drake. On Sep 20th Hannah Drake, wife of Isaac Drake, renounced executorship due to age and inability.*[1]

The Inventory dated Sep 24th 1741 was taken by John Blackford and John Pain, Appraisers.[2] His cash on hand was £9.02.11. The Bonds he held from others was startling. John Shilisay £19, Aaron Stark £9.10.00, Philip Drake £10, Martin Drake £30, Jonathan Dunham £34, Jeremiah FitzRandolph £10, David Drake £20, Abraham Drake Jr & Nathaniel Drake £23, Martin Dunham £10, Moses FitzRandolph £27.14.30, Ephraim Dunham £20, Samuel Moore £30 and Abraham Drake Sr. £5. = £247.24.30

Other items of interest were a Beaver Hat, a Broad Chest Coat, a Smocked Holland Vest, a Brown Vest & a Long Coat, a Duraye Hat, Coat, & Britches, a Flannel Wafre Coat, Ticken Britches, a Cotton and Wool Vest, a Watch Coat, Leather Britches, Kersey Britches, 5 Shifts, a Silk Handkerchief, Yarn Stockings, 3 pr shoes, Tobacco Box, Gloves, Mittens, Belt, and Cane. He was obviously well read with numerous books, a New Bible, 1 New Testament, a Psalm Book, 2 Large Annotations. Even some Allspice, tailor's sheers, Money Seales and weights, and the usual household goods, furnishings and food. Seems like everyone had Indian corn but he also had a beehive. For transportation there was male & female saddles and bridles. John and Rebecca's eldest son was:

John Drake who was born Jun 2nd 1678 m. Sarah Compton Dec 9th 1697 at Piscataway, NJ.[3] John and Sarah had five children born at Piscataway:

+1.   Mary b. Oct 10th 1698, m. John Martin Jul 16th 1716 at Piscataway.
2.   Nathaniel b. Oct 28th 1699.
3.   Abigail b. Jul 19th 1701.
4.   Sarah b. Jul 5th 1703.
5.   Josiah b. Jul 14th 1706.

---

1 Middlesex Co. Will Bk. C, p. 442
2 Pgs. 1303-05
3 Piscataway, NJ, Town Register

Ayres Pictures

Henry Cook Ayres

Augustus Ayres, Henry's older brother

Lydia Wood Ayres

Henry & Lydia's Cabin in Meridian, Michigan
L is son Augustus S. Ayres, R is Charles W. Ayres

1899 Photo of Cabin

Pvt. Charles Wesley Ayres at Camp Denison,
Ohio

Elizabeth Jane Ayres

Elizabeth Jane Ayres 1st husband
1st Sgt. James P. McCurdy
Co. G. Michigan Infantry Volunteers

Augustus Seymour Ayres
Son of Henry and Lydia

Watercolor of Hospital in Columbus, Ohio where Elizabeth Ayers worked in the 1860's by K Windwart

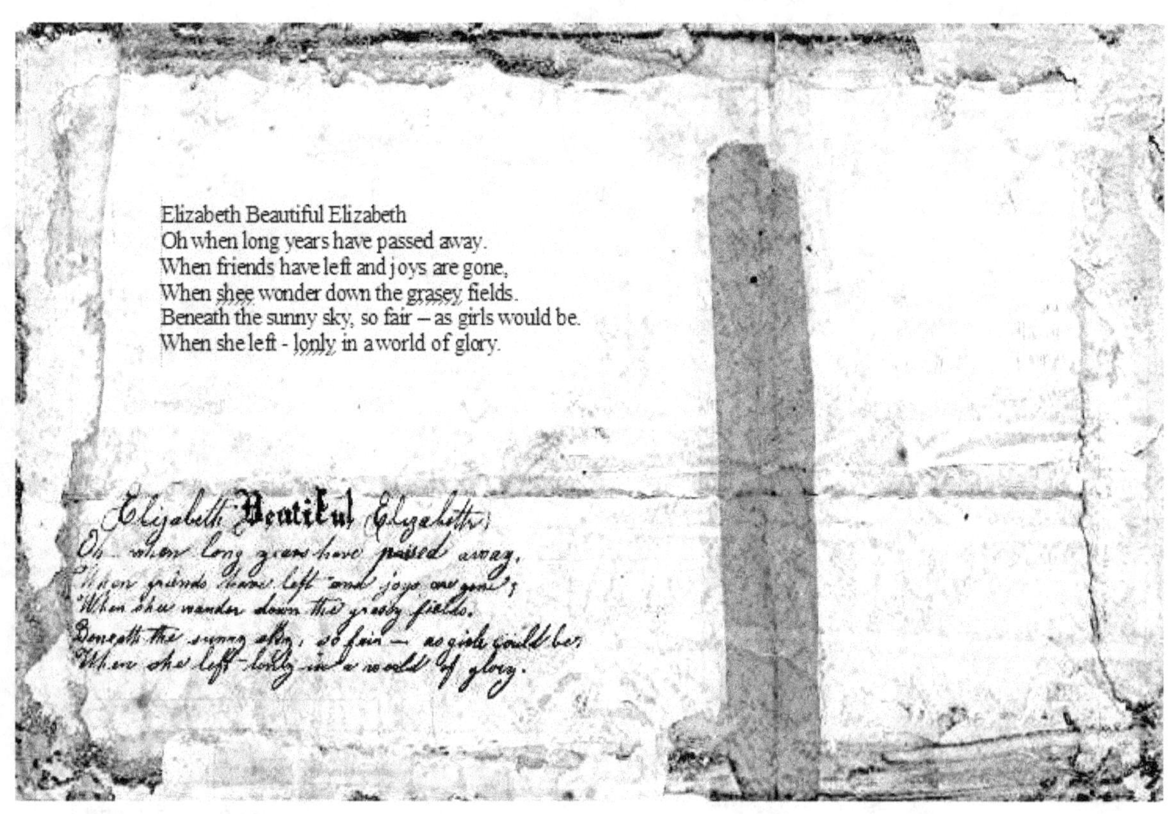

Reverse side of watercolor by Windwart

108

William Francis Ayres
Son of Henry and Lydia

Ella R. Smith, wife of William Francis Ayres

Frances Ellen Sutherland
First wife of Augustus Ayres

Seymour Augustus Ayres
Son of Augustus and Frances

Ayres Family Gathering July 4, 1920
Back Row: Phoebe Smith Burger, May McNeil Ayres, Belle Adams, Elizabeth Gordon Ayres holding Lucille Ayres.
Maude Woodcock Ayres holding Jean Ayres. Eno R. Ayres, Elizabeth Ayres McCurdy Champion, Augustus S Ayres.
Center Row: Ella Smith Ayres, William F. Ayres, Charles W. Ayres, Bina Smith Ayres.
Front Row: Alta Eston Townes

Siblings - Top - Augustus and Elizabeth Ayers
Bottom - William F. and Charles Wesley Ayres

Raymond Cleveland Ayres
Son of Wes and May

Elizabeth Rachel Gordon
Wife of Raymond

Eno Richmond Ayres

Eno and Maude

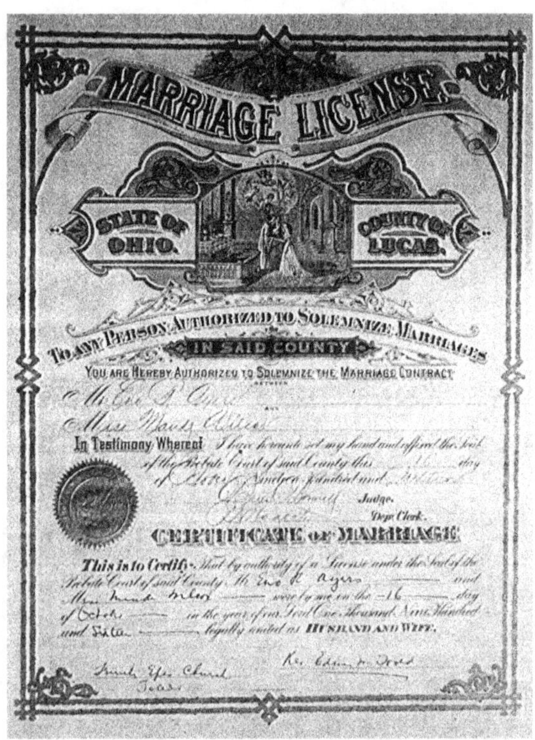

Eno R. Ayres & Maude Woolcock Ayres

Eno with grandchildren Rebecca and Todd
Children of Bob and Noreen Engle

Eno and boat *Ursula*

Camping at Chain of Lakes, MI, 1930
Back: Eno, Maude, Lucille - Front: Frances, Noreen, & Jean Ayres

Halloween Party of Polly Prim Club - 1933
2nd left: May with Granddaughter Noreen

This was the last photo taken by the elder son, Ray, of Charles W. Ayres in the fall of 1926.
Back row: Eno R. Ayres, Maude Ayres, Frances M. Ayres, Elizabeth R. Ayres, May F. Ayres.
Front row: Jean E. Ayres, Charles W. Ayres, Lucille M. Ayres.

Mary McNeil Ayres and Granddaughter Noreen
in1930 - Mary Frances died April 13, 1934

Last photo of May with Granddaughters Noreen
and Mary taken in fall of 1933

Compton Ancestry

Sarah Compton, John Drake's wife, was b. Jun 1st 1673 at Woodbridge, NJ, daughter of William Compton and Mary Wilmont whose family first settled in Ipswich, MA. William Compton, son of John and Mary Compton of Ipswich, arrived in New Jersey in 1668 from Gravesend, NY, when squabbles over land erupted between the Dutch and English in New York. William was patented 174 acres from the New Jersey Proprietors on Mar 10th 1671.[1]

William and Mary Compton's children were:

1. Mary b. Nov 1668 and presumed to be the first child born in Woodbridge. She m. Caleb Campbell Jan 1st 1695 and had daughter: Rachel b. May 20th 1697.
2. John b. Jan 2nd 1669, m. Mar 6th 1689 Elizabeth Munday of Piscataway, children: Mary, John, William, Elizabeth, Sarah, Rachel, David, Hannah, & Samuel.
3. Sarah b. Jul 25th 1670, d. Sep 16th 1670.
4. David b. Jul 21st 1671.
+5. Sarah b. Jun 1st 1673, m. John Drake.
6. Jonathan b. Dec 18th 1674, m. Sep 24th 1701 Esther Martin, son Jonathan b. Jul 12th 1706.

Sarah's father William Compton served as Constable in 1677 and was noted as a jurist from Woodbridge in the notable case of Capt. John Pike in 1684. Little is known about his wife, Mary Wilmont or Wilmot. William Compton died Sep 21st 1694 in Woodbridge at age 63. William's wife, Mary, and son Jonathan were administrators of his estate.[2] Mary W. Compton died in 1713 at Woodbridge at age 78.

After Sarah Compton Drake died, John Drake married 2nd Anne FitzRandolph around 1734. John's will dated Dec 12th 1744 was proved May 30th 1751. He made Anne his sole heiress, executors to sell all real and personal. The inventory taken May 29th 1751 provides a clue to his death date which was probably in late May 1751.[3]

John Drake and Sarah Compton's eldest daughter was:

1. Mary Drake, the 1st wife of John Martin, son of John Martin and Dorothy Smith. See Martin family

Thomas Ayers' Family Cont'd.

Women on an average at that time died sooner than men, often due to complications during childbirth. And so it was with Thomas' wife, Mary Ross Ayers. Thomas was willing to pledge $5 toward the building of a parsonage for Perth Amboy's Presbyterian Church in Sep 1809. This church later owned the property on which the Long Ferry Tavern was located in Amboy. Of course, New Jersey had taxes and kept very complete lists of householders from 1773-1822. Items taxed varied depending on the year they were taken. Acreage and value was the first item listed. Other items were horses, cattle, hogs, whether they were a householder, owned a mill, tavern, slaves, a riding chair, a sleigh, a sloop, or one's estate if deceased. The 1818 tax for Perth Amboy listed Thomas father Daniel's heirs, namely Thomas, Abraham, Daniel, and Moses Martin of Perth Amboy. In 1819 his son Abraham was added to the list as part of Daniel's estate.

Thomas was 43 years old when his father, Daniel, died in 1818, three years after his wife Mary. Like most men with a family and no wife, men went into another marriage. Sometime between 1815-1818

---

1 Middlesex Co. Deed Bk. 1, p. 122

2 Middlesex Co. Will Bk. B, p. 214

3 Middlesex Co., Will Bk. E, p. 526

Thomas married a woman named Jane. I have not be able to locate their marriage record. Shortly after his father's death, Thomas moved his family to Ohio. In regard to his real estate, New Jersey court records show that Thomas had inherited about 32½ acres in 1818 from his father's estate which he released in July 1821 to his brother, Abraham, for 50 cents. On Oct 4th 1821, Thomas sold to Thomas Salter of Elizabeth Town 53 & 19/100 acres in Perth Amboy township located on the north side of the Woodbridge road where his brother, Daniel Ayers' house was also located. The sale for $1,500 was recorded on Oct 17th 1821. Then Thomas purchased for $1,500 two parcels in the U.S. Military District in Delaware County, Ohio, from Thomas and Susan Salter. The Ohio lands were recorded on Jun 22nd 1822 as Lot 15, 16th range, 6th township, 2nd section containing 185 acres and 100 perches and Lot 17 in the same area containing 100 acres. In essence they exchanged properties. Salter's father had purchased enough Revolutionary land warrants to enable him to acquire the northwest quarter of Bennington township, which his son sold after his father died and also moved to Bennington. Who was handling these transactions is unknown but I doubt Thomas was making an arduous trip to Ohio and back to New Jersey to handle necessary paper work. Thomas' final two recorded land sales in New Jersey were on May 20th & 28th 1822 for a total of $85.

These early deeds were recorded as so many acres, "more or less" or "strict measure." More or less meant that no further surveying had been done since the land was initially laid out. Land was described in chains or links in a certain direction, such as north or south, in so many degrees and minutes with points of reference as a stone, stake, creek, or a specific type of tree or sapling, sometimes notched or marked, and running along or near a neighbor. One example is in the deed that Thomas sold to Sally R. Potter in May 1822.

> *Beginning at a persimmon tree standing in the line of land in the possession of Timothy Carhard which is also a corner of a lot of one half acre of upland belonging to Abraham Ayers then from said persimmon tree running south 46 degrees east 2 chains to a stake for a corner of a lot of land belonging to Abraham Ayers, thence with his line north 28 degrees 5 minutes east 14 chains & 86 links to a stake by the south side of Woodbridge Creek, thence along the line north 66 degrees west 3 chains and 44 links to a corner of daniel Ayers meadow, thence south 34 degrees & 45 minutes east 2 chains and 63 links, thence south 41 degrees and 10 minutes west 5 chains and 92 links to a stake, thence south 50 degrees west 1 chain and 45 links to a stake at a corner between the half a moiety set off to Abraham Ayers and the sd Thomas Ayers, thence south 13 degrees and three quarters west 3 chains and 66 links to the beginning, containing 5 acres bounded by meadow and land of Abraham Ayers, Daniels Ayers, Woodbridge, &...*

Small outlots were noted in breadth and length in rods, known as poles or perches. The chain of 100 links that equaled 66 feet that was used in measuring was invented in 1620 by the English mathematician, Edmund Gunter. Eighty chains equals one mile (80x66=5,280 feet) and 10 square chains equals 1 acre (66x66x10=43,560 square feet). The rod was known as a quarter-chain and equaled 16½ feet. These measurements are still in use today. The standard set for a length/section of a fence rail was 11 feet so that a fence-viewer could tell the size of a field by walking along the fence noting that 6 rails equaled 1 chain or 66 feet.

Prior to 1817 there were few settlers in the area where Thomas purchased his Ohio property. The large township of Bennington was formed on Apr 22nd 1817, a land of streams and forests formed by retreating glaciers. The soil was a fertile sandy loam, good for farming. Ages ago a large Indian mound was located west of Marengo near where Thomas settled. Several tribes of Indians had lived in the area for many years, one obviously the Delaware or Lenni Lenape (manly man) originally from the east coast. A grape grown in the area was named Delaware. Indians were attracted by a sulphur spring in the city of Delaware on today's Ohio Wesleyan University's campus which they called "Medicine Waters." Delaware Run, a small stream ran nearby. Mingoes and Wyandots also left their names attached to a park and lake in the area. Tribes had and still have their differences, one reason why the Delawares departed their eastern home. They did like Quakers because they were treated fairly by Wm. Penn. The story of a clash of two very different life styles developed early in the settlement of this country. The Indians eventually meeting their demise from the plow. Water was also vital for settlement. Walnut Creek, known as *Big Belly* ran through the western half of the area with all its branches. The creek ran through Thomas' property.

One story my father liked to tell was how his great grandfather, Thomas Ayers, traveled from New Jersey to Ohio and how Thomas' father, Daniel, fought in the American Revolution. It was said that Thomas won $1,000 in a New Jersey lottery and in 1821 walked to Ohio that summer from New Jersey, located and purchased a tract of land in Bennington township, Delaware County, Ohio. Ordering a log house to be built on that land, he then journeyed back home the same summer. The following spring, with oxen and covered wagon, his family and two other families from New Jersey made the overland trip to Ohio. Thomas settled in his new home near Marengo, Ohio, where he resided until his death. But how much truth is there in this family lore?

His land sales prior to leaving are more accountable as to how the land in Ohio was acquired. New Jersey had Lottery schemes as early as 1720. A decade later, a law was passed prohibiting lotteries and raffles for the disposal of goods. By 1748 most towns had lotteries for building and repairing churches, parsonages, bridges, public works and supporting colleges. Despite legislative action, lotteries existed in New Jersey after the Revolution. Although New Jersey newspapers printed lottery records, I have not been able to verify that part of the story. What is known is that Thomas Ayers and Robert Noe's families were living in Ohio by 1820 and possibly Thomas Salter.

The Noe and Ayers families were intertwined back in Woodbridge, NJ. According to Noe researchers, Marengo Cemetery Records, and my research: The children of this Daniel Noe of Woodbridge made an agreement in 1810 over the division of Daniel's estate that his sons Amos and John would get all his estate according to his will which was not executed. Daniel's children were: Robert Noe (b. 1772, d. Apr 18th 1861 age 89, bur. Marengo); Marsh who had a daughter who m. Samuel Crow; Benjamin; Amos; Elias d. Jan 1768, NJ; John; Mary wife of Chas. Gamberton; and Susanna wife of William Virity.

Robert Noe m. Mary Tappin in 1802 Madison Co., NJ. where Mary was born. They moved to Ohio with children:

1. Susan b. 1803.;
2. Elias b. 1805, d. NJ.
3. Mary Ann d. Apr 20th 1868, age 63y9m20d, m. Calvin Vining.
4. Samuel d. Mar 22nd 1831 age 23y10m11d.
5. William d. Jun 21st 1888 age 88y,4m. m. Abacina Crane 1837.
6. Margaret b. 1813, m. William Johnson 1833.
7. James H. b. 1815 m. Caroline Page 1840.
8. George T. b. Jan 7th 1817, d. Jun 14th 1901 m. 1844 Sarah S. Doty b. 1824, d. 1915.
9. Robert L. b. Oct 16th 1819 m. Fannie Morris Jul 4th 1849.

Thomas' son, Augustus, had gone to Wilton, Connecticut, for an education in hatting. On Jun 7th 1820, Thomas wrote to Augustus about the illness of Samuel Noe.

Samuel Noe has been so sickly that he has done no work of consequence for more than a year...even though he was a lad age 13.

So we know from this letter that they were living in Ohio by 1819. The winter of 1819/20 was particularly harsh with heavy snow and bitter cold. Food was scarce. Livestock became so hungry that they hung about the few cabins. All looked forward to spring. Thomas continued...

Samuel sent a letter to jersey and has had an answer. They write to him that a number of them talk of moveing out this way, one of them is dead [Oliver Drake] and some is married [his widow married Gage Inslee]. Joseph Catyers is married to gage inslees daughter.

Thomas had nieces, daughters of his brother, Daniel, who married into the Inslee family. Samuel Noe died on Mar 22nd 1831 at age 23 years 10 months and 11 days as noted in another letter dated Mar 29th 1831.

He tryed the steam docter, the apothecary docter, got medicine from the Root docter, but all would not cure him.

This also gives some idea as to what medical conditions were in Ohio in the 1820's. Only half of the populace could expect to live to age 45 due to the rigors of daily life, diet, and limited knowledge in medical care at the time. Diseases and epidemics took a toll on the people since germ theories of infections were unknown. Most depended on self-medication with home remedies and prayer. In all, that was probably not as bad as blood letting and purging which were more or less standard medical practice. So Thomas advised Augustus: *"to prepare for death for you have not got your life insured no more than Samuel Noe."* An 1830 map of Delaware County shows Salter's lot 14 is adjacent to Thomas' lot 15 with Walnut Creek running through both properties. Lot 3 east of the creek on both properties is owned by Salter. Lot 17 owned by Thomas connects with Lot 15 at its southwest corner. Further North of the two men is Noe's Lot 11. The number of adult male inhabitants in Bennington in 1834 totaled 133. Bennington was removed from in Delaware County in 1850.

Getting to Ohio

The proposed Cumberland or National Road, now Highway 40, ran from Baltimore to Wheeling closely following the earlier Braddock's Road. A bill for construction went before Congress in 1805, passed in 1806. Many people had already gone west before this road was started. By 1806 enough money had been collected to begin the survey between Fort Cumberland and Wheeling. The road was completed by 1811 from Baltimore to Fort Cumberlan, however, the war of 1812 delayed construction. By 1813 ten miles was completed, eleven more partially done. Construction was fully underway in 1815 and completed in 1818 to Wheeling. Travel by stagecoach was reduced from eight days to three. It would take longer by wagon and oxen. Three families set off on this road to Wheeling by covered wagon and oxen. Getting to Baltimore from Perth Amboy was another challenge. Perth Amboy was located across the river from New York City and travel from that area to cities of Trenton, Philadelphia, and Baltimore had long been established. Once at Wheeling, they had to take older turnpike roads to complete their journey to Bennington since it was after 1828 that the National Road was completed to Columbus, Ohio. Turnpikes were common back east in the 1790's but nothing like those we have today. They were trails through woods cleared by cutting down trees and leaving stumps low enough that would clear wagon axles. Bridges were made of wood and in need of constant repair. In spring these byways were muddy, and summer travel raised clouds of choking dust. Many preferred to travel in winter, if the weather was mild. Sleds moved more easily than wagons. The most one could hope to make was three or four miles an hour or twenty-five miles a day.

The National Road was to be a modern macadamized surface from end to end but the final hot oil treatment was never completed so it ended up a mostly gravel road. Since the road was never built to specifications, it was plagued with freezing trapped water that created large potholes. Nonetheless, it was by far the most comfortable road to travel for its day. All bridges along the road were built of stone rather than wood. Stagecoaches and commercial wagon traffic was heavy. Taverns and inns located throughout the states along the road catered to travelers where the latest news and politics were exchanged around roaring fireplaces. Inns were nothing like today's motels. In the East, most were framed 2½ story structures while those further west were built of logs. Meals were provided at reasonable rates as well as a stable for animals. Some travelers slept on the main floor by the large fireplaces. Others, if they could afford the extra expense, were put up in double-bedded rooms with pillows, blankets and quilts. If there were room in the wagon, some may have slept there. Later the

Delaware County Ohio property map - 1830

States of Maryland, Pennsylvania and Virginia became involved in a heated debate with Congress as to the road's maintenance. It took several years until the Supreme Court ruled that although the U.S. Government built the roads, the finished roads belonged to the states. Tolls they charge could pay for maintenance.[1] Once their long journey was over, Thomas' younger boys found plenty of land in which to roam and play. The wooded lands needed clearing for raising crops. This major undertaking for most settlers began with the girdling of trees. There were only hand tools available for this and other farm jobs. Thomas' father and grandfather were carpenters as well as yeomen and his older brother, Abraham, was a wheelwright so Thomas should have acquired some knowledge in the use of tools as

---

1 (William Dollarhide, *Wagon Roads to the Ohio Country*, 187-1820, Genealogy Bulletin, American Genealogical Lending Library Newslatter, No. 23 (Jul-Sep 1994): 7-9)

he grew up. Inventories taken after one died are a source of the kinds of tools that were necessary for farming. Among those I located were oxen and horse farm wagons. Tools included betty and iron wedges, grindstones, iron trammels, broad and narrow axes, forks, rakes, drawing knives, augers, spades, hoes, scythes and sickles, saws, plow irons, iron harrows, Leyden mill and press, and miscellanous other tools. The best description of most of these items and their uses are found in Eric Sloane's book, *A Museum of Early American Tools*. Most families carried needed tools on their wagons for purchases in the wilderness could be difficult and expensive. Thomas' younger boys helped their father on the farm. Enos was injured at age seventeen raising a cabin which affected his health for some time. The boys seemed not to be as interested in getting an education like their brother Augustus, Thomas wrote:

> *Enos and Henry both live home yet most of the time tho enos dont work much for me. he shoots dears and workes amongst the neighbors. he has but little learning i asure you he would not go to school. likewise henry dont no much. there was school last winter within about a half a mile of us. enos would not go to it. henry went. it appears to me that both of them are verry neglectfull about learning. they know but little and I gues they never will no much. they will do for farmers.*

And farmers they became like their father. His son, Augustus, was in Wilton when his father wrote to him on Jun 7th 1830 on the conditions at home in Bennington as well as to express concern for his behavior in response to a letter dated Mar 10th from Augustus:

> *.....I dont begrudge a phew quarter dollars in the corse of a year for letters. we can talk to each other by the way of letters tho at a great distance. this way of talking at a distance is a great satisfaction...we are some richer than we was when we come to ohio. we are on the gaining hand. we have had a tolerable plenty of provision ever since you left home. we kild a fat beef last winter, likewise some fat hogs. I only have thirty nine hogs that I kept threw the winter. i think its likely there will be more than one hundred by next crismas pigs and all. we are likely to have a good wheat harvest. I have some old corn on hand I gues more than one hundred and fifty bushels of ears. we have plenty of wheat flour in the hous. we have fruit this Season apples, peaches, plums cherries. I want you to write soon to let urs no how you...are making out...i remind you of one thing, be carefull how you conduct yourself, try and live in creddit. one of our neighbors when he heard that you worked at hatting, he calculated that you would not come to much for hatters are drunkards. he laid you out for a drunkard. I hope you will disappoint him. in your last letter you mentioned something about honour as though you had by a calculation that you could git a more honourable living than working at the hatting business. I want you to write how long you calculate living in Wilton. as for your talking about honour, I approve of such language as that for it is the honourable that is exsepted of into the kingdom of heaven as John the divine was talking of heaven, of the hevenly Jerusalum as it was revealed to him of the Lord by the angel that the nations of them that were Saved do bring their glory and honour into it. therefore it is a great thing to live in honour to be honourable. we may begin at Abraham of old and trace it down to the present day. it is the honourable and the riteous that is the first the greatest carrecters on earth those are the verry carrectirs that is exsepted of into the kingdom of heaven. Some of our neighbors has gone to a New Cuntry called Saint joseph...I dont calculate to move yet. this land is rich a nuff...I gues that i shal live and die here in bennington.*

Thomas seemed eager to have Augustus get into the teaching profession and give up the idea of the hatting business suggesting he might live longer.

> *...if you can git lerning anuff and have a gift to teach others, you can git a living without slaving the body, but it is a feteigue of mind to teach School. one of Squire Etons sons is a teacher in [?]Snactada colege, gits five hundred Dollars a year.*

It would be almost another year before Thomas wrote to Augustus on Mar 29th 1831 in response to a letter received the previous Jan. In it he passed on information learned last fall through a Mr. Henry Hampton that a number of inhabitants of Amboy and Woodbridge had died furthering his desire for his son to take care of himself. Also concern about the time spent on his education.

> *...therefore try and take care of number One that is yourself...how much longger you mean to go to School to the Cademy Teacher...by what you said in your last letter you wont git through with your learning till you are more than thirty years old...I dont see it would be of advantage to you unles you Should git to be a teacher and teach orthers.*

On Aug 30th 1832 Thomas and Jane sold fifty acres of the west end of Lot 15 to Clark Dwinells for $150. In the meantime his son Augustus moved to Newtown, Connecticut, and Thomas' letters continued on the subject of his education and vocation and trying to get him to return to Ohio.

> *Bennington, Ohio Nov 25th 1832*
> *My Son*
>   *I received the letter that was dated Mar the 13 wrote in Wilton. I also received the letter that was dated Aug 4th wrote in Newtown. I likewise received the letter that was dated Newtown Sep the 20. I confess I have neglected writing or answering either of those letters. You must not think hard of that for I asure you it seams to be an undertaking for me to being to write a letter. I am glad to hear from you so often. You must write again soon and tell urs how you do and whether you desine to come and see urs nex spring if you can make it convenient. David White and myself was talking about you not long ago. We think altogether likely it would be much to your proffit to come here in the State of Ohio. You can get education much cheaper here than you can in Connecticut. We presume there is a greate siminary in Worthington a little rising of twenty miles from where I live. The first teacher is a Connecticut man. He knows the lattin greek and french languages. He comes from Princetown Colledge New Jersey to Worthington teaching is five dollars per quarter board one dollar. The way I know this is an old gnetleman was at my house last sumer who was going about stablishing Sunday schools a presbeterian minister, he said his son was the first teacher. He is a religious man also he has license to preach. There is an establishment of Docters at Worthington also. Hatters wages is higher here than it is to the eastward as I am informed. Nath King was at my house who came from Milton, New Jersey, who owns a part of Salter section now lives in Granville, Ohio, who has got a son and son in law who carries on hatting in Newark, Ohio. His son in laws name is ?vorus come from Milton, New Jersey. I informed myself of Mr King about hatters wages he told me hatters wages was higher here than it was to the eastward though they don't pay all money, part mone and part store pay. Perhaps this store pay would answer your turn. Perhaps the teacher would take part store pay likewise pay your board out of the store. If I knew what was for the best I would tell you . I guess you had better come and try it. I think you will do well a*

nuff here in case you be sick you wont be far from home though you have been blest with health. You don't know how long it will last if you should be sick where you live now you would be in a verry poor situation. Health is a great blessing we ought to b verry thankfull to Almighty God for health for he can put urs in great pain in a verry short time. We ought to take a prudent care of our bodies and be verry thankfull to the Lord for preserving our unproffittable lives. We all know we are in his power therefore let urs be thankfull for all things. We are all I presume verry well at present escepting my self. I don't get rid Of the old complaint in my head but I am total Comfortable at present. I advise you it you setout to come here not to come by the way of the sail boats on the Lake. We hear of so many getting drowned out of those sail boats we believe it to be a verry dangerous way. The steam boat is more safe. Keep a good distance of the boiler. Concerning land I give you your share of land of what I have on hand to spare at present. I give Harriet fifty acres, Enos fifty acres. I have fifty acres for you. It would not be right to give one all and the rest none. The hundred acres that I would have given to you had you stayed here now I give the one half to Enos. See what you lose by going away but never mind that maybe it is all for the best. Yet I make no doubt in my mind you can attain to as great a bit of knowledge here as in Connecticut. I presume there is a school for Doctors here perhaps as in any State in the unighted States. There is a College near Mount Vernon as I am informed about one hundred and sixty students there but I should prefer Worthington. If you should come and rove about this state a little you can judge for your self where you think you can make out the best. Land is cheep here yet especially new land. David White and Harriet has sold the fifty acres I gave them for three Dollars per acre. That is as high as any new land has been sold for in this district of country. They will sell land for three dollars per acre with some improvement on those that are in want of money. Some two dollars per acre but land is on the rise and will be what money you have laid out for learning would have bought a great farm here. You might now be tolerably independant but still I suppose you think your learning is worth something. I think it is as healthy here and as it was in Jersey. I haint has a days sickness for ten years. My Docter bils put them all together for ten years has been about fifteen Dollars though not much of it on my account. We are all a live that was alive when you went away that is my family and David Whites. You must send urs a letter soon after you receive this and tell us what you are about and when you calculate to come and see urs. No more at present.

Thomas Ayers

Augustus was in South East New York, when Thomas wrote to him on Nov 25th 1833, after finishing up his fall work, in response to a letter written in Oct.

Enos has got so well that he can do light work though he hasn't done much for a number of years. He has tended a C[?]anging machine last summer. He is now about the neighborhood. I guess he will come to be a hearty man. He makes his home with me, likewise Henry lives at home yet he was twenty one years old in Oct. I expect Henry will continue to live with me and have a share of the profits of the farm. Somthing has been said about Henry's getting married but I guess he will put it off as you did. You enquired about our prosperity. We are on the gaining hand...I guess I am worth one thousand Dollars more than when I came to Ohio. I presume my Farm is worth five hundred

Dollars more. I am Confident I have five hundred Dollars worth of stock and other property more than I had when I came to the state. The people in general in this Country is a getting rich. That is prudent saving car[e]ful people that looks well to the right. Lazy idle drunken people dont make out so well. We have got a good flock of sheep between twenty and thirty. We make their wool into cloth. I guess about sixty yards of woolling and sixty yards of linen this year. Your Step Mother has bought a one Horse Wagon. Cost Forty Dollars. She had Fifty Dollars willed to her by a verry amiable old lady who Dyed on Staten Island in the state of New York. Jane Mofses Myers. She sent a power of attorney Signed by the Chief Judge of the Court of Knox County Ohio. This power of attorney was sent to a man by the name of Mikel Mundy. This Mofses Myers was a relation of hers. I have got a good horse to put before the said wagon. We can take some comfort in riding about. We calculate to go the the State of Indiana next summer if we live and prosper. Only on a visit likely begone a Month.

In response to Augustus' comment about coming to Ohio to study, Thomas wrote again of the higher wages for hatters, continuing his studies, and becoming a farmer would be good in Ohio. Despite some drop in farming due to the younger generations moving to the city to enter manufacturing jobs, America remained primarily a rural population until the beginning of the Civil War. Thomas wrote highly of the great schools in this state and noted a seminary near Athens plus a high school at Columbus for gentlemen and another for ladies. Also a great Academy at Worthington where board is one dollar per week and you can live and learn much cheaper here than you can in the eastern states. He suggested that Augustus stick to the hatting business till you can get money enough ahead to bear your expenses so as not to be pinched for money. I guess you would stand a much better chance to get in to be a school teacher in this Country than in the eastern states.

I think you had better make up your mind and come to this Country and try your luck here. If you conclude to come don't venture to early in the spring on the lake for it is a dangerous place. We hear of numbers of boats getting cast away and people losing their property and lives. The last of May would be as early in the season as I would like to risk my body on the lake.

Augustus did move back to Ohio. On Feb 24th 1835 Thomas and Jane divided 100 acres of the north half of Lot 17 between his sons Augustus and Enos. The typical farm at that time was small, about fifty acres, which was about all a healthy man could manage. This land was not cleared and it would be up to the men to make the land usable. Thomas and sons, Enos, Augustus, and Henry were among the 1835 list of 133 male inhabitants in Bennington twp. Augustus sold his 41+ acres on Oct 9th 1836 to Stephen Rosevelt. By 1840 Bennington's population totaled 1,051.

Thomas had no reason to celebrate his 70th birthday on Aug 16th 1845. Jane was his second wife to be buried on his birthday. Jane was sixty-eight and buried in the Vining Cemetery in Morrow County, now Fargo Methodist Church, between Samuel Noe and Abraham Wells. On Oct 10th 1846, Thomas was married 3rd to Abraham Wells' widow Abigail by John Doty, JP, in Delaware County. His children were not fond of Abigail. During that time Thomas, now living in Morrow County, made a deed to sons Enos and Henry plus a lease to Enos. Henry sold his to Edward Shotwell in 1850 with Abigail's approval. After Abigail died, Thomas considered marrying again but his children raised an objection to it as their father was in his 80's. There was some Debate and legal papers over real estate about whether Enos or Henry would move in with him in the frame. It was decided that Enos along with his wife, Mary Mifflin Ayers (1827-Apr 17th 1877 of consumption), and family would. Enos and

Mary were married Sep 29th 1839 by John Doty, JP. Enos d. Mar 4th 1889, a widower age 79 of old age. Their children were:

1. Priscilla Jane (1840-1903).
2. Thomas (1842-1892) m. Mary E. Horr, Oct 16th 1861 by Rev. Wm. King. Children: 1) Lizzie Belle b. Aug 1st 1870, Bennington twp; and 2) Josiah b. Jul 25th 1873, Peru twp.
3. John Mifflin (1845-?) a plaster mason m. Lucy ? (b. 1840).
4. Obediah (1847-?) a boot & shoe dealer, m. Sep 5th 1877 by Rev. O. Webster, Nettie Steen, (b. Ireland 1855).
5. David L. (?).
6. Harriet/Hattie (1853-?) m. Andrew C. Horr. Children: 1) Mary A. (Stella) b. Mar 23rd 1873; 2) Joseph Clarence Horr, b. Nov 30th 1875, Bennington twp; and 3) Claude b. 1876 Missouri. By 1880 they were living in Paola, Miami, Kansas where Andrew was working in a marble shop.
7. Cassius M. (1859-1944) m. Sep 5th 1877 by Rev. Webster, Cora Estelle Morton (d. Jun 24th 1943 age 91y6m8d of a fractured hip) and had a son, 1) Ralph Edwin (Dec 12th 1887-1968) who married Ida L. (1900-1972). This was the family my father Eno and his cousin, Seymour, visited in Ohio. After Enos wife died in 1877 he began deeding his land in Bennington to sons: 2) John Thomas and 3) Cassius.

Although Thomas Ayers lived within hearing distance of the railroads for fourteen years, he never ventured to see the RR cars. Thomas' journey to Ohio ended when he died Feb 16th 1864 six months before his 89th birthday at his home in Bennington. There is no record of Thomas' death in the courthouse or burial in any of the area cemeteries, so he was probably buried on his farm.

Following is a family generation graph of a portion of the previous information beginning with Thomas Ayers.

Thomas Ayers (1775 - 1864)
  Robert Ross (1731 - 1812)
William Ross (c1738 - 1796)
  Mary [—] (? - 1777)
Mary Ross (1780 - 1815)
  Jeffrey Manning (c1645 - 1693)
  James Manning (1674 - 1724)
    Thomas Andrews (c1570 - 1643)
    Joseph Andrews (c1597 - 1680)
    Hepzibah Andrews (c1640 - 1692)
Nathaniel Manning (1706 - 1766)
  John Laing (1654 - ?)
  Christian Laing (c1678 - 1724)
Benjamin Manning (1744 - 1801)
  Mary Harris (c1712 - 1793)
Mary Manning (17? - 1849)
  John Martin (c1618 - 1674)
  John Martin (c1650 - 1704)
    Gov. Thomas Roberts (c1600 - 1674)
    Hester Roberts (1628 - 1687)
John Martin (1691 - 1721)
  Richard Smith (c1665 - 1696)
  Dorothy Smith (c1677 - 1698)
    Anne Browne
Benajah Martin (1719 - 1788)
  Francis Drake (1615 - 1687)
  John Drake (1655 - 1741)
    Francis Walker (c1645 - 1701)
    Mary Walker (1625 - 1688)
John Drake (1678 - 1751)
  William Trotter (1630 - 1676)
  Rebecca Trotter (1652 - ?)
    Cutbury Gibbs (1628 - 1667)
Mary Drake (1698 - ?)
  William Compton (? - 1694)
  Sarah Compton (1673 - ?)
    Mary [---] (? - after 1694)
Mary Martin (1747 - 1772)
  Hannah [—] (1720 - 1797)

Ayers Family Continued

Henry Cook[7] Ayers/Ayres, son of Thomas Ayers and Mary Ross, was born a few months after the War of 1812 began. The day was Oct 9th in Middlesex County, NJ. His parents seemed to have a knack in naming their children that gives a researcher a challenge. It took me years and a trip to Philadelphia to discover that Henry Cook Ayers was named after the minister who married his parents, the Rev. Henry Cook of the Metuchen Presbyterian Church. The initial church began in Woodbridge whose minister would frequently ride on horseback to Metuchen to preach in private homes. The town of Metuchen decided to organize a church in 1767 which led to its unison with Woodbridge, whose minister alternated his preaching between the two. The Metuchen Society was known as the 2nd Presbyterian Church of Woodbridge or the upper congregation. Two hundred acres had been set aside for the ministry by the townsmen. Several years later a dispute erupted with the Episcopalians over this allocated land. Subsequently the Episcopalians filed a law suit against the Presbyterians. The 1776 Revolution ended that situation. The two Presbyterian churches officially separated in 1793. Metuchen hired Rev. Henry Cook from Morris County, NJ, as their minister. He was beloved by his congregation and served them for thirty years until his death in 1824 at age 55.[1]

Henry was a young lad of six or seven when his family moved around 1818/9 to Bennington Township, Delaware County, Ohio. The wooded land his father purchased was in the U.S. Military District. He enjoyed living among the trees and sleighing in winter. His passion for music led him to play the fife and flute. He taught singing school, a popular social function at that time. Years passed as Henry grew old enough to think about marriage. He fell in love with a *social butterfly* who abruptly ended their engagement by fleeing and marrying a very wealthy man. Broken hearted Henry did not trust his choosing a bride, so he asked neighbor Frona Hoar to select a wife for him. She chose a pragmatic Quakeress, Lydia Wood, daughter of Jonathan Wood and Martha Reynolds, members of Alum Creek Monthly Meeting. Henry was anxious to marry. Lydia, a spinner and weaver, wanted time to prepare her modest wardrobe. So she did and packed the items in a small wooden chest. Then they were married on Sep 19th 1840 in Delaware County by Shadrack Hubbell, JP.[2] Lydia was immediately disowned by the MM for marrying out of unity. I don't think it bothered her very much. Their children born in Bennington twp., Ohio were:

+1. Charles Wesley b. Apr 4th 1842.
2. Elizabeth Jane b. Jun 26th 1844.
3. Augustus Seymour b. Dec 21st 1846.
4. William Francis b. 1857.

Henry was also an avid reader and he and his older sister, Harriet White, wrote many letters, especially to their brother, Augustus. Harriet was about 17 when their father, Thomas Ayers, took his family to Ohio. Around 1824 she married David White who had come to Ohio from Virginia. They would have nine children:

1. James Madison b. Nov 12th 1824, d. Oct 18th 1889 and buried in Glendale Cemetery, Cardington twp. He m. Almeda Hore and had three children.
2. Francis M. born 1827, d. Dec 9th 1862 in Cincinnati after being thrown from a carriage. He m. Serena Lewis on Jun 11th 1855 in Cincinnati and they had two children.
3. William Collun b. Feb 1829, and in 1850 he left for Boonville, Missouri, becoming a peddler of books, then off to Louisiana to peddle clocks. By 1856 he was back in Ohio and took out a license to marry Harriet P. Wyant but it was never returned. Eventually he ended up in

---

1 *Woodbridge and Vicinity*, Rev. Joseph . Dally, Madison, NJ, Hunterdon House, 1967, pgs. 132,224-226

2 Delaware Marriage Vol.I, p.237

Cowley County, Kansas, with a wife named Phebe and witnessed the homestead papers of James and Elizabeth McCurdy.

4. Phebe Catherine b. 1834 d. young and buried in Stark Cemetery, Porter twp.
5. Elizabeth Jane was in high school in 1851 and was to teach the next year. She became a milliner and married Henry C. Carhart an attorney and had 4 children the last 2 born in Galion.
6. Mary C. b. c. 1835, d. 1855 of consumption and buried with her sister Phebe.
7. Margaret C. became a milliner and married S. Lyn Cooper in 1860, son of Elias Cooper & Mary Talmage, and had a son Claude.
8. Albert b. Mar 1844 d. from measles in spring 1864 while fighting in the Civil War. Buried with his parents in Oak Grove Cemetery.
9. Henry Augustus who married Laura A. Brainhard about 1881 at Gilead and had 3 children.

Many of the family letters provide a picture of the settlement in central Ohio. The earliest was dated Feb 2nd 1834 to their brother Augustus was from Harriet's husband David White who were living in Kingston, Ohio.

Dear brother

I take this opertunity to let you know that we are well at present thank to God for all his mercies to us and hoping that these few Lines will find you in Good health. I now tak my pen to Cribble a few Lines to you in anser to Same of yours. I have had three leters from you since you left. This and this is the third that I have rote to you. I have not enjoyed Good helth for near three years but it is much beter at presant. We have four Children three boys and one girl. James Madison and francis and William Collun and pheby Catherine. I have not made Great improvements on my farm for my health and Ability would not admit it but we are able to live well. Father's girls is all Married and betsy is Dead. Father Ayers and his famley is well escept Enos Ayrs and he is Complaining and Has been for Some years and Does but little and Henery is after the girls already. Father Ayrs want to See you as well as the rest of us. He wants you when you write to Set a time when you will Come and See us. We want you to Come by Next Spring if not Sooner. He thinks that you might as well spend Some time and money that way as eny other way and there is a good deal to be Lernt by traveling. You wanted to know if thare was any Schools in this part that Langues is taght in. There is a siminary in Worthing 6 miles North of Columbus and a Collage at Mount vernon and theare is others in the State and thare is the new Reformed medical College at Worthington which Sistom of practice is thought to be by meny the best mode of practise and the Reguinitions for Admitance first A Good moral Character, Second A Good English Education. The price of going through is 150 Dollars in advance or 175 at the Close of the term. Board Can be had att one Dollar A week if you wish to be a Docter. I think thet you had beter Come and attend that Some Can Go threw in a year. This Society is a branch of the Same Society in New york. Then come home my Lad and go to that. Sir in your Leter to father, you Said that money was the Root of all evil and you Said the Scriptures Said So. I Cant belive it tht A peace of Cold metle or paper can be the Root of all evil. Neither Does the Scriptures Say So. Search and See. There is Great improvements made here Since you Left. This part if you want to know we would Say Come and See. You can Come by water Nearly all the way. The canals in this state is nearly completed and our markets here grows beter this season. The wheet crops was very much injured and Corn Crops don't look as well as usel. You must tkae your time in Reading this Letter that you may git my meaning for it is poorly Cribbled in Deed for it is

*probible tht you have more tim to reed than I have to write. Nothing more at
presant but Remains you Efectionate Brother and Sister*
    David and Harriet White

On Jun 18th 1836 Henry, who was in Bennington, wrote to Augustus who was now in
Worthington, Ohio. Lacking in detail it mentioned why Carpenter and Dwinnell had not received their
back issues of medical papers from Augustus. By 1844 Augustus was in Jeffersonville, Indiana. Henry
wrote to him that the last news about him came from David White in regard to some papers and that
Caroline, his "wife", had stayed with David a year ago and was not remarried. Henry continued,
Father has begun to build a new house. I talk of going out west to the upper Mississippi River but the
river had a destructing deluge this year and I have not moved. The next early letter from Henry to
his brother is dated Apr 18th 1847 from Bennington. By then Henry and Lydia had three children,
their father had remarried, and other family members were well. In response to Augustus' inquiry
about Ohio, Henry wrote:

> *We have Railroads building and in contemplation in all directions through the
> State. There is a rail road nearly completed from Sandusky City to Cincinnati by
> way of Tiffin, Belfountain, Urbanna, Springfield, Zena, Lebanon and soon another
> road is completed from Sandusky city to Mansfield and is going to Mountvernon,
> Newark &c. One is going from Cleveland to Cncinnati by the way of Mansfield.
> Soon to Columbus. We expect it will go through Bennington. They surveyed it once
> through to Harmony, Bennington, Kingston and say itis the nearest and best
> route...Bennington has improved considerable since you was here last. We number
> about two hundred and fifty voters. F. P. Freeman moved from Rahway, New
> Jersey, on the lot north of Fathers on the hill...He has put up several frame
> buldings and is now building a large farm house on top of the hill. We made
> application for a county...Mount gilead has ben trying for twenty five years and
> cant comit. We have the strongest claim in the State. Freemans son is our main
> man...Most all our neighbors...has built frame houses...Spring ice froze last night
> nearly an inch thick...We had fine crops last summer...Wheat remarkably good,
> apples in abundence. Peach buds has just begun to swell...Soft maple is just blown
> out Apr 8th. So you can observe the difference between...Ohio and Arkansas. People
> here talk a good deal about the Mexican war. Some in favor and some against...We
> have just heard of the capture of Veracruce. Land here is ? to ten dollars for wood
> lots and there is not many farms for sale now. Five hundred dollars would buy 25-
> 30 acres.*

Harriet and her son' Francis and David made the following replies:

> *Feb 12th 1848, Bennington, Ohio*
> *My Uncle Augustus, Helena, Arkansas*
>   *Agreeable to your request to Father in the letter you sent Requesting
> information about the coledge at Delaware. Having been living in Delaware for
> some time past And went to school some, I have had the opertunity of becoming
> acquainted with the President & Professers. The [?] Edward I F [?] is [?]
> Literature. The [?] H. M. Johnson is Prof. of Ancient Language. The [?] H. M. Merie
> is Prof. of Science. The [?] L. D. McCab is Prof. of Mathematics. And Prof. Williams
> & Meirs Teacher in the Preparatory Department. Good Board can be had at
> Boarding Houses for/from $1.50 to 1.75 per week at Hotells from $2.00 - 2.50. The
> tuition Fee's amount to $30.00 per year. And where students room and board*

themselves in the coledge building, Board & Tuition will amount to But about one Hundred Dollars Per Year. I remain your Nephew   Francis White.

Sir after A delay I would tell you that we received your leter and was glad to hear that you are well. We are well at presant enjoing tolerabriel the [?]. we feel that we are growing older and the time will son be here when we shall be silent indeed to friends and things Here. I got a Lane in Bennington on my farm and is something in the Dressing bed Elss I ahve traided more for two years then Common for me. I have been over the mountains. Visited several of the Citties to East. I have Generly drived cattle. Father Ayers is well as common. He fails very much and complains of his Head. His wife was the widow of Abreham wells old and homely and loves her biters and I think in the presant station is not much comfort to him. Nor to her near Relations. Father no dout was depraved when he got her. She was no Aunt Jane but no more of that. Enos and family is well and Henerys two is well. Madison married Almeda Hore. Francis White startes to morow for Cincinta and expects to go into Bookkeping in that place. He has rote to you Respecting the Colage At Delaware as he was beter Aguated with things. I would just say that I believe it to be the best situation in our State. I have no heard enything from Caroline for a considerable time and cant tell you enything about her. We have been tring here to get it new county benington for the center and have not yet Luck too. I remin your friend and brother-in-law   David White

Dear Brother

I now think I will talk a litle to you. I thout when I received your latter I would write you a letter myself but David and Francis got ahead of me. I was glad to hear from you. I thank you for your present and you mentioned that you would like to have mine, the Children laughed And thought if you should see it you wouldent now who it was for I have lost all my fore teeth. I adsepct you would like to know something about the children. Madison is married and has one child. Francis has gone south. William is learning the sadler trade. Betsy thinks her self almost a young woman. Mary had fever and Ague all the fall and has not grown much. Margret is as fat as a pig. Albert is fore years old in Mar next. And that is all the children. And All I expect will be. The girls send thear best respects to you. David would like to have you come back. And have not forgot thear dol baby. Well I recognize you will think this noncence and I will stop. We commenced this letter on Sunday and it is now wensdy evening and I am all alone for the familey is all to bed. And I must bring my epistel to a close for the present. I want you when you receive this leter to write And tel us wether you ever think of Comming back or not. You dident say what business you was in. I should like if you can to try And see Francis if you could . He thout he would write you A leter when he got thear. So no more at present. But remain your Sister   Harriet White

Not knowing where to write his brother in Arkansas, Henry responded to a letter he received at Christmas. It is dated Dec 30th 1848. Henry was always fascinated by the stars and heavenly manifestations.

The phenomenon which you spoke of...was as bright here as there. I presume it was very light indeed and very red in spots but I thought no thing of it as such occurrances often hapen. [Was Henry was speaking of the northern lights/aurora borealis?] Father has deeded Enos ninety five acres on the south side of the farm which leaves a strip on the north side 20 rods wide containing about 30 acres. This he keeps in his own posession. Enos is to take care of Father as long as he lives. He has repaired the old cabin and lives in that. Father and mother lives in the frame...Henry seems to offer his older brother advice on where he would do better in land speculation...I should not wonder if you should get the gold fever and start for California in the spring. The fever rages very high all through the States and I expect thousands will take off before one year. I would not mind going if I had no family to take care of. I expect we all will soon be rich whether we go or stay at home...Our cities is more than twice as large as they was in 1840. Cincinnati has upwards of 100,000. Columbus 14,000, Cleveland 14,000 and all the rest in proportion. The legislature made us a new county last winter. Morrow is the name with the county seat at Mount Gilead...its improving very fast since...They had got a railroad under contract from Cleveland to Columbus then to Cincinnati. It goes through Gilead thence to Delaware...They will have it done in a year or so to...So you see we will soon be surrounded by railroads. Freeman has quite a village of is own. They have a post office there. Marengo is the name...Woodberry has not improved much. Direct you letter to Marengo, Morrow Co., O.

Augustus must have been thinking about going to California as Henry wrote on Apr 5th 1849 saying:

I would like to see you once more before you go to California. I think California is a great country. would like to go there myself very well but I don't expect I ever shall...I don't see any thing to hinder you from going. I should like the climate very much as it is a very mild climate. I should like to then pick up that root of all evil. There is a great many going from Ohio to the land of gold. There were the usual comments about relatives, weather with rain and little snow, and a bad wheat crop.

The following Aug 18th Henry responded to a Jul 28th 1849 letter from Augustus. Henry thought Augustus had started for Ohio and had died on the road with cholera:

...cholery is very bad on the rivers and large towns. It has been very bad in Columbus. 110 of the convicts in the penitentiary has died...very bad in Sandusky City. Out of a population of four to five thousand about one hundred left though they did not all dye, many of them fled to other parts. There has not been any of it nearer than Columbus with the exception of a few cases where they have fled...

Summer was dry with wheat a total failure. The topic of speculation in land seems to consume much of their thoughts. Henry stated that he knew of none less then $100 and one was bought at Mt. Vernon for that price.

Thomas Freeman sent to New York and bought eight or ten. He gave one hundred and thirty five dollars a piece. He is now in Illinois locating them...there is a great emmigration from the east to western states...Wisconsin, Iowa, and...Minnesota...a good many in Ohio in the northwestern corner. There is a good deal of Congress land there yet. Probably you can get them as cheap in Cincinnati or some where on the route...

Henry sold his 29 acres for $300 and moved the family to South Nankin Township, Wayne Co., Michigan sometime after Aug 1849 as shown in the 1850 census. Eventually his mail caught up with him for he wrote to Augustus next on Mar 16th 1851.

After the usual family news that came to him by mail, he noted that he lived close by the Michigan Central RR which does more business than any one yard in the west. This was followed by news in land speculation. There is no Congress land near here but plenty in the west and northwest in Michigan. Better deals are in Wisconsin, Iowa, or Minnesota, none in Illinois. Freeman has been speculating there for two or three years in Illinois, Wisconsin and Iowa and made a good deal of money. He bought land warrants for $134 each and sold 160 acres lots for $300 to $400 each in a short time and selling a quarter section for $200 to $300. It's a good business to make a quick sale without making any improvements. A railroad is being built from Chicago to Galena. Soon will have one from the Mississippi to San Francisco and Astoria. I don't think you could do much hatting as hats are all made east by machinery. I have forty acres and want to plant 5 or 6 in corn. Corn is 50 cents a bushel, flour $4.00 per barrel. There is a chance for a good market here as navigation is open on the lakes, boats running briskly. Our railroad and lakes is a great thorough fare. Uncle Daniel's [son] Joseph lives near Quincy City, Illinois.

On Jan 18th 1852 Henry wrote a brief letter from South Nankin to his brother in Helena, Phillips Co., Arkansas:

Respected Brother

I have been looking for a letter from you for a long time but have not received any yet. I want to hear from you very much so I thought I would send you a few lines. I have just received a letter from Madison White. He and his father is in Woodbury yet keeping store. They were all well when he wrote. Francis is in Cincinnati clerking in an iron store. He gets eight hundred dollars a year. He is a preacher of the gospel. He has been preaching about two years. William is in Missouri in Boonville. He has been there nearly 2 years. Father is living with Enos. He is quite smart yet. We have had a very cold winter so far it is not good sleighng. We are all well at present. I expect to rent my place this year and go down to Ohio a visiting. I want to do down in Apr. David's folks wants to hear from you. They think you are ded. I want you to write as soon as you receive this letter so I can receive it before I go to Ohio. Direct as usual...
Your friend and Brother Henry C Ayres
If you shouldent receive this in time direct to Marengo, Morrow County, Ohio. I expect to stay there a year at any rate.

Francis M. White wrote from Cincinnati to his Uncle Augustus the following on Nov 24th 1852:

Dear Uncle, It is so long perhaps since you have heard from me or known any thing about that perhaps you may have forgotten that there ever was such a boy. I was quite a boy when you last saw me. I have been here in the City now some five years, often during this time I have contemplated writing to you but have never got about it until now. I have resently paid the folks up in old Bennington a short visit. I found them quite well. The old farm looks quite forsaken. Grandfather is living with Uncle Enos. He was fully as smart as I expected to see him. I had not seen him for five years. Henry's folks have been living in Michigan for sum part of the time I left home. They have now returned and are living over the creek. Uncle H. said he had written to you some time since but had not yet received an answer. Fathers folks are all well. Mother begins to look quite old. Grandfather said I must write you and then let them know how you were. Enclosed you will find one of my

Henry returned to Ohio and moved back to Bennington where he bought a small farm. The weather for the next three years had it ups and downs with crops. On Apr 1ˢᵗ 1855 land was the major topic in Henry's letter. His recommendation to his brother was Omaha, Nebraska, suggesting he might join him there.

Get near steam boat navigation and where the great western Railroad will pass. Kansas is first rate but has too many slave holders. There will be war there yet. Oregon is probably good but a long journey.

Henry was aware of the Kansas-Nebraska Act of May 1854 that overturned the 1820 Missouri Compromise and sent settlers rushing to the territory each hoping to make it into either a slave or abolitionist state. The controversy erupted in May 1856 at Lawrence, Kansas. On Dec 22ⁿᵈ 1855 Henry acknowledge that he has received Augustus' letters including the one with $5 which was intended to buy something for his namesake, now 9 years old. Augustus was now living in Council Bluff, Iowa. Henry felt Augustus was in the center of the thoroughfare between the eastern and western states and felt he should buy more land if he could afford it.

I think you have made a good location though you got swindled pretty bad on the start that will serve as a warning to be on your watch. You must keep your eye peeled for these yankees...You could make money by raising cattle. I have long thought it I should go to Iowa I should steer for about where you are. Don't be discouraged. Henry then asked for the usual information where Augustus is living. Always with the chatter about moving there but his wife won't so he would just have to make a visit. Since Henry hadn't heard anything from Iowa, he wrote on Feb 5ᵗʰ 1857:

We heard that there has been a number of people fro:e to death this winter in Iowa. It has been cold here also with little snow. He mentioned a Solomon Brownell who didn't like Council Bluffs with its many sand hills and went back to Nebraska...we have another boy three months old. The letter ended with the usual question on how Augustus prospers. Henry got a reply which he answered on Mar 26ᵗʰ very briefly. Our baby is sick and Father is failing slowly. Times are hard with hope of a business revival this summer. Henry's next brief letter was dated Feb 19ᵗʰ 1858. Henry was disappointed to hear that his brother was still in Iowa. Sleighing is good with six inches of snow. The next short letter dated Aug 8ᵗʰ said summer was wet and crops poor. There is scarcely any fruit this year. Times are dull and money scarce. I received the Bluff Bugle you sent. Please send another when convenient as I like to read those papers.

The 1860 census was revealing. It noted that after secession the remaining 23 states in the Union had about 4 million men of combat age. Factories employed over a million workers, there were 20,000 miles of railroad and the banks held 81% of the nation's bank deposits and $56 million in gold. The eleven Confederate states population was about 9 million including nearly 4 million slaves. One hundred thousand workers were employed in 20,000 factories and there were about 9,000 miles of railroad tracks. The Union and Confederate states were not *one nation under God*, but two nations, divided by politics, culture and economics.[1] Newly elected Lincoln was on his way to his inauguration when word came that Jefferson Davis had been chosen provisional president of the Confederate States of America. Neither of these men were particularly popular with Lincoln getting 40% of the votes. The Confederate states fate had been decided by 854 men selected by their legislature. Of those, 157 voted against secession, leaving less that 700 mostly wealthy and upper-middle class men deciding the fate

---

1 Davis, 150-151

of 9 million people. Davis actually wanted a bid for the White House but knew he would never get northern support. At age 53 and in poor health he was elected on Feb 9th 1860 by the Confederate Provisional Congress, not the people.[1] Senator Jefferson Davis stated: *We are probably soon to be involved in that fiercest of human strife, a civil war.*[2] With Georgia's secession, its Governor called out for troops and the women began preparing their soldiers for war. Also in that census, Henry and Lydia were in Bennington twp. with four children, $800 in real estate and $200 in personal.

Wm. T. Sherman wrote to a southern friend:

> *....You people of the South don't know what you are doing. This country will be drenched in blood, and God only knows how it will end. ...You people speak so lightly of war; you don't know what you're talking about...You mistake, too, the people of the North. They are a peaceable people but an earnest people, and they will fight too. They are not going to let this country be destroyed without a mighty effort to save it...If your people will but stop and think, they must see in the end that you will surely fail.*[3]

The war began with the firing on Fort Sumter on Apr 12th 1861. Henry wrote to Augustus on the following Sep 20th: *The last time I wrote I said I was going to Missouri. I did not go and am not sorry. I have not sold yet.* He mentioned the boys' enlisting and that Elizabeth has been in Columbus a year working in the Lunatic asylum: Father is getting to be and old man and will be 86 this summer. It is dry here but crops are pretty good. Write soon and let me know how you are getting along."

On Aug 25th 1862 Henry sold nearly 33 acres in Ohio to James Culver. Then in Nov he purchased 74+ acres in Meridian Township, Ingham Co., Michigan. The last 50 acres in Ohio was sold to one of Lydia's relatives, Moses Gidley, on Jul 5th 1863 and they moved to Michigan. Come Nov they bought 30 more acres in Meridian from Benjamin Wood. Henry's sent the following letter to his brother, Augustus, on May 20th 1865 from Lansing.

> *Respected Brother. its ben a long time Since I corisponded with you. well you must excuse my negligence and I probably will do beter in the future. I have had so much care on my mind, so much writing to the Boys in the army and distant friends and exciting war news to read besides the care of seling, moving and setling again in the woods, all has kept me busy though I have not forgoten you. We are all well as comon hoping this to find you the same. I have ben to work pretty hard this winter and spring being alone, ben choping clearing spliting railes making fence and lately plowing and planting. Gus listed last Oct in the 12th Michigan infantry. he want eighteen yet when he listed. he got 400 from county and I took the money and bought him thirty acres joining us. With a litle improvement on it gave 450 for the lot. I have 75 acres. Gus has ben in Arkansas all winter garding the rail road from duvalls bluff to litle rock. they are mustering them out now, so we are lookin for him home before long. he is a noble boy stands plump six feet high and quite hand some. his hair curls beautiful. he is a great money maker, very industrous and saving. he wrote sometime ago he had made 52 dollars geting out railroad ties. one Boy from that regiment says he never saw Gus gamble or drink any whisky, but was most always to work his leisure hours, very good natured and fond of company, always singing or whistleing. you need not be a shamed of him for a nephew and name Sake. Our oldest Boy Charles Wesley got home in Mar. ben gone most four years through all the war. he has ben through many a hard siege and ben grased several times with rebel bullets. he has ben in the marine brigade*

1*Ibid.*, 154, 179

2Davis, 149

3 Michael Leavy, *Railroads of the Civil War*, 2010, Westholme Publishing, LLC, Yardley, PA, p. 140

on the Missippi river for the two last sumers. he is a faithful boy. one of the Soldiers that put down the rebellion, he was at the fall of Vicksburg. Well the rebellion is a bout wound up. they caught old Jef the other day runing away with his wifes dress on. I guess that wil be a bout the last scene acted in the grand drama of the great rebellion. Well its ben a long pull and a hard strugle but the old flag still waves over the land of the free and the home of the Brave. We would like to hear from you again and learn how you get along out there. Lib got a leter from you last sumer. We like this country first rate. we are scraching a long trying to make a living and clear up the woods. I came up here on purpose to get more land so as to give the Boys a chance to get a start in the World. We are only five miles from the capital Lansing which is destined to be a big city. Wesley has 40 acres which makes us 145 acres all together. its very good land here, crops looks nice here now. We have potatoes and other vegetables up and growing fine. Gus has a nice album and we would like to se your photo graph picture in it. our old Father died over a year ago. Well he was quite an old man and couldent take much satisfaction living. Enoses folks was all well the last I herd from them. David Whites folks lived in Delaware the last I herd from them. two of their Boys had died. our folks is going to town so I must stop. Write Soon and give all the particular news from your respected Brother.   H. C. Ayers

The following was written on a postcard that had the corner missing where the stamp had been cut out.

Feb 19th 1866, Lansing, Michigan
To: Augustus Ayers, Rocton, Kansas
*   Respect Brother I received your letter two ag[missing] Lizzie received one [missing]. We are all moderately we [missing] Some pictures taken and [missing] Sister Harriet lives in Cardington, Morrow Co. at presant with Madison. She has ben sick but was recovering last I herd from her. You must ben mistaken. I never got Fathers old Bible. Enos has it. I cant tell anything about Fathers and Mothers Marriages Berths or Deths. Father was born Aug 16th 1775 I think if I ant mistaken. Ant jane and our Mother was both berried on Fathers Birthday Aug 16 thirty years a part. ant jane died in 1845. mother must died 1815. Father died in 64 I believe. His last wife was old Abe Wellses widow. Brother of old Ike Wells Elias Willsons wifes mother. She was a ?-ken old of no account. its ben a warm winter for Michigan, hardly ben down to zero this winter. lots of rain. Several thunder showers, frogs all out new years day.*
*   H. C. Ayers*

This postcard was responsible for my father and his cousin, Seymour, to going to Ohio to get family information from this Bible. My understanding is was the Cassius Ayers family that they visited. Meanwhile back in Ohio, Harriet and David White's youngest son, Henry Augustus, wrote to his Uncle Augustus on Dec 6th 1868 from Galion.

Dear Uncle
*   I take this opertunaty to write you a few lines. We have not ben able until latley to find your whareabouts. Mother susposed you ware dead entil Uncle Henry wrote to a Mr. Shotwell in our town and sent your address to us.*
*   We are living in a town of 5 thousand inhabitents. I have 2 sisters and a brother living hear & prospering fine. Father & Mother is engaging good health for old folks.*

Ma looks as young as she did 10 or 20 years ago. I have ben clerking in a dry goods store for the last 3 years.

Uncle Enoses ware all well the last time we heard from them. They live so far back from any rail way that we don't see them very often.

We wought like to hear from you very mutch. Ma wants to know if you have ever married yet & so fourth. As it is church time and not knowing as this will find you, I will close to try and do better next time.   From   HAW

I am very mutch obliged to you for the $5.00 you have me for my name years ago. Father bought 5 sheep & kept them untill I grough up & then put them out on shares until they increased to over 1 hundred & sold them for 3.50 a head.

Please Answere

From Henry Augustus White

The following letter by Henry Augustus dated Mar 20th 1869 from Galion was the last one that survived from the White family.

Dear Uncle

We are all well as usual. All the children have had the meesles but are wll over them. Thare has ben more meesles in town & surounding cuntry that was ever known before. Other ways it is helthy hear. The weather has been very cold all this month. Thare is about 2 & 3 inches of know on the ground now. Business is very dull for some time. Back hear thare has been sem excitment about rail roads hear and citizens are wating to see. Waiting till thay are settled before thay do much building &c. I expect I will stay whare I am. I like the dry goods trade very much. As times is harde I do not know as I could do any better. When I get a little older I think I will try my fortune in the West or South.

William has jest got home from the South. He has a Cotten Plantation in Louisiana and has ben spending the winter thare. We heard from uncle Enos about a month ago by the way of Mr. Shotwell who is living in this town. Thay was all well then. I was out to Iowa City 2 summers ago. Is that neer your home. I think I would like it out thare if it was not so windy. Enclosed please find my foto which you will se is not very handsom. But Handsom is as Handsom does, So Says the old motto. Our foulks sends thair Serpect to you and Ma is verry anxious to see your picture. Write soon.

Yours Truly   H. A. White

Apr 3rd 1870, Lansing, Michigan

To: Augustus Ayers

Respected Brother. I thought I would send you a few lines asking a good many questions. Lizie and her man and Wesley has got the Kansas fever and I dont know but we all will get out there yet. I sent to Chicago got a leter and paper from C. N. Pratt, General agent of the National Land Company with a map of Kansas having all the Counties and towns marked along the road. I se you are in the 20 mile limet. We want to get all the information we can in referance to them parts. these long winters here I dont like where we have to feed 8 or 10 monts in a year. Snow ant all gone yet and the frost ant near out of the ground. Will have to feed a month yet or longer. Snow fell first in Oct and I guess ant all gone yet. Have you had any snow this winter and how long have you to feed catle. of course Horses wants feding longer. how early could you put in oats and spring wheat this spring. you know I supose that Kansas took the big gold medal at the pamological meting at Philadelphia last fall for having the best fruit there. thats a big cap for Kansas.

What can farmes be bought for with some improvements and orchard and tolerable buildings. as you have ben there now a year, you can se how you like the winter. My Sonenlaw wants to know what a good team of horses costs there. he wants to go with his team and what is a good new wagon worth comon two horse. he has a new one good span here worth about 300 three hundred dollars. which is worth the most there, geldings or mares. Lizzie wants to make butter out there. think she can make it pay, that seems to be her trade. I think I can get a living there a good deal easier than here. that Rail road will soon be a great thorough fare and farmes will sell high. We are all well as comon. My wifes helth is poor evry winter and spring. She is consumptive. I think her helth would be better there. She is always helther in warm wether. Lizzie is going to write some so I will stop. Write Soon as convenient. Your friend and Brother.

H. C. Ayers

P.S. how far west is that Pacific Railroad finished West and how far up Kansas river dose steamboats run.

Henry and Lydia built a log home and barn on their 75 acres in Meridian Township. They lived in it until their deaths. The family spoke of Chief Okemos' tribesmen coming to the log house for handouts. The 1880 census noted that Henry was 67, Lydia 63; their eldest son Wes, a carpenter aged 38, and youngest son William Francis [WF], a telegraph operator aged 23, both living with their parents. His son Augustus "Gus" and wife farmed nearby. Gus' son Seymour A. Ayres spent many hours listening to tales told by his grandparents and to him the family owes gratitude for his interest in writing some family history.

Henry died Apr 13th 1886, 4:13 p.m. at Meridian, MI, at age 73½ yrs.[1] There is no record of his death reorded in Ingham County Records. He was buried Apr 14th 1886 and later re-interred in Mt. Hope Cemetery, Lansing, MI, in a large gated crypt with his son's name *Augustus Ayres* over the door. Henry's wife, Lydia, son Augustus and Gus' second wife, Bina, are also buried there. Lydia died Jul 26th 1888, at Meridian.[2] Bina was a relative of WF's wife, Ella.

Land where the farm was located is now part of Michigan State University. Years ago there was a building called the girl's cabin which stood on the remaining wood lot of the farm. Within Henry & Lydia's log house was a hook made from a limb's crotch on which Henry hung his cap. Long after their deaths, one end of the house was removed to make a tool shed and Henry's cap still hung there undisturbed for many years. Phoebes, who return to nest in the same site each year, had built their nest in Henry's cap. Year after year the birds came back to nest. As the lower logs on the old cabin decayed and the split shingle roof gradually eased down to earth, Henry's cap came with it. Mother phoebe lost her nest.

Henry's wife, Lydia Wood, was about four years old when she first lived at Galway, Saratoga Co., NY, with her Quaker grandparents, Amos and Elizabeth (Mosher) Reynolds. Her parents lived at LeRay, Jefferson Co., NY, as shown in the 1820 census. It was here that Lydia learned to spin and weave from her grandmother. Lydia described her aging grandfather, Amos Reynolds, as a man who suffered from rheumatism and spent much time sitting before the fire in his later years. He died in 1832 at Galway. Lydia said her grandmother, Elizabeth (Mosher) Reynolds, was the business head of the family. Lydia was about age 20 when she returned to her parents in Jefferson County. There she was granted a certificate from LeRay Monthly Meeting to Alum Creek MM in Ohio on Jul 20th 1837.

Henry Cook & Lydia Wood Ayers eldest son:

Charles Wesley[8] Ayers/Ayres was born in a modest log cabin on a farm located in Bennington Twp., Delaware Co., Ohio. His grandfather, Thomas Ayers, was born in New Jersey and had purchased the land and settled decades earlier. Charles Wesley's birth was on a cool day in April

---

1 Ayers Family Bible

2 Ingham Co. Death Bk 2: 35

1842. The 4th to be exact. He was the eldest of four children born to Henry and Lydia Ayers. His mother, a former Quaker, came from New York state. His father came from New Jersey as a young boy. His only sister was Elizabeth Jane (Lib or Lizzie). Two brothers followed: Augustus Seymour (Gus) and William Francis (Will or WF). Wes, as he was called by his family, was expected to help with the chores in running a farm. His father had cleared the land enough to raise some crops. There were still ample trees left to supply wood for heating and cooking. The pleasant aroma of burning hardwood from the fireplace permeated the cabin. Any source of light inside was scant at best and night brought out the burning of kerosene lamp wicks whose odor mingled with the smell of burning wood. Winters in Ohio were snowy. Their horse with its ringing bells pulling a sleigh over the sparkling mounds of snow became the family's favorite winter recreation. Sounds of music also permeated the cabin as his father played the flute. Wes learned to play the violin and his fiddling brought a lifetime of pleasure to family and friends. Wes also learned the carpentry trade in his youth. His life spanned nearly 86 years. He died on Jan 21st 1927 and was buried in the family plot in Mt. Hope Cemetery in Lansing, Michigan, three days later. A GAR (Grand Army of the Republic) monument was placed at his grave. His eldest granddaughter born in 1918 knew him best of the three grandchildren known to him. She and her slightly younger sister would put his bent aging body in a little red wagon and pull him uptown to his barber. I was the first of three more granddaughters who only knew him through stories, letters and photos.

Wes was seven when his parents decided to move to Nankin township in Wayne County, Michigan. They traveled by rail from central Ohio to the Detroit area. Trains began sweeping over America in 1830. They were noisy and prone to breakdowns, yet faster than horses. Stubby four wheel steam engines pulling a load of wood for fuel was followed by cars for passengers or freight. They ran on wood rails covered with strap iron. During the family's trip a strap broke loose and penetrated the floor of one car creating chaos among frightened women as men tried to calm them. This was the cause of frequent accidents, some fatal, with this type of rail. Any chunks of wood that were too large to be used to fuel the engine were tossed along the side the tracks by the fireman. Curious boys sometimes get into trouble. Wes was one. He was standing too close to the fireman when he was suddenly hit with a chunk of wood that knocked him off the train. He fell into a pile of fresh manure by the rails. He got up, scraped his clothes as best he could, and jumped back on the train expressing how he didn't like that experience very much. One can only ponder what words he actually chose to describe his situation. After a few years of living in Michigan, the family returned to Ohio.

Years rolled on as differences between North and South over trade and slavery had been simmering like a witch's brew in a giant cauldron. Two diverse American societies had emerged. With new states came discord over the slave issue. Many Southern plantations were dependent on them. There was little concern by Wes' Quaker raised mother for some of her Wood relatives had been hiding negros in their wagons taking them from town to town to get them further north where they would be safe. The process was known as the Underground Railroad. Then came a string of Secessionists and shots fired on Fort Sumter.

A Call to Arms

On Apr 15th 1861 Lincoln called for seventy-five thousand volunteers. It was a cool overcast April day in Ohio when Wes responded to Lincoln's call. He and had just celebrated his 19th birthday on Apr 4th. The general naive thinking was that this rebellion would be quickly quelled. After saying goodbye to his grandfather, Thomas Ayers, his parents, siblings, and other relation and friends, Wes joined many men from this farm area and headed for the rails which could be heard at the family farm. Railroads became strategic in the war and created a path for years of fighting over great distances.

Southern women had been preparing their soldiers for the inevitable war. They gave their sweethearts embroidered slippers and all kinds of things. These young gentlemen brought their dress suits and a quantity of fine linen. Nearly every soldier had a negro servant and a wide selection of eating utensils. They planned to live elegantly in camp and make a pretentious entry when they reached the Northern Capitol. Unlike southern males, the Ohio men packed a few of their belongings and some food as they boarded a belching train. Their destination was Camp Jackson near Columbus.

These young volunteers had no concept of what war was like. Since there were few qualified men to teach them, they had to learn the "business" along the way. Almost every significant commander in the Civil War had been together in the Mexican War thirteen years earlier. Now they were divided between the northern and southern armies. Some considered the war a political struggle. Most felt it was over slavery. Some of its generals came from the ranks of political officials who lacked knowledge in things military. Today it's called political payback. Of the youthful West Pointers from the class of 1857 who served on both sides, ten rose to rank of general or its honorary equivalent, brevet general, despite little experience.

Wes' enlistment ranked him as a Private in Co. I, Third Regiment Ohio Infantry, for three months. Of the ninety-eight men and officers enlisted in Company I, forty-four mustered out in three months including five officers and one for disability. The Third Ohio Volunteer Infantry consisted of ten companies, A thru I and K and served under two separate enlistment terms. The first enlistment term on Apr 16th 1861 was for three months. The second enlistment term on April 21st was for three years consisting of Company A - Columbus, Franklin County; Company B - Belmont County & Columbus, Franklin County; Company C - "Ohio State Guards" (Color Company) Athens County; Company D - Springfield, Clark County; Company E - Zanesville, Muskingum County; Company F - "Hamilton Guards" Hamilton, Butler County; Company G - Cincinnati, Hamilton County; Company H - Newark, Licking County; Company I - Cardington, Morrow County; Company K - Wellsville, Columbiana County & Licking County.

Rigid drilling began immediately. Eleven days after inception Wes's regiment was mustered into U.S. service. An election by ballot was held for field officers. John Beatty of Morrow County was elected Lt. Colonel. Can you imagine today's military enlisted men electing their officers? On April 28th a group was sent to Camp Dennison, near Cincinnati, with orders to prepare a suitable camp. The camp was named after the current governor of Ohio. It was located on the estate of deceased Christian Waldschmidt, a German minister, who came to Ohio from Pennsylvania and started a paper mill. His fieldstone mansion was listed as a tavern in 1850 and it became the commandants dwelling in November 1861. One general found it insulting to live in a deteriorating house. Waldschmidt's daughter had lived in a cottage on the estate which became the camp's guardhouse. Over 30,000 men volunteered creating a challenge to feed, house, train and supply uniforms and weapons. The sight selected was a newly planted cornfield on the west side of a railroad. The regiment spent its first night of field service without cover or tents. The remainder of the regiment arrived on April 30th bringing lumber and tools for construction of quarters. The regiment stayed in this camp throughout May. Drill practice was without arms. Muster rolls reveal that payment to the men was sporadic.

On May 19th 1861 Wes wrote from Camp Dennison to his sister, Elisabeth, who was working at the "Lunatic Hospital" in Columbus.

> *Dear Sister*
>
> *I received an answer from you soon after it was mailed and was glad to hear from you. I am very well at present and have some very good times here now although we hardly have enough to eat which makes it rather hard. It is reported that we will have to enlist for three years or be sent home before the three months is out-although we do not know whether it is so or not.*
>
> *We have not received our uniforms yet and do not know when we Shall but expect them soon. We have received the arms. I will tell Something about military*

Although these men were officially mustered out in August, it appears from Wes' letters that they were sent home earlier. Before field orders were received, recruiting parties were sent out for volunteers for three years in the Regiment. Supplies arrived around the end of May, a motley collection of old flint-locks altered to percussion and some blouses and gray pants. On June 12th the regiment was re-organized. The same officers re-elected. Wes was mustered-in for three years on June 15th, officially noted as June 20th. He had written to Lizzie June 14th.

Training included the customary standing at attention, shouldering a musket, and the various right or left faces. Most training, as Wes noted, was getting into a line of battle, marching in column formations in which they could fight. Once in action however, necessary commands during skirmishes became difficult to hear due to the noise of firing. Camp Dennison served as a military hospital in addition to training men for battle. The Camp was deactivated in September 1865, its barracks dismantled and the Waldschmidt home ceased as a residence.

Raw Men Sent Into Battle

With less than two months of training, the Third Ohio was sent off to battle in western Virginia, which became West Virginia two years later. George Brinton McClellan, age 34, a handsome West Point graduate was chosen to lead the Ohio State volunteers and promoted to Maj. General. He had distinguished himself in the Mexican War but resigned his commission to become superintendent of the Illinois Central Railroad as well as President of the Ohio and Mississippi Railroad. His skill and perfectionism was thought to be the answer to southern Gen. P.G.T. Beauregard. The northern press dubbed him Young Napoleon. In early June 1861 Confederates had taken Rich Mountain in a night attack. The Union wanted this region to use as a base to invade the Valley of Virginia. On June 3rd a portion of McClellan's Ohio and Indiana forces routed a small contingent of confederates in the town of Grafton. McClellan's men then occupied Grafton where the important Baltimore and Ohio RR had a roundhouse and other facilities. Rail lines were considered vital to defense. Though the Rich Mountain battle was a small victory, an elated press enlarged it into a major victory.

On Jun 20th 1861 the first three years' men left Ohio. They were supplied with arms and uniforms and ordered to proceed to Grafton. They traveled by rail from Camp Dennison to Columbus, then eastward toward Bellaire by the Ohio River where they arrived on June 22nd. Crowds had assembled at every station along the rail route across the state to bid the soldiers well. After crossing the Ohio River, their travel by rail continued some eighty miles reaching Grafton the next day. They were quartered in deserted houses at Fetterman two miles north of Grafton. After two days at Fetterman, they proceeded west by rail to Clarksburg where camp equipage was supplied. On June 25th the Third Ohio was brigaded with the Fourth & Ninth of Ohio and Loomis' Michigan Battery, with Brig. Gen. Schleich of Fairfield County commanding. From Clarksburg they advanced on foot southeast to Buckhannon in Upshur County until July 5th without incident. McClellan said: *No prospect of a brilliant victory shall induce me to depart from my intention of gaining success by maneuvering rather than fighting. I will not throw these raw men of mine into the teeth of artillery and intrenchments if it be possible to avoid it.*

While West Point graduate and Confederate Gen. Joseph E. Johnston was keeping Robert Patterson in check in the Shenandoah Valley, an important event and one of some consequence to the Confederates occurred in northwest Virginia beyond the western ridges of the Alleghaney Mountains. Confederate Gen. Robert S. Garnett occupied a position at Rich Mountain in Randolph County with Col. Pegram occupying the mountain top with sixteen hundred men. Both sides divided their armies to defend the passes at Rich Mountain and Laurel Hill. McClellan's goal was to secure the western region of Virginia for the North. A scouting party of fifty of Company A under Capt. O. A. Lawson was sent to check the road leading to the rebel position at Rich Mountain. Approaching Middle Fork bridge, they discovered the enemy occupied it. One man was killed and five wounded in trying to dislodge the rebels. The wounded were taken back to camp. Several skirmishes occurred on Jul 6th & 7th 1861. Advancing several days later, they discovered the dead man's body and buried it. It was written that it was the body of private Johns, the first of the Third Ohio to die in battle. Pvt. Edward H. Johns was age 21 when he enlisted for three months, then three years in Company E. Another skirmish occurred on the 10th.

Gen. William S. Rosecrans troops were on a flanking march before daybreak on July 11th to dislodge the Confederates from the passes. The path up the mountain on an obscure wagon road was rugged. Weather was uncertain with heavy intermittent long showers and sun breaks that filled the air with sultry heat. Laurel thickets and slippery stones in the wet soil made climbing laborious. The artillery at the top of the mountain had little effect on the men in the brush and trees. Col. Pegram was caught in front and behind and sought to escape. Six of his companies escaped, the rest surrendered. When Garnett heard the result at Rich Mountain, he was determined to evacuate Laurel Hill to Huttonsville by way of Beverly. With that road blocked, he was forced to retreat by a mountain in Hardy County with Union forces nipping at his heels. At one of the fords on the Little Cheat River, four companies of a Georgia regiment were cut off and Garnett was killed in a rear guard skirmish, the first General to be killed in the war. Results for Confederates, though not monumental in killed or wounded, was its loss of artillery, about seven hundred casualties and prisoners, and loss of nearly all the command's baggage. The Third Ohio was part of the division to advance directly on the enemy works, but the fight occurred at the rear of the fortifications and the regiment saw little fighting. In pursuit of the fleeing enemy, they proceeded to Beverly on July 12th. Their success was due to a poor distribution of Confederate forces numbering forty-five hundred infantry.

Jul 14th 1861 Wes wrote to his parents about his first experience in seeing dead after battle:

> *As you deserve my letter more than anyone and not having much time to write I will occupy the time in writing to you and let you know that I am still alive and among the living and enjoying good health although I am a considerably tired today as I have Mared twelve miles with a heavy load which is no easy job-- We are at present camped about twelve miles from Beverly out the Richmond and*

Charles W Ayres | Civil War Record.

My first Enlistment as private in Co I, 3d O.V.I Apr 23 -1861 under Capt John Beatty in Cardington O who was later Commissioned to Brig General. Were first sent to Camp Jackson Columbus. May 1st was Transfered to Camp Denison near Cincinnati was then Mustered for 3 Months. was then in a few days reorganized and Mustered for 3 years. the 15 of June were soon sent to West Virginia under Geo B McClelland was at the Battle of Rich Mountain was sent South to Camp Elk water Where we remained until Near Winter were transfered to Louisville Ky then South to camp Jefferson Where we remained until Spring then under Command Gen O M Mitchell

In Early Spring of 62 Moved for a Southern climate until the Capture of Huntsville Ala Remained there during summer While there was detailed as Body Guard for Gen O M Mitchell. In the fall was sent to Chase Gen Bragg who was moving his Army toward Louisville Ky. We followed him to Perryville where He gave us a Sharp Engagement, our Ranks were greatly depleted and I came out With my Cap being Shot from My Head. He retreated to Cumberland Gap then we Made for Nashville was taken Sick on the way and Sent to Louisville Hospital Was sent from there to Cincinnati Hospital Where I had an opportunity to Enlist in the M.M.B Was sent to Benton Barracks St Louis Mo

Wes writes about his service in the Union Army

Wheeling Pike. We left that place yesterday and arrived here last night and while on the road we came across some Secession Cavalry but were unable to take them they fired at our guide-- We have been expecting a fight every day for about a week but have not had the chance yet and it is not very probable that we will Soon as they run as fast as possible and keep out of reach they are afraid of us. I was in hearing distance of the battle near Roaring Creek rally, the minor battle known as Carrick's Ford. We were placed in ambush to cut off their retreat whare we expected to fire into them every minute but they did not come near us. we took up our Mar the next morning after the fight and went through the battle ground-- where I saw a hard Sight-- whare dead men and bones lay Scattered over the ground. I saw twenty eight dead men piled up together for to be burried which was a hard sight. they were badly whiped. Their were over a hundred killed and a great many more wounded.

Unfortunately, medical care or knowledge had not kept pace with weapon development or camp life. The sick and wounded mostly relied on kindness and amputations. There was no knowledge of sterile dressings or what caused dysentery, typhoid, or pneumonia. Doctors did discover that camp cleanliness was related to the men on sick call, but sanitation was rudimentary, and water, if it looked or smelled okay, was thought safe. Wes continued:

The[y] took over six hundred prisoners and a great many ran away. They took four pieces of cannon, two Six pounders and two twelve pounders of rifled cannon and all their camp equipage. I have no time to write anymore at present. From your Son Wesley Ayres

Tactics for the infantry was based on the use of a smoothbore musket and cannon with limited range and accuracy making bayonets vital in close combat. But muskets used in the Civil War were rifled making an enormous difference resulting in hideous casualties. It took generals a long time to learn that a new approach based on rifled equipment was necessary.

The newspapers reported the victor of Rich Mountain was young Union general, George McClellan, even though he had little to do with the minor victory. McClellan understood the Civil War would be fought in newspapers as well as in trenches. He made certain that telegraph lines followed him wherever he went. McClellan initially proved a superb organizer with good rapport with his troops. To his troops he remarked: *Soldiers of the Army of the West, I am more than satisfied with you.* But he lacked the strength of character and single-mindedness like that of Grant or Farragut and was easily tricked by Confederate generals. McClellan was first fired by Lincoln after his failure to pursue Lee after Antietam. His second firing came after being within six miles of Richmond with a large, well-equipped army and failure to act. No matter how many troops he had at his disposal he would request more, swearing that the enemy had twice as many. His indecisiveness and caution would prove to be costly.

From there the Third Ohio went to Huttonsville and Cheat Mountain Summit where the pursuit was abandoned and they began fortifying the passes of the Alleghanies. The Third Ohio returned to the foot of Cheat Mountain where they engaged in erecting a telegraph line from Huttonsville to the post at Cheat Mountain Summit. On Aug 4th 1861 the regiment marched to Elkwater Creek in company with the Fifteenth Indiana Infantry and Loomis' battery and commenced building a series of fortifications across the valley. These activities kept the units occupied until Sep 11th. Meanwhile on Sep 4th Confederate Gen. Polk had ordered an invasion into Kentucky to take control of the Mobile & Ohio Railroad terminus at Columbus. Gen. Grant responded on the 6th by going into Paducah, KY, where he seized control of the north end of the New Orleans & Ohio Railroad and part of the Tennessee River. Wes, not having received a reply from his last letter written to Lizzie, wrote again from Camp Elk Fork on Sep 8th 1861:

Dear Sister   Having answered your letter which I received some time ago but not having an answer in return I begin to think that you had not received it and for fear I will write again and let you know that I am still among the living and enjoying pretty good health. I received a letter from father lately they are well at home...We have not received our pay yet but are expecting it every day. I am in hopes that I will get to go home this winter and if we should take up our winter quarters in or near Ohio, it is probable that I will. Thare has nothing happened of much importance Since I wrote last consequently I will not have much to write about. We are still at work on the fortification. Thare has several regiments came here lately. We are expecting to have a fight here pretty Soon as the Secessionists are advancing this way. Thare is a strong force on the other Side of them they will Soon have to fight or give up. Colonel Beatty has gone home to get Some new recruits for our company. They are beginning [to] think at home that I am home Sick. to be Shure I would like to See the folks but you need not think that for I could not content my Self at home to Stay. I will not write anymore this time and write more some other time but write to me as soon as you can. From Your affectionate Brother Wesley Ayres*
I will send you a laurel ring. Get some of the boys to finish it with fine Sand paper and not put it in water as it will rot it.* [Mountain laurel was prominent in this area. Its wood was used for carving.]

Confederate Gen. Robert E. Lee was sent to repair the scene of operations at Elk Water without delay after Gen. Garnett was killed in his retreat. Lee's force numbered about sixteen thousand. Their advance across the precipitous Alleghanies in deep mud was to engage the Union forces in Randolph County. Gen. John Reynolds held the approaches to Beverly with ten to twelve thousand men, the larger part entrenched at the junction of Tygart's Valley River and Elk Run, called by the Union Elk Water. The remainder held the summit at Cheat Mountain on the best road flanked by earthen and log entrenchments and protected on every side by dense abatis, an obstacle of trees with sharpened or bent branches directed toward the enemy rendering it inaccessible. Norman C. White of Wes' Company I was discharged for disability by Surgeon's certificate at Cheat Mountain Pass. Lee had received imperfect reconnaissance of the Union's position on Cheat Mountain and ordered his forces to move on Cheat Mountain and Elk Water. The weather was cold. After much physical effort, his forces were in place to make an attack on Elk Water. They waited for a signal from Col. Rust at Cheat Mountain. His assignment was to converge the widely separated columns. But Rust who found the area unapproachable, gave no signal. Lee made his advance on Elk Water Sep 11th. While coming up the Huntersville Road he met the Third Ohio, the Fifteenth and Seventh Indiana volunteers, plus a section of Loomis' Battery, who challenged the advance at Elk Water Junction in several sharp skirmishes. Lee abandoned all of it. The Third Ohio kept active until the rebels fled to Mingo Flats located about thirteen miles south of Huttonsville. On Oct 3rd two companies of the Third Ohio under Capt. McDougall scouted the area as far as Marshall. They were to make a reconnaissance at Big Springs on the 6th but found it abandoned. The Third was now indoctrinated to the hardships of marching in mud and pelting rain storms together with intense drilling and numerous skirmishes. 2nd Lt. Joseph D. Moore, age 27, of Wes' Co. I was killed at Elk Water.

It had been sometime since Wes' father, Henry, had heard from his brother, Augustus. He wrote him on Sep 20th 1861 from Marengo to tell him news of the family and the locals:

the last time I rote I told you I was going to missouri. I did not go and I am not very sorry. I have not sold yet. my oldest boy is gone to the war. Wesley he is nineteen. he listed with the first volunteers last Apr. he is in western virginia.

Augustus is going in a few days. he is young to go in the army but he is large of his age. he is not fifteen yet he is a first rate Boy. our Girl is at work at the Lunatic assylum in Columbus. She has ben there over a year So we will be left with one baby 11 years old. the war Spirit runs high here. there is over twenty listed from Bennington. Father will be 86 this summer. it has ben very dry here this summer but the crops is pretty good.

On Oct 7th Mary Chestnut wrote in her diary: *Uncle H writes, "All this Marching and counter Marching--it seems so aimless and futile. We take a place with heavy loss of men and ammunition, then retire. The enemy then takes it from the few we left to guard it, and then we have to go and capture it anew--at the same expense of life, &c".*

In western Virginia, the Third Ohio proceeding back to Clarksburg met with the paymaster and from there went by rail to Parkersburg and took steamers for Cincinnati on Nov 28th. It became evident that Wes would not get home for after their welcome at Cincinnati they embarked for Louisville, Kentucky. From there they marched to Camp Jenkins four miles from the city. Here the Army of the Ohio was organized under Maj. Gen. Don Carlos Buell, a cautious hard working disciplinarian whose opinions and bad temper made him unpopular. The Third Ohio was assigned to Buell's Third division. On Dec 7th 1861 they marched for Elizabethtown, Kentucky, and on to Bacon Creek or Camp Jefferson for winter quarters arriving on the 17th. Meanwhile Gen. Grant was engaging the Confederates at Columbus in Kentucky and New Madrid in Missouri on the Mississippi River.

A New Year

On Feb 22nd 1862 the Third division broke camp and marched into Bowling Green, Kentucky, with some forty thousand men as Rebels fled. The city was key to both sides. Then they moved into Nashville, Tennessee, as soon as it was abandoned by Confederate troops on the 25th. It was a great loss to the Confederates being their depot for supplies including ammunition, powder, leather, clothing, blankets, flour and bacon. The surrender of one made it necessary to abandon the other. Both Bowling Green and Nashville were on the major Louisville & Nashville rail system which was a logistical tool and passageway to enemy territory. From Nashville the Third Ohio marched southward as part of the distinguished Third Division. Tennessee was now in the possession of the North. Northern Alabama counties were harassed by the Northern Army.

The Third Ohio participated with Gen. Mitchell in the advance on Huntsville, Alabama, on Apr 11th 1862. Wes had turned twenty seven days earlier. On the 12th twenty Union volunteers led by a civilian scout and spy, James J. Andrews, seized the Confederate locomotive *General* at Big Shanty [Kennesaw] as it stopped for breakfast at the Lacy Hotel. Their objective was to head for Chattanooga, Tennessee. On the way they would burn bridges, tear up track, and cut telegraph lines. As the train's conductor, William A. Fuller, looked on in horror as his engine left town, he and two crewmen chased the stolen train for 87 miles across Georgia country by foot, hand car, and several different locomotives: notably the *William R. Smith* and the *Texas*. The *General* ran out of steam near Ringgold, Georgia. The men fled on foot. Andrews and his raiders were caught, some tried and later hung. Eight made it back to Union lines.

Union troops did succeed in capturing 23 engines and 3 trains belonging to the railways running into Huntsville from Athens, Decatur, and other Alabama towns. Their objective was to cut off troop reinforcements by rail from Chattanooga. What little opposition they met in Huntsville after it was occupied was mostly continuous skirmishes of guerrilla type warfare trying to destroy Mitchell's communications and supply.

This rail line ran from Memphis on the Mississippi River eastward to Corinth and Iuka, then across northern Alabama northeast back into Tennessee to Knoxville and on into Virginia just south of Richmond to Norfolk on the Atlantic coast. A spur ran north from Decatur, Alabama, to Nashville. Another spur ran from Chattanooga to Nashville. From Nashville it ran north to Bowling Green, then to Munfordville and Louisville. A short spur went near Perryville. Another spur at Louisville went eastward to Frankfort and Lexington, then north to Cincinnati.

Gen. Don Carlos Buell, now commander of the Army of Ohio, wanted the war waged in a "civilized manner." Buell was considered a headquarters general. His men only saw him briefly as he made blurry-eyed hurried inspections. Mitchell wrote to the Asst. Adj. Gen. that about two hundred prisoners, fifteen locomotives, passengers, box and platform cars, telegraphic apparatus and offices, plus two Southern mails were taken and that they had succeeded in cutting the artery of the railway intercommunications. Mitchell was one to hold the citizens responsible for destroying the railways, cars, and trestles. As "payment for these damages," some of his officers went to nearby plantations and took their cotton using their wagons to haul it to speculators. While under occupation, Col. John B. Turchin, a Russian, with the Nineteenth Illinois was angered by guerrillas who had fired on his troops. He allowed his men two hours to sack the wealthy town of Athens whose population was less that four thousand. This outraged Mitchell who reported the plundering and requested permission to hang the perpetrators. At Mitchell's suggestion, about forty-five Athens citizens filed for damages. He also requested of the War Department for permission to send prominent Confederate sympathizers to northern prisons, claiming that Gen. Clemens and Judge Lane had advised him. With the advance of Bragg into Tennessee, Turchin had to abandon Athens, and to the dismay of his officers, burned much of the city. The day before Buell ordered Turchin's discharge, he was promoted to Brigadier General Buell, enraged by these actions, held and reported that Mitchell was responsible. Mitchell was later charged at Washington for failure to suppress plundering and removed from his post.

Wes' letter to his sister gives a different perspective of Mitchell's actions:

Huntsville May 19ᵗʰ 1862
    Dear Sister I received your letter some time ago but on the account of no mail leaving her[e], It was useless to write but as the mail is going to leave in the morning I will try and send you a short letter which I Suppose will come more acceptable than none. I have just come from Athens today. I was guard on General Mitchells train. I have been staying at the Generals head quarters for nearly two weeks. I have been to Athens four times with the General, it is about fifty miles which makes a nice car ride in one day. Thare has nothing of much importance transpired Since we came back to Huntsville, consequently I will have nothing much to write about this time. I have not heard anything from the fifteenth regiment Since I left them at Nashville. I Suppose they had a fight at pittsburgh landing but I hope that no more than Hiram was hurt. Our Army is makeing a good progress towards Subdueing the rebellion. I hope we will Suceed in doing it Soon for I am getting anxious to see home once more--We have been in pretty tight place here and it has been prophesized that we could not hold it but we have held it So long and can hold it longer. They have had fights all around us here. Vegitation is getting quite a Start here. peach trees are loaded with peaches and are about the size of walnuts. Corn is Knee high the weather has been pretty hot for a few days past. I received a letter from Albert Platt the same time I did yours and was written before. Our mails are very irregular now. we hardly get a mail once a month but I hope you will not fail to write as I will get it some time. I have nothing more to add this time so I will quit for this time. as ever your Dear Brother. Wesley Ayres

Wes' sixteen year old brother, Gus, talked his parents into letting him enlist. On May 30ᵗʰ 1862 the brown hair, gray eyed, 5'9 ½" 16 year old enlisted for three months at South Woodbury, Ohio, as a private under Capt. Thomas L. Bunker's Co. C, Eighty-Fifth Regiment of the Ohio Infantry. He was appointed Musician on Jun 11th and mustered out on Sep 23rd at Camp Chase, Ohio, with the whole regiment whose purpose had been to aid in guarding a large number of Rebel prisoners in confinement at that camp. He returned to his parents Ohio farm after the three months. As the war raged, his parents left Ohio in the fall of 1862 and moved to Meridian, Michigan, located four miles from Lansing where 75 acres of timber land was purchased. Elizabeth left her job at the Central Ohio Asylum to move with her parents and two younger brothers. It was here that Gus would later enlist with the Twelfth Michigan Infantry and sent to Arkansas in 1864.

The Third Ohio's summer in Huntsville was consumed by scouting, foraging, and other duties while the Rebels were preparing for a larger campaign after the loss at Corinth, Mississippi, the end of May 1862. By June 10th the Union held Memphis and Tennessee west of the Cumberlands, northern Alabama and Mississippi, Missouri, and Arkansas north of the Arkansas river, plus the Mississippi river from Vicksburg north and from the Gulf to Port Hudson. Gen. Halleck, overall commander of the Union Army of the West, sights were set on Chattanooga. Gen. Buell and his Army of Ohio was to embrace Kentucky, Tennessee east of the Tennessee River except Forts Henry and Donelson, plus the northern portions of Alabama and Georgia. Buell was dispatched from Corinth eastward to take eastern Tennessee. Halleck wanted him to go by way of Chattanooga but Buell chose a route by McMinnville half way between Nashville and Chattanooga.

After the Confederate loss of Corinth on Oct 4th 1862, health problems caused Gen. Beauregard to request relief of his command. He was replaced by 46 year old fussy disciplinarian Gen. Braxton Bragg who was given orders to head northward to Nashville and pierce Gen. Buell's strung-out army. Buell planned to flank Bragg when he got in eastern Tennessee but he had to rebuild bridges and repair railroads with his dispersed army. He also had other problems. Since he was not particularly liked back in Washington, his requests and suggestions were not well received which cost him delays.

Confederate strength of fifty-six thousand men in the Army of the Mississippi were south of Corinth at Tupelo in addition to some troops at Vicksburg. The self centered, ambitious, and very independent Confederate Maj. Gen. Edmund Kirby Smith, age 38, who had led Johnston's troops at Bull Run was now at Knoxville with two small divisions. Buell's Union Gen. G.W. Morgan had flanked the Cumberland Gap and had controlled it since Jun 18th 1862. It was a big job for Buell to protect three hundred miles from the Gap to Corinth.

Bragg, a dour pessimistic Confederate, was a good strategist but had difficulty in making decisive action at the moment of climax. His subordinate, Gen. Smith, was responsible for Chattanooga and full of ambition. Smith's two divisions were located at Cumberland Gap and Chattanooga. Despite growing concerns over Chattanooga, Smith sent two cavalry commanders into Kentucky to disrupt the Federal supply line to Buell's army. One was the notable Col. John Hunt Morgan with his raiders, the other Col. Nathan B. Forest who escaped from Ft. Donelson and with one thousand troops captured Murfreesboro taking twelve hundred prisoners, fifty wagons and teams, a battery of artillery and supplies estimated to be worth millions. Confederate raiders created havoc for Union railroad men. Various methods were used for derailing trains. Isolated telegraph operators were tied up and their equipment used to send false messages. Some independent groups were fearless leaving destruction and death in their wake. Buell again was outraged when he heard news of the wholesale surrender at Murfreesboro. He sent a thirty-five hundred division there to stop Forrest. They quickly repaired the railroad but failed to stop Forrest. On July 21st Forrest struck again north of Murfreesboro destroying three railroad bridges and taking ninety-seven prisoners. The railroad was out of commission until July 29th. The outcome of the orchestrated distraction caused Buell to delay his operations.

While Morgan and Forrest were striking, Gen. Smith was scheming in Knoxville to invade Kentucky. This could only be accomplished if he could get released from his Chattanooga assignment. Painting a gloomy picture, he succeeded in getting Bragg to order the Army of the Mississippi to Chattanooga. Bragg arrived in Chattanooga on the morning of July 30th. Smith came down from

Knoxville to confer with Bragg on the best way to use thirty-two thousand men, his and Smith's, against a larger scattered Union force. A solution was found on Aug 1st. Smith would take on Buell's men at Cumberland Gap. It would require ten to fourteen days. If Smith was successful, both armies would head for mid Tennessee. Smith returned to Knoxville. He wrote Bragg that Federals were intrenched at Cumberland Gap and he wished to go directly to Lexington. Assembling his men, they marched on to Lexington, a difficult task getting by Buell. On Aug 14th his headquarters was established at Lexington. A cavalry force was sent to occupy Frankfort, Kentucky's capital. Out of ideas, Smith became defensive, waiting to see what Generals, Bragg and Buell, would do.

Abandoning the posts in western Alabama, the Army of the Ohio was concentrated at McMinnville, northwest of the Rebel stronghold at Chattanooga. Gen. Nelson arrived on Aug 3rd while Buell was preparing to cross the mountains at Altamont and invade East Tennessee. Confederate Morgan arrived north of Nashville on Aug 12th and captured Col. W.P. Boone and five companies of the Twenty-Eighth Kentucky Infantry. He went on to burn an eight hundred foot tunnel with a train loaded with supplies and a bridge with forty cars between Gallatin and Nashville. Buell sent Gen. Richard W. Johnson, a West Point graduate, with seven hundred men to get Morgan who was camped at Hartsville. Six miles west of Hartsville, Johnson, his staff and two hundred men were captured, sixty-four killed and one hundred wounded by Morgan.

After a few days resting, Union forces resumed their movements. Huntsville was evacuated on Aug 23rd. Wes' units marched to Decherd Station. A detachment from the Third Ohio was sent east of Huntsville to Stevenson by rail on Aug 27th to bring back some sick men and hospital supplies. When returning, the train met with gunfire and several were wounded. The march from Decherd Station to Louisville took a month due to severe hot weather, dust, little water, and scant rations. They reached Shelbyville, Murfreesboro, and Nashville without incidence. The Union Army waited at Green River. At nearby Munfordville Col. Wilder and his gallant little band were overpowered. On Sep 23rd Confederate Gen. Smith sent some of his cavalry on a raid in the outskirts of Louisville. Panic had already set in upon hearing news of Confederate advances into Kentucky. A bridge was built over the Ohio River to Indiana where many women and children fled to safety on the north shore. Upriver, Cincinnati was also aroused and martial law was declared. Gen. Lew Wallace was put in charge of the city's defense. Buell's advanced division of twelve thousand veterans and a half dozen batteries of artillery had arrived near Louisville on the 24th. It was the Federal supply center for Kentucky and Tennessee. The Third Ohio entered the city on the morning of Sep 25th as did Buell. Elated Buell wired department headquarters in Cincinnati that "Louisville is now safe. We can destroy Bragg with whatever force he may bring against us."

Mercurial Bragg had left Chattanooga for Kentucky on Aug 28th 1862 and concentrating on moving his troops by way of Richmond and Glasgow where he was headquartered. On September 15th, after a few days of resting his troops, Bragg left Glasgow with plans to capture the Union fort at Munfordville by the rail line at Green River. Buell had moved six Union divisions about thirty miles west of Glasgow to Cave City where he waited for Maj. Gen. George H. Thomas. Two armies were in close proximity and ill-tempered Bragg told his men that: *A powerful foe is assembling in our front and we must prepare to strike him a sudden and decisive blow.* Bragg left Gen. Leonidas Polk's wing north of Green River and had Buckner's division cut across Buell's front. Buell refused to be provoked. Bragg gathered his forces and resumed his march northward later reporting excuses for his inaction. All his forces arrived on the 16th, surrounded the fort, and signaled by flag to surrender. The next day, Col. Wilder surrendered over forty-two hundred men, ten pieces of artillery, rifles, horses, mules, and considerable stores. As Bragg left Munfordville he told a staff colonel: *This campaign must be won by marching, not fighting.* This unexpected event caused Bragg's delay in getting to Lexington.

Gen. Thomas finally arrived on Sep 20th and Buell pushed forward only to find the rebels gone. Suspecting Bragg was headed for Louisville, Buell followed at a slow pace fearing an ambush but hoped to strike Bragg's rear. But Bragg headed parallel to Buell toward Bardstown leaving Buell a clear path to Louisville. Since Bragg mostly maintained his troops from the land and populace and from what he captured, he moved in anticipation of productive land and sympathetic cooperation from the people. The terrain proved rough and unproductive. The people were cautious since he had no Kentucky troops. Bragg arrived at Bardstown on Sep 23rd. He planned on attacking Louisville from there. Bragg left Polk in command and went to Lexington to ask Gen. Smith to send supplies and join him. Since the plans were not made by Smith, he refused and left Bragg on his own.

Meanwhile the two opposing armies stumbled around the Kentucky hills groping for each other. Buell sent a twenty-two thousand man column southeasterly toward Frankfort as a larger contingent of fifty-five thousand moved toward Bragg at Bardstown. They arrived Oct 1st. Bragg underestimated the strength of a three-corps column heading for Bardstown and sent Polk two messages on Oct 2nd instructing him to strike the flank and rear of the column moving toward Frankfort. Received on the 3rd, Polk replied that conditions make "compliance with this order not only eminently inexpedient but impractical." One third of Buell's men were inexperienced new recruits including commanders known as "Squirrel Hunters." They were acquired at Louisville during a hasty reorganization.

On Oct 4th Bragg was in Frankfort to hear the new secessionist Governor Hawes of Kentucky give his inaugural address. He also hoped to get new enlistments from Kentucky. The ceremony was interrupted by the boom of Sill's Federals lobbing shells on the outskirts of Frankfort. Bragg sent a message to Polk: *the Enemy in heavy force advancing on us, only 12 miles out. Shall destroy bridges and retire on Harrodsburg for concentration and then strike. Reach that point as soon as possible.* Bragg, forewarned and not entirely surprised nor dismayed, evacuated Bardstown the next day and moved his headquarters to Harrodsburg on the 6th. The next day he ordered three divisions of Polk's corps to head to Versailles south of Frankfort. The orders were countered after getting information that Federals were at Perryville.

After a few days rest in Louisville, Federals resumed their movements. The first encounter of any importance would occur in Perryville. Bragg felt the attack would be at daylight on Oct 8th. Then he would head to Versailles after Polk defeated the Federals at Perryville. Bragg thought that Buell would not have time to assemble all his units for a sudden attack. But things were falling into place for Buell who had all his eight divisions collected except for Sill who was coming from Frankfort and Dumont's green division who was continuing a feint. There were fifty-five thousand infantry, artillery and cavalry under his command. Confederate forces under Bragg consisted of three divisions of infantry of fourteen thousand five hundred men plus two small calvary brigades of fifteen hundred, most from Tennessee.

Buell's three widespread columns under McCook, Gilbert, and Crittenden were heading toward Bardstown. Finding Bardstown evacuated, the columns trudged on. Buell had ordered a concentration near Perryville on Oct 7th where there was water. Maj. Gen. Alexander McCook was to move at 3 a.m. for Perryville and form on the left of Gilbert. Delayed by a bad road, he had to make camp eight miles short of the objective. Maj. Gen. Thomas L. Crittenden coming from Lebanon was delayed by a detour and stopped ten miles short. Only Gilbert's central column coming from Springfield arrived on time. Water was on the minds of men and commanders since their water situation had grown serious. Doctor's Creek located a few miles west of Perryville was vital to his troops. Summer's long drought had dried or shrunk any water. What remained was brackish and disagreeable to taste. Rebels were in strength at Doctor's Creek, a tributary of Chaplin River, and defended it with snipers. Gilbert's men, who made a dry camp in the woods, made several exhausting attempts at getting water on the 7th but were thwarted. In a grey dawn before sunrise on Oct 8th, Brig. Gen. Philip H. Sheridan, commander of a division under Gilbert, seized a stretch of Doctor's Creek as well as part of the heights. The 31 year old Ohioan, ten years out of West Point, had received his Star two weeks earlier and division command nine days previous. He had commanded a Michigan Cavalry regiment at Corinth and had to prove validity of the statements of his worth. Buell had been thrown from a horse earlier that day and was lame but not discouraged. His thoughts lay in finally having Bragg's army within reach. Sill was headed south to join McCook after the feint at Frankfort. It diverted Bragg's thinking. Buell's estimate of the enemy's situation was considerably mistaken. He thought he was facing the whole of Bragg's army. Bragg earlier had made a similar error.

Bragg waited at Harrodsburg through early morning of Oct 8th with ear cocked to catch the rumble of guns ten miles southwest, but hearing nothing, rode to Perryville arriving about 10 a.m. He found Polk reconnoitering high ground near the confluence of Doctor's Creek and Chaplin River with Cheatham on the left of the town. Bragg confronted Polk why his orders to fight immediately were not carried out. Polk gave several explanations. After conferring with Hardee, he decided to adopt a defensive offensive and did not regard Bragg's letter of instructions as a pre-emptory order to attack. Bragg took command from Polk approving some suggestions about divisions under Buckner, Anderson and Cheatham. Before Cheatham's preparations were complete, Federals opened a cannonade in his direction. Due to topography they had little effect. By 1 p.m., Polk was in attack formation without Union knowledge. Word was passed for both divisions to move forward. Cheatham and Buckner struck with a surprisingly immense force emerging from the woods. Hardee's commands overtook the music and the air filled with the sound of shot and shell.

In the opening action, Union's color-sergeant Wm. V. McCoubrie stood a bit advanced of the color-guard. Bearing the regimental standard in an exposed position instantly brought fire killing him. Five others shared the same fate until David C. Walker of Co. C, a boy of seventeen caught the colors before they touched the ground. His success in carrying the flag was rewarded by Col. Beatty making him a color-sergeant. Col. Lytle's brigade of the Third Ohio had taken position in an open field on the right of Perryville road, protected only by a rail fence. The Third stood its ground, returning volley for volley, until more than one-third of its number had fallen, both dead and wounded. The most stubborn resistance was in the center where Rousseau was assailed by Buckner. When it finally gave way, the line recoiled and Confederates held the entire battlefield. About two hours later Confederates were thrown into confusion by Sheridan's gunners.

Meanwhile, McCook reported to Buell that he had sent Generals Jackson and Terrill to advance his skirmishers to the river bank as soon as his troops were in attack position. Jackson was killed by one of the first volleys and within the hour Terrill's green men wavered when a bullet killed Terrill. Some fled, others fought but were steadily thrown back. When McCook returned from the rear he found two demoralized divisions staring at him and called for help from Gilbert. Confusion existed on both sides as intermingled units cried: *You are firing into friends.* Before the battle closed, the Third regiment, pressed by enemy, was ordered to withdraw to the second line where it remained until the close of the conflict. While in line, Gen. Rousseau rode up to the regiment and commented about the Third's conduct: *You stood in the withering fire like men of iron.* Even though the Federals were no longer responding with muskets, danger lurked on the Lebanon road into Perryville.

The sun set in a red brick sky in autumn's haze as a waning full moon rose opposite. The artillery on both sides kept up their fire which gradually slackened. Death lay everywhere. Tactically, it was a Confederate victory, strategically, a defeat. It amounted to a standoff. Darkness ended the duel to the relief of Perryville civilians. Sixteen thousand Bluecoats had challenged fifty-five thousand Yankees. Bragg reported that: *for the time engaged, it was the severest and most desperately contested engagement within my knowledge.* The night was moonlit. Some in the Union army favored launching a night counterattack. Buell attempted to get such an order underway but his messenger got lost until well after sunset. Communications between Buell, Thomas, and Crittenden were slow and unsatisfactory. The last order at 1:30 a.m. was to attack at daylight on Oct 9th. Morning came with no sounds of conflict. Three hours past dawn Buell queried: "What delays your attack?" Crittenden replied he had no orders to attack. Buell responded to get moving. But Bragg and his men were gone having pulled out after midnight.

Federal blunders and lack of communication cost them dearly, having far more casualties than the Confederates. Buell fought his first battle badly being outdone by an army under a third its size. McCook stated in his report that it was "the bloodiest battle of modern times for the number of troops engaged on our side." Both sides claimed victory. Neither gained much. Federals had 845 killed, 2,851 wounded, and 515 captured or missing. Confederate loss was 510 killed, 2,635 wounded, and 251 captured or missing.

The Third Ohio lost a third of its men. Two hundred fifteen men were killed or wounded including two company commanders. The Third drew special praise for its bravery. It was here that Wes had his cap shot off and although he mailed it home, it never arrived.

In Wes' Company I, among the 3 years men killed Oct 8th 1862 at Perryville were:

Capt. Henry E. Cunard, age 23 when enlisted as Sgt.
1st Lt. James St. John, age 21 when enlisted as 2nd Lt., aide-de-camp to Col. Lytle.
Cpl. Sidney J. Aldrich, age 25 when enlisted.
Cpl. Charles R. Merrill, age 21 when enlisted as Pvt.
Pvt. Alfred Fisher, age 28 when enlisted as Pvt.

Wounded at Perryville were:

Cpl. George W. Merrill, age 25 when enlisted as Cpl. Died Apr 3rd 1863 at Cincinnati from wounds at Perryville.
Cpl. Stephen Latsgo, age 34 when enlisted as Pvt. Discharged Oct 8th 1862 for wounds at Perryville.
Sgt. Simon C. Bennett, age 22 when enlisted as Pvt. Discharged for wounds.
Pvt. Byron Bunker, age 20 when enlisted.
Lyman M. Courtwright, age 18 when enlisted. Mustered out Jun 21st 1864.
Job Garberson, age 19 when enlisted. Mustered out Jun 21st 1864.
Daniel J. Long, age 19 when enlisted as Pvt. Mustered out Jun 21st 1864.
John Straub, age 22 when enlisted as Pvt. Mustered out Jun 21st 1864.
Alonzo Swisher, age 20 when enlisted Pvt. Mustered out Jun 21st 1864.
Henry Van Brimmer age 19 when enlisted. Lost his right arm at Perryville and discharged.

After the battle was over, Bragg learned he had been fighting the whole Army of Ohio. He also discovered that Buell was reinforced during the night. Quickly he retreated to Harrodsburg where he could counter any move by Buell. He expected Buell to pursue. Instead Buell destroyed mills from which Bragg was getting bread. This lack of action caused Buell to be replaced in command on Oct 23rd by Maj. Gen. Wm. Rosecrans as commander of the Army of the Cumberland. Known as *Old Rosy*, he was a brilliant strategist and brought a new spirit to the men fighting under him. He also had a lit firecracker temper. Pope and McDowell had been dismissed before Buell. It was a season of dismissals.

The same day of Buell's dismissal, Bragg ordered Polk to proceed to Murfreesboro, Tennessee. Already weary, further pursuit of Bragg's army to and beyond Crab Orchard, Kentucky, was fruitless. Union men marched back toward Nashville. Bragg also suffered some criticism. He left Kentucky with few recruits. But his army was stronger and in good form. Wes' ill-clad and dispirited regiment waited at the village of New Market just south of Lebanon, Kentucky, for a supply of clothing and camp equipage which had been left at Louisville. Upon its receipt, they resumed pursuit of Bragg encouraged by Buell's removal as commander. Wes was sent to the Benton Barracks hospital in Louisville when he became ill. Family history said he had pneumonia. He also suffered intestinal problems throughout life due to his war experiences. Wes' Company I went on to fight at Stones River near Murfreesboro where they lost Robert Glenn who died Feb 6th 1863 at Murfreesboro from his wounds, James Wright killed Jan 3rd 1863, Charles W. Wood who died Feb 21st 1863 at Murfreesboro from his wounds, Wendell P. Willets who died Jan 31st 1863 at Murfreesboro from his wounds and Sgt. Elias C. Nicholas who was discharged Feb 24th 1863 due to wounds on Dec. 31st 1862. Two days before Wes became ill on Oct 28th,

Sec. Of War Stanton notified Col. Alfred Ellet that the Gunboat Fleet was transferred to the Naval Department. The disposition of the Ram Fleet was left for further consideration. You will retain command until further notice. On Nov 6th Ellet was appointed Brig. General and summoned to Washington to discuss appointments of subordinates and details of the river brigade. The Navy, keeping a watchful eye, secured an order for Ellet to report to Rear Admiral David Porter for instructions and act under his direction until otherwise ordered by the War Department. From Nov 1862 to Mar 1863, Ellet, now a General, and his staff were engaged in forming the Marine Brigade and getting boats ready for use under the command of Col. Charles Rivers Ellet. Gen. Ellet was despatched to recruit convalescents for his Ram fleet. Those recruited would be discharged from their regiments.[1]

At the hospital in Louisville Wes was mustered-out of the Third Ohio pursuant to orders. It was noted that he was paid to Dec 31st 1862. His clothing account was never settled and given $11.00 for same. He was sent to Benton Barracks where on Jan 27st 1863 he was mustered-in the Marine Brigade for three years under Capt. Fisher and there made Corporal. His transfer was to Co. E, First Infantry, Mississippi Marine Brigade as a Corporal. Muster rolls show him present since Jan 31st. Wes now faced a new experience of life on the Mississippi River. George C. Wright of Wes' Company I, also transferred to the Mississippi Marine Brigade.

Fighting on the Mississippi - 1863

The next two paragraphs give a glimpse as to what kind of men were sought for recruitment in the Mississippi Marine Brigade. Orders were sent to Gen. Ellet from the Secretary of War stating the Marine Brigade is to consist of one regiment of infantry, two squadrons of cavalry, and one battery of light artillery to be called *Mississippi volunteers* with its officers commissioned by the President of the United States. The organization is connected with the Ram Fleet in cooperation with the Western Gunboats. It is believed that men best suited can be recruited from boatmen and rivermen on the Mississippi River and its tributaries. A mustering officer will assist you and you will select recruiting officers to submit for commission. The brigade should be organized as soon as possible. From your known capacity and energy much will be expected of you.

A letter dated Jan 7th 1863 at St. Louis, Missouri, from Gen. Ellet to Adm. Porter noted: *I am receiving men quite fast now as compared with the first few weeks and hope yet to be able to strike a blow to aid in the suppression of this rebellion with the Mississippi Marine Brigade. I shall not be able to leave here for weeks to come. My men must be well drilled before I can take them on the boats and it takes time and labor both to effect this. I shall lose no time. It was a great mistake that my command was not assigned me from troops already in the field. I could now be at work.*[2]

On Jan 22nd a list of recommendations for appointments in Command in the Infantry Regiment (eleven) and the Battalion Cavalry (twelve) was forwarded to the Sec. of War Stanton by Gen. Ellet.

At the end of January, Gen. Grant was operating about ten miles north of Vicksburg aided by a Union river boat fleet under Adm. Porter. It was here that he fruitlessly tried to dig canals on the Louisiana side of the Mississippi River to allow Union boats to bypass well protected Vicksburg. On Feb 3rd Confederate Gen. Joseph Wheeler tried to dislodge the Federals at Fort Donelson on the Cumberland River above Nashville. Col. A. C. Harding's, 83rd Illinois successfully defended it with about 750 men. Harding reported 13 killed, 51 wounded and 46 captured. That evening Wheeler moved south of Duck river. His losses were greater and included horses, mules and a transport loaded with provisions.[3]

Wes wrote the following: Feb 22nd 1863, Benton Barracks, St. Louis, Missouri To: Lizzie Ayres:

---

1 *War of the Rebellion Official Records of the Union & Confederate Armies, Series V, Naval Forces on Western Waters*, p. 140

2 Ibid.

3 Yoseloff, Vol.VIII, 223-224

Dear Sister

Your letter I gladly received last night which found me well and hearty but in answering, I am Sorry to inform you that furloughs have played out in this regiment. an order was read the other evening telling us that no more furloughs would be granted. I did expect one as the Colonel Said that we should all have one but as my chance has failed I dont think there is any use to cry about it but let it pass and hope for the future to bring it around all right yet. We had a grand review yesterday out in the city. this piece of print will explain it to you better than I can...I suppose that I am a little larger than when I left you. when I was in the hospital I weighed a hundred and thirty but now I only weigh one hundred and Seventy. I was getting to fat to play off on the doctor any longer, So I took my choice to come here or go to the Regiment. It appears to me as though it would be a dry place thare now for me as I like a good Suppy of young people and espcially the gender of the feminine....I want you to get Father to write Some next time and tell more about that land whether he has picked out a piece for me yet I shall want a piece of land of my own Sometime and one lot will not be enough for us all. We have had some nice warm weather for a week past untill last night thare came a little Snow consequently it is a little cool to day which you will perceive by the close of this letter the effect it has on my fingers I have nothing more at presant Write again Soon
I remain as your Brother   C W Ayres

The long dreary winter with heavy continuous rains was hard on field troops. Measles, smallpox and malarial fever broke out among the men. While Wes said he had gained 40 pounds during his hospitalization which ended in March, the Confederacy was having great financial problems as well as shortages. Its capital was tied up in land, slaves, and cotton in an embargo. Inflation was taking its toll as well as taxes imposed on goods and farm products to arm its military. Richmond was among the hardest hit cities. With a doubling of population since the war began, the crisis reached the breaking point on Apr 2nd. Hundreds of hungry women marched to Capitol Square. A small group grew into an angry mob shouting, "Bread! Bread!" They began smashing windows in the shopping district and took what they could. The mayor ordered police to fire on the women, but Jefferson Davis appeared in the midst of the riot and standing on a wagon chided the women telling them they had five minutes to disperse. They promptly did. Davis had the leaders arrested. A few were briefly imprisoned.[1]

The next day the Brigade fleet left Milliken's Bend to cruise in the neighborhood of Greenville, Mississippi. They landed on Wes' 21st birthday, Apr 4th, to scout at Lake City. Grant was at his Headquarters at Vicksburg and wrote to Acting Rear-Admiral Porter advising him that in view of massing forces of cavalry on Rosecrans to have Gen. Ellet send the Marine Brigade to the Tennessee River to defend that line: *If this brigade is sent, I would suggest that General Ellet be instructed to keep his fleet well together, destroy all rafts, flats, skiffs, and everything that can facilitate the crossing of the river. If on arrival at the mouth of Duck River it should be found safe to land with his small force, he might to advantage proceed up that stream for some distance and destroy the ferries, etc., that he would probably find.* Porter responded by telling Ellet that circumstances of a serious nature render it necessary to change your field of operations to the Tennessee River and to destroy all rafts, flatboats, skiffs, or canoes, and all means of transporting an army. Also sawmills and lumber to be burned.[2]

On April 9th Porter informed Sec. of the Navy that four rams would accompany the brigade.[3] On April 12th the brigade was sent to the Tennessee River to cooperate with General Ellet. A telegram was

1 Davis, pp. 284-285

2*Ibid.*, Naval Forces on Western Waters,V.24, pp. 76-77
3*Ibid.*, p. 79

sent to Gen. Rosecrans that the Marine Brigade of one regiment of infantry, one squadron of cavalry, one battery of light artillery and four guns and will depart Cairo tonight or tomorrow morning.[1] The steamers at this time under Ellet's command were the *Adams, Baltic, Diana, E.H.Fairchild, John Raine* and *Woodward*.[2] Gen. Ellet's son, Col. Charles Ellet, was commander of the *Diana*. More steamers were added later totaling fifteen. The brigade arrived at Fort Henry on the 15th having been detained at Cairo and Paducah for repairs and the arrival of Col. Streight's command. Ellet's fleet missed Gen. Grant's dangerous plan to have Porter's fleet run past Vicksburg beginning the night of the 16th. Ellet's fleet left Fort Henry on the 17th with Streight reaching Eastport on the 19th. The cavalry was sent out from Cerro Gordo Landing to destroy a mill and lumber being used for ship-building. They were forced to leave Eastport and landed at Savannah. Scouting parties were sent out to burn mills and commissary supplies. Three enemy pickets were captured. On the morning of April 26th they were attacked below the mouth of Duck River by the Sixth Texas Rangers commanded by Maj. R.M. White [Engagement at Duck River Island or Little Rock Landing, Tennessee]. They landed and pursued the enemy for twelve miles killing ten men including the Major and wounding many more. Most escaped due to the inability of landing at the point of attack. That day the Asst. Quartermaster forwarded a report to Gen. Rawlins, Dept. of Tennessee, listing the boats with their capacity of holding men, animals, and wagons for the embarkation of troops. He estimated 1,000 men, 200 animals, and 20 wagons. They arrived back at Fort Henry on the 28th with difficulty in navigating. The ram *Monarch* joined the brigade on the Tennessee River. The ram *Switzerland* was blockading the mouth of the Red River.

Lt. Wm. F. Warren, Acting Signal Officer, MMB on the Flag-ship *Autocrat*, wrote the following report on Apr 26th to Capt. O. H. Howard, Chief Signal Officer, Western Departmen:

Captain: I have the honor to report that the signal detachment of the Mississippi Marine Brigade has had an opportunity to test its efficiency and make itself useful, to some extent, in the following manner: At a few minutes past 8 o'clock this morning, while passing a point on the Tennessee River, a few miles below Duck River, where the direction of the current compelled us to run within 50 yards of the land, our fleet was opened upon by a field battery of four guns and a regiment of calvary. The Autocrat, being in advance, was the first to receive the fire. The Diana [3] came next, followed by the Adams, each receiving a raking fire at close range, but with very slight casualties. The Autocrat replied instantly with musketry, the Diana and Adams with musketry and field artillery. Our fire becoming too hot for the rebels, they immediately limbered up and fell back in great haste, out of musket range. The general discovering this, ordered me to signal the other boats to land their forces at once. The order was instantly understood, both by J. Q. Adams on the Diana, and Lieutenant Wilson on the Adams. This order was immediately followed by instruction about the position in which they should land. As a result of this signaling, the troops were ready to march out almost at the instant the landing was made. We have officers on each of the five large boats who are able to read signals quite readily, and I have the honor to say that I am reliably informed that they were all upon the hurricane deck during the engagement, with glasses and equipments, on close lookout for signals. The Diana and Adams were both hotly

---

1*Ibid.*, p. 80

2*Ibid.*, V.27, p. 147

3 There were also two other known steamers, *Diana*, which were used in this war. One was fitted as a ram and used as a gunboat of the Texas Martine Dept. for the defense of Galveston Bay. The other was reported to have escaped from Farragut's passage in Apr 1862 in New Orleans. The USS Cayuga took possession of the *Diana* on the 27th. On May 5th 1862 she went into service at New Orleans and became a transport on interior waters. Confederate troops in a two hour battle killed her commander and five other men plus wounding three. She was used as a gunboat by the Confederates but was hit on Apr 13th 1863 by a battery of Parrott guns. It managed to pull beyond range, made repairs and proceeded as support to Confederate troops. Badly outnumbered, the Captain abandoned and burned her to prevent capture.

engaging the enemy at the time their signals were given, and the Adams was receiving the fire of this battery. Officers and men deserve commendation for their coolness and close attention to duty. I am, captain, very respectfully, your obedient servant, W.F. WARREN

Warren's report to Capt. Howard, was forwarded to Gen. Ellet, U.S. Army commanding the MMB who wrote the following version to Hon. E. M. Stanton at Cairo, Apr 30th 1863.

I have the honor to report that, in compliance with instructions received from Admiral Porter, I proceeded with my command up Tennessee River to Eastport, Miss., without interruption from the enemy. Returning in consequence of low water, I made several raids into the country, and destroyed a number of important mills and considerable amount of subsistence and supplies belonging to the enemy. At the mouth of Duck River my boats were attacked by 700 cavalry, with two pieces of artillery, commanded by Major White of Sixth Texas Rangers. The fight was spirited for a few moments only. The enemy were driven back and pursued some 12 miles in the interior with the loss of Major White mortally wounded and left near the field, and 1 lieutenant and 8 men killed. They carried off a large number of wounded in wagons and on horses. We buried their dead. Our loss was 2 men killed and 1 wounded. The west bank of the Tennessee River was lined with refugees, who have been driven from their homes for love to the old Union. I exhausted my supplies in providing for their necessities. The Tennessee River is too low for my boats to operate in with safety. My orders from Admiral Porter do not provide for this emergency. I shall hope to receive instructions from the Department. ALFRED W. ELLET [1]

On April 30th Grant's army of 50,000 began to cross the river sending scattered Confederate troops back to Vicksburg. When Grant attacked Vicksburg on May 19th he received a rude welcome and his troops became pinned down. He lost 942 men that day. After a failed second attempt to take Vicksburg on May 22nd by storm, the bloody battle caused Grant to lose 3,199 men of which 502 were killed. Reluctantly he began a formal siege. Adm. Porter already had his gun boats and the Marine Brigade at Vicksburg to help Gen. Grant with its siege. The boats had difficulty navigating the falling waters. Admiral Porter began by cutting off communications and blasted the confederate batteries from the river while Grant's batteries hammered from land. A levee had been built on the river across from Vicksburg. It was here that Wes proved to be very capable in firing a 20 lb. Parrot, a small cannon that all too often exploded when fired killing or maiming its handlers.

The ironclad gunboat *Cincinnati* mounted with 14 guns was observed on May 27th by Confederate Col. Edward Higgins approaching their upper battery with four ironclads approaching he lower batteries. The resulting engagement resulted in the sinking of the *Cincinnati* and credit was given to Confederate Capts. J. P. Lynch and T. N. Johnston of the 1st Tennessee. For the next month these batteries were exposed to an unceasing fire of mortars, Parrot cannons and sharpshooters. [2]

By June's end Confederate Gen. Pemberton knew it was only a matter of time. Ellet's command now consisted of the *Autocrat, Adams, Baltic, Diana, E.H. Fairchild, John Raine,* and *Woodford* which operated between Vicksburg and Lake Providence. [3] Pemberton met with Grant on July 3rd to discuss surrender. July 4th marked the turning point in the war with Vicksburg's surrender and Union control of the entire Mississippi. Entering the fallen city, Union troops began distributing their bread and supplies to the starving Confederates. Vicksburg would not officially celebrate Independence Day until

---

1*Ibid.,* 90,91

2Yoseloff, Vol. VIII, 87-88

3Naval Forces on Western Waters, V.27, 220, 337

1945, the end of World War II.[1] Guerillas were still in the area. The boats and men continued chasing them on land along different areas on the Mississippi. Acting Rear-Admiral David Porter began a paper drive to get rid of the Marine Brigade as part of the Navy.

On the Flagship *Black Hawk* off Vicksburg, Porter wrote on July 13th to Gideon Welles, Secretary of Navy, that the Marine Brigade consists of a large number of vessels capable of transporting 10,000 men and recommend the vessels be turned over to Gen. Grant. *I find the Marine Brigade and army do not get along very well together when cooperating.* The brigade is now so small that it is not available against the bodies of guerillas which infest the Mississippi. He pointed out that the Brigade under Ellet could be better organized. If placed under Grant, he can use the vessels to put a body of 10,000 men at any place. I have offered this to Grant and recommend an order to make the transfer.[2]

On July 22nd Adm. Porter sent a memo to Gen. Ellet saying that Gen. Grant has requested assistance of the boats under command and you are to proceed to points he designates. When the general no longer needs your service, I recommend you look for guerrillas at Rodney, Cole's Creek, Fort Adams, Ellis Cliffs and other notorious places. Grant replied by telegraph to Gen. Washburn that: *the boats of the Marine Brigade will be up tomorrow. They will take 5-6 regiments with 5-6 wagons to each regiment. Have that number of Kimball's troops ready to embark, and start off immediately, to debark at Helena. Price is moving toward southeastern Missouri and Schofield is moving a force to drive him back. I am ordered from Washington to send a force from Helena to cut off all retreat.*[3]

Another memo on July 22nd from Lt. Comm. James Greer of *USS Benton* to Acting Ensign R.A. Turner of *USS Curlew* told Turner to proceed slowly up river as far as the head of Fairchild's Island. Examine closely every place that may seem to have been used for cattle crossing and destroy all flats and barges which can be used for that purpose. You may be able to ascertain from the negroes on the plantations if there are any cattle in large numbers in the vicinity. If so, and they can be obtained, return at once or send me a dispatch by a passing steamer and we will then, if possible, send up a transport for them. Be economical of fuel and do not tie up to the bank at night, but anchor. Do not allow your officers or men to stray from the vessel or to take any other property than what is *contraband of war*. Do not remain at the same place all the time, shift about. Return on Saturday to this place. Ellet wired the next day that all marine boats will be up but he will not consent to leave his boats but take up his whole command, horses and all.

Adm. Porter had received a letter from a John Routh of Louisiana, an owner of two plantations and manager of three others with over 500 negroes on them. He wrote: that with the approach of Grant's army the latter part of April, I removed over 400 negroes with my valuables to Mississippi where I remained until the 18th or 19th of July. On the 21st I was visited by a portion of the Marine Brigade, commanded by Capt. Crandall [Commander of the *Autocrat*], who broke into my storeroom and took nearly everything that I had stored. He went on to itemize the items which were marked with H. W., the name of my home place. He pleaded for the return and arrest of any of the men.[4]

Months later, Greer wrote to Adm. Porter claiming the Marine Brigade were taking cattle and livestock, negroes and salt from plantations. Grant wrote to Gen. L. Thomas, Adjutant General of the Army, on Aug 14th: Enclosed I send you a letter directed to Gen. Ransom from A.T. Bowen. This is but one of numerous complaints made of the conduct of the Marine Brigade under Gen. Ellet. *I think it highly probably the charges brought against the Marine Brigade are exaggerated* and that these boats in charge of the department commander *might be very useful* in transporting troops within the department, also in carrying troops to operate against guerrillas or transfer the brigade to land and take the boats for general use.

The Secretary of War did not approve of the men being converted to land use, but preferred alternate use on both land and water as circumstances require. On Aug 27th Gen. Halleck authorized Grant to detach and place on shore such portions as necessary for the good of the service but not to

---

1Davis, 310
2*Ibid.*, 293, 294
3*Ibid.*, 319
4*Ibid.*, V.27, 318

break up the brigade. Halleck later wrote to Grant saying that Ellet's brigade and boats was intended that each boat should carry a company of cavalry and a piece of artillery to land and pursue the guerrilla bands from the river and still believed to be the most effectual method of keeping the Mississippi open.[1]

On Aug 14th the Adj. Gen. wrote to the Secretary of War Stanton that Grant is desirous of having Ellet's command transferred to him for use of troop transport.[2] Adj. Gen. Thomas telegraphed the War Dept. requesting that Ellet's Marine Brigade be placed on shore duty. Halleck at the Headquarters of the Army in Washington, D.C. wrote to Grant on Aug 24th: *The Secretary of War does not approve conversion of the marine or river brigade into a land brigade but authorizes you to use any of Ellet's brigade for temporary shore duty. The brigade was organized and men enlisted as river men. They have already proved themselves valuable auxiliaries and can probably be used to great advantage against guerilla parties on the Mississippi and with expeditions up the Arkansas and Red rivers.*[3]

The decision was bantered around the Navy and War Department for several months. On Sep 20th Porter wrote again to Welles that he had been unofficially informed that Ellet received a telegram stating the Marine Brigade had been turned over to Grant. He went on to say that they were out of coal which they burned transporting troops and if the Army is to take the brigade, they need to supply fuel. Welles replied that the Department has received no information of any transfer. The Asst. Quartermaster informed Gen. Rawlins on Sep 26th of the boats readiness for embarkation of troops with most provided with fuel. The *Diana* was ready for carrying troops totaling 1,000 men, 200 animals, and 20 wagons; fifteen steamers could embark a total of 10,550 men, 2,610 animals, and 268 wagons. He revised his figures to Rawlins on the 28th to eleven boats with 6,905 troops assigned to the 2nd Division. An added P.S. noted: *I learn that the dispatch-boat Diana, sent up with Colonel Wilson, exploded her boiler at the mouth of White River. No lives lost.*[4]

The following day orders were sent to the Commander of the 2nd Brigade to embark units on three steamers to Griffith's Landing. The *Diana* was to carry 137 men of the 6th Iowa & transportation, 103rd Illinois & transportation, and 40th Illinois & transportation. The 15th Michigan & transportation was aboard the *Lancaster*. The *Groesbeck* transported Co. I, 1st Illinois Light Artillery.[5] The three steamers left Vicksburg Oct 1st arriving at Memphis on the 9th. Lt. Comm. E.K. Owen, reported: "The *Diana* going on dispatch business for General Grant broke down 9 miles above. I had her towed down, and repaired her at an expense of nearly $700." He also wrote to Porter that the men repairing the *Diana*, in need of food and beverage, went to the issuing room and took a small tin pot of ground coffee, sufficient for about 20 men, rather than awakening the paymaster'q steward on the *Sampson*. Owen reported later on Oct 19th that the owner of the steamer *Diana*, R.J. Tunstall, wishes to pay for the repairs done at Skipwith's Landing. Col. Charles Walcutt reported: the men aboard these boats left Memphis on Oct 11th for a long and arduous campaign, short of rations, scant and insufficient clothing, many barefooted, and duties performed without a murmur. Their satisfaction being part of the old 15th Corps from the Army of the Tennessee.

About this time Admiral Porter made an all out effort trying to rid the Navy of the Marine Brigade but not the Ram fleet. On Oct 3rd Col. J.H. Wilson wrote from Cairo to Adm. Porter that the Marine Brigade has been transferred by order to Gen. Grant. Will you be good enough to order all boats to proceed to Vicksburg.[6] On Oct 12th Adm. Porter transmitted a copy of a telegram order from the Secretary of Navy to Ellet informing him that Grant has ordered the Marine Brigade to Vicksburg, I declining issuing any orders until the usual steps are taken as customary.[7] The Secretary of War, Edwin Stanton, wrote to the Secretary of the Navy, Gideon Welles, that the War Department refused to transfer

---

1*Ibid.*,V.27, 696, 697

2*Ibid.*, p.299

3*Ibid.*

4*Ibid.*,Series I, V.30, Correspondence, pp.864, 908

5*Ibid.*, p.923

6*Ibid.*, p.296

7*Ibid.*

the fleet to Gen. Grant as requested by Adm. Porter.[1] The Navy Department's Secretary Welles' order to Adm. Porter at Cairo on Oct 21st noted receipt of your No. 160 and enclosures in reference to the Marine Brigade. You were informed of the transfer of the brigade to Gen. Grant *without the knowledge of this Department. Your connection with it has therefore ceased and, of course, you will not interfere with its movements.*[2]

Several days later Stanton, Secretary of War wrote to Gideon Welles, Secretary of Navy, an endorsement which stated: "War Department refused to transfer the fleet to General Grant as requested by Admiral Porter." However, the Secretary of the Navy wrote to Porter on Oct 21st that his connection with the Marine Brigade had ceased and Grant was in charge. On Oct 30th Porter wrote to Ellet that our official relations have ended, and that Porter expressed *his appreciation of the zeal you have always manifested in regard to public service.* On the same date, Porter added a P.S. to a memo written to Sherman stating: I just received notice that the Marine Brigade and Ram Fleet was turned over to Grant, and that is in your department. He said that he and the general had concluded that the brigade should be broken up, the vessels used as transports, and officers and men put on shore. *I can not tell you all the reports made to me against the brigade. Its robberies and house burning are shameful; and though I felt it to be my duty to report all the matters that came to my notice, yet a feeling of delicacy toward a branch of another corps prevented my so doing. Moreover, the Ellets have been guilty of some very dirty, underhand work toward myself in publishing contemptible articles in the papers, which I never noticed beyond exposing the parties to Gen. Hurlbut, and having the progress of the editor suddenly arrested...and was glad to get rid of the command. They are here doing nothing...I do hope you will break up the whole concern, as General Grant intended to do....*[3]

On Nov 1st the Secretary of War wrote to Gen. Ellet regretting the death of Col. Ellet and authorized 10 to 15 days leave of absence as your purposes may require. Col. Ellet had been the commander of the *Diana* and died Oct 29th at Bunker Hill, Illinois. On Nov 14th, Porter wrote to the Asst. Sec. of Navy that Gen. Ellet is in defiance of Grant's idea of using the brigade as transport. Five boats lay at Cairo doing nothing. Others below or near Vicksburg, reported as ordered, and Ellet dismissed their commanders. In case the Marine Brigade is taken from him, he will fall back on the Ram Fleet command again. The law of Congress prescribes that all vessels used for naval purposes be turned over to the Navy. *The Marine Brigade and Ram Fleet has been the most expensive affair...If it should be permitted to operate independently, the Navy would bear all the odium of its doings...I trust that you will use every effort to put a stop to this thing...*

On Nov 21st an order from the War Department to Ellet responding to a letter of the 22nd Ultimus, authorized Ellet to recruit your present command to the maximum strength conducted in Western States with consent of their Governors. Ellet was denied recruitment of two each additional companies of Cavalry and Artillery.

Wes was at Goodrich Landing, Georgia when he wrote on Nov 24th from Goodrich Landing, Georgia:

> *To: Miss Lizzie Ayres*
> *From: C. W. Ayres*
> *Dear Sister*
> *Your letter was received yesterday which pleased me verry much. while reading it the boys asked me what I was laughing at. I told them that if they understood it as well as I did they would probably laugh a little too. I also received a letter from Tryphemia which is the first I have heard from Bennington since I left Camp Dennison...Thomas Morehouse has never written to me as he promised to. I was glad to learn that you were all getting better once more for your Sickness...My getting home as I Supposed has played out Sometime ago and now I have no hopes*

<hr>

[1] *Ibid.*, p.297
[2] *Ibid.*, p.300
[3] *Ibid.*, p. 524

158

of getting home until my time is out and I don't know as I want a discharge anyhow for I will be liable to be drafted which I never want done on me in this war...Tell Will that Wes Says he would like to see him but Wes thinks that Will would not like him if he should come home and so he won't come. I don't think that they will take either Ben or Amos for either one of them are not fit for a Soldier...We have captured nearly one hundred rebels Since we left Vicksburg. We go out a Scouting nearly every day. Father must not get Scared about my going on land for we are not a going to be put thare. As this is enough to puzzle your brains, I shall stop. From your Brother   C. W. Ayres

1864

Wes next wrote from Grand Gulf, Mississippi, after the battle at Grand Gulf on Jan 16-18.

Jan 20th, U S Steamer Diana, Grand Gulf, Mississippi
To: Miss Lizzie Ayres
Dear Sister
I received your letter yesterday which you may be Shure I was not at all Sorry to receive for your letters do me more good than you can probily imagine. you have written me a good long letter and deserves a much better answer than I Shall probily be able to give you this time...I will try and write enough for you to under Stand that you still have a brother who occasionally thinks of the good things and happy times generally if I do not now have the privaleges of enjoying them occasionally but Still live in hopes that the time is coming when I can Share them with you. you only tantalize me in telling me of your good times but Still I am glad to learn that you are enjoying your Self. I am afraid that your Christmas and mine will not Stand much of a comparison. I enjoyed myself with a little of no kind of recreation and Scarcely anything to eat but a few hard tacks and cold water So you may know what a good time I had. We have had Some pretty cold weather down here for So far South. New year's morning was the coldest and the thermometer was not down to zero and Since then it has kept about an avarage of temperature. We have to Scout nearly every day. We had a fight last Saturday and one Monday and Several of the boys was wounded and taken prisoners but the rebels got pretty badly punished. We come acrost them nearly every time we go out but they try and manage to Keep out of our way. We came on the Diana as Soon as we came back from Vicksburg which place we left the day I wrote to father and we have been Scouting between here and Natchez every Since but I expect we Shall go up to Vicksburg before long and probably up to about Greenville as the Rebs are getting rather Saucy up there. The Adams has gone up to paducky to repair. I dont Suppose your wishes about me are any greater than my own for I think if I was home now I would try and See if I had enough enginuety left to put up a Sleigh and as we now have good horses we could more than enjoy ourselves...

James E. Geatman wrote to the Secretary of War, Stanton, a seven page letter on Feb 10th.

I take the liberty of addressing you on a subject of interest and importance just at this time, and one which requires prompt action. It is in regard to adequate protection to the Freed people and Lessees of Abandoned plantations, scattered along the Mississippi between Helena and Natchez. The care of these people and the leasing of Plantations has been assured by government and numbers of loyal men from the Middle, Western and Eastern States are flocking in to cultivate these lands and employ the laborers and thereby relieving the Government from the charge and care of these people. During the first year many thousand slaves have flocked into our lines and have been placed in camps along the Mississippi, where they have been furnished with food and protection, by the government. In a limited district, employment was attempted to be given on abandoned plantations some forty persons were found who leased plantations, under a system adopted by commissioners approved by you or those acting under your authority. Although the season was far advanced, fully six weeks beyond the usual time to commence cotton planting still as reported by General Thomas, it resulted satisfactorily to the Lessees, and gave support to men, women, and children who the government would otherwise have been obliged to support. Protection was given to the people in neighborhoods, where there was planting. At Goodriche's Landing there were three regiments of colored troops raised and located at Millikens Bend one, at Skipwith's Landing one. The general impression was that they were intended for the permanent guarding and protection of these people, and this growing and important interest. Sometime since by your order the whole subject relating to abandoned property, and the care of these people was turned over the the Treasure Department and in compliance with that order the Secretary of the Treasure sent Mr. Wm.T. Mollen special supervising agent of the Treasure Department to attend to the new duties devolving upon him. Through advertisements in the Public papers and by other means, large numbers have come forward to and the government in working these lands, and employing the people. A system has been devised by which these people will, not only, be relieved and rendered self supporting, but will add many millions to the Treasure of the United States and give a supply of cotton which will greatly reduce the price of this fabric. At the moment, that these plans, were being just into operation, important Military operations movements required that every available man should be brought into service. The colored troops were removed from the points where they have been located, which produced alarm in the minds of the Lessees, and freed people, heightened by the fact, that a portion of Quantrells band was hovering in the swamps, a short distance back. A perfect [illegible] took place, plantations were abandoned, and thousands of these freed people flocked to the river seeking protection under the cover of gun boats. Some outrages were committed, Cotton Gins burned, Negroes killed, and some carried off into slavery. In order to get these people to labor they must feel that they are secure from those that are vowing vengeance and destruction on them. If it was deemed a matter of sufficient Military necessity to bring these people into our lines, to break the relation of master and slave is it not a matter of equal military necessity that they should be protected, and cared for, let us do nothing to roll back the wave of freedom which is sweeping over this nation, but rather let us remove every obstacle and aid with all our might its onward progress. The breaking of the chains of slavery by the Presidents proclamation has been equal to many mighty battles.-- Should we hesitate now to protect that which has done so much for us. God forbid. I am one that would not for a moment retard any military operations, or dig the wheels of the army into legitimate work, the putting down and crushing out of the rebellion. But there are other interests which must be preserved and protected where it can be done, And the free commerce of the Mississippi which thousands of lives have been sacrificed in regaining should be protected, and there is no more effective way than by lining the shores of that river with loyal men -- which can *only be done by offering them some little protection until they get a foot hold in their new homes and can become accustomed somewhat to their new surroundings. What is required now is that you shall confirm the order of General Sherman who has assigned the Marine Brigade which he could not take with him, to the permanent protection of the Lessees on abandoned plantations and the thousands of freed people who are employed by them. The assignment has been made, but it is liable to be changed or removed any day. By your order or request it can be made permanent. The Marine Brigade numbers now about 1100, Six hundred of whom are mounted, it should be increased to 2000, and at least 2/3 if not the entire force, should be mounted with this Brigade, and the two colored regiments organized specially for Guard duty increased to 4 or 5 will afford adequate protection to this important interest. I am informed that you hesitate or are unwilling to issue any orders that would in the least degree interfere with the Military in the District. Gen. Sherman; now commanding in that department is a true noble gallant Soldier none more so, and one in whom I have every confidence but changes are constantly being made. The Commanders are in the field and one General may not know the empelling motive of another. The parties going into that country carry with them stock, provisions and farming implements amounting in the aggregate to many millions of dollars in value. They are unwilling to jeopardize their lives and property without having some assurance of permanent protection. The Rebel Government, can spare men to break up these planting interests, ours surely can to preserve and protect them. The matter now rests with you -- it is a great responsibility -- another year of idleness, and destitution, of suffering, and death, among these people must do uncalcuable damage. I earnestly intreat you that you will save these people. Let it not be said that the freed man cannot support himself - he can if he only has a fair chance, and such protection as is essential to all industrial pursuits. I crave your early and immediate consideration to the subject. Thirty thousand people stand tremblingly on the shores of the Mississippi awaiting your decision. Shall I return and speak words of life on earth to them -- Thousands of others have by this time pressed on to partake of the new born of freedom offered to them by the Presidents proclamation and tens of thousands more will follow -- shall they be forced back into Slavery? Shall this great problem be so soon solved and decided. The colored man is not fit for freedom's crush but for the hopes and hearts of the loyal men of the nation. All I ask is that you extend your helping hand, Ah! But your little finger of protection and all will be well. Prompt and immediate action is necessary and I trust you will give this subject your early and earnest attention. If I can be of any service to you in the way of offering information, I mold myself in readiness to answer any call night or day from you.* [No response to this letter was in the National Archive Folio.]

About March 1st Gen. Banks came up the Mississippi river with gunboats, transports, and an army of 30-40,000 troops. They started up the Red River. Confederates felt Federals wanted to reach the heart of Texas as it was reported the wagon train had scythes to reap wheat. Walker's and Martin's divisions and Tom Green's two brigades of cavalry delayed the March until Apr 8th giving time for a larger number of Texas troops plus Missouri and Arkansas troops under Price to come to their assistance.

Wes was present on the muster-rolls of Company E on Mar 5th when the Brigade fought in the battle of Coleman's Corner, Mississippi. Gen. Sherman was en route for Memphis when he wrote to Gen. Rawlins at Nashville on Mar 8th:

General: I had the honor to receive, at the hands of General Butterfield, General Grant's letter of Feb 18. I had returned from Meridian by the time I had appointed, but the condition of facts concerning the Red River expedition being indefinite, I took one of the marine boats, the Diana, and went down to New Orleans to confer with General Banks...I have inspected Natchez and Vicksburg and feel sure they can now be held safe with comparatively small garrisons, and the river is patrolled by gun-boats and the Marine Brigade.[1]

Wes' biography noted that he had participated in the Red River campaign in Louisiana. Following is a series of reports about the campaign to show the paper work involved in the command.

In early March, the fleet of transports sailed from Vicksburg at 7 p.m. Thursday with steamers *Hastings, Autocrat, John Raine* and *Diana*. They arrived at the mouth of Red River and reported to Adm. Porter on Friday noon. They went up Red River and Atchafalaya to Simsport on Saturday, where inspection, review, and drill by regiments were held. The infantry began marching at 7 p.m. Bridges were repaired thru the night. They bivouacked at 4 a.m. Roads were bad and swampy. They were eight miles from Simsport on Monday. From 6 a.m. on they marched until 11 a.m. when coffee was ordered for the men and animals fed. They resumed marching at noon through bayou and swamp. Then they came into a lovely prairie called Avoyelles, settled exclusively by French immigrants, many of whom had sought shelter under the French Flag. Pressing on they arrived at Marksville at 5:30 and formed a line of battle. The men had been earlier warned by deserters that the enemy was located on their left flank. Firing came from the fort. The commander had been warned that 6,000 Texans under Walker might attack our rear and left wing. The fort surrendered at 6:30, heavy pickets were posted, arms stacked, and bivouacked. A large amount of commissary and ordnance, 334 prisoners, and 24 officers were taken.

Friday March 11th found the convoy and fleet making a slow, devious progress up the tortuous windings of the Red River.[2] Much of the travel was at night and navigation, at the present stage of water, was difficult. Col. Risdon's report to Capt. Fisk said: Agreeable to instructions from post headquarters I embarked with my regiment on board the steamer *Diana* at 11 a.m., Mar 12, 1865, and proceeded down the river. On reaching Hard Times Landing I gave the signal for the gun boat agreed upon. I was not answered and I kept on to Grand Gulf...then down river to the mouth of Bayou Pierre, where I found the gun boat *Mound City*.[3] After conferring with Captain Paddock, we started up Bayou Pierre, the gun boat in advance. After running up some 3-4 miles the bayou became so narrow and trees hung so far over that the *Diana* could not proceed and I was obliged to return to the mouth of the bayou, then to Grand Gulf, disembarked with my command, and started overland for Port Gibson.[4] Lt. Comm. John Mitchell's log noted that on Mar 15th ten steamers and the hospital ship, *Woodford*, passed up thru the river's obstructions. Among them the *Diana*.[5]

Gen. T. Kilby Smith, US Army, 17th Army Corps report to his Headquarters Division on March 16th varied little from Adm. Porter's earlier report written above. He wrote:

....the detachment he had honor to command embarked on steamers Hastings, Autocrat, John Raine e:, and Diana and arrived at the mouth of Red River and reported to Admiral Porter on Friday noon. We sailed up the Red River and Atchafalaya at Saturday 10 a.m. On Sunday debarked and received marching orders at 7 p.m., Marching at 8 p.m. They rested two hours during the night and went on rapidly until 11 a.m. when coffee was ordered and animals fed. Resumed march at noon. Arrived at Marksville at 5:30, formed line of battle, then

---

1 *Ibid.*, Series I, V.32, Part III, Correspondence: p.40

2 Louisiana reported that on 11 Mar 1864, Adm. Porter entered the mouth of Red River with nineteen gunboats followed by 10,000 men loaned by Sherman. Conf. Gen. Taylor immediately evacuated Alexandria and went to Pleasant Hill. Alexandria was captured on the 15th by Porter. Fort DeRussy was captured on 14 Mar by A.J.Smith's forces who Mared unhalted up the whole valley of the Red River. Conf. Vol.10, Louisiana , pp.127, 129, 133

3 The *Mound City* with 13 mounted guns was blown up on Jun 17th by Arkansas batteries on the White River near St. Charles with 180 men lost.

4 *Naval Forces on Western Waters.*, Series I, V.49, Pt.1: p.85, 53rd US Colored Troops

5 *Ibid.*, V.26: p.774

commenced firing at the fort. At 6:30 the fort surrendered. The command had marched 28½ miles, built a substantial bridge 60' in length, repaired minor ones, and took a fort between sunrise and sunset. One brigade was actively engaged with two killed and 33 wounded. Prisoners numbered 334, 24 officers.[1]

On May 26th Col. Colton Green, C.S. Army reported to Maj. H. Ewing, Asst. Adj. Gen., that: *on several attacks at Adair's above Gaines Landing on May 24th, his second attack riddled the transports and caused them to be burned. In the 4th attack the boat Diana was seriously hurt, with some damage to the mosquito gunboat. Quite an alarm extended to the upper river, and the enemy has assembled a formidable fleet.[2]* Another report on June 8th reiterated that the fleet was engaged for near two hours, the gunboat disabled, the Diana roughly handled, with many killed and wounded, and the transport penetrated in many places.[3]

Wes was transferred to Co. F, Marine Regiment on June 30th and left the boat in July for Jackson and Grand Gulf.

On July 18th Halleck sent a letter to Gen. Canby, Natchez, Miss, in regard to the conduct of the Marine Brigade in carrying on trade with the rebels. Some months ago Grant made similar charges and recommended the Brigade be disbanded, officers mustered out of service. Authority was granted but he (Grant) left to take command in Chattanooga, the matter not acted on. You are now directed to examine these charges and if you concur with Grant the organization should be broken up with the boats turned over to the Quartermaster Dept. and transfer the men back to their regiments or put them in garrison, mustering out such officers as now required. Ellet will report in person to the Secretary of War after turning over his men and public property.

Asst. Quartermaster Brooks at New Albany, wrote to Gen. Meigs on July 19th in response to their meeting on the 8th, Brooks being requested to put the substance of his remarks about the Marine Brigade in writing:

> *The idea of such an organization was well conceived; it can do a work in keeping the river clear of guerrillas...When organized in Dec 1862, necessity was getting to work as soon as possible. Gen. Ellet was ordered to recruit men, but not those detached with another service. Being difficult and progressing slowly, an order was obtained to recruit from convalescents from the hospitals. This was done and to disadvantage. Many thought fit were found unserviceable. Others had contracted lazy and vicious habits...Notwithstanding these defects, I doubt if any portion of the Army, in proportion to cost of men and money to the Government, has accomplished more. I doubt whether, the navigation of the Mississippi could have been kept open. The boats have been running up and down the river, landing at points infested with guerrillas, following them into the interior, scattering and cutting them up...Where people have been known to harbor them [the guerrillas], their houses were burned. Where points have been particularly infested, one or more boats have been stationed to keep the river clear...This kind of service, though very necessary and useful, is not the kind which makes much noise in the newspapers...The brigade could be more efficient with the present number of boats by increasing the number of men with a large increase of expenditure.[4]*

---

1 *Ibid.*, Series I, V.34, Pt.I, Reports: pp.376,377, Red River Campaign
2 *Ibid.*, p.803
3 *Ibid.*, p.805
4 *Ibid.*, V.26: p.481

Wes' letter gives a good description of the brigades activities in early July, 1864:

Jul 26th, Omega, Louisiana
To: Miss Lizzie Ayres From: C. W. Ayres
Dear Sister

Your long looked for letter came to me two or three days ago and I now find the first opportunity to answer it. I have had a pretty rough time since I wrote to you before but still I keep well and hearty. The first of Jul we came aboard of our boats and took on a load of negro troops and went down to rodney and on the third we started out with three days rations. we went about fifteen miles and camped for the night. The next morning (the fourth) learning whare they were we started after them. we soon found them and fought them awhile but they did not stand long. then we followed them untill nearly night when we came back to our old ground and unsaddled for the night but it was not long before the pickets began fireing which rather vexed us as we was just getting our supper which we had to leave. We was soon in our saddles ready to fight or run. The rebels soon came up in pretty good force and commenced on a negro regiment. they had not been fireing long when a strong force of them came up and attacked us on the other side so we were completely surrounded and all we had to do was to fight our way out or surrender. So we went at it, the balls came from both directions over us for a while, but they found it rather too hot for them, they opened a road for us and we started for the boats. they kept fighting our rear guard until long after dark when we ambushed them several times and killed a good many of them. They soon found that they were getting the worst of it and they left us and we went on to the boats unmolested. we had two negro regiments with us thare was several of them killed. the loss in our regiment was light So you may know that we had a pretty high time in celebrating the fourth of July. we then came back to Vicksburg and soon started out toward Jackson with six day rations. we took a round about way and came in at Grand Gulf. we was out five days only. we had some light skirmishing with the rebels but nothing serious. we lay on Shore one night for thare to transport troops up the river in the morning---at daybreak they attacked us but we were ready for them and they got a little to far for all of them all to get back again. we killed a good many and took several prisoners, one was Colonel Wood, the man that commanded the rebels the fourth and also a major the next night. we got aboard and came to Vicksburg but they Soon put us off on Shore where we now are about thirty miles above Vicksburg. we came with ten day's rations for them to transport troops to Memphis we are expecting down now. I took a ride of fifty miles day before yesterday. I have given you a pretty good history So I will end this sheet of scribbling. Dont delay so long in answering. From your affectionate Brother   C. W. Ayres
the weather is verry hot just now it will almost singe the hair off my head. thare is plenty of peaches here now. thare was plenty of blackberries but they are all gone. we have greens come everyday and thare is no end to mellons. If father sells his horses I wish you would tell him to pay fifty dollars that he used of mine that I first drawed in towards my land for I think I have earned all of my money.

This letter written by Wes' father, Henry, is apparently the only one that he wrote to Wes that has survived. It paints a vivid picture of the news at home:

Jul 28th 1864, Meridian, Michigan

To: Wesley Ayres, Mississippi Marine Brigade, Steamer Diana, Co. C, Vicksburg, Miss.

    Dear Son   I received your letter some time ago. Lib wrote soon after So I will answer now. We was glad to hear that you was all rite yet whilst So many is coming up mising. Tom Crank was shot lately at PetersBerg in the head and killed dead. Elishur was all rite yet. I have ben poorly for a day or two but keep to work. The rest of us is all well. Gus is away to work in hay and harvest gets 2 to 3 dolars a day. But that wont get as much as fifty cents would before the war, everything is so dear. Shirting yard such as we used to get for 8 and 10 cents if fifty to sixty cents and everything else in the same proportion, calico 30 to 40 cents, flour 11 dollars a barrel. So you see it costs something to live. I am wearing some of your and Guses old duds that you called worn out. If I could [have] some of the clothes thats thrown away and wasted in the army I could use them to good advantage. I see congress has raised your wages private soldiers to Sixteen dollars a month from the first of May. Well 36 dollars a year is Something. I don't know how much longer the rebels will hang on. Grant is holding Lee level at Richmond. What the result will be no body nows but our army pressing them hard. I think Grant means to Starve Lee out this Sumer. I think will end the mess Some how or other there has ben Some terable hard fi[gh]ting around richmond. our men has done Some terrable Storming and the rebels fights with great desperation. some of the most desperate fi[gh]ting the world ever witnessed. Both Sides determined to konquer how many more brave men has got to fall God only nows and he wont tell. Another new call lately for 500,000 men. its begining to make some Squirming. Volunteering is prety much playd out So they will have to draft. there is no 300 dollar class now every man drafted will have to go or furnish a Substitute and Substitutes will come very high as they can ask just what they are a mind to. Some men will pay a thousand dollars before they will go. Well I want to see the big lofers fetched in the ranks. here to fore they have Stood back and let the poor lofers go but they have got to face the music now or pay pretty deer probably they cant get Substitutes anyhow. I would like to See Some of the Doctors, Priests and Lawyers and rich lofers have to lay off fine broad clothes and put uncle Sams apparel an take the musket and Step in the ranks. Well they have got to go if the call is made and the men must be had. the men is quite thin now and 500,000 more will thin the ranks a good deal. there is hardly any young men now cant get up much doings for want of men. all kinds of business building and farming goes with a drag for want of men. the war has used up all the lofers that used to loaf around the vilages and cities. Most every man is busy at Some thing and you will [see] a great many women out to work in the fields or gardens. they have to do it their men is in the War. its very common to Se Women driving horses to Wagons and Buggies. we have got our wheat stacked its nice wheat. wheat is first rate in this State. we will have 30 or 40 bushels a piece. we had 125 dozen. well thats good deal beter than to have to buy at 2.30 or 2.40 a bushel. we have nine acres of corn and looks well. we have half. its quite dry this Sumer all over the northern States. Grand father [Wood] and mother is here yet. they came the last of Jun. Grand father is underbushing and Slashing for Ben. he thinks Ben will never get it cleard so he has gone at it. General Sherman is near Atlanta has taken a good share of Georgia. Jonathon is with him he rote to us last they had drove the rebels 40 miles and was going to drive them to hell or Some other Seaport. Lib is home to work making Gus and Will Some clothes. She Says She is going to get Wills likeness and Send you before long. Will is going to make a master builder he is all the while a geting up Some machinery or implements. Mother is fixen up around with flowers it looks like home if it is in the woods. Gus and I worked your road tax. it was a little over 2 dollars. we cant get much time to clear yet have hard Scratching to

make a living. I would like to underbush considerable this fall. we have girdled considerable last Sumer and this So as to have the big trees a dying. I Supos you would like to be home this Sumer and girdle and underbush Some. Well maybe you will after a while. You have a rich lot of land no mistake if it was cleared up. I Supos you have had green corn and ripe peaches long ago. our corn is just tassaled and Silking. we will have roasten [e]ars before a great while but no peaches out here this year but plenty aples. we have had peas beans and new Potatoes Sometime. Me and Mother Gus and Will went visiting up to Vans in Jun. he has got sixty acres good land mostly cleard, good new frame barn, a good lot and frame house he has betered himself a good deal. the Boys was all well the last they herd George is with Sherman. Sele was somewhere in tennessee and Tom was out. they looking for him home every day. thats a firtle country where van lives old cleard up farms and rich farmers. they raise a host of wheat there great fields forty to sixty acres in a field one third the land in wheat and it looked Splendid. it will yield from 20 to 40 bushels an acre. Nate Marsh and perry Sebring has took up land and Setled near Marvins. Nate thinks its a fine country in the South of isabel the back woods is Setling up fast. Maby you dont care anything about Such connections. well tell what news you want to now and I will write it. I herd up at Vans that Albert White died in the army last spring with the measles. Lacretia's there at her fathers. Gus is in Tennessee at work for uncle Sam. he hired for six months and got a lot of fellows to go with him from Bennington. Steve Lasko was one. Well the sketers bites and I must quit they are prety thick here. have you any of them down there for comfort. 29th warm this morning. Amos and I are going to town today. Amos takes a load of hay. Hay is 16 or 18 dollars a tun. Lansing is growing prety fast. they are at work on the railroad from here to Jackson going to have it done a year from next fall. it wont go more than 2 miles from your lot. Grand father[1] Says he likes it better everytime he comes out here. he would like to live here if Moses[2] would Sell and come out. Will Says tell Wes he would like to have him come home. I expect he would be so tickled he wouldnt know how to act. Mother Says Send a lock of your hair in your next letter curls if you have any. Guses hair curls in a Solid mat. its prety Black if he was home I would Send Some. We will Send a lock of Wills. My whiskers is geting quite white. We have one litle crabaple, Siberian, with 8 aples on. I Set out 12 aple trees around the house, they are growing fine. Well good By for this time. Write Soon tell all the particulars.
    H C Ayres

Wes participated in the artillery engagement with Marmaduke at Greenville plus the battles at Port Gibson, Mississippi; Lake Village; the Red River expedition and other minor battles. He also served as a Special Order Clerk at General Dana's Headquarters.

Special Orders No. 106, by Major Gen. Dana, Vicksburg, Mississippi, on Aug 25th gave the following disposition of officers and enlisted men of the MMB:

All enlisted men who have been formally transferred from other organizations and whose original term of service has not expired, will be immediately transferred, the Cavalry and Infantry to the 58th Ohio Infantry and the Artillery to the batteries now stationed here, to be distributed by the Chief of Artillery of the District. All enlisted men now serving in the Brigade by original enlistment or by re-enlistment after discharge from regiment to which they originally belonged will be organized into Companies of the maximum strength. A full number of

---

1Jonathan Wood
2Moses Gidley

commissioned officers for all companies formed will be retained in service and attached to them, and Field and Medical Officers in proportion to the number of companies organized. Brig. Genl. E. W. Ellet is charged with the execution of this and will see that each man is provided with a descriptive roll and military history and will report progress to these Headquarters.

The following day orders were modified by General Dana as not to include the battery of Light Artillery with Captain Walling preserving the present battery organization and report with his command to the Chief Art'y of the District.

A group of enlisted men from Ohio on the U.S. Steamer, *B.J. Adams*, at Vicksburg wrote on Aug 26th to Governor Brough of Ohio:

We the undersigned members of Ohio organizations having been placed on detached service in the Marine Brigade on Jan 1st 1863 I have the honor to represent-- 1st -- That said organization has ceased to exist-- 2nd -- That the term of enlistment in the organization from which we were detached has expired. We desire an order from you to report to the HdQrs of our State to be mustered out of the service in order that we can reenlist in defense of our glorious old Flag, as representatives of the gallant State of Ohio. The following are the enlisted men from Ohio whose term of service has expired or nearly so. [The list of men signing the letter was missing from the records in the National Archives].

On Aug 27th Wes was confined to a Military Prison at Vicksburg. When news reached his family in Michigan, his father wrote letters of inquiry about his situation. Upon his release he was made a private again on Sep 1st by regimental order when he went on detached service as a Clerk at District Headquarters at General Washburn's Headquarters in Vicksburg.

General Dana wrote a lengthy letter from Vicksburg on Sep 3rd to Maj. Christensen, Asst. Adj. Gen. of the West Mississippi Military Division addressing the reasons why it was impracticable to carry out your orders literally with this peculiar organization in reply to Halleck's letter of Jul 18th 1864:

The organization was composed of a battery of Artillery which had neither armament nor horses, but was full of officers and men; a battalion of Cavalry of four companies, and a regiment of Infantry of ten companies. The battery was placed on shore in its former condition and is now serving here in the defences - The Cavalry was transferred into the regiment of Infantry forming ten maximum companies. This consolidation rendered super numerary a number of non commissioned officers, one 1st Lieutenant and one Asst. Surgeon who were mustered out of service in accordance with the rule embraced in General Order No. 86 War Department 1863. The regiment is now known here by the name of the Marine Regiment and I regret to give the opinion that it is demoralized, disaffected, insubordinate, and will probably as an organization be useless. I have not yet thought proper to issue arms to it, as I have been compelled to use harsh measures with it in its mutinous demonstrations on being reorganized. I have refrained from making report upon it till now because of its uncertain condition. I have now reduced it to submission and obedience, not however to discipline or to a condition where a commander can treat it with confidence - I have never expressed an opinion of this reorganization of this force and retaining it in service to any living soul but have insisted on a silent submission to orders and have enforced it. Now however to my superiors I feel that it is my duty and is expected of me that an opinion should be given - It is, that the feeling of the officers and men of the late Mississippi Marine Brigade, entertained unanimously to a man, that they have a just claim to be mustered out of the service; has so good a ground of entertainment as to be entitled to a respectful and careful consideration from the government. Further, that, as they are now retained in service, disaffected as they are badly disciplined with inexperienced and in some instances incompetent officers, they will be far more hurtful than useful. My advice is to muster out the whole organization but if it is not mustered out then it certainly should be dispersed under new officers and the officers and non commissioned officers discharged. To this end I would recommend that three companies be sent to Morganza, the privates distributed as recruits through the whole command and the officers and non commissioned then mustered out the same with three more companies to be sent via New Orleans to the Army of the Potomac, the same with four more to go to General Granger. These men feel that they have been induced into a special service under special promises; have forfeited and relinquished their bounties etc and that their contract is of such a kind that the government cannot now in good faith put them on shore where many of them who were gathered from hospitals claim that they would be unable to march a single march.

As of Sep 3rd, General Dana had 45 men in confinement, one shot by the guard which escorted them to daily work on fortifications. He yielded to their petition and released them on a promise of good behavior and detailed them for fatigue duty to test their sincerity. Enclosed were copies of his two orders directing the reorganizing of this force. Gen. Canby replied from New Orleans on Sep 14th that he was of the opinion that the circumstances under which these men were enlisted give them an equitable claim to be discharged. Gen. Ellet wrote to Col. Townsend on Sep 15th that in accordance to orders the Mississippi Marine Brigade has been consolidated into one regiment of infantry and one battery of light artillery and the boats turned over to the Quarter Master of the Dept. of West Miss. He noted great dissatisfaction among the men as many from other organizations sacrificed eighteen to twenty months of former service in hopes to be able to serve their country. But now when the MMB no longer regarded as necessary they feel that they are entitled to an honorable discharge. Many of them having served over three years from the period of their original enlistments and in most cases without any bounty. They do feel that great injustice is being done to them by thus being compelled to serve in the field the remainder of the time, that they enlisted to serve in the Mississippi Marine Brigade and consider the act of consolidation as one of bad faith on the part of the govt towards them and should be mustered out of service.

He earnestly hoped that it may be deemed advisable by the Department to muster the entire command out of service. As an act of justice to brave and good soldiers whose term of enlistment has expired with the expiration of the service into which they enlisted. Papers over this matter were being shuffled about the country.

There was considerable correspondence in the case of Acting Master Daniel W. Glenney, U.S. Navy, who was accused of treacherous conduct while commanding the *USS Rattler*, Sep 4th 1864. In direct violation of general orders issued by Adm. David Porter, Glenney directed his boats to land and the crew to proceed beyond the distance wherein he could protect or give assistance, thereby losing his men by death or capture which showed his lack of judgment and capacity. Glenney was also directed to return to his command, but proceeded to Vicksburg and Gen. Dana supported his unofficer like conduct. Lt. Commander wrote to Admiral Porter that Glenney was relieved of his command and placed under arrest. Glenney had come to Selfridge to report the loss of his men, and was reprimanded, and sent back on the *Empress* to his command. Instead he went on to Vicksburg where General Dana notified me of his whereabouts. He had been previously directed not to send armed parties ashore. It seems that from information received from negroes, Glenney sent the men out at night to the home of J. James to try to locate James' two sons, both rebel officers.[1]

On Sep 23rd, Samuel Breck, Asst. Adj. General forwarded the papers to Major General Canby. Despite Ellet's plea on behalf of his men, on Sep 29th, Halleck wrote to Gen. Canby at New Orleans orders from the Secretary of War that the men of the former Marine Brigade be transferred to other companies and regiments and officers mustered out except in such cases as you may deem it proper to dismiss them for neglect of duty in maintaining order and discipline subject to approval of the President. It was recommended *that these men be scattered far and wide ... where they can best be reduced to discipline as at the fort's near New Orleans, Mobile, Pensacola and Key West. Also to Hilton Head and Fort Monroe if deemed proper and without inconvenience or great expense. Those who continue mutinous or insubordinate should be confined or put in irons at night and be compelled to labor on the public works during the day till they yield to discipline as an example to others.*

Canby at New Orleans, wrote to Hd Qtrs. Div. of West Mississippi, that he endorsed the discharge from service of the men recently belonging to the MMB. On Nov 19th Secretary of War, Stanton, wrote to Gen. Canby at New Orleans requesting a report on the disposition of Ellet's marine fleet. A reply noted a list and location of the steamers and tugs. The *Diana* was at Morganza.

> *These boats were nearly all in bad condition when received from Marine Brigade. Several are at St. Louis being overhauled. They are all required for reserve transportation and post service at different points on the river.*[2]

Breck responded on Dec 2nd to the Secretary of War: Richard McCanney of 76th Ohio Volunteers and others now on detached service in the Marine Regiment together with others of that organization have applied for their discharge on the ground of expiration of term of service and that they were enlisted for duty on the water. He went on to state that: *the organization was authorized by the General-in-Chief on Nov 11th 1862 (copy enclosed) to act in connection with the Ram Fleet and in cooperation with the Western Gunboats by instructions from the General-in-Chief on Feb 10th 1863 (copy enclosed) with authority to General Ellet to recruit from convalescents in Hospitals who were to be discharged from their regiments upon enlisting in this organization... Ellet remarked: ...these men were induced to sacrifice their former long service and enlisted for three years more in this Brigade for the sake of lighter duty, that many have served over three years altogether, and since discontinuance of the organization the men are justly entitled to their discharge.*

Major General Dana recommends they be mustered out. Major General Canby recommends for their discharge in an endorsement on Oct 9th. Canby's papers have been lost in transmittal which is much regretted, as his views would have doubtless furnished much light on the subject.

> *It is evident that these men were enlisted for a special service on the water and the assignment of them to duty as land forces seems not to have been contemplated by either party on their enlistment unless the interests of the service required a temporary transfer to duty with land forces. The great inducement was that their services would only be required with the Ram Fleet for which consideration they were induced to forego their former services and enter into a new contract with the Government for three years additional service. To compel them now to perform permanent duty as land forces it is believed will not tend to subserve the best interests of the Government or do justice to these men who were doubtless correct in supposing that at the time of their muster in, the Government did not contemplate employing them in any capacity save that specified at that time. In consideration of these facts it is respectfully recommended that such of these men*

1 *Ibid.*, V.26: pp.536,537

2 *Ibid.*, Series I, V.41, Pt. IV, Correspondence: p.609

This was approved on Dec 3rd 1864 by order of the Secretary of War. (Sg'd) C. A. Dana, Asst.
Secretary of War. On Dec 5th, Special Orders No. 431 by order of Secretary of War:

Wes' letter to Augustus Ayres:

Dear Brother
    *I received a letter from Father this morning and for the first time received
information that you was a Soldier in Uncle Sams Army, and learning that you
was so*
*near by I thought I would write to you and find out how you are getting along.
Father has not heard from me for a long time. He has been very uneasy about me
he wrote to Washington and to Columbus and to our Colonel to find out whare I
am but I have written to him some time ago, and suppose he had not received it
when he wrote to me. He told me that they were all well and said that Uncle Moses
had bought a farm near us and was a going to move up thare. Hazin had enlisted
and was at Nashville the last heard from him. Jonathan was all right.I am detailed
at General Washburns Head Quarters as Clerk. I have very good place and get
twelve dollars more a month, and have good liveing and a nice house to live in. We
are expecting orders from the war Dept to have us mustered out of the service of
the U.S. and I think that I will be on my way home in month or two. I would try
and get liberty to go and see you if I was at the Company but I could not leave
now. My Company is at pawpaw Island above the mouth of the yazoo River on the
Mississippi guarding a wood yard. The weather is rather cool just at presant. I
have nothing else to write you at presant, so I will terminate this by requesting you
to write as soon as you receive this. If you hear from home let me know. I shall
write another letter to Lib today.*
Your Brother Wesley Ayres
Address to, District Head Quarters
Vicksburg Miss
PS. Give me the letter name of your Company

Wes wrote to his brother Augustus on Jan 6th 1865 from Head Quarters District of Vicksburg,
Mississippi:

Dear Brother
    *I received your letter several days ago but had forgotten to answer it until
today. I was verry glad to hear from you and learn that you were all right and
hope you will continue to keep so. I was sorry that you enlisted for I hoped to see
you soon as I expect to have the privilege of being home before long. The order*

came here about a week ago from Washington to muster us out of the United States service and they are making preparations as fast as they can, and I expect the last of this week or the first of next I will be on my way up the River. I should be glad to get to see you before I go but I suppose that is impossible, but nine months will soon pass away and then we can get together once more. I expect that Father Mother Lib and Will will more than rejoice to get to see me once more and I dont suppose that I will be verry sorry to see them. I expect that I will almost freeze to death up there it has been so long since I have seen any cold weather but I think that I can stand it before Fathers fire. I will try anyhow. I suppose you are just beginning to find out what a nice thing Soldering is. I suppose you find it as nice as you expected and probily a little nicer but wait until you get to Marching through the mud then you will find where the nice part comes in. It has been verry muddy for the last two days it rained hard all day yesterday. General Grierson came in yesterday with a large Cavalry force they started from Memphis some time ago. They brought in between seven and eight hundred prisoners. it was a hard sight to see them Some of them all covered with mud Some wadeing through the mud barefooted with their pants up to their nees. I am going to Ohio before I go home it will not be much farther out of my way and I want to see the folks in that Country once more. I received a letter from father and one from Lib since I wrote to you. They have fine slieighing there now. They were all well when they wrote. I dont know as I have anything more to write at present that would interest you so I shall stop with my scribling for this time. you need not answer this for I would not receive it. I will write when I get home.

As ever your Brother   Wesley Ayres

The Company muster-out roll stated Wes was mustered-out at Vicksburg on Feb 1st 1865, having last been paid Aug 31st 1864. He was due $100 and $38.07 for clothing.[1]

When Wes entered the Mississippi Marine Brigade January 1863, his old unit, The Third Ohio, continued to serve in the Western Theater after Wes' hospitalization on Oct 28th 1862. After the Battle of Perryville they wintered in Murfreesboro. Some units were in Alabama on Apr 30th 1863 involved in fights at Day's Gap in Sand Mountain, Crooked Creek, and Hog Mountain. Others were part of Streight's Raid on Rome, Georgia, from Apr 26th to May 3rd. Near Rome many were captured on May 3rd. Officers and men were sent to Belle Isle and Libby Prisons where they lived in tents with sparse rations. Later that month many were exchanged and sent northward to Camp Chase in Columbus, Ohio, to reorganize. In June, they helped quell the Holmes County Rebellion. Morgan's cavalry crossed the Ohio River into Ohio on July 9th beginning their raids. Ohio men were now on home turf. Morgan lost half his men on the 19th. He surrendered on the 26th. On Aug 1st those in the south were transported to Nashville, then Bridgeport, Alabama, where they were on rear guard duty under Nathan B. Forest. On Nov 27th they were sent to do garrison duty at Chattanooga until June 1864. Orders came on June 9th to return to Camp Dennison where they mustered out Jun 23rd 1864. During its service, they lost 4 officers, 87 enlisted men killed and mortally wounded. Three officers and 78 enlisted men were lost to disease, totaling 172 fatalities.

Wes left Vicksburg and headed to central Ohio to visit his relatives there. His family in Michigan were anxious to see him. On Mar 20th 1865 his father wrote:

---

1 The preceding came from family letters, copies of Wes' Civil War papers in the National Archives in Washington, DC., and information located in the published volumes of the War of the Rebellion Official Records. I had difficulty acquiring his papers in the Archives due to his records filed under Ayers or Ayres; Wesley, Wesley C., Wesley J., and C. Wesley. Success came after I found his pension application number. When the Archives sent copies of his papers, it was suggested that due to his being a clerk for generals, I might come to D.C. and check out one particular file. That occasion arose much later. By then it had been given a different file number. In the reading room I unfolded, read, copied, and refolded a large collection of original documents which were at my disposal to use in this book.

Wes got home at last and we was glad. He is Wes yet, only he has some mustaches on his chin and upper lip and brought home a big trunk full of things in a box he made. He bought a new suit of citizens clothes in Cardington worth $50. He brought a double barrel gun, his Colt gun and a very nice fiddle worth $30. Also 3 blankets, a coverlet and rubber blanket, 3 pair pants, 3 drawers, 2 shirts, 2 pair socks, 2 vests, 2 jackets, 1 dress coat and an overcoat and cap. Also 3 Hunter case silver watches. Wes tried on his brother's linen coat and offered to buy it since Gus had outgrown it. Yesterday a man offered him $1,000 to go as his substitute.

Earlier Wes had sent money to his father to buy some land for him. Wes occupied himself improving his forty acres on Forest Road near Meridian township, helping his relatives, and doing carpentry work in the Okemos area. He played his fiddle at dances with a guitarist named, Bascom. Later he and Lib's family headed for Kansas.

The Historian

Published by the Society of the Survivors of the Ram Fleet and Marine Brigade.

Oct 1919 - Annual No. 38
Charles Wesley Ayres
The 33rd reunion of the Society was held at Columbus, Ohio, Sep 9th 1919, the results printed in this issue. A brief biography of Brigadier General Alfred W. Ellet, Commander of the Mississippi Marine Brigade and the Ram Fleet, was noted on page five. Memorial services were held at the 9th Annual Reunion at Louisville, Kentucky, on 11 Sep 1895. Ellet had died the previous 9 Jan. Beginning on page three was an item in memory of Capt. Warren D. Crandall, our beloved Historian. Crandall had authored in 1907, The History of the Ram Fleet and the Mississippi Marine Brigade. This appears to be the only publication about this group serving in the Civil War. It was available in 1919 for $5.00 plus $1.50 postage in facsimile which did not guarantee the graphics or charts in the original.

The following article on Charles W. Ayers was printed on page nine.

Comrade Charles W. Ayers has quite an extended and varied war service to his credit. His first enlistment, Apr 23rd, 1861, was in Co. "I", 3rd, O.V. Inftry, and was sent to Camp Jackson, Columbus, Ohio. May 1st, was transferred to Camp Dennison, near Cincinnati and mustered for three months service. On the 15th of June following, his command was re-organized and mustered for three years. Was then sent to West Virginia, under the command of Genl. McClelland. Participated in the battle of Rich Mountain, and then was sent south to Camp Elk Water, and remained there until the approach of winter and was sent on south to Camp Jefferson under command of Genl. Mitchel, where he remained until the following spring, '62, and then going south again with his command, which captured Huntsville, Ala., and remained there during that summer. Was detached as "body guard" to Genl. Mitchell, and with his army proceeded to intercept Genl. Bragg, who was moving his army on Louisville, Ky. Encountered him at Perryville, where a sharp engagement ensued in which the Union forces were greatly depleted. In this engagement, Comrade Ayers lost his cap by a "Johnny" shot, but saved his head. Proceeded then to Nashville, but on the way became ill, and was sent back to the hospital in Louisville, and thence to a hospital in Cincinnati. On recovering his health, he enlisted in the M.M. Brigade, and was sent to Benton Barracks, Mo., and mustered again for 3 years. Was assigned to Co. "E," Capt. Fisher commanding, made a Corporal and later a Sergeant. With the fleet proceeded to Vicksburg, where it cooperated with Gen. Grant in the siege of that city. It was here at this time that Comrade Ayers took a very active part with the 20-pound Parrot gun, that was placed in the levee opposite the city, and did such effective work to the wonder of the Confederate artillerymen. He also participated in the artillery engagement with Marmaduke at Greenville, also the battles at Duck River, Port Gibson, Coleman's Corners, Lake village, the Red River expedition and several minor battles. After leaving the Marine Boats at Vicksburg, he was detailed as Special Order Clerk at Genl. Dana's headquarters, afterwards Genl. Washburn's, retaining this position until he was mustered out with the Brigade in '65. Comrade Ayers resides at Lansing, Mich. His photo is No. 8 in the group.

Following is Wes' Mar 5, 1895 recollection of his war record written thirty years after his discharge and noted to be given to his son, Eno, as his Mother's Secret Gift.

My first enlistment as private in Co. I, 3rd, O.V.I. Apr 23-1861 under Capt. John Beatty in Cardington, O, who was later commissioned to Brig. General. Were first sent to Camp Jackson, Columbus, May 1st was transferred to Camp Denison near Cincinnati. Was then mustered for 3 months. Was then in a few days reorganized and mustered for 3 years the 15th June. Were soon sent to West Virginia under Geo. B. McClelland. Was at the Battle of Rich Mountain. Was sent south to Camp Elk Water where we remained until near winter. Were transferred to Louisville, KY, then south to Camp Jefferson where we remained until spring then under command Gen. O. M. Mitchell. In early spring of 62 moved for a southern climate until the capture of Huntsville, Ala. Remained there during summer. While there was detailed as Body Guard for Gen. O. M. Mitchell. In the fall was sent to chase Gen. Bragg who was moving his Army toward Louisville, Ky. We followed him to Perryville where he gave us a sharp engagement. Our ranks were greatly depleted and I came out with my cap being shot from my head. He retreated to Cumberland Gap, then we made for Nashville. Was taken sick on the way and sent to Louisville Hospital. Was sent from there to Cincinnati Hospital where I had an opportunity to enlist in the M.M.B. Was sent to Benton Barracks, St. Louis, Mo. Then re-mustered for 3 years. Was appointed corporal but was soon raised to the Sargent list. The new organization was then drilled a few days and fitted for active service and our Co. was known as Co. E, Capt. Fisher Comdg which was assigned to the Steamer Diana. Everything being in readiness we started for the seat of war and kept our course until Vicksburg hove in sight. Then took the wisest plan to halt. Grants siege was in operation. A scheme was then designed to place our 20 lb. parrot in the levee opposite the city. It was a very perilous undertaking but was successfully done very quietly after night. I had an active part in the affair. The gun was kept in position until after the surrender and was a wonder to the Confederate Artillerans. We had many incidents that I participated in. The engagement at Duck River, Greenville, Lake Village, Columbus Corners, the burning of Austin, Red River Expedition, Port Gibson, and several minor affairs too numerous to mention. After leaving the boats at Vicksburg to the

Wes' Brother Augustus Seymour Ayres

There was no internet or even fast mail service in the country during the Civil War. Meridian township had begun a program of paying $100 war bounties to volunteers in Jan 1864 crediting the township. Citizens who had contributed earlier to the cause were reimbursed and bonds issued to volunteers payable in two years. This was amended a few times as the President put out a call for more men. Some of the men that Augustus spoke of in his letters were among those that received a $100 bond. The last amendment was on Feb 4th 1865. Volunteer enlistees would be paid $200 and drafted men $100.

As Wes was waiting at Vicksburg to be mustered out he found out his brother was also serving in the south. Wes' brother Gus kept a daily log with few details of note. His letters and military records are more revealing. Gus volunteered on Oct 7th 1864 mustering in for one year on Oct 10th receiving a $100 bounty bond. He had grown to 6' since his first enlistment, his complexion noted as brown due to outdoor farming. He was sent to Duvalls Bluff, Arkansas, with the returning 12th Michigan. Under Lt. Col. May they were to guard the 5½ foot gauge Memphis & Little Rock Railroad and wireless communication lines. Their location was Buttermilk Station.

The railroad had only 38 miles of track from Hopefield (later West Memphis) to Madison completed and operational by May 6th 1861. Prior to Union occupation, the railroad's machine shop at Hopefield was used to modernize rifles. Confederates also used the railroad to transfer its soldiers to Memphis on the Mississippi River. At year's end the western section of the railroad from Little Rock to DeValls Bluff was completed. The latter located on the White River. This was a significant southern railroad construction that took place during the war. Steamboats carried needed supplies up the Mississippi into the White River to DeValls Bluff where they were railed to Huntersville (North Little Rock). It was 133 miles in length. The railroad fell into Union hands in June 1862. Federal troops burned the shops, depot, and engine shed at Hopefield on Feb 19th 1863. There were frequent guerrilla attacks on the railroad but none kept it out of service for long. Ashley's Station was attacked by Confederate Gen. Joseph Shelby with 2,500 men on Aug 24th 1864.

Gus wrote a few lines to his father on Nov 1st 1864 requesting a box of things be brought back by a Michigan soldier who was on furlough. Henry's reply to Gus was dated Nov 21st 1864, from Meredian, Michigan:

Well Gus as Lib has riten a leter to you, I will send you a few lines too. I went over today and got litle Bossy. Reve Kent had her in his field. the other two calves is runing out yet. I cant keep them her till snow comes. We killed the hogs last week. they was pretty fat, I keep the sow. I think she will have pigs this winter. got the corn all husked some time ago. I sold Polly to Herman Huls for ninety dollars payable in one year maby sooner. will that do. you know I couldent keep them and they was poor. Polly has got a good home and plenty to eat, so has old Sal. Ben likes his team first rate. I can get along as Ame and Ben[1] both has teams. When you get home we will need a yoke of steers. I think I made a good trade for you buying Bens place and its all paid for. its worth a good deal more to us being joining ours and there is 2 or 3 hundred dollars worth of timber on it. I took the windows all out and fetched them home. We are going to have a road through from our corner out east through on ames north line in sted of going the other way upon the town

---

1 Amos and Benjamin Wood

line. they can make a road much esier and it will be just the thing for our farm,
fech all the travel by our house make it handy to get out east or west. Joe Smith got
home last week, he and his wife was here visating yesterday. Sabina is here
tonight. She sends her love to you. Hasty is home to[o].
We hant herd anything from Wesley yet. I am going to town tomorrow, if I get any
news from him, I will leave this open and tell you. I think he has ben taken
prisoner. Corporal Wardel stoped here and had quite a chat. Said he was coming
back this way. We had a big rain week before last. it filled up the swamps prety
well. our well is filling up now and I guess we will have plenty of water from this.
Lib is going to send you her photograph picture in this. in town, just got a leter
from ruth. they are going to move up in Mar. got no word from Wesley yet. Moses
hant bought Linden bergers lot yet, he asks 1000 dollars. Write soon.   H. C. Ayers

1865

Gus wrote to his sister on Jan 5th 1865 stating that Wes was still at Vicksburg and a clerk for Gen. Scofield and getting $12 more per month. Gus began keeping a brief log of his activities on Jan 8th. Most of Union men's time seemed to be spent on guard duty, skirmish drills, chopping wood and making Railroad ties, repairing and washing clothing, and daily playing a game of ball or sow and pigs and pitching quates. On Jan 27th his shanty caught fire. Several men shared a shanty. They supplemented their diet by hunting rabbits. On Mar 17th he was paid $40 for his share in making the ties and sent half of it to his father. Lib replied on Jan 20th 1865 the following of what it was like on the home front:

Dear Brother,

I received a letter from you today and was very glad to hear from you. It was
the first letter we had received from you for about a month. We have answered
every letter that we have received from you. Perhaps they are at the Bluff and you
may get them when you get back there. I wrote the last one Christmas night– I
believe. We are all as well as common. Mother was down here this afternoon. I am
at work for Truman. This is the fourth week I have been here. I like to work here
the best of any place around here. We are looking for Wes home any day. He rote
us a letter Christmas night - he said he expected to be home in a month from that
time which time will be up in five days more. I shall be so glad when he get home.
I went to Williamston to a New Years party. Thcar was 114 numbers sold. We had
a verry good time. I went in company with Aron and Ell. They had a suprise at our
house and are going to have another when Wes gets home. It has been nice
sleighing here for some time. It came on about three weeks before Christmas and
is good yet. But I miss you to take me sleigh riding. We got a letter from
Grandfather today. He intends to be here the 9th of next month. He said I do not
exspect to stay there long for we are looking for Wes every day and when he come
money would not hire me to stay away for a while at least. Tom [and] Agnes has
got a boy. Nate Marsh has sold his claim to Hank Hance and goone back to Ohio.
Grandfather is going to start for Michigan the 8th of Feb. We have got nine pretty
little pigs about a month old. Father saw Max Jennison yesterday. He said
Wardells brother got home the day before he said Joe had got back so I supose you
have got the things before this that we sent you. Father has signed for a lot of fruit
trees to be delivered in the sping. Will is busy from morning till night making cants
and bobs and everything he can think of. Mother says she begins to want to see Gus

about as bad as Wes. I am so nervous today that I cannot wright fit to be seen but I hope you can read it. I sent you my photograph in a letter. Did you get it.

His father wrote again on Jan 23rd 1865 from Meredian:

Well Gus I will send you a few lines. I am pecking around a litle a taking care of the catle cuting wood work out some. Ame and I hawled me a load of foder over yesterday, the first. the foder from terrils is most gone. guess I will have enough to get through the winter. the catle looks very well. Bessy is very harty. I feed them all a litle corn evry day. the nine pigs is all smart and lively. they will eat corn like hogs. it will pay big to keep them. next fall they will fat in the woods and make us meat and not cost much. I am lone some with you gone but I expect wes will soon be home, then we will be all rite and have plenty of music. he said he had a double barrel gun, one shot, and the other rifle and a good fidle to fech home with him. Grandfather will be here soon, then all the rest of them. So I guess we will have plenty of company. I helped Ame cut and saw wood seven days. Sawed about sixty cord. I helped Ben 1 1/2 days saw last week. john and Peter Bennet has got them a wood saw. Dingman and Bene has one, so we have plenty of wood saws now. its ben good sleighing ever sence the first of Dec and nice winter wether, not very cold. the roads is smooth as a plank. Lib got a leter from jont, he said they had just ben giving the rebs hell from the word go. his regiment took a batery of 4 guns turned them on the rebs and made them more than clime. jont is one of the Boys. Gus I have lined up for seven dollars worth of aple trees pear and grape to come next Apr. Send me some money to pay for them. It will keep me busy to split rails and fense in the lot to set them out in time. We have got the road laid through to Ames that will fech us all rite. all the travel will go along here. you can build rite over on your lots south side. good building spot and be handy to the barn and orchard. Gus I have ben thinking it will be the best for us to cut all our wood in 18 inch and three feet wood and cord it up and sell it on the ground. I could get a dollar a cord this winter here for seasoned wod. that will pay the best. we have got to clear the land any how. George Grove is paying a dollar a cord for choping 3 foot wood down here on his lot. hired a man to put up 50 cord. that would pay us here prety well, dollar a cord, and he clearing the land. they are going to making salt next sumer. that will take the wood. they have moved a big building down on the railroad crosing, built a plat form. it begins to look like a depo. they are pushing the jacks on railroad rite a long. Wel Gus one third of your time will soon be gone. they are trying to fix up a peace now, but I dont now how they will make go it if they succeed. you wont have longer than spring to stay. two men to come out of maridian they say to fill the last call. Well Wilson wont trouble me this time I guess. Joe Smith and his wife was to Ames visating yesterday. joe is a first rate fellow. Ame got the School house inclosed and there is stands. Gus Miss Cannon enquires after you evrytime I am in to Biases. guess she would like to see you. Well She is a first rate girl. they are geting in lots of logs to the mill over here. I expect joes Brother will come out and se us. Nate Marsh and Alf all went back. Hank Hance bought nates land. Hank has bought over 300 acres up there. he will be a rich man in a few years. Write often   H. C. Ayers

Well try and take care of your self, be care full with your gun and dont shoot your self. I dont now when the war will end but the way they are using up the rebels lately they cant last long. there wont hardly be a greese spot left of them by spring. I dont se how they can hold out a nother sumer. old Generl Tomas has usd up hoods army at nashville and Sherman is making a clean sweep in Georgia. they are going to arm their negroes now and that will be the end of rebeldom. the negroes wont shoot the yankies. I dont think you will have to stay all next sumer. Joe I supose is there. We sent a sausage, dried charries and aples, diary, 20 stamps and envelopes paper. joe said he would let you have some of his buter and honey as he had forty pounds of buter. give my best respects to joe. I wish him much joy and a big Boy, but he went off so quick after geting marrid I dont now as he got the boy made. My respects to Huls Martin and all the rest of the boys. We sent a botle of ague cure, 2 boxes of pills and pair of socks. keep your medicin carefull. maby you will have the chills in the spring, then you wil need it. Write often and try and improve in writing and spelling all you can. you do first rate.   H. C. Ayers

Lib's next letter was dated Jan 29th and included one from his mother.

Dear Brother   I received a letter from you last night. I was glad to hear from you but sorry to hear that you did not get your things for I had been thinking how glad you would be when you got them. Thear was a big sausage, one bottle of Ague cure and a diaria that I believe was all we sent that you did not get. We did not send you butter because Joe said he had about 40 pounds and he would share with you. Mother says thear was a quire of paper and 25 envelopes. Its very strange that anyone should steal your things and no one else's and why didn't they take all of them while they was about it. Its my pinion that some of Joe's friends have had a chance in his box and accidentally or on purpose helped themselves to your things for who would steal a sausage but a hungry soldier. It you want us to send you some things by express, wright and tell us what you want and send us money to get them with and we will try again. I don't know but Father could scare up a little money but its something scarce. I guess my Kitty got sick and died last week. I am done making at Trumans for the present. Aleanniette has got home again. I have no news to wright for it is only a week today since I rote to you. We haven't heard any more from Wes yet. Gus, them verses you sent me about the dead soldier boy are very pretty but they made me cry for I thought how I should feel if my pretty curly haired Brother was in his place but I hope you will not be for I do not know us I think more of you but I should miss you more than eny of the rest. I have answered every letter I have received from you and one or two more. From Sister Lizzie

Well Gus mother wants to see her poor soldier boy. The time begins to seem long and lonely but the time has already one quarter of the time has expired. We are all well and hope you are the same. Lib got a letter from you last night stating that you had not got many of them things I sent you. Did you git the invelopes. They was dun up with the paper. I took your socks and knit new heels to them and sent them to you and put a leter and two boxes of Ayers pills in them. They was the ones that you got knit on the machine so you will know them if you see them. The two boxes was both dun up together. A paper put round them both and your name rote on them . I sent one bottle of Ayers ague cure one diria and rote your name in it and put a paper around it and rote your name with a pensil. The sausage was made up in a white cloth rote on with a pensil your name. In the letter I sent sixty cents worth of postage stamps. I think you had beter go and look a gain. Mabey you have overlooked them. From Your Mother Lydia Ayres

His father writes:

Mar 2nd 1865, Maridian, Michigan
To: Augustus Ayers
thursday evening

Well Gus we got your coton seed letter to night. Amos was to town. we had to pay six cents for the leter. it was marked six cents due at memphis and your leter with the part in was the same 12 cents. I paid for the two leters. if you send such big leters put on two stamps or none. your one stamp they dont call anything. we are all well as comon. Lib is over to Bens to work yet I have sent you two or three leters sence Lib and Mother wrote theirs. told you all the particulars how I get a long. you suposed wes was home by this time. well he ant home yet. its now Mar dont that beat you. we have ben looking for him six monts. well we herd he got to Cardington two weeks ago last Saturday. I expect he is visating there and will wait to come with Moses if he dont come before. Grandfather said Moses was going to start the first of Mar. Grandfather, Mother and Mary is keping house in the kitchen nice as you please. I helped him saw out the door and windows in the big house yesterday. Moses and Wes will be along soon, then we will be all right. Well Gus, the rebels is prety near usd up. We have got all the Seaports Charleston and old ft. Sumter again. Sherman will soon make a sweep and clean the Bord. they hant but a few more cards to play out. their men is leaving them by hundreds evry day. I dont think you will have to stay all sumer. take care of your clothes, get what you can cheap. you now how good they come up here. its thawed considerable today. Sleying is playd out. there hant any frogs hallowing here for some time. Swamps all froze sollid. its ben a nice winter and there has ben a host of work done in Michigan for the number of hands. Well Gus I got my wood sawed tuesday. Ben Anne Charly and I hed to set the machine in the morning. Sawed four logs in the fore noon, seventeen in the after noon. one that big sugar you cut out on the south side of choping 24 feet long. got a nice lot wood all maple. I have ben making railes. Split up evrything that will make railes. I split one cut off of the big elm down back of the well. made nice rails. all the rest into wood so I get rid of that log prety easy. Well I am doing all I can. when it comes night I feel like an old broken down stage horse but I have to keep moving. they give me a hard one sawing day. I split most of the Blocks. I miss you Gus to take the but end. Will has made 1 1/2 pounds of sugar and sold it to Abe truman today for three shilling.

Friday evening Mar 3rd Well Gus I must finish your leter and send it to town tomorrow. Well I have ben luging rails today and building a fence to keep the cows in while we are making sugar sap run a litle to day, but its to cold yet and to much frost in the ground. Will sugard off a pound today. it was nice. Lib went to a dance the 22nd at Okemos. She said they had a nice time. Sold over 50 numbers. they had a first rate Band, four or five musitions there. want but one girl there that she ever seen before. they came from Williamston, Delhi and Lansing. I hant seen Polly sence I sold her but they say she looks well. I must go up and se if Lambert has any money to let me have. has herman sent any home. Maccurdy told Lambert Polly had fits and it scard him bad but she hant had any fits i guess. Somebody told Mc curdy maby you can guess hoo it was. Ame and I are going to tap next week. we shall look for Moses and Wes next week. Will sold Grandfather one of your Pigs for a Dollar. they wanted a pig. We have 8 yet that will do, the sow is prety well sucked out. She ant quite as fat as she was when you left. Well Gus you have put in nearly five monts a redy. I shall plant potatoes around your old house. Bens wheat will look nice when the snow gets off. I have the Straw. I will have him hawl it up here to stack then hall our share from Ames home. then we will have a straw stack for our catle next winter. our wheat looked nice when the snow fell. it ant bare yet. I guess we will have a nice piece of wheat. its ben a good winter for wheat dont you think we had beter Bens lot again next fall get the potatoes off early and sow the hoal peace, then we will have the whole and if we could get the corner cleard out it will make quite a wheat field. I like the idea of having all of the crop soon as we can get land cleard so we can. Will and I masured up on your southline sixty rods so as to now how far east your thirty acres goes. Grandfather choped far enough plenty and two or three rods more, but its all the beter for your field. I shall girdle them big Beeches next Jun so as to have the roots a roting. H C Ayers Mar 4th this is to be a big day all over the north. I am going to town, write often. Lib hant wrote in sometime. H C A

Mar 20th 1865   To: Augustus Ayres

    Well Gus, I must send you a few lines. Amos and Moses is going to town in the morning to get Moses folks some bedsteds and other things. they got here last week. Well Wes got home at last and we was all glad. he is Wes yet, only he has got some mustashes on his chin and uper lip. he feched home a big trunk full of things. he bought him a suit of clothes in cardington. he has a double barel gun, one rifle barel, its a nice gun and a very nice fidle. he plays nice. there was a man here yesterday oferd Wes a thousand dollars to go as a substitute but he hant concluded to go. Well Gus the draft went off last week and some of them keched it. they drafted 22 and 11 has to go. Ame is clear. I will tell you some of them. Aron Laphans, Lambert Hulse, Rene Kent, all three of the Chatertons, Bill Marble, Bob Heiset, Stanton Stevens. Stanton has skedadled, the rest I dont know. Dingman and Rene hired for six monts and gone to nashville. Amos and I are making sugar. Wes feched home three blankets, one bed spred, whet blanket and a lot of things. Well it seems like old times to have Wes home to fidle for us and it seems nice to have Moses and Grandfathers folks here to go and see. its ben very warm today, the frost is most out. We had a thunder shower this morning but it will be sometime yet before the frogs can get their noses through the ice. Wel Gus I have got the catle through so far...let Ame have half the hay stack, got my part home. guess I will have a nuf to get through. Moses sold his team and wagon and come out on the cars. it was so mudy there that they had to put two span to a wagon to get their things to Cardington. he is going to buy a team. Lib is home She and Wes must send you a leter soon. Gus our wheat looks first rate. its ben coverd up all winter with snow. I guess we will have a good crop. I hope you will get home in time to help me cut it. hands will be scarcer than ever this sumer if the war dont close but I am in hopes they will use the rebels all up soon. we have all the seaports now and I think Shrman and Sheridan will soon run them to Hll. We got your pencil. I paid six cents for your three last leters. I had to pay six cents a piece for when you send such hevy things put on two stamps. I am out of money. When you send home some, send by express, its safer I think. Mother says the frogs begins to peep tonight. Well we will soon have sumer again. I was to Mack curdyes yester day. they just got a leter. Wels he said you was well. Wes says he saw Lot in cardington sick with the measles. Adam Hance and his folkes is going to move up to Michigan again next fall. its bed time and I must quit.   H. C. Ayers

The following notes were included with the previous letter.

Monday night. Well Gus its after 10 oclock but I will wright a few lines. our folks have just come to the house with their syrup. they think they have got enough to make 50 pounds. Wes got home thursday night. he seems just like he used to onley he puts on a little more style. I am so glad he is home at last but I shal feel better when you get here too. good night for I am sleepy. Lib.
Will is feeling prety well, he has got Wes to sleep with.

Tuesday morning. rained last night, its very warm this morning. the grass will soon start now. peaches is killed but there is going to be lots of aples. they are driving the railroad along to jackson. the ice has gone out of the rivers, no Briges gone out as I now of. James and T. Davis is going to farm colege this sumer. Moses I guess is prety well pleased with his place. there is such a nice lot of timber on it. Grandfather has got the large room almost finished, so they will soon be all in order. Wise and Stanton is both cleard these digins my potatoes comes out all right. I am going to plant potatoes around your old house. Well your time will be half out in a few days. take care of your self. Well gus we hant forgot you if Wes is home.   H.C. Ayers

Mar 31ˢᵗ 1865, Lansing, Michigan
To: Augustus Ayres
*   Well Gus I was to town yester day and got your leter with a 20 dollar green back. Well I could work out and make some money but there is so many things that ought to be done that I hate to leave. its quite necesary that I clear off a piece here South of the house and set out my aple trees and plant a pach of corn and potatoes. I have ben spliting railes, I have got the old dry oak most split up. it makes nice railes. I am going to make a litle loging, get it cleard off some around. I have usd up considerable many of the logs for wood. Gus its ben a nice day, its spring again. I dont think we will get much sugar making. the roads is geting dry and dusty. I have ben up to help Aron Lapham raise a log barn. Aron has to go to jackson next tuesday and all the drafted men to se hoo goes in the army. Mother and Will has ben to uncle Moseses today. Mary came home with them tonight. it semes nice to go over to uncle Moses again. Wes went over to lees this morning to help split Blocks after the wood saw. I expect he will get thick with them old maids. it seems clever to have wes home again. he fidles real nice, he has a splendid fidle. he got a good gun, fine stub twist barrels worth 30 dollars. I will be as saving of the money as posible. I think you are doing first rate geting out ties. Well get out all the ties you can and make all the money you can so you make it honorable. your time will soon be half out, that will be 96 dollars. Well uncle sam will pay you before long, be saving of your money. you will need it. your time will soon be out anyhow but I guess the war will soon end. three monts will use up the rebels, they are fixing to make a big strike soon. Elisher has got to Lansing, Ame and Samy went down after him yesterday but he was away visating, so they dident se him. the rebels dident quite starve him to deth. Ame, Ben and Wes has ben twice a fishing but they dident get many. the fish is geting scarce, the rivers has ben very high but is got down now. Moses has bought a span of Mares and Wagon for 300 and 45 dollars. goods is going down fast and every thing else. gold will soon be par with green backs. Gus our wheat looks well, I think it much beter than last year. the pigs grows, they will make good hogs by fall if there is plenty of acorns next fall. they will make a nice lot of pork and wont cost much. Will says he ant much afraid of Gus puting him through for seling his pig. I have had the rheumatism in one*

*shoulder for some time and its hurts me to chop or split railes but I keep pecking
a way. there is no time to rest, so much to do, must keep diging away sick or lame.
I want do all I can and make it look like home. I am glad we hant got to move this
spring. I want to get all I can done before you get home again. the sooner we can
get our place cleard up, the sooner we can begin to live at home. this working land
on shares dont suit me if I can do beter.*

*Saturday Morning Apr. Well Gus its ben a year sense we moved here. it looks a litle
beter than it did then and I am glad we are at home on our own land and hant got
to move this spring. we have got to use economy and work our selves into a nice
home. it froze a litle last night but is plesant this morning. Moses and his folks are
well suited. I guess Moses has got his things the other day, Ame hawled them all up
at one load over ??21 hundred. Moses said it took eight horses to hawl that load
from Cardington to where they lived. Hazen has ben in 8 monts and hant got any
pay yet. I supose you was pleased to se all come in to your company. give my best
respects to all the Boys. Well I must quit scribling and go to work. I am geting some
beter of my rheumatism. Moses folks is all going over to Bens visating tomorrow.
Our old cow will have a calf the first of Jun, so we will have to wait 2 monts yet for
milk and buter. the 2 heifers ought to come in next spring. Moses has bought them
two cows. if you feel any simtoms of chills go to taking your ague cure. you may
have a turn of it this spring. Write often.*
  H. C. Ayers

Gus wrote his sister Lib on Apr 8th stating that we are still on the railroad and got some new
recruits. The regiment is now 1,225 with more coming and he didn't know what all of them are going
to do. With extra men more shanties had to be built. They are enlarging their fort and erecting a
stockade. He earned $2.55 that morning making ties. Lorenzo Mosher has the mumps and three in our
shanty have them. Word came today that Richmond was taken.

Gus wrote his father:

Apr 14th 1865
*Dear Father   We just got news that Lee surrendered. The bushwhackers tore up
the track a while ago about twelve miles west of here and run the cars off but did
not hurt them much or any folks on them. There were 35 of the rebs. They charged
the train but the guards kept them off. They shot one of their rebs horses and they
left. Six of us went up there in the hand car to help fix the railroad. I saw three of
them come out toward us but didn't fire on us. We got the road fixed and cars on
it by night...* Gus earned another $2 that day. He closed by saying he has a headache
and guesses he is getting the mumps. He was excused the next day from duty because
of mumps.

Apr 20th
*Dear Father   I am well and over the mumps. We drawed our pay last Sunday and
I drawed $75 dolars. I had $50 dolars coming to me from the boys and I got it all
so I will send $100 dolars to yo. I was down to the bluff today and got it expressed.
I have got $40 dolars left. I will keep it so if I should git sick I would have som
money to halp my self with. I want yo to take my money and keepe it till I git home
then I hope it will do me som good then...lib spoke about takeing the doors out of
my house and the partition. Yo can take the partition out if yo want to but I guess*

yo had better leave the doors in. Yo said yo wanted one of my curls but I jest got my har shingled the other day so I cant git one long a nough to send.

Gus wrote to his father on Apr 26th at the same time his father was writing him.

Dear Father Our first lieutenant started for the bluff a couple of weeks ago. When he got about one mile from camp six bushwhackers rode up to him and got him on a horse. They took him in the woods, took his coat, hat, vest, money, exchanged boots with him and let him go. Then they came up to our camp and shot at two of our boys but did not hurt them. We went after them but couldn't find them. There was a captain that came to the bluff the other day with 25 men and surrendered. The rebs are all glad to surrender. I guess they say they are whipped and want to quit. There was a lot of old Jackson's men went past here on the car yesterday going home.

Apr 26th 1865, Lansing, Michigan
To: Augustus Ayres, Co. B 12th Mich. Inft., Devalls Bluff, Ark.
Beloved Gussey. I must scrach you a few lines again and let you know how we are geting a long. we got your leter last week. you said you was geting the mumps. we will be anxious to hear how you get a long with them. jimmy had them very bad. we herd took cold. they are not very troublesome if they dont get cold. you will be over with them before you get this. So I need not give advice. Well I have to keep pecking a way as usual. We have the lot South of the door all fenced and plowed. Wes helped plow it with Ames horses and I have sat out 18 aple trees on it and sat a row of peach trees around the fence. I have just planted the pach back of the house with potatoes. the trees is leaving out, grass and wheat is groing fast, our wheat looks well. Gus it begins to look a litle more like living around here. Mother and I have got most all the stumps burnt off around here. our flowers and trees will look quite nice this sumer. Wes is working for Moses now cuting rail timber. its lone some to have him gone. it seems rite good to have one boy home again. Moses is slicking up that place rite fast. they will soon make rite nice. Moses sat out 100 aple trees and several pear trees. there is going to be lots of fruit here all but peaches. they are winter kiled. Well Gus I guess you wont have to stay all sumer for the rebels is all usd up, hook and line bar and sinker. they wont make much killing old Abe for Johnson put them through sharper than Lincoln did. Well poar Leishur [Elisha B. Mosher 1831-1865, buried Mt. Hope Cemetery, Lansing] *had to leave us to. that was bad but if cant be helped. Leishur was a good fellow and we expected to soon have him liveing with us again. he had the camp fever. they said Wells McCurdy got home last week but I hant seen him yet. I saw frank going that way today. Maby she was going up there. the old cow begins to make bag some. We will have some milk again after a while our meat will last us till we get milk and buter and I guess our wheat will last till new wheat comes again and we will have potatoes enough till new ones comes. So I guess we will get a long comfortable. it seems nice to have Grandfather and uncle Moses folks here. We go down there every Sunday. Gus I have ben quite poorly this spring with the rheumatism but I had to keep diging away. So much to do but I hant done much but I begin to feel some more like work. Ame has got the school house most done. Emily Lee is going to teach our school. Wes got a leter the other day from Albert Platt. he was at Knoxville Tennessee. jont and Hazen was well not long a go. this patch back of the house plowed up first rate. I look for a big crop of potatoes this sumer and Wes and*

I plowed this south of the house pretty well considering how new it is. I was all around stoping the fence on your lot today to keep the pigs out. I am going to plant potatoes there. Mother and I planted some peas there. Bens wheat is up half leg high. I should hate to take six hundred dollars for the lot now. Lois wrote that Shotwell was about Seling. if he does I shall look for him up here. I dont think of much to rite. 27 Morning. I am going to town this morning. the aple trees will soon be blown out now but I expect its a month earlier thare than here. I dont se as there wil be any need of keeping you boys a great while longer. the rebels armies is most all taken and all their Sea ports. So they are done. they have ben making the old cannons boom big for a few weeks back. the taking of Richmon then lee, and his army, made the people all most crazy. Such times as they have had in the cityes dont often hapen but the shooting of old Abe turned their tunes. Well I guess they can finish up the job with out him. Jonson will fetch them up to the Scrach I guess. our folks are all well. I believe Marilla has got prety smart again. Well take care of your self and be a geting redy to leave. you may get discharged before long. look out sharp for the money due you or you will lose some.
  H.C. Ayers

On Apr 29th this brief letter was sent to Lib.

> *We are still on the railroad but guess we won't stay here much longer. I don't know where we will go unless north for there isn't any fighting to do here. The rebs have almost given up. Several bands came in the past two weeks and gave themselves up and have gone home, so there ain't any rebs in Arkansas. This railroad has been sold.* [Records indicate the railroad was returned to control of the company on Nov 1st 1865, several months after Gus noted it in this letter] *Two in our company died this week. They were new recruits. Spring is a bad time to come here. I went to the bluff last night on the hand car. We are now getting mail twice a week.*

Weeks rolled on for Gus with the usual routine of going to the bluff and trying to guess when or where they will go next. May brought hotter weather. He never mentioned anything about Lincoln's assassination, Johnston's surrender to Sherman, Smith's surrender to Canby or other national events in his letters or "diary." Little changed until June 7th when they packed their things and marched to Duvall. The next day they marched to the cars and went to Little Rock where they camped by the river. They fixed a shanty on the 9th and 10th and began inspection with firing of guns. A grand review was held on the 12th. The next nine days found them daily packing, marching, and camping at night on their way to their destination of Washington, Arkansas.

Gus was on guard at the Washington Hotel on Jun 22nd when he wrote his father that evening noting they were the first troops to come here. He said there were lots of rebs getting paroled. A supply train came with us, 60 wagons. We will start for Camdon tomorrow for supplies. It is 60 miles from here. Washington shows the effects of war. There are no stores and the people are glad it is over. It is pretty nice country with lots of corn, peaches, and apples. He stopped the letter as he didn't have a very good pencil. On June 30th they mustered for pay.

There was little to do except a bit of gun cleaning, inspection, guard duty, and dress parades. They went into town to talk with girls and eat either a breakfast or supper. July 7th found Gus writing to his father from whom he hadn't heard for over a month. He gave a good description of life near Washington, Arkansas.

Four companies were ordered to march to Camden on July 8th. It was their regimental headquarters located about sixty miles from Washington, Arkansas. They arrived on the afternoon of the 11th and camped in an old building. They did a bit of washing and fishing in the river. Gus reported sick on Jul 20th & 21st. Then it was back to guard duty. On the 25th he visited the graveyard in town. Peaches were ripe and added to their diet. The next day he wrote to his father saying he was over having the ague. We don't do much now. Company's A, B, C, & F are here, the rest in Washington. A note to Lib said the reb girls don't have much to say to us, saying they are rebs to the back bone. Reb soldiers are here now. The rest of July and early August was much the same. They acquired apples and peaches from a man named Lee who had come from Ohio. He gave us all the fruit we could eat. He said he would rather be home cutting wheat and hay than do nothing but lay around here. We only guard once a week now. A negro regiment arrived today and it is expected they will take our place. August rolled into September. He wrote his father on the 6th. This place is sickly with half the boys having chills and fever. It sounds like the regiment will have to stay here all winter. You wanted me to buy some clothes but they are more costly here than in the north. When I leave I will get some if they are cheap. He enclosed some posey seeds called hollyhock for his mother in the letter. You don't have to plant them every year. I think they are very pretty. The next day he helped dig a grave for Sgt. Ed Sutten. He was from Benton, Michigan, and later buried in the National Cemetery at Baton Rouge, Louisiana, Grave #1626.

By October it had cooled a little and was cloudy. On Saturday the 7th 1865 Gus, Lorenzo Mosher, James W. Terrill, John Donahoe and William Thatcher were mustered out. Sunday and Tuesday was spent getting some persimmons and hickory nuts with Albert and Lorenzo. He was discharged at Camden on Oct 12th by virtue of expiration of service term and due $66 & 66/100 from his bounty. He and his buddies fended their way home, camping in old buildings along the way. They made 20-30 miles per day. On the 16th they arrived at the arsenal and got payed. In the morning they took the cars to Duvall's Bluff where they took the boat *Rowena* for Memphis for $5. There they changed boats for Cairo. The *Marble City*, cost $3. It got stuck on a sand bar on the 20th delaying arrival. They got into Cairo at 11 pm on the 21st. After breakfast on the 22nd they rode the rails all night and most of the morning to Calumet, Michigan. After dinner they left at 6 pm on Oct 23rd for the town of Jackson. He never said when he reached home. He bought 30 acres from his uncle, Ben Wood, which was across the road from his father. There he built a frame house. On Nov 26th 1868, he married Frances Ellen Sutherland, a local music teacher. They had one son, Seymour Augustus, who was born Jul 27th 1875. His mother died a few years later. Young Seymour was past age 6 when he entered school. He was 11 when his grandfather, Henry Cook, died in 1886 and from then on spent most of his time with his grandmother, Lydia, in the old log home until she died two year later. Then he went back home and helped on the farm until 1894 when he went to work for Pliney Olds.

Homesteading in Kansas

When Wes' grandfather left New Jersey for Ohio in 1822, his eldest son, Wm. Augustus, went to Connecticut to learn the trade of hatting. He later moved to Ohio to join the family. In 1835 his father deeded him 50 acres for $150. He became a teacher in the neighborhood. Each student agreed to pay him $1.75 per quarter and to board and work for him. The school would provide a school room, books, and other materials. Classes consisted of: orthography, grammar, writing, reading, geography and arithmetic. During that time he studied to become a doctor which at the time took one year. He received two letters in 1836 and 1837 addressed to Doct Augustus Ayers/Ayres. In 1836 he married Caroline in Knox Co., Ohio, but apparently left her a few years later. He and Caroline made three land sales in Delaware County. In Oct 1836 they sold a little over 40 acres for $140. Another sale was made on Jan 30th 1837 for 39+ acres for $80. Their last joint sale of 72 acres was on the following Apr 2nd for $360. When Delaware County residents sold him military bounty land in Arkansas on Jun 5th 1838, he set out to speculate in land there until 1855. He made sixteen land transactions during those years. He continued this activity in Iowa, and lastly Kansas. He saved his correspondence which made it was easy to trace his movements. Initially, he did well financially. He sent coins to Ohio to commemorate the births of new nephews and nieces. Eventually all the trading put him in a financial hole. He wrote to family members requesting help. Augustus died in 1878 at age 71 in debt leaving two nephews his depleted estate in a will. He did manage earlier to convince his nephew Wes and niece Lib to homestead in Kansas.

Wes' sister, Elizabeth, had married James Perry Wells McCurdy on Jan 27th 1866 at Ord, Clinton Co., Michigan. He was born on Mar 20th 1836 in Fayette County, Pennsylvania, son of Thomas and Eleanor McCurdy. Their large family moved to Morrow County, Ohio, before moving to Meridian twp. in Michigan in 1850. Two of their sons joined the 12th Michigan Infantry, Company G. James' younger brother, Thomas M. died of dysentery at Little Rock, Arkansas on Nov 23rd 1863. James P. W. mustered on Dec 19th 1861 at Niles, Michigan. The 12th Michigan fought in numerous battles in Arkansas. In Aug 1863, James P.W. was promoted from 4th Sgt. to 2nd Sgt. at Little Rock under Gen. Frederick Steele. Between battles, the troops spent days marching in knee deep mud. On Mar 6th 1864, James P. W. was made 1st Sgt. at Niles. He proceeded to Little Rock with the new recruits just missing the Red River campaign. The month of May was spent moving on foot or steamers to Pine Bluffs, Brownsville, Springfield and Little Rock. There James reported sick, his only absence. On June 1st James P. W. was promoted to 2nd Lt. to fill the vacancy of Lt. Simeon M. Babcock who resigned. The regiment continued to move about on the Arkansas and White Rivers and Devall's Bluff. On Mar 17th 1865, James P. W. wrote to Lt. Col. John Levering the following letter:

Colonel:

I have the honor to tender the immediate and unconditional resignation of my Commission as 2ᵈ Lieutenant 12th Michigan Veteran Infantry for the following reasons.

Viz.

My Father and Mother are both old people and have been very sickly during past Fall and Winter and unable to attend to their own wants and as they are dependent on my for their support - and I am the only one they have to assist them.

I deem it an imperative duty and only Justice to my Parents to be with them having already been in the Service three years and four months.

I am not indebted to the United States Government on any account what ever.

I have made and forwarded all reports and returns of Ordnance and Ordnance Stores and other public property.

There are no charges against me.

I was last paid by Major Wilson to include the 30th day of Jun 1864 and am
responsible for no Government property what ever.
I am Colonel
Very Respectfully
Your Obedient Servant
James P. W. McCurdy
2^d Lieut 12th Michigan Vet Inf. Company G

James P. W. was discharged from service at Camden, Arkansas, Mar 21st 1865 by the order of Maj. Gen. Reynolds.

Early in this country's history Osage Indians had left Virginia's Piedmont region for the Ohio Valley. The Osage were a linguistic speaking Dhegid Siouan like their Omaha, Otoe, Poncas, Konzas and Quapaw relatives. In 1804 the Louisiana purchase was divided into the Territories of Orleans and Louisiana and Osage lands were transferred to the United States. The government then sought to move eastern tribes including Cherokees to these lands. That led to conflict between the two tribes. The Osage were living in Missouri and Arkansas and hunted buffalo on the plains of Kansas and Oklahoma. Hides were traded with the French. Then in 1812 Kansas became part of the territory of Missouri. Several treaties followed before the 1825 treaty in which the Osage ceded all their lands except a reserve in southern Kansas. The reserve began 50 miles west of the Missouri border, ran west 125 miles (approximately now the southern border of Kansas to the 100th meridian, and extended roughly 50 miles south to north. The treaty stated they could hold it as long as they chose to occupy it. The rest called Indian Territory, the eastern part of Kansas, would be available for eastern tribes and Euro-American settlers. The Kansas-Nebraska Act of May 30th 1854 opened Kansas to settlers who would hopefully determine whether the area would be slave or free. Land was given "free" as "squatter sovereignty." The major flaw in the Act was there was no land legally available for settlers. The situation was messy. In 1861 Kansas became a state. That April southern states made an alliance with the Osage. Not all of them were in total agreement with the south. Only two bands remained loyal to them in the Civil War. Two hundred Osage Indians led by Chetopa joined the 2nd regiment of the Indian Brigade for the Union. It was like a stab in the back when Kansas authorities demanded the Osage cede part of their reserve for settlement. Before the 1862 Homestead Act was passed, earlier squatters hoped to grab land by preemption. Railroad companies fought each other for the preemptive land. Settlers lost to the railroads. The Homestead Act that Wes referred to in this letter permitted citizens age 21 and over to acquire 160 acres if improved and lived upon for five years. The $1.25 per acre came from the Preemption Act of 1841. The end of the Civil War brought a new wave of settlers. Wes and his sister, Lib McCurdy, settled in Cowley County. Its borders were surveyed in 1867 and consisted of some 1,144 square miles. It was opened to settlement on Jan 1st 1870. Ten thousand Native people were removed from land that was theirs to be held in perpetuity. Few remained.

On Jun 9th 1870 Wes settled on a homestead claim in Cowley County, Kansas. His official Patent Certificate No. 985 for 160 acres was in the SW quarter, Section 5, Township 31, Range 4 E. It was dated Aug 1st 1872 and recorded on Aug 30th 1876,[1] the year Wes sold his claim. Wes' letter to his Uncle gives a good description of surveying difficulties at the time:

Sep 4, 1870, Arkansas City, Kansas
To: Mr. Augustus Ayers, Alma, Wabaunsee Co., Kansas
Posted: Sep 5, 1870 at Arkansas City, Kansas
Respected Uncle
*   I rec'd your letter dated Augt 19th last night. I wrote one and sent to you last*
Sunday which gave you near all of the particulars. I have rec'd all the letters you
sent me & rec'd one from home last night they are all well. Father talks of coming

---

1Cowley Co. Patent Bk B: 140

out here and taking a claim. Brother in law will not come until next summer if he comes at all. They are looking for Aunt Harriet out. I dont wish for you to go to any unecessary troble to pay the note it would come verry exceptable now but if you have no way of getting it just now, I will try and get along without it. When I get the house done and get my pay I can get along verry well. Mr. Lee has the note to keep for me. I was afraid I might loose it here. You seem to think it risky in settleing on this land. I am pretty well posted in all the objections you discribe. This was the Osage Indian lands until recently a bill passed congress that this land shall be sold to actual settlers at $1.25 pr acre payable in one year. No R.R. has any thing to do with the land yet. My claim is only 7 miles from the Butters County line and a surveyed line has been run through south within half a mile of mine so I almost know my lines one way and I know where a section corner is on the line so all I have to do is to take a tape line and run until it strikes mine. then I can tell within a few rods where my four corners are. they have all taken their claims large enough and they will move to the section lines after the survey and they will all follow each other. I dont care which way I go. It will not hurt me any. I would a little rather be moved a little either way from my lines. They claim that they can straddle a section line. What is your opinion. If that can not be done it will be a pretty big move for some. but they will all move alike so they will get their allowance. It will discommode some and better some. Every letter settler will hold the 40 that his house is on and they generally break on that and take enough surrounding to make 160 acres. I have put up a log house 14 x 16 and have 4 acres broke. but when the survey is made I will move my house where I want it. I will not put on any more expense than necessary. Perhaps you will get this before you answer the one I wrote last Sunday. So I will make you out quite a letter to answer.

On Sep 18th 1871 Wes' Affadavit was filed for his Osage Indian Land Claim of 160 acres located at the SW quarter, Section 5, 31 S, Range 4 E. He stated that he had a hewed log house 14 x 16, one story high, one door, one 12 light sash window, board floor, and roof covered with clapboard. Two witnesses, L.P. Sieker and Thomas G. Ragland, stated that Wes had a hedge row all round the 160 acres one rod wide and had a half acre of potatoes planted but destroyed by stock before it was fenced. They valued the improvement at over $150. Osage Cash Entry No. 985.[1] Wes wrote to his uncle:

---

1 National Archives and Cowley Co. Patent Bk B: 140

entered under the preemption law which I presume you know what this is. I paid for my claim some three months ago. there are but a few that have proven up yet consequently there have back but a few sales. There was 120 acres sold lately joining mine for 800 dollars. I consider mine worth $1000 dollars at least. It is well located and is on the State road. We feel there of a Rail Road inside of two years, then I expect a good price for it. It will not be Aug until I shall see you then I will give you the particulars.
Respectfuly Your Nephew   C. W. Ayres
I could not get any papers to send you now. I do not take any and I should have to go to Winfield to get any as soon as I go there I will get you some and send. C.W.A.

Post War Blues

The first sign of financial trouble occurred on Sep 8th 1873 when the New York Warehouse and Securities Company closed its doors. A week later financier Daniel Drew's firm of Kenyon, Cox, and Company followed suit. On Sep 18th 1873 Jay Cooke and Company failed. That sent Wall Street into a panic. Jay Cooke was an honest and cautious man who had marketed government bonds during the Civil War and made substantial profits. He also caught railroad fever and the failure of his Northern Pacific Railroad caused his financial house to collapse. Two other prominent firms closed the same day and 37 more on Sep 19th. The Panic with subsequent depression had several underlying causes due to post Civil War inflation, rampant speculative investments in railroads, a large trade deficit resulting from the Franco-Prussian War, and property losses in Chicago and Boston fires that put a massive strain on bank reserves that plummeted in New York City during Sep and Oct 1873 from $50 million to $17 million. Unable to meet payment demands, many banks and financial institutions closed their operations. History has a way of repeating itself.

On Dec 26th 1875 Elizabeth wrote to her Uncle in Kansas:

Respected Uncle
I have thought I would write to you ever since we left Kansas but have kapt waiting for plenty of time which I do no think I shall have again very soon so I will wait no longer.
We are all well but Mother her health is verry poor most of the time. Fathers health is uncommon good this fall. We came back on account of Mothers poor health but I guess it was a good thing for we got away before the grasshoppers made it such hard times for you thear. We sent a box weighing 450 pounds of provision and clothing to the neighbour hood that we came from. They had verry hard times thear. We had a good claim thear but could not rent it for only enough to pay the taxes they were so high. We had a chance to trade it this fall for city property here so we traded. We have it now whear we can rent it for $75 dollars a year or trade it for land here. We think we can make money faster and easier here than we could thear. We have such good markets here no matter how much we raise it always fetches a reasonable price and money seems to be much plentier here than thear but people here complain of hard times and I think if they would go thear and stay a while they would find out what hard times are. I liked it verry much while I was thear but since I have got back I have no desire to return. Our Kansas boy will be four years old next Mar. He is the largest boy of his age I ever saw. He has dark hair and verry black eyes. Guess he must look like his Great Uncle as thear are no black eyes in my husband's family or mine. Our girl is seven. They are all we have. Brother Gus's wife has a boy five months old, their first one.

Wes has been working at his trade all summer. He gets all he can do here and is called an extra carpenter. He still keeps his land in Kansas.

We are having a very warm winter here so far it has been raining all day. We haven't had snow enough for sleighing yet. All kinds of crops were good here this year. Wheat is worth $120 per bushell, potatoes and oats 30 cents, corn shelled 75 cents, apples 50, onions 50, butter 30, eggs 25 cents, dressed pork $750 per hundred.

I sent you two Mason papers last spring which told considerable about our country, presume you got them. I cannot think of anything more that I think would interest you so I will close hoping to hear from you when convenient and how you are getting along. Direct to Okemos, Ingham Co., Mich   Lizzie McCurdy

There was no surviving correspondence during that period. Wes returned to Michigan in 1875 and sold his homestead in Kansas the following year. He became a very active member of the Charles T. Foster Post G.A.R. Still single, he kept in touch with his Uncle Augustus in Kansas. Wes was working as a finish carpenter about this time in the House of Representatives wing and on the original library in the new Michigan State Capitol which was under construction and completed in 1879. The Capitol was completely restored over a century later. Much of the old carved doors and window casings that Wes worked on were duplicated in a non wood product. The effect is similar as when originally built but lacks the warmth of wood. The old library was converted and does not look as it did originally, but it is certainly worth a visit to see this marvelous structure. On Mar 20th and Dec 7th 1876 Wes sent his Uncle in Kansas $30, the last by registered letter. Augustus' plea for money seemed unending. On Mar 20th 1877 Wes sent his Uncle who was at Rocton, Kansas, the following letter:

Your letter was rec'd some time ago. We have not been able to attend to fixing your matter yet. I am getting material together to build with and it keeps me pretty well drained, but we will fix you out pretty soon. Father has gone to Ohio expect him back this week. We found nearly four acres of the old homestead has never been deeded. He sold his share & Aunt Harriet gave him her share. You will probably get 35 or 40 dollars for your share as soon as you have a chance to give a quit claim. When Father gets home we can tell more about it. Snow is about 18 inches deep & good sleighing. I will write again soon.
Your Neph.   C. W. Ayres

On Wes' 35th birthday he wrote his Uncle followed with a brief comment by Wes' sister in regard to requesting more money. Interest was at the time 24%.

Respected Uncle
I suppose you are anxiously waiting for some money but your call caught us unprepared to comply with your demand. I have your letter to Lizzie with will which causes some dissatisfaction as it was expected that your will would be made directly to the source of your assistance. I do not care so much about it but gus does not see it in the same light that I do. but as we are running all responsibilities and trouble in assisting you we should share the full benefit of the reward. Lizzie is not able to help you any in time of need and was not expecting any such favor from you. Therefore by her request we would ask you to change it leaving out her name as it would probily be better for your interest as a united effort to help you by us two. It would be more satisfactory. In the condition it is in now we are doing the most and have the promise of the least as we have nothing to show to exact what

we are letting you have from what you have promised. Father has got back but did not bring any money. He is looking for one share to come evry day which amounts to thirty dollars. I intend to send this to you when it comes which you may notify your creditors to have a little patience and it will be all right. I can not get money only from the Bank by paying 24 per cent and that I dont like to do unless really necessary. please write back as soon as possible and let us know what the probabilities are.
Your Respect Nephew
C. W. Ayres
Respected Uncle
change your Will and give it all to the Boys as I cannot help you and Gus will not unless you do and I do not want you to lose on my account. will write to you in a few days.　　　　　　　　　*Lizzie McCurdy*

Additional letters Wes wrote to his uncle follow:

Sep 11th 1877, Lansing, Michigan
To: Augustus Ayers, Rocton P.O., Wabaunsee Co. Kansas
Resps Uncle
*　　I received your letter yesterday and as I am in town to day I will enclose Fifteen dollars for you. Gus brought down a load of wheat got 1.35 pr bushel. Our folks are all well. Aunt Harriet made us a visit this summer. She looks young for her age. Will is going to teach school next winter has one engaged. I have been away all summer working at my trade. Am going to build a small barn and finish up my house.*
I am glad to learn that prospects are good with you this season. I guess you will come out all right. We have good crops this season - wheat was extra. We have been having a good deal of rain lately. Our state house is almost done - it shows up big. I would like to hear from you occasionally.
From Your Nephew
C. W. Ayres

Jan 12th 1878, Lansing, Michigan
To: Augustus Ayers
Respct Uncle
*　　I enclose you ten dollars & since by req. letters hope you will receive it in due time. How would you like to trade your land for some land near us and live here where we can attend to your wants. I think you are getting to old to live where there are no friends to rely on in case you need assistance. I don't know but what I might help you to a trade as there are some here that have quite a notion of going to Kansas. I think if you was here we could visit and you would enjoy life much better. please write how you feel about it..*
We are all well. No sleighing yet.
I rec'd your card.　　　　　　　　　*Yours Respectfully C. W. Ayres*

May 14th 1878, Lansing, Michigan
To: Augustus Ayers
Respected Uncle
*　　Your letter came to hand a few days ago asking for fifteen dollars so I enclose*

the amount for you today hoping you will receive it in due time. I believe that I had not better take that land as I am some in debt now and I do not care to get in any deeper until I can see my way out. I will try and send some one to buy it if possible. Please send a receipt for what we have sent you with each amount separately and dated if you can. Yours Respt's   C.W.Ayres

James P. W. McCurdy died Mar 9th 1880 of chronic diarrhea and lung disease contracted in military service and buried in Mt. Hope Cemetery in Lansing. His heartbroken father, Thomas, after losing two sons due to the Civil War, died at age 74 on Mar 3rd 1896 and buried in the Okemos Pioneer Cemetery with his wife, Eleanor A. and daughter, Agnes. James' widow, Elizabeth, married widower Andrew Jackson Champion on Aug 7th 1881 who was born Dec 18th 1828 at Delhi, Hamilton Co., Ohio. They had two sons: William C. and Ralph Waldo Champion. Dad referred to the family as his, hers, and theirs. Andrew J. died May 11th 1914. Elizabeth died Jan 17th 1926. On Jul 1st 1881 Wes sold to Mason D. Chatterton for $1800 on note the Northwest ¼ of the Southeast ¼ of Section 25 in Township 4, north of Range 2 west in Lansing. It was discharged Apr 9th 1886.[1] Wes had been investing in mining stocks, most becoming worthless.

Wes was age 39 when he married Mary (May) Frances McNeil Dec 20th 1881 at Lansing, Michigan. May was age 28, born May 15th 1853 in Milton Center, Ballston Town, New York. George S. Heickey, Minister, performed the ceremony. Witnesses were friends E. J. and Belle Adams of Lansing.[2] Wes met May when his sister, Elizabeth McCurdy Champion, had hired her for sewing. It was often customary then for a seamstress to live with the family until the work was completed.

Wes was operating a cider mill in 1884 when May was pregnant with her first child. Their son Raymond Cleveland was born on Nov 3rd 1884. Two years later they were running the *Farmhouse* at Michigan Agricultural College. It was a boarding house for students.[3] One day their toddler, Ray, came up missing and the students helped search for him. He was found in the power house watching the fly wheels. He loved moving things and when riding with his mother would say, *Mama, winmill, see winmill.* On May 21st 1887, Wes sold the forty acres to Charles Goritz for $1,000 subject to a mortgage.

The following amusing letter was sent to them from their dear friend, Belle Adams, who had moved to Kansas.

Nov 20th 1887, Kirwin, Kansas
Dear Friends Wes and May.
Again you hear me addressing you, althou you have not answered my last, but I write when I please just the same as I used to visit you. Now Wes - I want you to please transact a little business for me and will pay what ever it is worth to you, if I did not bother you once in a while you would forget you had a Belly.
Mr M. and I are corresponding right along. I took the liberty to say to him that, you and May were two of my witnesses and Should he wish to see and talk with you he could find you at said no. 119. Also that if there was any other business to be attended to, to inform you, and you would attend to it for me. And I dont think there will be, but Should the Gent call on you in person or by mail, please be equell to it and charge same to me. Am I asking to much, I hope not, and am anxious it should go on. be plain and frank with me please and dont let Mr M. bluff you. bear this in mind.

---

1 Ingham Co. Deed Bk 57: 165.

2 Ingham Co., Michigan Marriage Certificate

3 Located in East Lansing, the college underwent two name changes: Michigan State College and Michigan State University.

I have no idea of what business she was asking Wes to do.

Wes was living in Lansing Township in 1888. The Thomas Bradman Feed Mill stood on the eastern corner of River and Kalamazoo Streets in Lansing, Michigan, in 1888/9. The Grand River flowed by the back of the property. The mill was owned and run by Thomas Bradman and Charles W. Ayres, my grandfather, who ended up owning the property. On it he first built a two story wooden framed home. During this time Wes was trying to obtain evidence in his case in the Pension office for his disability in the Civil War. He received the following letter from J. W. Blue of Delaware, Ohio, dated 25 Jan 1890:

> Dear Sir.
>
> *I am in receipt of a letter from C. Ranne asking for evidence in your case now in the Pension office. My father (Joel G. Blue[1]) died Feby 3d 1889 in N.Y. City with Pneumonia Brights disease. I can refer you to several of the boys. Wm. Stiver,[2] Cardington, Ohio; Charley Benedict,[3] Cardington, Ohio; Philander Powers,[4] Cardington, Ohio; Jesse Snyder,[5] Cardington, Ohio; Wm. Williams,[6] Lima, Ohio; H. B. Shotwell,[7] Marengo, Ohio; Charles Hiskett,[8] Lindley, Missouri. Can give you names and address of nearly all the Co.*
> *Yours in F. C & L. J.W. Blue* [These were 3 mos. men who remustered for 3 yrs.]

A barn had been built on the back of the lot close to the river. On its left side wide double doors opened for their horse and buggy. On the right was Grandpa's carpenter workshop with all its pulleys, benches and assortment of woodworking tools. It became one of my favorite places to hang out when Dad worked in the shop. My grandparents' buggy was put in the loft when an auto was purchased. Plum, pear trees and grape vines were located left of the barn. Just before Dad was born they moved into a new brick home that Grandpa had built next to the frame home in front of the barn. It consisted of three apartments, then called flats. Theirs was the largest facing River St. The other two faced Kalamazoo St. The structure was completed in Nov 1894. May delivered her second son on Feb 22nd 1895. She wrote that day to her Spiritualist leader, Olney H. Richmond, in Boston suggesting a name for her son. He replied on Mar 9th stating that his astral name was Eno and that Richmond could be his middle name. And that was how my Dad acquired his name, Eno Richmond Ayres. His mother would take little Eno to church and put him in a small trunk while she spoke.

In those early years River Street ran parallel to the Grand River. Industries were located by the river. There was a three story Mineral Well House and Spa, Smith Floral Greenhouses, Bakers Boathouse, and the workshop of Pliney F. Olds and Son (Wallace S.), founders of the company. The Olds shop was located at 221 River Street. The Olds families lived on Cherry Street which ran diagonal off River and Kalamazoo Streets. Wes and May's son, Eno, attended the one room Cherry

---

1 Joel G. Blue, age 21, remustered for 3 yrs Jun 15 1861 in Wes' Co. I, 3rd Ohio Volunteer Infantry. Promoted to 1st Lt. 1862, captured Rome, GA. POW May '63. Mustered out Jan 5 1865.

2 William Stiver, age 21, remustered for 3 yrs Jun 15 1861Co. I, 3rd Ohio Volunteer Infantry. Corp. To Sgt. Mustered out Jun 21 1864

3 Charles W. Benedict, age 18, remustered for 3 yrs in Co. I, 3rd Ohio Voluntary Infantry, Pvt. Mustered out Jun 21 1864.

4 Philander Powers, age 18, remustered for 3 yrs in Co. I, 3rd Ohio Voluntary Infantry, Pvt. Mustered out Jun 21 1864.

5 Jesse Snyder, age 21, remustered for 3 yrs in Company I, 3rd Ohio Voluntary Infantry, Pvt. Mustered out Jun 21 1864.

6 William Williams, age ?, entered service on Sep 2 1861, Co. I, 3rd Ohio Volunteer Infantry. Sgt. Jan 1863, transferred to 24th Regt. O.V.I. Jun 8 1864 by order of War Dept..

7 Hudson B. Shotwell, age 18, remustered for 3 yrs in Co. I, 3rd Ohio Voluntary Infantry as Musician. Mustered out Jun 21 1864.

8 Charles S. Hiskitt, age 23, remustered for 3 yrs Co. I, 3rd Ohio Voluntary Infantry, Pvt. Mustered out Jun 21 1864.

Street School which was located not far from this intersection. The Olds family is mentioned as they were neighbors to Wes and May. May was a seamstress and she sewed for the Olds family. Also their nephew, Seymour Ayres, worked for Pliney Olds beginning Dec 4th 1894. So the family knew the Olds family very well. Seymour lived with Wes and May and continued to work for the Olds family as they were developing a gas engine. Seymour was working on the carburization. The first experimental horseless carriage was completed in 1896. Seymour wrote that: *I put this car on the test stand in the spring of 1898 and took the bugs out of it.* He continued to work for Pliney Olds until he noted in his memoirs: *when the trouble came.*

Pliney's son, Ransom E., worked as a machinist for his father and brother. After several changes in ownership and management within the company, Ransom (R.E.) gained control of the business. May said the two sons had differences over labor practices and she did not speak well of Ransom who had created a partnership with his father leaving out his brother. Wallace moved his family from the area. Later he returned and continued to work as a machinist for his father who remained president of the company. Ransom would test cars early in the morning. When an engine would not run, he would get Wes out of bed and have him help push the auto back into the shop. By 1900 Ransom had formed the Olds Motor Works located at 221 River Street and brought in the Smith brothers as officers in the company. The shop was moved to Detroit where it burned. Meanwhile Seymour went to Bay City and got a job with the Industrial Works. It was there he met his future wife. He returned to Lansing in December 1898 and began to develop the gas engine he had designed. Seymour was living with his Uncle Wes and family. In 1900 Wes and Augustus' younger brother, Will, and wife, Ella, had returned from San Francisco and moved to Saginaw and started a gas engine company based on what he saw his nephew, Seymour, was developing. Wes could not find money with which to build so he moved to Saginaw, Michigan, to work for his youngest brother, Will, making wood patterns.

Will was now age 33 and he and his Canadian born wife, Ella, had moved to San Francisco by 1890. He was working as a teacher when his older brother, Augustus, father of Seymour, traveled to California to visit them. Will had started the Ayres' Typewriter Renting Agency in the Safe Deposit Building on Montgomery Street. The business bought, sold and rented all kinds of typing machines and provided a corps of workers to type transcripts. By mid-1900 Will and Ella had left San Francisco, moved back to Michigan, and were living with his brother, Augustus. On Nov 19th 1900 Ella purchased six lots north of Case Street in Saginaw. They moved to Saginaw and lived at 905 N. Michigan Ave. On Dec 16th 1901 A. W. Wright Lumber Company sold two parcels of land, block 64 of Smith & Hayden addition, at Hamilton and Bristol streets with its building to the Ayres Gasoline Engine and Automobile Works. The land lay westerly of the Michigan Central RR Company right of way and its building. The Ayres company was located at the corner of Hamilton and Bristol streets. Wm. F. was President and General Manager, Seymour Ayres, Sup't. of Construction, and Charles W. Ayres, patternmaker. In 1902 Herman Pistorius was added as secretary, and Herman Goeschel, treasurer. By 1903 there was no mention of the two Hermans.

Wes' residence in Saginaw was 1027 N. Harrison St. in 1902-3.[1] Wes and May's son, Raymond, had stayed in Lansing working for Olds Motor Works as a machinist. He roomed in one of the his father's flats. Later that year Ray came to Saginaw to work for the Saginaw Whistle Company. About this time Henry Ford came to Saginaw to see if Will would move his plant to Detroit to make his engines. Dad said he was on his way to watch the logging at the waterside below the plant. His Uncle Will stopped him to enquire where he was going. After telling his uncle his intentions, he was told to be careful. Dad remembers his uncle Will was usually impeccably dressed and somewhat concerned that Ford was clothed in coveralls. Despite his appearance, his uncle took Ford to lunch at the popular five story Hotel Vincent at the corner of Washington and Germania. The hotel was noted for its dining and buffet service. It was Seymour's patents that had impressed Ford and after Will rejected Ford's proposal, things began to decline. Seymour found different employment with the Pere Marquette RR Company but Wes stayed with his younger brother Will. In 1904 there were five gasoline engine manufacturers listed in Saginaw. The next year the gasoline engine manufacturers had dwindled to

---

1 Saginaw City Directory

two, Ayres and National Engineering Co. Only two automobile manufacturers were listed in 1906, Ayres and Emendorfer, and one gasoline engine manufacturer, National Engine Co. No mention was ever made in the family that an automobile had been manufactured. Seymour, now married, stayed with the RR until 1906 when he returned to Lansing and worked at The Kneeland Engine Company for a year, then Olds Motor Works for five years, then R.E.O. that was started by Ransom. By 1907 all family members had left Saginaw except Will and Ella. On May 7th 1907 the Ayres Gasoline Engine and Automobile Works was sold to Clark L. Ring. Will's wife Ella had begun selling the lots in 1905. They were living in Highland, Oakland Co., Michigan when more lots were sold. In 1910 they were renting at West Palm Beach, Florida. They purchased the Oyama Hotel in Daytona Beach, later changed to the Daytona Beach Hotel where they owned a yacht *Ellayre* offering chartered fishing parties at $10 per day. Two more Saginaw lots were sold in 1914. The last lots were sold in 1915 when they were living at Daytona Beach. Eventually they moved back to Lansing and owned a large Queen Anne style home . At some time they had traveled around the world and their home was filled with their numerous purchases. It was like stepping into a museum. Will died Jul 16th 1922, the youngest and first of his siblings to die. Ella died in 1953. Ella was close to Wes' wife, May, and many of Ella's letters to May have survived.

Ayres Gasoline Engine and Automobile Works
Saginaw, Michigan

Following is information gleaned from the company's catalog:

The "Catalogue of Ayres Gasoline Engine and Automobile Works" is an interesting historical document. The pamphlet starts out by noting that the Twentieth Century has dawned and "....we may expect another era of improvements such as the world has no conception." It's too bad that Seymour could not have lived to see what really happened. The first page goes on to explain how the everything on the market is the product of machines and that the Ayres Gas Engines are useful in Marine, Stationary and Automobiles applications.

Seymour went to great detail describing the: "General Design", "Valve Movement", "Igniter", "Generator", "Governor", "Easy Starting", "Economy", and "Guarantee" of these engines. Of interest is how the terminology has changed since this was written. It's perhaps not hard to understand that the word "Igniter" refers to what is now called the ignition system. It takes a little more stretch of the imagination to realize that the "Generator" is what is now known as the carburetor. At least that was what it was called before it became so sophisticated.

The pamphlet includes illustrations as to how the engine can be used to power various commercial applications such as: elevators, feed mill, printing press, and blacksmith shop. Specifications as to horsepower, RPM, fly wheel diameter, etc. are given for their line of stationary and marine gasoline engines.

A copy of this catalog is included as Attachment B.

Ayres Family Continued

Meanwhile back in Lansing, another major flood occurred in late March 1904 that took out the metal Kalamazoo St. bridge next to the flats and flooded the areas next to the Grand River. Shortly after that, River Street was renumbered and Wes and May's home was changed to number 345 which it retained until it was demolished.

Around 1904, the Olds company split into the Olds Gasoline Engine Works on River Street and Olds Motor Works located at the Old State Fairgrounds. Ransom had severed his ties with the Olds companies and started REO. He had a massive multi-story mansion built on the corner of S. Washington and Main. During the Depression we children thought it would be a great place to trick or treat on Halloween. After climbing about ten wide stone steps onto a porch, its roof held up by eight tall columns, a door bell was rung. Shortly a maid dressed in black with a white cap and apron opened the door, silently counted the number of waiting children, then closed the door. Returning later, she carried a silver tray with the exact number of pieces of white divinity candy as there were children. In contrast, a man lived nearby in a large white Victorian home setting on a corner of Cherry and Lenawee streets. He had a Chinese servant who answered the door bell's ring. Children were invited into a parlor where bushels of various fruits were placed around the room. But there was a catch. Before one could partake of this treasure trove, each child had to sing, recite a poem, dance, or perform something for the owner as his servant hid chuckling behind a curtain. Even the poorest of the poor in this area would give out pennies. The Olds mansion was demolished in 1957 to make way for a freeway.

Wallace Olds returned to live at 210 E. Kalamazoo Street which was half a block from Wes' property. Wallace's gas engine manufacturing plant was named W. S. Olds Air Cooled Motor Company and located at 508 S. Hosmer Street. By now father Pliney was deceased.

Wes' family was settled back in their home in Lansing. He was now 64 years old and continued working as a carpenter. May advertised herself as a seamstress in addition to preaching at the Spiritualist Church. Its members presented her with a gilt-edged Bible in 1927. We still have that Bible, Henry Cook's Bible and the McNeil family Bible. Wes was six when Spiritualism arrived in Ohio. I doubt his family had much to do with the local medium. But Wes' wife was a Spiritualist.[1] The Spiritualists first met in Lansing in May 1880. They promoted free thought and spiritual philosophy. May had became involved with the group before her marriage. It was locally popular with notable families attending. At the time May was living with her brother, George McNeil. When she was young, she was hit in one eye by a stray arrow which developed into a traumatic cataract. It didn't deter her ability to sew or crochet or her spiritual interest and card reading. Eventually she became a preacher.

Wes' mother's side of the family enjoyed family reunions that continued many decades. They were known as the Wood-Gidley Reunions. One was photographed beside the brick flat on Kalamazoo Street. Wes, now bent with age, was seated with his siblings in the front of the group. All I knew about this grandfather came from family stories, letters, and my research since he died the year before I was born. He was also the last of his siblings to die.

Wes and May's younger son:

Eno[9] Richmond Ayres was born Feb 22nd 1895. He was a young blond haired toddler when he would wander up the streets. I say up because the main avenue was uphill from where he lived. He was 3½ when the sounds of drums and fifes were blaring nearby. A corps was playing on Grand Avenue one block north of his home. So Eno set off to see what was happening. Musicians were playing as a large banner flew overhead. They were recruiting men for the Spanish-American War. That war set off a depression which closed banks and left people out of work. On another occasion Eno meandered off several blocks away to the Michigan Avenue Bridge. Then it started to rain. A friend of the family, George Whitcomb, spotted him and asked: *Young man, what are you doing?* and proceeded to tuck Eno under his raincoat and take him home. Dad never lost his desire to explore. As dementia set in around age 80 and mother was deceased, he would wander down the main road on Casey Key in Florida well after midnight. A kindly policeman on patrol would pick him up in his car and drive him home.

One winter when Eno was young, a female neighbor asked May if she could take Eno with her to

---

1 Grandmother Was A Spiritualist, © 2005, Noreen Ayres Craig

where there was skating on the river. After donning her skates and starting out to meet other skaters, Eno followed her onto the ice. He fell through a thin spot but managed to keep himself from going under the ice by extending his arms over the ice until he was rescued. May was furious.

Very young boys at the time were still wearing dresses. Dad grew to dislike his dresses and his long blonde curls so one day he pleaded for a hair cut and to be allowed to wear pants. His blonde curls were cut off and saved in a little box. Occasionally when he was older and his dark hair was thinning, he liked to show them off so he must have been proud of them.

He was five when his father moved from Lansing to Saginaw and had just started kindergarten in September. He was put into first grade in Saginaw since there was no kindergarten. He enjoyed living in Saginaw where its logging industry provided much to see. He liked watching logs being floated on the river on their way to a mill. His uncle Will warned him to be careful in his wanderings since his mother did not spend all her time with the family in Saginaw as shown in the following letter:

> *Apr 7th 1904, Saginaw, Michigan*
> *Dear Mamma,*
>   *I thought I would write you a few lines. I do not think I will pass. The teacher is reading us a story of "Mrs. Wiggs of the Cabbage Patch."*
>   *I think I will go to the Bliss School next year. I think this will be all for this time. Your loving son. Eno*

Eno continued his education through the 5th grade in Saginaw. With the Ayres plant in duress, he and his father moved back to Lansing. Their home was rented so his father lived in the barn. Eno stayed with his mother's brother, George McNeil. Dad wrote to his mother again who had joined her son, Raymond, in Saginaw:

> *Oct 12th 1905, Lansing, Michigan*
> *To: May F. Ayres, 608 Bristol St., Saginaw, Michigan*
> *Dear Ma:-I thought I would write you today and tell you how things were getting along. I went back to the fifth grade at the begining of the week. I think the fifth grade is easy as pie, and I get a hundred (=A) in every lesson pretty near. Pa tole me to write when Mrs. Scott moves out, she has a house and is going to move into it saturday. I hope you are getting along all right. Have you got everything packed. We had snow yesterday and it was bitter cold my feet, ears, and hands was about froze. I am staying at Uncle George's. I am getting along allright but I wish I had some clothes, my cap, some underdrawers. I guess I will close for today. don't forget some under wrists. Your son Eno*
> *I thought I would write you because you told me to. I have been so busy. I wish that Mrs. Scott would move out. I dont like to live on bread and milk. George told me that he wanted you to send down Ed's address he said that he had lost it. I dont want you to show everybody in the neighborhood this letter.*
> *Your son, Eno*

Eno completed 6th grade at Cherry Street School while living with his Uncle during its first session. The one room school was about half a block away from the brick flats. Later he attended Townsend Street School in the 7th- 8th grades after which he was given a Certificate of Promotion to Lansing High School in 1909. His 8th grade textbooks are so very different from what are used now. The *New Educational Music Course* seems to have bored him as he was playing with the words lemon and revolver turning them into names of streets, townships, towns, county and states. A hole was drilled into the back cover with drawing of faces on the pages, the holes serving as mouths. On some pages he made the notes into dancing people. The areas of music covered in the book is taught today at college level in an Introduction to Music course. Another book was *Selections from the Sketch-Book by Washington Irving.* Inside the back cover is pasted "For External Use Only." *Graded Lessons in Physiology and Hygiene* has an extensive college level study on health and the human body. Numerous dried 3 and 4 leaf clovers are tucked in many pages. The other two books are: *A German Grammar for Beginners* and *Horne's Pennsylvania German Manual.* The grammar book has a small hole on the cover with part of the fabric torn out in the shape of a shield. I do know he enjoyed the last two books as he spoke some German on occasion. He also completed Algebra IX. Comparing these 8th grade textbooks with today's, one could say despite the excessive amount of tax dollars poured into our educational system, there has been a continual "dumbing down" process. Eno had to drop out the second half of 9th grade high school in April 1910 due to his mother's illness. That fall he started classes at the local manual training school to learn the trade of tool and die making. He was allowed to drive the family car to school and piled all the students in it he could. When fall arrived the teachers needed some corn shocks for decorations so Eno volunteered to drive the car to the nearby small village of Bath to acquire some. After three flat tires, he finally returned at 5 p.m. to an anxious crew of teachers.

In Jan 1911 Eno toyed with the idea of becoming a dealer for N.S.U. Motor Company selling their motorcycles. The next month he received a letter from a friend who was attending St. Francis College in Cincinnati suggesting Eno move to Detroit where this friend was living. But Eno stayed in Lansing working for Olds Motor Works in the office getting parts for customers, the only place where one could acquire spare parts. On one occasion he was carrying a battery when the strap broke and spilled acid on his shoes. He ran to the boiler room to put water on them. After showing his discolored shoes to his boss, he was sent to the janitor who put ammonia on them. His red shoes magically turned back to their original color. He left that job shortly to work in their tool crib. Eventually he ended up in the tool room where he was able to practice tool and die making.

He was working at the Reo Motor Car Company in 1912. Then he drove for Smith Floral delivering flowers until winter came. Having frozen his toes bobsledding when living in Saginaw, he couldn't stand cold weather for a long time thereafter. Years later he somehow managed to bundle up and ice fish at Clifford Lake where a cottage had been purchased. His odd jobs included making mail boxes, selling clothing, and clerking in an electric store. There he purchased for his parents 25th anniversary a large Tiffany style grape patterned lamp shade which hung over their dining room table until the brick house was sold and razed for a city parking lot. In 1913 he moved to Detroit to work at Chrysler Motor Car Company. The next year he switched to General Aluminum and then the Cadillac Automobile Company which was formed from Henry Ford's bankrupt Detroit Automobile Company. Ford had nothing to do with the Cadillac Company since he had started the Ford Motor Company. It was about this time that Dad began smoking and going out with the boys. His favorite drink was a strawberry flip. And of course, there were girls to date. He returned to Lansing in 1915 and became a night inspector for the Michigan Crank Shaft Company. He said that job "really got me down" so he went back to REO staying there until 1918 when he began working again at Olds Motor Works. After a year he returned to REO.

Eno met his future wife at his home when her older sister had come for a "card reading" from his mother. Clara Maude Woolcock waited in the parlor while her sister Esther was upstairs in May's "Temple Room." The room was kept dim by a dark green shade covering the single slim window. At some point earlier she had "circles" because his Aunt Ella had written to her that she missed having them. May's gilt edged Bible lay atop a typical simple wooden church pulpit. Cards and other mysterious things in frames were hung on the walls. Her card reading incorporated astrology and occult sciences with each birth date having a personal card and ruling planet. An individual's card is a key to one's life plan and relationship to the past, present and future. The medium interprets the cards for an individual. It is all too complex to try explain in more detail.

The Grand River behind the barn has flooded more than once. It also provided Eno a playground. He liked water and acquired a speed boat to race up and down the river. He also owned a board on which he rode while being towed by his boat, Ursilla. Wallace Olds, who lived across the street, found it an interesting name and told Eno he would name a daughter after it if he had one. Wallace did have a daughter that he named, Ursula. She married Phil Walters. The river also afforded Eno a means to go courting. He would dock near Moores Park, then walk through the park to Maude's parents home on Bradley Avenue. Eventually he persuaded her to go to Toledo to marry. On Oct 16th 1918 Eno Richmond Ayres and Clara Maude Woolcock were married in Toledo's Trinity Episcopal Church by Rev. E. W. Todd. Eno was not working at the time and needed to get a job. He went back to REO Motor Car Co. making $5 a day. It was considered "big money" at the time. After he was laid off he went back to Olds' tool room. Later he acquired the same job at REO.

Eno and his brother, Raymond, lived in the frame house that was vacated when Wes and May moved into the brick flats. It was remodeled to have two entrances and two apartments. Raymond and his wife, Elizabeth, lived upstairs. My folks lived downstairs. On Sundays the families gathered for their noon meal in the brick flat. The table was set in an elegant Victorian style with fine China and silverware engraved with a fancy A on the handle. Many a good meal has come from its kitchen, not a fancy one by any means. A diagonal cupboard for cookware was built in on one corner. The dining room china cabinet was similar only fancier with glass doors. A long porcelain sink with hot and cold faucets hung beside a door next to the cupboard that led into a small room with a toilet. The kind with an overhead box that held the water for flushing. A porcelain ball hanging on a chain connected at the box was pulled to discharge the water. The ball was always falling off to Dad's annoyance. Next to the sink was a white porcelain gas range standing on four legs. It served multi purposes. Besides baking and cooking, water in a large copper boiler was heated for laundry. Its small pilot light served as a place to heat a curling iron. Dad hung his razor strap on a handle below the oven door and near the sink. One day it came up missing. Several years passed before one of my sisters admitted that she had thrown it into the river. I can't recall that he ever used it other than to sharpen his razor. He was patient, often spending part of his evening helping that sister with her math homework. The wall opposite the sink faced outdoors. Its uninteresting view was one side of the grey painted frame house. A white porcelain topped work table stood below the window. It had a built in bin for flour with a sifter, a cabinet and some drawers. It was here that dishes were washed and wiped. Two pans were placed on top, one for washing, the other rinsing. Dish towels were used to complete the job. When a friend, an only child, of my next eldest sister came over at dish washing time and we usually sang as we worked. Dish washing and drying could also evolve into a "getting even time." Some older sisters could be bossy and to counter that, you could say "I'm not going to wash the dishes" or "I'm not going to wipe cooking pans." Anything to arouse mother. Of course, the oldest always got the blame. We may have had our pecking order squabbles at home but we would protect our siblings from anyone else. Next to the work table was a door that opened to a small back porch. Here a small wood coffee grinder hung next to the door. An insulated wooden ice box kept food items cool. It was not very efficient but better than nothing. We always looked forward to the ice man's delivery to beg for a small chunk to nibble on.

In June 1921 Eno purchased lot 34 in Cedar Acre Subdivision. One side of the lot was next to the old inter-urban line that ran on Washington Avenue from one end of Lansing to the suburbs. With building restrictions waived the following October, he was allowed to build a mercantile store. The land sloped slightly downhill from the old track bed. A basement was dug, the earth used to create a flattened area. Dad's father, Wes, was now age 79 but helped construct a grocery store on Rockford Rd. The building was symmetrical with a center slightly receding entrance. One side held the fruits and vegetables, a meat display case, butcher's block, walk-in cooler and kitchen. A check out counter separated it from the canned and packaged goods area. At its rear behind the candy case, a lift-up trap door led to the basement where potatoes, bananas, and such products were stored. Large windows were on each side of the front entry. Vegetables on ice sat in front of one window. The other side had a place to sit and display non perishable items. Initially, Eno continued working at REO while he hired Maude's sister Esther and other family members to run the grocery for a couple of years. After his 8-5 weekday job, he would drive to the store to close it at 7 pm. His Saturdays were also spent there. Work hours were long and he survived on little more than five to six hours of sleep most of his adult life. In 1923 he quit REO to work at the grocery full time. Maude's father had worked at REO since moving to Lansing from the Michigan's Upper Peninsula.[1] He was due to retire in 1927. The company fired him just before his retirement so they wouldn't have to pay him any retirement. Many family members were embittered over this. Eno and Maude's two brothers took on the added responsibility of financing Maude's parents.

It was the Roaring Twenties and the country was thriving. Then came the crash in 1927 with the coming Depression. Eno's brother Raymond lost his job so he joined Eno as a partner in the grocery store. He and his wife, Elizabeth, would winter in Florida until he died in 1932. As a youngster he had a severe case of measles which left him with poor vision and a heart problem. An inventory of the store was necessary and completed on Jul 27th 1932. Assets were: Cash on hand $361.53; Stock approximately $1,000; Fixtures & Equipment $971; and Accounts Receivable $1,324.76, its size due to the Depression. People from Kentucky, Indiana, and numerous distant cities and states purchased on credit from this little out of the way grocery. Many gave nothing more than a name and city or a state as their address. It reminds me of hoboes long ago marking houses where they could get a handout. Dad was trusting and sympathetic to those whom he felt must be hurting from the Depression. Thus, most of those accounts were never collected.

Dad's unmarried cousin, Orno Lester, lived with us and also worked in the store. By now there were five girls, my parents and the cousin crammed into a two bedroom lower apartment. Raymond's widow, Elizabeth, lived in the upper apartment. A crib was kept in my parents' bedroom for the youngest and moved into the dining room at night. Three or four of us slept in a small bedroom or at grandma's on occasion. The small bedroom had nothing more than a tiny closet and a double size bed. The room was barely large enough to hold it. Orno slept in an alcove off the living room. French Junior High School was located not far from the grocery store and my two oldest sisters were allowed to attend it so they could help in the store after school. Mother's parents also lived somewhat near that area. My oldest sister Jean often helped our maternal Grandmother do her laundry. After Dad's mother died on Apr 13th 1934 we moved into her home.

In summer much of the fresh produce for the store was purchased at the local City Market. It consisted of several rows of greenhouse like covered buildings where local growers displayed their products. Dad had his preferred growers. Although I was very young, I was allowed to go twice a week with Dad in summer. It meant getting up at five in the morning to get to the market, make purchases, and get to the store in time for a seven am opening. I later realized the importance of not buying too much. Fresh produce when passed its prime or bruised fruit was brought home. Mother made wholesome stews and soups from the vegetables. Fruits were made into pies or canned. My oldest sister was her helper. We also had a pear tree next to the barn that bore large saleable fruit. I was a tomboy and had no difficulty in being asked to climb the tree and carefully pick and place one Bartlett pear at a time into a sock tied on the end of a long pole that Dad held. In back of the frame house was a large green gage plum tree. I picked that fruit for Uncle Raymond's wife, Aunt Elizabeth, who made it into jam. Because we lived "downtown" relatives would drop in after church, often unannounced, or Sunday evenings. That meant more family to feed. Dad called Mother a miracle cook because she always managed "to whip up something out of nothing" to feed relatives.

Christmas meant putting up a floor to ceiling tree and the ceiling was HIGH. Once every year we could "Oh & Ah" looking at the prized old ornaments. Dad handled the lights. In the basement he had rigged up a method of testing individual bulbs and replacing bad ones before putting them on the tree that I thought was clever. The bulbs were connected in series so when one bulb failed none of the lights in the string worked. Once decorated and finally lit in the evening, we could count the days until Christmas morning. The large family gathering was always at mother's parents home. A fun day with many cousins and lots to eat. I liked to spend some of the time with Grandma Woolcock in the kitchen but she would tell me in her Cornish accent to "gosalong." All too soon came New Year's Day. It was

1 *A Cornish Heritage*, © 1996, Noreen Ayres Craig

the day for taking inventory at the grocery, a tedious job counting every item I remember so well. On one occasion Dad explained to me that one can in a case of goods was his profit. That's why part of my job was to see that nothing was taken without paying. There were pranksters too. A box of individual mouse traps sat on the top shelf of the bread rack. Boys would set the mouse traps so an unsuspecting person could get their fingers nipped. I had the job to check the mouse trap box. Some pranksters called on the telephone asking the question: "Do you have Prince Albert in a can?" If you were naive enough not to hang up and answered "yes," the caller would say "Why don't you let him out?" Since I liked being near my Dad and sister Jean, I was happy spending time at the store. It certainly was a hands on education. I learned much about trade and marketing, prudent shopping, bookkeeping, and dealing with the public. Most of this was during the Depression when there was little money. Products were often obtained by exchange. The potato man who had lost one hand in a farm accident and wore a metal "claw hand" would exchange his potatoes for eggs or other food products. And so it went with others who had farm produce to trade. Dad's cousin, Orno, went into the poultry business after he married which provided a good place for Dad to purchase his chickens and Thanksgiving turkeys. It meant a fun trip to his farm. His poultry were immaculately cleaned. To this day, I have never seen poultry as clean as Orno's in <u>any</u> store. Costly Federal Government regulations put him out of business. If all the chickens didn't sell immediately, Dad put them in two quart glass jars and processed them in a large pressure cooker. This was long before Swanson's canned ones came on the market. Cleanliness was vital and the store and equipment were kept spotless with cloroxed water. Some packaged goods were different. Bulk cookies came in square cardboard boxes that fit into a rack with covered glass doors. I was appointed to look out for cookie snatchers. A parent would never admit that their darling stole a cookie. An example of grocers prices in 1935 comes from a Symon Bros. bill, wholesale merchants in Jackson, MI: a case of 24 boxes of Wheaties cost Dad $2.44, a case of 36 cans of Del Monte Crushed Pineapple $2.55, and a case of 9 oz. French Mustard $4.80. Interesting that mustard was so expensive.

About this time Dad was told to quit smoking by his doctor or else. He quit cold turkey. A surgeon had just removed one kidney. I was about age eight when he began building a travel trailer after dinner. At the time, it was my favorite time to be with Dad. I could fetch his tools or just watch him at work. I can't recall exactly when it was completed but it afforded the family time at various lakes. On one weekend he left my mother and we three youngest daughters at a nearby lake while he went back to work. I never wore anything more than my little swim suit around the clock at a lake. As the weekend neared for Dad's return on Sunday, I was unaware that our food supply was scarce. I had just gone to bed when I heard a commotion outside the trailer. Curiosity set in and I went out to see why all the chatter. A couple of men had just come in from fishing bearing a large washtub full of fish and were giving them away. Hastily I ran to tell Mother. She got out of bed and gave me a large pan to get some. I cleaned them the next day for mother to cook. Mother then told me there was nothing for us to eat until Dad returned on Sunday. The Lord and good fishermen provided.

Sunday's were the one day Dad could sleep late. Being an early riser, I would pick up the newspaper lying on the porch, spread it on the living room floor to read, then carefully put it back as delivered. When I would hear Dad stir, I would tiptoe into his bedroom to ask him for some change for church and Sunday School collection before heading off to church. About the only time I didn't attend my church was when we were camping or I stayed with Aunt Elizabeth and we would go to her church.

Since age five I had also been singing in the local youth choir on Saturdays at the Strand Theatre. We were on the local radio station WJIM. We met early Saturday mornings to rehearse. After the radio show at noon, we could watch the world news and the movie afterward. When we moved to the Oldsmobile Auditorium, we practiced Saturday mornings. We were served lunch on a noon break. Just before we went on air Sunday Dec 7th 1941, we were told of the bombing of Pearl Harbor. We were all aware of Europe's situation and after tears and hugs of what we knew lay ahead for our country, we composed ourselves, dried our tears, straightened our robes and sang our program with gusto to a weeping audience to whom the announcement had been given. After that, the Olds plant was converted to produce small cannon and shell casings. I recall seeing stack upon stack of bomb shell casings in one plant located near the auditorium where the choir sang. All areas were restricted and off limits. When I was in junior high I helped at the store after school, Saturdays, and in summers. It was a very long walk from school to the store. As the war went on I entered high school. It had a program where interested students could help farmers with their livestock and picking crops. I assisted in this program in addition to gathering metal for the scrap drive. Dad had a huge collection of large old keys that he graciously contributed to the scrap drive. Fats from meat trimmings in the store were saved and converted for making explosives. Earlier they had been collected by a soap manufacturer. Each Christmas a box of fancy fragrant soap was delivered to the store to my mother's delight. Due to the grocery business, we did have ample gas. That made it possible for my sister Jean to take Grandmother Woolcock for occasional Sunday outings.

Dad had the coal stoker removed from the store and put to use in the basement of the brick house. Before that Mother stoked the furnace at 5 AM, then put oatmeal in a double boiler to cook for breakfast. Ice blocks and milk were always delivered to the house even though the grocery sold milk. The cream was always reserved for coffee or tea and occasionally hand whipped cream. After Jean returned to Lansing, she worked in a plant making airplane wings. My Dad's love of water never ended. He acquired two cottages and a Florida home by the inland waterway. In 1951 a brick home was built on Berkeley Drive in Lansing. The two houses Grandpa Ayres built were sold to the city whose interest was to turn the land into a large parking lot. They went down fast with a swinging ball. March 1952 brought the sale of the store building. It later came into the possession of the Prayer and Healing Temple, Inc. with Rev. John Sheerin and Joseph Sheerin. The City of Lansing's Fire Marshall directed the Sheerins in 1958 to rehang doors, fix roof supports, quit placing ashes in combustible boxes, replace the furnace smoke pipe with a proper draft and check controls plus replace the rear steps. The Sheerins contract became muddled and owed my folks $7,396.23. In Oct 1961 Dad entered into a contract for the store with the Water of Life Tabernacle, Inc. Oct 1966 brought the celebration of my parents 50th wedding anniversary. Retirement years were spent between Pickerel Lake near Petoskey, MI, and the home in Florida.

Dad wrote:

> *The Amiotte family lived across the street from the grocery store. In 1940 Maude had been quite ill from eating some bad chocolate eclairs from Arbaugh's bakery and was on the mend. The Amiotte's daughter, June, was a close friend of our oldest daughter, Jean, and had graduated from high school together. The family came to see Maude and during the conversation the question of work was brought up. I had mentioned that I was a tool and die maker and Mr. Amiotte said that they were hiring in the Experimental Machine Shop at the Oldsmobile plant. Since the depression had made quite a bit of grief in the food business, I thought it would help to stabilize the business to bring in some outside funds to fill in the slack. So I went over to talk with the Foreman and it happened that he had worked for my brother, Ray, when he had been in charge of the department and said you can go to work tomorrow. I said I would have to have some time to get adjusted so how about bringing my toolbox in Friday and start Monday afternoon. He said okay so I did and the afternoon shift worked out real good as I could spend most of the day in the store helping Jean. This worked alright until Jean got married. Food rationing had started increasing paper work as well as food shortages and Jean wanted to be with her husband in Missouri. I put on a big sale and closed the business but still kept my job at Olds eventually retiring after some twenty years of service. The building was later sold and became a church.*
> *The Clifford Lake cottage[1] had been sold and another built in Petoskey,*

---

1 The cottage was purchased in mis May 1945 and located in Montcalm County and sold in May 1959.

Michigan, in 1958. We had been vacationing in Florida in a trailer park. In 1957 a lot was purchased on Casey Key with expectations of building a retirement home there. I retired on January 1, 1961, and we spent our summers in Michigan and winters in Florida until Maude became too ill to travel beyond Lansing. Her brother and I got her settled in Haslett while I went up to the summer cottage with the idea of selling it. I knew we could never enjoy it like we did so I got our personal things packed to take to Florida and sold the cottage on August 11, 1973. While there she took a turn for the worse and was hospitalized in Carson City under the care of my son-in-law. She was eating better and transferred to a nursing home where I could often visit. I made on last quick trip to Petoskey and upon returning found she had a stroke. I visited with her every day and upon improvement, I made a necessary quick flight to Florida to settle some affairs when word came she was in a coma. I flew back to Lansing where I ended up in the emergency room myself and while there word came that Maude had died. This was January 21, 1974. It is hard to realize how anyone feels after so many years close together when suddenly you are separated and the lonesomeness makes you feel you have nothing more to live for. However, you have your own life to live and must make the best of it. Amen. I lived in the Florida home with a housekeeper until she was eventually discharged when my daughter, Lucy, moved to Venice and looked after me while I lived alone.

PART TWO

Wood Ancestry

★ ★

Pilgrims, Puritans, Quakers

The term "Pilgrim" was coined by William Bradford in reference to those who came from Leiden on the *Mayflower*. It wasn't until 1789 during a Forefather's Day Celebration in Boston that the Pilgrims of Leiden were eulogized. A year later a poem was written that used the term Pilgrim Fathers. Not all on the *Mayflower,* were Separatists (Pilgrims). That group consisted of eighteen married couples, fifteen with children, six married men traveling without their wives, four with sons, plus eight servants. Richard Warren left his wife and five daughters in England. Francis Cooke with his son, John, was among the married men without wives but had his son with him. The Strangers, non Separatists, referred to by Bradford consisted of seven married couples, six with children, one married man traveling without his wife, and five servants who boarded the *Mayflower* in London. Three women aboard were pregnant adding to their travails at sea. One had a son delivered at sea who later died during the early sickness. Another was stillborn, another male lived to old age.

William Bradford's journal *Of Plymouth Plantation* was written around the time of settlement of New England in 1620. It offers an historical insight into the settling on a new continent. *Mourt's Relation, A Journal of the Pilgrims of Plymouth* was penned later by the mysterious G. Mourt and based on Bradford's writings. I have interjected in script applicable quotes from Bradford's *Of Plymouth Plantation* written in the phonetic spelling of that time in history.

On the eve of Easter 2008, I was watching History Channel's "The Protestant Reformation." It was stated that those who came on the *Mayflower* were Puritans and the 1630's arrival under John Winthrop were Pilgrims, Did I hear correctly? I suspected that I would next hear that the Massachusetts Bay Colonists started the Congregational Church. Many other groups opposed practices of the Catholic Church and the Church of England for various reasons; some persecuted for their actions. Puritans wished to reform or purify the Church of England. The Separatists (Pilgrims) sought change in the church. There is considerable difference between reform and change. Too often it seems the only time Pilgrims come to light in our educational system is at Thanksgiving with its less than factual tales about men dressed in Puritan, not Pilgrim, garb feasting with Indians.

In the year 1624 Capt. John Smith wrote his description of the settlement at "New Plimouth". The Colony was midway in its first decade of settlement when James I died bringing an end to England's bloodiest years under the Tudor-Stuart reigns. Charles I became King of England in 1625. This further unsettled the English Calvinists or Puritans as they feared a return to Catholicism. In protest, they took on a somber mode of dress which would be brought to America by some Puritans. Others would arrive more elaborately dressed. Having paid their own passage, they were not indebted to any Adventurers. As for Quakers, also in the year 1624 at Leicestershire, England, George Fox was born to a pious mother and father, members of the Church of England. The settlers of the Plymouth and Bay Colonies had no way of knowing what impact this humble birth would have on the future of religion in New England.

The early settlers on Cape Cod who joined the Society of Friends movement did not arrive in New England as members of that sect. The Society of Friends were called Quakers in derision, yet the term survived for centuries without the early connotation. Due to governmental treatment and new laws, especially in the Bay Colony, those who were not members of acceptable churches soon joined the movement. Puritanism evolved into age of religious bigotry, intolerance, and persecution.[1] The Bay Colony often brutally enforced the iron rule of conformity. When Governor Winthrop died, he lamented the part he had played in the persecution of those considered heretics which had little effect on those who later punished the Quakers. As Plymouth Colony grew, their more tolerant religious belief became diluted and like the Massachusetts Bay Colony, passed laws requiring church attendance and financial support. Communities became alienated, especially in Sandwich where Quakers gained an early foothold. They would suffer more than Anabaptists who along with Puritans and Presbyterians were supported by Oliver Cromwell, leader of England's Roundheads, when he

---

1 Richard P. Hallowell, *The Quaker Invasion of Massachusetts* (Bowie, MD, Facsimile Reprint Heritage Books, Inc., 1987) p.130

became Lord Protector of the Commonwealth of England on Dec 16th 1653. This concluded the mass emigration of Puritans into New England, but left the followers of George Fox and similar Christian sects in England facing imprisonment for their refusal to swear allegiance, pay tithes, or bear arms for England. These people are found in this family history. Their lives will encompass their ventures in government, business, family life, religion, and customs.

Tracing Lydia's Pilgrim Roots

A couple of decades ago my husband, Robert, my sister, Jean Wells, now deceased, and I joined a genealogy group to tour England and Scotland. After a week in London, we departed the group. Armed with booklets and a large road atlas, we rented a car and struck out on our own. Our first major stop was the charming city of Salisbury from which we could easily tour nearby villages and cities. On a pleasant, but cloudy Sunday, Southampton, a city that lay southeasterly past the city of Romsey, was our goal. We arrived in the small village of Whiteparish where one ancestral family had been married in the Anglican church. We were invited in to participate in viewing local children conducting the services that day. After the service as we were looking at the monuments on the church wall, the Vicar's wife graciously invited us to tea. Due to our limited schedule we had to decline the

Wall at West Gate in Southampton

West Gate at Southampton

offer. The next brief stop was in the town of Romsey before arriving at Southampton located in the water inlet north of the Isle of Wight.

Southampton was the place of departure where the *Speedwell* would join the *Mayflower*. We found the old part of Southampton still had its ancient stone walls, gates, and structures. The West Gate was where the Pilgrims came and went before their departure. Beyond the gate was the west quay where they embarked on August 15th 1620. Like many cities on England's southern coast, Southampton suffered much ruin in WWII from German bombs.

The following day we left our B&B in Salisbury taking a coastal southerly route through the subtle rolling hills of Dorsetshire dotted with numerous English channel inlets on our way to Plymouth, Devonshire. We made another stop in Bridport where we had lunch at a pub near the

Friend's Meeting House. With summer flowers in full bloom, a festival was being held that day. Saint Mary's Church chancel was resplendent with fragrant floral arrangements. We bypassed Dartmouth where in August 1620 the two ships had departed after the *Speedwell* was checked out by shipwrights. We made no more stops on our way to Plymouth except briefly viewing the interesting coastal town of Lyme Regis.

We took a short rest at our B&B before undertaking the crowded streets of Plymouth. It too had suffered considerable damage during WWII. On March 20th 1941, thousands of incendiaries fell like n unexpected hailstorm by showers of high explosive bombs. As Britain suffered from German bombs, it wouldn't be until the following December 7th that Pearl Harbor was bombed by Japan.

The area in Plymouth known as Barbicon was where the *Mayflower* and *Speedwell* had tied up in 1620. It was filled with tourists munching on the popular fish and chips served in a container made of folded brown paper. Their chips were made of un-peeled potato chunks, nothing like the thin pared strips of our French fries. Numerous plaques commemorate the Pilgrims, one listing all the passengers who boarded the one hundred eighty ton *Mayflower*. Plymouth had become another inadvertent stop caused by the *Speedwell*'s condition and it was here that the ship was abandoned before the long voyage. These delays put the *Mayflower* in jeopardy as it slipped away from its sheltered harbor near the center of town on September 6th 1620 in a fine small gale having been kindly entertained and courteously used by divers friends there dwelling. Despite fair weather at the moment, the Atlantic would threaten with increasing storms and chilling weather for these passengers.

Financial backing was a hurdle. Bradford noted *They were perplexed with the proseedings of the Virginia Company.* One of Virginia Company's acquaintances, Mr. Thomas Weston, went to Holland to confer with Mr. Robinson and others telling them *not to medle with the Dutch, or too much depend on the Virginia Company; for if that failed,...he and such marchants as were his freinds (togeather with their owne means) would sett them forth.* Weston, an ironmonger (hardware

One of Southampton's oldest structures

16th Century Elizabethan House at Plymouth
retaining most of original architecture

dealer) and small capitalist, whose only interest was making money on the enterprise, convinced them to accept his Merchant Adventurers offer, the first of many mishaps with Weston. He was determined to make the Pilgrims ishermen to cash in on north Atlantic fishing. Financial articles were drawn up and agreed. John Carver, a member of the congregation, was sent to London with Robert Cushman to receive the money and acquire provisions for the voyage. An agreement was made to hire the *Mayflower.* Previously noted, *A small ship was bought, & fitted in Holand, which was intended as to srve to help transport them, so to stay in the cuntrie and atend upon fishing and shuch other affairs as might be for the good & benefite of the colonie.* Weston created another problem by demanding a change in is Leiden agreement. Two agents were again sent to London. On July 1st 1620, eight changes were inserted into the agreement. Cushman, upset with Leiden's discontent, wrote them a lengthy letter outlining the two groups' positions. He with Carver, Bradford, Brewster, Winslow and Allerton led in this decision. After considerable travel and debate, things were ready and provided.

A last religious service was held on July 20th 1620. Some members sadly departed leaving family members behind, others still anxious over Weston's dealings. Travel in Holland was unrivaled with its canal boats traveling almost every hour in "ditches" with inexpensive passenger rates. From Leiden they passed Delft with its azure and red clay tiled roofs atop stone structures. Beyond Delft and before embarking on the *Speedwell* on July 22nd, sixteen men, eleven women, and nineteen children gathered for another religious service in the Oude Kerk in Delftshaven near Rotterdam. *Truly dolfull,* said Bradford, *was ye sight of that mournful parting, to see what sighs and sobbs and praires did sound amongst them, what tears did gush from every*

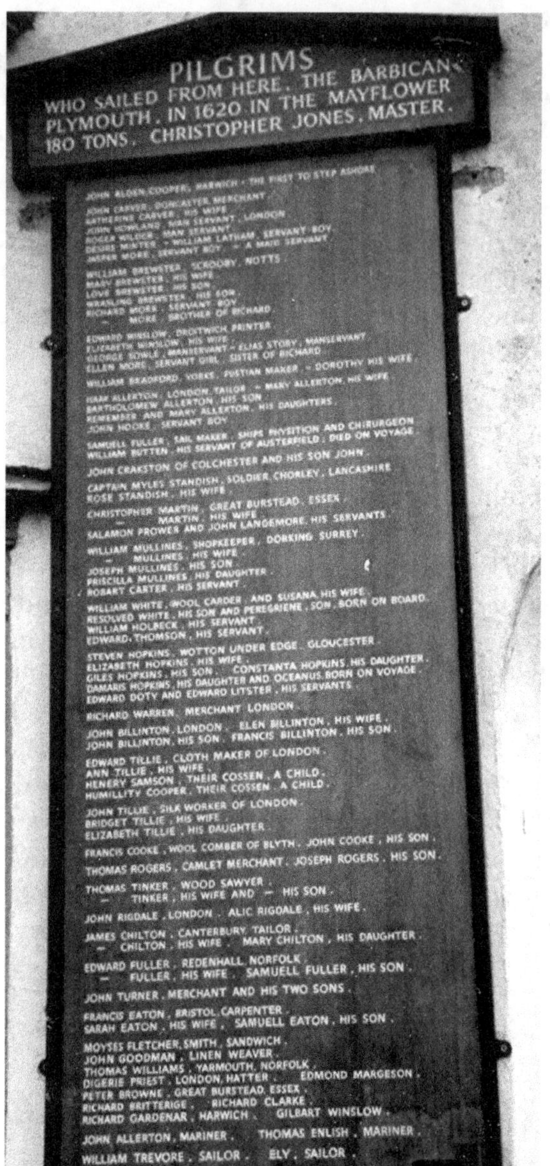

Plaque at Plymouth with names of the
Mayflower Passengers

eye, & pithy speeches peirst each harte. Robinson falling down on his knees with watrie cheeks commended them with most fervente praiers to the Lord and his blessing. And then with mutuall imbrases and many tears, they tooke their leaves, one of an other, which proved to be the last leave to many of them. Bradford added: *So they lefte that goodly & pleasante citie which had been their resting place near 12 years; but they knew they were pilgrimes, & looked not much on those things, but lift up their eyes to the heavens, their dearest cuntrie, and quieted their spirits.*

The Merchant Adventurers felt the group too small to settle a plantation so they added ninety people in London before the *Mayflower* set off for its rendezvous with the *Speedwell* at Southampton. There were thirty-eight freemen, five hired laborers, and eighteen male and female indentured servants. Bradford noted that those shuffled in upon them by the Merchants were heard to brag that once ashore they would be outside English law and would do as they please. The Separatists were in no mood for mutiny. Some of these Strangers would become pillars of the Colony.

The *Mayflower* was lying ready to sail when the *Speedwell* arrived at Southampton. After a joyful welcome, the men began to discuss the alterations of Weston's agreement with their agents. Carver claimed he didn't know what was done. Cushman expressed it was done of necessity. Due to the amount of beer and ale aboard, they had to locate a cooper. John Alden, a Welsh cooper, signed on. Weston came to Southampton from London to see that his new terms were met. Refusing his altered terms, he cut off further funding for their basic necessities. To meet expenses, they were forced to sell 4,480 pounds of butter to pay £100 for the *Mayflower's* port dues. Cushman, disgusted with "bloodsucker" merchants, wrote to a friend in London: *If we ever make a plantation, God works a miracle, especially considering how scant we shall be of victuals, and most of all disunited among ourselves and devoid of good tutors and regiment. I pray you prepare for evil tidings of us every day. But pray for us instantly, it may be the Lord will be yet entreated one way or other to make for us.*

After repairs were made to the *Speedwell*, the two ships left but additional problems forced them to put in at Dartmouth. Underway again, the *Speedwell* sprung a leak which obliged them to enter the harbor at Plymouth, England. There the *Speedwell* was abandoned. Robinson and nineteen others, including Lydia Wood's husband's ancestor, Thomas Blossom, and his son returned to Leiden. It bothered the Pilgrims to lose Robinson but they had survived for many years under elders and deacons. The last known reference to their functioning as a religious group in Leiden was in 1644. Some members complained about lack of proper religious exercises and sought church membership in the Dutch Reformed Church. Mrs. Robinson after the death of her husband joined the Dutch church.[1] Robinson's son, Isaac, later came to Plymouth Colony. Through cunning, deceit, and probable sabotage by the ship's captain, Mr. Reinolds, the *Speedwell* proved to be a bad purchase.[2] They later learned Reinolds had plotted and feigned the ship's problems to free himself and his crew from a year's stay in New England. The *Mayflower* set sail on September 6th 1620. Bradford noted that day: *These troubles being blown over, and now all being compact in one ship, they put to sea again with a prosperous wind, which continued divers days together, which was some encouragement unto them.*

The *Mayflower*

The staunch three masted ship with a prominent beak and bowsprit was not built to carry passengers. She was ninety feet long and at her broadest, twenty-five feet wide. The middle part of the main and upper decks where most of the passengers lived was open to weather but covered with canvas *waist cloths* to keep sea spray off them and their possessions. Beds were set up since there were no bunks or hammocks. A few wealthier individuals had cabins and brought some luxuries of sugar, lemons and a few bottles of wine or French brandy. Below was general stores with tools, supplies, cordage, canvas, canon shot, and powder. The stern had a high wooden superstructure known as sterncastle which housed the poop deck over the Captain's cabin. Behind the main mast were pens for livestock. More cabins were further aft. The forecastle on the upper deck contained the galley, boatswain's store, and crew quarters. The galley was so small the passengers did their cooking elsewhere. Beneath the main deck was the water supply, barrels of biscuit and flour, cargo and supplies including barrels of beer, dried salt beef and pork, and dried peas or beans. The passengers were fortunate in that Captain Jones had skippered the *Mayflower* for twelve years as a *sweet ship* used only for wine trade. There was no smell of garbage and rotting cargo, only the fragrance from leaking wine casks.

They brought a copy of John Smith's book about his 1614 New England voyage which included a map of New England's coastline. Smith offered himself for hire but they felt his book was cheaper than he. Besides New England was not their destination. Despite a fair wind and their troubles behind them, many suffered from sea-sickness and drenchings. Some male passengers helped sailors haul ropes in fair weather. Others were allowed to get some fresh air but none were allowed aloft in foul weather. Tensions below decks were eased by playing games like Nine Men's Morris, a medieval or earlier board game, reading, telling stories, and singing. Those who were ill were daily profanely

---

1 Sprunger, pp.123-130

2 Dowsing

cursed by a haughty young crewman who *hoped to help to cast halfe of them over board before they came to their jurneys end and to make mery with what they had.* Half way in the voyage he suffered a painful disease and died and was thrown overboard. They feared drowning as streams of icy water poured over them. Prayers were uttered as the ship creaked and groaned under cross winds and stormy seas. A main beam cracked causing the main deck to leak dousing those below. They helped the crew repair the beam with aid of an iron screw brought from Holland. During westerly gales, sails were hauled in to drift with the wind. In one such instance Bradford noted:

Seeing endless seas they prayed. Others jeered complaining that God's wrath would descend on them. And in one of them, as they thus lay at hull, in a mighty storm, a lusty yonge man (called John Howland) coming upon some occasion above the grattings, was, with a seele of the ship thrown into sea; but it pleased God that he caught hould of the top-saile halliards, which hunge over board, and rane out at length; yet he held his hould (though he was sundrie fadomes under water) till he was haulled up by the same rope to the brime of the water, and then with a boat hook & other means got into the shipe again & his life saved; and though he was something ill with it, yet, he lived many years after, and became a profitable member both in church & commone wealthe. In all this voiage ther died but one of the passengers, which was William Butten, a youth, servant to Samuel Fuller, when they drew near the coast. Separatists weren't intimidated by Strangers any more than they feared England's king. After a weary sixty-six day trip, twice as long as a normal trip, land was seen at dawn on November 9th. Everyone excitedly rushed to the upper deck to catch a glimpse of New England. Seeing land comforted them and they rejoiced praising God. Few aboard knew their northern Virginia patent destination on the Hudson River. A discussion among knowing males ensued with Captain Jones. It was decided to tack about and head southward. Bradford wrote: *After they had sailed the course about half the day, they fell amongst dangerous shoals and roaring breakers, and they were far entangled therewith as they concerned themselves in great danger; and the wind shrinking upon them withal, they resolved to bear up again to the Cape, and thought themselves happy to get out of those dangers before night overtook them as by God's Prvidence they did.* So they put ashore in territory allocated to the Council of New England knowing their patent was void.

On the outer arm of Cape Cod near today's Provincetown, Bradford cited: *Being thus arived at Cap-Cod on 11. Of November in a good harbor and brought safe to land they fell upon their knees and blessed the God of Heaven, who had brought them over the vast & furious ocean, and delivered them from all the periles & miseries therof, agine to set their feete on the firme and stable earth, their proper element...They had no friends to wellcome them, nor inns to entertaine or refresh their weatherbeaten bodys, no houses or much less townes to repair to...But necessity called them to look for a place of habitation.* All they could see was desolate wilderness and an ocean behind them. The bay was so shallow the nearest they could get to land was three quarter of an English mile. Jones' long boat could not be beached so they were forced to wade when the tide was out to reach shore. Many went to refresh themselves resulting in coughs and colds in frigid weather. Uncertainness was everywhere. Captain Jones' sailors were near mutiny. Some of the Strangers were so discontented they felt no one could tell them what to do once on land. Jones was anxious to locate a place to settle and repair their shallop, a small open two-masted rowing boat with lugsails that holds about thirty to forty men used in shallow waters. The leaders also knew they had no authority for settlement at Plymouth as they were beyond the bounds of their Virginia Company patent.

Observing these issues, a few Separatist leaders met to discuss the situation. Others held their own discussions. The Dutch Motto: "Een dracht maegt macht" (Unity makes strength) stirred them into action to offer terms that assured everyone of fair treatment in governance. Thus, the *Mayflower Compact* was born. At a general meeting its terms were read and signing began. Would the Strangers sign? In all forty-one adult males signed. After the signing, Carver was selected Governor. They would have to deal with a land patent later.

Tale of Plymouth Rock

An interesting tale originated at Plymouth's Old Colony Club and was verbally passed on by someone who claimed to hear it from a person in the audience. It related that ninety-five year old Elder Thomas Faunce, son of John Faunce who arrived in 1623 on the *Anne*, said that he was driven to town in an open wagon from the Eel River and taken to Plymouth Rock. He told the people gathered there how he had talked to John Howland and his wife, Elizabeth Tilley, John Alden, Giles Hopkins, George Soule, Francis Cooke and his son, John, and Mrs. Cushman, nee Mary Allerton. All of these told him that upon that very rock they had stepped ashore. John Winslow's wife, Mary Chilton, came there on her seventy-fifth birthday and said she was the first woman to have stepped on it.[1] From this story Plymouth Rock acquired its name. Faunce, born about 1647, married at Plymouth on December 13th 1672, Jane Nelson. Faunce died in 1746, short of one hundred years old.

Where to Settle

Locating a place to settle occupied much of some men's time. It wasn't until Dec 18th that others went ashore to see their choice. After several days of bad weather as many as were able went ashore on the 23rd. The 6th person died that day. Construction began on building housing on the 25th by two carpenters, one fustian maker, two printers, one tailor, one woolcomber, one cooper, one merchant, one soldier, four seaman, two tradesmen, one hatter, one blacksmith, one physician and ten adult servants. A meeting house was completed and on Jan 7th 1621, they held a religious service. It also served as shelter for some passengers. Then disaster struck one Sunday when a spark flew into the thatch roof of the meeting house burning all but the frame work as they watched in horror. Food was sparse so fishing was of necessity. Forty-five died from November through March. Eight married couples died leaving four children orphaned. Six children lost one parent. Crew members refused to help each other. Only the passengers still on the ship offered them help. Bradford noted about the illness in January and February, *being the depth of winter, and wanting houses & other comforts: being infected with the scurvie & other diseases...so as ther dyed some timed 2 or 3 of a day...that of 100 & odd persons, scarce 50 remained.* Early spring brought birds singing in the woods, lightening and thunder storms with rain and planting time. Squanto[1] taught them how to plant, where to fish and procure commodities. Early April the *Mayflower* set sail for England with letters to family and the Adventurers. Late summer 1621 Bradford noted that the surviving sixteen men, four women, and twenty-three children ... *begane now to gather in the small harvest they had, and to fitte up their houses and dwellings against winter, being all well recovered in health and strenght, and had all things in good plenty; for as some were thus imployed in affairs abroad, others were exersised in fishing, aboute codd, & bass, & other fish, of which they tooke good store, of which every family had their portion. All the sommer ther was no wante. And now begane to come in store of foule, as winter*

---

1 Eugene Stratton, *Plymouth Colony, Its History & People* (Salt Lake City, UT, Ancestry Publ., 1986) p.291

Wickapedia says that Squanto was of the Patuxet, a Native North American people living on the western coast of Cape Cod Bay, that had been annihilated by an epidemic infection. Six years before the Mayflower's landing, in 1614 Squanto was abducted by an English adventurer, Thomas Hunt, who was part of a commercial fishing and trading venture commanded by Captain John Smith. After Smith left for England with his cargo, Hunt, who was to take his dried fish cargo to Spain, kidnapped 27 Natives, including Squanto and sailed to Spain to sell them into slavery. Squanto escaped from Spain, perhaps with the help of Spanish friars, and went to England where he lived with a merchant involved in a project to exploit and settle Newfoundland. He eventually was sent there and lived with the Pokanoket, some say as a prisoner. No records exist of his activities from that time until his famous encounter with the Mayflower settlement in 1621. Squanto's chief fame resulted (Squanto con't) from his efforts to bring about peaceable contact and alliance between the English Separatists and other colonists who had come aboard the Mayflower and the Pokanoket. Owing to his facility with English, Squanto played a key role in the early meetings in March 1621. He soon became attached to the English settlers, whom he assisted in planting native vegetables, obtaining trade with local peoples and dealings with other native tribes, in at least one case endangering his safety in the process.

approached, of which this place did abound when they came first (but afterward decreased by degrees). And besids water foule, ther was great store of wild Turkies, of which they tooke many, besids venison, &c. Besids they had aboute a peck a meale a weeke to a person, or now since harvest, Indian corne to the proportion. Which made many afterwards write so largly of their plenty hear to ther friends in England, which were not fained, but true reports. With all the shooting and celebrating over their good harvest, Massassoit and ninety braves curiously and unexpectedly appeared. They were welcomed as noted in a letter of Edward Winslow published in *Mourt's Relation* in 1622. *Our harvest being gotten in, our governor sent four men a fowling, that so we might after a special manner rejoice together after we had gathered the fruit of our labors. The four in one day killed as much fowl as, with a little help beside, served the company almost a week. At which time, amongst other recreations, we exercised our arms, many of the Indians coming amongst us, and among the rest their greatest king Massasoyt, with some ninety men, whom for three days we entertained and feasted; and they went out and killed five deer, which they brought to the plantation, and bestowed on our governor, and upon the captain and others. And although it may not always so plentiful as it was at this time with us, yet by the goodness of God, we are so far from want that we often wish you partakers our plenty.* The men may have acquired the food but it was up to the four women Elizabeth Hopkins, Eleanor Billington, Susannah Winslow and Mary Brewster to coordinate the three day festival. The Pilgrims English way of Thanksgiving would have been somber with prayer and fasting. The welcome harvest was certainly blessed but sensitivity to their situation and Indian guests changed the custom.

Pilgrim vs Puritan Attire

It is a disservice to Pilgrims, Leiden Separatists, and unfortunate that artists have stereotyped them, generation after generation, as Puritans from England who protested court dress, wore somber clothing, mostly black, and carried a bell-mouth blunderbuss which could only scatter shot at short range. Puritan males wore short coats with a wide plain collar and tall wide brimmed black hat over short cut hair. Women wore a chemise covered with plain dark colored dresses. A large kerchief, nearly the size of a shawl, was worn over the shoulders of a dress. A long linen apron was vital to protect their dresses. Hooded cloaks protected them from inclement weather. Their hair was held into tight buns over which they wore a linen cap. Any hat was worn over the cap.

In contrast, most Pilgrim males owned a fifteen pound muzzle loaded smooth bore six foot long matchlock musket, a birding piece, a sword or cutlass, and wore metal helmets and breastplates in European style. Standish had an extensive number of weapons. Having lived in Holland, the Pilgrims came dressed in rich brightly colored Dutch clothing with ruffed collars, hats with sashes, and shoes lacking buckles. Women dressed like Dutch wives of New Netherland settlers. They had received fashionable clothing allotments from those who financed their voyage. Clothing was valuable and often given in wills. Inventories of some who died in 1633 showed the following items: A complete suit of doublet, breeches and cloak, satin suit, red wool lining for a doublet, caps with silver lace, sky blue garters, red, violet, "mingle-colored" petticoats, violet waist coats, blue aprons and stockings, linen or beaver felt caps, and hooded cloaks. Only one listed a black suit. Bradford had a red cloak and waistcoat, a lead-colored suit with silver buttons, and hats of color. Brewster had a violet cloak and blue cloth suit, a pair of green drawers, lace & red caps, and a green waistcoat. Like any social class, some dressed according to their means. Fabric was saved from worn garments as well as laces and trims for future use.

Male and female children wore dresses until boys were five or six. In baptism, infants were wrapped in a scarlet blanket embroidered with biblical verses and trimmed in gold lace. A bit superstitious, they felt red kept an infant safe. Children's clothes were usually made from recycled adult fabric in similar or newer styles. Ruffs were changed to softer stand-up or turned down collars. Boys' hair was combed straight back while girl's hair was long and curly. Older children of both sexes wore corsets.[1] Their

---

1 Estelle A. Warrell, *Children's Costumes in America 1607-1910* (New York, Charles Scribner &s Sons, 1980) p.21

clothing was not austere but time, hard labor, and need for trade items took its toll in Plymouth's earliest years.

Family Reunions & Newcomers

The good harvest of 1621 was shared with their Indian friends, but Weston dumped lazy and unruly sailors onto them and problems developed with the Narrangansets so they felt it necessary to build a fort. Tribal jealousies hindered trade in 1622, their corn was gone, news of the fate of the *Fortune* arrived, and more of Weston's beach bums sponging off them, things continued to look foreboding. When the *Anne* and *James* arrived in July they were seen as a desperate looking group. Some wept at what burden lay ahead for them and wished they were back in England. They saw *Many were ragged in apparell, & some litle better than halfe naked.* Only a few peas for soup, lobster or fish was available and spring water to drink. The old planters were concerned *that their corne when it was ripe, should be imparted to the new-comers whose provissions which they brought with them they feared would fall short before the year wente aboute* (as indeed it did). These ships raised the colony's numbers to ninety-three persons. After three years of separation, some families joyfully reunited. Aboard the *Anne* was Francis Cooke's wife, Hester, daughter Jane and son Jacob; Bridget, the 3rd wife of Dr. Samuel Fuller; Elizabeth, wife of Richard Warren, with daughters Mary, Anna, Sarah, Abigail and Elizabeth; plus other wives and children of those in Plymouth, some useful persons, and some so bad they were sent home the next year. As bad as the situation was there was no lack of humor. The following ballad was composed around this time and passed down by word of mouth for generations until written as uttered by a woman aged ninety-four.

> The place where we live is a wilderness wood,
> Where grass is much wanting that's fruitful and good:
> Our mountains and hills and valleys below
> Being commonly covered with ice and with snow;
> And when the northwester with violence blows,
> Then every man pulls his cap over his nose;
> But if any's so hardy and will it withstand,
> He forfeits a finger, a foot, or a hand.
>
> When the spring opens we then take the hoe,
> And make the ground ready to plant and to sow;
> Our corn being planted and seed being down,
> The worms destroy much before it is grown;
> And when it is growing, some spoil there is made
> By birds and by squirrels that pluck up the blade;
> E'en when it is grown to full corn in the ear
> It is often destroyed by raccoons and deer.
>
> And now our garments begin to grow thin,
> And wool is much wanted to card and to spin;
> If we can get a garment to cover without,
> Our other in-garments are clout upon clout;
> Our clothes we brought with us are often much torn,
> They need to be clouted before they are worn;
> But clouting our garments they hinder us nothing,
> Clouts double, are warmer than single whole clothing!

If fresh meat be wanting to fill up our dish,
We have carrots and turnips whenever we wish;
And, when we've a mind for a delicate dish,
We repair to the clam-bank and there we catch fish.
For pottage and puddings and custards and pies,
Our pumpkins and parsnips are common supplies;
We have pumpkin at morning and pumpkin at noon;
It 'twere not for pumpkins we should be undoone.
We must be contented, and think it no fault;
For we can make liquor to sweeten our lips
Of pumpkins and parsnips and walnut tree chips.

Now while some are going, let others be coming,
For while liquor's boiling it must have a scumming;
But we will not blame them, for birds of a feather,
By seeking their fellows are flocking together.
But you whom the Lord intends hither to bring;
Forsake not the honey for fear of the sting;
But bring both a quiet and contented mind
And all needful blessings you surely will find.
If barley be wanting to make into malt.

[1]Clouting was an old English term for patching or mending clothing with a piece of cloth. There garments had become tattered from hard work in building and planting. Indian corn became their dietary mainstay. Breakfast consisted of cornmeal porridge made of pease, corn, and coarsely ground samp (today's cornmeal) cooked in liquid. Juice from corn stalks was made into candy. Thus, corn became more precious than silver and was used in trade for small items. A large meal was eaten mid-day, and for supper sops (soup) and bread. Once their supply of molasses ran out, puddings were sweetened with honey or syrup tapped from birch or maple trees. Sugar was made by further boiling. All kinds of berries grew wild in addition to onions and plants such as treackleberry, sorrel, yarrow, purslane and sweet marjoram. Cranberries were avoided due to their unfamiliarity.

They ate with their fingers, sopping up their ford with bread on wooden or pewter trenchers and eating directly off knife blades. They were not aware of the lead content in pewter as being a health hazard causing lead poisoning often resulting in death. Highly acid foods such as tomatoes leached the lead into food. One reason why tomatoes were considered poisonous for centuries. Spoons were made of wood or pewter. Porridge and soups were served in pewter porrigers. Table forks were rare. An iron fork was used for toasting. Six wills written before 1630 noted silver spoons worth 5 shilling each. Bottles were made of leather. The preferred beverage was warm beer which everyone, including children, swilled from shared goblets. Sweets were served with the rest of the meal. It was left to the children to serve the food and clear the table. *Let faire young uns do the dirtie work.*

Knowing the need, the new arrivals brought seeds for kitchen gardens and wheat seed that failed for several years. It wasn't until 1624 that dairy cattle became available and milk, custards, and cheese was added to their diet.

---

1 Morison, pp. 97-99

A Failing Experiment

The experiment tried under a communal condition was: the taking of property into a common wealth would make them happy and flourishing. For this group, it bred confusion, discontent, and retarded employment. Those able and fit did not want to work for others without compensation. The equal division of goods among the strong and weak was thought an injustice. The aged, who ranked with the young, felt it was indignant and disrespectful to them. Wives ordered to work for other men felt it was slavery. *Upon the poynte all being to have alike, and all to doe alike, they thought them selves in the like condition, and one as good as another; and so, if it did not cut of those relations that God hath set amongest men, yet it did at least much diminish and take of the mutuall respects that should be preserved amongst them. And would have bene worse if they had been men of another condition. Let none objecte this is man's corruption, and nothing to the course it selfe. I answer, seeing all men have this corruption in them, God in his wisdome saw another course fiter for them.*

This would not be the only experiment in communistic societies in what would become the United States. Most notable were Shakers, established in the east around 1784, and the midwest around 1808 that lasted eighty years. Others were Rappists, Bäumelers, EbenEzers, Bethel Communes, Oneida Perfectionists, Icarians, Amanas, and Aurora Communes consisting of approximately seventy-two communes, Shakers the largest. Why did they fail? Each began with some form of diverse religious belief not necessarily Christian. Some were celibate. Political systems varied. Leaders were usually elected or appointed for life. Manual labor, frugalness, and early hours were required. Submission and self-sacrifice became irksome to some. They lived in isolation even lacking communication between their own communes. Being debt free was necessary. Wealth was not divided equally, older communes getting the larger share.[1]

Disheartening News

Word arrived in Plymouth that Captain Standish had returned from England in early Apr 1626. A shallop was sent to Monhegan to bring him to Plymouth. The customary route to and from England from Plymouth Colony was on fishing vessels out of Maine. Though greatly welcomed, his news was disheartening over their financial losses. Also word of the suffering of their Holland friends, some disabled, some dead of the plague, and the deaths of Mr. Robinson, King James of England, Prince Grave Mourise of Holland, and their friend, Mr. Cushman.

Settling A Debt

Since, after seven years, their debt was due to expire, Allerton was sent to England to make settlement terms with the Adventurers. Forty-two Adventurers sold their interests for £1,800 in an agreement negotiated by Allerton on Nov 15th 1626. Before Allerton was sent again to England, the Governor and some assistants consulted on how they might end the debt that lay heavily on the Colony and find means to bring their Leiden brethren to Plymouth. An adventurous method to free them of the £1,800 debt and other debts of £600 was contrived. Calling the Company together, the debt was explained and a plan for solving the problem. After considerable debate in July 1627, seven articles of agreement were drawn up between the Colony and the Undertakers, a group of eight Plymouth men and four Adventurers.
1.   The Colony was discharged of debts due for the purchase as of this date.
2.   The Undertakers are to have the last built pinnace, the boat at Manamett (Manomet), and the shallop called the Bass-boat, with all implements in store of the said company, with all the stock of furs, corn, wampum, hatchets, knives, etc.

---

1 Charles Nordhoff, *The Communistic Societies of the United States* (New York, Dover Publ. ,1966) pp.29,70,100,131,201,260,307,326,335

3. The Undertakers have the whole trade to themselves for six years beginning the end of the coming September.

4. In further consideration of the discharge of debts, every Purchaser shall pay annually for the term of six years, three bushels of corn, or six pounds of tobacco, at the Undertakers choice.

5. The Undertakers shall during the term provide £50 yearly in hose and shoes to be sold for corn at six shilling per bushel.

6. At the end of six years, the whole trade shall return to the Colony as before.

7. Lastly, if the Undertakers after acquainting the friends in England with these covenants, resolve to perform them and discharge the debts of the Colony according to the intent and stand in full force, otherwise all things remain as they were, and an account to be given to the Colony of the disposal of all things.

Twenty-seven Plymouth men signed the document that allowed Bradford, Standish, Allerton, Winslow, Brewster, Howland, Alden, and Prence and four London Adventurers: James Sherley, John Beauchamp, Richard Andrews, and Timothy Hatherly to become Undertakers. These men were willing to assume the risk, some motivated by the desire to bring more brethren from Leiden. That in itself made some Plymouth men unwilling to sign as they had no desire to pay their transportation.

The 1627 Distribution

A group known as Purchasers consisted of heads of families and single free able young males formed a partnership that made them privileged regarding future distributions. Men were needed for strength and defense and most had born their share of miseries, thus considered equal to take part in better conditions. Keeping a strict distribution of lands was necessary so new arrivals could participate. At a gathering of all the company, it was decided that trade would be managed the same to pay debts. Those named could purchase shares for each individual in his family, servants getting only what their masters give them. This became the land distribution of 1627. The Governor and four or five special men were given the houses in which they lived, the rest were valued and equalized so every man kept his own house. Each person was given an additional twenty acres added to what they had. Said land was to be laid out five acres in width by the water side and four acres long, except for nooks and corners. Meadows were reserved for the community with seasonal appointments made where they could mow according to their cattle proportion.

The population now numbering one hundred fifty-six, not the one hundred eighty estimated by Smith, was divided into twelve groups of thirteen individuals for a separate division of animals. *The first lot fell to ffrancis Cooke & his Companie Joyned to him his wife Hester Cooke. Also, John Cooke, Jacob Cooke, Jane Cooke, Hester Cooke, Mary Cooke, Moses Simonson*, a Leiden Separatist who had come on the *Fortune* in 1621, *Philllip Delanoy*, a Huguenot member of the Separatist Church in Leiden who also arrived on the *Fortune, Experience Michaell*, born in Leiden, who had arrived on the *Anne* in 1623 and married Cooke's daughter Jane, *John Ffance, Joshua Pratt* who arrived on the *Anne*, and *Phinihas Pratt.* who had arrived on the *Sparrow* in 1622 as part of Weston's advance group but remained in Plymouth. *To this lot fell the least of the 4 black heyfers Came in the Jacob, and two shee goats. The ninth lot fell to Richard Warran & his companie joyned with him his wife Elizlabeth Warren, Nathaniell Warren, Joseph Warren, Mary Warren, Anna Warren, Sara Warren, Elizabeth Warren, Abigall Warren, John Billington*, who came on the *Mayflower* with his parents, *George Sowle*, who came on the *Mayflower* as a servant to Edward Winslow, *Mary Sowle*, his wife, *Zakaraiah Sowle.* his son. *To this lott fell one of the four black Heyfers that came in the Jacob called the smooth horned Heyfer and two she goats.* This altered the Colony's initial concept of a church-state colony but its non-Separatist population prevented implementation. The Colony's land policy was unique compared to Jamestown, VA. Plymouth Harbor's size prevented it from becoming important.

Abused in Their Simplicity

In 1621, the Merchant Adventurers had promised to raise £7,000. The common stock was to be repaid from all the colony's produce with dissolution after seven years. In 1629/30, the Colony received a patent defining their boundary. Ten years later, a major change in policy occurred with the Bradford Patent which put all land rights of Plymouth Colony under Bradford and his associates. He governed with a small group among whom were Undertakers and Purchasers (old comers). This small group controlled the distribution of land and were more privileged than others when it came to awarding future lands and in forming new towns. Of the fifty-eight Purchasers in 1626, there were five Adventurers, four who became Undertakers. Many had came on the *Mayflower*. Bradford wrote... *it was by the Courte desired that William Bradford should make a surrender of the same into their hands. The which he willingly did, in this manner following* which was written in considerable detail. During bargaining, Bradford assigned his governing rights to the whole body of freemen on Mar 2nd 1640/1.[1] Due to mishaps and mishandling of funds, Bradford later stated: *to draw a conclusion of that long and tedious business*, the Undertakers Winslow and Prence would have to sell their houses in 1648, the others their lands to pay off this wrongful inflated debt. *Thus, they were abused in their symplicity.* Allerton had been sent to England to deal with the Adventurers. He could best be described as a corporate raider. He had run up Colony's debts into many thousands, as James Sherley, like Allerton cheated his London partners as well as the Colony. Allerton's accounts *were so larg and intrecate, as they could not well understand them, much less examine & correct them, without a great deale of time & help.* Three years would pass before an imperfect accounting was made. Allerton had married 2nd Fear Brewster, daughter of their beloved Elder Brewster. Bradford noted: *Yea, he scrued up his poore old rather in laws accounte to above 200.*

Richard Warren Family

One Purchaser was Richard Warren, a prosperous merchant from Greenwich and London, and was associated with the Merchant Adventurers who financed the voyage. He came on the *Mayflower* without his family. Bradford referred to him *as Mr* but wrote little of him and described him as grave Warren. He was considered a man of integrity, upright, honest, and a devoutly religious person. In July 1623 his wife and five daughters: Mary, Anna, Sarah, Elizabeth, and Abigail arrived on the *Anne*. Two sons, Nathaniel and Joseph, were born in Plymouth. Richard was well thought of and served as Assistant Governor beginning in 1624 until his untimely death. Nathaniel Morton wrote, in *Memoriall*, *This year died Mr. Richard Warren, who...was an useful Instrument and during his life bare a deep share in the Difficulties and Troubles of the first Settlement of the Plantation of New-Plimouth.* After his death, his wife Elizabeth[2] was granted unanimously by law the unique distinction of being the only female Purchaser, *shee dying before he had performed the bargaine, the said Elizabeth performed the same after his decease.* Accompanying this new economic structure was taxation and widows were not exempt. Records show that the widows Warren, Blossom, and Harding were taxed in 1633. Warren remained a widow, Blossom remarried, and Harding died that year. The next year Elizabeth Warren was taxed as were widows Adams, Brown, and Fuller. These tax records note male deaths during the disease outbreak at that time. The Warren's 500 acres was located on the north side of town adjoining the gardens of those who came in the *Fortune*. Their house was built on Eel River meadows later known as Wellingsley or Hobshole. Land was also owned along the shore that became Warren's Cove. The fertile and lush Eel River meadow with underground springs was a select place for grazing cattle, raising pigs and growing vegetables.

---

1 Stratton, p.399

2 Elizabeth Warren, said to be daughter of Augustus Walker whose will dated April 1613 stated: to my daughter, Elizabeth Warren wife of Richard Warren and children Mary, Ann, and Sarah. Elizabeth chr. 1583 in St. Mary's Church, Baldock, Herts., married April 14th 1610 at Great Amwell, Herts., St. John the Baptist Anglican Church..

Elizabeth appeared at court on July 5th 1635, when her servant, Thomas Williams, was accused of speaking profane and blasphemous speeches against ye majesty of God. Thomas confessed to swearing during the court hearing. It was decided he spoke in passion and distemper and the court let the case pass after he humbly acknowledged his wrongdoing although the Governor stated he would have him punished with bodily punishment as the case required.[1] Elizabeth was in court again on January 5th 1635/6 in which Thomas Clark accused her of taking his boat which was lost in the Eel River where she left it. Clark demanded £15 in payment but the jury acquitted Elizabeth on grounds that the boat was borrowed and put in a safe place. For other considerations, Clark was given 30 shilling.[2] On March 14th 1635/6, the court made an order that Mrs. Warren, Richard Church, Thomas Little, and Robert Bartlett, all three her sons-in-law, could mow where they did last year, and they to provide for John Fans (Faunce).[3]

In 1650 Bradford wrote: *Mr. Richard Warren lived some * 4 * or * 5 * years, and had his wife come over to him, by whom he had * 2 * sons before dyed; and one of them is maryed, and hath * 2 * children. So his increase is * 4 * But he had * 5 * doughters more came over with his wife, who are all maried, and living, and have many children.* Elizabeth gave lands to her sons-in-law upon marriage some of whom had differences that were settled in court. On Mar 7th 1652, her son-in-law Robert Bartlett petitioned the court to settle a dispute from those, not named, who claimed to be heirs to the land at Manomet Elizabeth had given him when marrying daughter, Mary, and are keeping him from building and fencing. The court decided Elizabeth had the power to dispose of lands based on previous court orders, she being a Purchaser, and her other land gifts valid. Elizabeth and son, Nathaniel, quarreled over lands bequeathed him by his father, both appearing in court on June 11th 1653. Petitions were presented by Jane Collier in behalf of her granddaughter, Sarah Walker, wife of Nathaniel Warren and by Robert Bartlett requesting justice. All parties deferred the decision to the bench selected by each. Elizabeth chose William Bradford and Capt. Thomas Willet; Nathaniel and Jane chose Thomas Prence and Myles Standish, each in bond of £100 with a fifth person to be selected in case there was no agreement.[4] Since the outcome of this case does not appear in court records, one can assume it was settled out of court. Elizabeth survived her husband by forty-five years dying at Plymouth on October 2nd 1673 above age ninety, *whoe, haueing lived a godly life, came to her graue as a shoke of corn fully ripe. Shee was honorably buried on the 24th of October aforsaid.*[5] It was interesting to discover that some of these early settlers lived to a very old age despite the hardships they suffered.

Francis and John Cooke

Elizabeth Warren's son-in-law, John Cooke, and his Purchaser father, Francis, had acquired upland and meadows at Rocky Nook on the south side of the Jones River as it entered Plymouth Bay. Court records in 1640 refer to it as "old Cookes Holes." The Court ordered that Francis, John, and three other men be allotted six acres each at the north meadows of Jones River on October 17th 1642. Francis' son, Jacob, received some of his lands.[6] Francis sued John Browne, a former Assistant and Magistrate, for abusing his cattle. He was awarded £3 damages and 13s6p in costs. Browne, refusing to pay, was ordered by the Court three months later to pay Cooke. Since no further Court record was entered, Browne probably paid the damages and costs. On October 3rd 1650 the Court noted that Miles Standish and John Alden had been ordered in 1640 to lay out lands and meadow at North River with two islands to John Cooke, Francis Cooke and John Rogers. They were later sold to Thomas Tilden,

---

1 Plymouth Colony Court Orders, Vol. I, p.35

2 *Ibid.,* p.36

3 *Ibid.,* p.62

4 Plymouth Colony Court Orders, Vol. III, p.19

5 Plymouth Town Records

6 Plymouth Colony Deed Bk. 1, p.307

Moris Truant and William Macomber, the latter two having a falling out. Standish and Alden said in court they could not remember if there were any meadows attached to the islands. The Court ordered that once the bounds are established, half the meadow laid out to John Rogers be divided equally between Macomber and Truant and they to pay Richard Garrett to lay out the bounds on the other half which was completed and presented at Court on March 13th 1650/1.[1] Francis was part owner of the 5th lot in the Majors purchase near Namassakett Ponds (now Middleborough). Its cedar swamp was divided after his death on October 14th 1671.[2]

Bradford's account of Francis in 1650 states: *Francis Cooke is still living, a very olde man, and hath seene his childrens children have children; after his wife came over, (with other of his children,) he hath * 3 * still living by her, all maried, and have * 5 * children, so their encrease is * 8 * And his sone John, which came over with him, is maried, and hath * 4 * children living.*

Francis, a quiet and reserved great grandfather, died at Plymouth on Apr (seauenth) 7th 1663.[3] His will written on 7th tenth month [Dec]1659 was simple in that he gave his wife, Hester, all moveable goods and cattle of all kinds: *neat Cattle horsekind sheep and swine to be att her Dispose,* plus *his upland and meddow lands to enjoy during her life* and made his wife and son, John, executors. Ephraim Tinker and William Crow inventoried his estate on May 1st 1663 and valued his goods and chattel at £86.11.01. Eventually Francis' surviving children made an agreement to dispose of the lands after Hester's death. On Jun 8th 1666, Richard Wright of Plymouth and Thomas Mitchell of Duxbury equally divided sixty acres of upland and meadow near the Jones River, Mitchell stating the land was given him by his grandfather, Francis Cooke.[4] In 1672, Thomas sold this land to Wright, husband of Francis' daughter, Hester.

John Cooke Marries

John Cooke was too young on arrival to become a Purchaser but managed to acquire a substantial amount of land. At age twenty-seven he married Sarah Warren on Mar 28th 1633/4.[5] Sarah was a young girl when she arrived at Plymouth with her mother and sisters in 1623. The Warren's had been able to see John grow from a teen to adult. In recognition of their marriage, Elizabeth deeded John land at Eel River which was exchanged with his brother-in-law, Richard Bartlett, on Nov 11th 1637. From 1634-1651 John and William Paddy served as a Deacons for Plymouth Church under pastor Ralph Smith who came from Salem and leaned toward Separatism....*the beginning of this year [1629] ...Ther was one Mr. Ralfe Smith, & his wife & familie, that came over into the Bay of Massachusetts, and sojourned at presente with some stragling people that lived at Natascoe; here being a boat of this place putting in ther on some occasion, he ernestly desired that they would give him & his, passage for Plimouth, and some such things as they could well carrie; having before heard that ther was liklyhood he might procure house-roome for some time, till he should resolve to setle ther, if he might, or els-wher as God should disposs; for he was werie of being in that uncoth place, & in a poore house that would neither keep him nor his goods drie. So, seeing him to be a grave man, & understood he had been a minister, though they had no order for such thing, yet they presumed and brought him. He was accordingly kindly entertained & housed, & had the rest of his goods & servants sente for, and exercised his gifts amongst thenm, and afterwards was chosen into the ministrie, and so remained for sundrie years.*

1 Plymouth Colony Court Orders Vol. II, pp. 149-150

2 Plymouth Colony Deed Bk. 3, p.216

3 Plymouth Town Records

4 Plymouth Colony Deed Bk. 3, p.73

5 Plymouth Colony Court Orders, Vol I

Clerk of Court vs Cooke

Nathaniel Morton, born in Leiden about seven years after John Cooke' birth, arrived at Plymouth with his parents in 1623. Bradford was his uncle who took him in after his father died in 1624. Morton served as Clerk of the General Court from 1645-1684. Church Deacons Cooke and Paddy with James Hust deeded Morton a house and land on Mar 21st 1646/7. Nathaniel, a very orthodox church member, was intolerant of anyone who opposed his views as shown in his two writings about Plymouth's Church. Morton grew to dislike Cooke when he wrote the following: *troubles Came on apace Not to mension againe the troubles which were occationed by some of the Church at Barnstable which was blowne up by John Cooke and others...By Reason or occation of the before mensioned devision and decention of the Church of Barnstable one of the Church of Plymouth whoe was formerly a deacon thereof: fell into the error of Anabaptistry and falling in with some of those that Carried on that Scismaticall devision: att length was Called in question by the Church; and Continewing in his obstanacle and sequestration from the Church Comunion att times of sollemne worshipp was alsoe Cast out of the Church and soe Remaineth untill this day. This John Cooke although a Shallow man became a Cause of trouble and decension in our Church and Gave Just occation of theire Casting of him out.* Morton's attitude did not hamper John's political life. John served as a representative to General Court for many years and elected to serve as a deputy from 1641 to 1656, the very Court where Morton served as Clerk.

Cooke's Business Affairs

On Nov 18th 1648, Isaac Abraham of Enchusen in Holland sold to John Cooke planter of Plymouth and Robert Scott merchant of Boston, the thirty ton barque called the *Bride* with all its masts, sails, sailyards, anchors, cables, ropes, cords, tackle, boat apparel and furniture for an undisclosed sum which sale was declared a true sale by Gov. Endicott on Jun 12th 1651.[1] Was this the barque that brought single young women to Virginia in the early 1600's?

The Indian chiefs Wesamequan and Massassoit, plus his son, Wamsutta, conveyed by deed dated Nov 29th 1652 to William Bradford, Capt. Standish, Thomas Southworth, John Winslow, John Cooke, and other associates all the land lying three miles eastward from the river called Cushenett to a certain harbor Acoaxet to a flat rock on the westward side of the harbor. This conveyance included all waterways, meadows, necks, and islands that lay within it. Metes and bounds were not clearly stated but considerations were more clearly outlined. Disputes arose concerning the title since forests, meadows, and streams were neither valued highly nor mentioned. There were settlements established in this area as early as 1652, one being Dartmouth on Oct 5th 1652. John Cooke was buying and selling land during this time.[2] On Jun 8th 1664, Plymouth's General Court ordered a tract of land called Acushena, Ponagansett, and Coaksett be made a township and its inhabitants have liberty to make such orders for the common good in the town's concerns and said town be called Dartmouth. It's location in the county's southern part was bounded on the north by Fall River and Freetown, east by New Bedford and Buzzard's Bay, south by Buzzard's Bay and west by Westport. Massassoit had died three years earlier and replaced by son Wamsutta who died within a year. Massassoit's younger son, Metacomet or Philip of Pokanoket, became leader and not having been consulted started annoying Dartmouth's settlers.

Nathaniel Warren and John Cooke were appointed on Oct 3rd 1665 to meet with Metacomet for the purchase of land and set out boundaries after which Metacomet gave a quit claim. The large tract was divided into thirty-four shares, two of which were sub-divided, so original proprietors numbered thirty-six persons, three of whom were women. Not all its original proprietors settled in Dartmouth which was

---

1 *Suffolk Deeds, Lib. I., 138* (Boston, MA, Rockwell and Churchill, City Printers, 1880)

2 Plymouth Colony Deed Bk. 1, p.350, Bk. 2, pp. 68, 74, & Bk. 3 :p82

common due to buying for speculation or investment. Another purchase was made with Metacomet in June 1669. Shortly thereafter Metacomet began to raise some issues that lead to his being at Plymouth court. His manner was: confess and repent. In 1671 he requested Massachusetts Bay Colony represent him at Plymouth court which resulted in his having to sign a loyalty pledge and pay a heavy fine. Things were uneventful for several years.[1]

John Cooke's Move to Dartmouth

Around this time, John Cooke moved to Dartmouth where he was granted fifteen acres of meadow near Dartmouth by the General Court on Jun 8th 1664 with liberty to purchase it from Indians providing it was not already granted to others. Dartmouth was settled in part by the Cooke, Delano, Howland, Soule, and Spooner families and by Baptists or Anabaptists and Quakers who objected being taxed to support the Congregational ministry in other towns. John had paid to purchase a part of the island of Nakatay for others. The court ordered on Mar 6th 1665/6 that if payment is not made to Cooke, the land will be given to him. John served as deputy to represent Dartmouth in General Court in 1666 where Morton still served as clerk. On Jun 5th and Jul 1667, John was appointed at General Court to solemnize marriages in Dartmouth and appointed a pre-trial magistrate to give oaths at grand inquest and trial cases. Debts due often ended up in court. On Mar 5th 1677/8, the court authorized John Cooke, John Russell, and Lt. Smith or any two of them to call the town together to make rates for defraying debts due by the town to cover such bills due to Symon Cooper for curing William Dyer and his trips to Plymouth requesting payment. The court ordered that £16 in silver money be paid to Cooper. Other sums ordered paid were to: Jonathan Delano, 40 shilling; Thomas Taber £2.10.00; the same to William Spooner, John Cornwell, and Phillip Taber; Samuel Jenney £12; and Eliezer Smith, 5 shillings to be paid in marketable pay and an account to be given at June court.[2] John continued to serve as selectman and representative to General Court for many years and later issued warrants.

The Court appointed John to build a ferry between Dartmouth and Rhode Island. John also had a long and continued difference with Dartmouth's inhabitants and purchasers. The representatives at court for the Purchasers were John Smith, Samuell Hickes and Peleg Tripp. The court made its determination on Jul 1st 1672. It was ordered that John could keep possession of Ram Island and the town would pay him the £11 plus £3 in damages in pork, beef, and corn in equal portions that he had paid out on the town's behalf. In return he would deliver deeds for other lands to the town. They also determined that the bounds would be according to a deed given by Metacomet, the sachem. As for Dartmouth, the court ordered £15 paid to the constable in current money for not paying church support for two years.[3]

From Separatist to Baptist

John became an adherent to the teachings of Roger Williams and Obadiah Holmes. On at least two occasions by invitation, he spoke at Boston's Baptist Church. Despite his position, John was not immune to law and was fined ten shilling on Oct 29th 1670 for unnecessary traveling on the Sabbath. In all probability he was traveling on his circuit as a Baptist preacher. On May 24th 1686 he was among the 45 men who took the freeman's oath. Included were many who will be found in this paper such as: Wood, Shearman, Tripp, Taber, Soule, Jenney, Earle, and Wilcocks. With John's associates, a Baptist Church was formed in Dartmouth in 1684 where he was its preacher until his death in 1695. John Cooke and Sarah Warren's had five daughters:

---

1 Morison, pp.248-249

2 Plymouth Colony Court Orders, Vol. 8, p. 254

3 Plymouth Court Orders, V. 7, pp.97-98

1. Sarah who married Arthur Hathaway, Nov 20th 1652.
2. Elizabeth who married Daniel Wilcox, Nov 28th 1661.
+3. Mary who married Philip Taber, c1667.
4. Hester who married Thomas Taber, c1667.
5. Mercy who married Stephen West, c1683.

Deeding Rest Estate

John and Sarah began deeding land to their family members as well buying and selling other lands in Acushanett (Dartmouth), the last purchase appearing to be on Jul 20th 1694. John exchanged land with his brother, Jacob, on Jul 4th 1672. Two tracts of land were deeded on May 21st 1672 and Nov 28th 1673 to Thomas Taber, a mason at Dartmouth who married daughter Hester.[1] On Jul 17th 1673 fifty acres at Dartmouth with all the meadow belonging to it was deeded with "love and affection" to Phillip Taber and daughter, Mary Taber.[2]

Arthur Hathaway, another son-in-law of John and Sarah was deeded land Jun 26th 1674 and on Jun 4th 1686.[3] Daniel Wilcox, a yeoman of Dartmouth and husband of their daughter, Elizabeth, was deeded land at Mackatan Island on Jul 10th 1674.[4] Son-in-law, Stephen West of Portsmouth, RI, was recipient of land on Jul 8th 1686.[5] On Feb 27th 1693, the heirs of Phillip Taber were rightfully confirmed by John.[6]

On Apr 6th 1693, John's petition from Dartmouth in Bristol County was read in Council in the providence of Massachusetts Bay.

That your Petitioner one of the Antientest Inhabitants in this Province who arrived from England in the County of Plim° Anno Dom 1620 with his Father who was one of the first Purchasers and Old Comers who layd out and expended a Considerable Estate in setling the first Plantation, and your Petitioner being much conversant with the Sachems Papamoe, Machacom, Achawannomet who had a considerable Tract of Land situate between Dartmouth and Sandwich the chief of them being Papamo was indebted to your Petitioner and by reason of the obligation he had to and kindness he had for your Petitioner did often in his life time by word and deed and before his Death will the said land to your Petitioner and Mr. William Bradford and entrust them requiring & desiring our care of his Children But he said Land is kept away from your Petitioner & the said Papamos Children who have had no benefit thereof altho they were very serviceable in the Late Indian Warr against our Enemies under ye Command of Major Church and have received the Christian Faith and notwithstanding there was a Reserve or Exception of the said land when the rest about it was Surrendered as being Indian or English mens rights which hath administred Occasion of Offence to the Indians Some reflecting on your Peticoner as not being faithfull to his trust, which is ground of Trouble to your Aged Peticoner and if not Remedied desires that he may be satisfactorily discharged of his trust and he will then desist tho grieved that he cannot doe as he ought for them.

And Further May it please your Excell[y] & the Honourble Councell your Peticoner did by Peticon obtaine of the General Court of Plimouth a Grant that if your Peticoner could find out any land undisposed of and not Granted to others he should be accommodated with the same as by reference to the said Grant bearing date July 1683 being had doth fully appeare Now so it is your Petitioner doth here by certify that there is a little Island called Little Island of 2 or 3 acres of land which lyes neer Dartmouth & the said Indians Land which if with some part of the same may be conferred on your Peticoner for the good of your Peticoner and his [Papamoe] children.

---

1 Plymouth County Deed Bk. 3, p. 324. Bk. 5, p. 388

2 *Ibid.*, Bk. 3, p. 324

3 *Ibid.*, Bk.5, p.12; Bk.6, p. 44

4 *Ibid,* Bk.3, p. 325

5 *Ibid,* Bk.6, p. 70

6 *Ibid,* Bk.3, p. 339

John Cooke's Will

John's will dated Nov 9th 1694 named his wife, Sarah, sole executrix; mentioned son-in-law Arthur Hathaway and wife, Sarah; son-in-law Stephen West and wife, Mercy; Jonathan Delano; grandson Thomas Taber; and granddaughter Hester Perry. Hathaway was given land at Dartmouth near the burying place purchased from John Russell, West a third share of his lands in Dartmouth with housing and orchards after Sarah's decease; Delano a third share of meadow called Freemens meadow in Rochester township; Thomas Taber the little island lying in the Cushnet River in Dartmouth with a third of Freemans meadow plus John's gun and sword; and Hester a feather bed and bolster. To Sarah, wife, the rest of the estate to dispose as she sees good. John Cooke died on Nov 23rd 1695 in Dartmouth. The inventory taken Dec 7th by Thomas Taber and Arthur Hathaway totaled £299.19.00. John was buried in its upper village of Oxford in an unmarked site.[1] On Apr 16th 1696, it was judged necessary to take a deposition from Sarah, she being *Very Antient* and unable to travel. There is a Tablet in Cooke Memorial Park in Fairhaven, MA, that reads:

> *Sacred to the Memory of John Cooke Who was buried here in 1695 The last surviving male Pilgrim Of those who came over in the Mayflower The first white settler of this town And the pioneer in its religious Moral and business life A man Of character and integrity And the trusted agent for this Part of the Commonwealth Of the Old Colonial Civil Government Of Plymouth.*

Mayflower Descent

Richard Warren m Elizabeth - Francis Cooke m Hester Mahieu

Sarah Warren	m	John Cooke
Mary Cooke	m	Philip Taber II
Joseph Mosher	m	Lydia Taber
Philip Mosher	m	Abigail Tripp
Caleb Mosher	m	Elizabeth Wilbur
Eliz. Mosher	m	Amos Reynolds
Jonathan Wood	m	Elizabeth Reynolds
Lydia Wood	m	Henry Cook Ayers

Cooke Sisters Marrying Taber Brothers

Two of the John Cooke daughters, Mary and Hester, married Taber brothers. It is Mary Cooke Taber who carried on the family line. The Taber brothers father was Philip Taber, sr., born 1605, son of Thomas Taber from Kilmington Parish, Somersetshire. Their mother was Lydia Masters, daughter of John and Jane Masters from Aldenham, Hertsfordshire. Philip, sr. is first noted as being in Watertown when he pledged on Apr 1st 1634 to provide two hundred feet of four inch planks for building the city's sea fort.[2] The following May 14th he gave bond to testify against someone who sold commodities against the law. After admission to Watertown's church he was declared a freeman and granted thirty acres on Jul 25th 1636.[3] Many left Watertown finding Puritan tenets too strict. Carpenters also moved around seeking work, so Philip moved to Mattaccheeset (Yarmouth) where as an original proprietor, was made freeman on Jan 7th 1638/9. Yet he remained a member of Watertown's church. The following March 5th Philip sr. was ordered by the General Court to be added

---

1 Stratton, p.271

2 Massachetts Bay Court Records, Bk. 1:114

3 WRBOP 5

as a commissioner to help make the first division of planting land. He also served as deputy to Plymouth General Court on Jun 4th 1639 and Jun 2nd 1640. [1] His father in law, John Masters, died in Yarmouth on Dec 21st 1639.

The previous June Mattakeeset (Barnstable) had been incorporated. The well admired Rev. Lothrop left the town of Scituate and went to Barnstable the end of June. It was due to "great dissensions" between church and government matters. Barnstable had no meeting house so parishioners met in homes or outdoors in pleasant weather. Philip sr. and Lydia Taber took two children to be baptized there on November 8th 1640. Three more Taber children including Philip, jr. were baptized there in Feb 1645/6 just before a meeting house was completed. Lothrop noted they lived at Yarmouth and their father was a member of the church at Watertown. Sometime after that Philip, sr. left the Bay Colony for New London, CT, and from there to Rhode Island where on Feb 14th 1655/6 he was received an inhabitant and made freeman at Portsmouth on May 20th 1656.[2] After his wife Lydia died, he married on Dec 21st 1659 Jane Latham daughter of Nicholas Latham. They moved around living in Newport, Providence, and lastly Tiverton, RI, when Jane, deposed on Jun 10th 1669 that Taber's youngest son, Joseph, was her son-in-law (step-son).[3] She died sometime after that since Philip, sr. died a widower at Tiverton in 1672.

Philip Taber, jr. and wife, Mary Cooke, seemed content to live in Dartmouth, MA, on the fifty acres the Cooke's had deeded him. Following is an accounting of the children of Philip Taber and Mary Cooke, all born Dartmouth.[4] A quick glance will show just how these families wdre interconnected.

1. Mary Taber, b. Jan 28th 1667/8, m. Thomas Earle.
2. Sarah Taber, b. Mar 28th 1670/1, m. Thomas Corey.
+3. Lydia Taber, b. Sep 28th 1673, m. Joseph Mosher.
4. Philip Taber, b. Feb 29th 1674/5, m. Margaret Wood, daughter of William Wood and Martha Earle. This Philip was one of five tax payers protesting a £700 tax on Dartmouth's citizens. As a selectman, he refused to assess the tax and was imprisoned with others in the Bristol County jail for about eighteen months. On Jun 2nd 1724 the court of St. James ordered the obnoxious taxes dismissed and the men released. The Governor and officers of the Bay Colony were also notified to yield to these orders.
5. Abigail Taber, b Oct 27th 1678, never married.
6. Esther/Hester Taber, born Feb 23rd 1679/80, married Thomas Brownell.
7. John Taber, b. 1684, married Susanna Manchester.
8. Bethiah Taber, b. Apr 18th 1689, married John Macomber, Sep 11th 1711.

Little is known of Philip Taber, jr. except his unexpected death early in 1692/3. Dying intestate, an inventory of his estate totaling £231.14.6 was presented Mar 4th 1692/3 by Thomas Taber, Joseph Tripp, and widow Mary. That day a committee was appointed to make a division of his estate, completed on Nov 27th 1693 by Thomas and Joseph Taber, Jonathan Delano, Joseph Tripp and George Cadman all of Dartmouth and attested by five commissioners on Sep 13th 1694 before Jn° Saffin, Probater. The division follows. Mary received her third of real and personal, ie. the lower room in the new house plus the cellar, the southern end of land and meadow with its orchard bounded on the south by land of Mary Timberleg (Timberlake). His eldest son, Philip, received the upland, ½ of marsh by the upland, and ½ of all undivided lands formerly belonging to his father. Also ⅔[rds] of housing, the whole amounting to £50, he to pay his sister, Esther, £14.7.7 when age eighteen. Son John, the remainder of divided land, with the other ½ of marsh lying at the north end of his brother Philip's marsh, and the other ½ of undivided land, the whole amounting to £30, he to pay his sister, Bethiah,

1 Stratton, p. 66

2 Portsmouth Town Records 69

3 Robert C. Anderson, *The Great Migration Begins,* Vol.III, P-W, (Boston, MA. New England Historic Genealogical Society, 1995, pp. 1791-1793

4 Dartmouth Vital Records

£12.3.8 when eighteen or married. £17.16.4 each to five daughters: Sarah, Lydia, Abigail, Esther, and Bethiah. To daughter, Mary Earle, £7.16.4 to make up her portion equal to the rest. On Nov 16th 1694, daughters Lydia Taber, Sarah Taber, and Mary Earle receipted to their mother now, Mary Davis, administrator for full payment. Mary had married 2nd Aron Davis before Mar 1692/3.[1] Their mother, Mary Cooke Taber Davis, died between Apr 1708 and Jan 1715.

It never ceases to amaze me how these families were so intermingled. Lydia, daughter of Philip Taber and Mary Cooke married into the Mosher family. This family will carry down for several generations to Lydia Wood's grandparents. Lydia Taber, third child of Philip Taber and Mary Cooke, was single when she signed a receipt to her mother for her share of her father's estate. Sometime after that she married Joseph Mosher at Dartmouth, born about 1670 son of Hugh Mosher. There are three possibilities to Hugh Mosher's parentage which follow.

1. Nicholas Moger, christened in 1596, brother of Hugh Moger, gentleman of Wincanton, Somersetshire, left in his five page will dated Jul 9th 1656, probated at Prerogative Court of Canterbury in Jan 1657, folio 228, "to brother Tristram Moger, 20 shillings with no condition...I give unto my godsonne Hugh Moger the sonne of my brother Nicholas Moger fiue pounds of good money of England if hee shall come to Wincanton and lawfully demand the Same of my Executor hereafternamed..." Wills that have people living outside England are probated in Canterbury Prerogative Court. Hugh Moger was christened in 1609 and came to Boston in 1632, then moved to Maine settling at Saco on Cosco Bay. Two of his sons, John and James, departed Maine to settle at Brookhaven, Long Island, NY.
2. It was also recorded in Sep 1616 that a William Mosher was living in Manchester, Lancashire, England. He died four years later leaving a will that noted his children, Mary and John, as well as brothers John, Thomas, Stephen and George, three having sons named Hugh.
3. Other's state Hugh was the son of Nicholas Mosher christened in Cucklington, England and married in Portland, Maine, dying in Tiverton Feb 2nd 1718.

From Blacksmith to Preacher

Culturally we annually celebrate birthdays. Many of these early settlers were not sure of their birth date probably due to recording of Christening dates which didn't necessarily happen at birth or shortly thereafter. Hugh Mosher was among them when he gave testimony on Mar 4th 1662/3 that he was about age thirty. Just prior to that, Hugh with five other men purchased land on Jan 29th 1660 at Misquamicut (Westerly) from the Indian sachem Socho who had acquired the land for driving off the Pequots in 1637. Hugh was apportioned his share and subsequently became a freeman. By Apr 1668 Hugh lived near Portsmouth, RI. The following July he bought a house from Thomas Lawton and was to maintain sufficient fencing between his land and David Vaughan's corner. Even though he and Vaughan mutually agreed to void the contract, Vaughan filed a complaint against Ensign Hugh Moisser claiming Hugh fenced off more land than his right. Fencing and land disputes were common court cases. The two appeared in court Oct 10th 1673 to settle differences but it took until Feb 14th 1675/6 for a verdict which favored Vaughn.

Hugh's wife, Rebecca Maxson, was the daughter of Richard and Rebecca (?) Maxson. Richard was granted 31 acres in Portsmouth, RI, which his widow sold to Richard Morris who sold it to Thomas Brownell on Jan 15th 1657. Then Rebecca Maxson married John Hardnell of Newport who in his will dated Feb 9th 1685 referred to Rebecca Mosher as his daughter-in-law (step-daughter).

Hugh did his appointed duties on the grand jury and court of trials. Some of his deeds state he was a blacksmith so it seems a well versed blacksmith can become a preacher. The Baptist Church in Tiverton hired Hugh as their pastor proved by his being taxed £1.3.1 in 1680 as pastor. To make ends meet he undoubtedly had to keep up the dirty job of blacksmithing. His Church attendees came from

<hr>

1 Gary Boyd Roberts, *Mayflower Source Records*, (Balt, MD, Genealogical Publ. Co., 1986) p. 52

Dartmouth, Tiverton, and Little Compton. With his wife's consent, he sold his dwelling house, barns and orchards located within both Newport and Portsmouth, RI, to Henry Brightman on Jan 28th 1689 for £230 then moved to Dartmouth where Rebecca died before 1709. Hugh and Rebecca had nine children noted in his will written Oct 12th 1709, probated Dec 7th 1713. In addition was a grandson, Hugh, son of Nicholas and other grandsons not named. Birth dates are not known. We do know that son Nicholas was said to be 81 when he died on Aug 14th 1747. Hugh Mosher and Rebecca Maxson's children were:

1.   James Mosher, m. Mary Davol May 22nd 1714.
2.   John Mosher, d. Aug 1st 1739 at Bristol Co., MA, m. Experience Kirby Mar 5th 1691/2.
3.   Nicholas Mosher, b. c1666. d. August 14th 1747 at Tiverton, RI; m. Elizabeth Audley 1689.
+4.   Joseph Mosher, m. Lydia Taber
5.   Daniel Mosher, d. 1751 in Bristol Co., MA.
6.   Hannah Mosher, m. Stephen Cornell.
7.   Ann Mosher, m. Peter Lee.
8.   Mary Mosher, m. Joseph Rathbun May 19th 1691.
9   Rebecca Mosher, m. John Kirby.

Hugh's estate inventory dated Jun 6th 1715 totaled a comfortable £290.17.02 which included £12 from his second wife, widow of Rev. John Harding of Newport who died in 1716. Next in line was Hugh and Rebecca's son:

Joseph Mosher is known mostly through his many land transactions as a mason from Dartmouth. Recorded in Bristol County deeds portions of his homestead were deeded to heirs of Philip Taber (1714/5), and to sons: Philip (1723), Joseph (1724), Jonathan (1723,1729,1735), James (1729), and Benjamin (1733), plus daughter: Ruth Tripp, wife of William (1729)[1] and other individuals. Joseph's wife Lydia Taber, was granddaughter of Francis Cooke and Richard Warren, and daughter of Phillip Taber, jr. and wife Mary Cooke.
Joseph and Lydia Mosher were parents of nine children born at Dartmouth, MA.

1.   Rebecca Mosher, b. Dec 28th 1695, d. bef. Nov15th 1743, married Daniel Tripp.
+2.   Philip Mosher, b. Dec 20th 1697.
3.   Jonathan Mosher, b. Mar 13th 1698/99, married Esther Potter
4.   Joseph Mosher, b. Jun 23rd 1701, d. young.
5.   James Mosher, b. Dec 14th 1704, married Sarah Davol.
6.   Ruth Mosher, b. Sep 17th 1707, married William Tripp.
7.   Benjamin Mosher, b. Feb 22nd 1708/09, d. bef. Nov 15th 1743, married Sarah Tripp.
8.   William Mosher, b. Jul 29th 1713, d. young.
9.   Lydia Mosher, b. Jun 11th 1717, married Timothy Davol.

Joseph's lengthy will dated Nov 15th 1743, probated May 7th 1754 at Dartmouth, named his wife, Lydia; sons: Philip, Jonathan, James, and Benjamin, deceased; daughters: Ruth Tripp, Lydia Davol, the seven children of daughter Rebecca Tripp, deceased (Hannah, Constant, Rebecca, Daniel, Joseph, Thomas and Charles) and granddaughter, Rebecca Mosher, daughter of son Benjamin, deceased. His wife was given the use and improvement of all moveable estate, not otherwise disposed, for her maintenance since she ails at certain times of the year, the best room in their house and a cow to be maintained by son James, in lieu of power of thirds. Joseph expressly wanted his Executors, namely sons Phillip, Jonathan, and James, to look after their mother. On Mar 23rd 1754 a petition was presented at Dartmouth by Lydia Mosher she thinking otherwise. *Whereas I do not accept of What*

---

1 Bristol County Deeds: Bk.15, pp.602, 605; Bk.16, p.16; Bk.17, p.210; Bk.20, p.72; Bk.27, pp.158,258,525; Bk.28, p.151; Bk.32, p. 120

My Late Husband Gave me in his Last Will in Leiue of my thirds but being far advanced in years Even to Eighty and upward and under decays of Nature and at Sume times past have Ben Disordered in my Mind of sences and probably may be so again tho at Present am of Perfect mind Thanks be to God for it but I Say the Reasons above Makes incapable of Maniageing my own Busines whereupon pray your honour Would be pleas to appoint My Loveing son Phillip Mosher and my Loveing son in Law Timothy Davel to be Guirdeans to take Care of me and my Estate and your petitioner as In Duty bound Shall Ever pray. Signed with a mark. "Lidia Mosher Refusell of her Husband will" was written on the back.[1] What the judge determined is not known. Joseph and Lydia's eldest son:

A Cooper in the Clan

Philip Mosher was born Dec 20th 1697 in Dartmouth, MA. His 1st marriage around 1719 was to Abigail Tripp, the only daughter of Jonathan Tripp and Martha Brownell. Abigail was born May 8th 1701 in Little Compton, RI.

Abigail's mother, Martha Brownell, was born May 24th 1678, daughter of William Brownell, son of Thomas and Anne Bourne. William Brownell, their sixth child, married Sarah Smiton at Portsmouth where he was admitted a freeman on Apr 9th 1675. They left Portsmouth for Little Compton, RI, where a son was born in Aug 1682. Their eleventh child was born there in Dec 1695. William died in Dartmouth, MA, in 1715. His will dated Nov 16th 1714 was proved on Aug 1st 1715.[2] All land mentioned was in Little Compton. Two of William and Sarah's daughters, Martha and Anne Brownell, are ancestors. Martha married: 1st Jonathan Tripp, 2nd Samuel Hart. Anne married Benjamin Davol, son of Jonathan and Hannah (Audley) Davol. William's grandfather, Thomas Brownell, was born 1535 and married Oct 20th 1560 Margaret Gilbert-Hayse. Of their four children son Thomas Brownell jr. was christened June 5th 1608 at Ryecroft, Rawmarsh Parish, Yorkshire West Riding. He married Anne Bourne at St. Paul's Wharf, London, Mar 20th 1636/7. They left England for Portsmouth, RI, where their ten children were born, the eldest a daughter Mary was born in Apr 1639. Land was purchased for settling and Thomas participated in town duties, lastly voted a deputy to general court on Apr 27th 1664. Thomas died the following Sep 24th while riding his horse and running into a tree. His granddaughter Martha Brownell's first husband, Jonathan Tripp, was born in Tiverton Oct 5th 1671 son of Joseph Tripp and Mehitable Fish.

Anne Bourne, Thomas Brownell' wife, was christened Dec 15th 1607 at St. Michael Cornhill, London, daughter of Richard Bourne and Judith Cowper/Cooper. All nine of Richard's children were christened in that church. Richard was christened Jan 18th 1565 at Bobbingworth Parish in western Essex, son of William Bourne of Bobbingworth and Margaret Ryse. Richard died Mar 11th 1631/2 in London. Richard Bourne's grandparents were John and Margaret Bourne.

William Brownells' wife, Sarah Smiton, was the daughter of William Smiton of Stepney Wapping, Middlesex, and his wife Sarah Lloyd, daughter of William Lloyd of Bristol, Somerset, and his wife Agnes Noke, daughter of John Noke of Offley, Herts. William Lloyd, William Smiton, a member in a troop of horse, and Thomas Brownell jr. all died at Portsmouth, RI.

---

1 Bristol County Probate, Bk. 14, pp. 194,197

2 Bristol Co., MA, Probate, Vol. 3, pgs. 230-321, 298-299

In an effort to provide clarity of the relationship of these families the following chart is offered:

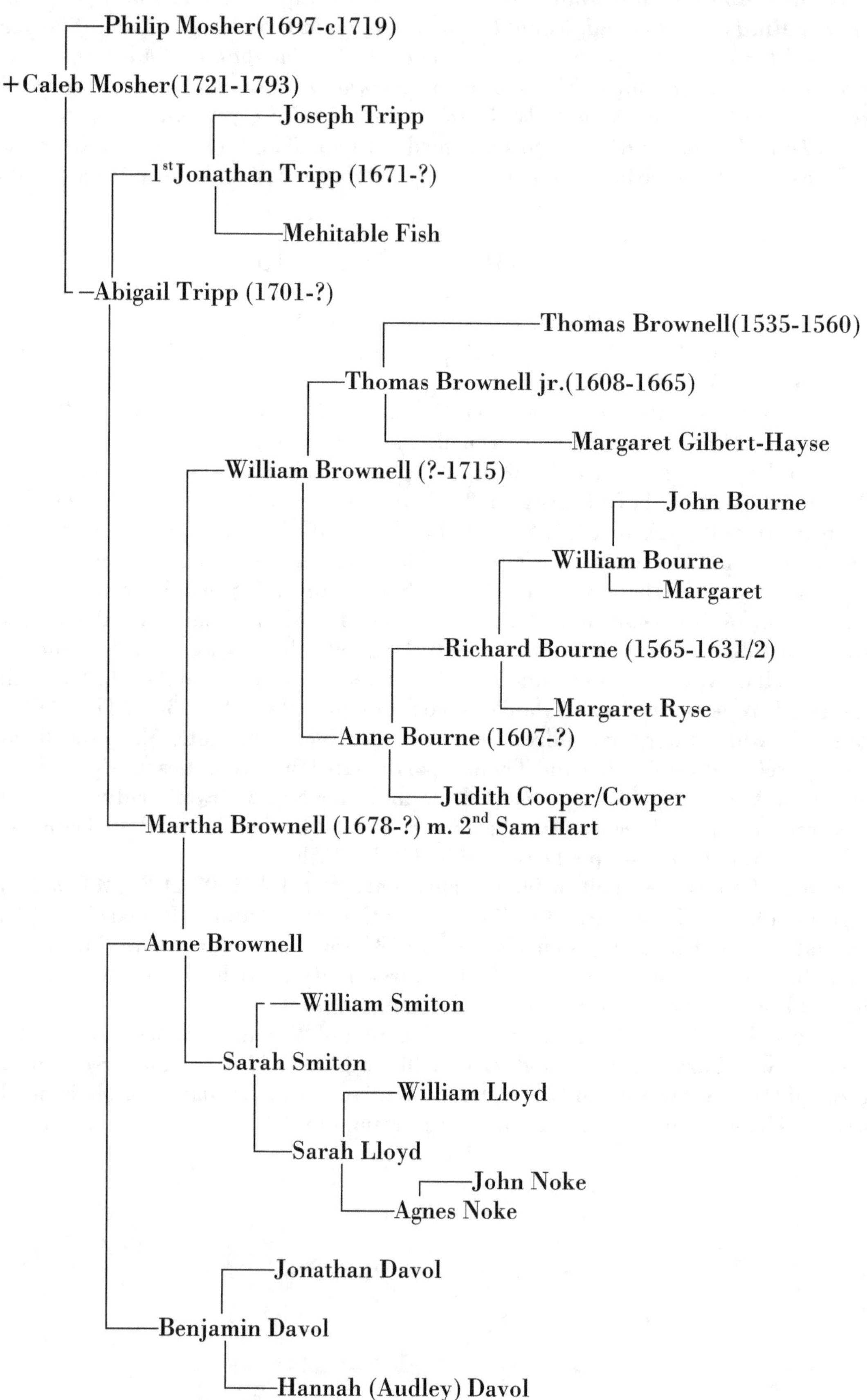

Philip Mosher and Abigail Tripp had the following nine children:

1. Israel Mosher, born May 20th 1720.
+2. Caleb Mosher, born September 8th 1721.
3. Maxson Mosher, born January 13th 1721/2.
4. Martha Mosher, died young.
5. Abigail Mosher, born September 4th 1730.
6. Philip Mosher, born May 8th 1734.
7. Benjamin Mosher, born April 21st 1735. He was on the Nine Partners/Crum Elbow tax list 1773-1779.
8. Lydia Mosher, born July 27th 1738, died young.
9. Martha Mosher, born December 28th 1745.

Philip was a cooper as noted in his many deeds. Unlike Miles Standish who was hired to look after the casks of liquids aboard the *Mayflower*, land coopers needed wood, a shop, and numerous tools peculiar to the trade. In very small villages a traveling cooper would carry enough tools to repair wooden pails or vessels. In towns large enough to support a cooper he would make casks, pails, and other household items in his shop. His wood supply would be large and varied especially those that were non porous like cedar which came from swampy lands and used mostly in making barrels and small boats. With increased buying and selling of land, prices were escalating. After cutting usable timber the land would be sold which accounts for his many land deeds. Most of his deeds were for salt meadows or cedar swamp.

Philip's first deed on record was a purchase from Benjamin Davol for swamp land in Cranberry Neck, Dartmouth, on Feb 7th 1724. On Mar 7th 1729/30 he sold fifty-four acres in Dartmouth to Benjamin Davis. Jeremiah Davol sold Philip the salt meadow bought of Nicholas for £360. Howland Salt meadow was used for grazing and growing hay. In May William Sherman sold him for land in the sixteen acre division in the Quanapog Great Swamp for £40. The next month, Philip sold part of this to Timothy Maxfield for £13.6s on Jun 27th 1734. The following Jan 24th 1734/5 he sold more of it to Joseph Mosher. Three years passed before he and Abigail sold the meadow bought from Jeremiah Davol on Aug 27th 1737. In Aug 1738, Philip sold more of the swamp to Samuel Borden of Tiverton for £10. Joseph Mosher bought more of it for £27.10s on Dec 29th 1740. Seven years passed before Philip and Abigail sold to William Davol, his homestead farm in Dartmouth for £140 on Mar 5th 1747. Half of twenty-five acres to Philip's son, Israel, a cordwainer (shoemaker) for £20 on Jan 31st 1759, the other half to William Gage. On Feb 16th 1760, Philip sold twenty acres to Jacob Anthony which was half the lot bought of Joseph and Elinor Tucker.[1]

His wife Abigail died before 1759 for on Jan 20th 1759 widower Philip published at Dartmouth his intention to marry Elinor Huddlestone, widow of Isaac Huddlestone.

Time to Move Further West

Caleb Mosher, son of Philip and Abigail Mosher, was born Sep 8th 1721 at Dartmouth, MA. His intention to marry Elizabeth Wilbur, daughter of Samuel Wilbur and Elizabeth Carr, was published at Little Compton, RI, on Nov 26th 1743. They were parents five sons and three daughters:
1. Tripp Mosher, b. 26 Oct 1744. He was on the Nine Partners/Crum Elbow Tax List 1772-1779.
2. Philip Mosher, b. unknown.
3. Samuel Mosher, b. unknown. He was on the Nine Partners/Crum Elbow Tax List 1775-1779.
4. Esek Mosher, b. 19 Mar 1756.

---

1 Bristol County Deeds: Bk.15, p.603; Bk.20, p.75, Bk.28, pp. 79,80; Bk.23, pp. 456,458; Bk.28, p. 316, Bk.42, p.90; Bk. 44, p.403; Bk.47, p.163; Bk.56, p. 362; Bk.71, p.217

5.   Martha Mosher, b. 18 Jun 1757.
    6.   Israel Mosher, b. 14 Oct 1760.
    7.   Abigail Mosher, b. unknown.
 +8.   Elizabeth Mosher, b. 1764.

Land was getting scarce so Caleb Mosher thought the time was ripe for moving further west. He was located next on the Nine Partners/Crum Elbow, Dutchess, NY, tax lists beginning June 1746-1778 with two sons. Other Moshers on the tax lists were: Adley, Benjamin, Ephraim, George, Hugh, and William.[1] Crum Elbow became Charlotte in 1762, later Washington in 1788. Caleb's brief will dated Feb 8th 1786 hints he was a profitable miller. Millers were necessary to a settlement and much favored. Caleb's will was probated Sep 19th 1793 at Charlotte Precinct, NY, with some noted changes. His wife, Elizabeth, to receive all household goods, and after her decease to his daughters: Martha Palmer, Abigail Finch, and Elizabeth Reynolds one cow each. To sons: Tripp, Philip, Samuel, Esek, and Israel Mosher all the farm whereon I now dwell with the mills, profits, privileges and appurtenances and all remaining part of my moveable which I have not given away heretofore to be equally divided between them and they to pay their mother four pounds a year or the value thereof in gold during her natural life in lieu of dower and she provided comfortable rooms. My son, Samuel, to pay my three daughters £15 each. Sons Tripp and Esek, were named executors. Witnessed by Benjamin Church, William White and Ira Gardner. An account of the estate was presented on Aug 1st 1793.[2]

Wilbur/Wilbore Ancestry

Caleb Mosher's wife, Elizabeth Wilbur's family line, takes us back to northeastern England where Thomas Wildbore/Wilbore was born in the 1480's when Henry VII became the first Tudor king. Thomas moved south to the old Roman capitol Camulodunum (Colchester) in Essex, where the wool trade was still profitable. The court rolls at Colchester dated September 30th 1549 state Thomas Wildbore was born at Royston, West Riding, Yorkshire where he was a tailor and made justice of peace. On September 6th 1555 bailiffs were elected for the common council. On the head ward was Thomas Wilbore, William Simpson, John Jankyn, and John Dethick. On this date Richard Wilbore was admitted a burgess, born in Notton, Yorkshire, a sherman or shereman, the surities being Thomas Wilbore and Richard Whale. On September 30th 1562, Thomas and his wife, Alice, made a deed for the consideration of £26.13.0 4 paid to them by William Ram of St. Peters parish in Colchester, and sold and confirmed to *said Wm Ram all that tenement with garden adjoining, formerly of John Holmes and afterwards of Thos Lawrence and later of James Cole and Ellen his wife, situate in Holy Trinity parish, beyond Le shire gate between the lot called Berishane on the north side, and the highway leading towards a certain grene called St. John's Grene on the south side which tenement and garden I had myself from Henry Asshely, late of Colchester, shereman and Joan his wife as can more fully be seen by deed of Jan. 7, 1558. To have and to hold by William Ram and Markion his wife*, dated September 30th 1562. On January 20th 1564 Thomas Wylbore was in court against Thomas Vincent for trespass, 4d. The following June 22nd Alice Wilbore, widow, and adm. of the goods of Thomas Wilbore, deceased vs. George Wright for debt £00.11.04.

Of three known children, son Nicholas Wildbore, became a prominent woolen draper (dealer in cloth) in nearby Coggeshall. Nicholas' will shows he held considerable land in Stisted, Bocking, and Braintree where he pastured sheep at Skitts Hill. He sold a house in Braintree to his brother, John and his wife, Alice. Nicholas' will dated November 27th 1582 was probated September 26th 1583. It detailed his considerable real estate holdings. His wife Ann gave birth to these children: Ann, +Joseph, Susan, Mary, Thomas, William, Robert, and Nicholas.

Their son, Joseph Wildbore, lived in Braintree on a passageway south of St. Michaels church

1 Galway MM Death Records, Lydia's Wood Bible
2 Dutchess County Probate: Bk. A, p.366

given him by his father in addition to Hollis Grove which lay partly in Braintree and Bocking. The Manor Rolls of 1622 show his widow, Mary, living there. She died in 1623 leaving Hollis Grove to their sons Nicholas, John, and William; son Joseph deceased. Records of 1642 show the three sons were again admitted to Hollis Grove. Of their four known sons two are of interest in this family history. Joseph's son Nicholas married twice and had a son Samuel who married and moved to New England. Joseph's son John, of Braintree married Joan Drane, August 6th 1616, at Felsted, Essex. Their first son, John, was born and died in 1617. Joseph's son, William Wilbur, according to the Manor rolls bought land from Jonas Webb on March 30th 1647, selling it on January 2nd 1649/50 to Thomas and Mary Rowell before he departed for New England a single man.

Moving to New England

William Wilbur, a weaver, settled in Rhode Island where his "cousin"[1] Samuel Wilbur lived with wife Ann. Samuel was more politically active in that he was disarmed and banished from Massachusetts in 1638 for "having been seduced and led into dangerous error" by radicals who were protesting against the church in Boston. Like others he left for Portsmouth, RI, where he was among the men who signed the Portsmouth Contract on the 7th day of the first month 1638. Samuel deeded William ten acres on Jul 10th 1654, then returned to Boston where he died in 1656. His will written at Taunton and valued at £282.19.06 was recorded in both Massachusetts and Rhode Island due to his land holdings in both colonies. Cousin William was one of the overseers of Samuel's will.

William Wilbur married Martha by whom, according to his will, they had the following ten children:

   1. Joseph who married Ann Brownell,
   2. John,
   3. Benjamin,
   4. Thomas,
   5. Daniel who married Ann Barney,
+6. Samuel who married Mary Potter,
   7. Mary wife of Joseph Mowry,
   8. William,
   9. Martha wife of Wm. Sherman, and
  10. Joan wife of Nathaniel Potter.

On Dec 27th 1687 William deeded his son Joseph 30 acres in Little Compton. In 1692 Joseph and his brother, John, with eighteen men rebelled about paying Little Compton tax rates but gave in on December 13th. Son, Benjamin, was deeded his dwelling house, orchard and lands in Portsmouth plus 70 acres in Swansea on Feb 23rd 1705. The following May 7th he deeded 250 acres in Kingston to his minor grandson, Samuel son of Thomas, with its income to be for Samuel's sisters, Mary and Martha Wilbur, until Samuel reached age 21.

William Wilbur's will dated March 1st 1710 was probated the following Aug 15th at Little Compton, RI, with son Joseph Executor, sons John and William overseers. Wife Martha was deceased. The will gave to son John Wilbur's two children, John Wilbur and Mary Records, £30 equally due by bond from son John. To son Daniel, land at Shawamoke Great Neck. To son Samuel £43 for his children equally. To daughter Mary Mowry's grandchildren £20 due from her. To son William, £50 and son Joseph £100. To son John £20 and son Benjamin, the money due me by bond from Daniel Wilcox, deceased. To daughter Martha Sherman £10 and daughter Jone £10 and the great iron kettle. To four sons, John, William, Joseph and Samuel, all my land in Little Compton equally. To all grandchildren, equally, the rest of estate. On Jul 13th 1711 William Sherman gave receipt for legacy for wife Martha. On Oct 1st 1712

---

1 Cousin is a term used to denote a family relationship, not as we use the term today.

Nathaniel Potter of Little Compton gave receipt for wife Jone. William and Martha Wilbur son:

Samuel Wilbur was born in 1664 at Little Compton. He built a two room house in 1690 a year after he married Mary Potter, born 1666 daughter of Nathaniel Potter, jr. and Elizabeth Stokes of Portsmouth, RI. This house had a long life with five remodels to become a fifteen room house by 1870, the west half an "L" shape added around 1776. It was occupied by the Wilbur family into 1940's and is now preserved by the Little Compton Historical Society. Little Compton vital records have most of the births, deaths, and marriages of these families which include Samuel and Mary Wilbur's eleven children, five sons and six daughters:

1. Mary Wilbur b. Oct 22nd 1690.
2. Samuel Wilbur b. Nov 7th 1692.
3. William Wilbur born January 6th 1695.
4. Martha Wilbur b. Oct 29th 1697.
5. Joanna Wilbur b. Jun 8th 1700 married John Taylor.
6. Thankful Wilbur b. Jun 8th 1700.
7. Elizabeth Wilbur b. Dec 23rd 1702.
8. Thomas Wilbur b. Dec 29th 1704.
9. Abigail Wilbur b. May 27th 1707.
10. Hannah Wilbur b. Feb 9th 1709.
11. Isaac Wilbur b. Aug 24th 1712.

Samuel's will probated June 17th 1740 gave his eldest son Samuel <u>his now</u> dwelling house, land and £100; his son William <u>my now</u> dwelling house so we can assume that William and his twelve children occupied the historical home. Since his wife Mary was not mentioned in his will, she undoubtedly had died earlier and was buried in the cemetery behind the Wilbor/Wilbur home where Samuel requested to be buried. From the inventory of his estate we learn they were also making cloth of wool and linen. There were cards for combing fleece, 2 wheels for wool and 1 for linen in addition to 15 cows, 4 yearlings, 3 calves, a mare, bonds of £217.05.03, £2,000.00.00 homestead and £800 for other lands and houses plus other items. His estate was valued at a sizeable £5,344.13.03. Even his wearing apparel was worth £25.06.

Lydia Wood, wife of my great grandfather Henry Cook Ayers, was born into a Quaker family. What follows is her Wood family ancestry with its lateral branches through their marriages. The earliest ancestors were not of Quaker faith. Some joined the Quaker movement, others did not.

Since this Wood ancestry has so many males in the family named William Wood, I found it interesting that one by that name came to New England in the 1630's and wrote extensively of the conditions, habitat, and of the Indians among other things. He returned to England and published a book in 1634, printed in London by Thomas Cotes for John Bellamie, titled: *New Englands Prospect. A true, lively, and experimentall defsciption of that part of America, commonly called New England: difcovering the ftate of that Countrie, both as it ftands to our new-come Englifh Planters; and to the old Native Inhabitants.* Apparently there was considerable curiosity in England about the place known as New England, Wood wrote the book to enrich the knowledge for any future voyager. Little is actually known of William but he spent four years in New England gathering data and returned to England in August of 1633. I would sure like to know if he was related in some manner.

My eldest sister give me a copy of the Jonathan Wood Genealogy that included a copy of the following letter written at Dartmouth, MA, on April 2nd 1895 by Edward G. Wood, son of Joseph and Angelina (Deryshire) Wood, to his mother, sister and brother David in Ohio. It included the names of Jonathan Wood and Peace Davis.

> *I have traced our ancestry on father's side back to William Wood whose first child*
> *Mary was born, as you will see, in 1689. Of his children, Jonathan, was a minister*

for twenty years among Friends, was our ancestor. I think you will readily understand the plan I present. Of Jonathan's children Daniel was our great grandfather. I have taken this from the records of Dartmouth and Westport monthly meetings down to David, 4th child of grandfather David. Grandfather's first four children were born here and recorded in records of Westport. I have seen the marriage certificates of Jonathan and Peace, Daniel and 2nd wife Susanna Wood, and David and Rest. We are descended from Daniel Wood's first wife, but I could not find out her maiden name. A removal certificate was issued for David Wood and Rest his wife and four children: Peace, Ruth, Jonathan and David 16,1,1796 to Saratoga, New York. You will see names of grandmother's parents and brothers and sisters. I have been preaching to a lot of 2nd cousins nearly three years and didn't know it. They are descendants of grandfather's sister Esther, who married Robert Allen and lived and died in Westport; and also grandmother's sister Susanna was grandmother to a number of people here. Of course there won't be any nearer than second cousins left here. I don't know whether the Wood preachers of Ohio are descended from grandfathers brother Stephen or Jonathan. Perhaps this is enough of this for the present...Lovingly yours, E. G. Wood.

Back in Massachusetts was a researcher of the Wood family named Bertha Clark. In her diligent research, she provided the link that took my Wood family back to John Wood, mariner, and made it possible for my research to take my Wood family further back. The Wood ancestry begins with one named John Wood.

John[1] Wood was born about 1590 in England and became a mariner. As to his seafaring days of buying, selling, and transporting goods, some letters follow regarding these adventures. On May 16th 1636 at Quineticut, John Winthrop wrote:

Sir, John Wood being returned without any Corne I shall now desire that I may be supplied by the first shipping that arrive with any store of provision[s] with 10, or 13 Hogs[hd] of meale 5 or 6 hogs[hd] of pease 2 or 3 barrells of oatmeale 2 hogs[hd] of beife. for

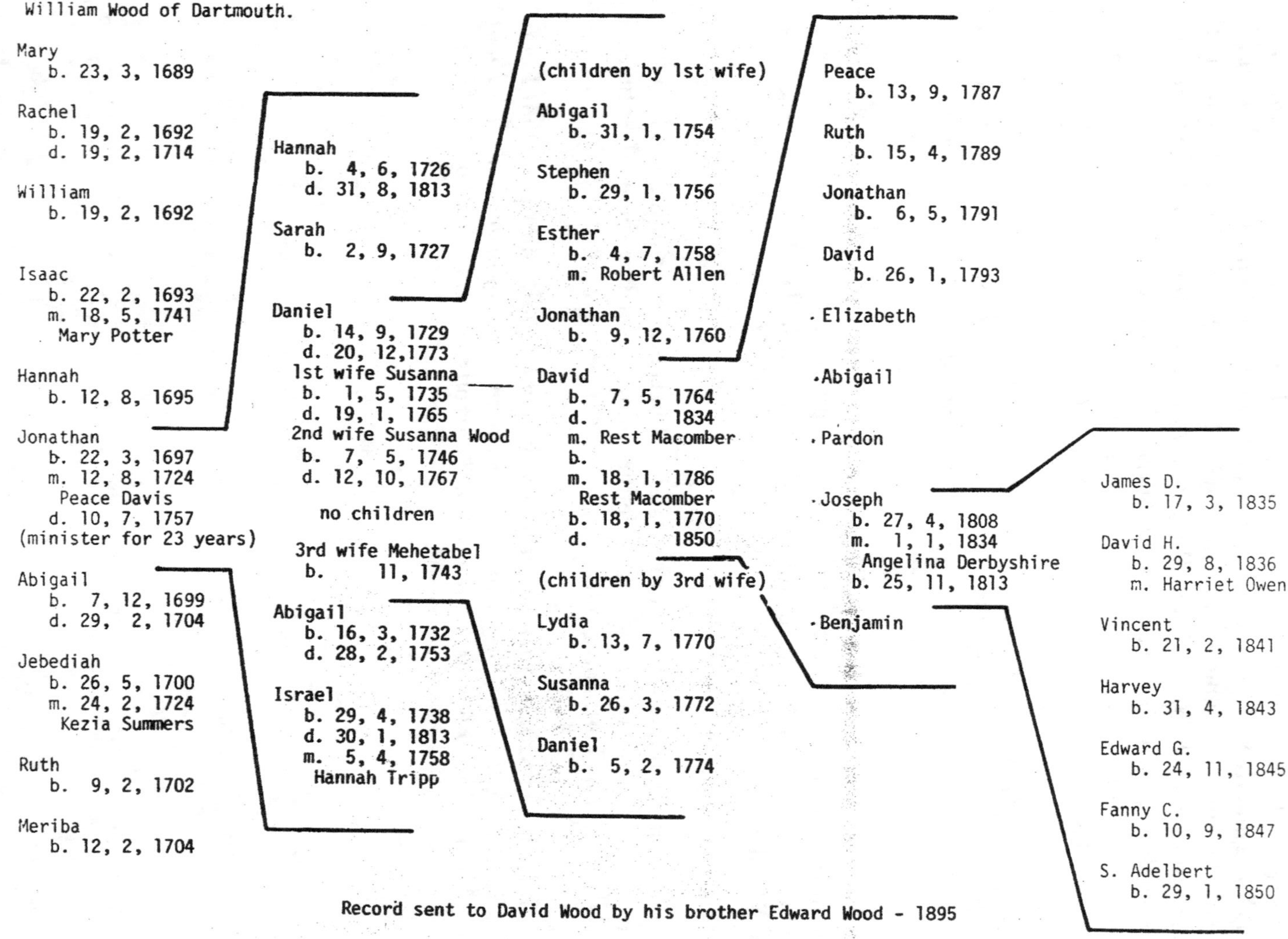

William Wood of Dartmouth.

Mary
    b. 23, 3, 1689

Rachel
    b. 19, 2, 1692
    d. 19, 2, 1714

William
    b. 19, 2, 1692

Isaac
    b. 22, 2, 1693
    m. 18, 5, 1741
    Mary Potter

Hannah
    b. 12, 8, 1695

Jonathan
    b. 22, 3, 1697
    m. 12, 8, 1724
    Peace Davis
    d. 10, 7, 1757
(minister for 23 years)

Abigail
    b. 7, 12, 1699
    d. 29, 2, 1704

Jebediah
    b. 26, 5, 1700
    m. 24, 2, 1724
    Kezia Summers

Ruth
    b. 9, 2, 1702

Meriba
    b. 12, 2, 1704

Hannah
    b. 4, 6, 1726
    d. 31, 8, 1813

Sarah
    b. 2, 9, 1727

Daniel
    b. 14, 9, 1729
    d. 20, 12,1773
    1st wife Susanna
    b. 1, 5, 1735
    d. 19, 1, 1765
    2nd wife Susanna Wood
    b. 7, 5, 1746
    d. 12, 10, 1767
    no children
    3rd wife Mehetabel
    b.   11, 1743

Abigail
    b. 16, 3, 1732
    d. 28, 2, 1753

Israel
    b. 29, 4, 1738
    d. 30, 1, 1813
    m. 5, 4, 1758
    Hannah Tripp

(children by 1st wife)

Abigail
    b. 31, 1, 1754

Stephen
    b. 29, 1, 1756

Esther
    b. 4, 7, 1758
    m. Robert Allen

Jonathan
    b. 9, 12, 1760

David
    b. 7, 5, 1764
    d.   1834
    m. Rest Macomber
    b.
    m. 18, 1, 1786
    Rest Macomber
    b. 18, 1, 1770
    d.   1850

(children by 3rd wife)

Lydia
    b. 13, 7, 1770

Susanna
    b. 26, 3, 1772

Daniel
    b. 5, 2, 1774

Peace
    b. 13, 9, 1787

Ruth
    b. 15, 4, 1789

Jonathan
    b. 6, 5, 1791

David
    b. 26, 1, 1793

· Elizabeth

·Abigail

· Pardon

·Joseph
    b. 27, 4, 1808
    m. 1, 1, 1834
    Angelina Derbyshire
    b. 25, 11, 1813

· Benjamin

James D.
    b. 17, 3, 1835

David H.
    b. 29, 8, 1836
    m. Harriet Owen

Vincent
    b. 21, 2, 1841

Harvey
    b. 31, 4, 1843

Edward G.
    b. 24, 11, 1845

Fanny C.
    b. 10, 9, 1847

S. Adelbert
    b. 29, 1, 1850

Record sent to David Wood by his brother Edward Wood - 1895

236

if we should want I see noe meanes to be supplied heere, and a little want may overthrow all our designe. [A hosghead is a large cask that holds 63-140 gallons of liquid. Apparently they were also used for dry ingredients.] *I sent home the 'Bacheler', and desire your helpe for her disposing. I must of necessity have her returne heere for I may shortly have much vse of her: but I desire they may goe for shares and victuall them selves, which John Wood, and his company are willing to doe. I cannot find that the miscariage of his voyage was through his default but Contrary winds therefore I am desirous he should and that Company goe still in her, so they will goe for shares and vicuall themselves. the Blessing I would sell if any will buy her at £160 or 150 she Cost 145 besides some new saile, and rigging and a new Cable above £20. the Cable is speciall good, except you should foresee any occasion that she should rather be kept still: or if their be implyment to Sable for her: but if she continues still to goe vpon any designe I desire she should goe likewise for her share the men to find themselves, otherwise I would have her laid up at Boston till further occasion. the men I desire should be discharged as soone as ever they Come ashore, and their wages paid them: I thanke you for the bread you sent. you write of 800 but there is not above 300 and an halfe at most delivered, besides 100 they keepe still aboard the rest I cannot learne what become of it but that it hath beene wastfully spent: they had besides halfe an hogshead of bread of their owne which was likewise spent and they were but [torn] eleven persons they say most of that tyme. [torn] for they pillaged her the tyme they had her to Salem pittifully that she hath neyther blockes nor braces nor running ropes, which the Bolt Will sayth that mr. Holgrave cutt them of he saw him. therfore I have agreed with John Wood Fredericke and George to take her to thirds. thus with my duty remembred I rest your obedient Son   John Winthrop[1]* [John's eldest son was named George. Was Frederick another son or a brother?]

A letter delivered to John Winthrop, Jr. at Ipswich from Francis Kirby, London merchant and dated, 10 April 1637, stated:

> *Kind Sir, I receiued yours dated 28th January and haue deliuered the inclosed to Mr.*
> *Kefler, and haue receiud the glasses and the water from him and haue packed them carefully in a runlet with 5 or 6 packs of salt, and deliuered it abord the "Hector" to John Wood masters mate who is my Cosen James Downeings acquaintance. I haue made him acquainted with the nature of the water and danger of it. he hath promised*
> *to be careful of it. Thus with my harty praiers to God for the preseruation of you and yours I rest Your lo frend Fra: Kirby[2]. London this 10th of May 1637 Sir, I wrote you lately per the Hector wherin I sent a runlet marked with your marke conteyneinge some things your son did write to me to send him. John Wood masters mate did promise mee and James Downeinge that he would be carfull of it and deliver it to you.... To John Winthrop at his house at Boston[3].*

John also became involved in some land adventures for on Nov 20th 1639, Thomas Bescher leased to Abraham Newman and Pieter Breyle, afterwards to John Wood, a house and tobacco plantation.[4] Between 1624 to 1639 there were 45 tobacco plantations on Manhattan Island according to VanWinkle, *Manhattan 1624-1639*. Thomas Bescher owned two plantations, one where present day Greenwich Village is located, the other at Gowanus. It was customary to use Indians and Negroes for labor at that time. On Mar 5th 1640, John Wood [Johannes Wodt] hired this date Thomas Bescher's tobacco farm at Gowanus.[5] It is assumed that someone ran this plantation for him, possibly one of his sons, for the following shows he was still sailing.

<hr>

1 Winthrop Papers 3:260

2 TRP 3:385

3 TRP 3:409-10

4 NY Calendar of Dutch Manuscripts, 1:16

5 Bergen: Early Settlers of King's Co, LI, p.391

A letter dated, Jul 6th 1640, from George Fenwick at Saybrook to Winthrop in Boston:

After the death of my servant, I sent another for Engl. to bring me some returnes, who was forced to goe about by Spaine, and I heare noething of him, though I haue a letter from John Wood, who mentions prouisions he hath to bring for me from some freinds but mentions not my man.[1]

Memorandum that John Wood of Nuport bought and purchased of Robt Jeoffreys a parcel of land about fifty acres more or less for a valuable consideration giuen and receiued and is laid forth at the Hermitage alias Middletown bounded on the eastern end by land off M[r] Sanfords on the northern side by Edward Robinson on the western end by the hieway 5 acres granted by the towne added the water at the western end and one the southern side by the land granted to M[r] Vaughan, also a parcel of land of 3 acres bordering upon M[r] Hutchensons land is by the town consigned to the s[d] John being in number 56 and is the proper inheritance of the said John and his heirs for ever. Teste William Dyre Rec[r], 1640[2]

New Amsterdam, Apr 27th 1641. Thomas Bescher's *widow*, Nanne Beets, entered into a marriage contract with Thomas Smith and John Wood became their security for the payment of the many debts for which they found themselves responsible.[3] On Aug 1st 1641, Ambrose Lonnen gave note for 200 guilders to John Wood for a house and plantation belonging to said Wood and situate on Long Island at the Bay of the North River.[4]

At Newport on June 7th 1643, An ac[t] of John Richman agst John Wood of same Towne in an ac[t] of Trespass; Refer[rd] to m[r] Easton in £8 a peice to abide the arbitr[mt] of all causes Also, An ac[t] of Trespass by David Greenman agst John Wood of the same Towne Referred .[5]

On Mar 7th 1643/4, *The debt of John Wood of twenty pounds is respited for two years in regard of his great losse.*[6] In February of 1643 the Dutch of New Amsterdam under the direction of Kiefft attacked an Indian settlement taking their corn and killing two males. In retribution, the following September the Indians attacked the Dutch settlements taking cattle and horses and burning the properties. Mespath, a place located about ten miles from Gowanus, suffered greatly. In was described by Riker in his *Annals of Newtown* as one in which all those who did not make the fort were killed and all dwellings burned. M[r] John Winthrope, Jr, was granted on Nov 13th 1644 y[e] hill at Tantousq, about 60 miles westward in which the black lead is and liberty to purchase some land there of the Indians. Colonists knew about this mine as early as 1633 located near the Connecticut border at Sturbridge, MA.[7] John Winthrop Jr, was deeded Blacklead Hill by W. Bucksham and his son on Jan 30th 1644/5. Five Indians and five settlers witnessed this paper, among them was John Wood.[8]

At the March 1645 Quarter Court held the first Tuesday: Griffin his sureties in 10£ Itt the ac[t] prosecuted by the Towne ag[st] Ed. Robinson, the Jury found £4.8s in arrears and 20s damage + the charge of the Court 28s, Ed Robinson bound to his good behav[r] to appeare the next Sessions in £20 John Wood + Robt a peec.[9] On Sep 18th 1645, John Wood of Nuport Road Iland bought & purchased of John Cranston of the same isle a parcel of land contayning 14 acres more or less for a valuable consideration given and received vpon which surrender all claime or title therto of the said John Cranston is annulled and is laid forth by a parcel of land granted by the towne aforesaid to the said John Wood Teste by William Dyre Rec[r] Recorded Sep 15th 1646.[10]

---

1 Winthrop Papers 4:261

2 RI Archives: Colonial Records Part I,Vol.I,p.10

3 NY Calendar of Dutch Manuscripts, 1:15

4 *ibid.* 1:16

5 Chapin: Doc. History of RI, 2:141-2

6 MA Bay Records: 2:63

7 *Ibid.*, p. 82

8 Winthrop Papers 5:5

9 Chapin: Doc. History of RI, 2:154

10 RI Archives, Colonial Records Vol.I, Part I, p.10

Memorandum that the towne of Nuport granted to John Wood 30 acres of land which he hath satisfied for the Threas[y] together with ten given to John Cranston as a servant as-?- for which allowed 14 in Nuport of a house lott is laid forth 5 acres by his 50 bought of M[r] Jeoffrey the rest amounting 39 acres more or less is laid forth 80 poles squar, the southern side bounding on Weedens land at the northern corner therof, the eastern by the hieway going between Carrs land & the said Weedens & the western & northern by the Common. His land so butted & bounded is for ever impropriated to the s[d] John Wood his heires & assignes for ever,...Teste William Dyre Rec[r.1] An action of the case com by William Withington plaintiff of Nuport ag[st] John Wood of the same upon 20 nobles damag, 1646, Delayed till next Court find for the defendant costs.[2]

John moved from Newport to Portsmouth about this time for on Jul 10th 1648, John Woode was declared *Freeman* of Portsmouth along with Samuell Jenne, Thomas Bordin, ffrancis Borden, Mr. Tho Cornell, Richard Bordin, Cornelius Joanes, Mathew Grenell, John Parker, John Cooke, Ichabod Sheffell, Capt. Morris, Jeames Badcock, Thomas Brookes, John Roome, William Hall, and John Brigs.[3]

"This present deede bareinge date this first day of the March in the yeare of our lorde sixtene hundred fortie nine witnesseth that I Nicholas Browne of the town of Portsmouth in Roade Iland for a valuabl Consideration in hand receiued haue bargained and sould unto John Woode Senior of the same towne and place, a parcell granted to me by the towne, being fortie fiue ackers more or lesse lyinge within the boundary of Portsmouth neer Nuport line bounded on the East with a parcell of Thomas Lawtons lande, together with my house there on, and all other priuiledges thereunto belonging I the aforesayd Nicholas doe for my selfe my heiers exsequetors or administrators resigne up all my rite title and interest in every parte and parcell of the forenamed bargained premises vnto the aforenamed John Woode his heirs administrators or assignes for euer, so that neither I myself nor any other by or from mee. shall Claime any rite title or Interest in any parte or parcell of the bargained premises in witness here of I haue hereto sett my hand and seale the day and date aboue written   Witnessed by Philip, Sarah and Eber Shearman   Nicholas Browne his marke.

This property in 1962 was known as Jepson's Lane, a short distance from the Middletown line or the old Newport line.[4] On May 20th 1649 John Wood was one of the twelve jurymen who served on Generall Court of Tryals houlden at Warwick, May 26th & 27th.[5] John wrote the following letter on Apr 16th 1650:

To Mrs. Elizabeth Winthrop at Boston in New England per a friend C.D.G. Wellcome. I salute yo kindly, + am glad to heere of your happiness. I could haue wished your tobaccko had proued to better acco[tt] We came to miserable lowe price for it. + after I had carryed it all the Straite over + the longer the worse, I keept it. I am allmost ashamed to give yo acco[tt] of it. However it hath produced these small things yo aduised me to buy for yo: to say, six rush leather chaires, some showes But you must excuse me. I haue been badlye dealt with about them. I spooke for them, + he putt me of till last, + now they proue not to my mind nor to yours neither, w[ch] is worst of all. I intended one paire for your selfe + one paire for your mother + one paire for your grandmother, +

---

1 *Ibid.*.

2 Chapin: Doc. History of RI 2:p.157

3 TRP, p.. 38

4 TRP pp. 300-1

5 RI Court Records 1: pp. 5-6

John first married about 1611. (On Jan 28th 1610/11 at St. Saviour's, Southward, London, a John Wood married Margaret Carter. This is possibly his first marriage.) His known children were: George, John, Thomas, Susanna, Margaret, and William. By his 2nd wife Elizabeth (?) they had Susannah and Elizabeth. John Wood died intestate in March 1655 in Portsmouth, Newport, RI. In April 1655 the Town Clerk recorded the widow of John Woode and the said Woodes children, John, Thomas, and William, requested an inventory be made of his goods, the sons choosing their mother, as administratrix. She gave unto daughter, Manchester, an ewe goat and son-in-law, Samuel Jennings, an ewe kid. Sons John to have the land in his possession and Thomas to have the 40 acres next to Robert Spinkes land. William to have the lands and house and each son to give their sister, Manchester, an ewe goat. The Town Council of Portsmouth met on May 7th 1655 for the legal disposing of his estate and John Coggeshall, Thomas Cornell, Jr., James Badcock and William Hall were chosen to appraise the lands, buildings, fences and other appurtenances of the deceased. Already accounted was £45 in hands of John Wood, £20 in hands of Thomas Wood and £50 in the widow's hand. An inventory of goods and cattle taken by Thomas Cornell, Sr., John Roome, James Badcock, Obadiah Holme, John Gould and Edward Thurston presented to the Council totaled £16. Then William Baulston, John Roome, John Briggs and Philip Shearman presented the following disposal of the estate: To John Wood the land in his possession and paying unto his sister, Manchester, £8 in account of silver, £4 presently and £4 the 29 September next. To Thomas Wood the land of his father's lying in Newport by the farm of William Weeden, it being 40 acres. To William Wood the land which the widow lives upon, 10 acres laid out to him on the side of the brook next to Clement Weaver, the brook to be the bounds at that corner until one comes to the swamp, then to run as Richard Borden and William Hall see convenient and they to lay out the land. The crop of corn presently growing on part of this land to the widow with the exception of the ten acres and she to have the rest of the land for the term of her life and she to pay to George Wood the eldest son £4 in silver account. The widow also to pay to the two young children of the deceased, Susanna and Elizabeth, £8 each in silver account at the age of 16 years or upon the widow's decease. William Wood to enjoy all that parcel of land now in his mother-in-laws [step-mother], possession and he to pay the £8 each to the young children if he comes into possession of said lands before the children are 16 years. The £16 of cattle and goods to be given to the widow to bring up the young children. Also ordered the if one of the daughters died before age 16 the legacie to go to the survivor. The widow, Elizabeth Wood, appointed sole executrix. John and his 1st wife Margaret's son:

William[2] Wood was born about 1633 and married about 1661, Martha Earle, daughter of Raulphe Earll and Joan Savage. William was the youngest son of his father, John, and of age as noted in the settlement of his father's estate in 1655. This helps approximate his birth date as well as becoming a freeman in 1658. He was noted as being a planter at Portsmouth, RI. Like others he dealt in land transactions. At Plymouth in 1668 he received his ear mark for his cattle. He sold his land in Portsmouth in 1673 for land in Dartmouth where he became constable before 1685. In 1689 he wrote a will that was never accepted for probate. William died on February 3rd 1696 at Dartmouth, MA. Since his wife, Martha, was not mentioned in the settlement of his estate, she must have died before her husband. The following reveals the complexity in distributing an estate. On Jan 4th 1696/7, the first inventory of William's estate was entered and taken by Aaron Davis, William Macumber, Jonathan Davol and Increase Allen. Its value was £411.13.02. Included was shoemakers working geer which leads one to wonder if he was a cordwainer. On Feb 3rd, Increase Allen entered a land addition of a sixth part of undivided land in Dartmouth. The same day sons, William and George, attested that the inventory was true and just to the best of their knowledge. Several days later sons, Joseph and Daniel, selected their guardians requesting the Court also accept them for their younger brothers, Josias and John. The

---

1 Mass .Hist. Soc., series 5, pp.1:372

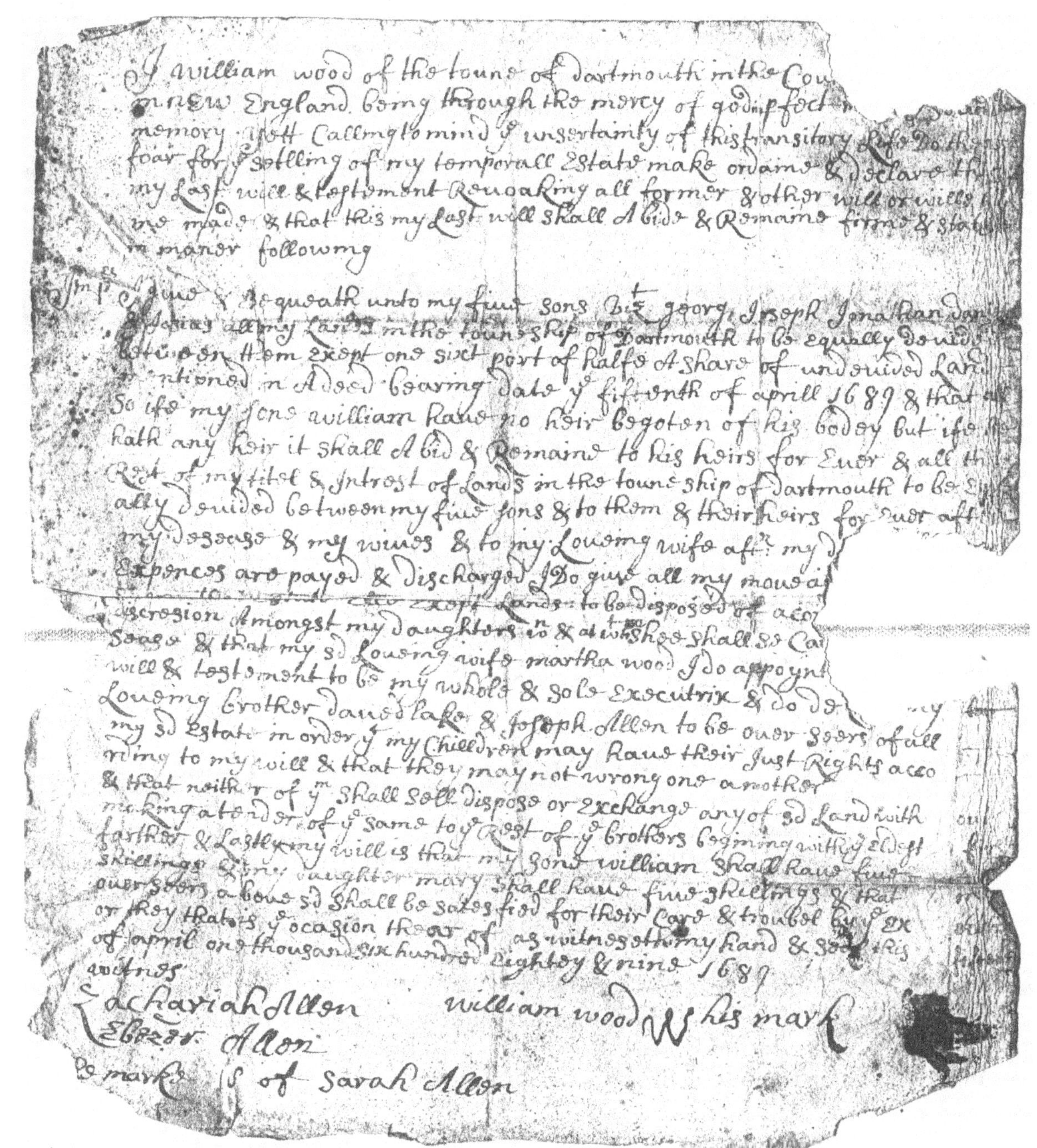

Will of William Wood not accepted for probate

following day William and George were appointed administrators and bonds were posted. Two weeks later another addition to the inventory was added valued at £4.13.06. On Apr 14th 1697, William Fobes, Joseph Taber and Christopher Allen entered the value of the houses and lands at £226 with a recommendation for the division of the estate. The total estate was valued at £1046.15.00. After debts, there remained £370.04.04 which divided among ten children amounted to £33.00.13 each. William, the eldest, was given two shares (the double portion rule): the house and 100 acres with meadow already laid out, also ¼ of the half share of land after 300 acres are laid out to George, also two guns, the whole amounting to £168.10.00, sd William to pay Josiah, Daniel, and John Wood £33.13.00 each. To son George 300 acres to be laid out, also ¾ if the undivided lands belonging to the half share of land, one loom and one small bed, the whole amounting to £67.06.00, he to pay Joseph £33.13.00. To Mr Mallets wife a bed at marriage with cattle and household goods amounting to £33.13.00. To Sarah, cattle and household goods amounting to £33.13.00. To Margaret and Rebecca the same. In Mar 1698, William and George presented the receipts for the distribution which were discharged by the Court that day. The following May, Guardian Receipts were entered.[1] One final entry was made in Nov 1701 when George turned over to his brother, Joseph, now of age, his share of the estate.

Children of William Wood and Martha Earle were: William, Mary, George, Sarah, Margaret, Joseph, Daniel, Josiah, Jonathan, and Rebecca.

Martha Earle's Ancestry

Raulphe Earll was married on August 25th 1605 at St. Michael's Church, Bishop's Stortford, Herts, to Margaret[2] Browne, daughter of George[1] and Margaret Browne. Raulphe was one of organizers of the company to settle the colony. The church's records started in 1431. Their children were christened in St. Michael's Church, namely:

+1.   Raulphe chr. Feb 9th 1606/7.
  2.   Samuel chr. Aug 27th 1608 3) John chr. Apr 19th 1610.
  4.   Dorothy chr. Aug 23rd 1612.
  5.   Margaret chr. Oct 9th 1614.
  6.   George chr. Dec 25th 1616.
  7.   Jonas chr. Jan 18th 1616/7, d. 1619.
  8.   Elizabeth chr. Aug 15th 1619.
  9.   Richard chr. Nov 1st 1620.
 10.   Mary chr. Nov 1st 1622.

Raulphe married on Jun 29th 1631 at St. Michael's, Joan Savage, d/o Richard Savage and Mary Isacke. Joan was chr. Feb 18th 1609/10. After the birth of two sons, they arrived at Boston in 1634. They settled on Aquidneck Island at Newport where he was admitted an inhabitant in 1638. On Apr 30th 1639 records show he declared himself a subject of King Charles. By 1646 he was of Portsmouth and like many early settlers was buying and selling land often ending up in law suits. He served in various offices with other members in this family history. In Nov 1650, his home became an inn and house of entertainment and he an innkeeper. Being under government control, he was ordered in 1655 to place a conspicuous sign outside his inn to attract strangers. He joined a Troop of Horse on Aug 10th 1657, later becoming its Captain and served twenty years. He was sixty-eight when he assisted Dartmouth, MA, in King Philip's War in July 1675.

Dealing with King Philip

There was such a fury over King Philip's actions that the General Court ordered the whole lot of Indians be shipped too Spain. Whether this actually occurred is speculation. Repeated raids occurred in the towns of Taunton, Middleborough, and Scituate as others were left in ashes. Capt. Benjamin Church recalled that on a march on June 30th as they passed burned houses in Swansea, they witnessed a gruesome sight...*they exercised more than brutish barbarities, beheading, dismembering, and mangling them and exposing them in the most inhuman manner, which gashed and ghostly objects struck a damp on all beholders...at a place called Keekkamuit, where they took down the heads of eight Englishmen that were killed at the head of Metapoiset Neck and set upon poles...*[2] For over a year Indians that had allied with Philip burned and massacred the inhabitants up and down New England's coast. Captain Church, weary and worn from fighting, decided to visit his wife who was living

---

1 Bristol Co. Probate Records, Vol. I. pps. 167-8,178-9, 198, 216-218

2 Stratton, p. 111

in the Sanford house in Newport, Rhode Island. He barely saw his wife when word came from an Indian deserter that Philip was camping on a hummock in *Miery Swamp* at Mt. Hope. Under the cover of night Church and his men, both English and Indian, approached the area. Near dawn, Philip was telling his counselors that he dreamed he had fallen into enemy's hands. When the first shot was fired Philip threw his haversack, powder horn and gun over his shoulder to face his enemy. Two shots killed him on August 12th 1676 as he fell into muddy water. Philip's "great captain" who had escaped to Rehoboth, was captured two weeks later. Annawon and Tispaquin, Philip's brothers-in-law, were condemned to death. Church pleaded in vain to spare them. With the death of Philip and his great Captain, Annawon, the war in southern New England ended. Some of Philip's subjects fled westward through Iroquios country to what is today Indiana.[1]

Raulphe Earle was seventy when his will was written on Nov 19th 1673 and entered and recorded at Portsmouth, RI, on Jan 14th 1677. His wife, Joan, died in 1680. They were parents of five children:

1. Ralph Earle chr. Apr 22nd 1632 at St. Michael's church, m. Dorcas Sprague, d/o of Francis and Lydia Sprague of Duxbury and had children: John, Elizabeth, Ralph, William, Joseph, and Dorcas.

2. William Earle chr. May 11th 1634 at St. Michael's church, m. 1st Mary Walker, had children: Mary, William, Ralph, Thomas, and Caleb. By his 2nd wife Prudence, had: John and Prudence. His will was probated Feb 8th 1713/4.

3. Mary Earle born about 1636 married 1st William Cory and had children: John, William, Mercy, Anne, Thomas, Margaret, Mary who married Thomas Cook, Caleb, Roger, and Jane Cory who married a Taylor. By her second husband, Joseph Timberlake, she had a daughter Sarah Timberlake who married Thomas Jeffreys. Her will probated April 14th 1718 mentions sons John, Caleb, Thomas and Roger Cory. Daughter Mercy Gonsales Moreno and children, Sarah Jeffreys wife of Thomas Jeffreys, Anne Bennett, Jane Taylor and Mary Cook. Grandsons William Cory son of son John, Caleb Cory son of son Calbeb, brothers Michael and William Cory, granddaughters Anne & Mary of daughter Anne Bennett, grandson Samuel Chaplin who rec'd cupboard at decease of dau. Jane Taylor.

+4. Martha[3] Earle married William Wood.

5. Sarah Earle m. 1st Thomas Cornell as his 2nd wife, son of Thomas and Rebecca Cornell. Thomas was chr. Oct 21st 1627 at Saffron Walden, Essex, England. Thomas and Sarah had three children: John, Sarah, and Innocent Cornell. The last name has significance in that Thomas was convicted of his mother's death. Rhode Island MM records state: *Rebecka Cornell widow was killed strangely at Portsmouth in own house, was twice viewed by coroners inquest, dug up and reburied the 8th 12th mo 1672 on own land.* Sarah Earle Cornell married 2nd David Lake by whom she five children: Sarah, David, Jonathan, Joel, and Joseph Lake.

William[2] Wood and Martha Earle's eldest son, William[3] Wood was born about 1663 at Portsmouth, RI. He and his brother, George, administered their father's estate in 1697. He seemed to be busy buying and selling land in Bristol County, MA. On Jan 18th 1707 for £13 he bought from John Wilcox the land next to his own in Dartmouth. Two more parcels were purchased in 1708. On May 4th 1709 he witnessed the will of Robert Millard of Rehoboth and served as an appraiser. He also was an appraiser for the estate of Joseph Hix of Dartmouth Aug 9th 1709 and Capt. John Brown of Swansea on Dec 17th 1709. He and Nathaniel Soule bought Dartmouth land from Zachariah Allen on Feb 1st 1710. A year later he sold his share of land purchased with Nathaniel to William Soule. Twenty nine acres were bought from his brother-in-law Philip Taber on Jan 28th 1713 for £29. He bought 30 acres for £15 from Jeremiah Devol and more land on March 14th 1717/8 of Jeremiah Devol for £58. The following Jul 30th he sold land for £9 to Benjamin Gifford. That seem to end his land deals. He witnessed Increase Allen's will Oct 31st 1722 and served as appraiser on Jul 6th 1724 at Dartmouth. With Nathaniel Soule, William Macomber and Jedediah Wood he witnessed John Macomber's will on Oct 7th 1723. On Dec 20th 1728

---

1 Morison, pp.277-279

he sold to to his son Jonathan Wood, 1 acre & 48 rods of his Dartmouth homestead for £61:14:00. His will written Dec 12th 1748 was witnessed by Nathaniel Sowle, William Macomber, and Giles Tripp, and affirmed Mar 2nd 1756. He called himself a yeoman of Dartmouth and bequeathed to his three sons William, the eldest, two parcels in Dartmouth on the westward side of Nenecompsh cedar swamp and on the east side of Noakechuck River containing thirty-four acres plus the sixty-five acres on which he resides in ponagancet village and two parcels already given to him by Deed of Gift. To Jonathan the dwelling house where he lives with the rest of my ancient homestead farm all in Dartmouth with all buildings on it and one half of two acres and forty rods of ceder swamp which formerly belonged to Edward Wing. To son, Jedidiah, my new dwelling house & farm land bought of Jeremiah Dauol plus land bought of William Soule and that bought of Zachariah Allen of nine or ten acres as it is already fenced and part joining to son, Jonathan's meadow with drift way to and from at ye most convenient place with least damage to his brother, Jonathan's land. Also one half of two acres and 40 rods of ceder swamp. To the heirs of son, Isaac, deceased, three parcels of land and meadows in Dartmouth, one piece of one hundred and twenty acres at ye fork of Noakachuck River, the other of one hundred and aces of meadow on shiprock flat on Coakset River and the third, of one hundred and twenty five rods joining to a pond and creek at ye great flat. To three daughters: Abigail Youen, Ruth Stafford and Meribah Roan, all my household goods, all my silver and bills of credit or bonds for bills of credit free and clear, to be divided equally, except Thomas Youens bond of £400 which is to go to grandson, Benjamin Youen, after the decease of his parents, if living, and if not, to be divided among all his grandchildren. To his three sons also his clothing to be divided as well as his husbandry tools and tackling of every sort for out doors use for farming. Son Jonathan to be executor. The inventory dated Jan 27th 1756 for £3.18.1 was taken by Humphry Smith, John Soule and Gabriel Hix and presented by Jonathan. No real estate valued. His wife, Mary, had preceded him in death.

These children of William and Mary Wood were born in Dartmouth, MA:

1. Mary[4] Wood, b. May 23rd 1689; died Jan 27th 1706/7 in Dartmouth, unm.
2. Rachel Wood (twin), b. Apr 16th 1691, d. Apr 19th 1715 in Dartmouth.
3. William Wood (twin), b. Apr 16th 1691, d. Mar 6th 1772 in Dartmouth, m. May 14th 1730 in Flushing, LI, NY, Keziah (Liza) Hedger, d/o of Joseph Hedger. Four children born in Dartmouth.
4. Isaac Wood, b. Apr 22nd 1693, d. Jul 18th 1741 in Dartmouth; m. Jun 12th 1722 in Dartmouth, Mary Potter, daughter of Nathaniel and Joan (Wilbur) Potter. Witnesses were: William Wood; Nathaniel and Jesse Potter; William, Jonathan, and Jedediah Wood; Nicholas Lapham; Mary Soull; Rebecah Tripp; Hannah, Abigail, Ruth, and Maribah Wood; Ann Manchester; Eliashim Smith; James Tripp; Mary Wilbur; Job Almy; William Barker; Samuel Gaskel; Elizabeth Slocum; Daniel Wood; Peter Allen; Josiah Merrehoo; George Layton; Robert Kerby; Isaac and Mary Wood; Two children born Dartmouth.
5. Hannah Wood, b. Oct 12th 1695, d. c. 1728; m. Feb 16th 1724/5 in Dartmouth, Nicholas Davis, his 2nd wife. Intentions published Jan 23rd 1724 in Rochester, MA. Witnesses were: William sr., William jr., and Isaac Wood; Stephen Wing; John Walker jr.; Shubal Barker; Jonathan, Maribah, Abigail, Kesiah and Ruth Wood; Judah Smith; James Trip; Josiah Mariho; John Tucker jr.; Peleg Trip; Nathan Soule; Joseph Mosher; Benjamin Wing; John Borden; William White; Elizabeth Trip; Hannah Cadman; Dinah and Mary Smith; Mary Lapham; Rebecah Soule; and William Macomber. No known issue. On Jul 5th 1729 in Rochester, Nicholas married 2nd Ruth Tucker, daughter of Abraham Tucker. Witnesses were: Henry Tucker, Abraham Tucker, Jonathan Wood, Phebe Tucker, Mathew Wood, Ruth Tucker, Elisabeth Barker, Hannah Tucker, Patience Tucker, John Tucker, Adam Mott, John Howland, James ?Beuker, Thomas Smith, Isaac Howland, Joseph Russill jr., Joseph Russill, Joseph Tucker, Benjamin Thomas, John Tucker, jr., Judah Smith, Mary Lapham, Anne Mumford, Mary Howland, Silvester Barker, Rebeckah Russell, and John Smith.[3]

48

Marriage Certificate
Jonathan Wood and Peace Davis

+6. Jonathan Wood, b. May 22nd 1697; d. Jul 10th 1757 in Dartmouth; m. Oct 12th 1720 in Dartmouth, Peace Davis, d/o of Timothy Davis, dec'd, of Rochester, MA.

7. Abigail Wood, b. Feb 7th 1698/9, m. in Rochester, MA, Thomas Youen. Intentions Mar 18th 1731/2. One son, Benjamin Youen, b. May 24th 1734 in Rochester.

8. Jedediah Wood, b. Jul 26th 1700, d. after 1758; m. Feb 16th 1724/5 in Rochester, MA, Kezia Summers, d/o of John Summers, deceased. Witnesses were: William sr., William jr., and Isaac Wood; Steving Wing; John Wilber jr.; Shubel Barlow; Jonathan Wood; Maribah Wood; Nicholas Davis; James Tripp; Judah Smith; Josiah Mariho; John Tucker jr.; Peleg Trip; Nathan Soule; Joseph Mosher; Benjamin Wing; John Borden; William White; Hannah Cadman; Hannah Davis; Peace Davis; Abigal Wood; Elizabeth Trip; Dinah Smith; Mary Smith; Mary Soul; Rebecah Soul; and William Macomber. Five children born in Dartmouth, MA. Their son, John of Dartmouth, m. Feb 27th 1744/5, Hannah Wing, d/o Benjamin and Content Wing. Witnesses were: Benjamin Wing, Jedidiah Wood, Kezia Wood, Henry Tucker, William Wood, Kesia Wood, James Barker, Jonathan Wood, Rebecca Russell, John Tucker, John Lapham, John Mosher, Barnabas Howland, Nathaniel Potter, John Russell, Peleg Smith, Daniel Russell, Jonathan Ricketson, William Barker, John Ricketson, William Gifford, Henry Hedly, John Howland, John Parke, Christopher Gifford, Abraham Tucker, Phebe Ricketson, Elisabeth Barker, Penelope Allen, and Joanna Craw.

9. Ruth Wood, b. Apr 9th 1702; m. Sep 13th 1739 in Dartmouth, Abraham Stafford, s/o Josiah

Stafford of Tiverton. Witnesses were: William Wood; David Irish; William jr., George jr., Isaac and Jedidiah Wood; Thomas Youin; Richard Hart; Daniel Tripp; Joseph Tripp; Benjamin Shearman; Lot, Jonathan, and Ebenezer Tripp; Nathaniel Potter; Stephen Willcock; Othaniel and Abial Tripp; Christopher Gifford; Mary Laton; Mary Potter; Eunice Goddard; Peace Wood; and Mary Soule.

10. Maribah Wood, b. Apr 12th 1704; m. 1st Apr 23rd 1730 in Dartmouth, Moses Shearman, s/o Daniel and Sarah (Jenney) Shearman of Dartmouth. Witnesses were: William, Jonathan, Abigail, and Ruth Wood; Isabel and Rachel Shearman; Isaac Wood; David Irish; John Lapham; Robert Kerby; John Tucker jr; Jonathan Divol; Nathan Soule; Increas Allan; Christopher Gifford; Eliashib Smith; James Tripp; Henry Healy; Stephen Willcock and Jabez Barker. She married 2nd Dec 27th 1736 in Dartmouth, John Roan.

William[3] and Mary Wood's son:

Jonathan[4] Wood was b. May 22nd 1697 at Dartmouth, MA. He married Peace Davis, daughter of Timothy Davis and Sarah Perry, on Oct 12th 1720 at Dartmouth. Witnesses were: Isaac Wood, Joseph Tripp, Jedediah Wood, Thankful Fish, Hannah Wood, Abigail Wood, William Wood, Nicholas Davis, Savia Fish, William Wood, jr., Joseph Taber, James Tripp, John Tucker, jr., Robara Carby, John Wilber, Vollentine Huddlestone, Phebe Tucker, Elizabeth Trip, Nathan Soule, John Irish, Kesia Summers, Mary Soule, Ebenezer Tripp, and Mary Youon.

Children born to Jonathan and Peace Wood in Dartmouth, MA, were:

1. Hannah[5] Wood, b. Aug 4th 1726, d. before 1756; m. Jan 11th 1746/7 in Dartmouth, William Barker, s/o William and Elisabeth Barker. Witnesses were: William Wood; James Barker; Jonathan Wood; Peace Wood; William Wood, jr.; Abraham Barker; John Wood; Daniel Wood; John Russell; Caleb Tucker; Stephen Willcock; Peleg Tripp; Ebenezer Tripp; Jonathan Sisson; Jedediah Wood; Increas Allen; Benjamin Wing; Christopher Gifford; Jacob Mott; Nathaniel Potter; Edward Cornell; Wm. Gifford; Othaniel Tripp; Walter Cornell; William Sisson; Richard Gifford; David Cornell; Susanna Cornell; and, Mary, Lydia and Hannah Potter. Children: Peace and James Barker.
2. Sarah Wood, b. Nov 2nd 1727; m. Dec 7th 1752 in Dartmouth, Philip Tripp, b. Apr 3rd 1725, s/o Joseph and Elisabeth (Smith) Tripp of Dartmouth. Witnesses were: Joseph Tripp; Jonathan Wood; Jedidiah Wood; Benjm. Tripp; Joseph Tripp, Jr.; Daniel Wood; William Barker; Dinah Tripp; Hannah, Ruth and Abigail Wood; Hannah Tripp; Isaac Wood; Elisabeth Cornell; Eunice Wood; John Davis; Othaniel Tripp; Christopher Gifford; Benjm. Shearman; Ewd Cornell; Wm Gifford; John Mosher; Ichabod Karby; Thos Cuoe; Joshua Cornell; John Macomber; Joshua Barker; Ezekl Cornell; Abigail Kerby; Ruth White; Ruhamah Kerby; and Sarah Deuil.
+3. Daniel[5] Wood, b. Nov 14th 1729, d. Dec 20th 1773 in Westport, MA; m. 1st Jul 30th 1752 in Swansea, MA, Susannah Chase, d/o Stephen and Esther (Buffington) Chase. Five children: Abigail, Stephen, Esther, Jonathan, and David. Daniel married 2nd Jun 30th 1767 in Dartmouth, Susannah Wood, b. May 7th 746 in Dartmouth, d/o Esek and Sarah (Tripp) Wood who d. Dec 12th 1767, in Dartmouth. No issue. He married 3rd Oct 5th 1769 at Dartmouth, the widow Mehitable Thurston Coggeshall, d/o Jonathan and Lydia Thurston, b. Nov 13th 1741. Known issue: Lydia, Susanna, and Daniel. After Daniel died, Mehitable m. Benjamin Chase Feb 19th 1777 in Dartmouth.
4. Abigail Wood, b. May 16th 1732; d. Feb 28th 1753 in Dartmouth.
5. Israel Wood, b. Jun 29th 1738, d. Jan 30th 1813 in Westport, MA; m. Apr 5th 1758 in Dartmouth, Hannah Tripp, b. Aug 13th 1728, d/o Joseph and Elisabeth (Smith) Tripp, both deceased. Witnesses were: Peace Wood, Joseph, Philip and Benjamin Tripp, Jedidiah Wood, Ruth Cornell, Daniel Wood, Sarah and Daniel Tripp, Ichabod Eddy, Christopher Gifford, John

Mosher, John Macomber, Peter Deuol, Benjamin Wing, Joshua Cornell, Stokes Tripp, John and Henry Brightman, Constant Tripp, Job Potter, Abial Macomber, Obadiah Mosher, Mary Potter, Mary Gifford, Abigail Tripp and Sarah Mosher.

Jonathan was a yeoman and Quaker minister for twenty three years. He served as executor of his father's will. Peace was also a Quaker minister. Following is a copy of Jonathan Wood and Peace Davis' marriage certificate.

Peace Davis' Ancestry

Peace Davis, wife of Jonathan Wood, was born Apr 14th 1702 in Rochester, Plymouth, MA, daughter of Timothy and Sarah (Perry) Davis. Peace was the fifth of six children. She became a Quaker minister and preached for twenty-one years. Peace died July 4th 1763 in Dartmouth, MA.

Peace's father, Timothy Davis, was born about 1666, son of John and Hannah (Linnell) Davis. He married Mar 7th 1689/90, Sarah Perry, daughter of Edward and Mary (Freeman) Perry of Sandwich, Plymouth, MA. Timothy was a Quaker who lived at Sandwich and Rochester and belonged to the Quaker Church in both communities. *At a Town meeting of inhabitants of town of Rochester regularly assembled and warned to be on the 21 day of Mar in ye yr 1700 to Chasotown - Officers as the Law Dyreck on which day choice of sundry officers was made as followeth: Timothy Davis, John Randal and Peter Blackmor chosen for Selectmen for the present year.*[4] He served again the following year. Timothy died in 1723 in Rochester, MA.

Timothy's mother, Hannah Linnell, was born about 1629 in England, daughter of Robert Linnell and his first wife. Hannah married John Davis on Mar 15th 1647/8 in Nocett, Barnstable, MA. Hannah's father, Robert Linnell, was born about 1584 in England and died on Feb 27th 1662/3. In his will he gave to John Davis, who married my daughter, my two oxen and to find my wife wood and to mow my marsh and plow my ground for her for two years if she remains a widow, if she married before two years then to be free. After arriving in New England, Robert Linnell joined Rev. Lothrop's church in Scituate on Sep 16th 1638 by letter of dismission from the church of London. He was declared a freeman in Scituate in Dec 1638. The following year the men of Scituate were granted land at Mattacheese, now Barnstable, where he appeared in 1640 on the list of townmen and voters. He was granted ten acres as a house lot, three acres of planting land in the Commons, three acres of meadow at Sandy Neck, nine acres at Scorton, and a great lot of sixty acres with rights of commonage, thus, making him among the owners of large land holdings. He had two wives, the latter named Penninah Howes who on Oct 20th 1669 complained to the Court that her step-son, David Linnell, had possessed himself of the house and land given to her by her deceased husband. Timothy Davis' wife, Sarah Perry, was the daughter of Edward and Mary (Freeman) Perry. There is some question if Mary Freeman was the daughter of Edmund Freeman by either of his two wives who in his will dated Feb 24th 1678 named his son, Edward Perry. Two researchers, Rosemary Canfield and Henry J. Perry, addressed this situation and their articles were recommended to be submitted jointly to *The Second Boat*. Mr. Perry's conclusion is that Mary, baptized on Apr 16th 1630 in St. Mary's Parish, Pulborough, Sussex, England, was the daughter of Thomas Freeman who was on the ship's list with Edmund. Thomas seemed to vanish, possibly dying during the voyage leaving a daughter to be taken in by her uncle. Mr. Perry has found no evidence to the contrary. He also addressed the parentage of Edward Perry of Sandwich in which he located in the Petworth Parish Register, Sussex, England, Edward Perry, son of Thomas, who was chr. Apr 13th 1596; plus Edward Perry, son of Thomas, who married Sarah Rader, Oct 10th 1624; and Edward Perry, Gent. who was buried July 28th 1630. This would leave Mrs. Sarah Perry, a widow with probable children or related children when she arrived in Sandwich about 1644 with five children: two males and three females. This is only one of many quandries in which researchers find themselves today as many old publications made assumptions based on evidence as slight as similarity of names in English families or other undocumented information.

Edmund Freeman, nonetheless, was an interesting individual who provided Mary a comfortable home for the time and a non-conventional attitude about church and other affairs. He was one of ten men of Saugus who agreed to settle Sandwich in April 1637. He became a large land owner and served as Assistant to the Governor for six terms beginning in June 1640. His brother-in-law, John Beauchamp, an adventurer was owed money by the undertakers and he gave Edmund power of attorney to collect £400 due Beauchamp. The colonists suffered from demands by the adventurers for more money and goods and Edmund suffered for helping Beauchamp. Edmund's liberal attitude toward church attendance plus being more sympathetic toward the Quakers, found him being called to account on more than one occasion. He was brought before the Grand Jury on Mar 1st 1642 for loaning a gun to an Indian. Edmund was chr. Jul 25th 1596 in St. Mary's Church, Pulborough, Sussex, England, son of Edmond and Alice (Coles) Freeman. He died in 1682, and his second wife died in 1676, both buried on the original farm in Sandwich.

As written by Amos Otis, the Friends of Sandwich were aware of the magistrate's dislike of Quakers. Christopher Holder and John Copeland, two Quaker preachers, were arrested on Jun 23rd 1658 on their way to a meeting in Sandwich. They had been banished from the Colony the preceding Feb 2nd and whipped at Plymouth on the 8th for non compliance. Marshall Barlow had to keep them for six days in his house before he brought them before Thomas Hinckley, one of the newly elected magistrates. They were tied to an old post and given thirty-three stripes with a tormenting whip of three cords with knots at the ends that were made by the Marshall himself. This was not as bad as the early Roman's whips that had either bits of metal or bone, or small lead weights attached to the end of the cords. All were despicable. Some spectators were anguished and wondered why they left had England for this. When Barlow went to arrest Edward Perry in 1659, it was said that he was drunk, and that he often stole from the Quakers. He lived on the spoils of the innocent but died a poor miserable drunkard with no one to mark where he was buried or feel any remorse.

Edward Perry, who was wealthy and well educated, resided in East Sandwich and joined the Friends of Sandwich. Nine men were disfranchised by the Colony Court on Oct 2nd 1658 for being or sympathizing with the Quakers. Robert Harper had his house, lands, and nine cattle confiscated. Thomas Johnson, a poor weaver, was stripped of all he had, namely his house and land. Edward suffered more than most and was among thirteen men who were fined £10 each for refusing to take the oath of fidelity and again fined £5 on Jun 4th 1659. These fines continued for several years. A statement of the amount of fines taken for three years from the Quakers from 1658-1660 totaled £679.02s for livestock only. Cattle numbered one hundred twenty-nine, three horses and nine sheep. The Court did return one steer to Edward on Jun 10th 1661. During this period he suffered seventeen cattle confiscated, was tarred and feathered, and paid a total in fines of £89.18s. With similar feelings existing in England, New England was only echoing the opinion of Puritans in the mother country. For obvious reasons, several of Edward's children later moved to Rhode Island. On Jun 5th 1671, Edward and his older brother, Ezra Perry, were appointed to represent Sandwich "to view the damage done to the Indians by horses and hogges of the English." The Sandwich Friends noted in their records in 1672 and in 1675, that Edward was listed among the Sandwich men who have just right to town privileges. Edward's will dated Dec 29th 1694 named his wife, Mary, and eldest son, Samuel to have his now dwelling house. To son, Edward, the remaining part of the tenement on which I dwell lying on the westerly side of lands given to Samuel. To youngest son, Benjamin, all lands lying on Scoton Neck, but wife to have use of all these lands during her natural life. To daughters, Peace and Rest, £20 each to be paid by son, Samuel, within one year after my wife's decease. Also £20 to daughter Deborah to be paid by son, Edward, also Benjamin to pay within one year after he becomes twenty-one £10 to daughters, Dorcas and Sarah, and £5 to Peace and Rest and daughter, Mary, to have £5 paid by her mother besides what she hath already had and £6 to granddaughter, Hannah Easton. In researching Quaker records it is interesting that all his daughters were married in the Society.

Peace Davis' grandfather, John Davis, was the son of Dolar and Margery (Willard) Davis and was born about 1626 in Kent County, England. John was married on Mar 15th 1647/8 in Nocett, MA, by Mr. Prence, to Hannah[2] Linnell, sometimes called Lynnitt, daughter of Robert Linnell. The births of John and Hannah's first eight children, which included two sets of twins, were recorded in Barnstable records. Four more children were born but not noted in this particular record. John brought goods from Weymouth to Sandwich in 1637 and he was on the list of those "Able to Bear Arms" in Barnstable in 1643. John Davis, like his father, Dolar, was a farmer and house carpenter. His houselot, containing eight acres, was the first on the west of Baker's Lane, Hyannis Rd. The lot was originally laid out to ancestor Edward FitzRandolph, who sold it to John Chipman on Jun 1st 1649. This was an unrecorded deed, but executed on Aug 13th 1669. In 1656, John was a surveyor of highways. The following year, he took the oath of fidelity at Barnstable. In Jan 1658, he sold six acres of his house lot to Samuel Norman which was reconveyed on Feb 26th 1665 but bore the name of Norman's Hill. John also owned thirteen acres on the east side of Hyannis road, three acres in the old common-field, and two acres in the new field, and a half acre on the north side of the county road opposite his house with orchard and garden. In addition, a quarter acre bought of Henry Cobb, four acres of meadow at Sandy Neck, and two acres bounded westerly by Rendevous Creek. John Davis was one of the witnesses to Captain William Hedge's will at Yarmouth on Jun 30th 1670. He served as surveyor of highways in 1671, 1672, 1675, and 1677. He owned considerable land and portioned it to his sons during his life including his father's house and land in Concord. He served on the Grand Inquest in 1682. John died about 1702/3 in Barnstable, MA. His will dated May 10th 1701 was proved Apr 9th 1703. He gave his eldest son, John, lands in his possession estimated to be fourteen acres with the condition that he pay £30 to the executors with what he has already paid to be deducted. To daughter, Mercy, £20 for her tender care and £5 a year if she continues to attend me and her mother and her diet, washing and lodging at her brother Benjamin's, plus some livestock, and at her mother's decease some household stuff and bedding, plus the southward end of the house so long as she remain single. To son, Samuel, a yoke of oxen and a great chain. To son, Benjamin, nearly all his estate in consideration of taking care of his parents during their life. Also named sons: Dolar, Timothy and Jabez, and daughters Ruth Linnell, Mary Hinckley, and Hannah Jones' five children; son John's four eldest sons, granddaughter Mary Goodspeed and grandson Joseph Davis. Son, Benjamin, executor. Witnessed by: Joseph Lothrop, James Cobb, and Samuel Sargeant. The inventory was appraised at £268.12.04 by James Lewis, Jeremiah Bacon, and Edward Lewis.

Dolar Davis, John Davis' father, was born about 1595 in Kent County, England. Dolar married 1st Mar 22nd 1624 in Kent County, England, Margery Willard (Recorded as Margerye Wilerd), who was chr. Nov 7th 1602 and died about 1665, probably in Concord. She was the daughter of Richard Willard by his 2nd wife, Margery of Horsemonden, Kent, England, who died in 1608. Richard died in Feb 1617 willing to his four daughters and son, Simon, who was Margery's brother. Dolar sailed for New England in 1634. His wife, Margery and three children, John, Mary, and Elizabeth, left London Sep 17th 1635 on the *Elizabeth*, William Stagg, Master, to join Dolar.

Dolar had left England in the company of his brother-in-law, Simon Willard, a founder of Concord. On Aug 4th 1634, Dolar was granted twenty-five acres on the west side of the Charles River in New Towne (Cambridge), MA, which was settled in 1629. Also a house-lot of half a rod [1.8 acres] more or less within the palisade on the northwest corner of Water (Dunster) and Long (Winthrop) streets on Jun 4th 1635. It is doubtful if Dolar actually settled in Cambridge for on Aug 25th 1635 he sold his land to Richard Girling, and his house-lot on Water Street to his brother-in-law, Simon Willard, and went to Duxbury, located about ten miles north of Plymouth on Plymouth Bay. Simon resold it in 1639 to Edward Mitchelson. At Duxbury, Dolar took the oath of fidelity and on Mar 5th 1638/9 declared a freeman. The family were members of the church at Duxbury. On Apr 6th 1640, he and seven others were granted lands by the Court of Assistants at Plymouth that lay on the northwest side of North hill in Duxbury with the farmlands and meadows of Christopher Wadsworth to be divided among them and with the liberty to "sett corne at Namasacussett," plus mow grass for their cattle and build a house on the south side of the brook. On Aug 31st 1640 the Court granted Dolar fifty acres of upland on Namasacusset River with some meadows. Dolar farmed and was also a master house carpenter which accounts for his many moves.

Plymouth Colony records note the following dated events. On May 3rd 1641 Dolar was among those of Scituate who posted bond for George Willard of Scituate who had spoken disrespectfully of the magistrates. Scituate lies on the Atlantic Ocean about fifteen miles north of Duxbury. Dolar served as a juror at General Court at Plymouth on Mar 1st 1641/2. The people of Scituate were divided over baptism methods and Rev. John Lothrop removed with many from the town to Barnstable. Dolar also departed Duxbury for Barnstable and was listed in 1643 with four sons who were "able to bear arms" ie. males 16 to 60. Barnstable had been officially incorporated in Sep 1639 under a land grant from Plymouth Colony and is located a few miles northwest of Hyannis near Barnstable Harbor. Early industry included cranberries, shipbuilding, lumbering, oysters, and extraction of salt from the ocean. Sea trade was of importance and members of this family were in that occupation.

Dolar and Margery joined the Barnstable Church on Aug 27th 1648 being dismissed from the Duxbury Church.[5] On Jun 4th 1645 Dolar was sworn in as a member of the Grand Inquest of Plymouth, marked as sick. That same day he was propounded to become a freeman and admitted on Jun 2nd 1646. Dolar served as surveyor of highways in 1652 and constable in 1654. They left Barnstable with the younger members of his family in 1655 and moved to Concord, northwest of Boston, where his three younger children married and settled. Roger Draper of Concord conveyed one hundred fifty-two acres to Dolar, husbandman, on Aug 20th 1655 which included his house and house-lot. This deed was witnessed by Josiah Willard and James Hosmer and acknowledged on Feb 23rd 1657/8 before Simon Willard. Dolar was one of the original proprietors of Groton and served on its first Board of Selectmen for two years beginning in May 1655. However, on Apr 9th 1656 Dolar called himself of Concord on a receipt. He took the oath of fidelity at Duxbury in 1657. The next year, he completed the sale of forty acres of his Barnstable lands to Abraham Blush describing himself as a house carpenter late of Barnstable. This house lot stood near the water mill called Old Mill Creek and other lands at Stoney Cove opposite Mill Creek. His son, Nicholas, owned land next to the mill. His great lot of sixty acres was sold to Thomas Allen who resold it on Feb 22nd 1665 to Roger Goodspeed. Dolar's farm in Concord remained in the possession of his descendants for at least 225 years. He stayed there about eleven years but apparently did not sever his ties with the Barnstable Church. He moved back to Barnstable where he married in 1666 the widow Joanna (Hull) Bursley, daughter of Rev. Joseph Hull and widow of Captain John Bursley. Rev. Hull was driven from Plymouth Colony for preaching without a license. Joanna's brother, Capt. Tristram Hull, was fined for befriending Quakers. Joanna was living in 1683 on the old Bursley homestead in Barnstable.

Amos Otis wrote of Dolar in *Barnstable Families, Perhaps among all the families which came to New England, not one can be selected more deserving of our esteem and unqualified approbation than that of Dolar Davis. As a man, he was honest, industrious, and prudent; as a Christian, tolerant and exact in the performance of his religious duties; as a neighbor, kind obliging, and ever ready to help those who needed his assistance, and as a father and head of his family, he was constantly solicitous for the welfare of all its members, cultivating those kindly feelings and amenities of love, which render home delightful. His sons and grand-sons followed in his footsteps. They were men whose characters stand unblemished. It is pleasant to read their wills on record, and note the affection with which they speak of the members of their families, and their desire to provide not only for their immediate wants, but for the future prospective misfortunes or necessities of any of their kindred. The latter remark, however, will apply more particularly to Samuel of whom a more particular account will be given.* Dolar wrote his will on Sep 13th 1672 and died in June 1673 in Barnstable. The inventory was dated Jun 19th 1673. His son, John, was sole executor and the will was proved Jul 2nd 1673. Having already provided for sons, Simon and Samuel, his son, John, was given his house and land in Concord and his carpenter tools, serge suit and cloak. The inventory totaled £125.05.07.

The Ancestry Chart of Peace Davis follows:

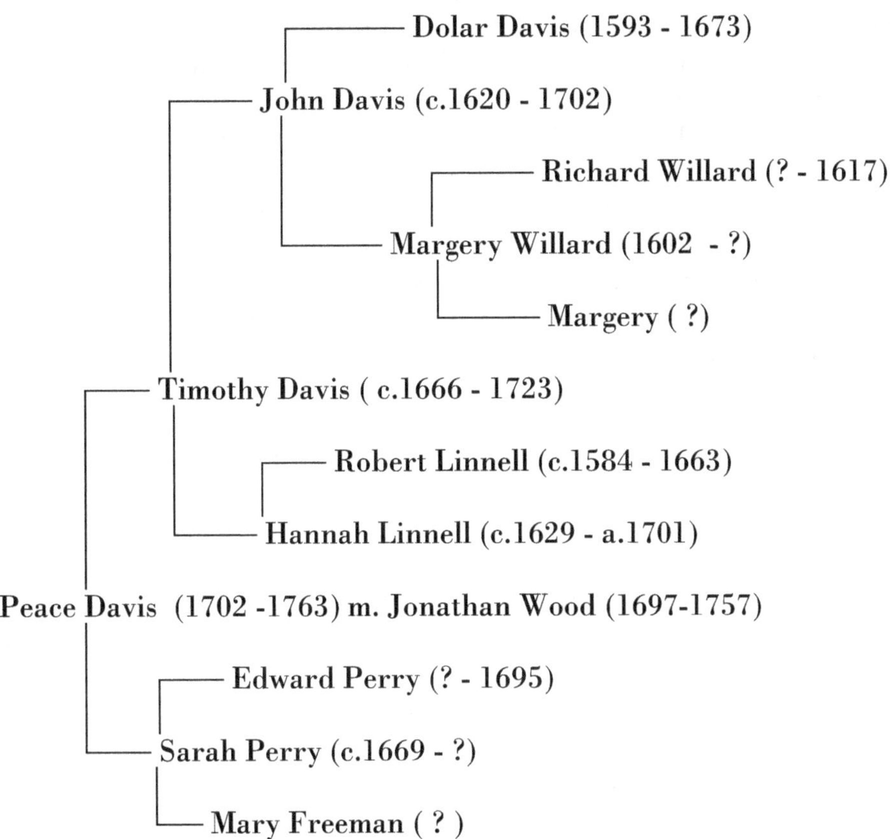

Peace Davis' husband, Jonathan[4] Wood, late of Dartmouth, wrote his will on Jun 12th 1756 witnessed by William and John Macomber and Joshua Cornell, which was affirmed by them at probate "being to the people called Quakers" on Aug 2nd 1757 before George Leonard. The inventory was dated Jul 26th 1757 and presented by his wife. To wife, Peace, a choice of my horses with side saddle and bridle plus two cows and a feather bed with sufficient bedding. To daughter, Sarah Tripp, a feather bed with bedding plus my book called Sewels history. To son, Daniel, land bought of Edward Winslow and ye house upon it in which he resides plus a piece of salt meadow bought of Nathan Soule together plus all the real or personal lying in the government in New York State, also my Great Bible. To son, Israel, my homestead farm that my father willed me with the piece of land bought of William Soule and buildings excepting ye privileges hereafter given to my wife, but not to be given to him until age twenty-five. He also to have a horse and 2 cows on his farm at his own charge, winter and summer, for his mother so long as she remains my widow. When he comes into possession he to provide his mother with one hundred fifty weight of beef yearly and every year so long as she remains my widow plus ten bushel of corn yearly and sufficient firewood yearly. To granddaughter, Peace Barker, when she arrives at age twenty one, one feather bed with bedding plus all moveables which I took into my care when her mother, Hannah Barker, deceased. To grandson James Barker one year and vantage heifer when twenty one. To my wife a half part of my dwelling house, half of the cellar, and use of half of orchard and garden for use and improvement plus privilege of ye run of swine yearly. Also use and improvement of all real estate given to son, Israel, until he is twenty five and use of the remaining part of my personal estate not disposed of, in lieu of her right of dower, and at her decease to be divided equally among my surviving children, this to allow her to bring up Israel until age twenty five and granddaughter, Peace Barker, until age twenty one or marriage. His wife, Peace, was executrix. Jonathan[4] Wood and Peace Davis' son:

Daniel[5] Wood, son of Jonathan[4] Wood and Peace Davis, was born Nov 14th 1729, at Dartmouth, MA. Daniel was a member of the Friends Society and referred to himself as a yeoman in his will. He was forty-four years old when the Stamp and Quartering Acts were imposed on the colonies by the British in March 1765, but it news didn't reach Massachusetts until September. The Quartering Act had little impact other than in New York where most of the British troops were stationed. The Stamp Act required revenue stamps to be affixed to all official documents and printed matter. This would impact the buying and selling of real estate, wills, and other legal matters. It probably had some impact on the Friends. Even though the initial reaction was peaceable, nine delegates from various colonies drew up a Declaration of Rights and Grievances in October. The populace chose of policy of nonimportation of English goods and to break off the custom of wearing black while in mourning since this clothing was generally of British manufacture. The inhabitants agreed to eat no lamb during the year to increase production of wool, but this met with little success. The Stamp Act wasn't repealed until March 1766. Then came the Townshend Act of June 1767, a new series of taxation. A tax was imposed on paper of all kinds, painter's lead, glass, tea, and many other things which caused a lot of grumbling among the colonists. The British established the American Board of Customs Commission and within two days, thirty-two ounces of silver came out of the hard earned money and a hungry Massachusetts economy. Bostonians resisted with a war of published words with the subsequent formation of the Sons of Liberty. Before its repeal, thousands of pounds of currency made its way into English coffers. Daniel died at age 44, four days after the Boston Tea Party which left his family to face the Revolutionary War.

Daniel married 1st Jul 30th 1752 in Swansea, MA, Susannah Chase. Witnesses were: Jonathan Wood, Stephen Chase, Job Anthony, John Hathaway, Joseph ?Flood, Jonathan Luther, Edward Upton, Thomas Church, Isaac Pearce, Jacob Hathaway, John Shove, Elisha Chase, Thomas Dawes Jr, James ?Gubbon, Philip Tripp, Joseph Buffinton, Joseph Shearman, Abigail ?, Ruth Stafford, Abigail Buffinton, Sarah Wood, Sarah Shove and Esther Chase.

Susanna Chase was born Nov 1st 1735, in Swansea, MA, the fourth of eleven children of Stephen (Joseph[3], William[2,] William[1]) and Esther (Buffington) Chase who married in Swansea Nov 11th 1728 and was witnessed by: Benjamin Buffington, William Chase, William Buffington, Benjamin Buffinton, Susanah Buffington, Mary Chase, Lydia Davis, Nicholas Davis, Isaac Chase, William Wood, Abraham Anthony, Oliver Earl, Samuel Baker, Edward Slead, Daniel Baker, Nicholas Otis and Job Chase. Susanna died at Dartmouth Jan 19th 1765

Children of Daniel and Susannah (Chase) Wood born at Dartmouth, MA, were:

1. Abigail[6] Wood, b. Jan 31st 1754; m. Jan 23rd 1778 John Wanton in Dartmouth, MA.
2. Stephen Wood, b. Jan 29th 1756; m. 1st Oct 1st 1780 Deborah Allen in Dartmouth; m. 2nd Jun 21st 1784. m 3rd Elizabeth Cornell in the First Stanford Church, Bangall, Dutchess, NY. Stephen d. Sep 13th 1827, in Washington, Dutchess, NY.
3. Esther Wood, b. Jul 4th 1758; m. May 14th 1778 Robert Allen at Dartmouth, MA. She d. Jul 28th 1824 in New Bedford, Bristol, MA.
+4. Jonathan Wood, b. Dec. 9th 1760 at Westport, MA. He married. Rachel White; b. Jan 18th 1764.
+5. David Wood, b. May 7th 1764; d. Sep 26th 1824. He married Rest Macomber.

Daniel married 2nd Jun 30th 1767 in Dartmouth, MA, Susannah Wood, born May 7th 1746 in Dartmouth, daughter of Esek and Sarah (Tripp) Wood. She died Dec 12th 1767, in Dartmouth having no children.

Daniel[5] married 3rd Oct 5th 1769 at Dartmouth, the widow of Cornelius Coggeshall, Mehitable (Thurston) Coggeshall, daughter of Jonathan and Lydia Thurston. She was born Nov 13th 1741. Cornelius was the son of John Coggeshall and Elizabeth Timberlake, daughter of Henry and Mary Timberlake. After Daniel died in 1773, Mehitable married 3rd Feb 19th 1777, in Dartmouth, Benjamin Chase, son of Stephen and Esther Chase, formerly of Freetown, late of Nova Scotia.

Children of Daniel and Mehitable Wood were:[6]

6. Lydia Wood, b. Jul 13th 1770 in Dartmouth, MA. On Jan 17th 1789, she removed on certificate from Acoaset, Massachusetts to Rhode Island. She left Rhode Island MM for New Bedford MM,

a single woman on Aug 19th 1794.
7. Susanna Wood, b. Mar 26th 1773 in Westport, MA. She removed from Acouset, MA, to Rhode Island on Oct 17th 1795, a single woman.
8. Daniel Wood, b. Feb 5th 1774, in Westport, MA, after his father's death.

Daniel's will dated Jul 1st 1773, says much about his character, literacy and occupational abilities. Oh, to see his ivory headed cane. To his wife, Mehetabel, all the household furniture she brought with her with my best bed and furniture, my best horse, my best cow, ten of my choice sheep, and one swine. To son Stephen, all land bought of Timothy Davol, he paying hereafter mentioned, my Great Bible, my small grindstone, my best saddle and all my shoe making implements. To son Jonathan, all that part of my homestead farm as noted and one half of my cedar swamp, my watch, my next biggest Bible, my gun, my great grind stone, my ivory headed cane, and my next best saddle. To son David, the remainder of my homestead together with my salt meadow and one half my cedar swamp, he performing hereafter mentioned, plus my Dictionary, all my mathematical instruments and books with the residue of my estate except that further given. My debts and funeral charges to be paid with my money & credits so far as they extend, the remainder from livestock not disposed of. To my three sons the remainder of my live stock & all my farming utensils to be equally divided after my son, David, arrives at lawful age, my wife using them until that time. To my two daughters, Abigail and Esther, all household furniture that was their mothers to be equally divided. To Abigail my side saddle and one marked silver spoon. To Esther my Pileon & one marked silver spoon. To four daughters, Abigail, Esther, Lydia & Susanna all the remainder of my household furniture to be equally divided. To Abigail & Esther the use of the westerly half of the dwelling house that I gave my son Stephen, together with a privilege in the well and oven so long as they remain single. To daughter-in-law [step-daughter], Elizabeth Coggeshall, & my daughters Lydia & Susanna, the privilege of living in the northerly end of my now dwelling so long as they remain single. To my sd wife the use of all my estate, real & personal, until each of my children arrive at lawful age, provided she provide for such as shall need support. Also during her widowhood, the use of the northerly half of my now dwelling house with privilege of well, cellar & oven and the use of my new garden and orchard with the keeping of one cow, one swine, two ?, and her father & mother, brother & sister's horses when they come to see her at any time on that part of my land given to my son, Jonathan. Also three pound yearly after my son Stephen be of lawful age to be paid by my son Jonathan, also the keeping of six sheep yearly with their increase yearly until the tenth day of the twelfth month on that part of my land given to my son, David. The aforesaid gifts are in lieu of dower or power of third. Also to enable her to support my children in their minority. To my three sons my wearing apparel to be distributed to them at the discretion of my executrix. To my two daughters, Abigail & Esther, thirty shillings to be paid to them by my son, Stephen, at their marriage. Daniel died Dec 20th 1773, at Westport, Bristol, MA. Daniel's first wife, Susanna's ancestry follows.

Susanna Chase's Ancestry

William[1] Chase was born in England about 1595. William, his wife Mary Townley and son William from Wivenhoe, Essex, departed England in 1630 with the Winthrop fleets. He settled in Roxbury until 1637 before moving to the newly formed settlement at Yarmouth where he participated in the land division and was appointed constable on Mar 5th 1638/9. At the time William contracted to build a house for Thomas Starr who sold it before completion to Andrew Hallet, jr. It was agreed to be delivered *thatched, studded, and latched, daubing excepted* for ten pounds. Twenty-nine acres of land were included in the deal. Houses at the time were usually daubed with clay in the crevices and oiled paper used at windows. A daughter Mary was born at Yarmouth who died at age fifteen. A son Benjamin was born and later married Hannah Sherman, daughter of Philip and Sarah (Odding) Sherman. William and his son, William, were on the *Able to Bear Arms* list in 1643. He took the freeman's oath in 1657. Shortly after writing a will he died May 1659 in Yarmouth, MA. His youngest son Benjamin was given one heifer calf and two steer calves a year or more old. His eldest son William who hath had of me already a good portion, 5 shillings, if he demand it. To wife Mary, rest of goods with house, land and appurtenances bought of William Palmer during her natural life. If she continues a widow and decides to dispose of a third, the other two parts to our son Benjamin. William and Mary's eldest son:

William[2] Chase was born about 1622 and came with his parents to New England about 1630. In Yarmouth they lived on the east side of the Bass River near the Herring River. William took the oath of fidelity in Yarmouth in 1657. He died Feb 7th 1685. The General Court ordered on Jun 2nd 1685, Capt. John Thacher and Mrs. Barnabas Lothrop to settle his estate. Apparently he had more than one wife but some of the town records were destroyed. It is known that William was the father of eight children:

1. William m. Jun 25th 1704 Sarah Carter d/o Robert at Swansea. (Probably his 2nd.)
2. Jacob whose wife was Mary (?).
3. John m. Elizabeth Baker 1674. 4. Elizabeth m. Daniel Baker May 27th 1674.
5. Abraham m. Elizabeth (?).
+6. Joseph[3] m. Sarah Sherman Feb 28th 1694.
7. Benjamin m. Ammie (?) Sep 21st 1696; dau. Hope d. Feb 14th 1715 at Tiverton.
8. Samuel m. Sara Sherman 1699. Children b. Swansea: Phebe, Martha, Susanna, Elisha, Samuel, & Eliezer.

William's eight children would become associated with the Society of Friends. William's son:

Joseph[3] Chase was born about 1665 in Portsmouth, RI, the sixth of eight children of William[2] and Mary Chase. As a yeoman he participated in the Shewomet Purchase. In 1681 he became a member of the Sandwich Monthly Meeting and the Rhode Island Friends at Portsmouth from 1688 until he moved to Swansea. His marriage to Sarah Sherman on Feb 28th 1693/4 was recorded in the Rhode Island Monthly Meeting records. Joseph and Sarah's children were:

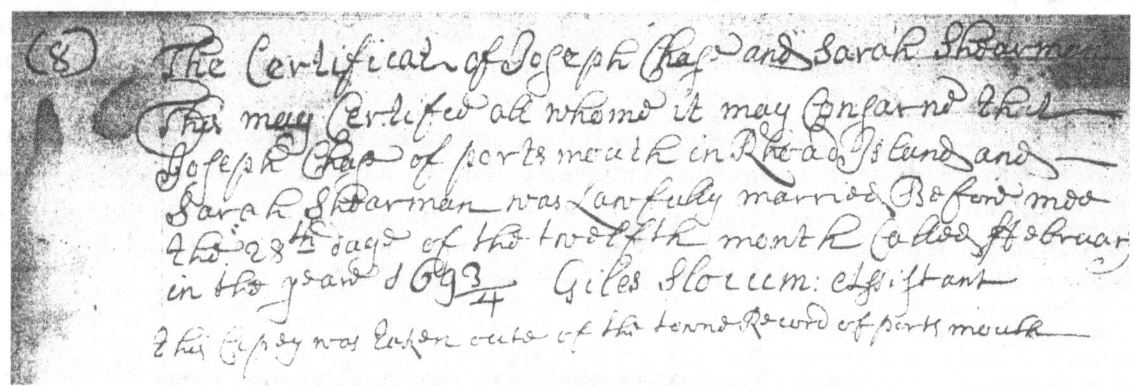

Marriage Certificate of Joseph Chase and Sarah Sherman

1. Abigail b. Jul 5th 1695 in Portsmouth, RI, m. Aug 27th 1730 John Davis; children Mary, Job, Eben & Amey Davis.
2. Lydia b. Oct 28th 1696 in Portsmouth, RI, m. Mar 4th 1716/7 Thomas Davis; children: Thomas, Alice, Joseph, Lydia, Benjamin, Job, Moses, Aaron, & Stephen Davos.
3. Job b. Oct 21st 1698 in Portsmouth, RI; m. Nov 6th 1718 Patience Bourne at Swansea; children: Job, Susannah, Joseph, Ebenezer, Jonathan & Ichabod Chase.
4. Alice b. Sep 16th 1699 in Wickapimsett.
5. Ruth Chase b. Apr 15th 1702.
6. Sampson Chase b. Apr 2nd 1704.
7. Isabel Chase b. Oct 6th 1705, m. Aug 8th 1726 Benjamin Buffington; children: Sarah, Benjamin,

Moses, Stephen, Elizabeth, & Hannah Buffington.

8. Joseph Chase b. Jul 11th 1707.

+9. Stephen[4] Chase b. May 2nd 1709; m. Nov 11th 1728 at Swansea, Esther Buffington d/o Benj. & Hannah Buffington.

10. Sarah Chase b. Aug 14th 1711; m. Nov 20th 1730 at Swansea, George Shove, s/o Edward & Lydia Shove of Swansea; children: George, Sarah, Stephen and Ruth Shove.

11. Silas Chase b. about 1713 in Swansea, MA; m. 1st Dec 20th 1733 at Swansea, Hannah Buffington; children b. Swansea: Silas, Uriah, Daniel, Elizabeth, Hannah, Esther, & Patience Chase. Silas m. 2nd May 27th 1774 at Swansea, Sarah Tucker Chase, d/o of Moses & Sarah Tucker, widow of Elisha Chase.

12. George Chase b. about 1715 in Swansea, MA; m. Feb 8th 1736, Lydia Shove d/o Edward & Lydia Shove; children b. Swansea: George, Edward, Benjamin, Micajah, Paul, Sarah & Huldah Chase.

13. Ebenezer Chase b. Swansea, MA.

14. Moses Chase b. about 1718 in Swansea, MA; M. Mar 25th 1742 at Swansea, Alice Sherman d/o Samuel and Martha (Tripp) Sherman. Children: Samuel, William, Elizabeth, Grissel, Moses, Joseph, Sarah, Mary, & Alice Chase.

Their father, Joseph Chase, died at Swansea in Dec 1724.[1] His wife's Ancestry follows:

Sherman Family History

The name Shearman or Sherman surname derives from their occupation. Sarah Sherman's ancestors were located in Essex County east of London where the known Celtic Trinovantes tribe used the dye from the woad plant to paint their faces. The city of Colchester became the Roman capital in Britain. It was the blue dye of woad that centuries later created a wealthy merchant class who dealt in woolen and linen cloth until indigo crushed the woad trade. Woad, now extinct in England, is the biennial plant *Isatis tinctoria*, its leaves producing the dye. Flemish weavers had come to England in the 1300's bringing their superior methods of making cloth. Local weavers adopted these more advanced methods in cloth making. In 1628, John Endicott of Massachusetts Bay Colony imported woodwax or Dyer's Green weed *Genista tinctoria* whose leaves produce a yellow dye that was needed for the colony's wool and flax cloth. Eventually the plant became invasive around Salem where it covered the meadows and hills and is still found in the area's woods. Mixed with woad it produced a rich green dye.

During Saxon days there were sheep in Essex, its wool used in weaving. Prior to 1506, Britain depended on importing superior cloth even though Flemish weavers had settled as early as 1300 at Sudbury about ten miles from the town of Dedham. The town lies next to the narrow but navigable Stour River located about six miles from Colchester. Much later Henry VIII allowed English weavers to sell cloth retail as well as wholesale accelerating a rise in the wool market creating a new class of wealthy merchants.

Henry[1] Shearman or Sherman the elder had been apprenticed in the shearman's craft. A shearman did not shear sheep. Clothiers or shearman were middlemen who bought lengths of cloth from cottage weavers, dressed (sheared) and dyed it, sorted it for quality, baled and marked it with his trademark, then carted it to a Colchester warehouse for market. A clothier's residence was combined with a counting room, woadhouse, and storerooms. At the time most were built in Tudor style with a Flemish designed business attachment, like a large leanto.

The shearman or clothier trade was good to Henry Sherman. In 1554 he became a copyholder of Dedham Hall and paid large sums in taxes to Henry VIII's increasing demands in filling the royal till. The manor court rolls of 1561 show Henry living at "Woodowse." Woadhouses were dye-houses important to wealthier clothiers who performed this task for those that did not have the facility. Like

---

1 Bristol co., MA, Probate Vol. 5, pp. 8, 37-39, 449-450.

many prominent men, Henry's family held civic positions.

In a deposition taken on October 11th 1574 at Dedham in the case of Seckford v. Forth, Henry established his age as 62 or there about and had only lived in Dedham for eleven years. Henry's statement determined that he was born approximately in 1511/12 in Catholic England and moved to Dedham about 1534 when Henry VIII declared the Act of Supremacy followed the next year by the beginning of the dissolution of monasteries and other church properties. Henry Shearman married around 1540 Agnes Butter and had seven children, two dying before his will was written. Dedham Manor records of 1548 noted that on Wednesday, Easter week, Henry should *remove rubbish from the footway against his house.* After the King's death, the news was who would get the throne. Eventually Elizabeth I became Queen and granted Thomas Seckford the manors of Netherhall and Overhall in 1562. Maps presented showed Henry Shearman's land parcel at Netherhall.[1] Henry's wife Agnes was buried Oct 14th 1580. Henry married 2nd at Dedham on Jun 5th 1581, the widow Maryan Wilson.

The April 12th 1581 manor rolls show that Henry surrendered one messuage and dwelling house and twenty acres of land and meadow called Summers to the use of his son, Henry, the son paying his father £8 yearly during his father's lifetime. He made a similar arrangement on Oct 7th 1583 with his son Edmund, twelve acres having been purchased from Seckford. Henry moved to Colchester where he died in 1590 and was buried in the parish church at Dedham as requested in his will dated Jan 20th 1589 with a Codicil dated the following Feb 16th.[2]

It is a wonderful lengthy will in that he not only names his children and grandchildren but sets the stage for costs of living, dedication to church and poor, one's wealth and language use at the time. To Dr. Chapman, the preacher of Dedham, £6 to be paid within six months after my decease. To Mr. Parker forty shillings to be paid at the same time. To the poor of Dedham £20 to be *contynewall* stock for the poor to the world's end and the benefit of it go to the poor. My will is that it shall be ordered at the discretion of the governors of the free school of Dedham or the greatest part of them to take security for the principal. His son Henry was bequeathed his Shearman's crafte in addition to the house and household goods already in his possession. His grandchildren of son Henry: Henry, Samuel, Daniel, John, Ezechiell, Phebe, Nathaniel, and Anne were given £5 each at age twenty-two for the boys and twenty-one for the girls. To his grandson, Edmond, son of Edmond, £13.13.04 at age twenty-two or divided between his siblings Richard, Bezaliell, and Anne if he dies before age twenty-two. The siblings were also given forty shillings when at the ages previously mentioned. His son, Edmond was given his best cloak. £20 was bequeathed to his son-in-law William Petfeild and £6.13.04 to Petfeild's children, Richard, Susan and Elizabeth in like manner. To my wife, Margery, £22 to be paid within three months after my decease and all the household stuff she brought me and that household which we renewed and bought since we married. Also twenty shillings plus £12 due from Fendring if my executors can recover it from him. My wife also to have two years of dwelling in that part of the house we now dwell, that is the lower parlor and two chambers next to Mr. Ruddes and part of the *backehouse* if my son Robert do enjoy the house. If the house is redeemed then Robert shall pay Margery £4 for two years dwellings. Margery to have my tipped pott for the term of her life, then to daughter, Judith. If Margery make claim or title to thirds or any part of that house wherein I now dwell, she shall be *frustrate* of the £22 and it to be divided between my sons, Henry, Edmond, and Robert. Also she shall put in bond to my Executors before she receives my part of her legacy that she will not molest my executor or son Robert. To son Robert, three score pounds which I give for the state of the house wherein I now dwell, lately Richard Kings, Beerbruer of Colchester. If the three score pounds is not paid according to bargain and sale in time appointed, then I give the aforesaid house with yards and appurtenances to my son, Robert. Also Robert to have the copyhold called the Heckells, or known by any other name, containing an estimated fifteen acres with barn and cottage and two acres called Byrdes, now in occupation of William Petfeild. Also to Robert, £40 to be paid to him within six months after my decease to be divided between the living children of Robert when they come of age. Also to Robert the household stuff I had before I married Margery, that is, beds, featherbeds, cupboards, bedsteads, pillows, brass, pewter, hangings, together with the great cupboard in the parlor and the sealing with the three tapestry cushions. Also

---

1 Bertha L. Stratton. *New Light on Henry Sherman of Dedham, Essex, England,* 1954, pp. 3, 34

2 Essex County England Wills, D/DCmF1/165

three pair of sheets and all other household implements, my silver and gilt goblet, my best gown, one sword and belt. To daughter, Judith Petfeild, the chest and linen upon the *Soller* (three pair of sheets excepted those given to Robert. To son, Henry, twelve silver spoons. To son-in-law, Nicholas Fynce, four shillings. To the poor of Allhallows parish six shillings, eight pence. To son Robert the *typped* pot which he has, to son Henry all my arms except those given to Robert. If the £40 due unto my by the administrators of Richard King, beerbruer be recovered, then it to be equally divided between my five children. To daughter, Judith my side saddle and cloth to it. To son Robert, my saddle. To William Petfeild, my best gown save that given to Robert. To Henry my best cassock hat and nightcap. To Christopher Stone a cloth doublet. To Caser an old pair of hose. To Richard Fycher my old gown. To each of my sons twenty shillings in gold and to their wives the same. Also to daughter, Judith. The half year rent due at my decease of all my lands and tenements shall go to the performance of my will. To my three sons all goods un-bequeathed to be equally divided. The Codicil was for some respit of paying legacies by my Executors. That £20 for the poor shall be paid at our Lady day next twelve months. I will that Dr. Chapmans £6 be paid the same time. Also that Nicholas Fynce's forty shillings be then paid. Son Robert to have £5 paid to him next Lady day and £10 the next midsummer, and £35 at Lady Day come next twelve months. The legacies for son Edmond's children to paid at our Lady day come twelve months. That Petfeild have £40 paid him next midsummer. Whereas the £20 given to the poor was appointed to be ordered by the governors of the free school at Dedham. Now my mind is that my son Henry shall have the occupying of it to be bestowed in woolen and linen cloth. My executors to pay son Robert use for £35 for the latter half year. Sons Henry and Edmond, Executors.

According to his father-in-law, Thomas Butter's will dated Aug 20th 1555, proved May 7th 1556, Thomas made Henry Sherman co-executor with William Butter. Thomas Butter bequeathed Henry Shearman's wife a silver pott. Butter's wife was named Marion and his daughters named in his will besides Henry Shearman's wife were: Agnes Rolffe, Alice Percival and Alice Butter his youngest daughter. It was not uncommon at that time to give the same name to children. The only record located of Henry's children was the christening of his son, Robert, at St. Mary's Church in Dedham whose church records began in 1560. Henry and Agnes' son:

Henry[2] Sherman, jr. was born about 1546. He married Susan/Ann Lawrence Jun 14th 1568 at Moze, Essex, daughter of John Lawrence, who was chr. May 21st 1548 at Moze. Her brother, Thomas, was chr. May 21st 1551. These dates are located in the parish records. The names Ann and Susan at that time were usually synonymous. Henry continued his father's shearman trade living a comfortable life style.

Susan's brother Thomas Lawrence died in 1614 possessing the Mark Tay property which was mentioned because John Lawrence sold a third part of lands held by his father, Thomas, to his brothers Thomas and Robert on Nov 8th 1555. The Lawrence lineage is: Thomas Lawrence who possessed the Mark Tay property had sons: John, Thomas, and Robert. John had two children: Ann/Susan who married Henry Shearman and Thomas Lawrence of Esthorpe.

Henry Sherman Jr.'s will dated Aug 20th 1610 was as lengthy as his father's will. He was buried at Dedham eight days later. His wife, Susan wrote one Aug 31st 1610 and was buried Sep 13th 1610. Henry and Susan had eleven children whose baptisms are found in Dedham records. They were Phebe Fenne, Henry, Samuel, Susan/Anne Wilson, Daniel, Sarah, Nathaniel who died age two days, John, Ezekiel, Edmund, and Mary who died young.

Susan's will bequeathed the personal luxury items and furnishings given to her by Henry plus her mare and clothing to her children, grandchildren, great grandchildren, her brother and a cousin's daughter. Henry's will mentioned his brother Lawrence and brother-in-law Gilbert Hills. Susan has been noted as Susan Lawrence/Hills. "My brother Lawrence" refers to Susan's brother, Thomas Lawrence or Esthorpe, who was sued in 1600 with Henry. Gilbert Hills could be a husband of a half-sister of Susan to whom she would feel closer than Henry or a half-brother. Both referred to Edmund Galloway as a cousin which leaves one to ponder the exact relationship. Henry and Susan's son,

Samuel[3] Shearman was chr. Jan 11th 1573 at Dedham. He married around 1598, Phillipa Ward, daughter of Lancelot Ward of Lexden, Essex, and Mary Upcher. Lancelot was chr. Feb 4th 1550 at Dedham, son of John Ward and Margaret Parson. Phillipa Ward's parents, Lancelot and Mary had children: Phillipa, Upcher, Robert and John Ward.

Samuel and Phillipa Shearman had seven children baptized in Dedham: 1) Mary, 2) Samuel who died in Boston, MA, 3) Henry who died young, 4) Henry who died in Boston, 5) Martha, 6) Sarah who died young, and +7) Philip. The surviving Sherman children grew up during the reign of James I as problems simmered over taxation and religion in England. Before young Philip became of age in 1632, a new king was crowned and the wool trade had collapsed, Plymouth Colony had been settled for over a decade, and Puritans were flooding into New England. For Samuel's sons opportunities looked brighter across the Atlantic. Samuel[3] died in Feb 1615 at Ardley, Essex. We learn more about Samuel from his will. He inherited considerable land and appeared to be a landlord as shown in his will made Jan 20th 1615 shortly before his death.

> *To wife Phillippa all my lands, tenements, houses, edifices, buildings, yard Orchards, gardens with the appurtenances lying within the parish of Dedham, or elsewhere during her natural life. Son Henry to receive my copyhold called Hardings in Dedham with houses, barns, orchards, etc. where Thomas Cole now dwells with two acres adjoining on the north side and two fields, one lying next the heath called Dedham Heath, containing four acres, the other a close or field called Poppes field of an estimated four acres after my wife's decease. Sons Samuel and Phillip five closes of land occupied by Lionel Cheute an estimated eight acres and those lands late occupied by John Wrench after my wife's decease. If either Samuel or Philip depart this life before age twenty-two and without issue then to son Henry together with the close Poppes field and meadow in Coxepittd after my wife's decease. If either Samuel or Phillip survive, all lands, etc. called Hardings to the survivor, if neither to son Henry. To daughters Mary and Martha "XL4i" at age twenty-one. My wife to have profits and all goods to bring up children in a good manner. If she dies before all children are age twenty-two, the executor to enjoy same to bring up my children. To the poor of Ardley fifteen shillings. To Mr. John Rogers of Dedham, twenty shillings. Wife Phillipa and John Upcheire of Dedham, my brother-in-law,* executors. Here again is another confusing brother-in-law. Samuel and Phillipa's son:

Philip[4] Shearman was chr. Feb 5th 1609/10. He left England about 1633 settling in Roxbury, MA. There he married Sarah Odding, daughter of George and Margaret (Lang) Odding. Their first two of eight children were born in Roxbury where he was admitted a freeman on May 14th 1634. He became sympathetic to Anne Hutchinson, the daughter of a clergyman, who criticized ministers and was one of the Roxbury men ordered disarmed, then all were banished from the Bay Colony on Oct 2nd 1637. The men departed from Boston to settle in New Hampshire. Finding the climate too severe they headed south for the island of Aquidneck, later Portsmouth, RI, in Narragansett Bay. Upon arrival, Roger Williams advised the men to purchase land. On Mar 7th 1638 nineteen men signed an article of incorporation known as the Portsmouth Compact for purchasing land from the Indian chief, Aquetnet. The sale was completed Mar 24th. A government was formed Jul 1st 1639 with the disbursement of land to follow. So a new life began settling in this area. It entailed keeping the peace, rating taxes, keeping Newport men from intruding on their lands, auditing books, preventing the embezzling of wood from the Commons, preventing sheep being driven into the Commons, and laying out highways. Philip was chosen as the Rhode Island Colony's first Secretary, later town clerk. It is said he used his Shearman Crest on neatly written town records, land leases, family papers, deeds and monuments. At a town council meeting on May 16th 1651 it was ordered that Philip be paid £5 for the five years he served as clerk plus 5 shillings for writing out general court orders. He contributed greatly to Rhode Island's settlement.

Philip Shearman's will was dated Jul 30th 1681, proved Mar 22nd 1686/7.

First, wife, Sarah, the use and her dwelling in the first room at the west end of my dwelling house, bed and bedding with its furniture. His son, Samuel, executor, to see that his wife is maintained with food and raiment and all necessities during her natural life. Also ten good ewe sheep for her sole use for yearly wool, and kept by my executor without any charge to her. To eldest son, Eber, that already given him, ten acres of land in Portsmouth called Briggs swamp that joins to a parcel of his land and all my horse flesh in Narrangansett except one mare, the second best, I give to Thomas and Peleg Mumford my grandchildren. To son Peleg five ewe sheep. To son Edmund a quarter share of meadow and a 16th part of a share of upland lying in Ponagansett with the township of Dartmouth. Also my whole right in the purchase of Squamscutt now called Westerly by the Colony. To son Samson after the decease of my wife his half of the breadth of my farm I now dwell from the west end to the sea and three rod more in breadth of the whole length bounded south upon a straight line to a land mark about a rod short of the cart way that goes by my dwelling house to my barn in Portsmouth. And from said land mark a third of any hay and grass yearly. Sons Samson and Samuel to have equal privileges in the arable land of my farm during my wife's natural life. Son Samuel all the remaining of my farm with dwelling house and all buildings upon the part of the land lying south of the other part of my farm now given to son Samson after the decease of my wife and two parts of the grass and hay during her natural life. Also all my neat cattle, horse kind, sheep kind and swine except two oxen and a fatting cow. Also all moveable goods, excepting two great chests with locks and keys, which I give to my wife, Samuel my executor paying the legacies herein specified. To son Samson one white faced mare with her foal and those four Indians which we jointly bought. To sons Samson and Samuel my draught horse and two draught steers equally between them. To son John my bay mare. To son Benjamin, the remaining part of my land at Brigg's Swamp where upon Benjamin's house now stands, be estimation twenty acres. To daughter Sarah ten ewe sheep paid one year after my decease. The same to daughter Mary. Daughter Hannah five pounds New England money for proper use of her and her children one year after my decease. Also five ewe sheep one year after my decease. My son Edmund providing Benjamin Clarke with sufficient food and clothing until he becomes of age.

About this time the spelling of the name became Sherman.

The fourteen children of Philip Sherman and Sarah Odding were: 1) Eber, 2) Sarah Mumford, 3) Peleg, 4) Mary who died age 5, 5) Edmund, +6) Samson, 7) William who died age 3, 8) John, 9) Mary Wilbur, 11) Hannah Chase was b. 1647 and m. William Chase, +12) Samuel, 13) Benjamin, and 14) Phillipa Chase. Sons Samson and Samuel married into the Tripp family. This is where the intermingling of these families began.

Samson[5] was born in Apr 1642. He married Isabel Tripp, Mar 4th 1673/4 at Portsmouth, RI, by Joshua Coggeshall, Asst. She was born 1651 at Portsmouth, daughter and eighth child of John and Mary (Paine) Tripp. Samson served as a juryman and that dreaded position of constable serving at grand inquests. Samson died in 1718. They were parents of seven children: 1) Philip, +2) Sarah Chase, 3) Alice Howland, 4) Samson, 5) Abiel, 6) Isabel Baker, and 7) Job Sherman. Members of this family became Rhode Island Friends.

Samuel[5] Sherman, son of Philip[4], was born in 1648, married Martha Tripp, Feb 23, 1680/1, daughter of John and Mary (Paine) Tripp. Their seven children were: Sarah, Mary, Mehitabel, Samuel, Othaniel, John, and Ebenezer Sherman.

Sarah[6] Sherman, daughter of Samson[5] Sherman, was born Sep 24th 1679. She married Joseph Chase, Feb 28th 1693/4 at Portsmouth. Joseph Chase was born about 1665. He participated in the Shewomet Purchase. In 1681, he was a member of the Sandwich, MA, Friends. He moved to Portsmouth about 1688, later to Swansea, MA, where he wrote his will Nov 8th 1724, inventoried Dec 22nd 1724. He made his wife, Sarah, and son, Job, executors. legacies paid to: Abigail Chase, Lydia Davis, Alice Baker, Isabel Chase, Ruth Chase and Job Chase plus monies paid to Sarah Chase as guardian of Sarah, Stephen, Silas, George, and Moses Chase. His sons were: Job, eldest, Stephen, Silas, George, Ebenezer and Moses under age twenty-one. Daughters were Abigail Davis, Lidia Davis, Alice, Sarah and Ruth Chase.

t was their son, Stephen Chase, who married Esther Buffington, Nov 11th 1728 at Swansea, MA, in a Quaker ceremony.

Chase Family Continued

Stephen[4] Chase was born May 2nd 1709 at Portsmouth, RI, the ninth of fourteen children. He married 1st Nov 11th 1728 Esther[4] Buffington at Swamsea, witnessed by: Benjamin Buffington, William Chase, William Buffington, Benjamin Buffinton, Susanah Buffington, Mary Chase, Lydia Davis, Nicholas Davis, Isaac Chase, William Wood, braham Anthony, Oliver Earl, Samuel Baker, Edward Slead, Daniel Baker, Nicholas Otis and Job Chase.

Esther was b. Oct 30th 1712, eldest child of seven children born to Benjamin[3] and Hannah Buffington. Esther's grandfather, Benjamin[2], was the eldest child of Thomas[1] Buffington who d. in Swansea in 1729. Thomas' will dated Feb 16th 1726 was proved Nov 11th 1727. It said he was aged and son Thomas was deceased. Also mentioned son Benjamin and daughter Abigail King. Esther's father's will was proved Feb 4th 1739/40 and said he was a husbandman with an estate valued at more than £434. No wife was mentioned in either will. Four of his children married into the Chase family. Stephen and Esther had eleven children born in Freetown, Bristol Co., MA:

1. Hannah b. Feb 22nd 1739; m. Jul 25th 1747 Joseph Slade.
2. Sarah b. Nov 18th 1731; m. Nov 18th 1742 Jonathan Luther.
3. Esther b. Oct 5th 1733; m. Nov 11th 1753 Thomas Earle.
+4. Susannah b. Nov 1st 1735.
5. Benjamin b. Jan 29th 1737.
6. Stephen b. Apr 3rd 1740.
7. Joseph b. Apr 13th 1742.
8. Asa b. Aug 4th 1744.
9. Jethro b. Jun 13th 1746.
10. Peace b. Aug 5th 1748, m. Nov 26th 17767 David Baker.
11. Comfort b. Jul 10th 1750, m. Feb 18th 1773 Samuel Upton.

Esther Buffington Chase d. Jul 14th 1750. Stephen Chase m. 2nd Basheba Stafford Apr 20th 1751 & d. about 1763. Stephen m. 3rd Aug 3rd 1764 Abigail Porter at Nova Scotia. He was last known to be in Nova Scotia dying Jun 23rd 1790.

Susannah[5] Chase was born Nov 1st 1735 in Swansea, MA, the fourth of eleven children born to Stephen[4] Chase and Esther Buffington. She married Daniel Wood in Swansea Jul 30th 1752. Susanna died at Dartmouth Jan 19th 1765. Their son:

Wood Family Continued

Jonathan Wood, b. Dec. 9th 1760 at Westport, MA. He married 1st Sep 28th 1783 in the First Stanford Church, Bangall, Dutchess, NY. Rachel White; b. Jan 18th 1764. At a Monthly Meeting held at Nine Partners, NY, Jul 14th 1784, Rachel was disowned for marrying by a Priest, *contrary to the rules of Friends after being Precautioned...until by admission of her error she shall Condemn the same to the Satisfaction of that meeting.* Jonathan and Rachel White Wood were parents of twelve children:

1. Phebe, b. Feb 16th 1785; m. Thomas Nichols Feb 6th 1800 at Peru, Clinton, NY.
2. Esther, b. Dec 3rd 1786; m. Israel Irish at Peru, NY. He d. Apr 18th 1861 at Lynn Co., IA.
3. Daniel, b. Jan 19th 1789; m. 1st Apr 30th 1812 at Peru, NY, Phebe Benedict d/o Reuben Benedict & Anna Stephens. He settled in Peru Twp., where the east branch of Alum Creek ran diagonally and was surveyed and plotted as South Woodbury. Its first cabin was built by Joseph Horr.
4. Amy, b. Feb 22nd 1791, m. (?) Peasley.
5. David, b. Dec 19th 1792; m. Sep 2nd 1819 Alum Creek, OH, Esther Mosher d/o Asa and Bethia Mosher. Asa Mosher settled just south of today's Mt. Gilead and Cardington where he built a grist and saw mill.
6. Susannah, b. Feb 7th 1795, m. (?) Kingman.
7. Israel C., b. Apr 14th 1797; m. Dec 30th 1819 in Delaware Co., OH, Mary H. Thurston.
8. Lydia, b. May 5th 1799; m. Sep 30th 1819, David Osborn.
9. Jonathan, b. Sep 1st 1801; m. Jan 29th 1824 Columbiana Co., OH, Mary Ashton.
10. Reuben, b. Dec 3rd 1803; m. Feb 11th 1826 Morrow Co., OH, Anna (?) b. VT.
11. Rachel, b. Dec 2nd 1804; m. 1st Nov 1823, Caleb Hathaway; m. 2nd (?) Washburne.
12. Matilda, b. 1808; m. Dec 28th 1826, Slocum H. Bunker s/o Isaac Bunker and Mary Smith.

22nd 6th mo. 1793 Acouset. Beloved Friends -- These are to inform that Jonathan Wood now living at Danby [Danby MM, VT, was formed from Easton MM in 1795] within the verge of your meeting was formerly a member of our meeting but for some misconduct was dismissed and hath since made Friends Satisfaction and is restored to membership with us. Therefore as a member of our religious Society we hereby recommend him to your Christian love deferring his growth and prosperity in the Friends. Signed in an on the Behalf of our s[d] meeting by John Mosher, Clerk. On Mar 3rd 1818, Jonathan, Rachel and children Israel, Lydia, Jonathan, Reuben, Rachel and Matilda were received from Peru MM, NY, dated Sep 25th 1817, endorsed by Short Creek MM, OH, Feb 24th 1818, at Alum Creek MM, OH. Jonathan was 58 when they settled on Section 14 in Gilead Twp. with Asa and Bethia Mosher and their family having traveled in winter as far as Cleveland by sled where they acquired wagons to complete their travel. Jonathan's wife, Rachel, d. Sep 26th 1824.

Jonathan was reported married 2nd in Delaware County, Ohio, Feb 2nd 1826, to Desire (?) Osborn.[7]

Alum Creek MM was a stronghold in the Underground Railroad. Some *conductors* in this family were Jonathan, his son Daniel Wood, Joseph Mosher, Aaron L. Osborn, Daniel Osborn, and William Osborn. In Bennington there was three stations where Samuel, Jonathan, and William Wood; Joseph, John and Gideon Mosher; and Reuben, Aaron L. and Dick Benedict served as conductors. *Stations*, (safe houses) were about 10-20 miles apart where the fugitives, were housed, fed, and then transported at night hidden in a spring wagon to the next station.

Desire Wood died Jul 26th 1832, age 70, in Marion County, Ohio. She is buried with Jonathan and Rachel at Gilead Friends Cemetery, Morrow County, Ohio. The Will of Desire Wood, dated Jun 13th (or 30th) 1832, was witnessed by Jonathan Wood Jr. and Griffith Lewis. *I Desire Wood of Marion County and State of Ohio thinking it right to make my will and settle my estate while in health of Body and in soundness of both mind & memory Therefore I give and devise the same in manner and form following Imprimis--I give and devise unto Charles Osborn (the son of Henry Osborn deceased) and to his heirs and assigns forever, a certain piece and parcel of land situate in the first quarter of the sixth township and seventeenth range of the United States Military lands in the State of Ohio, being the northwest corner of lot no. fourteen according to the survey of said quarter, lying on the west of Alum Creek and Bounded on the north by the land of Reuben Benedict on the west by the land belonging to the heirs of Ezra Thern dec'd, and eastward by said Alum Creek containing by estimation thirty acres. Item. I give and bequeath unto Mary Davis my feather bed, Bedding-Bedstead and cord as a free gift. Item. I give and bequeath unto Daniel Osborn, Azar Osborn, Dorcas Osborn, David Osborn Jr. and Charles Osborn all the money and notes of hand which I may have at my decease to be equally divided between them. Item. I give unto Esther Osborn, the widow of Henry Osborn, all my wearing apparel together with all the rest and residue of my estate not herein otherwise disposed of. Finally I hereby nominate and appoint Daniel Osborn Executor of this my will...Signed - sealed and declared by the said Desire Wood* (seal) *Delaware Co., Ohio.* In the May Term 1833 the last will of Desire Wood was produced in open court and proved by testimony.

Jonathan was reported on Oct 24th 1833 to have married 3rd in Delaware Co., OH, Rhoda Mullinix. Jonathan d. May 7th 1839 at age 79, in Delaware Co., Ohio. Buried in Gilead Friends Cemetery, Morrow, OH, with his wives, Rachel and Desire. His tombstone reads: *Jonathan Wood b. 2nd mo 9th day 1760. d. 5th mo 7th day 1839.* Thirty-one Wood family members are buried in this cemetery.

Daniel Wood and Susannah Chase's son:

David[6] Wood was born May 7th 1764 in Dartmouth, MA. David was received at Swansea from Acushnet MM by certificate on Jul 4th 1785. His marriage intention was dated Dec 5th 1785 at Swansea. In early January, the women's monthly meeting found nothing to hinder Rest Macomber's marriage to David and to proceed. David was of Dighton when they married on Jan 18th 1785/6 in Dartmouth. Rest Macomber, daughter of Abiel and Rest (Davol) Macomber, was born Jan 9th 1770 in Westport, MA.

Rest Macomber Ancestry

A Thomas Locke was fined in 1497 for feeding some misguided followers of Perkin Warbeck as they passed Locke's farm in Brockampton, Buckland Newton Parish. Warbeck was a Flemish imposter who tried to claim he was Richard of Shrewsbury, 1st Duke of York, son of Edward IV of England. Edward IV had died suddenly in 1483 and his brother became Richard III who died fighting ending the War of the Roses in 1485. Henry Tudor then claimed the throne ending the reign of the Plantagenets. Warbeck had challenged Henry for England's throne. Once the imposter was caught, he met his demise by execution.

William Locke married 1st a woman named Elizabeth that had several children, among them was Edith born in 1587 and her sister, Elizabeth, who was buried in 1603 at Bridport. William Locke's will written and proved in 1611 stated that he desired to be buried in Cerne Abbas Church. His 2nd wife, Alice Harte Locke's will proved the next year mentioned her brother, Thomas Harte, and requested her brothers-in-laws (step-sons) Thomas and Nicholas Locke as overseers.

Edith Locke married John Macomber on Jun 8th 1607 in St. Mary's Parish Church in Bridport. They had eleven children christened in that church. Bridport was one of our stops after we left London for Cornwall. Its parish church was having a floral festival that day. Across the street was the Friends Meeting House. William[2] Macomber was christened Mar 25th 1610, son of John[1] and Edith (Locke) Macomber of Bridport, Dorset, England. Edith's father William Locke was a tanner from Cerne Abbas Parish, Dorset, located fifteen miles northeast of Bridport. Bordering it northerly is Buckland Newton Parish in which many named Locke lived in earlier centuries.

Young William Macomber left Dorset for New England where he married Jan 16th 1633/4 Ursila Briggs, daughter of Walter and Mary Briggs of Brigg's Harbor, Scituate, MA. We know that he was in Plymouth on Apr 2nd 1638 when it was recorded *Will'm Maycumber, of Dorchester, cooper, is lycensed to dwell within this gov'ment, at Plymouth or elsewhere, upon the testymony of his good behavior hee hath brought with him.*[1] In Sep 1638, he *...is graunted an island lying on the north side of Powder Poynt, & contayning about three or four acres of land, provided that the committees of Duxborrrow doe consent-therevnto, and that he doe not stop the townes cattle from the fresh water thereupon. Liberty is graunted...to fetch tymber tomake hoopes offor vessels for the colonies use at Clarks Island and Sagaquash.*[2] On Aug 3rd 1640,*...is graunted the wood fitt for coopery growing vupon Wood Island, to be used by him so long as he followeth his trade, and forbidding all others to cutt there except for the loading of boats and vessells to carry away the hay.*[3] By 1643 William was living in Duxburrow among those listed as *Able to Bear Arms.* He was sent out to bring in his brother, John, at Taunton for making allarum. In 1650 he and two other men bought land at the North River from Francis and John Cooke. William moved to Marshfield where he was appointed surveyor in 1653 and made a sworn statement on Mar 1st 1655 that he was 45 years old. John Cooke also sold William a quarter part of land in Dartmouth that had been given to John by his father.[4] This land is known as the Village of Westport Point, its boundary on the west branch of Westport River. William's home in Marshfield became a garrison house built of brick ends and wood for protection. It stood near the old railway station in Marshfield Hills where it burned during Revolutionary times. The land stayed in the hands of a descendant until 1908 or later. William and Ursila had eight children, two in this family genealogy, namely William and Hannah. This will not be the first of two or more children in one family that became ancestors.

William[3] Macomber, jr. was born about 1647 and married Mary around 1672, surname unknown. He followed his father's cooper trade. In 1674, the Court found him guilty for "breach of the Sabbath" and he was summoned to appear on July 7th to answer. *Att this Court Willam Maycomber appeered, being summoned to answer for his breach of the Sabbath in a high degree expressed by his goeing to an Indian house on the Sabbath day to demaund a debt, and otherwise abusing two old Indians, is fined forty shillings to the vse of the collonie, accoording to the law, or be publickly whipt.*[5] I bet he paid the fine. All their seven children were born in Dartmouth, MA, according to their vital records. William was among the householders in Dartmouth that signed a petition to the Governor on October 18th 1708. Three years later his will of Apr 1st 1711 was proved Jun 2nd 1711.[6] It named his wife and children. Their son, William Macomber III is noted below.

William Macomber jr's younger sister Hannah was born about 1650 and married Joseph Randall in Scituate, MA, son of William and Elizabeth (Barstow) Randall. William Randall left England on April 24th 1635 for Providence, RI, on the *Expectation.* He moved to Marshfield, then Scituate by 1643. William Randall was a bit feisty and fined on occasions for abusing the constable and breaking the King's peace. Constables were the arm of law most commonly interfacing with people making the position undesirable, especially when taxing people for Magistrates' meals, maintaining ministers, or the harsh treatment of Quakers. Randall's fines were paid in shoes so he was probably a cordwainer. Their son, Joseph Randall, was born in March 1642 at Scituate, baptized there on Nov 23rd 1645. He married Hannah Macomber of Marshfield in Oct 1672. Of their eight children, the first were twin girls, Elizabeth and Ursula born Jul 3rd 1673. Elizabeth Randall married her first cousin, William III Macomber, at Scituate March 9th 1697/8.

William Macomber III, the third child of William II and Mary Macomber, was born at Dartmouth on Dec 24th 1674. He married his first cousin, Elizabeth Randall, on Mar 9th 1697/8. He became a tanner making leather for his wife's family. He also signed the petition to the Governor with his father in 1708. Elizabeth had inherited land in Scituate which was sold on May 10th 1722. William's will dated Jul 17th 1759 wasn't proved until April 6th 1767. It named his children but no wife. He and Elizabeth had ten children born in Dartmouth. The third was a son named William:

---

1 Plymouth Colony Records, V. I, p. 82

2 *Ibid.*, p. 95

3 *Ibid.*, p. 159

4 Plymouth Deeds, V. 3, p. 169

5 Plymouth Court Orders V.7, p. 152

6 Bristol Co., MA, Probate, V.3, pgs. 51-53

William Macomber IV, was born at Dartmouth Mar 29th 1701/2. Little is known of this William except he witnessed the will of Jonathan Wood. William[4] and Lydia Tripp were published to marry Apr 2nd 1728. Lydia Tripp was the daughter of Abiel and Anna (Davis) Tripp. William died at Westport on Feb 3rd 1800 in his 98th year. Both he and Lydia were buried on their farm in Westport. They had ten children, the eldest Abiel:

Abiel Macomber, eldest son of William IV, was born Dec 3rd 1729 at Dartmouth. Abiel married Rest Davol, daughter of Peter Davil and Susanna Tripp in a Quaker ceremony on May 27th 1756. Witnesses were: Peter Davil, William Macomber, William Davil, Joshua Davil, William Davil, Timothy Davil, John Macomber, Peleg Cornell and Benjamin Davil, Jonathan Wood, John Mosher, Joseph Tripp, James Mosher, Philip Tripp, William Gifford, Benjamin Shearman, John Macomber, Othaniel Tripp, Jedediah Wood, Lydia Macomber, Mary Cornell Peace Davil, Abigail Tripp, Desiah Macomber, Ruth Cornell, Eunice Wood, and Susannah Cornell.[8] Abiel and Rest had nine children all born at Westport, MA, according to town records. Westport Vital Records state that Abiel died Jul 27th 1812 at Westport age 72yr 9mo and buried on his farm at Westport Point. The most common spelling for the name Davil is Davol, pronounced as the word "duel". To complicate matters in the Tripp family, Rest Davol's mother was Susanna Tripp and one of three of Lydia's great grandmothers that came from the Tripp family. The others were Lydia and Abigail.

Rest Macomber, the seventh child of Abiel and Rest, was born Jan 9th 1770. She married David Wood, son of Daniel Wood and his first wife, Susannah Chase, at Dartmouth on Jan 18th 1786 in Quaker style. According to Westport Vital Records David was of Dighton, MA. David and Rest removed to Acushnet on Jul 15th 1786. Another certificate was granted on Jan 16th 1796 for their removal to Saratoga MM, New York. It was noted in a Saratoga meeting in 1806 that they were about to remove to Coeyman MM in Greene, New York.[9] On Jun 21st 1812, David requested a certificate from DeReyter MM in Madison County, NY, to Sippio MM for himself, wife Rest, and children David, Lydia, Susanna, Daniel, Abigail, Pardon, Elisabeth, Joseph and Benjamin. In 1828 they were living in Madison County, NY, with sons Joseph and Benjamin. David Wood and Rest Macomber's children were:

1. Peace[7] Wood b. Sep 13th 1787 in Westport, MA; requested a certificate from DeRuyter MM in Madison County, NY, having removed to Sippio MM on Mar 25th 1812 with her brother, Jonathan, and was clear of marriage engagements and her affairs were in satisfaction.

2. Ruth Wood b. Apr 15th 1789 in Westport, MA; m. Gershom Mosher. On 16 Apr 16th 1806 Gershom Mosher, about to remove to Coeyman MM in Albany Co., NY, is clear of marriage. On Dec 3rd 1818 Gershom and wife, Ruth, and children: Joseph, Samuel, Daniel, David W., Julie Elma, Allen Seneca, Harriet, Pauline and Dennis, were received on request from DeRuyter MM, NY on Jan 21st 1818, endorsed by Short Creek MM Nov 24th 1818. Another entry was dated April 30th 1828. From 1828 through 1848, Alum Creek MM records indicate their children had numerous records of being disowned. Gershom and Ruth Mosher had thirteen children: Joseph W., Samuel, Daniel, David W., Julie Elma, Allen, Seneca, Stephen who died age two, Harriet, Perlina/Paulina, Dennis, Cassander, and Manford Mosher. The births from Seneca to Manford are recorded in the Alum Creek MM Records. Gershom and sons, Samuel and Daniel, were listed as male inhabitants in Peru twp., Delaware Co., OH in 1835.

+3. Jonathan Wood, b, Jan 6th 1791 in Westport, MA; m. Martha Reynolds. Children were: Lois, Lydia, Samuel, Eliza, Ruth Rest, David, Catherine, Amos, and Benjamin.

4. David Wood, b. Jan 26th 1793 in Westport, MA; m. Esther Hunt. He d. Dec 24th 1866 in Dutchess Co., NY, late resident of Washington, Nine Partners.

5. Lydia Wood, b. Jun 6th 1796, in Saratoga Co., NY. On Mar 13th 1816 having removed to DeRuyter MM, Madison Co., NY, she requested certificate from Saratoga MM and she was clear of marriage and her affairs settled. She m. after 1816, Phineas Hunt.

The friend to attend the Marriage of Jonathan Wood &
Martha Reynolds report they attended and did [...]
ver but that it was [n]orderly conducted

Jonathan Wood & Martha Reynolds appeared in this
Meeting and desired an answer to their Proposal of
Marriage and Nothing appearing to obstruct they Left
at Liberty to Decently Consummate the Marriage at a
Suitable Season between this and our Next Meeting Martha
Pettit and Lois Howland are appointed to attend the Mar[riage]
and see that it be orderly Conducted and report

Jonathan Wood and Martha Reynolds Friends Meeting Request for Marriage

6. Susannah Wood, b. Jan 9th 1798 in Saratoga Co., NY; On Oct 12th 1818 at Indian River, LeRay MM, Charles Gardner and Susannah Wood expressed their proposal of marriage, their parents consenting. On Jul 1st 1819, they appeared again expressing continuance of their request and were left at liberty to accomplish their marriage. Receipt acknowledged Nov 2nd 1819. Married between July to Nov 1819 in LeRay, Jefferson, NY; Five children born at LeRay: Seth, Lewis, Dennis, John, and Edwin Gardner.
7. Daniel Wood, b. Jul 29th 1801 in Saratoga Co., NY; m. Mary Peasley; certificate of removal from DeRuyter MM dated Jul 21st 1824 was read and accepted at LeRay Monthly Meeting.
8. Abigail Wood, b. Aug 28th 1803 in Saratoga Co., NY; m. (_) FREEMAN. In Apr 1826, DeRuyter MM forwarded a complaint to LeRay MM against Abigail Freeman formerly Wood, for outgoing in marriage contrary to disciplines requesting them to take necessary care and inform them of any proceeding, she now residing within limits of LeRay MM. Noted in the women's mm in May 1826 at LeRay, the committee talked with Abigail Freeman and decided to leave the matter under the care of DeRuyter MM. In Sep 1826 LeRay sent a memo to DeRuyter and accepted her acknowledgment. In Apr 1827 a certificate of removal was granted to Abigail Freeman from DeRuyter.
9. Pardon Wood, b. Sep 26th 1805 in Saratoga Co., NY; m. 1st about 1827 in Jefferson Co., NY, Mary Derbyshire; d. before 1849. Four children born in Jefferson Co., NY: Henry, William, Charles, and Eliza. Pardon m. 2nd May 16th 1849, Sarah Cooper, at LeRaysville. Children: Mary Eliza and Persis Alberta. Pardon d. Aug 24th 1876 in Jefferson Co., NY.
10. Elizabeth Wood, b. Jul 30th 1807 in Saratoga or Albany Co., NY.
11. Joseph Wood, b. Apr 27th 1809; m. about 1840 in LeRay, Jefferson, NY, Angeline Derbyshire, daughter of Daniel and Fanny Derbyshire; b. Nov 23rd 1813; On May 13th 1852, Angeline and her son Vincent, a minor, were received at Rollin MM, MI, from Scipio MM, NY. Her three minor children, Edward, Fanny, and Stephen were received on Feb 7th 1857 as members at Rollin at their parent's request. She became an Elder at Rollin on Apr 9th 1870 and requested release of same on Dec 14th 1878. Joseph and Angeline Wood had six children who were active in Michigan MM: Vincent, James D., Edward G., Fanny Catherine, Stephen Adelbirt, and David H.[10] Joseph d. Mar 26th 1888. Angeline d. Mar 9th 1905.
12. Benjamin[7] Wood, b. Jun 6th 1810; m. Lydia Gage. No further information.

Their father David Wood died Sep 26th 1824 in Delaware Co., OH, at age 60. ??His eldest son:

Jonathan Wood, son of David and Rest Wood, was born Jan 6th 1791 at Westport, Bristol, MA.[1] He married Martha Reynolds, daughter of Amos Reynolds and Elizabeth Mosher, between January 20th 1813 and February 24th 1813 at Galway, NY.[2] Martha was born February 2nd 1787. These were Lydia Wood's parents. Jonathan was rather tall for the times, had a long oval face with wavy hair, deep set blue eyes and worked as a carpenter. He removed from DeRuyter Friends Society in Madison Co., NY, to Scippio Friends Society as a single male on Mar 25th 1812. The following Dec 12th he and Martha appeared at a Galway Friends Meeting requesting to be married having their parents consent. After attending meetings on Dec 23rd and Jan 20th 1813 they were given clearance to marry. Members were appointed to attend the marriage to see that it was properly conducted and report. On Feb 24th 1813 it was reported that the marriage was orderly conducted from which one can conclude they were married after Jan 20th and before Feb 24th. When a copy of marriage certificate has not been recorded this three step process presents the only evidence of a Quaker marriage. The top copy was dated Dec 23rd, the following Feb 24th.

Before Apr 12th 1815, Jonathan and Martha had moved from Galway to Jefferson Co.. NY. At Indian River Monthly Meeting held February 8th 1816, Thomas Townsend and Jonathan Wood were appointed to attend the ensuing quarterly meeting and report. On Jan 8th 1818, Pleasant Creek Preparative Represent stated the friend appointed to superintend the building of the meeting house at LeRay, reported on Jan 8th 1818 that there was a difficulty of money

Jonathan and Martha Reynolds Wood

to the amount of $390.68. Therefor this meeting appoints Musgrove Evans, Sylvanus Gardner, John Brown, Jonathan Wood and Thomas Townsend to take the subject into view and consider the most proper method to be adopted to make up the deficiency and report to next meeting.[3] Jonathan Wood, John Townsend, Joseph Child Jr., Rufus Spencer and Edmund Tucker were appointed on Oct 8th 1818 to bring forward names for Overseers at next meeting. At the August 5th 1819 meeting, friends appointed to attend Burials, have the care of Burying goods, and report were Benjamin Hillman, William Barber, Benjamin Kirkbride, Jonathan Wood and John Townsend for one year. A new committee was appointed in October 1825 to have care of Burying goods and attend Burials, and report: David Mosher, Jonathan Wood, Joel Haworth, Samuel Child, David Hillman, Thomas Townsend, Zecheus Hill, Medad Comstock, James Powell and John Crega were appointed.

New York State has interim censuses which are different from the national census. In 1825at Jefferson County, NY, Jonathan Wood had a daughter born the preceding year. He had 35 acres of improved land, 4 meat cattle, 2 horses, 8 sheep, 8 hogs, 12 yards of fulled cloth made by domestic means the preceding year, 8 yards of flannel or other woollen cloth made as preceding and 17 yards of linen, cotton or thin cloth made as preceding. Ten years later his improved acreage was reduced to 30. He owned 8 meat cattle, 2 horses, 23 sheep, and 8 hogs.

Women held separate meetings. In Jan 1826, they voted to disown Mary Mosher if the men concur. The same day David Mosher, Jonathan Wood, Sylvanus Gardner and Moses Child were appointed overseers of the poor for one year. At the January 1828 meeting, Jonathan Wood, Samuel Rogers,

---

1 Westport Monthly Meeting Records

2 Galway Meeting Records

3 LeRay Meeting Records

Joseph Child Jr., and Joel Haworth were appointed to collect the account of births and deaths for the preceding year and hand to the recorder and report.

On May 20th 1834, Jonathan Wood and Martha, his wife, of LeRay, Jefferson, NY deeded to William Clark of the same place for $300 a piece of land that Jonathan had bought on May 28th 833 from David and Charlotte Petrie of Little Falls, Herkimer, NY, known as in lot No. 371 of the Macomber purchase containing 25 and 70/100 acres. An indenture made Jul 11th 1836 between Jonathan and Martha Wood to Andrew Isdell of Stoke, Montgomery county, for $1,250 land lying in the town of LeRay being the NW quarter of lot No. 605 of great Lot No. 11 of Macomber purchase containing 107 and 60/100 acres except for the SE 53 & 93/100 acres that Amos Reynolds conveyed to Reuben Palmer. This was the land that Martha's parents deeded to her and her spouse. They were getting ready to move to Ohio for on Oct 26th 1837, Jonathan and ch: Samuel, Eliza, Ruth R, Catherine, Amos and Benjamin were received on certificate from LeRay MM, NY, at Alum Creek MM, OH.[1] The family was listed in 1840 living in Bennington twp., Delaware Co, OH. After twenty-five years in Ohio, they moved to Michigan. Jonathan and Martha were granted a certificate on Jan 19th 1865 to Rollin MM in Michigan. Later they moved to Ingham County where they were buried in the Okemos Cemetery on M16. Jonathan died Oct 6th 1870 at Ingham Co., MI. His stone reads age 79y-9mo-2dy. Martha died Jun 12th 1876. No stone remains for her. This small cemetery has been badly damaged over the years with lost records. Their daughter, Ruth Rest, and her first husband are located next to them.

The children of Jonathan Wood and Martha Reynolds were: Louis (Lois), Lydia, Samuel, Eliza, Ruth Rest, Catherine, Amos and Benjamin F. I will go into more detail here on Lydia's siblings due to some misinformation in the Jonathan Wood Genealogy compiled from family records by Beulah Komjathy. It was unfortunate that my father did not look at his father's letters from the Civil War for Wes was corresponding with two of Lois Wood Travallee's daughters. It was stated in the book that she had no children. While this work was being done, I was living in the area where the family first settled in Ohio and had access to the court house records and cemeteries in both Morrow and Delaware Counties, the latter in which I was living at the time. I later did research in those courthouses and found among many other things, the marriage records of my great grandparents, Lydia Wood and Henry Cook Ayres.

Lois Wood, eldest child of Jonathan and Martha Wood, was born Dec 31st 1813 in Saratoga Co., NY. She married John J. Travallee about 1836 in Jefferson Co., NY. He was born Feb 8th 1813. He died Apr 2nd 1855 after their move to Morrow County, OH, at age 42. After his death as executrix she sold on Sep 2nd 1856 two parcels in Morrow County to B.G. Fisk and G.H. Trace for $41,143.33. The first parcel of 12 & 3/16 acres located in a part of section Two, twp. Six, range Sixteen U.S. Military land commencing in the center of big Walnut Creek along the lines of Job Chase. The second 48 acres in the same area commenced at the SE corner of Lunds formerly Abner Morchouse to lands formerly owned by Job Chase. She was still living in Bennington in 1860, working as a gardener with her five children at home. Her daughter, Martha, was employed as a housekeeper. On Oct 3rd 1865, Lois sold for $260 to Peter Coulthbury, four acres known as lot 11 in the same township and range. This was her last transaction before moving to Michigan. She and John deeded land in Delaware Co, OH, Mar 10th 1849, to her brother-in-law, Moses Gidley. My grandfather, Charles Wesley Ayres, corresponded with two of Lois' daughters during the Civil War.

Children of Lois[8] Wood and John J. Travalee were:

1. Son Travalee born and died in Jefferson Co., NY.
2. Tryphenia Travallee was born in 1841 at Bennington twp, Delaware, OH.
3. Martha Travallee was born in 1843 at Bennington twp, Delaware, OH. She worked in the boarding hall at Michigan State Agricultural College in 1870.
4. Permelia Travallee was born in 1847 at Bennington twp, Delaware, OH. She was a domestic

1 Alum Creek Monthly Meeting Records

with her sister, Martha, at the college. She married about 1880, Hubert N. Lamphere, born about 1855. They were living alone in 1910 in Windsor, Eaton, MI. They had two daughters: 1) Martha Lamphere was born about 1882 and married (?) Eldred, and had five children. 2) Lois May Lamphere was born about 1883/4, married Richard A. McPhee born about 1873 in England and immigrated in 1878. His father was born in Scotland. The McPhee sons were: 1) Edwin was born about 1901, and 2) Evan H. was born about 1903. They live in Windsor, MI.

5. Melvin D. Travallee was born in July 1850 at Bennington twp, Delaware, OH. About 1882, he married Rosa E. Lamphere and had three children: 1) Bessie Lois Travallee born about 1884; 2) Merritt D. Travallee born in August 1886; and 3) Guy Adelbert Travallee born June 26th 1890 in Michigan according to his WWI Draft Registration Card. Before the turn of the century Melvin and Rosa were living in Windsor twp, Eaton, MI. Daughter Bessie Travallee married George Earl Gilbert, born Feb 1884 son of John G. And Flora A. Gilbert of Potterville. Their daughter Fern C. was born about 1908. Bessie and G. Earl lived in Benton and Potterville area of Eaton County, MI. Her father was living with them in 1930. Melvin, Rosa, and their two sons moved to Lansing before 1910 where they ran a boarding house at 628 St. Joseph St. in Lansing in 1920. Their sons were living with them. Merritt was an electrician and Guy a student who was married to Aina G. Helthenen born about 1893 in Michigan whose parents were from Finland. They had a son, Guy jr., born Jul 19th 1918 who moved to California before 1951. Guy jr., died Jul 27th 1994 at Sunnyvale, CA. At some point Melvin and Rosa moved to Potterville, MI.

6. John S. Travallee was born in 1855 at Bennington twp, Morrow, OH. He was a farmer who died of paralysis on Aug 31st 1913 in Lansing, MI.

Lydia Wood, daughter of Jonathan and Martha Wood, was born Jun 20th 1816 at LeRay, Jefferson, NY. She was received on certificate from LeRay MM, Jefferson Co, NY at Alum Creek MM, Delaware Co, OH, on Jul 20th 1837. She married Henry Cook Ayres on Sep 19th 1840 in Delaware Co, OH, solemnized by Shadrack Hubbell, JP.[1] So Lydia was disowned on Apr 22nd 1841 by Alum Creek MM for marrying contrary to discipline. Henry was the son of Thomas and Mary (Ross) Ayers of New Jersey. Mary died after the birth of their last son as did the child. Thomas eventually sold all his lands in New Jersey and came to Ohio bringing a second wife and his children by Mary. Henry died April 13th 1886 age 73 and Lydia died Jul 26th 1888 in Ingham Co, MI, age 72. Both were initially interred in Meridian and after the death of their son, Augustus, they were moved to a large vault in Mt. Hope Cemetery, Lansing, MI. Henry and Lydia had three sons and one daughter born in near Marengo, Bennington twp, Ohio. Their family history appears in Part I with the Ayres family.

Samuel Wood, son of Jonathan and Martha Wood, was born Oct 7th 1817 at LeRay, Jefferson, NY.[2] On Dec 22nd 1842, Alum Creek MM granted Samuel certificate to marry at Gilead MM, OH. He married his second cousin, Priscilla H. Wood, daughter of Israel Wood and Mary C. Thurston of Vermont, on Feb 1st 1843 in Delaware Co, OH. Priscilla was born Mar 19th 1821 in Delaware Co., OH. Samuel and his sons were carpenters. On Aug 26th 1852 Samuel was dismissed for disunity. Samuel died Feb 12th 1855 at age 37. Things were difficult for widowed Priscilla having to work and raise six children. On Jun 21st 1856, Priscilla and her six children were granted a certificate to Gilead MM from Alum Creek MM. The 1860 census in Gilead twp. listed Priscilla employed as a weaver, age 39, with four minor children. Her youngest child died in 1863. Before 1870 she moved to Delhi, Ingham, MI, with her five children and daughter-in-law Emma Wood. Still associated with Quakers, Priscilla and four children were granted on Jun 16th 1874 a certificate to Rollin MM, MI, and received on certificate from Gilead MM, OH, to Rollin MM, MI, on Oct 10th 1874. With her were Mary Frances, Israel, Sarah Ellen and Catherine. The family moved to Holt, MI. According to Ingham records, she died Sep 13th 1887 at age 66 in Holt, Delhi twp., Ingham, MI, of a liver complaint.

Children of Samuel Wood and Priscilla H. Wood were:

---

1 Recorded 5 Oct 1840; Delaware County Marriage Records, Vol. 1, p.237;
2 LeRay Monthly Meeting Records

1. Libeus Wood was born Feb 25th 1844 in Delaware Co, OH.[1] Libeus, was granted a certificate to Rollin MM from Gilead of Feb 16th 1864. On Apr 9th 1864, he was received on certificate from Gilead MM, OH at Rollin MM, MI. He married Emma S. Kidney Jul 22nd 1870 at Mt. Gilead, OH. She was born in 1846. He was granted certificate to Long Lake MM, MI, where he was living, from Rollin MM, MI, on Octr 25th 1884. The following Nov 1st he and Emma were received on certificate at Manton MM, residing Manton, MI. He died in 1927 in Oregon, probably St. Johns. Their two children born in Ingham Co., MI, were: 1) Amos D. Wood born Oct 2nd 1878 and 2) Carrie B. Wood born Apr 20th 1880. Amos D. Wood married Bertha Schram May 1st 1898 at Grand Traverse, MI[2] and had children:[3] 1) Harold L. Wood born Jul 16th 1899 in MI; 2) Hazel C. Wood born Jan 2nd 1902 in MI; and 3) Elizabeth Esther Wood born Feb 25th 1905 in Oak Grove, Clackamas, OR.

2. Mary Frances Wood was born Nov 17th 1846 in Delaware Co, OH and died Oct 27th 1888 at Holt, MI, age 41.

3. Israel Wood was born Mar 15th 1848 in Delaware Co, OH. He married in 1887, Augusta Mulliken who was born about 1860, daughter of Rhoda Mulliken. Their five known children were: 1) Alice Wood born 1889, 2) Mary Wood born 1891, 3) Alfred T. Wood born 1894, 4) Daisy B. Wood born 1895, and 5) Earl M. Wood born 1897. They lived in Delhi, Ingham, MI. Augusta's mother was living with them in 1900. Israel died Feb 2nd 1938 at age 89.

4. Sarah Ellen Wood was born Apr 28th 1850 in Morrow Co, OH and died Aug 21st 1935 age 85.

5. Catherine Wood was born Apr 20th 1852 in Morrow Co, OH. On Jun 16th 18874 she was granted a certificate to Rollin MM from Gilead although she had been listed with her mother on an earlier certificate.. On Sep 12th 1894, she removed to Rollin MM from Traverse City MM, MI. She died Jun 1904 age 52.

6. Mary Elizabeth Wood was born May 20th 1855 in Morrow Co, OH and died there in 1863.

Eliza Wood, daughter of Jonathan and Martha Wood, was born Jun 3rd 1819 at LeRay, Jefferson, NY. Alum Creek MM, OH, disowned Eliza for disunity on Dec 26th 1839. She was married to Eli Platt on Jun 20th 1840 in Delaware Co, OH, by Barton Whipple, JP. Eli was born Apr 16th 1814 in Canada, son of Eli and Eleanor (Winchell) Platt. Eli had married first, Clarissa Beach, on Jul 22nd 1836 by Joseph Scott, JP, in Delaware, OH. He and Eliza lived in Bennington, Morrow, OH. They sold fifty acres for $100 to Moses Gidley on Sep 22nd 1855 a part of lot 13 in the 6th quarter, 6th twp., 16th range US Military land. Eliza died Aug 6th 1889 at Newaygo Co, MI, age 70. Eli died there Nov 7th 1889. Both are buried in Croton twp. His father, Eli, Sr., acquired 174 acres of government land in Michigan about 1815 and was buried in Croton Twp. Dec 26th 1839.

Children of Eliza[8] Wood and Eli Platt were:

1. Albert Platt was born Apr 30th 1843 in Delaware Co, OH. He married 1st, Selinda Bacon, Jun 13th 1853 who died Jul 31st 1873. They had a daughter, Melissa born Apr 15th 1870 and died in Apr 1872. Albert married 2nd Mary Jane Barnes, born Oct 11th 1856 in Lansing, MI. Their children were: William James, Charles Edmond, Mary Elizabeth, Evelyn Rocellia, Edna Mae, Loretta Eliza, Lena Bell, Ada Melissa, twins Nellie and Nettie, and Laurence Alfred Platt. Albert fought in the Civil War in Co. A, 10th Regiment, Michigan Cavalry. He enlisted Aug 25th 1863 and was discharged a corporal on Nov 11th 1865. He died Mar 4th 1898 at Newaygo Co, before his 55th birthday.

2. Clarion Platt was born Nov 13th 1845 in Delaware Co, OH.

3. Ellen Platt was born May 10th 1847 in Delaware Co, OH. She married Peres Miner Pickett Oct 8th 1865 who was born Jan 30th 1843, son of Peter and Theda (Norton)Pickett of Onondaga Co., NY. Ellen and Peres Pickett's children were: Ella, Flora M., Warren M., Edwin Orange, Emma, Elsie, Lauren W., and Roy Pickett. Only Flora, Edwin O., and Roy are known to have lived to adulthood. Ellen died Jan 7th 1915 at Newaygo Co, MI, age 67. Peres died Mar 27th 1933, age 90, the last surviving member

---

1 Alum Creek Monthly Meeting Records

2 Traverse City Monthly Meeting Records

3 *Ibid.*

of GAR Samuel Judd Post having served in 2nd Michigan Cavalry. A 2nd wife and his three children survived him.

4. Sarah Louise Platt was born Apr 29th 1848 in Delaware Co, OH. She married Lafayette F. Pickett in 1866 who was born Jul 30th 1846 in MI. Their children were: Esther, Eli, Theda, Babe stillborn, John, Mary, Alice died age 2, and Jennie Pickett. Sarah died Apr 13th 1921, age 72. Lafayette died from carbon monoxide on Jan 21st 1922. He had served in 10th Michigan Calvary for 3 yrs. Both died in Newaygo Co, MI.

5. Minerva Platt was born May 29th 1850 in Morrow Co, OH. She married Daniel H. Bement about 1872. Their children were: 1) Julia May born Jan 30th 1873; 2) Melissa born 1875; 3) George D. born 1880; 4) Lena Rebecca born May 10th 1886; and 5) Harry E. Bement born Apr 13th 1890.

6. Jonathan Platt was born Jan 31st 1851 in Morrow Co, OH. He married Jan 21st 1883 in Newaygo Co, MI, Achsah Mila Doty born Jul 7th 1865 in Clinton Co, MI, daughter of Enoch and Hannah (Kimball) Doty. Their children were: 1) Lucinda Ellen born Aug 28th 1884 in Newaygo Co, MI; 2) Lizzie born Jul 15th 1888 in Newaygo, MI; 3) Edwin Dee born May 21st 1891 in Port Angeles, WA; 4) Frances Olive born Aug 30th 1893 in Port Angeles, WA; 5) Eliza Jane born Feb 16th 1896 in Juliaetta, ID; 6) Ruth Edith born Nov 27th 1897 in Melrose, ID; twins: 7) Dallas Martin and 8) Alice Martin born Oct 29th 1900 in Melrose, ID; and 10) Inez May Platt born Feb 28th 1905 in Melrose, ID. Jonathan Platt died Aug 12th 1929, age 78 at Clarkston, WA. Achsah had divorced Jonathan and married 2nd (?) Ricketts. She died Jan 26th 1934.

7. Emma Ida Platt was born 10 Nov 10th 1855 in Morrow Co, OH. She married Gus Force. Children were: 1) George born in 1881; 2) Dee born in 1886; and 3) Ralph Force born in 1894. They lived in Newaygo Co, MI.

8. Ruth Elizabeth Platt was born Jun 3rd 1859 in Morrow Co, OH. She married as his 2nd wife on Jan 22nd 1884 at Hanover, MI, William Mills who was born May 1st 1850 in NY State, son of Thomas and Deliara (Luch) Mills. Their children were: 1) Esther born Feb 4th 1886; 2) Earl born Jul 19th 1890; 3) Floyd John born Apr 11th 1893; and 4) Lawrence Mills born Apr 4th 1898. Ruth died Dec 21st 1941 at Hillsdale, MI. William died there on Sep 25th 1930.

9. Mary Catherine Platt was born May 10th 1861 in Morrow Co, OH. Died Sep 19th 1879 in Newaygo Co, MI, age 18.

Ruth Rest Wood, daughter of Jonathan and Martha Wood, was born March 19th 1822 at LeRay, Jefferson, NY. Alum Creek MM, OH, disowned Ruth for disunity on December 26th 1839. She married first Moses Gidley, January 30th 1840 at Delaware Co, OH. Moses was born November 22nd 1815, son of William Gidley and Phebe Mosher. He died October 12th 1866 at Meridian, MI. His simple tombstone reads: M. GIDLAY; 1815 - 1866. Ruth married second Nathan Newlon on March 23rd 1878 in MI who died May 4th 1897. She died on September 23rd 1898 in MI age 76. Besides their eight children noted, she and Moses had two that died in infancy.

Children of Ruth Rest Wood and Moses Gidley were as follows:

1. Jonathan Gidley was born Jan 30th 1842 in Delaware Co, OH. He died Jul 30th 1924 at Saginaw, MI, age 82.

2. Mary Ruth Gidley was born Aug 2nd 1844 in Delaware Co, OH. She died Sep 4th 1921at Grant, Newaygo, MI, at age 77.

3. Hazen Gidley was born Nov 29th 1845 in Delaware Co, OH. He died Dec 15th 1923 in CA, age 78.

4. Phebe Gidley was born May 4th 1848 in Delaware Co, OH. She died Apr 16th 1920 in MI at age 71.

5. Susan Jane Gidley was born Jul 22nd 1852 at Marengo, Morrow, OH. She died Mar 30th 1923 in ND, age 70.

6. Elizabeth Gidley was born July 25th 1854 at Woodbury, Morrow, OH. She died Apr 29th 1930 at Grand Ledge, Eaton, MI, at age 75.

7. Henry Gidley was born Oct 20th 1856 at Woodbury, Morrow, OH. He died Mar 8th 1922 in MI, age 65.

8. Robert Comfort Gidley was born Jul 26th 1865 in Ingham Co, MI. He died Apr 11th 1940 at Grand Ledge, Eaton, MI, age 74.

There were no children of Ruth Rest Wood and Nathan Newlon.

Catherine Wood, daughter of Jonathan and Martha Wood, was born August 9th 1824 at LeRay, Jefferson, NY. Alum Creek Monthly Meeting disowned Catherine on September 19th 1842 for joining another society without permission.

Amos Wood, son of Jonathan and Martha Wood, was born Feb 29th 1828 at LeRay, Jefferson, NY. He married Amelia King about 1847. Amelia was born on May 2nd 1834 in New York State, daughter of Edgar King. On Jul 26th 1847, Alum Creek MM, OH, disowned Amos for disunity. Amos was a carpenter by trade. In Morrow County, OH, he purchased on Sep 27th 1849 from his sister Ruth and her husband, Moses Gidley, two acres and one hundred twenty-eight rods on the north side of the forty acres owned by John J. Travallee. He was in Meridian, MI, when he and Amelia deeded to his brother, Benjamin F. Wood of the same place, all of Meridian, Ingham Co., MI, for $210, thirty acres off the West end of the North half of the SW fractional quarter in Sec. 30, Twp.4, north of range one West on Feb 4th 1856. My Dad wrote: "In 1895, Amos Wood had the farm across the road from my grandfather [Henry Cook Ayres in Meridian twp., Ingham Co, MI] and was taken over by Robert Gidley." The 1913 reunion was held at Amos and Amelia farm near the [Michigan Agricultural] College Grounds. Robert Gidley obtained the farm before 1915 where a reunion was held that year. Amos died Oct 9th 1912 age 84, Amelia died in 1919. Both buried in the Okemos MI Cemetery off Hwy. M16.

Benjamin F. Wood, son of Jonathan and Martha Wood, was born Mar 5th 1831 at LeRaysville, Jefferson, NY. Alum Creek MM, OH, disowned Benjamin on Jul 26th 1849 for disunity. He married Marilla Vining on Dec 25th 1853 in Morrow Co, OH. On Apr 25th 1861, he joined the 3rd Regiment, Co. I, Ohio Volunteer Infantry for three months. He mustered out with the Company, Aug 22nd 1861. He died Mar 21st 1917 at Newaygo Co, MI, age 86.

Children of Benjamin F.[8] Wood and Marilla Vining were:

1. Charles Wood b. Oct 21st 1855 in Morrow Co, OH. He d. Jul 7th 1940 at Newaygo Co, MI, age 84.
2. Arvilla Wood was born Jun 1st 1858 in Morrow Co, OH. She died Jan 31st 1931, age 72.
3. Francis H. Wood was born Nov 17th 1859 in Marion Co, OH. He died Jan 8th 1955 at Harrison, Clare, MI, age 95. He also went by the name of Frank.
4. Ansel Ellsworth Wood was born Sep 17th 1861 in Marion Co, OH. He died Oct 23rd 1956 in Kent Co, MI, age 95.

Appendix A

Civil War Diary of Augustus Ayres

During the time Gus[1] was in Arkansas near Devall's Bluff in the Civil War, he kept a dairy in a small book that has been saved. Except for a few days at the beginning of the diary and a few days at the end, when Gus was on the way home after being discharged, the diary has been abbreviated so as to only include those entries where known members are mentioned. This copy is in the original phonetic spelling. Where necessary, for clarity, periods have been inserted.

Sunday, 8 Jan 1865

I com of from garde this morning and got som wood in the fore noon and in the after noon wrote a letter to marthy trevaly[2] - plesant to day

Monday, 9 Jan 1865

raind most all day monday Set a Guard in the Shanty most all day and a long torge night I and lorenzo[3] went to the bluff and got our things from home. got a letter from home.

Tuesday, 10 Jan 1865

tuesday rote a letter home in the fore noon and rote a letter for Scofield[4] to in the afternoon. halp git up som wood. plesant all day.

Wesnesday, 11 Jan 1865

Cold but plesant all day. wensday Stood one trick of guard in the fore noon on the post no 1. halp git in som wood in the afternoon. on picket at night. the counter sign was grogris landing. fixt my diary to night and had a sing.

Thursday, 12 Jan 1865

thursday com off from guard this morning. after breakfast went to the bluff. went a foot and saw wardell[5] and got the rest of my things and come back on the cars. very plesant all day.

Friday, 13 Jan 1865

got a letter to night from premelia trevallee[6]

friddday layed around the Shanty most of the four noon and the rest day git up som wood in the after noon. went over to old galeses. plesant all day.

Saturday, 14 Jan 1865

plesant all day. Saturday went out in the woods and dug som brier roots for pipes. after noon toke the hand car and went up the railroad after the rations. I was on picket last night. the counter sign was milageville.

Sunday, 15 Jan 1865

very plesant all day. this fore non washed and Shoer myself and went on sicurety worning. inspection this after noon. wrote a letter to Ohio and Lorenzo and I took a walk out in the woods. a Sing tonight.

Monday, 16 Jan 1865

monday went on drill this morning and then went over round by old gales and sen the girls. this after noon I was on Scurmish drill and lade around the rest of the day. vary plesant all day.

Tuesday, 17 Jan 1865

this fore noon washed my cloths and went on drill this after noon. went on Scurmish drill and

---

1 Augustus Ayers/Ayres. Enlisted Co. B, 12th Michigan Infantry, 10 Oct 1864, at Meridian for three years, age 18. Mustered same day. Discharged at expiration of term of service at Camden, Arkansas, 12 Oct 1865.

2 Martha Travalee, his cousin, daughter of John J. Trevalee and Lois Wood.

3 William Lorenzo Mosher of Meridian. Enlisted Co. B, 12 Michigan Infantry, 10 Oct 1864, at Jackson for one year, age 21. Mustered next day. Discharged at expiration of term of service at Camden, Ark. 12 Oct 1865.

4 Lorenzo D. Scofield. Enlisted Co. B, 12th Michigan Infantry, 27 Sep 1864, at Oronoko, for one year, age 32. Mustered next day. Discharged at expiration of term of service at Camden, Ark. 9 Sep 1865.

5 Wardell. Either John A. Wardell of Lansing, Michigan. Enlisted Co.G, 12th Michigan Infantry, 10 Dec 1861, at Lansing for three years, age 18. Mustered 19 December. Discharged Devall's Bluff, 7 Jan 1865. Or Joseph C. Wardell, veteran, of Lansing. Enlisted Co. G, 12th Michigan Infantry, 28 Nov 1861, at Lansing for three years, age 20. Mustered 19 Dec 1861. Reenlisted, 9 Feb 1864, at Little Rock, Ark. Mustered same day. Mustered out at Camde, Ark., 15 Feb 1866.

6 Permelia Travalee, younger sister of Martha Travalee.

then got us som wood. I got a letter from wesley[1] today. vary plesant all day.

Monday, 23 Jan 1865

clouday all day. I went a hunting this fore non and gorge brown[2] went with us. we ketched 4 rabbits. I had som fride for supper. I went out and halp ketch a con and run up a whele barrel of wood. Got three loads of wood to day.

Tuesday, 24 Jan 1865

this fore non I fixt my boots, drove som nales in them. then wrote a letter to lib[3] this after noon. I fixt lorenzos[3] boots. cold but plesant.

Monday, 30 Jan 1865

mary wahte. I wrote two leters this fore non, one to mary[4] and one to walter[5]. this after noon I went and plade a game of ball then cut som wood and then went on drill. clouday all day. I wrote a letter for Scofield[4] to night.

Wesnesday, 1 Feb 1865

rany all day. I wred som this fore noon and lade a round the rest of the four noon. this after noon fixt coon skin then went up after the rations. wrote a letter for king[6] to night.

Monday, 6 Feb 1865

this four noon I fixt albert litles[7] boots, that is all. this after noon I sode som fur on my gloves, then plade a game of ball. plesant all day.

Friday, 10 Feb 1865

this four noon I wred som in the testament and clend out the fireplace. this after noon I wrote a letter to almira baldwin[8]. had a dance to night. vary plesant all day.

Saturday, 11 Feb 1865

plesant all day. this four noon I and james terril[9] went a hunting. we ketched one rabbit. this after noon went out and plade a game of ball. then pitched a game of quates, then halp git up som wood. we had a dance to night. I went out and stode one trick of guard with Lorenzo[3].

Monday, 27 Feb 1865

I got out tyes this four noon and this after noon we plade a game of ball. after supper had a dance to night. I got a letter from walter cook[10] to night and wrote a letter home to night.

Thursday, 2 Mar 1865

went down to duvalls bluff to day and went up to the ridgement and toke diner with H. hults[11] and got my watched fixt and com back on the cars. rained most all day and most all night.

Sunday, 5 Mar 1865

I sweep the shanty and shaved and put the seets in my ring this four noon. this after noon pitched a game of quates. albert mosher[12] com to day. on guard to night. the counter sign was

---

1 Charles Wesley Ayres, Gus' older brother. Fought with 3rd Ohio and Mississippi Marine Brigade.

2George Brown. Enlisted Co.I, 12th Michigan Infantry, 5 Sep 1864, at Buchanan, Michigan for one year, age 39. Mustered 5 Sep 1864. Discharged at Camdem, Arkansas, 9 Sep 1865.

3 Elizabeth Jane Ayres, Gus' older sister.

4 Mary White, cousin and daughter of Gus' Uncle and Aunt, David and Harriet (Ayers) White

5 Walter Cook. No further information.

6 George King. Enlisted Co. G, 12th Michigan Infantry, 8 Dec 1863, at Berrien, Michigan for three years, age 19. Mustered 23 Dec 1863. Mustered out at Camden, Ark., 15 Feb 1866.

7 Albert Leidle. Drafted for one year, 24 Oct 1864, from London, Monroe Co., Michigan, age 33. Mustered same day. Assigned to Co. B, 12th Michigan Infantry. Discharged at expiration of term of service at Camden, Ark. 9 Sep 1865.

8 Almira Baldwin.

9 James W. Terril of Meridian. Enlisted Co. B, 12th Michigan Infantry, 10 Oct 1864, at Meridian for three years, age 19. Mustered same day. Discharged at Camden, Ark. 12 Oct 1865.

10 Walter Cook

11 H. Hults/ Harmon Hulse of Lansing. Enlisted Co. G, 12 Michigan Infantry, 13 Aud 1862, age Lansing for three years, age 24. Mustered 13 Sep. On duty with 11th Ohio Batterh, 10 Jan 1864 to 9 Apr 1864. Discharged at term at Little Rock, Ark., 30 Sep 1865.

12 Albert P. Mosher. Enlisted Co. B, 12th Michigan Infantry, 14 Feb 1865, at Lansing for one year. Mustered same day. Mustered out at Camden, Ark. 15 Feb 1866.

willmonton. plesant.

Monday, 6 Mar 1865

I choped ty timber this four noon. this after noon split ty timber and plade a game of ball. got a letter from father[1] to day. vary plesant all day.

Wednesday, 19 Apr 1865

I and ketcham[2] toke a walk and picked som flours then I slep the rest of the four noon. this after noon I stode one trick of guard for cavender[3]. it rained som to day.

Tuesday, 6 Jun 1865

I laid a round camp this four noon. this after noon I and turnors[4] went and got som berries. hot and clouday.

Monday, 26 Jun 1865

I and Charly trumble[5] went down town and had a talk wit the girls this four noon. this after noon I laid a round till night then went on picket. hot.

Friday, 30 Jun 1865

I and james Cavender[6] went down town and bought som meal for breakfast. this after noon musterd for pay then we moved in our shanty and built our bunks. clouday to day.

Wednesday, 12 Jul 1865

I and albert[7] and James[8] went down town and got som bread this four noon. this after noon we went up in the fort. hot and clear.

Thursday, 13 Jul 1865

we went down to the river and toke a wash this four noon. this after noon I and James cavender went a fishing down the river. hot and clear.

Monday, 17 Jul 1865

I laid a round camp this four noon. I and lorenzo[9] went down town and got som peeches. wrained som to day.

Thursday, 7 Sep 1865

I was detaled for fategue this morning to halp dig a grave for ed sutten[10] a Sargent. warm and clouday.

Friday, 8 Sep 1865

I and james terril[11] went over to old lees and got som peeches this four noon. this after noon I washed my cloths. wrained som to day.

Monday, 11 Sep 1865

---

1 Henry Cook Ayers, his father.

2 Florence D. Ketcham. Enlisted Co. B, 12th Michigan Infantry, 10 Feb 1864, at St. Joseph for three years, age 17. Mustered same day. Mustered out at Camden, Ark. 15 Feb 1866.

3 James Cavender of Bunker Hill, MI. Enlisted CoB, 12th Michigan Infantry, 15 Feb 1865, at Bunker Hill for 1 year, age 44. Mustered 22 Feb 1865. Mustered out at Camden, 15 Feb 1866.

4 William Turner, veteran of Buchanan, Michigan. Enlisted Co. C, 12 Michigan Infantry, 20 Oct 1861 at Buchanan for three years, age 18. Mustered 19 Dec 1861. Reenlisted, 24 Dec 1863, at Little Rock, Arkansas. Mustered same day. Mustered out at Camden, Ark., 15 Feb 1866.

5 Charles H. Trumball of Burlington. Enlisted Co. B, 12th Michigan Infantry, 25 Mar 1865, at Jackson, for one year, age 24. Mustered, 27 Mar 1865. Discharged for disability at Little Rock, Ark. 23 Nov 1865. Died, 7 Apr 1889. Buried at Diamondale, Michigan.

6 James Cavender of Bunker Hill. Enlisted Co. B, 12th Michigan Infantry, 15 Feb 1865, at Bunker Hill, for one year, age 44. Mustered, 22 Feb 1865. Mustered out at Camden, Ark. 15 Feb 1866.

7 Albert Mosher

8 James Cavender of Bunker Hill. Enlisted Co. B, 12th Michigan Infantry, 15 Feb 1865, at Bunker Hill for one year, age 44. Mustered, 22 Feb 1865. Mustered out at Camden, Ark. 15 Feb 1866.

9 William Lorenzo Mosher

10 Edward Sutton (Veteran). Enlisted Co. B, 12th Michigan Infantry, 17 Oct 1861, at Benton for three years, age 19. Mustered, 19 Dec 1861. Re-enlisted as Corporal, 28 Dec 1863, at Little Rock, Ark. Mustered same day. Made Sargeant, 22 Feb 1865. Died of disease at Camden, Ark. 7 Sep 1865. Buried in National Cemetery at Baton Rouge, Louisiana, Grave #1626.

11 James W. Terril

I laid a round camp this four noon. this after noon I and Shep trumbull[1] went after som musk lines. wrained som to day.

Thursday, 28 Sep 1865

I washed my cloths then I made a badge and cut out another one this four non fore J terril. this after noon I made a ring for D bele[2]. warm and clouday.

Monday, 2 Oct 1865

I made a ring for M Driskle[3] this four noon. this after noon I laid around camp. warm and clouday.

Saturday, 7 Oct 1865

I laid a round camp this four noon. this after noon I and lorenzo mosher and James terrill and John donahoe[4] and thacker[5] was mustered out. cool and clouday.

Tuesday, 10 Oct 1865

I and loranzo went and got som hickery nuts this four noon. this after noon I laid a round camp. cool and plesant.

Wednesday, 11 Oct 1865

I laid a round camp this four noon. this after noon I went down town and sene the trane come in. cool and cloudy.

Thursday, 12 Oct 1865

I went down to the river last night and stade ther all night and most all the next day then we crost over the river and camped in a old house.

Friday, 13 Oct 1865

we went about twenty five miles to day and camped in a old chool house.

Saturday, 14 Oct 1865

this four noon we went about 15 miles. we pased through prinston this afternoon. we com 28 miles and camped in 4 miles of t[h]e Salean and slep in a citizens house. I was sick to night.

Sunday, 15 Oct 1865

this four we com 10 miles. toke dinner in a little crick bottom. this after noon we com 10 miles and camped under a pine tree. plesant day.

Monday, 16 Oct 1865

we got up and started at 12 o clock at night. we com 8 miles and toke breakfast by a crick then com 18 miles which brought us in little rock. I went over to the arsnel then got pay and discharged and crosed the river and slep in the store house.

Tuesday, 17 Oct 1865

this morning we toke the cars and went to duvalls bluff. this after noon we toke the boat rewena for memphis. fare $5 dolars. wrained som to night.

Wednesday, 18 Oct 1865

we wrode all day and all night. cool and plesant to day.

Thursday, 19 Oct 1865

we got to memphis this morning then we changed botes. we got on the marble city for cairo. fair $3 dolars. we started out this after noon. cool.

Friday, 20 Oct 1865

---

1 Shepardson Trumbull. Enlisted Bo. B, Michigan 12th Infantry, 10 Mar 1865, at Burlington for one year, age 21. Mustered same day. Mustered out at Camden, Ark. 15 Feb 1866.

2 Richard H. Bell (Veteran) of Berrien County. Enlisted Co. B, 12th Michigan Infantry, 29 Mar 1862, for three years. Mustered same day. Taken prisoner, 20 May 1863, at Middleburg, Tenn. Re-enlisted, 30 Dec 1863, at Little Rock, Ark. Mustered same day. Returned to Regiment, June 1863. Mustered out at Camden, Ark. 15 Feb 1866.

3 Noah Driscoll/Driskell of Porter. Enlisted Co. B, 12th Michigan Infantry, 13 Feb 1864, at Porter for three years, age 21. Mustered, 16 Feb 1864. Made Corporal, 22 Jan 1866. Mustered out at Camden, Ark. 15 Feb 1866.

4 John Donahue (Veteran) of Watervliet. Enlisted Co. B, 12th Michigan Infantry, 7 Oct 1862, at Coloma, age 18. Mustered, 20 Oct 1862. Re-enlisted 30 Dec 1863, at Little Rock, Ark. Mustered same day. Discharged at Camden, Ark. 12 Oct 1865.

5 William H. Thatcher (Veteran) of Watervliet. Enlisted Co. B, 12th Michigan Infantry, 7 Oct 1862, at Watervliet, age 18. Mustered, 20 Oct 1862. Re-enlisted, 28 Dec 1863, at Little Rock, Ark. Mustered same day. Discharged at Camden, Ark. 12 Oct 1865.

we run all day and till night then the boat got fast on a sand bar. dident git off till morning. cool and plesant.

Saturday, 21 Oct 1865

we wrode all day and till 11 o clok at night which fetched us in cairo. cool and plesant.

Sunday, 22 Oct 1865

I got my break fast then run a round town a while then toke the cars for calamet. warm and plesant.

Monday, 23 Oct 1865

we wrode all night and most all the fournoon which fetched us to 100. we got dinner and stade till 6 o clock then toke the cars for Jackson. cooll and cloudy.

The back pages of this booklet held recipes for medical treatments for various problems that people encountered. One hundred plus years ago doctors spent little time in training in medicine compared to today's standards. One thing evident in reading these treatments was the use of a tincture of opium, roughly 1-2 oz per recipe, obviously readily available. In 1866 he had an account with a Doctor Miller showing he was charged $10.00 for curing an ulcer. He had other miscellaneous accounts with individuals, some itemized, others not itemized. One was with his brother W.F. Ayres listing such items as butter, eggs, potatoes, flower [flour], and crocks. It would be interesting to know in what relationship these were made. Gus, however, according to his sister, Elizabeth, was most careful with his money and contracts.

Appendix B

Ayres Gasoline Engine and
Automobile Works

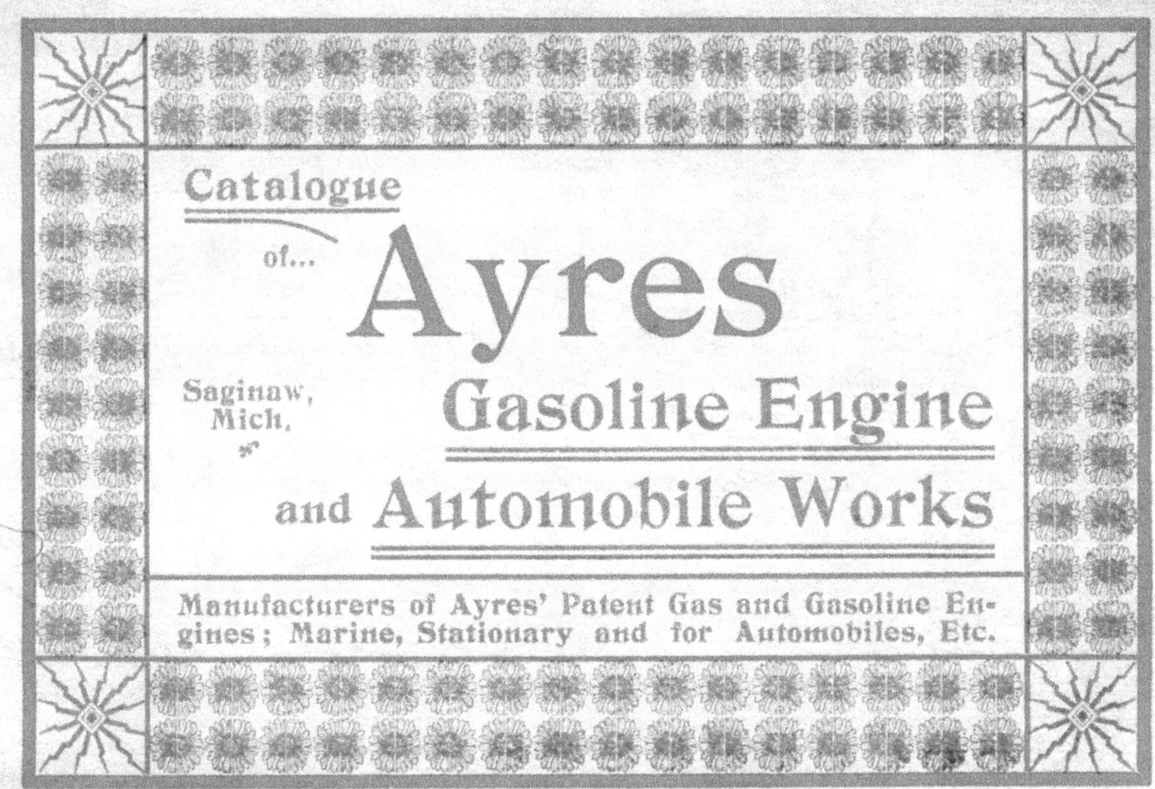

Ayres

20th Century
Gasoline Engine

THE Twentieth Century has dawned upon a progressive people, and with it we may expect another era of improvements such as the world has no conception of.

Turn back history's pages to the beginning of our past century and examine the systems of production adopted by our forefathers aud we may readily realize the truth of the statement that ...

THE WORLD MOVES BY MACHINERY.

There is not an article upon the market that is not the product of some machine, the varieties of which are almost without limit, but behind each we find that which is more important than the instrument itself, its propelling agent.

Steam and the horse have performed their work nobly, but it is a fact that they are both being replaced by the Hydro-Carbon Motor, better known as the Gas or Gasoline Engine, which generates its power from the force of an explosion, utilizing the force direct, not through the expansion of other bodies, thus making it the most economical of all power generating agents, and here we wish to state some of the latest developments in this line.

In presenting this catalogue of "Ayres" Gas, Gasoline and Oil Engines, attention is respectfully called to the fact that all the illustrations herein are from photographs of engines in actual use.

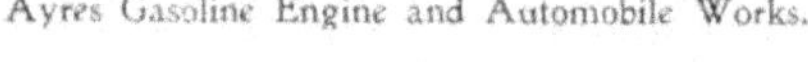

Ayres Gasoline Engine and Automobile Works.

This is the style of our 18, 25, 35 and 50 **H. P.** Stationary Engine, except they all have two Balance Weels.

This is the style of our 5, 8, and 12 H. P. Stationary Engines. The Simplicity and Positiveness of its Valve Movement is remarkable, particularly adapted for all kinds of weather and climate.

Ayres Gasoline Engine and Automobile Works.

General Design

There are certain portions of mechanism pertaining to the Gas or Gasoline Engine which may operate automatically and which are allowed to do so by the majority of our mechanical engineers but which are the source of great unreliability on the part of the machine.

To cause such operations to become mechanical requires a certain amount of extra movements. The inventor fully realizes this fact and has never lost sight of same in the designing of his recent developments.

The Ayres Gas or Gasoline Engine is an extremely positive machine, there being no automatic movements in its operation, and such can only be appreciated by those who have had years of experience with the unpractical as well as the practical. Notwithstanding this fact the Ayres Engine is extremely simple, neat and compact in its construction, having no unsightly portions of mechanism projecting from various parts of the machine. The foregoing cut proves for itself as to the truth of this statement, which is an exact representation of the engine as it is in operation, not with 90 per cent. of its mechanism absent to show simplicity as the majority of this class of machines are represented.

The gasoline engine of today is practically a new device upon the market and naturally possesses many unpractical undeveloped points which have heretofore been the source of an endless amount of annoyance to the public at large, so much so that many who have been the victims of some worthless article of this class have condemned all, forgetting that a worthless machine does not disprove the good qualities of a practical one.

The inventor has for many years been in a position to thoroughly investigate all points pertaining to this line of motors, has adopted the practical and avoided the unpractical, has overcome all difficulties which have been the source of so much annoyance, and has placed upon the market a machine that can be guaranteed to give complete satisfaction under proper care, at a price within the reach of the consumer.

Valve Movement

In no one class of machines do we find so wide a variety of mechanical movements to reach the same results as we do in the four-cycle hydro-carbon motors, which if properly designed, are the most economical of all power generating devices.

The general type of engine possesses two valves—inlet and exhaust, which are operated upon every other revolution, thus demanding an alternating principle in their opera-

tion. The great variety of type possesses spur, bevel or spiral gears, reducing the amount one half.

The eccentric has stood the test of many ages in all classes of mechanical devices and is universally known to be a most simple neat and durable movement where such may be applied.

But few types have adopted the eccentric principle owing to the alternation necessary in the operation of the valves and these types allow the inlet valve to take care of itself which is a sad mistake on the part of the inventor in designing engines of this nature and is the source of a large portion of trouble derived from motors of this class. But to have an inlet valve means an extra amount of mechanism and the average designer comes in contact with so many obstacles in giving the valve its proper alternation and governing properties that he generally gives it up for a bad job and allows the inlet valve to take care of itself.

The inventor fully realized this fact and in designing the valve operating mechanism, the operation of both inlet and exhaust valves mechanically and by eccentric principle, was ever held in view. This was triumphantly accomplished by a neat rock arm, as shown in the following cut, having operative arms pivoted to the ends of the same, to act upon the inlet and exhaust valves, to be placed into and out of alignment for the opening and alternating of same, which device is strongly protected by letters patent No. 632,888, granted Seymour A. Ayres, November 12th, 1899, by the United States Patent office. This is the only Hydro-Carbon motor ever placed before the public, having an inlet valve opening mechanically by the eccentric principle.

GENERATOR AND VALVE MOVEMENT.

Ayres Gasoline Engine and Automobile Works.

THE most important feature of a gasoline or oil engine is its Generator, for upon this depends its reliability in starting, economy in the consumption of fuel, positiveness in operation, and equalization of charges.

Many Generators of the past have been the source of great annoyance in the positiveness of the engine and equalization of charges, for upon this depends its economy. It should be understood that the greatest force from an explosion is only attained by a perfect mixture of gasoline and air and in proper proportion.

If this proportion does not remain unchanged during the operation of the engine and cannot be regulated very minutely it at once becomes a very extravagant and unreliable article. The Ayres engine possesses a Generator entirely different from the various types now before the public. There being a separate chamber adjoining the air passage way wherein the gasoline or oil enters through a needle point valve and comes in contact with a gate situated within said chamber, which allows only that amount of fluid to enter said air passage way necessary to give the charge its proper generation. The overflow is not in connection with the air passage way as in other devices of this kind and only the necessary amount of gasoline enters the passage and that amount is placed in such position as to never fail to evaporate as the air enters the engine through the inlet valve.

This principle is strongly protected by Letters Patent No. 632,509 granted September 5th, 1899, by the United States Patent Office and in possession of the inventor.

This Cut Shows the Way the Igniter is Attached.

Ayres Gasoline Engine and Automobile Works.

Igniter

A very important feature in explosive engines is the construction of the Igniter The hot tube and electric spark constituting those in general use, the latter being by far preferable as its use insures an ignition at the proper instant, is always ready for operation at a moments notice, and is much more economical in its cost of operation than either hot tube or flame Igniters.

In the judgment of many its reputation is poor owing to a great variety of unreliable Igniters found among the various types of engines in public use. The preceding cut shows great simplicity in the construction of the Ayres Electric Igniter which embodies those principles necessary to make it a most durable and positive device, which principles are thoroughly understood by the inventor, and nothing has been neglected along this and other lines.

Governor

There is no class of engines requiring a more sensitive Governor to insure a uniform motion than the Hydro-Carbon Motor, owing to the intense pressure of the explosion at distant intervals in its operation.

Many engines possess pendulum governors, which, to be plain with the expression, are altogether too delicate to be practical.

It is a well known fact among mechanical engineers that no device equals or exceeds the high speed centrifugal governor for accurate work.

The Ayres engine possesses a governor of the above type which never allows a second impulse to follow directly after a previous one when working less than half capacity and assumes a perfect alternation in its impulses when working at one half its full capacity.

This governor being of special construction and extremely sensitive, is in every respect a perfect device.

When working very close to full capacity in the operation of other types, two revolutions of the engine are required after the governor has taken effect, before a release thereof can be effected, whereas with the Ayres engine but *one* revolution is required as its load may demand. The construction of valve operating mechanism being such as to allow a release of the governor at any revolution, it not being essential that such release should be effected on any alternate number.

In no other type where an inlet valve opens mechanically can this principle be found, and with but one or two exceptions this is the only engine that possesses this point.

⁂ ⁂ ⁂ ⁂

Easy ⁂ Starting

It is a well known fact that the gasoline engine of the past has given an endlesss amount of trouble in starting, especially in low temperature.

We are proud to state that the Ayres engine has never failed to be in operation less than one minute after same received its first charge even in

temperatures registering 10° below zero, showing its positiveness in the operation. This is due partly to the positive operation of the valves and to the special construction of the Generator shown in Patents No. 632,509 as previously described, in which it is impossible for the gasoline to fail to evaporate.

One of the greatest obstructions in starting engines of this class is passing the crank by the compression which, at the highest point registers about 60 lbs. per sq. in. on the face of piston. This is reduced to a certain extent by relief cocks, valves and other devices, but requires an exceedingly large amount of exertion on the part of the operator.

The most convenient method of starting especially large types, is, after the engine has received its first charge and commences to compress same, allow the engine to reverse, which it does automatically owing to the piston acting upon the partly compressed charge, thus bringing the crank on the opposite quarter for its second light compression. At this point the crank is in position to receive the impulse of the explosion without passing the highest point of compression or allowing the charge to escape through a relief cock.

With but one or two exceptions the Ayres engine is the only machine that can be operated by this method and is the only engine having an inlet valve operated by mechanism that can be started in this manner.

All engines having valves operated by spur, bevel or spiral gears, cams, etc., must be given a continued revolution of the balance wheels in starting, requiring much exertion and anxiety.

An 18 H. P. Ayres engine can be started with ease by a boy of fourteen. 35 and 50 H. P. types may be operated by one person with equal success.

Economy

The cost of running Ayres engines depends upon the amount of work performed, as each is fitted with a sensitive governor which allows gas or gasoline to be used only in proportion to the energy exerted, thus producing the power with the lowest possible gas or gasoline consumption. When running the consumption ranges from *one-twelfth* of a gallon per horse-power per hour in small engines, to *one-fifteenth* of a gallon per horse-power per hour in the larger sizes.

Guarantee

Every engine is thoroughly tested before shipment and is guaranteed to be capable of delivering the actual horse-power for which it is sold. We also agree to send, free of cost, duplicates of any parts found defective in material or workmanship, within one year from date of shipment, the defective part to be sent to us for inspection.

TERMS:

Net cash, F. O. B., Saginaw, Michigan.

Twenty-five per cent. to accompany the order, balance to be paid when engine or launch is ready for shipment. No extra charge for drayage to boat or cars.

temperatures registering 10° below zero, showing its positiveness in the operation. This is due partly to the positive operation of the valves and to the special construction of the Generator shown in Patents No. 632,509 as previously described, in which it is impossible for the gasoline to fail to evaporate.

One of the greatest obstructions in starting engines of this class is passing the crank by the compression which, at the highest point registers about 60 lbs. per sq. in. on the face of piston. This is reduced to a certain extent by relief cocks, valves and other devices, but requires an exceedingly large amount of exertion on the part of the operator.

The most convenient method of starting especially large types, is, after the engine has received its first charge and commences to compress same, allow the engine to reverse, which it does automatically owing to the piston acting upon the partly compressed charge, thus bringing the crank on the opposite quarter for its second light compression. At this point the crank is in position to receive the impulse of the explosion without passing the highest point of compression or allowing the charge to escape through a relief cock.

With but one or two exceptions the Ayres engine is the only machine that can be operated by this method and is the only engine having an inlet valve operated by mechanism that can be started in this manner.

All engines having valves operated by spur, bevel or spiral gears, cams, etc., must be given a continued revolution of the balance wheels in starting, requiring much exertion and anxiety.

Economy Compared to Steam. ✿ ✿ ✿

The following is actual cost of running Gasoline Engine as compared to steam. The costs are actual, and computed by those using them who have given them a personal test:

12 H. P. ENGINE RUNNING FULL LOAD FOR TEN HOURS.

12 H. P. STEAM ENGINE.			12 H. P. GASOLINE ENGINE.		
Coal, 1½ Tons, @ $3.50	$5.25		Gasoline, 6 Gallons,	$ .51	
Water, - - -	.25		Water, (with cooling tank)	.00	
Oil and Waste, -	.06		Oil and Waste, -	.06	
Attendance, - -	2.00	$7.56	Attendance, - -	.10	$ .67

For cooling cylinder the same water may be used by means of a circulating tank. The cost of operating a steam engine is based on a man's time at $2.00 per day, and coal at $3.50 per ton; gasoline engine on gasoline at 8½ cents per gallon.

Our method of using gasoline (as described on another page) renders it perfectly safe, in fact insurance companies allow it as will be seen by following specifications taken from permit of Underwriters Association.

Specifications to which all Gasoline Engines must Conform in Order to be approved, and for their Installation.

1. Storage tank of gasoline shall be located under ground outside of the engine room and below the level of the inlet valve of the engine, and not less than 10 feet away from any building. Gasoline must be drawn from the general supply tank either to the engine or to the auxiliary or secondary resevoir or receptacle into which the pump discharges and out of which the gasoline is fed into the engine. The overflow of said auxiliary or secondary reservoir or receptacle must lead back to the main storage tank and be of four times the capacity of the pump.

2. Pipes leading from storage tank to engine must be put together at every joint, metal to metal; supply pipes to incline towards storage tank and to be so arranged that any surplus gasoline shall drain back to tank from engine when not in operation. Storage tank must always be filled by daylight, and all attachments between supply wagon, tank car, or barrels shall be tight-fitting screw connections. A vent-pipe provided with screw cap must be attached to tank, said pipe to be open during filling; and a valve in supply pipe of engine rear tank must be provided; said valve shall be closed when filling tank.

3. ANY FORM OF CARBURETOR OR VAPORIZER, (that is, engines with a carburetor or vaporizer so constructed that by the passing of air over or through the gasoline the explosive mixture is formed **within the carburetor or outside of the engine cylinder,**) **is prohibited.**

failed to be in operation less than one minute after same received its first charge even in

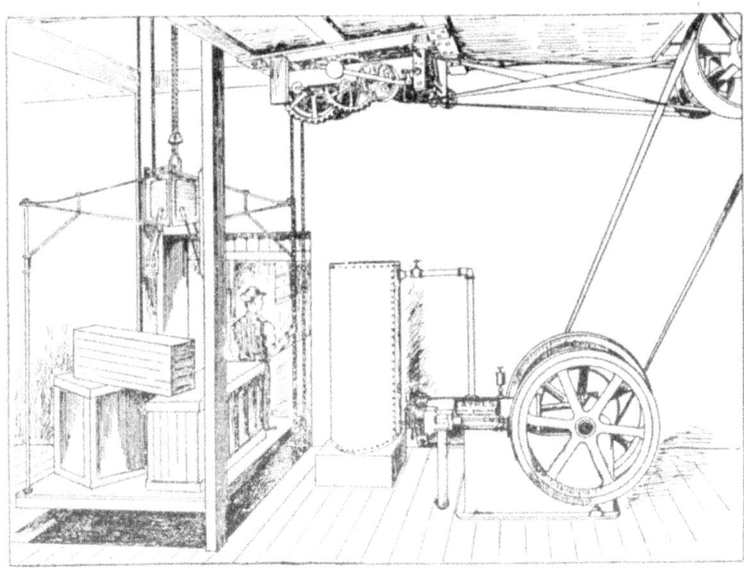

The Ayres Engine is always ready to elevate you in time of need. It has no equal for running elevators.

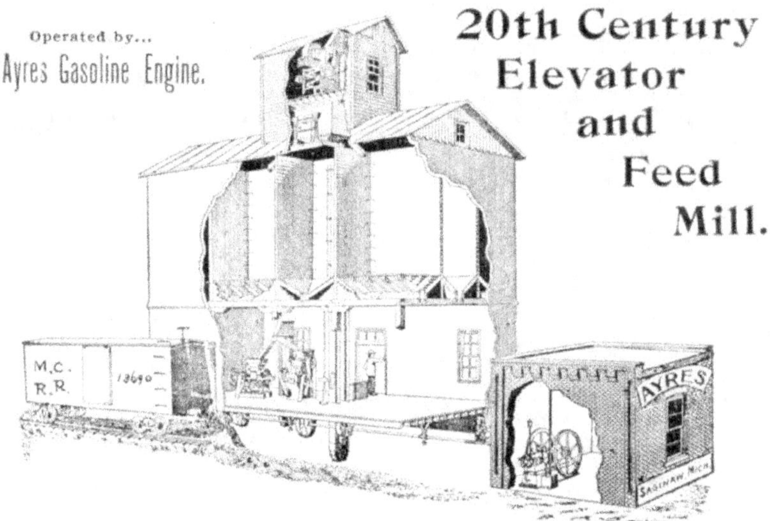

Nothing is equal to Ayres Gasoline Engine for Running Elevators, as they are always ready, easy to start and uses no fuel when you are waiting for a load.   Farmers always like to go where they can get their grain unloaded in a hurry and those who use Ayres Engine please the trade and get the business.

Why use old foot power when you can do as much more work with one of Ayres' Gasoline Engines.   The wise printer who puts in one of these engines is sure to double his business, as people always patronize an up-to-date business man.

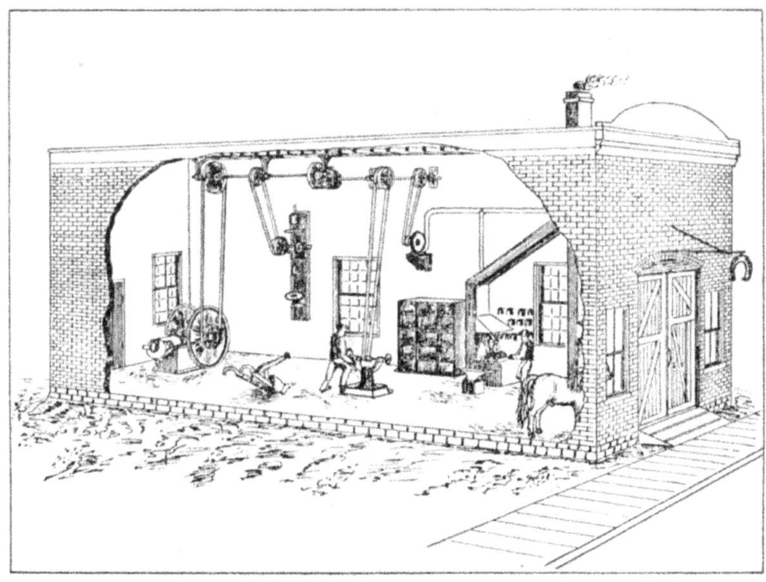

This wise and far seeing Blacksmith and Wagon-maker is always busy, because he put in one of Ayres' Gasoline Engines to run his shop with. He does more work with less help and as easy again as by the hand power, in fact work is a dream to him now. Be a 20th Century man and "Go Thou and Do Likewise!"

Ayres Gasoline Engine and Automobile Works.

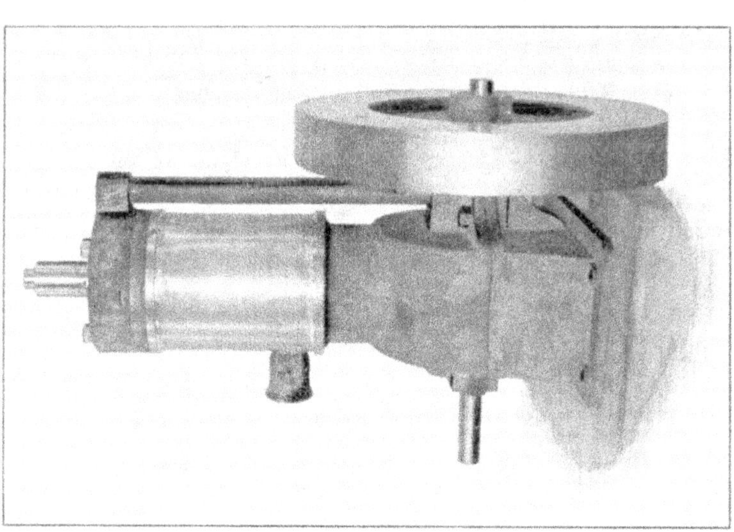

MARINE TYPE.

These Engines are made in sizes 1, 2, 3, 5, 8, 10 and 15 H. P., with a choice of a three Blade Reversable Propeller our latest patent, or a Solid Propeller with a Reversable Gear.

Marine

There is no pleasure exceeding that from the yacht and launch and there is no propelling agent equal to the practical two-cycle gasoline engine for that purpose.

Steam power is bulky, requiring much attention and a licensed engineer in its operation, besides never being free from dirt or danger. Electric power is burdensome and expensive as well as giving more or less annoyance in battery charging, etc.

A properly constructed gasoline engine is by far better adapted for launch and yacht work than any other propelling force. It being the most economical, requiring no attention after starting, absolutely free from danger, may occupy an exceedingly small space at the stern, leaving the body of the boat for the enjoyment of passengers and requires no licensed engineer to operate. Under proper conditions it propells a boat with a degree of steadiness equal to any steam or electric force.

The most important feature of the two-cycle engine is in the construction of its Generator and in which many types fail to give complete satisfaction. The Ayres Generator is especially adapted for two-cycle as well as four-cycle types. Being very accurate in its operation, it supplies high speed as well as low speed engines with equal success.

On the Atlantic and Pacific coast, all small schooners are being fitted out with engines of this type as auxiliaries to be used in case of storm or accident, which is becoming

Ayres Gasoline Engine and Automobile Works.

one of the necessary fixtures of small crafts. Our marine engines are of the same type as those used in the construction of our Automobiles.

We are also in a position to quote prices on Launches of any size and dimensions.

Marine Gasoline Engines

Engines Complete, including Stuffing Box, Stern-Bearing, three Blade Reversable or Solid Propeller, with Reversable Gear, Propeller Shaft, Spark Coil, Battery, Switch, Exhaust, Ejector and Wrenches.

Actual Horse Power	Revolutions Per Minute	Diameter Fly Wheel	Diameter Propeller Wheel
1	450	12 in.	12 in.
2	400	14 in.	16 in.
3	375	15 in.	16 in.
5	350	20 in.	20 in.
8	325	25 in.	28 in.
10	300	30 in.	28 in.
15	275	35 in.	30 in.

Spark Dynamos furnished and provision for their connection to engine made for extra price of $20.00.

All prices F. O. B. Saginaw. Terms, 25 per cent. on placing order, balance when ready for shipment.

We take every precaution in boxing and packing, but transportation must be at purchaser's risk.

No Instructions in the operation of our Gasoline Engine is ordinarily needed, but where specially desired we will send a man for that purpose at the expense of the purchaser.

The engine can be set up by any competent mechanic under the instructions furnished.

Appendix C

The Questionable Ayers Ancestry

It ain't necessarily so as the song goes. Even the best researchers can make mistakes. My family and others were caught in a web that still persists today in believing what other researchers had published long ago was fact. As a youngster, the glorious fairy tale began with Humphrey le Eyre, a knight, who came with Duke William to conquer England in 1066. Years later after a decade of research on that English Eyre family, I went on a genealogical trip to England in 1993. Excitement mounted as I looked forward to spending several days in Salisbury, Wiltshire, visiting the ancestral site to learn the history of St. Thomas church and its connection with my Ayer family. As I gazed at the dusty fractured dark oak stained alabaster memorials in Our Lady Chapel of Thomas Eyre, his wife, Elizabeth Rogers, and their fifteen children and the separate one of his son, Christopher, a wealthy London merchant adventurer who paid for these memorials, I wondered which figure was John Ayer who had settled in Massachusetts along the Merrimac River.

The initial building on the church site was a small wooden chapel constructed as a place of worship for the men working on the new Salisbury Cathedral which was dedicated to St. Thomas Becket about 1220. The chapel was replaced by a small stone church which has undergone numerous changes. Our Lady Chapel evolved from the reconstructed St. Stephen's Chapel which was destroyed in 1447. The Eyre memorials were moved to Our Lady's Chapel from their original site in the chancel. Despite their condition they are still impressive pieces of carving. Mostly any Eyre family member would love to claim this family as theirs.

In visiting the nearby village of Whiteparish on a Sunday side trip from Salisbury, we attended church services at All Saints Church. In conversing with the vicar's wife she said that a descendant of Giles Eyre, a younger brother of John Eyre, still resided in the Giles' home called Brickworth. A brass plaque on an outer wall in the church is dedicated to Giles. A well known landmark, the Pepperbox, was built by Giles Eyre in 1606. It was on high ground northwest of Whiteparish village and used by his lady friends to watch hunting parties. This was also the church where some of my Pike ancestors were christened and married.

As I did further English research on the Eyre family, several things began to perplex me about John Ayer who settled lastly in Haverhill, Massachusetts. The spelling of the family of Eyre changed little, if any, over the centuries in English records. And why was there no Christening for John recorded in St. Thomas' church records supposedly born in Sep 1582? Their records date from 1570. Why was there nothing recorded in the Chrysom books where wives gave a chysom offering after the birth of a child? Why was there no contact between John Ayer and the notable Rev. Charles Chauncey in Massachusetts, since Chauncey had married a daughter of the eldest son, Robert Eyre? What was the source of the birth date of John Ayer? Lastly, why the spelling change?

So I researched Eyre family wills and found that each Eyre male had carefully named his siblings, male and female, and other family members in them. The most common source cited for that family came from Hoare's Modern Wiltshire, Volume V published in 1837.[1]

There are three references in Hoare's massive two volumes that are vital here. Volume V had two pedigree charts for the Eyre family. One is a two page insert between pages 56 and 57. It was noted as taken from the Visitation of 1623, published family documents and papers, and parish registers. A John was listed as baptized on 20 Sep 1582. This pedigree was inserted in an article on the Giles Eyre family of the Hundred of Frustfield in Whiteparish. Another pedigree was entered on page 107 and taken from the College of Arms, Wills, Parish Registers and other evidences. Only twelve of the fifteen children were named and no John was among them.

The third and most important reference is contained in Volume VI, in the Appendix on page 835. Noted is the following on the Eyre's Charity, Parish of St. Thomas.

John Eyre, son of Thomas and Elizabeth (Rogers) Eyre, died in July 1599 as established by his will and other sources.[2]

John Eyre, by will dated Jul 13, 1599, gave for the use of the poor people of the parish of St. Thomas, all his lands and tenements at Alderbury. By an award of the Commissioners for the Alderbury

---

1 Sir Richard Colt Hoare, *Modern Wiltshire, Old and New Sarum or Salisbury*, (London, John Bowyer Nichols & son, 25 Parliament St., Vol.V 1837)

2 Hoare, Vol.VI, 1843

inclosure, made in 1809 with the consent of Jacob Earl of Radnow, and the then trustees, two pieces of land in Hornham were assigned in exchange for the charity property at Alderbury. [Alderbury is about 24 miles southeast of Salisbury and halfway to Whiteparish.] The rent, which at the time of the Charity Commission of Inquiry, amounted to £15 yearly, clear of all deductions, had been laid out in bread, and distributed on alternate Sundays to certain persons, of whom a list was kept. Vacancies, when they occurred, were filled by the Church wardens.

Going a step further, the Abstracts of Wiltshire Inclosure Awards and Agreements, published in 1971 made the following reference on Alderbury on page 12. Under the Award 2 Dec 1809 (enrolled 24 Jul 1816), it was stated under Allotments made: trustees of Eyre's charity for St. Thomas's, Salisbury; Samuel Whitchurch; John M. Eyre.[1]

The Churchwarden's Accounts of St. Edmund & St. Thomas, Sarum, published in 1896 were more rewarding. The following appear on pages 353-355: An Account of the Wills Deeds Plate &c. May 22, 1736.

Mem. Acknowledgment before Edmd. Pitman Esq. and W. Stone Oct. 22, 1735 by T. Langley baker of St. Edmund's that he had seen in his father's custody the lease of the houses &c. in Alderbury given by John Eyre to the poor of St. Thomas' by virtue of which he now sends 28 penny loaves every Sunday there; that his father told him it was for three lives viz, the father's brother's (both Dead) and his son. He himself has no writing but believes that J. Jennaway of Chichester who was his fathers executor and died about 30 years ago had all his father's writings. Further he now lets the premises at £10 a year...Bread 6.15.4d.[2]

John Eyre gent' second son of Tho. of New Sarum gent and who died at Lewes in Sufsex (in his journey from Sarum) and was buried in the parish church of St. Thomas in the cliffe there, have at his death five brothers viz. Robert Gyles Xpofer Thomas and William and five sisters viz. Elizabeth Katherine Anne Melior and Rebecca whom he made his Executors and gave by his Will all his goods and lands to the use of the poor, and as the lands were not sufficiently given by his Will Robert Eyre his brother and heir by his deed carried the said intention into effect.[3]

In the name of God Amen. The 13th day of July 1599. 41 Eliz. I, John Eyre of New Sarum in the County of Wilts being sick of Body but of sound Remembrance praised be God for it Do make and Ordaine this my last Will and Testament in manner and form following viz. first I bequeath my Soul to Allmighty God my Saviour and Redeemer in whom I trust to be saved through his meritts and my body to the Earth to be buried in the Church of St Thomas in new Sarum aforesd If it pleaseth the Lord that I make my departure near the same Item I give to the poor People of St Thomas where I dwell all That my Lands and Tenements lyeing & being in Alderbury in the sd County of the use and good of the sd poor for ever Item I also give to my Brothers and Sisters whom I make my Executors in equall porcōns all That my moveables goods and Chattells [everything other than land and tenements] whatsoever to the value of ffive hundred pounds more or less Item I will to the poor in Salisbury at the time of my Buriall in bread to the value of fforty shillings to be given them Item I appoint my ffather Thomas Eyre my Brother in law Gyles Tooker Esq. and Thomas Hooper of Boridge in Dorset my Overseers of this my last Will & Testament made the day and year above said. In Witness of the truth I have hereunto sett my hand & seal in the presence of these persons hereunder named. One other Clause yet forgotten I will that my Copyhold Liveing in Stoford that William Burstoe have the forsakeing of it before any man According to my promises And if he refuse it That then one Rawden Southery have it at the price I bought it of him. John Eyre Witness hereunto this my last Will & Testament John Harman the elder Thomas Oliver. Peter Stout Scr[4]

My efforts in locating the original will and that of John Eyre's father, Thomas, who died in 1628 proved fruitless.

---

1 R. E. Sandell, Ed., Abstracts Of Wiltshire Inclosure Awards And Agreements, (Devizes, 1971) 13

2 Henry James Fowle Swayne, *Churchwardens' Accounts of S. Edmund & S. Thomas, Sarum, 1443-1702*, (Salisbury, Bennett Brothers, Journal Office, 1896) 353, 354

3 *Ibid.* 354

4 Swayne, 354

An Indenture made Dec. 2. 45 Eliz. [1603] by which O. Powell and R. Roberts, in consideration as above confirm to T. R. G. Chr[r] T. and W. Eyre and Gyles Tooker and their heirs &c. for ever the above mentioned Tenements, in trust to dispose the ifsues & profits therof to the use of the poor &c. according to the intent &c. of the said J. Eyre. Sealed &c. and seisin delivered to T. Eyre in the presence of Js. Haviland mayor, E. Rodes, H. Mors, W. Wigan, Wr. Culley, J. Newman.[1]

The preceding initials refer to his father, Thomas, and brothers: Robert, Giles, Christopher, Thomas, and William. It is apparent that little was known of John Eyre, son of Thomas and Elizabeth, because he did not marry and leave issue. Many later English publications have contributed to this dilemma, but the settling of his estate leaves no doubt that he was the only son named John of Thomas and Elizabeth. The children of Thomas and Elizabeth follow: (Those with * denoted in John Eyre's estate.)

1. Robert.* Buried 8 Aug 1638 age 69 in St. Thomas Church, Salisbury.
2. John.Died Jul 1599. No issue.
3. Catherine.* Chr. 28 Feb 1570, in St. Thomas Church, Salisbury. She married Thomas Hooper of Boveridge, Dorsetshire.
4. Giles.* Chr. 27 Feb 1572 in St. Thomas Church, Salisbury, will 4 Jan 1655; died Jan 1655, buried in Whiteparish, Wiltshire. Founder of Brickworth and Irish branches in Galway. His brother, William, conveyed to Giles all his lands in Brickworth in 1628. There are numerous publications on this family.
5. Nicholas. Chr. 5 Dec 1573, and buried 6 Dec 1573 in St. Thomas Church, Salisbury. 1574, Thos. Eyers wyf off., 1d.
6. Elizabeth.* She married Giles Tooker of Maddington, Wiltshire.
7. Thomas.* Chr. 14 Sep 1575; buried 27 Sep 1575 in St. Thomas Church, Salisbury. Mr. Thomas Eyers wyfe her offerynge 11/2 d in 1575 during the Feast of St. Mychell unto the Feast of the Nativitie.
8. Francis. Chr. 20 Feb 1576; buried 8 Jun 1590 in St. Thomas Church, Salisbury.
9. Christopher.* Chr. 25 Apr 1578 in St. Thomas Church, Salisbury; will Jul 1617, died 1617, buried in St. Stephen's Church on Coleman Street, London. Thomas Eyres wyffe churched, 25 May 1578.
10. Margaret. Chr. 18 Jun 1579, in St. Thomas Church, Salisbury. Died before 1599.;
11. Thomas.* Chr. 24 Aug 1580, in St. Thomas Church, Salisbury; died 1633. Mr. Thomas Eyeres wyfe churched 19 Sep 1580, her crisome 7d, her offring 8d. He became Mayor of Salisbury in 1610, lived South Newton, Wiltshire.
12. Anne.* Thomas Eyres wyfe churched the last of Aprl 1584, her crisom 8d, her offring 5d. She married John Swayne of Gunville, Dorsetshire.
13. William.* Chr. 25 Nov 1585, and buried, 30 Aug 1638, in St. Thomas Church, Salisbury. Mr. Thomas Eyres wife churched, 23 Dec 1585, her chrisom 4d, her offring 1d. William was a Barrister-at-Law of Bonhams. He bequeathed his estate to his great-nephew, Samuel Eyre.
14. Melliore.* Chr. 9 Aug 1587, in St. Thomas Church, Salisbury. Thomas Ayers wiffe churched, 5 Aug 1587, her crisoms 10d, her offring 2d. Died after 1599, d.s.p.
15. Rebecca.* Chr. 22 Feb 1588, in St. Thomas Church, Salisbury. Mr. Thomas Eires wiffe churched, 19 Mar 1588, her crisom 4d, her offring 6d. She married John Love of Basing.

Of the numerous English publications printed after Hoare's, including Burke's, *Landed Gentry of Great Britain*, 1906, and later re-publications, *The Landed Gentry of Ireland*, 1958, *The Commoner's of Great Britain & Ireland*, 1977, p. 291, *Dormant and Extinct Peerages of The British Empire*, 1978, p. 193, that I have researched, little or no information is given on John, son of Thomas and Elizabeth Eyre. These also include, *A History of the Wiltshire Family of Eyre*, by Mary Richardson Eyre, 1897; *Signpost To Eyrecourt*, by Ida Gantz, undated, and *The Family of Eyre of Eyrecourt & Eyre of Eyreville*, by Rev. Allen S. Hartigan, 1899, most of whom gave sketchy vital information but noted the

---

1 *Ibid.* 354,355

1582 baptism of John. An Illustrated Quarterly Antiquarian & Genealogical Magazine has been compiled and bound as *Wiltshire Notes and Queries* in many volumes and cover many topics.

Previous reference has been made to The Chrysom Book of St. Thomas, New Sarum (Salisbury). This unique original book consists of sixty pages dating from 1569 to 1592 and consists of offerings for weddings, christenings, and church offerings. The Chrysom Book was transcribed in volumes 5 and 6 in *Wiltshire Notes and Queries*. Most articles are noted "To be continued" but no reference is made to page or volume which makes them difficult to locate. Fortunately, there was indexing. In vol. 5, dated June 1905, there was scanty information on the family of Thomas and Elizabeth in which John was noted as baptized on 20 Sep 1582 with no further information. The males were listed first, followed by the females with spouses. A. S. Hartigan appears to be the individual who provided this information which has added to the confusion. I feel that we descendants of John Ayer have been misled by one not very well documented pedigree chart in Hoare's. There were authors such as Sidney Perley, Editor of the *Essex Antiquarian,* and the *Colonial and Revolutionary Lineages of America,* V. 2, 1939, who made no such family claims in England.

Index